The St. Martin's Guide to Teaching Writing
Seventh Edition

CHERYL GLENN
PENNSYLVANIA STATE UNIVERSITY

MELISSA A. GOLDTHWAITE
SAINT JOSEPH'S UNIVERSITY

BEDFORD / ST. MARTIN'S
Boston ◆ New York

For Bedford/St. Martin's

Developmental Editor: Karrin M. Varucene
Associate Production Editor: Kellan B. Cummings
Senior Production Supervisor: Dennis J. Conroy
Executive Marketing Manager: Molly Parke
Copy Editor: Wendy Polhemus-Annibell
Indexer: Melanie Belkin
Permissions Manager: Kalina K. Ingham
Art Director: Lucy Krikorian
Cover Design: Marine Bouvier Miller
Composition: Westchester Book Group
Printing and Binding: RR Donnelley and Sons

President, Bedford/St. Martin's: Denise B. Wydra
Presidents, Macmillan Higher Education: Joan E. Feinberg and Tom Scotty
Editor in Chief: Karen S. Henry
Director of Development: Erica T. Appel
Director of Marketing: Karen R. Soeltz
Production Director: Susan W. Brown
Associate Production Director: Elise S. Kaiser
Managing Editor: Shuli Traub

Manufactured in the United States of America.

8 7 6 5 4
f e d c b

For information, write: Bedford/St. Martin's, 75 Arlington Street, Boston, MA 02116 (617-399-4000)

ISBN 978-1-4576-2263-2

Acknowledgments

Preface

There it is in black and white. You've been assigned to teach a college writing course: first-year composition. Sentences, paragraphs, essays. "Me—teach writing? I never took a writing course in my life, except first-year English, which I barely remember. What am I going to do?" This book was written to help you plan your writing classes and help you teach your students to become better writers. The theories, techniques, and methods discussed in the following chapters are based on our own teaching practice; they have been classroom-tested and as a whole represent the greater part of our current knowledge—both theory and practice—about teaching writing.

The St. Martin's Guide to Teaching Writing, Seventh Edition, is informed by three principles. First, writing is teachable; it is an art that can be learned rather than a mysterious ability that one either has or does not have. Second, students learn to write from trial-and-error writing and almost never profit from lectures, from teacher-centered classes, or from studying and memorizing isolated rules. Third, the theories and methods included here should represent strategies that work in the classroom. Therefore, this book is not a complete introduction to composition studies; some important composition and education theories are not covered here because they don't immediately lend themselves to classroom use.

This book is divided into three parts: "Classroom Issues," "Rhetorical Practices," and "An Anthology of Essays." If you're teaching writing for the first time, Part I offers you the nuts and bolts of teaching composition, with chapters ranging from "Preparing for the Course" (Chapter 1) to "Evaluating Student Essays" (Chapter 5). This part will help you prepare for, set up, and teach your first writing course. In this edition, we have paid close attention to the ways changing technology affects classroom practice and the composing process, which is increasingly multimodal. We have also expanded coverage of difference in the classroom and teaching multilingual writers.

If you're a more experienced teacher, you may want to begin with Part II on the theoretical background of the composition process and its application. Also covered here are the traditional canons of rhetoric—not only invention, arrangement, and style, but also memory and delivery. Each of the chapters in Part II consists of an introduction followed by discussions of specific theories and classroom activities. These activities have been successful for us and for other teachers. We hope that they work for you—and that you will help to improve them.

Part III includes a collection of essays, most of which are new to this edition, that explicitly attempt to link theory and practice with society at large. All of the essays interanimate one another, fusing classroom issues with social ones. We start with readings that concentrate on classroom practices and pressures and then move to essays that interrogate social conditions and expectations. Not surprisingly, the selections converge in rich and complex ways: The essays toward the end of Part III inform those at the beginning, and those at the beginning provide concrete illustrations of classroom practices that grow from and need to be revised by the exigencies explored in the later essays. Although we've loosely categorized the essays, we see them as richly overlapping in terms of their application to writing courses — both first-year writing and basic writing — based in contemporary essays, multimodal writing, and student writing. We believe these issues and topics will inform and vitalize your teaching, writing, and research, whether your work takes place at a two-year college, four-year college, or research university. We hope these essays will lead you to conduct research in your own classrooms.

ACKNOWLEDGMENTS

We wish to thank many people who helped with this book. We're especially grateful to our colleagues at Bedford/St. Martin's, Nancy Perry, Erica Appel, Karrin Varucene, Kellan Cummings, and Shuli Traub whose editorial support made this revision possible. Special thanks go to the reviewers for this edition: Elizabeth Berlinger, City University of New York; Joshua Keller, Temple University; Michael Keller, South Dakota State University; Alyse Knorr, George Mason University; Cindy Moore, Loyola University Maryland; Mary Lou Odom, Kennesaw State University. Throughout the text, we rely on the expertise and materials of many successful teachers, especially Andrea A. Lunsford. We're also grateful to the instructors who allowed us to quote them in our epigraphs for each chapter: Sarah Summers, Susan Weeber, Colin Hogan, Michael J. Faris, John Belk, Nathan Redman, Jessica O'Hara, David F. Green Jr., Craig Rood, Heather Adams, and Laura Michael Brown. We thank both the teacher-researchers who shared their syllabi and those whose work constitutes Part III of this book for their kind permission to reprint their essays.

Finally, we wish to acknowledge Robert Connors — teacher, scholar, researcher, and writer extraordinaire — whose work and personality shaped the first five editions of *The St. Martin's Guide to Teaching Writing*. We recognize his influence and honor his contributions to both the field of composition and to this book.

As the preceding paragraph suggests, teaching writing is always collaborative — and this book is no exception. We're all in this together, and one of the most satisfying parts of teaching writing is the way we all help one another out. We want to welcome you into our community, and we hope this book helps you get ready for your first — or your twenty-first — adventure in the writing classroom.

Cheryl Glenn
Melissa A. Goldthwaite

Contents

Preface   *iii*

PART I CLASSROOM ISSUES   *1*

1 Preparing for the Course   *3*

FINDING OUT ABOUT THE COURSE   *3*
CHOOSING THE TEXTBOOKS   *6*
MULTIMODAL LEARNING TECHNOLOGIES   *7*
LINKS TO COMMUNITY ENGAGEMENT: SERVICE LEARNING,
    COMMUNITY-BASED LITERACY PROJECTS, AND PUBLIC
    WRITING INITIATIVES   *9*
CREATING A SYLLABUS   *10*
SAMPLE SYLLABI   *14*
WORKS CITED   *43*

2 The First Few Days of Classes   *45*

THE FIRST CLASS   *45*
Bureaucratic Tasks   *46*
The Syllabus   *48*
Introductions   *48*
Dismissal   *49*
THE SECOND CLASS   *49*
Bureaucratic Tasks   *49*
Diagnostic Essay   *50*
Dismissal   *51*
After the Second Class   *51*
THE THIRD CLASS   *53*
LESSON PLANS   *54*
WORKS CITED   *58*

3 Everyday Activities   *59*

CLASSROOM ORDER AND GROUP ETHOS   *59*
CLASSROOM ROUTINES   *60*
Limiting Lectures   *61*

Leading Effective Class Discussions   *61*
In-Class Writing   *65*
Teaching in Wired, Wireless, and Hybrid Classrooms   *66*
COLLABORATION: WORKSHOPS AND PEER RESPONSE   *70*
Whole-Class Workshops   *71*
Peer-Response Groups   *72*
Tasks for Peer-Response Groups   *73*
Online and Electronic Peer Response   *77*
Evaluating Peer-Response Groups   *78*
Understanding Cultural and Multilingual Differences in
    Peer-Response Groups   *78*
STUDENT CONFERENCES   *79*
Scripting the Conference   *81*
EVERYBODY'S ISSUES   *83*
Absenteeism and Tardiness   *83*
Late Essays   *84*
Class Cancellations   *84*
Use of Personal Technology in the Classroom   *85*
Disruptive Students   *85*
Disabilities and Learning Differences   *86*
Plagiarism, Intellectual Property, and Academic Integrity   *87*
WORKS CITED   *93*

4 Successful Writing Assignments   *95*

ASSIGNMENTS   *95*
Defining Good Assignments   *97*
Assignment Sequences   *99*
Research Assignments   *100*
Web Assignments   *114*
Assignments Delivered Orally   *115*
Assignments That Call for the Use of Visual Components   *117*
Multimodal Assignments   *118*
Creating Assignments and Explaining Them to Students   *119*
REVISION   *120*
WORKS CITED   *124*

5 Evaluating Student Essays   *125*

STANDARDS AND EVALUATION   *127*
Formal Standards   *127*
Standards of Content   *129*
Evaluating Formal Standards and Standards of Content When Responding
    to ESL Student Writing   *130*
GENERAL ROUTINES FOR EVALUATION   *131*
MARGINAL COMMENTS   *133*

TERMINAL COMMENTS   *135*
THE GRADE   *137*
METHODS AND CRITERIA FOR GRADING   *138*
Course-Based Grading Criteria   *138*
Rubrics   *139*
Contract Grading   *144*
Portfolio Grading   *146*
HANDLING THE PAPER LOAD   *153*
THE END OF THE TERM   *154*
Final Grades   *154*
STUDENT EVALUATIONS OF COURSE AND TEACHER   *158*
AFTERWORD   *159*
WORKS CITED   *159*

PART II RHETORICAL PRACTICES   *161*

6 Teaching Invention   *163*

BRINGING THE RHETORICAL CANON OF INVENTION
    INTO THE WRITING CLASSROOM   *164*
HEURISTIC SYSTEMS OF INVENTION   *166*
Using Heuristic Strategies in the Classroom   *166*
CLASSICAL TOPICAL INVENTION   *167*
Using Classical Topical Invention in the Classroom   *169*
JOURNAL WRITING   *172*
Using Journals in the Classroom   *173*
Evaluating Journals   *177*
BRAINSTORMING   *178*
Using Brainstorming in the Classroom   *178*
CLUSTERING   *179*
Using Clustering in the Classroom   *179*
FREEWRITING   *180*
Using Freewriting in the Classroom   *181*
The Benefits of Freewriting   *183*
WORKS CITED   *184*

7 Teaching Arrangement and Form   *186*

RHETORICAL FORM   *186*
CLASSICALLY DESCENDED ARRANGEMENTS   *168*
The Three-Part Arrangement   *188*
Using the Three-Part Arrangement in the Classroom   *191*
An Exercise for Small Groups   *191*
The Four-Part Arrangement   *192*
Using the Four-Part Arrangement in the Classroom   *195*

The Six-Part Arrangement   *197*
Using the Six-Part Arrangement in the Classroom   *198*
OTHER PATTERNS OF ARRANGEMENT   *199*
Arrangements for Rhetorical Methods   *199*
Arrangements for Creative Nonfiction Essays   *201*
Using Arrangements for Creative Nonfiction Essays in the
    Classroom   *202*
An Exercise for Linking Invention and Arrangement   *204*
Arrangement and Multimodal Writing   *204*
Considering Arrangement for New Media in the Classroom   *205*
TECHNIQUES OF EDITING AND PLANNING   *205*
Using the Outline in the Classroom   *205*
Using Winterowd's "Grammar of Coherence" Technique in the
    Classroom   *208*
WORKS CITED   *209*

8 Teaching Style   *211*

STYLE: THEORY AND PEDAGOGIC PRACTICE   *212*
Milic's Three Theories of Style   *212*
A Pedagogic Focus on Rhetorical Choices   *214*
Choosing a Rhetorical Stance   *215*
Considering the Audience for Student Essays   *217*
LEVELS OF STYLE   *218*
EXERCISES FOR DEVELOPING STYLE   *219*
IMITATION   *220*
Using Imitation Exercises in the Classroom   *220*
LANGUAGE VARIETY   *222*
Teaching an Awareness of Language Variety   *224*
Language Varieties and Varying Syntax   *226*
ALTERNATE STYLES: GRAMMAR B   *227*
Using Alternate Styles in the Classroom   *228*
Evaluating Alternate Styles   *230*
WORKS CITED   *231*

9 Teaching Memory   *234*

MEMORY AND COMPOSITION STUDIES   *235*
REMEMBERING AND MAKING WRITING MEMORABLE:
    TEACHING MEMOIR AND PERSONAL WRITING   *236*
Invention   *237*
Memory as Communal   *238*
Research   *238*
Experience, Image, Idea   *239*
COLLECTIVE MEMORY   *240*

Considering Collective Memory in the Writing Classroom:
   A Multimodal Approach   *241*
WORKS CITED   *244*

10 Teaching Delivery   *246*

DELIVERING WRITING, DELIVERING PEDAGOGY   *246*
THE CHANGING NATURE OF WRITING, READING, AUDIENCE,
   AND CONTEXT   *247*
Establishing Goals — and Delivering on Them   *248*
Other Options for Exploring Multiple Modes of Delivery   *250*
UNDERSTANDING MULTIPLE LITERACIES AND THEIR EFFECTS
   ON DELIVERY   *252*
One Approach to Considering Multiple Literacies: Defining
   Computer Literacies   *252*
Using Selber's Approach in the Classroom   *254*
Expanding Consideration of Multiple Literacies in
   the Classroom   *255*
DELIVERING PEDAGOGY: EXTRATEXTUAL SPACES   *256*
One Approach to Delivery in Extratextual Spaces   *257*
Using Taylor's Approach in the Classroom   *257*
WORKS CITED   *259*

11 Invitation to Further Study   *261*

WAYS INTO THE SCHOLARLY AND PEDAGOGIC
   CONVERSATION   *261*
COMPOSITION/RHETORIC AND ITS CONCERNS   *263*
CENTRAL CONCERNS   *263*
The Content of First-Year Writing and Transfer   *263*
Disciplinarity and Assessment   *264*
Diversity and Difference   *264*
ANOTHER INVITATION TO FURTHER RESEARCH   *265*
WORKS CITED   *265*
SUGGESTED READINGS FOR TEACHERS OF WRITING   *267*
Bibliographies and Other Reference Works   *267*
Rhetorical History, Theory, and Practice   *267*
Composition History and Theory   *268*
Composition Practice and Pedagogy   *269*
Literacy Studies   *269*
Axes of Difference   *270*
Computers, Technology, and New Media   *271*
FY Writing Programs: Models and Administrative
   Practices   *273*
Pedagogic Issues for College Teachers   *273*

PART III AN ANTHOLOGY OF ESSAYS *275*

INTRODUCTION *275*

WORK CITED *277*

Douglas Downs and Elizabeth Wardle, *Teaching about Writing, Righting Misconceptions: (Re)Envisioning "First-Year Composition" as "Introduction to Writing Studies"* *278*

Donald M. Murray, *The Teaching Craft: Telling, Listening, Revealing* *305*

Wendy Bishop, *Helping Peer Writing Groups Succeed* *309*

Muriel Harris, *Talking in the Middle: Why Writers Need Writing Tutors* *318*

Nancy Sommers, *Responding to Student Writing* *333*

Andrea A. Lunsford and Karen J. Lunsford, *"Mistakes Are a Fact of Life": A National Comparative Study* *342*

Amy J. Devitt, Anis Bawarshi, and Mary Jo Reiff, *Materiality and Genre in the Study of Discourse Communities* *365*

Mike Rose, *The Language of Exclusion: Writing Instruction at the University* *381*

Jacqueline Jones Royster, *When the First Voice You Hear Is Not Your Own* *401*

Stephanie L. Kerschbaum, *Avoiding the Difference Fixation: Identity Categories, Markers of Difference, and the Teaching of Writing* *412*

Ilona Leki, *Meaning and Development of Academic Literacy in a Second Language* *436*

Paul Kei Matsuda, *The Myth of Linguistic Homogeneity in U.S. College Composition* *449*

Bruce Horner, Min-Zhan Lu, Jacqueline Jones Royster, and John Trimbur, O*PINION: Language Difference in Writing: Toward a Translingual Approach* *463*

Cynthia L. Selfe, *Toward New Media Texts: Taking Up the Challenges of Visual Literacy* *481*

Anne Frances Wysocki, *awaywithwords: On the Possibilities in Unavailable Designs* *507*

Cheryl Glenn, *2008 CCCC Chair's Address: Representing Ourselves* *514*

Acknowledgments *530*

Index *533*

Classroom Issues

CHAPTER

1

Preparing for the Course

*Before teaching my first composition course, I visited my classroom ahead of time,
and I imagined myself running through the syllabus with my students. I stood in front
of the U-shaped arrangement of tables and briefly rehearsed what I might say and
do. The first day of class went just as I imagined until I turned around and realized I
had spelled my name wrong on the board, omitting the final "s." I felt my face flush
in embarrassment. But I laughingly pointed it out, and it became a running joke that
my students and I shared for the rest of the semester. I might have been a little
nervous that day, but so were my first-year students. A silly mistake ended up being
a chance for all of us to laugh and relax a little.*

—Sarah Summers

FINDING OUT ABOUT THE COURSE

The first thing any new teacher must do is gather information. You have been
assigned to teach a writing course, but writing courses, even first-year (FY)
writing courses, come in many varieties. Before you can make intelligent and
useful plans, you'll want to find out some of the definitions and vital statistics
concerning your course. Such information may be presented in the form of an
orientation session for new teachers. Indeed, some departments organize special colloquia for new teaching assistants, and new instructors are usually
welcome to sit in. Such an introduction will provide you with all the information you need. If your program does not offer an orientation session, the writing
program administrator (WPA) or the chair of the department can undoubtedly answer most of the questions raised here. Some of your most important
questions concerning unwritten practices may be answered by experienced
teachers; at many schools, their wisdom is a vital element of the program. But
your WPA is the most reliable source for official departmental policy.

The first details you should find out about are the number of credit hours
the course carries and the number of times the class meets each week. A three-
credit course that meets three hours a week provides far less time for reading
and writing than, say, a five-credit, five-hour course; students willing to write
ten essays and fifty journal entries for five credits may object to doing the same
amount of work for three credits. As you plan your syllabus, adjust the number of writing assignments according to the number of credit hours.

Second, ask how many sections you will be teaching and how many students
you should expect to have in each class. The National Council of Teachers of
English (NCTE) recommends that each graduate student teach only one undergraduate section each term and that the maximum number of students in a

class be twenty (or fifteen in a basic writing course). Most English departments try to adhere to these recommendations, keeping the numbers within reasonable limits (from twenty to twenty-five students). Of course, the fewer students you have, the fewer papers you'll be reading and evaluating, the fewer conferences you'll be conducting, and the more time you will be able to devote to each student and your class preparation. If you are willing to teach at 8:00 AM or 5:00 PM, you may get a smaller class than if you teach at a more popular time slot, such as late morning or early afternoon. Nonetheless, you should count on having the maximum allowable number of students in your class. Information about your class size will help you organize assignments and plan a syllabus.

Third, find out whether there is a standardized departmental structure for the course. The structure of composition courses is shaped by pedagogical goals and curricular concerns. You'll need to find out how many composition courses students are required to take at your school. Some schools, for instance, have one term devoted to learning various rhetorical methods of development (such as narration, description, and argument) or different forms and genres of delivery (such as personal essays, analyses, reports, evaluations, speeches, Web writing, and multimodal assignments), and another term devoted to studying literature and composition or writing research papers. Other programs require just one composition course — sometimes a themed course (such as a writing-about-writing course or a course in which students write about popular culture, food, education, or another timely topic) or a capstone writing course in the student's major.

Since the structure of composition courses varies widely, knowing early on what your department expects and how the curriculum is shaped will help you plan the appropriate course. Many departments have official policies that new teachers must follow, and such policies and standards (which are very often linked to University Senate approval) will inform your own course arrangement. For instance: Must students write and submit a certain number of essays? across a variety of genres? produce a certain number of words? Must they keep journals or reading logs? Is there an official policy with regard to revisions? peer evaluation? teacher conferences? evaluation and grading? Is a portfolio or an exit exam required?

Finally, make inquiries about the academic level of the students you will be teaching. If your college or university has open admissions, then the range of your students' abilities will probably be wide. Some FY students may be basic writers with reading and writing abilities far below that expected of the average incoming student, whereas other students may be strong writers, accomplished and sophisticated products of hard-driving college-prep programs or their own natural ability and interest. Naturally, you must gear your preparation — from textbook selection to syllabus design — to the abilities and interests of your students. Find out whether incoming students write English placement essays and whether the school has a basic writing (BW) program, an English as a second language (ESL) program, and a writing center (WC). You will also want to know whether there are different levels of FY courses — an honors section, perhaps, or special-interest or themed sections — or whether all FY students are placed in the same course. Try to find out whether students from all years and levels can be placed in FY English; if that is the case, then you may have some more experienced students in your class.

Try at this point to find out all you can about the backgrounds of the students you are likely to encounter. Our students have different mother tongues and different levels of fluency in edited American English (also called Standardized English). Some come to us as native speakers of English but hail from other countries. And, now more than ever before, there is a huge range in their ages and life experiences. Find out what you can about your students' gender, ethnicity, age, and so on. You'll find that planning a course aimed mainly at Euro-American eighteen-year-old, able-bodied students from suburban high schools is very different from planning one for a group that includes urban minorities, recent immigrants, students with disabilities, and returning or part-time students. Especially if your course meets in the late afternoon or evening — that is, after the workday — be prepared for more diversity in your students and, correspondingly, more diverse demands on you. (See the scholarship by Ball and Lardner; Brueggemann et al.; Bruch and Marback; Davis; Lewiecki-Wilson and Brueggemann; Redd; Richardson; Trainor; and Watkins cited at the end of this chapter; see also the article by Leki in Part III of this book, starting on p. 436.)

If your school has a BW or an ESL program, you may want to find out its entrance and exit requirements and its relation to the standard FY writing course. Also try to find out about other writing programs on campus — not only to get a better picture of the entire writing program but also to know where to send your students for help. You may be surprised at the number of support systems your school offers. Some schools have writing centers that will work with students at any stage in the writing process and will send representatives into classrooms to give mini-lessons on such topics as process writing, writer's block, and essay exams. In addition, some schools have reading centers, where reading and comprehension problems can be diagnosed and helped. Your school may also have an office of disability services where learning disabilities (such as dyslexia, dysgraphia, and attention deficit disorder) can be diagnosed and treated. Such offices will also provide procedures for accommodating students with documented physical disabilities. By asking questions and talking with representatives of the various academic support programs on your campus, you will be much better prepared to guide your students through their writing course. When they have problems you cannot solve, you will be ready to send them to the specialists who can help.

At times, a student might exhibit behavioral or emotional issues that disrupt schoolwork or even the classroom. Your school likely offers psychological support to these students. If such a student acts out in class in a way that might be dangerous, immediately call campus security. Such situations are rare. It is not rare, however, for students to need counseling or support for substance-abuse problems, eating disorders, or other psychological issues—especially when such issues interfere with the student's ability to focus on schoolwork. Many teachers talk to and listen to students in crisis, but often these students will need professional help; in these cases, refer the student to the campus counseling center.

CHOOSING THE TEXTBOOKS

After you have discovered all you can about the nature of the courses you are to teach and the kinds of students you can expect, the next step is to investigate your textbook options. Since the textbook you use will underpin a number of important elements in your course, you will undoubtedly want to make use of it in as well-informed a manner as possible. Many writing programs require that all teachers follow certain texts and a common syllabus for a certain period, especially during the first year; others specify a primary text and allow teachers to choose the supplementary ones; and still others allow teachers to choose from a list of approved texts (so long as their syllabus meets all the course requirements). The freedom you have in choosing textbooks will depend on your school and its program as well as on the needs and interests of your students. In general, you may choose from among three types of textbooks: (1) rhetorics, which explain the step-by-step techniques of writing the various genres or methods of development and can include argument, research, online writing, and readings; (2) readers or anthologies, which provide selections of readings that are usually accompanied by analyses, discussion questions, and suggestions for writing; and (3) handbooks, which give guidance about style, grammar, punctuation, documentation, and the writing process. Many textbooks combine two or more of these purposes. A three-in-one textbook, for instance, includes features from the rhetoric, the reader, and the handbook.

Increasingly, publishers are offering custom-published books, which instructors can design themselves by selecting from a database of readings, discussion questions, and ancillary materials—including those created by the instructor. (Visit **bedfordstmartins.com/select** for an example.) Such an option might be especially welcome once you have a few years of teaching experience, allowing you the freedom to choose both the content and structure of the text.

Begin your consideration of textbooks by finding out which ones have been used with success and examining those texts carefully. Most departments that allow teachers some freedom in textbook selection maintain a small library of texts for teachers to examine. In order to make sense of the books you find there, you may wish to do some background reading on textbooks; several review articles and bibliographies provide an overview of the world of textbooks. *Composition Studies* and the *Journal of Teaching Writing* often carry textbook reviews. Publishers' brochures, catalogs, and Web sites are another source of information about the textbooks they offer. Book fairs, if your department or school organizes them, provide opportunities to see and compare a range of texts from different publishers. Through publishers' Web sites and book fairs you can get in touch with representatives who can help advise you about the texts available from particular presses. If you're seriously considering the adoption of a text, most publishers will provide a free or low-cost examination copy.

When examining textbooks, keep in mind the question of structure: How much do you want the structure of the textbook(s) to inform the structure of the course? If the textbook's order of topics is invention, organization, diction, style, and paragraphs, will you design your course around that structure and plan to spend a week or two weeks on each chapter? Or will you structure your course differently and organize textbook readings according to your syllabus, a course theme, a rhetorical method of development, types of argument, or some other plan? Perhaps you will find a book whose organization or thematic schema is congenial to you; however, you may decide to reorder the topics or to use only certain sections of a book.

Talking with experienced teachers in your program about textbooks can be helpful at this point. Get several teachers' opinions about a book before you make your choice, and don't decide hastily. Remember, for the next ten to fifteen weeks, you — and your students — will be living with your decision (or the decisions of a textbook selection committee). Make sure you're comfortable with the texts you use and with your plan for teaching from them.

Ask your WPA if your program offers pedagogy meetings or a Web site with sample syllabi and assignments; such examples can be especially valuable as you structure your course and choose your textbooks. Finally, be aware that there is no substitute for personal experience with a textbook. After teaching from a text, you may or may not want to continue to use it. Have your students evaluate each textbook; their responses will make your future choices easier. In any case, choose your first text carefully. *this will be extremely helpful in ESL courses*

MULTIMODAL LEARNING TECHNOLOGIES

Whether you teach at a school that has computer-supported classrooms, require students to create projects that include visuals and audio, or simply use e-mail to contact your students, you can use various technologies to support your pedagogical goals. Depending on the resources and support your school offers, you may be able to make such technologies a significant part of your classroom. Some schools offer online writing labs (OWLs) where students can send a draft and receive an online response to their writing. Many schools provide computer-supported classrooms and specialized software. Talk with your WPA about the technology and support your school offers. The following section provides an overview of some of the specific technologies writing teachers have found useful both inside and outside of the classroom. Keep in mind that the quickest way to learn how to incorporate these technologies into your own class is to sit in on the class of an experienced teacher. (See the CCCC's Executive Committee's Position Statement on Teaching, Learning, and Assessing Writing in Digital Environments; Hawisher and C. Selfe; Palmeri; Selber; R. Selfe; and Wysocki, cited at the end of this chapter. Also see Chapter 3, which includes a section on teaching in wired, wireless, and hybrid classrooms.)

In a computer-supported classroom, each student and teacher has a computer on which to compose, respond to, and revise drafts. Such classrooms generally provide Internet access as well as other technological resources, such as a document camera and DVD player. Whether you teach in a computer-supported classroom or not, however, you can make use of various technologies.

Increasingly, schools are providing a Web-based software package, such as Blackboard, Moodle, or Angel, which allows teachers to manage course materials online. These course-management systems provide areas for announcements, updates, and reminders; a space for course information, including the syllabus; staff information, where you can post your contact information and office hours; an area for course documents, where you can post additional readings or lecture notes; a communications section, where you can mount online discussions, chat, or e-mail links; and other spaces for external links or various tools. Even without a course-management system, however, you can most likely put your syllabus online and use other Web-based programs for pedagogical purposes.

Even if you don't have access to a fully equipped computer-supported classroom, you'll have access to e-mail through your college or university—so some part of your class work can be conducted online. There are obviously problems inherent in attempting to make complex connections through e-mail, especially if some of your students do not have easy access to the Internet or the time to use it. Students who are working full-time or who do not have a home computer may not be able to take advantage of e-mail, for instance. Even so, e-mail allows you to communicate easily with your students away from class, allows students to share drafts with each other, and allows them to send drafts to you for comment.

Many teachers also use Web-based discussion pages for conversation outside of class. A Web-based discussion page is a kind of private electronic bulletin board that allows you and your students to post messages and receive responses on the same thread or to start new threads. An advantage of Web-based discussion is that the discussion is stored and archived on the Web and can be accessed from any place you or your students have an Internet connection. If your school does not provide a Web-based discussion page for you, you can set one up yourself at www.free-forums.org.

Other technological support for your pedagogy might include using online textbooks or supplementing printed texts with online articles or essays. Many publishers that sell composition textbooks, including Bedford/St. Martin's (**bcs.bedfordstmartins.com/select**), also allow you to create your own custom reader online by choosing from a substantial list of readings. In addition, many textbooks have companion Web sites that offer support and information for both teachers and students, including interactive exercises, sample assignments, and model student essays. In addition to book-specific sites, many publishers provide helpful general resources for teachers and students.

Increasingly, composition teachers are asking students to create multimodal projects, ones that incorporate visuals and audio. Note, for example, the final assignment in Jessica Enoch's sample syllabus included in this chapter (pp. 15–30). Enoch builds on more traditional writing assignments by teaching students skills of argumentation, awareness of rhetorical situations, and support and by allowing students to use all available means of persuasion as they present their projects to the class. (For specific assignments and resources for multimodal composing, see Cynthia Selfe's *Multimodal Composition*, cited at the end of this chapter.)

LINKS TO COMMUNITY ENGAGEMENT: SERVICE LEARNING, COMMUNITY-BASED LITERACY PROJECTS, AND PUBLIC WRITING INITIATIVES

The past twenty years have seen burgeoning interest in the idea of service learning, community-based literacy projects, and public writing initiatives — combining standard classroom work with the movement of students out into the community, where they engage in various kinds of writing and community service as part of the course activity. Such initiatives have gained considerable momentum as a result of the power of Mike Rose's *Lives on the Boundary*, a book that movingly details the struggle for literacy that underprepared students must engage in. Service learning, community-based literacy projects, and public writing initiatives foster connections between students and local communities. Public writing initiatives also give students valuable professional writing experience. (See, for example, the Penn State Public Writing Initiative in the list of useful Web sites at the end of this chapter.) Community service by college students is a particularly promising concept in writing courses, which are always involved with seeking meaningful issues for students to write about. A number of respected writing programs at both state and private schools have incorporated community service and community-based literacy projects as an important part of some of their first-year courses. (See Adler-Kassner, Crooks, and Watters; Deans, Roswell, and Wurr; Flower; Herzberg; Mathieu; and Schutz and Gere, cited at the end of this chapter.)

There are many ways for students to involve themselves either in a community literacy outreach program or in writing for businesses, civic groups, or other organizations. Literacy outreach activities can include working in a variety of off-campus educational settings ranging from public schools to homeless shelters, community centers, social-service offices, public libraries, and the Internet. Students involved in such projects may work with businesses, schoolchildren, welfare clients, adults struggling with literacy issues, single parents, or second-language speakers trying to improve their English. Some may gain experience writing grants and Web sites. The placements students seek will depend largely on your pedagogical goals and the kinds of learning and writing experiences that will best meet those goals. Placements can also be influenced by students' interests and available sites.

A writing program that has a vital community-engagement component can be exciting for both teacher and students because it invests the whole course with an identifiable purpose and gives every student experiences to detail in writing. Writing assignments suggest themselves almost automatically, and involvement in the literacy practices of others helps students reflect on their own writing. When community engagement works, as Bruce Herzberg says, students' writing shows "a sense of life as a communal project, an understanding of the way that social institutions affect our lives, and a sense that our responsibility for social justice includes but also carries on beyond personal acts of charity" (317). Working with people who are less educated and often less fortunate can be a true revelation for first-year college students, many of whom have never been discriminated against. Especially in schools with a multicultural population, service-related values can help define what a writing program is about.

If your program has a community-engagement component, you will probably need to ask your WPA about working within it. Even writing programs that include community service and public writing initiatives as important parts of their work may not ask or even allow first-time teachers to take part in the service component, preferring to work with more experienced teachers. Speak with your WPA about making community connections for your students. If your program does not have such a component, perhaps you can work up some interest in starting one. Successful community partnerships require tight and effective coordination between a teacher or program and community organizations, and experience shows that firm relations between the agency and writing program must be established *before* the program begins in order for it to be effective. Some shelters or community centers will accept any sort of tutoring or teaching, even if it is only short-term, but many ask that tutors agree to work with their clients over longer terms. Community engagement is best accomplished in the context of a program that believes in and has committed to it. So if you feel drawn to working with your local community as part of your course, plan to get involved for the long haul. (For online resources, see the Web sites for Campus Compact, ABCD Books, National Service-Learning Clearinghouse, and National Writing Project Resources, listed at the end of this chapter.)

CREATING A SYLLABUS

Writing the syllabus is your next major task. The syllabus provides an overview of, and a plan for, the entire course: the forms your classes will take, the sorts of writing assignments you will require, the order of the material you plan to teach, and so forth. After you have read through this book, talked with your colleagues, and carefully looked over your chosen texts, you should be ready to make a rough draft of your plan. Formalized, this draft will be the basis for the central document of your course, the syllabus.

The syllabus for college courses originated as a list of the books for which every student was to be held responsible. Now, a syllabus is more encompassing. The syllabus for a FY writing course states the responsibilities of the teacher and the students as well as the standards for the course. Everyone concerned, from your department administrators to the parents of incoming students, may want to know your exact plans and expectations. Such a written document has other uses: For instance, it shows a student, who feels maltreated or wants special privileges, your position on the issue in question, whether it is your attendance policy or your due-date policy. To protect yourself and your students from potential misunderstanding, a detailed syllabus that clearly spells out your purposes and policies is best.

The syllabus also informs the structure of the class, explaining what the course will cover, when it will be covered, and what your qualitative and quantitative expectations are. In other words, the syllabus saves you from having to repeat explanations of course policies, goals, and dates. It is also the first written expression of your personality that you will present to your students. Although many elements of the syllabus will be constructed by the requirements of your program, writing it also gives you a chance to reflect philosophically on what you are asking of your students and why you are asking it. What does it mean that you are asking for six five-page essays rather than three ten-page essays? Why are you (or your department) refusing to allow more than three absences? What do you want students to gain from using an anthology? a handbook? Your syllabus asks you to answer those questions in a practical way.

Syllabi for writing courses usually need to be detailed for a number of reasons, not the least of which is that few students have developed a set of expectations and intentions for composition courses. Just as important is the fact that students deserve to see their assignments written out. If you write out the assignments, you take the time to explain what it is you want your students to do and be able to do. By following the outline presented here, you should be able to create a syllabus that fills all your major needs and answers all your students' major questions. This outline will not lead you to produce an exhaustive syllabus, but it is a good model for first-time teachers because of its simplicity and schematic development. Keep in mind that although few teachers adhere unconditionally to their syllabi, fewer still depart from them seriously. (See the two sample syllabi in this chapter, pp. 15 and 31.)

1. *Your name, the course number, your office address, classroom location, your office hours, your e-mail address, and your office telephone number.* Office hours are those periods when you must be in your office so that students may drop by without an appointment. If your department does not require a minimum number of office hours, a rule of thumb is that you should schedule as many office hours as your course has contact hours — hours you are in the classroom with your students.

For example, if your class meets five hours a week, set aside five hours a week for your office hours. (In a conferencing system, these would include hours spent in conference. See pp. 79–82 for more information on conferences.) Although teachers can generally choose their office hours, immediately before or after class can be the most convenient times for teachers as well as students. Try to schedule office hours on two successive days so that students who come in only on Mondays, Wednesdays, and Fridays or only on Tuesdays and Thursdays have a chance of seeing you.

2. *Course description goals.* Whether this is a departmental statement that must be included in the syllabus or a personal definition of your objectives for the course, some statement of goals should be included. It should mention the number of graded assignments, the basic skills that will be expected of each student by the end of the course, the importance of student participation, and the level of competency in writing each student will need to demonstrate in order to pass the course. You can also include a personal message about the course and its expectations.

3. *Information about the textbooks.* This includes the author, title, edition, and publication information for each text. You should also note whether there is an e-reader version of the textbook — and which version you would prefer your students to have with them in class. If you wish students to purchase any supplementary materials (course packets, for example), purchasing details should be included.

4. *Course policy.* Include in this section your policies on the following:
   a. Attendance — how many absences you allow and what you will do if that number is exceeded. You'll need to see whether the department has a policy on this before making your own.
   b. Tardiness — what you will do about students who consistently come to class late.
   c. Participation — how much, if any, of the final course grade will depend on classroom participation.
   d. Late papers — whether and under what conditions you will accept written assignments after their due dates.
   e. Style of papers — what you will demand by way of the physical format for graded assignments: what format students must use for citing sources (usually MLA), whether papers must be single- or double-spaced, and so forth.
   f. Reminders — include a statement asking students to turn off cell phones and disruptive electronic devices before entering the classroom.
   g. Plagiarism policy — Most colleges and universities have an official statement about plagiarism and academic honesty. Be sure to make students aware of such official statements and the consequences of academic dishonesty.

5. *Course requirements.* Discuss the following features of written work:
   a. The number and length of essays to be submitted for grading; your policy on revision.
   b. The requirements for keeping a journal or reading log, an explanation of the assignment, and how or whether it will be applied to the final grade (optional).
   c. Any explanation of a policy on ungraded homework, in-class writing assignments, drafts, online discussion postings, and so forth and how or whether ungraded work will apply to the final grade.
6. *Grading procedures.* Here you set forth the procedures you will follow in evaluating and grading written work. You do not have to discuss the standards that will be applied; you may merely detail how you will deal with assignments in order to arrive at final grades. Include a listing of the percentage value of each piece of written work as it applies to the final grade and, if you are using a revision option, a detailed review of how it works. The statement needs to be spelled out in detail; otherwise, students may be confused and may not do the required amount of work.
7. *Grading standards.* This section is optional; many teachers do not like to spell out the standards they will use in any quantitative or prescriptive way. Nevertheless, many departments have created grading standards that must be used by all teachers, and they may require that these standards be published in the syllabus. If a section on grading standards is included, it can contain the following:
   a. Standards of content — the levels of semantic and organizational expertise (a clear thesis, support of assertions, coherently developed paragraphs and arguments, and so forth) that must be apparent in a passing essay.
   b. Standards of form — the impact of serious syntactic errors (sentence fragments, comma splices, run-ons, and so forth) and of lesser errors (in spelling, punctuation, and usage) in "acceptable" essays.
8. *Meetings.* Specify how many days per week the course will meet, on which days, and any special information about specific events — for instance, workshop meetings, in-class writing assignments, or regular due dates that will always fall on the same day of the week.
9. *Additional information and resources.* Your department may designate a director of writing or an ombudsperson for handling students' questions and complaints. If so, you may be required to list the pertinent information on your syllabus: names, office numbers, office hours, official capacity, policy on confidentiality, and so forth. In this section, you can also list additional resources for students, including information on the writing center, the office of disability services, the study skills center, and other resources available at your school. You should make clear in this section that you will make reasonable accommodations for students with diagnosed disabilities.

10. *Course calendar.* Course calendars may be simple or complex. The only essential element is a listing of the due dates for reading and writing assignments. The calendar can also contain detailed information on skills to be worked on, goals to be met, and a host of other information. Whether you choose to include this more detailed material will depend on the degree to which you want to structure your course beforehand.

The preceding ten points make up the essential elements of a composition syllabus. Other sections can be added, of course, but these are the ones needed for your protection and for your students' understanding of the course.

To have your syllabus ready for distribution on the first day of class, avoid the inevitable rush and get your photocopying done as early as possible. Make more copies than there are students on your roster; a rule of thumb is to increase the number by one-third: If you have twenty-four students on your roster, make thirty-two copies of the syllabus. Students who drop the class will carry off their copies, and students who join the class late will need copies; others will lose theirs and ask for new ones. If you plan to use a course-management system, you should also post your syllabus online.

SAMPLE SYLLABI

Following are two sample syllabi for FY writing. The first one, written by Jessica Enoch for a FY writing class at the University of Maryland, uses a handbook and readings posted on a course-management site. It includes all the basic information — plus much more: resources, assignments, and a course schedule. The second syllabus, prepared by Paul M. Kellermann for an honors FY writing class at Penn State University, uses a rhetorically arranged reader, readings available through a course Web page, a style guide, and a book about argument. In addition to a course description, policies, and schedule, Kellermann's syllabus provides a glimpse of Kellermann's personality: note the humor and simultaneous seriousness. We have abridged these syllabi but left much of the important information that will give you ideas for preparing your own syllabi.

Sample Syllabus 1.1   **ACADEMIC WRITING**

Academic Writing
English 101

Professor: E-mail:
Meeting time: Office:
Meeting place: Office hours:

Course Description

What does it mean to be an effective communicator? While this question has
both invigorated and plagued thinkers for (literally) thousands of years, one
theorist's answer has proved particularly compelling. In the fourth century BCE,
Aristotle posited that effective communication was grounded in rhetoric: the
"art of observing the available means of persuasion." For Aristotle and many
after him, to be a successful communicator (or rhetor) meant that one first
assesses the context of a communicative moment — the rhetorical situation —
and then makes use of the *available* persuasive strategies that suit that context.
Through reading the rhetorical situation, the rhetor considers her audience's
interests and expectations, the distinctive resources she can make use of, as
well as the constraints that impinge on the rhetorical transaction, and then
she tailors her writing accordingly.

Thus, whether a rhetor is composing an essay about the Civil War for
his history professor or creating an iMovie about crime prevention for his UMD
peers, he will most likely create a strong composition when he begins his work
by asking and answering rhetorically inflected questions such as these: Who is
my audience? What are the audience's expectations? What are my goals and
objectives? What is the context of this writing task (academic, civic, personal)?
What genre of writing (report, position piece, multimedia essay) will best help
me to reach both my goals and my audience's expectations?

Over the course of this semester, you will fine-tune your rhetorical skills
by addressing questions such as these. To take up this work, you will identify
an issue that interests and excites you, and then you will spend the semester

experimenting with various ways to discuss this issue with an audience of your choice. Your goal for each assignment will be to observe the means of persuasion available to you and then to make use of the rhetorical strategies that best suit your interests, the context, and your audience's expectations. By semester's end, you will have had multiple opportunities to gain rhetorical expertise, and this expertise should provide the foundation for effective communication throughout your academic career and beyond.

Course Text

Glenn, Cheryl. *The Harbrace Guide to Writing*. Concise ed. Boston: Wadsworth, 2012.

Class Policies and Procedure

Requirements:

You will be expected to

- attend all class meetings and conferences, prepared (see attendance policy below);
- participate in class discussions;
- participate in all draft workshops;
- complete all course readings;
- compose and submit all Blackboard posts;
- compose and submit all proposals for major projects;
- compose and submit each course writing project;
- present your multimodal essay during the final week of classes;
- submit all work **<u>on time</u>** (on the hour/day it is due; **late papers will normally be docked one letter grade per day**, unless you get my approval for an extension before the due date).

Attendance:

As noted above, regular attendance is required. You are permitted a total of **two** absences over the course of the semester. If you miss a third class, your final grade will drop by one letter. For example, if you were going to earn a B in the class but were absent three times, you would earn a C instead.

If you miss four classes over the course of the semester, you will fail the class.

Regular attendance also means that you come to class on time and that you attend all scheduled conferences. I take attendance at the beginning of each class session. If you are more than five minutes late for class, you will be considered absent for that day and that absence will count toward your two excused absences. We will also have scheduled office conferences throughout the semester. If you miss a meeting, I will count it as a class absence.

It is your responsibility to get the assignments, class notes, and course changes from a classmate if you do miss a class. It is also your responsibility to keep track of and complete the missing work. In-class work cannot be made up. If you miss class on the day a written assignment is due, make arrangements to send it along with a classmate. As mentioned above, every day the paper is late the grade drops by one letter grade.

Grades:

To pass this course, you must complete five major writing projects and post all of your response posts. Your attendance and class participation will also affect your final grade for the course.

Blackboard Posts:	5%
Assignment #1/Annotated Bibliography:	10%
Assignment #2/Report:	20%
Assignment #3/Position Argument:	20%
Assignment #4/Proposal:	20%
Assignment #5/Multimodal Essay:	20%
Class Participation:	5% — lowest I've ever seen.

unless participation isn't impt to goals

If you have any questions about a grade, please see me during office hours, and I will be happy to discuss your grade with you.

Office Conferences:

Think of my office as an extension of the classroom, and use my office hours to discuss any aspect of your reading or writing. Come to my office with questions concerning course readings or class discussions, writing techniques or strategies, writing projects you're working on, ideas you wish to develop, and so on. During my open office hours, you may stop in my office whenever you like. I am also happy to schedule another time to meet if the office hours conflict with your schedule.

We will most likely have scheduled one-on-one meetings in my office, and these meetings are **mandatory**. If you cannot attend a scheduled meeting, please e-mail me at least two hours before our planned time. If you miss a meeting without e-mailing, I will count it as a class absence.

would we have one?

Writing Center:

All students should consider visiting the tutors at the university Writing Center as a way to improve the overall quality of their writing. The Writing Center is for all student writers — including those who see themselves as strong writers. It is an excellent resource for you; please take advantage of it.

Cell Phone Policy:

Please turn off your cell phone during class and put it in your schoolbag. Texting during class will not be tolerated. If you are found texting, you will be counted absent for the session.

University Policies — *Does Sant'Anna have these?*

1. Students with disabilities should contact the instructor at the beginning of the semester to discuss any accommodation for this course.
2. The University has approved a **Code of Academic Integrity** (www.shc.umd.edu/code.html) that prohibits students from cheating on exams, plagiarizing papers, submitting the same paper for credit in two courses without authorization, buying papers, facilitating academic dishonesty, submitting fraudulent documents, and forging signatures. Plagiarism policy: All quotations taken from other authors, including from the Internet, must be indicated by quotation marks and referenced. Paraphrasing must be referenced as well.

3. Religious observance: Please inform your instructor of any intended absences for religious observance well in advance.

4. Regular attendance and participation in this class are the best way to grasp the concepts and principles being discussed. However, in the event that a class must be missed due to an illness, the policy in this class is as follows:

- For every medically necessary absence from class (lecture, recitation, or lab), a reasonable effort should be made to notify the instructor in advance of the class. When returning to class, students must bring a note identifying the date of and reason for the absence, acknowledging that the information in the note is accurate.

- If a student is absent more than two times, the instructor may require documentation signed by a health care professional.

- If a student is absent on days when tests are scheduled or papers are due *[or other such events as specified in the syllabus]*, he or she is required to notify the instructor in advance and, upon returning to class, to bring documentation of the illness signed by a health care professional.

Course Assignments

Blackboard Posts (5%; 400 words):

In addition to the five major projects for the course, you will post writing to the discussion board on our course-management page. These posts enable you to reflect on course readings, plan for writing projects, and prepare for class discussion. This is a pressure-free writing zone. You will not be graded on your ideas or your writing in the individual responses. Rather, your grade for this component of the course is strictly dependent on your dedicated participation in these online discussions.

You can find the prompts for the posts on the discussion board page on Blackboard and at the end of this document.

Your posts are due by 10 AM on the day designated on the course schedule.

Assignment #1: Annotated Bibliography (10%; no page range):

Your first project for the semester will enable you to identify and learn more about the issue you will engage for the entire semester. Since you will be writing about this issue for almost four months, approaching it from different angles, you want to choose wisely and be sure this issue is one that not only interests and excites you but also one that can sustain a long-term discussion. Assignment #1 should ensure you that you've made a wise choice. Here you will identify ten sources that enable you to learn more about your issue and compose an *annotated* bibliography for these sources.

It is of vital importance that you choose your resources wisely. Identify resources that extend your understanding. Each source should offer a new perspective.

Your annotated bibliography should follow the example below. In each annotation you should (1) cite the text of your choice in perfect MLA format; (2) summarize the text or article; and (3) discuss how the text will help you gain a deeper sense of the issue and how you might use the source in Assignment #2, the report.

hooks, bell. *Feminism Is for Everybody: Passionate Politics.* Cambridge: South End P, 2000. Print.

> hooks's text works to define what feminism is to an uniformed, and possibly resistant, audience. Her goal is to dispel negative perceptions of feminists as "men haters" and instead to offer a new, more positive explanation of this political position. Feminism, for hooks, is a "move-ment to end sexism, sexist exploitation, and oppression," and she notes that anyone can be a feminist if he or she works toward this end (viii). Her chapters — "Our Bodies, Ourselves," "Feminist Class Struggle," and "Global Feminism" (just to name a few) — reinforce her overall aims, as hooks attempts at every turn to explain feminist issues to readers in a generous and welcoming tone. This semester, I plan to re-define feminism for students here at UMD. Her definitions of what feminism is will be particularly important for my purposes in the report.

Due: Friday, Feb. 2; posted to Blackboard by 5 PM (with reflective memo)

Assignment #2: Report (20%; 4–6 pages):

Writers use reports in a variety of situations to explain an issue to an invested audience. When a writer feels the need to educate readers about an issue and delve deeply into the concerns that issue raises for his audience, the genre of the report is often a good one to choose. And while genres such as reports are certainly not templates for writing tasks, they do often work toward certain objectives. The genre of the report, as *The Harbrace Guide to Writing* explains, has the following features:

- A report defines an issue in precise terms.
- A report makes clear why the issue is one that needs to be investigated.
- A report provides convincing facts to help readers understand how the issue affects different groups.
- A report uses direct quotations to vividly convey the perspectives of various groups with a stake in the issue.
- A report clearly identifies the conclusion readers should reach about the issue (166).

Your work for Assignment #2 is to compose a report on the issue of your choice for the audience of your choice. Your annotated bibliography should provide you with the research necessary to compose your report, and, of course, you are welcome and encouraged to continue researching your issue as you work on the report and as the semester progresses. Whether you are informing UMD students about innovative ways to "green" their dorm rooms or writing to members of your community about an upcoming local election, you want to use this opportunity to explain your concerns for your audience and persuade the audience members that this issue should capture their attention.

Due: Friday, Feb. 24; posted to Blackboard by 5 PM (with reflective memo)

Assignment #3: Position Argument (20%; 4–6 pages):

Rhetorical situations call for position arguments all the time. Faced with the threat of more development in the community, a resident might compose a position argument that challenges the invasion of big businesses and asks other residents to protest additional building. Concerned by the university's unstated support of sweatshop labor, a student might write an editorial to the

school newspaper or a petition to the university president that calls for the
university to rethink its corporate sponsorship and university apparel provider.
And of course students are asked to offer their "positions" or arguments all
the time during final exams or for writing projects (such as this one!) as a
way of enabling professors to gain insight on student engagement with
course topics.

For Assignment #3, you will compose a position argument regarding
the issue of your choice, writing to the audience of your choice. As *The
Harbrace Guide to Writing* explains, position arguments often feature the
following:

- Arguments vividly describe a problem or issue.
- Arguments are directed toward an audience with a clear connection to
  or investment in the problem being addressed.
- Arguments include a concise statement of the writer's point of view.
- Arguments provide reasons in support of the writer's position, and each
  supporting reason takes into account the audience's beliefs, attitudes,
  and values.
- Arguments contain specific evidence — details, examples, and direct
  quotations — to back each supporting reason.
- Arguments describe the benefits that will be achieved by responding
  to the writer's position in the intended way or the negative situation
  that will result from ignoring it. (205)

In creating your position argument, you'll want to explore each of these
genre features, identifying ways for you to compose the strongest argument
possible. Expanding your research from the annotated bibliography and report,
you also might identify opportunities for observation (see pp. 376–86 in *HGW*);
to prepare for Assignment #5, the multimodal essay, you may choose to video-
record your observations. Finally, as you compose your argument, you will want
to offer a perspective that builds on, but is distinctive from, the work you did
in Assignment #2, the report. You want to sustain a conversation with your
audience members by offering them a fresh, new perspective here.

Due: Friday, Mar. 16; posted to Blackboard by 5 PM (with reflective memo)

Assignment #4: Proposal (20%; 4–6 pages):

Like the report and position argument, proposals are used by writers every day to accomplish very specific ends. Making use of the genre of the proposal, writers attempt to solve problems by mapping out steps for readers to follow. For instance, if a student wants to solve the problem of unsafe social options for her peers, she might propose a set of safe (and fun) Friday night events for her campus community. Here, she would need to consider questions of *feasibility.* That is, in addition to thinking about the kinds of events the university should hold, she would also need to consider where these events take place, how much they would cost, who would pay for them, and how they would be advertised. By addressing questions such as these, the student would compose a proposal.

On p. 247, *The Harbrace Guide to Writing* elaborates on the features of a proposal:

- There is a clear, identifiable problem that the proposal seeks to resolve.
- This problem is of concern to a significant number of people.
- The proposed solution will resolve the problem in a way these people will find acceptable.
- The proposal contains specific details about the costs and benefits of the solution.
- The proposal is directed to the appropriate audience and demonstrates a good understanding of that audience's needs and interests.
- The proposal clearly explains the steps or processes required to enact the solution.

As you compose your proposal, you'll want to draw from the work you've accomplished in Assignments #1–3, creating a piece that underscores not only the fact that there *is* a problem but also that you've identified a way to solve it. In the process of exploring ideas for your proposal, you might also consider what *other* people or institutions have done. Going back to the example above, the student interested in creating a safer campus social life might investigate how peer institutions have addressed this issue. What, for instance, has the University of Delaware or Penn State done? What kinds of activities has the

University proposed and carried out? Such examples will reinforce the feasibility and acceptability of the plan for students here at UMD.

Finally, for this assignment, we'll also be considering possibilities for interviewing as another mode of research, so you may identify possible interview subjects, generate questions, and then interview. As you did in Assignment #3, you may also ask permission to video-record these interviews to use them in Assignment #5, the multimodal essay.

Due: Friday, Apr. 13; posted to Blackboard by 5 PM (with reflective memo)

Assignment #5: Multimodal Essay (20%; 2–3 minutes to view):

For each of the projects you have completed this semester, you have explored how to engage a particular rhetorical situation and speak to a particular audience about a particular issue. You're doing the same work here in Assignment #5. However, instead of accomplishing these ends through traditional means of delivery (typed papers), you'll create a *multimodal* essay that speaks to your audience about your issue.

Like Assignments #2–4, you'll draw on your past work to create a new rhetorical intervention for your audience. This time, however, you'll experiment with the ways audio and image can enhance your ends. Using platforms such as iMovie, you'll create a multimodal essay that engages your audience members and captures their attention in a new way. As Chapter 10 in *The Harbrace Guide to Writing* makes clear, when composers create multimedia projects such as this one, they still need to address the basic rhetorical concerns of audience, rhetorical situation, available means, and constraints. Your work will be to explore how your past experiences with the report, position argument, and proposal (as well as with observation and interviewing) can be translated and elaborated on in this multimodal essay. Thus, in this assignment, you will choose what your particular intervention might be; whatever it is, you want to make sure it is purposeful and effective.

You will present your multimodal essay to the class during the final week of class. This presentation is a mandatory part of the assignment.

During finals week, you will submit your final essay, along with a reflective memo that explains your rhetorical decisions for the project.

Note: There will surely be varying degrees of student expertise with media and video. The final weeks of the course are designed to help students learn the basics of iMovie and to work from their level of comfort and expertise.

Due: Either Wednesday, May 2 or Monday, May 7 (in class)

Course Schedule   *love this organization*

DAY	SESSION TOPIC	READING DUE	WRITING DUE
Week 1 M 1/24	Course Introductions; What Is Rhetoric?; Issues on Campus; Assignment #1: Annotated Bibliography; and Assignment #2: Report		
Week 2 M 1/30	Exploring Issues on Campus; Understanding the Rhetorical Situation; Report	*HGW*, pp. 1–24	Bb Post #1
W 2/1	Reports; Proposal	*HGW*, pp. 142–58	
F 2/3			Proposal for Assignment #2 Due by 5 PM (post to Bb)
Week 3 M 2/6	Reports: Researching the Issue, Exploring Databases	*HGW*, pp. 363–75	
W 2/8	Researching the Issue; Writing an Annotated Bibliography	*HGW*, pp. 407–14 **Bring to class five potential sources for Assignment #1**	Bb Post #2

DAY	SESSION TOPIC	READING DUE	WRITING DUE
Week 4 M 2/13	Annotated Bibliography to Report; Audience Analysis	*HGW*, pp. 158–77 *bolded imp + assignments* (handwritten)	**Assignment #1 Due + Reflective Memo** (post by 5 PM and bring to class)
W 2/15	Annotated Bibliography to Report; Rhetorical Methods of Development; What Is a Draft Workshop?	*HGW*, pp. 306–14	
Week 5 M 2/20	Draft Workshop for Assignment #2: Report	*HGW*, pp. 403–07	Draft Assignment #2; Group 1 Submit Drafts by 5 PM Sunday 2/19
W 2/22	Draft Workshop for Assignment #2; Introduce Assignment #3: Position Argument	*HGW*, pp. 403–07 (start with "Paraphrasing"); pp. 205–13	Draft Assignment #2
F 2/24			**Assignment #2 Due by 5 PM + Reflective Memo** (post to Bb)
Week 6 M 2/27	Assignment #3: Position Argument	*HGW*, pp. 178–204	
W 2/29	Assignment #3: Position Argument; Conducting Research; Proposal	*HGW*, pp. 376–86	Bb Post #3

DAY	SESSION TOPIC	READING DUE	WRITING DUE
F 3/2			Proposal for Assignment #3 Due by 5 PM (post to Bb)
Week 7 M 3/5	Assignment #3: Position Argument; A Fitting Response; Audience Analysis	*HGW*, pp. 205–13	
W 3/7	Outlining Position Argument; Defining a Thesis	*HGW*, pp. 318–20	Bb Post #4
Week 8 M 3/12	Draft Workshop for Assignment #3		Draft Assignment #3; Group 2 Submit Drafts by 5 PM Sunday 3/11
W 3/14	Draft Workshop for Assignment #3; Introduce Assignment #4: Proposal		Draft Assignment #3
F 3/16			**Assignment #3 Due + Reflective Memo** (post by 5 PM to Bb)
Week 9 M 3/19	Spring Break		
W 3/21	Spring Break		
Week 10 M 3/26	Assignment #4: Proposal	*HGW*, pp. 224–41	Bb Post #5
W 3/28	Assignment #4: Proposal	*HGW*, pp. 241–52	

DAY	SESSION TOPIC	READING DUE	WRITING DUE
F 3/30			Proposal for Assignment #4 Due by 5 PM (post to Bb)
Week 11 M 4/2	Conducting Research (Interviews); Audience Analysis	*HGW*, pp. 386–92	
W 4/4	Process Analysis; Feasibility	*HGW*, pp. 314–16	Bb Post #6
Week 12 M 4/9	Draft Workshop		Draft Assignment #4; Group 3 Submit Drafts by 5 PM Sunday 4/8
W 4/11	Draft Workshop; Introduce Assignment #5; What Makes a Good iMovie?		Draft Assignment #4
F 4/13			**Assignment #4 Due + Reflective Memo** (post by 5 PM to Bb)
Week 13 M 4/16	Assignment #5: Multimedia; Drawing from Assignments #1–4; Audience Analysis	*HGW*, pp. 328–48	Bring Assignments #1–4 to Class
W 4/18	What Makes a Good Multimodal Essay?; How to Make a Multimodal Essay; Creative Commons	TBA	Bb Post #7

DAY	SESSION TOPIC	READING DUE	WRITING DUE
F 4/20			Proposals for Assignment #5 Due
Week 14 M 4/23	Planning; Storyboard Workshop; Drawing from Assignments #1–4		Bring Storyboards for Assignment #5 to Class
W 4/25	Lab Day		
Week 15 M 4/30	Draft Workshop		Draft Assignment #5
W 5/2	Presentations: Group 1		Group 1: Send essay to me by 9 AM Weds.
Week 16 M 5/7	Presentations: Group 2		Group 2: Send essay to me by 9 AM Mon.
Finals Week	Final Assignments Due		**Assignment #5 Due + Reflective Memo** (post to Bb); Group 3: Send essay to me by 9 AM Mon.

Blackboard Prompts

Below please find the prompts you will respond to on our discussion board page.

Bb Post #1 (due 1/30):

Identify five pressing issues that you might consider writing about this semester. Write about each issue, explaining what the issue is and why you're interested in it. Also note the audience you might speak to regarding this issue.

Bb Post #2 (due 2/8):

What are you learning from the sources you've identified thus far? What other information are you looking for? What kind of help would you like regarding research processes? What questions do you have?

Bb Post #3 (due 2/29):

Use this Blackboard post to consider your possibilities for your position argument. (1) Identify two possible arguments you might make regarding your issue and write about them here. (2) Identify four new research sources as well as one observation opportunity.

Bb Post #4 (due 3/7):

Use this Blackboard post to continue working on your position argument by considering the following questions: What is your claim? How is this a claim that can be argued and responded to? How will you create common ground with your audience? What kinds of ethical appeals might you make? What kinds of logical appeals might you make? What kinds of pathetic appeals might you make? How might you integrate examples into your essay? What questions and concerns do you have?

Bb Post #5 (due 3/26):

Go to p. 241 in the *HGW*. Respond to questions 1–7 under "Analyzing the Rhetorical Situation."

Bb Post #6 (due 4/4):

Use the discussion on *HGW* pp. 314–16 to guide your work in this post. How might you break your ideas for your proposal into a series of ordered steps? How does the discussion here help you invent possibilities for your proposal?

Bb Post #7 (4/18):

Review the multimodal essays for this session. What do you find to be the qualities that support an effective multimodal essay? What do you admire here? What concerns you?

Sample Syllabus 1.2   **HONORS FRESHMAN COMPOSITION**

English 30
Professor:

Office:
E-mail:
Phone:
Office Hours:

Course Policies and Procedures

Course Texts

Primary Texts:

Cheryl Glenn, *Making Sense — A Real-World Rhetorical Reader,* Third Edition
William Strunk and E. B. White, *The Elements of Style*
Anthony Weston, *A Rulebook for Arguments*, Fourth Edition
Penn State University Policy Statements

Additional Texts:

The New York Times
The Centre Daily Times
The Daily Collegian
USA Today
The world around you

Suggested Resources:

William Zinsser, *On Writing Well*
A good college dictionary
An open mind, copious curiosity, and a thirst for knowledge

Course Description

P. T. Barnum famously said: "There's a sucker born every minute." But are
suckers born or made? And what, if anything, can we do to avoid slipping into
suckerhood? In this class, we will explore the rudiments of argumentation by

examining the rhetoric of everyday life — the profound, the mundane, and most things in between. In between. *Don't be fooled by cheap imitations.* In this class, we will sharpen our rhetorical acumen by learning to communicate with a *coherent* sense of purpose and audience (through a *strategic* deployment of argument and design). *It's new and improved.* In this class, we will approach composition as a process — a process that begins with listening. And understanding. *It's old-fashioned.* Instruction will be based on the Socratic method of inquiry with copious discussion, considerable reading, and incessant writing. And rewriting. And rewriting. And rewriting. *It's just that simple.* English 30 asks not simply for self-expression but for *participation* in the public discourse. *Void where prohibited.*

Requirements

To pass this course (with a grade of C or better), you must satisfactorily fulfill the following requirements:

<u>Write four papers</u>. Each paper must be submitted *in a folder*, along with rough draft(s), signed peer-review comments from draft workshops, and all other materials that represent the stages of the paper's development (including photocopies and printouts from any research sources used), along with a revised argument proposal. Papers must be handed in *on time*. Late papers will be docked one letter grade per day, unless you get my approval for an extension *before* the due date. In addition, you will submit a soft copy of each paper to the designated drop box on Angel *before* the paper is due.

<u>Complete the Library Research assignment.</u>

<u>Participate online</u>. Each week, you will post a meditation (100–200 words) on Angel by Friday at 6:00 PM. Most weeks, I will provide you with writing prompts to stir your creative juices. You will respond to at least two of your classmates' postings (by Sunday at 11:59 PM). In addition, there will be open discussion boards and targeted forums for you to exchange ideas with classmates. Engagement is the key, and I encourage you to engage your classmates in lively discussion. But I also expect your postings to be thoughtful and prepared with due diligence. Sloppy posts containing misspellings, poor mechanics, and random capitalization will only serve to damage your credibil-

ity. Toward this end, I suggest that you compose your messages in a word-processing program and then copy and paste onto the discussion board.

Be here. I take it as a personal insult when students don't show up for my class. If I don't see a classroom full of smiling faces, I tend to become ornery. Come to class; I'll try to make it worth your while. *You will be allowed three unexcused absences; any more and your grade will suffer.* If you miss a class, it is your responsibility to get the assignments — hint: You might try e-mailing me with a lame excuse in a show of feigned sincerity.

Be here on time. Tardiness will not be tolerated.

Come to class prepared and *participate*. A reading assignment and/or a writing assignment will be due for every class. You will be expected to come to class with *all* your assignments completed. You will also be expected to take part in frank, free, uninhibited, open (yet civil) discourse. Your opinion counts; everyone's opinion counts. Be unabashed, be forthright, but be courteous. If it is apparent that you have come to class unprepared, I will ask you to leave.

Listen attentively. More than most, this course requires you to hone your listening skills. I expect you to listen carefully to your instructor (me) and your classmates — being a successful participant requires you to be a successful listener. As such, your participation grade will be assessed qualitatively, taking your listening skills into account. Students who refuse to listen courteously to their classmates or instructor will be asked to leave.

Participate in peer review. Not only is feedback crucial to you as a writer, but reading critically and offering constructive criticism to peers are skills essential for any writer to possess. For each major assignment, we will devote one class period to critiquing each other's drafts. Participation is mandatory. *Papers that have not been peer reviewed will not be graded.*

Enjoy yourself. It's later than you think.

Grades

To pass this course, you must satisfactorily meet *all* requirements. Grades on individual assignments reflect the quality of the work and will be assessed in accordance with the Department of English grading standards. Please note: English 30 is a cooperative experience, not a competitive one. Helping your classmates succeed will only help your grade. Your final grade will be computed as follows:

Paper #1 (This I Believe Essay)	10%
Paper #2 (Definition Essay)	15%
Paper #3 (Rhetorical Analysis)	20%
Paper #4 (Recommendation Essay)	25%
Online Meditations and Responses	15%
Library Research Assignment	5%
Participation, Homework, and Peer Review	10%

This class maintains a strict no-whining-about-grades policy. If you wish to discuss your papers and how you might improve your work, I will gladly meet with you. But the moment that you begin complaining about your grade, the discussion will end.

In fact, this class maintains a no-kvetching-about-anything policy. If you have a suggestion on how class can be improved, feel free to propose it (along with support on why your suggestion will lead to improvement). But please be aware that incessant grumbling damages your credibility and alienates the audience you are trying to persuade.

Office Conferences

Think of my office as an extension of the classroom, and use my office hours to discuss any aspect of your reading or writing: problems, questions, papers you're working on, ideas you wish to develop, strategies you'd like to try, and so on. I'm here to help you; I suggest you take advantage of my generosity. If you can't make it during my office hours, set up an appointment for some other time.

E-mail

I expect you to have an e-mail account and to check your e-mail daily. I often send additional assignments, corrections, clarifications, cancellations, announcements, and the occasional pep talk over e-mail. In addition, you will use e-mail to submit your argument proposals and some homework assignments. Argument proposals may be pasted into the e-mail message or sent as file attachments. Feel free to e-mail me any time about anything (within reason, that is); you can (generally) expect a prompt reply.

Format

Keep in mind that formats are rhetorical decisions but that normally your papers should be typed or word-processed, using blue or black ink, double-spaced, with 1-inch margins. Please use a standard 12-point serif font, and make sure the print is dark enough to be legible. Unless otherwise specified, no separate title page should be used. Place your name, the date, "English 30," and my name (Paul Kellermann) in the upper left-hand corner of the first page. In the upper right-hand corner, put the name of the assignment, the draft, and the word count. Place your title above the text on page 1 and double-space beneath it. The title should not be underlined. Page 1 need not be numbered, but page numbers should be placed (along with your last name) in the upper right-hand corner of all subsequent pages. Fasten the pages with a paper clip or staple. I expect all papers to be spell-checked (and the spell-check to be verified with a good old-fashioned dictionary) and to be relatively free of grammatical mistakes and typos. In other words, proofread your papers before you hand them in — or better yet, have someone proofread for you. *Your papers should be submitted in a folder with all earlier drafts and peer review/workshop comments.*

Paper Submission

You will submit *both* hard and soft copies of each paper. Hard copies are due at the beginning of class on the days listed on your syllabus. Soft copies should be uploaded to the designated dropboxes on Angel and turnitin.com *before* the hard copy is due.

Plagiarism

Penn State defines academic integrity as the pursuit of scholarly activity in an open, honest, and responsible manner. All students should act with personal integrity; respect other students' dignity, rights, and property; and help create and maintain an environment in which all can succeed through the fruits of their efforts.*

Dishonesty of any kind will not be tolerated in this course. Students who are found to be dishonest may receive academic sanctions and be reported to the University's Judicial Affairs Office for possible further disciplinary sanction.

Talking over your ideas and getting comments on your writing from friends are *not* plagiarism. Taking someone else's published or unpublished words and calling them your own *is* plagiarism: a synonym is *academic dishonesty*. As an academic exercise, students will submit soft copies of all papers to turnitin.com and view their papers' originality reports.

For further information, please consult the Department of English Plagiarism Policy and the Appendix in *Making Sense*.

Note to Students with Disabilities

Pennsylvania State University encourages qualified persons with disabilities to participate in its programs and activities. If you anticipate needing any type of accommodation in this course or have questions, please tell me as soon as possible.

A Seemingly Unnecessary Warning

This classroom is a cellular-free zone. I do not want to see cell phones, and I certainly don't want to hear them. Do yourself (and everyone) a favor: Disconnect before coming to class, and stow your phone away where it won't be a distraction. *If your cell phone rings during class, you will be asked to leave. If I see your cell phone at all, I will ask you to leave.*

I Can't Believe I Even Need to Mention This

Class is only seventy-five minutes long. Most healthy adults should be able to maintain for this length without taking a bathroom break. Nevertheless, you might consider attending to your bodily needs before class begins and/or waiting until class ends. If you have a medical condition that requires you to take frequent bathroom breaks, please inform me immediately.

*University Faculty Senate. "Academic Integrity (49–20)" in *Policies and Rules for Undergraduate Students*. Penn State. http://www.psu.edu/ufs/policies/47-00.html#49-20 (Revised July 6, 2011).

Have fun!

Course Schedule

Week 1: In the beginning . . .

Tuesday	Course Introduction Fumigation of Preconceived Notions
Thursday	*Making Sense*, Chapter 1 (pp. 3–34) *A Rulebook for Arguments*, Introduction (pp. xi–xiv) *The Elements of Style*, Introduction (pp. xiii–xviii) Majora Carter, "This Is Home" Albert Einstein, "An Ideal of Service to Our Fellow Man" Studs Terkel, "Community in Action" Bill Gates, "Unleashing the Power of Creativity" Read Assignment #1 (This I Believe)

Week 2: The second week

Tuesday	*Making Sense*, Chapter 2 (pp. 45–67) *The Elements of Style*, Rules of Usage 1–4 (pp. 1–5) Malcolm X, "Prison Studies" (*Making Sense*, pp. 68–72) David Sedaris, "Me Talk Pretty One Day" (*Making Sense*, pp. 81–85) Brian Eno, "The Key to a Long Life" Robert Fulghum, "Dancing All the Dances as Long as I Can"
Thursday	*A Rulebook for Arguments*, Chapter 1 (pp. 1–7) *The Elements of Style*, Rules of Usage 5–8 (pp. 5–9) Penn Jillette, "There Is No God" John Fountain, "The God Who Embraced Me When Daddy Disappeared" Elie Wiesel, "God Is God Because He Remembers"

Week 3: Sometimes I have a great notion . . .

Tuesday	*Making Sense*, Chapter 3 (pp. 119–41) *The Elements of Style*, Rules of Usage 9–11 (pp. 9–14) Stephanie Disney, "Seeing with the Heart" Susan Cooke Kittredge, "We All Need Mending" Gregg Rogers, "I Am Capable of More than I Think I Am" Tony Hawk, "Do What You Love"
Thursday	*Making Sense*, Chapter 1 (pp. 34–44) *The Elements of Style*, Principles of Composition 12–15 (pp. 15–20) Gilana Tahir, "The Importance of Remembering" Chris Brearly, "Making the Bed" Brittany Russo, "I Believe in Caring" Ryan Moraski, "Blaze Your Own Trail" Lyndsie Wszola, "I Believe in Eating My Convictions" William Zinsser, "Simplicity" and "Clutter" (Angel)

Week 4: Panic, the first paper's due . . .

Tuesday	Peer Review #1
Thursday	**Paper #1 Due: This I Believe Essay** This I Believe Readings

Week 5: You don't need a weatherman to know which way the wind blows

Tuesday	*Making Sense*, Chapter 9 (pp. 563–83) *The Elements of Style*, Principles of Composition 16–18 (pp. 21–26) Judy Brady, "Why I Want a Wife" (*Making Sense*, pp. 596–98) Paul Theroux, "Being a Man" (*Making Sense*, pp. 600–603) Ben Zimmer, "Truthiness" Read Assignment #2 (Definition)

Thursday	*A Rulebook for Arguments*, Appendix II (pp. 81–86) *The Elements of Style*, Principles of Composition 19–22 (pp. 26–33) Briane Greene, "Put a Little Science in Your Life" (*Making Sense*, pp. 584–88) W. L. Rathje, "How Garbage Got to Be an -Ology" (*Making Sense*, pp. 590–93) Lewis Thomas, "Humanities and Science" (Angel)

Week 6: One for the money, two for the show . . .

Tuesday	*Making Sense*, Chapter 4 (pp. 203–23) *A Rulebook for Arguments*, Chapter II (pp. 9–17) *The Elements of Style*, A Few Matters of Form (pp. 34–38) Brent Staples, "Just Walk on By: A Black Man Ponders His Power to Alter Public Space" (*Making Sense*, pp. 224–28) Barack Obama, "Memorial Day, Abraham Lincoln National Cemetery" (*Making Sense*, pp. 241–44)
Thursday	*Making Sense*, Chapter 5 (pp. 267–89) *The Elements of Style*, Misused Words and Expressions A–E (pp. 39–46) Bill Bryson, "Varieties of English" (*Making Sense*, pp. 291–302) Amy Tan, "Mother Tongue" (*Making Sense*, pp. 330–35)

Week 7: Awop-Bop-a-Loo-Mop Alop-Bam-Boom . . .

Tuesday	*Making Sense*, Chapter 6 (pp. 339–59) *The Elements of Style*, Misused Words and Expressions F–L (pp. 45–52) *A Rulebook for Arguments*, Chapter III (pp. 19–22) Bill Bryson, "Swearing" (Angel) Malcolm Gladwell, "The Order of Things: What College Rankings Really Tell Us" (Angel)

Thursday	*Making Sense,* Appendix (pp. 759–73)
	A Rulebook for Arguments, Chapter IV (pp. 23–30)
	The Elements of Style, Misused Words and Expressions M–S (pp. 53–58)

Week 8: Second verse, same as the first . . .

Tuesday	Peer Review #2
Thursday	Read Assignment #3 (Rhetorical Analysis)
	The Elements of Style, Misused Words and Expressions T–W (pp. 59–65)

Week 9: Ethos and pathos and logos . . . oh my!

Tuesday	**Paper #2 Due: Definition Essay**
	Library Research Assignment due
	Making Sense, Chapter 10 (pp. 633–55)
	Charles B. Rangel, "Bring Back the Draft" (*Making Sense,* pp. 678–80)
	Wall Street Journal, "Uncle Charlie Wants You" (*Making Sense,* pp. 689–90)
Thursday	*A Rulebook for Arguments,* Chapter VI (pp. 37–47)
	The Elements of Style, An Approach to Style (pp. 66–69)
	Charles Moskos and Paul Glastris, "Now Do We Believe We Need a Draft?" (*Making Sense,* pp. 681–87)
	Maggie Koerth, "Women in the Draft: A Necessary Part of the Quest to End Discrimination" (*Making Sense,* pp. 693–95)
	Will Bardenwerper, "Party Here, Sacrifice Over There"

Week 10: Coming for to carry me home . . .

Tuesday	Statement by Alabama Clergymen
	Martin Luther King Jr., "Letter from Birmingham Jail" (Angel)
Thursday	Martin Luther King Jr., "Letter from Birmingham Jail" cont'd (Angel)

Week 11: The dogs on Main Street howl 'cause they understand . . .

Tuesday	*Making Sense* (pp. 653–54)
	A Rulebook for Arguments, Appendix II (pp. 73–79)
	The Elements of Style, An Approach to Style, Reminders 1–4
	  (pp. 70–72)
	Malcolm Gladwell, "Small Change: Why the Revolution Will Not Be
	  Tweeted"

Thursday	Individual Conferences

Week 12: Papa-oom-mow-mow

Tuesday	Read Assignment #4 (Recommendation Essay) *The Elements of Style*, An Approach to Style, Reminders 5–8 (pp. 72–73)
Thursday	Peer Review #3

Week 13: Same as it ever was

Tuesday	*Making Sense*, Chapter 8 (pp. 463–84) Malcolm Gladwell, "The 10,000-Hour Rule" (*Making Sense*, pp. 515–23)

Thursday	**Paper #3 Due: Rhetorical Analysis**
	A Rulebook for Arguments, Chapter V (pp. 31–36)
	The Elements of Style, An Approach to Style, Reminders 9–12
	  (pp. 73–76)
	"Deliberation in the Midst of Crisis"
	Jerry Sandusky, "Grand Jury Presentation"
	Michael Weinreb, "Growing Up Penn State"
	George Vecsey, "The Dangerous Cocoon of King Football"
	Kate Dailey, "Penn State: Would You Do Better than Joe
	  Paterno?"

Thursday	Michael Weinreb: "The Culture of Unrest at Penn State" Maureen Dowd, "Personal Foul at Penn State" Ryan Kristobak, "May No Act of Ours Bring Shame: The Riot That Never Should Have Happened" LaVar Arrington, "Joe Paterno Fired: This Is Not How It Should Have Ended" David Brooks, "Let's All Feel Superior" Joe Nocera, "Penn State's Long Road Back" Video: Penn State Student Rally Video: *The Daily Show* on the "Penn State Riots"

Thanksgiving break

Week 14: Rhetor without a cause

Tuesday	*A Rulebook for Arguments*, Chapter VII (pp. 49–57) *The Elements of Style*, An Approach to Style, Reminders 13–17 (pp. 76–80) Claudia Wallis, "The Multitasking Generation" (*Making Sense*, pp. 540–49) Nicholas Carr, "Is Google Making Us Stupid?" (*Making Sense*, pp. 551–59) Bob Herbert, "Tweet Less, Kiss More"
Thursday	*A Rulebook for Arguments*, Chapter VIII (pp. 59–65) *The Elements of Style*, An Approach to Style, Reminders 18–21 (pp. 80–85) Fareed Zakaria, "How to Restore the American Dream" Thomas L. Friedman, "Time to Reboot America"

Week 15: And in the end . . .

Tuesday	Peer Review #4
Thursday	**Paper #4 Due: Recommendation Essay** Course Evaluation Tearful Good-byes

WORKS CITED

Adler-Kassner, Linda, Robert Crooks, and Ann Watters, eds. *Writing the Community: Concepts and Models for Service-Learning in Composition*. Washington, DC: American Association for Higher Education, 1997. Print.

Ball, Arnetha, and Ted Lardner. *African American Literacies Unleashed: Vernacular English and the Composition Classroom*. Carbondale: Southern Illinois UP, 2005. Print.

Bruch, Patrick, and Richard Marback. "Race, Literacy, and the Value of Rights Rhetoric in Composition Studies." *CCC* 53.5 (2002): 651–74. Print.

Brueggemann, Brenda Jo, et al. "Becoming Visible: Lessons in Disability." *CCC* 52.3 (2001): 368–98. Print.

CCCC Executive Committee. CCCC *Position Statement on Teaching, Learning, and Assessing Writing*. Urbana, IL: NCTE, 2004. http//www.ncte.org/cccc/resources /positions/digitalenvironments.

Davis, Lennard. *The Disabilities Studies Reader*. New York: Routledge, 1997. Print.

Deans, Thomas, Barbara Roswell, and Adrian Wurr. *Writing and Community Engagement: A Critical Sourcebook*. Boston: Bedford, 2010. Print.

Flower, Linda. *Community Literacy and the Rhetoric of Public Engagement*. Carbondale: Southern Illinois UP, 2008. Print.

Glenn, Cheryl. *Making Sense: A Real-World Rhetorical Reader*. 3rd ed. Boston: Bedford, 2010. Print.

Hawisher, Gail E., and Cynthia L. Selfe, eds. *Passions, Pedagogies, and Twenty-First Century Technologies*. Logan: Utah State UP and NCTE, 1999. Print.

Herzberg, Bruce. "Community Service and Critical Teaching." *CCC* 45.3 (1994): 307–19. Print.

Horner, Bruce. "Discoursing Basic Writing." *CCC* 47.2 (1996): 199–222. Print.

Lewiecki-Wilson, Cynthia, and Brenda Jo Brueggemann. *Disability and the Teaching of Writing: A Critical Sourcebook*. Boston: Bedford, 2008. Print.

Lunsford, Andrea. *The St. Martin's Handbook*. 7th ed. Boston: Bedford, 2011. Print.

Mathieu, Paula. *Tactics of Hope: The Public Turn in English Composition*. Portsmouth, NH: Heinemann, 2005. Print.

Palmeri, Jason. *Remixing Composition: A History of Multimodal Writing Pedagogy*. Carbondale: Southern Illinois UP, 2012. Print.

Redd, Teresa M. "A Cultural Perspective: Teaching Composition at a Historically Black University." *Strategies for Teaching First-Year Composition*. Ed. Duane Roen et al. Urbana: NCTE, 2002. 21–34. Print.

Richardson, Elaine. "'To Protect and Serve': African American Female Literacies." *CCC* 53.4. (2002): 675–704. Print.

Rose, Mike. *Lives on the Boundary*. New York: Free, 1989. Print.

Schutz, Aaron, and Anne Ruggles Gere. "Service Learning and English Studies: Rethinking 'Public' Service." *CE* 60.2 (1998): 129–48. Print.

Selber, Stuart. *Multiliteracies for a Digital Age*. Carbondale: Southern Illinois UP, 2004. Print.

Selfe, Cynthia L. *Multimodal Composition: Resources for Teachers*. New York: Hampton P, 2007. Print.

Selfe, Richard. *Sustainable Computer Environments: Cultures of Support in English Studies and Language Arts*. Cresskill: Hampton P, 2005. Print.

Trainor, Jennifer Seibel. "Critical Pedagogy's 'Other': Constructions of Whiteness in Education for Social Change." *CCC* 53.4 (2002): 631–50. Print.

Watkins, James Ray, Jr. *A Taste for Language: Literacy, Class, and English Studies*. Carbondale: Southern Illinois UP, 2009. Print.

White, Linda Feldmeier. "Learning Disability, Pedagogies, and Public Discourse." *CCC* 53.4 (2002): 705–38. Print.

Wysocki, Anne. *Writing New Media: Theory and Applications for Expanding the Teaching of Composition*. Logan: Utah State UP, 2004. Print.

Useful Web Sites

ABCD Books
www.abcdbooks.org

Campus Compact
www.compact.org/resources

Daedalus Integrated Writing Environment: Overview
www.daedalus.com/products_diwe_overview.asp

National Service-Learning Clearinghouse
www.servicelearning.org

National Writing Project Resources
www.nwp.org/cs/public/print/doc/resources.csp

Penn State Public Writing Initiative
pennstatelearning.psu.edu/public-writing-initiative

2

The First Few Days of Classes

During the first few days of class, I try to show my students that I am interested in them and excited about teaching. My job is to make the classroom environment a safe learning community, a space in which everyone feels empowered to contribute, a space that is both comfortable and challenging, that stretches and engages everyone.

—SUSAN WEEBER

THE FIRST CLASS

Although you may begin to feel anxious as the time approaches for you to walk into your first class meeting, know that the nervousness you feel is natural and that every good teacher feels something of it on the first day of every new class. Even if you're a new teacher, teaching a subject that you've never taught before, your education, experience, and training have prepared you for this moment. You've seen effective teachers and communicators, and no matter what area of English studies you specialize in—rhetoric and composition, literature, creative writing, or film—you know a lot about good writing and strong reading strategies. You've also likely had experience speaking or performing in front of groups of people. Remember that teaching is a performance in the full sense of that word. The teacher is instructor, coordinator, actor, facilitator, announcer, pedagogue, and ringmaster, working to provide an environment where students can participate fully and actively.

Teaching style, the way you carry off your performance, is determined partly by conscious decisions that you make and partly by personality factors over which you have little control. It is difficult to control completely the manner and tone with which you naturally address the class as a whole, the way you react to individual students on an intuitive level, the quick responses you make to classroom situations as they come up, and the general public self you exhibit in front of the class. You cannot change who you are, nor should you try.

This is not to say, however, that teachers have no control at all over how they appear. Although your essential style may not be amenable to change, you can consciously modify other variables. You can control what the class does with its time, the order in which you present material, the sorts of skills you will concentrate on—all the content-oriented material that is at the heart of every class. You can also make an effort to control those aspects of your style that you want specifically to change or suppress. If your personality tends toward sarcasm or intimidation (intentionally or not), you can carefully and consciously reconsider your comments so that they convey encouragement; if you tend toward too much modesty or passivity, you can work toward speaking up more and taking a more active approach.

As you think about your own teaching persona, consider both what makes you feel most comfortable and what helps you facilitate classroom interactions. Many younger, female teachers find it helpful to establish authority by wearing professional clothing — especially toward the beginning of the term and when handing back graded essays. Others do well with establishing a more informal persona. Anne Curzan and Lisa Damour, in *First Day to Final Grade,* provide (in addition to other practical advice) lists of pros and cons for dressing up or dressing more casually. They note that while dressing up can make you look and feel more professional, helping you establish your authority, it can also be expensive, be less comfortable, and create distance between you and your students (104). Finding an appropriate and comfortable balance is key.

There are many questions you'll need to answer for yourself: what you will wear; what you'll have your students call you; whether you'll stand up in front of students behind a podium, move around the classroom, or sit among the students in a circle. Whatever configuration you decide on (the shape and size of the classroom will limit your options; see Chapter 10 for more on how the physical space of the classroom can shape your teaching and students' learning), make sure you're in a position to make eye contact with every student. The class will have a personality of its own, and your persona will likely be shaped in part by your level of comfort, but your persona — the choices you make in presenting yourself and interacting with others — will also shape the feel of the classroom.

More important than anything else, you should try to evince the two most important traits of a good teacher: humanity and competence. If students believe you to be kind and to know your stuff, they will, for the most part, be receptive. Humanity and competence, however, cannot be demonstrated in one day. They show themselves over time, not by how many jokes you tell or how hard you grade, but by the total picture of who you are and how you feel about your students, their successes, and their trials as beginning writers. If you are humane and know your subject, you and your students will, over time, build a common ethos based on mutual respect and trust. (For further reading on college-level teaching, see Boothman; Curzan and Damour; Davis; and Haswell and Lu, cited at the end of this chapter.)

Bureaucratic Tasks (10 minutes)

On the first day of classes, teachers often do little more than distribute syllabi and show the texts; writing teachers, however, have a good deal to get done on the first day. You'll likely spend the first ten minutes of the first class in an undemanding routine. Put your materials on the front desk and greet the students present. Students will continue to come in, even well into the class hour. (For further reading on getting started, see Haswell and Lu, Chapter 2,

"Beginnings"; Curzan and Damour, Chapter 2, "The First Day of the Term"; and Davis, Chapter 3, "The First Day of Class.")

Write your name, office number, and office hours on the blackboard, and then arrange your books, notes, and handouts so they are within easy reach. Look up every few seconds, trying to maintain eye contact with the students—it is natural to avoid their eyes until you speak to them in an official capacity, but eye contact establishes a friendly connection. Since you will probably want to begin teaching while standing up, check to see that the classroom has a lectern that you can use, or set up your satchel or briefcase so that it will hold your papers.

Your students are learning their way around campus, so some of them will almost certainly continue to drift in during the first fifteen minutes. Give most of the stragglers a chance to come in before you call the roll. Introduce yourself, the course, and your office number and hours. These first few announcements, routine though they are, are the most difficult. Speak slowly, and remember that you have everything planned, that you are in your element, that you will perform well. Meet the students' eyes as you speak and try to develop the ability to take in large groups of students as you move your gaze about the classroom. You may be surprised at how young some of them look. This may be their first day in college, and depending on the time of day, you may be their first college teacher. If you feel nervous, remember that your students probably feel the same way.

Describe the add-drop policy of your college or university. There may be specific school or departmental policies you are expected to announce: It usually pays to repeat the add-drop policy at least once. Finally, call the names on your class roster, marking absences. You will want your students to raise their hands if present and to tell you if you have mispronounced their names or if they have a nickname they would prefer you to use. Note the preferred name and pronunciation on your roster, and try to make eye contact with each student as you call the roll. Attempt to connect names with faces as soon as possible.

After you have called the roll, ask for a show of hands of those whose names you did not call. There will always be a few, usually students who have registered late or who have shown up hoping they can add the class. Now is the time to announce that, after class, you will talk to those students who wish to add or drop the course. After class, then, you can attend to them and decide whether you can handle more students in your class. Often there is a maximum number of students established by the department, and only the director of the writing program, the department chair, an advisor, or scheduler can give permission for an overload. If the ultimate decision about accepting more students is yours, keep in mind that each student whom you accept over the limit means that less of your time and energy will be available for the rest of the students. If the decision is not yours, do not make it. Send the student to the appropriate person.

The Syllabus (15–20 minutes)

Hand out copies of the syllabus. After every student has one, read through the important parts of it aloud. On this first reading, stress the textbooks — display your copies in class so students will know what to look for at the bookstore — and discuss attendance and lateness policies, the form for written assignments (double-spaced or single-spaced, citation style, and so forth), the number and length of required essays, and the policy on keeping a journal or writing log. You will also need to explain due dates — that on a syllabus, the assignments listed for a particular day are due that day (they are not homework for the next class, which might have been the case in high school). If you are using a revision policy, go over it in detail, giving examples of how it should be used. During this initial explanation of the syllabus, you will actually start to teach students that revision is an integral part of the writing process. Some students will initially think of revision as punishment or as simply editing for a cleaner copy — instead of the normal process of expanding thinking and polishing writing. There is inevitably confusion about the revision policy and how it works (and you will be explaining revision for the first few weeks of the course). Go over the calendar of due dates, and mention the grading standards you will be applying.

It is important, as you explain the syllabus, not to back away from or undercut any of the policies it states. Sometimes you will sound harsh to yourself as you explain the penalties for absence, lateness, plagiarism, or failure to do work on time, but do not apologize. You will find that it is far simpler to ease up on harshly stated policies than to tighten up lax policies. After you have gone through it, ask whether there are any questions about the syllabus. Finally, you will want to tell students about the diagnostic essay that you have scheduled for the second day of class.

Introductions (15–20 minutes)

Next, you might try to get to know some basic information about your students. Hand out index cards and ask students to provide specific information:

1. Name
2. E-mail address (and how often they check e-mail)
3. Phone number (and whether they wish to be included on any contact list you'll be making and if there are other specific instructions, such as a time after which it is too late to call students who work night shifts or have small children)
4. Any other information you need about students (such as their major, goals for the class, interests, favorite authors, and so on)

You can keep these index cards in a file, referring to them if you need to contact a student outside of class. The answers to the final question will help you get to know your students better and learn about what is important to them.

After you've collected the index cards, have students introduce themselves to the class. You can do these introductions in any number of ways. For instance, you could have students pair up and introduce themselves to each other and then have one partner introduce the other to the class. You could give the students a prompt: "The most interesting thing I've ever done is . . ." or "Writing for me is like. . . ." Their answers to prompts or how they introduce themselves or each other will help you begin to connect faces with names. If you give students a prompt—such as "I'm the one who . . ."—to use as an introduction, be prepared to introduce yourself in the same way. During these introductions, students will see glimpses of your personality, and you will see glimpses of theirs. Through this process, you will begin to develop an environment in which students feel comfortable speaking and listening to each other.

Dismissal (5–15 minutes)

Before dismissing the class, ask your students to write down any questions about course policies that they want to talk about during the next class. Announce your assignments, including the reading of the syllabus. If there are no final questions, dismiss the class.

You will undoubtedly be surrounded by a post-class swirl of students wishing to talk to you—students who only a moment ago had no questions. Some will want to add the course: Tell them whether they have a chance, and send them to the appropriate office. Some will have completed add or change-of-section forms; add those students' names to your roster. Some will have questions that they were too shy to ask in class; speak to them. As you resolve each situation, the crowd will diminish, and eventually the last petitioner will leave. You will be alone. This first day of class is over.

THE SECOND CLASS

Bureaucratic Tasks (10 minutes)

On the second day of class, there are still some bureaucratic tasks to be cleared away—you will need to call the roll again (make eye contact and see whether you can begin to remember students' names), and perhaps you will want to make a short speech about the add-drop policy of your school. Check whether wait lists are processed electronically by the registrar or if your department chair or writing program administrator handles wait lists and course overrides. If new students have registered for the class, as will probably happen on the second and third days, give them copies of the syllabus and ask them to speak to you after class. Ask the class for the questions they wrote down about the syllabus and course policies; answer their questions, clearing up any confusion.

Diagnostic Essay (30–40 minutes)

Some schools have only one writing class that all students take. Others have many levels of writing classes and place students — often on the basis of SAT, ACT, or Advanced Placement scores — before the term begins. Still other schools allow students to do directed self-placement. You'll need to find out how students are placed at your school. (For more on placement and assessment, see Chapter 5 in Edward M. White's *Assigning, Responding, Evaluating*.)

If you want a sense of your students' strengths and weaknesses as writers, you might wish to assign a diagnostic essay (sometimes called a "placement essay") today. If your school offers a BW, an ESL, a tutorial, or an honors program, the diagnostic essay serves to alert you to students who might best be supported by one of these other programs. If your school has a writing center, learning disabilities center, office of disabilities services, or center for language acquisition, your students can take advantage of a number of resources, and you can guide students in finding such help and enrichment. Writers are helped most when they receive an evaluation early, and the diagnostic essay allows you to begin to gauge the level of writing each student is capable of and to calculate your own pace in teaching each student and the class as a whole. Additionally, some students know what they need, and you can use this opportunity to ask them about the strengths and weaknesses they perceive in their own writing.

This exercise gives you an idea of how prepared your students are as writers. Ask students to take out paper and pen and to write on a topic that allows for narrative or descriptive responses. (You can bring paper with you and pass it out, or if your classroom has computers or students use laptops, they can submit their essays electronically.) The best topics for the diagnostic essay are those that (1) can be answered in a relatively short essay and (2) ask students to rely on their own experiences.

Here are three options:

1. In a short essay, discuss the reasons why your best (or worst) high school teacher was effective (or ineffective).
2. In a short essay, discuss the best, most worthwhile, and most valid advice you have received about adjusting to college life so far. What advice stands out most to you in your first week?
3. In a short essay, describe the role social networking sites play in your social life. Do such sites enhance your connections with others? Do they present any challenges?

Introduce the diagnostic essay to the class for what it is — an exercise that will give you an idea of how well students are writing now. Stress that the essay will not be given a letter grade and will have no effect on the final class grade. But remind students that you will be looking at form and content, at their ability to organize a piece of writing and develop it with specific examples. Explain the methods of rhetorical development you want them to use. If you want students, for example, to write a descriptive essay, provide examples that help illustrate the difference between general assertion and specific, sensory detail.

Ask students to try to write as finished a piece of work as possible in the time allowed. Make certain that they put their names on the essays and that they note whether they have already taken BW or ESL courses or if they have a documented disability that affects their ability to write in class. Write the diagnostic assignment on the board or display it on a screen; and then give the class the rest of the hour to think and write. Announce the amount of time remaining once or twice so that no one runs short of time. Near the end of class, give students a few minutes to write a paragraph about the strengths and weaknesses they detect in their own writing, including the writing they have just done in class. Finally, collect the essays or have students e-mail them to you or post them electronically.

Dismissal (5–10 minutes)

After you collect the essays, explain that you will talk more about the diagnostic essays next time and remind students of the reading they must do before the next class. Ask students if they have any questions. Once you have answered their questions, dismiss the class, but ask new students to stay for a few minutes to discuss the syllabus with you.

After the Second Class

You will have several tasks to accomplish after class or that evening, the most important of which are marking and evaluating the diagnostic essays. The range of writing skills evidenced by these essays may be wide. Some essays will be well organized and include fitting details; others may be marked by generalizations, many formal usage errors, and mechanical problems. Even if you find many errors, however, note that they usually fall into just a few patterns. (For more on the most common errors in student writing, see Lunsford and Lunsford on p. 342 of this book.)

Having prepared yourself, plunge into the pile of essays. Keep in mind that students had only twenty to thirty minutes to write these pieces and no advance knowledge of the prompt. Since good writing generally takes time and revision, it's best not to expect beautifully crafted prose or flawless standardized English, but you may be surprised by how well some of your students write already. Most of the essays will be short — two or three pages in length. Aside from some nearly illegible handwriting and inventive spellings, most essays should be readable. It is a good idea to scan each essay quickly, trying to get a sense of the writing as a purposeful whole. Then, in a second reading, mark the essay, looking for the following three specific areas of skill (listed here in order of importance):

1. Knowledge of and ability to use paragraph form, specific details and examples, and a well-supported and well-developed controlling idea.

2. Ability to write a variety of grammatically correct (according to standardized English) and interesting sentences.
3. Ability to use language — including grammar, usage, punctuation, and spelling — in a relatively standardized fashion.

To get a sense of how these three skills are demonstrated in an essay, you may have to read the essay two or three times — but since each one is not very long, this task is not as time-consuming as it sounds. By the time you reach the bottom of the pile, you should be spending about fifteen minutes on each diagnostic essay, noting the mechanical problems and writing a short comment at the end.

As you read the diagnostic essays, look especially for patterns of divergence from standardized English — a continual inability to use commas correctly, a continual confusion about verb endings, a continual tendency to begin fragments with relative pronouns. Chart such patterns carefully, for they will be your concern in the future and they can provide important information for tutors at the campus writing center, learning disabilities center, or center for language acquisition.

Whether or not you decide to use some form of portfolio evaluation, you may want to create a computer file in which to keep semester-long records, noting the progress of each student's writing. (See Chapter 5, "Evaluating Student Essays," for a detailed discussion of portfolio evaluation.) With such a record, you can chart each student's strengths and weaknesses as they appear in each major piece of writing. The first entry would cover the diagnostic exercise. Note whether the student grasps organization, can use sentences, has control of usage, and so forth. A short, three- to five-sentence description of each student's writing strengths and weaknesses, consulted and added to as you evaluate each new writing assignment, can be of great help in setting individualized goals for students and in discovering the particular kind of practice writing each student needs. These notes on students' progress will also help you when you confer individually with students.

The diagnostic essays and the way you respond to them will shape your students' perceptions of you as much as your classroom attitude will. As always in grading and evaluating, take the time to consider how students will feel upon reading your comments. Will they come away thinking they have problems they can deal with, or will they be overwhelmed? Try to balance critique with encouragement; find something to praise, and treat errors and problems as signposts pointing to needed work, not as dead-end signs. In your response to this first assignment, you are modeling ways of reading and response. As Nancy Sommers writes in "Responding to Student Writing," included in Part III of this book, teachers "comment on student writing to dramatize the presence of a reader, to help our students to become questioning readers themselves, because, ultimately, we believe that becoming such a reader will help them to evaluate what they have written and develop control over their writing" (p. 333). Even this first response demonstrates your pedagogical values. (Before you write detailed comments, you may want to read "Grading" in Curzan and Damour;

"Evaluating Students' Written Work" in Davis; and "The Writing" in Haswell and Lu, cited at the end of this chapter.)

Before the next class, you must decide whether any of your students might benefit from switching to another course or working with a tutor at the writing center. If you feel that a particular student should be enrolled in the BW or ESL program instead of FY writing, now is the time to make the necessary arrangements through either the director of composition or the director of one of these other programs. Do not feel you are betraying a student by recommending BW or ESL; you want your students to thrive under your guidance, not merely survive. If you think a student would benefit from the services of the writing center, learning disabilities center, office of disability services, or center for language acquisition, you might talk with a consultant at the appropriate center to find out how the student can enroll and how you can work with the writing tutor to best help the student.

For students with especially good writing skills, the diagnostic essay may provide pleasant news: Some schools exempt strong writers from FY writing courses or place them in honors sections. If that is the case at your school, make the necessary arrangements. Often, though, placement has already been determined by an earlier diagnostic essay or by a student's experience in high school. If this is the case, don't worry: Even already strong writers can become better writers, and many of these students will be a pleasure to work with, contributing much to the class.

After reading both the diagnostic essay and the student's reflection, note whether you have concerns about the level of a specific student's writing and whether that student might be underprepared or overprepared for your class. Write a note requesting a meeting with the student after class. Often, in talking with students, you can learn more about their level of preparation. Sometimes, too, you may discover unusual circumstances that affected their performance on the diagnostic essay. After talking with the student, you will have a better sense of ways you might help that student thrive in your class, or—if your school allows students to transfer to other writing classes—help the student find the appropriate class.

After you have read the diagnostics, marked them, and recorded your comments, you can put them aside and turn to the other task of the evening: planning the next class. The third class will be your first real class, the first class that demands a prepared lesson plan. Be certain that you know what you want to introduce and accomplish.

THE THIRD CLASS

Before the third day of class, you need to prepare a lesson plan that includes your objective for the class as well as planned activities that will help you achieve that objective. You will also need to reserve class time for discussing the diagnostic essays that you will be handing back to students.

Begin by taking attendance, and then announce that you will talk about the diagnostic essays at the end of the class. This is a good way to introduce the policy of not returning assignments until the end of a period. Such a policy keeps attention on the day's lesson and keeps students' reactions to their grades and your comments from coloring the class period.

As you begin your first day of actual teaching, introduce and state the goals of the first lesson. You may decide to connect the work you begin today with the first writing assignment. No matter what your objectives are, however, remember that you are there to lead the class, not to do all of the work. Early in the course, get students talking—to you, in pairs or small groups, and in whole-class discussions. The more comfortable students are with class discussions and group work, the more comfortable they will be with peer-response and whole-class workshops on their writing. (See Chapter 3, "Everyday Activities," for detailed information on leading class discussions, peer response, and workshops.)

Fifteen minutes or so before the end of class, make your assignments for reading and homework, and return the diagnostic essays. Before you dismiss the class, ask students to read over the comments you've written on their essays, and ask those who need to talk with you after class to do so. Since some students will have to get to their next class, dismiss your students at least ten minutes early so you'll have time to spend with those who need to talk with you.

If your school does provide opportunities for students to transfer to other writing classes, you'll need to help students make arrangements for transferring to a different course, which often requires special forms and approval from a department chair or dean. Students whose writing is so advanced that they may be exempted from your course should be congratulated. Students who need to work at one of the support-services centers on campus while they take your course should be encouraged to schedule an appointment with a representative of that center and to take their diagnostic essay with them to that appointment. Students who will not be able to do the level of work required in your course should be moved to the BW or ESL program. (You should speak to these students privately. Ask them to come back to your office during the remaining class time, and explain the situation to them there.)

LESSON PLANS

Leading a class of college-level writers may at first seem like a daunting prospect. You may have heard composition referred to as a contentless or a skills-only course, and many new teachers fear the prospect of running out of material. Therefore, it is best to prepare your classroom time for the first two weeks with extra thoroughness. Carefully think through the structure for each class; it is always better to carry some of your lesson plan over to the next class than to take the chance of coming to the end of your prepared notes with half an hour of class time left. At first, it might be difficult to gauge how long an activity or discussion will take, and sometimes a discussion will lead the class in a new, productive direction, causing you to discard part of your plan. Even so, it's always best to be prepared and go from there.

With experience, you will find that the classroom offers more teaching possibilities than you can take advantage of. By dipping into the following chapters you can get a quick idea of some options. As you'll see, teaching writing is so activity-oriented that with a little preparation, you'll never run out of material.

When drawing up plans for a class, always make sure you note the goal or purpose for each assignment and activity. The amount of other material you include in a lesson plan is up to you. Some teachers, at the beginning of their careers, prepare full paragraphs and detailed notes, whereas experienced teachers often work from notes made up only of key words or passages marked in the textbook. Make certain that you add to your notes cross-references to pages in the textbook or reader you are using.

Example 2.1   **SAMPLE LESSON PLAN: INQUIRY ACTIVITY**

Inquiry Activity 1

Day 6 [Day 5 was "responding to the visual" in terms of "The Deer at Providencia."]

- Before class, look over the rough drafts; see what problems and successes students have had, making brief comments on their drafts where appropriate. Select one or two examples from students' writing for class discussion, asking the students ahead of time for permission to use passages from their drafts.
- Have students read the sample description(s). Ask the other students to identify the dominant impression they get from the written description. Ask them to identify the features of the writing that make it easy or difficult to connect the visual with the essay. Discuss. (15–20 minutes)
- Look at the visual again. Discuss how each student's essay could be improved in terms of emphasizing the main point of Dillard's essay, particularly in terms of the accompanying visual. As a part of the discussion, examine the roles that establishing a purpose, establishing an audience, conveying a quality or an atmosphere, including sensory details, and organizing descriptions play in descriptive writing. (15–20 minutes)
- Have students begin revising their drafts. (25–30 minutes)

- Collect the revised drafts; remind students of the assignment for the next class. (3–5 minutes)
- After class, make brief comments on drafts, especially on their use of details to picture and support the dominant impression. Assign each draft a check, a check plus, or a check minus.

Example 2.2   **SAMPLE LESSON PLAN: OBJECTIVE SUMMARY WRITING**

Before class, assign "On Eating Meat" by Andy Kerr. After reading the essay, students should be prepared to write an objective summary of it, and, to that end, they should have read it carefully in order to gather information for their writing assignment. When you assign the essay, ask students to consider the following as they read: (1) the title of the piece, (2) what they already know about the topic, and (3) the main point of the essay. Also, as they read, they should mark places in the text that are confusing to them, that identify key points and terms, and that they question.

In class, ask students to identify in writing (1) the central issue of the essay, (2) the writer's point of view, (3) the organization of the essay and its connection to the purpose of the essay, and (4) the assumptions on which the writer's views are based.

- Encourage students to compare their responses and to talk among themselves about "On Eating Meat." After they have compared notes for five minutes or so, ask them each to write an objective summary of the essay. Students should aim to write an objective summary that:
  1. is one-third the length of the original essay.
  2. foregrounds the main idea (the thesis statement), includes key words and phrases, and mentions the supports for the author's main point or argument.
  3. is in their own words, avoiding plagiarism.
  4. follows the author's pattern of organization.
  5. uses only the information in the original essay.

6. avoids coloring the information with personal opinion.

7. lists the source of the original essay.

- Remind students that an objective summary conveys information, not opinion.

Examples 2.1 and 2.2 show two kinds of daily lesson plans. Example 2.1 outlines an inquiry activity, which asks students first to respond to a photograph of a badly burned student, wrapped in bandages, and then to draft an essay explaining how the visual enhances the accompanying essay, Annie Dillard's "The Deer of Providencia." Students are asked to bring their drafts to class for peer review and then to begin revising them. Notice how the teacher describes her objective in the first sentence: "Look over the rough drafts; see what problems and successes students have had, making brief comments on their drafts where appropriate." Her objective drives her carefully ordered and carefully timed classroom activities. Example 2.2 is based on an assigned reading, "On Eating Meat" by Andy Kerr. If, like this teacher, you are using a rhetorically arranged reader, you will naturally want to draft lesson plans that incorporate material from your textbook. In preparation for an upcoming writing assignment, this teacher wants his students to master the art of writing objective summaries, starting with a summary of "On Eating Meat." But before students begin writing, the teacher wants to talk about the genre of summary and the trouble students might encounter with the word *objective*. So he outlines important points he wants to hear students talk about: the central issue of the essay, the writer's point of view, how the progression of the essay relates to its purpose, and the assumptions on which a writer's views are based. Then the class turns to another essay and talks through the same points, discussing the problems with any claim to objectivity. Only toward the end of class does the teacher specify the practical elements of the assignment, saying, perhaps, "Use only the information in the essay. Try hard not to color your summary with your opinions or with extra information. An objective summary means you are conveying information and not opinion."

Until you know how effective your examples will be and how much time you will devote to each item on your lesson plan, for every concept you introduce and exemplify (plagiarism, for instance), you should have two or three other examples in your notes and ready to use. It's always better to be slightly over-prepared with examples.

While working out your classroom strategies and preparing your lesson plans, you may wish to annotate your textbooks, noting material you plan to discuss in class. Annotating your textbook is a way of inhabiting it; underline and mark in it if doing so will make your teaching life easier. Textbooks are a raw material, and they may be with you for years. Make sure they serve you and save you from repetitious work in the future. Annotate any part of the rhetoric that you feel may need more explanation, and mark the exercises you plan to use. If any exercises fail, note the problem and the potential reasons for it. Your marks need be no more than checks or underlines, so long as they are meaningful to you. You should be able to open the book to a page and know immediately what you wish to accomplish with it.

WORKS CITED

Boothman, Nicholas. *How to Make People Like You in Ninety Seconds or Less.* New York: Workman, 2000. Print.

Connors, Robert J., and Andrea A. Lunsford. "Frequency of Formal Errors in Current College Writing, or Ma and Pa Kettle Do Research." *CCC* 39.4 (1988): 395–409. Print.

Curzan, Anne, and Lisa Damour. *First Day to Final Grade: A Graduate Student's Guide to Teaching.* 3rd ed. Ann Arbor: U of Michigan P, 2011. Print.

Davis, Barbara Gross. *Tools for Teaching.* 2nd ed. San Francisco: Jossey-Bass, 2009. Print.

Haswell, Richard H., and Min-Zhan Lu. *CompTales.* New York: Longman, 2007. Print.

Lunsford, Andrea A., and Karen J. Lunsford. "'Mistakes Are a Fact of Life': A National Comparative Study." *CCC* 59.4 (2008): 781–806. Print.

White, Edward M. *Assigning, Responding, Evaluating: A Writing Teacher's Guide.* 4th ed. Boston: Bedford, 2007. Print.

3

Everyday Activities

The composition classroom is often a frenetic environment, filled with so many choices that every instructor has to make. How much time should students spend working individually, in groups, or as a whole class? What is the right balance of instruction, discussion, and other activities that practically put to use the material we have covered? What kinds of activities will engage and stimulate students' thoughts, and how will these thoughts inform the decisions students make while writing? How do I appeal to a diverse classroom of different learning styles, experience, and backgrounds? When I plan my classes, however, I try to keep in mind the most important question of all — how will these activities improve my students' writing? With this objective, day-to-day planning becomes a little less daunting, and my class takes shape around the needs and interests of my students.

–COLIN HOGAN

CLASSROOM ORDER AND GROUP ETHOS

The primary management issue you will deal with as a teacher is that of classroom order. *Order,* of course, is a relative term; very often an orderly writing class is abuzz with discussions of rhetorical choices, editing, language diversity, and correctness. Order does not mean silence. It does, though, signify that you and your students are "on task," engaged in a progression of meaningful activities. It's your responsibility not to let that progression be disrupted. Whether students are taking part in a class-wide discussion, listening to your explanation, or working in small groups, certain protocols should be observed. One of your functions is to demonstrate these protocols to make the progression of activities possible. But students also need to take some responsibility for meaningful progress in class.

In the best of all teaching situations, the class members develop a group ethos, a feeling that they're all in it together, depending on one another for support and direction. When you use class discussions as a way to help students talk with and listen to one another and not just to you; when you set aside class time for group work and peer editing; when you encourage students to call, visit, and e-mail one another about their assignments and their writing; and when you expect and demand that students are respectful of one another regardless of race, class, clan, religion, ethnicity, sexual orientation, physical ability, political affiliation, appearance, and gender, you can feel fairly confident that your class will develop a positive group identity. Still, even the best, most experienced teachers can teach two sections of the same course, using the same materials in the same ways, and find that one group has coalesced better than the other. Unless you're teaching ESL, basic writing, or honors sections of FY writing, your class will be composed of a random grouping of students. But as soon as your students meet and begin to know each other and you, the class will develop subgroup personalities and then a class personality.

It is important for any teacher to know and recognize the subgroup personalities in a class. Most FY writing classes have pleasant and flexible group dynamics, and your main task will be to keep willing (and sometimes overawed) students working productively. All teachers are familiar with the hardworking, enthusiastic group at the front of the class, whose hands go up before you finish posing questions. Most of the material in this book is based on the premise of such a student attitude. When students are working together with mutual respect and on task, a classroom feels taut, sometimes even exhilarating. Though it's difficult to describe, you will know when the class is coming together productively by the atmosphere of satisfaction and achievement that fills the room.

However, in some classes you may have a back-of-the-class group, whose responses are less apt to be raised hands than whispers or snickers. In this case, you'll want to strive even harder to establish a sense of inclusivity for your entire class, including the group in the back. The worst thing you can do is get angry or exclude those back-sitters. The best thing to do is to ask them direct questions, to watch for a flicker of interest or knowledge, to invite them to speak to you and the others as often as possible, and to ask about their absences in private.

Inclusivity is one of the most important reasons to stress attendance: Your class needs everyone, every day, because writing classes work best when students engage in lively conversation and participate in collaborative learning activities. Your class ethos might also benefit from some rearranging: On occasion, you can ask those front-sitters to take seats in the back so that there's a kind of seat rotation, or — if the chairs are not fixed to the floor — you can arrange them in a circle. As your class begins to witness your inclusive practices, they will come to believe that they have something to learn from everyone — and that everyone in the class (including and especially the teacher) has something to learn from them. Each student must feel like a necessary and important part of the class, of class discussion, of deliberations on assignments and due dates, of group work. As you read further in *The St. Martin's Guide to Teaching Writing*, you'll see that we offer you a number of ways to facilitate positive group dynamics in your class. (For further study of classroom dynamics, see Curzan and Damour, Chapter 4, "Running a Discussion"; and Brookfield and Preskill, cited at the end of this chapter.)

CLASSROOM ROUTINES

Many new teachers of writing are used to the classroom routines they grew up with — lecture by the teacher or teacher-directed classroom discussion. These are the routines many of us know best, and we are sometimes tempted to rely on them in writing classes as completely as we have in literature classes. Unfortunately, however, they cannot be used successfully as the only methods of classroom instruction in a writing course; in fact, they cannot even hold center stage. The writing teacher must use a much larger array of classroom activities that bring students' writing — not their talking, listening, or note-taking — to center stage.

Limiting Lectures

An old standby of classroom routines, one with which most new teachers are familiar, is the lecture. Many of us admire teachers who deliver brilliant lectures in literature courses. Lectures in writing classes, however, tend to be less helpful to students. They must consist of the application of abstract rhetorical principles; and as the thesis of this book suggests, students simply do not learn to write — or to practice any art — by studying abstract principles. As the philosopher Michael Polanyi writes,

> The aim of a skillful performance is achieved by the observance of a set of rules which are not known as such to the person following them. . . . Rules of art can be useful, but they do not determine the practice of art; they are maxims, which can serve as a guide to an art only if they can be integrated into the practical knowledge of the art. (49–50)

In this case, the "practical knowledge" of writing cannot be gained by listening to lectures on the rules and protocols of writing; nor can it be gained by lectures on the beauty of literature. It can be gained only by actually writing and performing writing-based activities.

We're not suggesting that you cannot tell your students anything about writing or that explaining material to students is somehow invalid; after all, the very act of teaching is predicated, as rhetorician Richard Weaver says, on the idea that one person can know more about a specific subject than another and that knowledge or skill can be transmitted. Your explanations will be validated by students' writing or their writing-based activities. After explaining, exemplifying, and pointing out the major components of a skill, you'll want to set up a learning situation that allows students to practice the skill — and the sooner the better. Only in this way are "lectures" in a writing class truly beneficial.

Leading Effective Class Discussions

Classroom discussion is probably the teaching method most congenial to new writing teachers. Teachers do not "lead" the class in any authoritarian way; instead, they guide the discussion, and everyone in class has a chance to contribute. Inexperienced teachers of composition usually envision themselves using classroom discussions, but the essential component of discussion — content — is much more complex in a composition course than in other courses. History, biology, and psychology courses are all about "knowing that," but composition courses are concerned not only with "knowing that" but also with "knowing how." Therefore, the content of a composition class is often practical as well as theoretical. The theory is best discussed in practical terms, as it applies to a student's piece of writing or to an article, essay, short story, or poem students have read.

This is the hard truth about discussion in writing classes: "knowing how" cannot be practiced without "knowing that," and emphasizing one at the expense of the other risks turning discussion into talk for its own sake. If the content of essays is discussed, it should be applicable to the content of the students' own writing. Students aren't usually interested in talking about sentence fragments or three-part organization unless the fragments and the organization are in their own writing. Therefore, to be useful and interesting, classroom discussions must be carefully planned and directed. You can, of course, assign essays or short stories and then spend the class time discussing them — but such use of class time is more appropriate to a course in creative nonfiction or literary appreciation than to a writing course, unless you manage to connect the reading of the literature to issues that students can work on in their own writing.

Discussion plays two important roles in the writing classroom. The first is relatively traditional: Classroom discussion of an object, idea, or situation is a prewriting activity that can give students ideas about content that they might wish to use in their writing. Fifteen minutes of discussion on different kinds of computers, for instance, might allow students access to ideas for their own essays about using computers in college. Such discussion needs to be limited and carefully directed, however, because it can easily take up more class time than it is worth. (In other words, such discussion should not be used in place of the invention activities described in Chapter 6, "Teaching Invention," but as a supplement to them.)

The second valid use of discussion in a composition course involves classroom conversations about different stylistic and organizational options available in the forms and genres you're teaching. (See also the descriptions of classroom discussion in Chapters 6–10 on teaching specific features of good writing.) Such discussion can be a valuable element in helping students make formal and stylistic choices about their writing. Any discussion of form, however, must focus on concrete examples of stylistic choices; otherwise, students may try to engage in arguments over abstract concepts but will not be able to apply their ideas to their work. Examples printed on handouts, drawn on a chalkboard, or projected on a screen often successfully supplement this kind of discussion by making the concepts concrete.

So how *do* you lead successful discussions? Important keys are knowing exactly what you wish students to gain from a discussion and having quick access to the specific materials in the reading that will apply to your purpose. For this reason, you must know the reading materials very well and have marked and labeled in your copy each line, sentence, and paragraph that you may need to call to the class's attention. If, for instance, you want to point out how the author of an essay moves from narration into argument smoothly, you must underline at least two or three examples of exactly where such a movement occurs. If you want to uncover the structure of an explanatory organization hidden by expert transitions, you need to write notes in your copy that allow you to demonstrate it. You will never regret making good directive notes in your teacher's copy; even if you have an excellent memory, notes allow you to have quick access to what you want to exemplify and thus to avoid what feels like the endless gaze of all your students while you search page after page for your lost example.

Once you have determined what you want the class discussion to accomplish and have prepared your own copy of the readings, you can look over the apparatus that usually follows most readings in anthology textbooks. These questions and issues developed by the textbook's author or editor may serve your purposes, but most often the apparatus will be only partially useful. You know what you need from the text, and the book does not, so feel free to ignore the apparatus. If you find helpful materials, mark them.

Leading classroom discussion itself is a complicated skill that improves with practice. It consists of orchestrating a few sub-skills that move within the discourse triangle of text, students, and teacher—with attention, too, to context. You must be able to frame questions that are concrete enough to be answered by a good reader but not so simple that they are condescending or can be answered with one or two words. You must be able to sequence those questions so that potential answers will continue toward the issue you want to explore. You must be able to build verbally on the answers students give so as to move the discussion along in fruitful directions or to move it back from tangents to task. And you must be able to read the tenor of the group as you go along in order to encourage some students, calm the ardor of some, start others from passivity or silence, and draw still others out. In the ideal discussion, every student participates, responding not only to you but also to other students, and though teachers seldom achieve that ideal, they always try to approach it.

One way to make sure students will have something to say about an important point of discussion is to give them time to write about the issue before you discuss it as a class. Beginning the class session with a short in-class writing, telling students one class period earlier what they'll be discussing in the next class so they can take notes, or starting the conversation as a Web-based discussion are all ways of making sure students have something to say. Some students are understandably nervous about speaking on the spot; but if they've expressed their ideas in writing, they have a starting place. If conversation begins to lull, you can ask a quiet student, "What did you write about?" Or you can ask the class, "Did anyone take a similar or different position from John on this issue?"

Stephen D. Brookfield and Stephen Preskill, in *Discussion as a Way of Teaching*, offer several types of questions that help keep class discussions moving. Questions that ask for more evidence encourage students to consider the sources for their interpretations and opinions. Questions that ask for clarification help students refine their ideas by expressing them in different ways or by providing additional examples to explain their points. Brookfield and Preskill also discuss

"What do you mean specifically?" Also ask them in their language, it's not completely clear?

hypothetical questions, which "ask students to consider how changing the circumstances of a case might alter the outcome" (87). Related to hypothetical questions are cause-effect questions. You can ask, for example, "What would be the effect of ending this essay where it begins, or moving this section over here?" Particularly useful in composition classes are open questions and linking or extension questions. Open questions, Brookfield and Preskill note, often begin with *how* or *why* and draw on students' problem-solving abilities (86). Instead of asking questions that elicit a yes/no answer or that encourage only one student to respond, try beginning a question with "Why do you think. . . ." This question format encourages more than one response because it assumes that students might actually have different thoughts on an issue. Open questions then can be extended by linking questions, such as "Is there any connection between what you said and what Susan said earlier?"

One of the most demanding skills involved in leading class discussions is learning to cultivate your own silence. There will be times when you can choose a hand from a number of enthusiastic hands, but there will also be times when all eyes are cast downward and you must call on students by name to get any response. Don't expect that a lack of immediate response to a question means you must answer it yourself; let the silence build for five or ten seconds, and then ask the question in a different way rather than answering it yourself. (As a colleague of ours says of post-question silences, "Keep quiet. They'll crack before you will.") If students are still quiet, point them to a particular place in the text you're discussing and give them a chance to write an answer to the question you have asked. Providing time for writing helps students compose their thoughts and reaffirms the important role that writing plays in learning. Finally, you will need to acquire the skill of knowing when you have achieved all you can achieve from discussing a text and how to recap the main points through summary and synthesis questions and then move on.

Example 3.1   **DISCUSSION ACTIVITIES**

1. <u>Collaborative Talking</u>: Allow students to help one another out with their class participation. If student #1 raises an issue that she doesn't fully understand, encourage student #2 to amend or address her thoughts. If student #2 almost nails the issue, encourage student #3 to do the final nailing. In other words, let them help one another out. (This procedure is particularly important if you expect them to respond to one another's writing; if they trust and respond to one another in class, they'll do the same out of class.)

2. <u>Believers and Doubters</u>: Early on in the term assign a "believer" and a "doubter" for each reading assignment. Expect the believer to start off the discussion by very briefly (2–3 minutes) explaining the main points the author wants to make. Then the doubter can offer one or two compelling questions (doubts) about the author's argument. Class discussion follows. Make sure that each student has the opportunity to play both roles during the term.

In-Class Writing

In-class writing activities can take a number of different forms, but they all have one thing in common: They involve students in practicing the skills of planning, writing, revising, and editing. Most of the classroom material in the following chapters is based on this sort of in-class activity approach, according to which students may work alone, with one other student, or in a group. At first, the writing-centered classroom may seem appallingly disorienting, accustomed as we are to the teacher-centered atmosphere — especially in literature, history, and political science classes — of our own education. It may take you some time to get used to the meaningful chaos of a writing classroom, but as you do, you will begin to see how discoveries take place within the busy buzz.

In-class writing assignments, an important part of the writing-centered classroom, can take the form of writing short essays based on the instructions of the teacher, freewriting in response to a prompt, practicing sentence or paragraph patterns, or editing drafts according to specific guidelines. What use you make of writing-based activities will depend on the skills you are trying to teach. Example 3.2 provides some activities that can be used with excellent results.

Example 3.2   **IN-CLASS WRITING ACTIVITIES** — *potentially could use there in the classroom*

1. <u>Opening</u>: Pose a question that allows students to synthesize or explore the topic at hand. Give them five minutes to write. Ask them to read aloud their responses and encourage them to respond to one another.

2. <u>Middle</u>: If students seem uninterested or perplexed (or bored), stop talking for a minute and ask them to focus their thoughts. If you can pose a question that forces them to assimilate the reading assignment

or problem at hand, you're on your way to getting the class back on track. For instance: "What prior knowledge does this writer expect from you?" or "What was the hardest thing to understand about today's reading?" "What's your biggest doubt about today's lesson? And what information could assuage that doubt?" "What does this reading make you think about?" "Describe this scene/setting/problem from a minor character's/the object's/the experimentation subject's point of view."

3. <u>Closing</u>: Near the end of class, ask students to write out (1) what they learned in class today that they didn't know before they walked in and (2) how today's learning connects with yesterday's — or will connect with tomorrow's.

Teaching in Wired, Wireless, and Hybrid Classrooms

Teaching in a computer-supported classroom provides for a class routine different from the one in a traditional classroom. Most writing courses in computer-supported classrooms are structured so that class time is spent writing, workshopping, conferring, and revising on-screen, so such classrooms are often quiet. The traditional buzz of classroom talk is much less often heard in an environment where students' comments are usually text-specific and written rather than spoken. In addition, students work on each other's drafts much more consistently and seriously than non-linked environments allow, and therefore such work seems and feels much more socially constructed. Depending on the software package being used, interaction with a text can involve one other person, a small group, or the whole class, and the teacher can choose to play various roles. This is a fascinating and quickly developing part of composition teaching; if you are interested in computer-supported teaching and your program does not offer it or have access to computer-supported classrooms, you may wish to speak to your WPA about future plans and possibilities and indicate your interest.

If you are teaching a course in which digital rhetoric, multimedia composing, or online work is essential, you'll need to think carefully about the ways that technology supports your pedagogy. As Janet M. Eldred writes in "Pedagogy in the Computer-Networked Classroom,"

> *Networking can work* in a writing classroom because it can be used to stress composing as a social, collaborative act, as an act of synthesizing and negotiating knowledge. But networking will work for us *only if* we plan carefully how we will use it in our classrooms, how we will take advantage of its strengths and downplay its weaknesses. (239)

Eldred goes on to provide "four areas that must be attended to if the full potential of networking is to be reached: (1) Choice of Technology, (2) Ease of Use, (3) Participations, and (4) Audience Awareness" (240). Technology changes quickly; in fact it has changed dramatically since Eldred's article was first published in 1991, yet attentiveness to these four areas of concern will help you use available technology in ways that support your pedagogical goals and values. Choose technologies that best fit your goals and that are not too complex for you and your students to use. When you do incorporate a particular technology, you should require all students to use it regularly, and you should help students gain awareness of their audience (whether you're asking them to write for just you and the class or for a larger audience).

If you are teaching for the first time in a computer-supported classroom, try to focus on one or two technologies that will best support your pedagogical goals and can be supported by your technological expertise. If you try to do too much in one term, to learn and teach too many technologies, you're likely to get overwhelmed — as are your students. The first time you teach in a computer-supported classroom, for instance, try to learn all you can about word-processing features, in particular the "track changes" and "comment" features of Word for peer response. Or use word processing for in-class writing and incorporate Web-based discussions through your course-management system. The next term, once you're more comfortable, add a technology or two: Teach online research and create a collaborative course Web site, or have students create their own blogs. If you add one technology at a time, you'll have time to learn what works and what doesn't, and you'll spend less class time trying to deal with the inevitable problems caused by trying to do too much.

As an alternative to traditional class discussion, for example, Web-based discussion can be used for a variety of purposes, including posting announcements, allowing students to serve as resources for each other, and preceding or extending classroom conversation. Web-based discussion works best when all students in your class can log on several times a week or at least once before each class meeting. Preceding a class meeting, you can provide a prompt or other guidance on what students should focus on in the reading or ask students to post questions about the reading that can be discussed online and then in class. If a conversation begins online, you can use the online postings as a starting point for classroom discussion, drawing those who have posted into the conversation ("As Katie mentioned in the Web-based discussion. . . . Katie, can you explain that idea further?"). Likewise, Web-based discussion works well for extending classroom discussion, for making connections or additions after the class period is over. Sometimes you and your students will leave class and think, "I wish I had said. . . ." Web-based discussions allow you to fulfill that wish. You can encourage frequent access by requiring a certain number of weekly posts, asking each student to start one thread and respond to one thread each week, for instance. Some students will do so more often on their own. Your WPA may be able to point you to the person who can help you set up a Web-based discussion page that is password protected and reserved for your class only.

You don't need to teach exclusively in a computer-supported classroom in order to make effective use of technology. Some writing programs will allow you to set up one or two class meetings in a computer lab in order to teach specific research skills or participate in real-time chat sessions. In addition, since some of your students will have access to computers—in an on-campus lab, at home, or in their dorm rooms—you can set up a Web-based discussion site or course Web site to support the work you're doing in an otherwise traditional classroom.

If your school offers technology workshops, sign up for ones that will help you learn about the technologies supported by your institution. For example, many schools offer course-management or learning-management systems, such as Blackboard, Angel, Desire2Learn, or Moodle. Such systems allow you to post your syllabus and course materials online, and they provide interfaces that allow you and your students to send e-mail to one another, participate in online discussions, and post additional resources. A course-management system—if you know how to use it effectively—allows you to incorporate a number of technologies in a central location. It's a place where you can post images, URLs, and videos; where students can create blogs or journal entries; and where classes can participate in online discussions. The system can be used both inside or outside the classroom—and in traditional, hybrid, or online courses.

As you explore and consider your options, remember that you don't have to do everything, and computers or other digital technologies don't have to be—and shouldn't be—the focus of the class. If you're not asking students to use outside sources for their papers, don't teach online research. The technology should support—not determine—your pedagogical goals. Just because computers can be used for peer response doesn't mean they *have* to be: You can have students print out their papers and talk face to face.

Since you're in the class to teach writing, not technology, you'll need to take a few steps to prevent the technology from taking the focus away from your goals. If you ask students to do an assignment that involves computers, be sure to prepare a written handout beforehand that takes them through the process step by step. Although some students will know far more than you do about technology, many will know far less. Written handouts help students follow along—and they keep you from having to run around the room, answering the same questions repeatedly. Also, experienced classmates can be an excellent resource for students who have less familiarity with computers. When asking students to work in small groups, make sure at least one student has a good deal of experience with the technology. And if you're assigning computer work as homework, remember that not all students will have easy or reliable access to a computer or the Internet.

Even when technology supports your pedagogical goals, remember that it sometimes fails, and you'll need to have a plan to fall back on. You may have prepared an elaborate PowerPoint presentation on invention techniques, but if the digital projector breaks down, you'll need a backup plan. Printers jam, networks go down, and computers freeze. At such times you can gracefully turn to something else, rather than spending twenty minutes trying to fix a fitful computer. When computers become distracting — through the interruption of instant messaging, the lure of surfing the Web, or the droning buzz and hum of the machines — you can always turn them off.

Example 3.3 **CONSIDERING STUDENTS' TECHNOLOGICAL LITERACY: A WRITING ACTIVITY**

Drawing on the work of Gail Hawisher, Dickie Selfe, Karla Kitalong, and Tracy Bridgeford, Cynthia Selfe provides a technological literacy activity in *Writing New Media*. This activity, simplified and excerpted here, encourages students to consider the literacy practices and values they bring with them to the composition classroom (59). Here are just a few of the questions Selfe asks students to answer in writing (for the full activity, see pp. 59–62 in *Writing New Media*, cited at the end of this chapter):

Early Literacy Development

- What stories can you tell about when, where, how you first came in contact with computers? (including mainframe computers, personal computers, computer games)
- What stories can you tell about when, where, how you first learned to use computers to read or write? To speak or listen to others? To view/ interact with/compose texts? Where did this take place? Did anyone help or encourage you?

Current Literacy

- Do you (or your family) own a computer(s) now?
- What specific kinds of reading and writing, speaking and listening, viewing/interacting and composition do you do now in computer environments at home? At school? Elsewhere?
- What are your favorite kinds of projects/activities in online environments? Please explain. (Wysocki et al. 59–61)

Asking students to write in answer to these and other related questions and to
share their responses with you and their classmates can help you gauge their
level of comfort and expertise with computers and other forms of technology.
Such knowledge, then, will help you structure additional classroom activities that
draw on what students already know in order to help them become better writers.

COLLABORATION: WORKSHOPS AND PEER RESPONSE

Students need guidance for their collaborations to be beneficial. A composition teacher, for example, cannot simply assign students to peer-response groups
and expect them to function successfully. To ask one student to read another's
essay and respond to it is to invite the disappointment of noncommittal comments such as "I really liked it" and "It flows really well." Given the traditional
emphasis on individual effort and the enforcement of student passivity in many
secondary school classrooms, FY writers are often unprepared and initially ill
at ease when placed in collaborative learning situations. For collaborative learning to succeed, then, it must be gradually cultivated and always supported.

Even before doing whole-class workshops or establishing peer-response
groups, you can organize collaborative activities that help students become
more comfortable working with each other. For example, you might ask your
students to select a satisfying passage (of fifty to one hundred words) from one
of their essays and to read it aloud to two other students. Because the intended
audience in the traditional classroom has usually been the teacher, this practice may seem unusual to many students. The students who are to listen should
be instructed to offer no comments at first, for they will best learn to practice
effective listening by suppressing both vacuous praise and harsh criticism.

After this simple shared reading, Peter Elbow and Pat Belanoff suggest that
the listeners (the response group) employ the "sayback" technique: After listening to the draft, the response group tries to restate the effect of the text on the
audience in the form of a question. Responses like "Do you mean . . . ?" and
"Are you trying to show . . . ?" serve as invitations for the writer to continue
developing or even inventing ideas (13). When the writer replies, "Yes, I was trying to explain . . ." and expresses the text's ideas with newfound clarity, then a
more conversational model of writing has been enacted.

In *Sharing and Responding*, Elbow and Belanoff offer several more demanding
response techniques. Descriptive responding consists of "pointing" to memorable or striking features of a text; then "summarizing" the piece, focusing on
the main meaning and suggesting ideas "almost said" but undeveloped or
even unstated; and then locating the "center of gravity," the point or idea most
important to the piece (15–16). For more persuasive or argumentative writing,
analytic responding involves noticing how the writer initially gets the reader
"listening" and interested in the subject; identifying the main claim, the reasons provided, and additional or counter-supports; and considering the tone

of the text, the intended audience, and the assumed attitude of the audience. Both response techniques are designed to encourage peer comments on broader issues of form and style and the content of the text, rather than a premature concentration on mechanical correctness; consequently, peer *response* should not be confused with peer *editing*, which involves proofreading.

Many kinds of collaborative activities are possible, such as submitting a student's draft for comments by the entire class (workshopping) and having the class respond in small groups during class, at conferences, outside class at mutually convenient times, or online—and each variation can be valuable for helping students work together.

Workshops and peer-response groups allow writers to have control over their work but give them the benefit of several readers' responses. Sometimes the peer reviewers align their judgments, sometimes not; but whatever the situation may be, the writers will want to choose among the possibilities for revision (ideas they might not have generated on their own) to revise accordingly. Workshops and peer-response sessions allow writers to see their work through the eyes of their readers and help them gain distance so they can improve their ability to evaluate their writing on their own.

Whole-Class Workshops

The whole class can act as an effective workshop group. Before setting up small groups, some teachers prefer to run several whole-class workshops in order to train students in the process and to get to know them as readers. In whole-class sessions, you will provide guidance on tasks through your questions and comments. The following techniques can help make whole-class workshops positive learning experiences:

1. Present strong student-generated work so the class can easily recognize its strengths. Readers will learn the techniques that work for their peers; writers will gain confidence from well-deserved praise and from recognizing what in their drafts is working. (Be sure to ask for permission ahead of time before using a student's text as your example.)

2. A day or two ahead of time, hand out copies of the essay to be discussed to give students a chance to read it at their own pace. Ask them to write comments in the margins as they read, indicating points of strength and confusion. Finally, have them write a note to the writer, giving their reaction to the overall content, describing the work's strengths, and offering one or two specific suggestions for improvement. Ask them to sign their name to their comments.

3. Begin the workshop by asking the writer or another class member to read aloud from the draft. This practice helps students focus on the essay and remember it. Readers should then be prepared to ask about the background of the piece: "How long have you been working on this?" "What are your concerns?" "Do you already have plans for revision?"

After learning about the background, readers can comment on the positive features of the draft: what worked and what they admired. After establishing the strengths, readers can then move on to discussing what needs to be strengthened in the draft — and specific ways to build those strengths. Ask the writer to take notes on what her classmates are saying rather than to try to defend her work. After listening to the comments of her classmates, the writer should be allowed to ask for specific advice or clarification of what a reader has said. In this process, all students will get some idea about the kind of feedback that is helpful.

4. At the end of the workshop, you should recap some of the strengths that were mentioned and point to two or three elements that the writer can work on in revision, summarizing those comments that seem most salient. You should then have readers hand the writer their signed comments. Let the class know that after the writer reads the comments, you will also read them (in order to record students' progress as readers).

Peer-Response Groups

If you use whole-class workshops as a training ground for talking constructively about writing, then your students may be able to move directly into peer-response groups without much further preparation. However, many teachers prefer to use peer-response groups from the start because beginning writers, whose self-confidence may not be high, tend to be more comfortable in smaller groups. In addition, with several peer-response groups meeting simultaneously, more essays can be discussed in a given period of time. A final advantage of small peer-response groups is that they often evolve into support groups, especially when their members make contact outside the scheduled meetings, either in person or electronically. Many peer-response groups become familiar, intimate, and trustworthy groups for all involved and survive long after the FY writing class itself, especially if you've encouraged students to swap names, e-mail addresses, and phone numbers so they have easy access to one another. (In preparation for setting up peer-response groups in your class, read Wendy Bishop's "Helping Peer Writing Groups Succeed" on p. 309 of this book.)

Small groups meet during class to accomplish specific tasks: discussion of an essay topic, analysis of an upcoming assignment, editorial work on one another's drafts, advice about one another's problem areas, division of a research project, and other mutual-aid endeavors. The expertise of group members usually evolves over the course of the term as students become better readers, questioners, and revisers — especially if you initially help them understand what exactly they are expected to do for one another.

Should you assign students to peer-response groups, or should they form their own? How many students should there be in a group? Should membership rotate or remain intact week after week? Should groups deal with one essay in depth during a session, or should each student receive feedback each time? Should you drop in on the groups (even those held outside of class), participate actively, or stay away? The answers to these and similar questions will depend on you, your students, the dynamics of your class and the groups, and the task at hand. The answers will also change as the term progresses and the class changes, but some general guidelines are provided here.

The size of the groups—and they should be created by the second week, if possible—depends on the amount of time you have and the complexity of the tasks to be accomplished. After all, the more group members, the longer it will take the group to go through the written work. Asking a group of three people to share thesis ideas in twenty minutes is realistic; asking a group of six is not. Keep in mind that groups seem to work best (more inclusively) when there are no more than four students in each—and when the group is balanced in terms of writing ability, race, age, personality, and gender. The best writing groups are usually made up of students who don't know one another well enough initially to talk about anything but the writing assignment. In fact, by waiting until the second week of class to form groups, you will have had the opportunity to see who is friends with whom and then assign friends to different groups.

Assigning tasks to small groups early in the term shows students what kinds of activities might be useful, gives groups a shared set of goals and objectives, and builds camaraderie. Later in the semester little instruction is needed if students are already used to working in groups: Students who are working well in their groups will respond naturally and in a variety of useful and supportive ways to one another's needs.

Membership in groups can be rotated purposely during the term to allow students to make contact with new peers, but some rotation will occur naturally if you move students around to replace absentees. How often you want to reconstitute your groups is up to you, of course. Rotating the makeup of groups every three weeks or so allows members a chance to move beyond introductions and to trust one another, but not to become so predictable in their behaviors as to be unhelpful. Often, though, a group will work so well that the students will ask to remain together. Most teachers will respect such a request.

Tasks for Peer-Response Groups

The ideal peer-response group—a number of motivated students who know how, and are willing, to talk about writing in progress—responds to the questions of the writer honestly, tactfully, specifically, and more successfully than a teacher could alone. Initially, students may be hesitant to critique one another's work because they don't know how to do so constructively or because they think they're supposed to criticize. Therefore, the tasks you assign must model appropriate reading and evaluation. By seeing different stages in one another's essays, students will develop a sense of the plasticity of prose and how changes can help. Finally, peer judgments make the teacher's evaluation seem less arbitrary. Once students learn these lessons and techniques and know what is expected, all you have to say is, "Writing groups, one hour, go to it," and they will.

In the beginning, though, you will want to offer detailed instructions, which may change from session to session as you train students to take on increasingly sophisticated tasks. For example, the first workshop might be a simple exercise in reading aloud: each group member reading a draft to the others, who simply listen, concentrating on the work. Through reading aloud, writers gain distance: They hear strengths and weaknesses they hadn't noticed before; they hear the draft with new objectivity, as though someone else had written it. Just as important, group members get to know what others are working on, gain a sense of how their work compares, and learn to give the most useful advice.

In subsequent sessions, the groups might be asked to work on the following tasks:

1. Without rereading, recall the most memorable points. ("This is what struck me as I listened/read.")
2. Jot down ideas or questions you want to raise.
3. Summarize the writer's point. ("This is what I think you're trying to say.")
4. Respond honestly and thoroughly to the writer's specific questions.
5. Talk through ideas for essays.

Although peer-response groups are capable of performing many tasks, their primary use lies in providing advice about revising and practice in editing. Several days or a week before a written assignment is due, have students meet in groups to discuss rough drafts of the assignment. Have them pass around and respond to their peers' writing. Better than having two students trade drafts, the system of peer-response-group revision allows each draft to be considered by at least two readers. Problems not spotted by one member of the group are usually caught by others, and every writer may hear a variety of responses to a piece of writing. In addition, better writers get the opportunity to assist poorer ones, weaker writers witness the behaviors of stronger writers, and all students get an idea of how others approach an assignment.

Example 3.4 provides guidance for students doing peer response on a written assignment, one that may or may not use visuals. If you're asking students to develop a multimedia project or one that depends especially on visual elements, see Cynthia L. Selfe's "Toward New Media Texts: Taking Up the Challenges of Visual Literacy" in Part III of this book. Selfe's essay includes reflection sheets for the composer/designer as well as for the reader/viewer that can guide students in their peer responses.

Example 3.4 **HOW TO RESPOND IN HELPFUL WAYS TO A PEER'S DRAFT**

Keep this list of questions by your side as you're reviewing your classmate's draft — or your own. Please know that these questions are suggestions or ideas to help you think of encouraging, truly helpful ways of responding. Responding does *not* mean criticizing — it means helping your classmate do his or her best work. In addition, by answering these questions about your peer's draft, you'll improve drastically and quickly your ability to answer the same questions about your own draft.

1. The Assignment. Does the draft carry out the assignment? How might the writer better fulfill the assignment?

2. The Title and Introduction. Does the title tell the reader what the draft is about? Does it catch the reader's interest? What does the opening accomplish in terms of hooking the reader's interest, establishing common ground, and establishing the writer's ethos? How else might the writer begin?

3. The Thesis and Purpose. Paraphrase the thesis as a promise: "In this essay, I will. . . ." Does the draft fulfill that promise? Why, or why not? What is the writer's purpose? How does the draft fulfill (or not fulfill) that purpose?

4. The Audience. Who is the audience? How does the draft establish goodwill with the audience? How does it capture the interest of the audience? What values does the audience hold that are different from the writer's?

5. The Opportunity for Writing. What is the situation (or context) that calls for this writing? Why is it timely or important?

6. The Rhetorical Stance. Where does the writer stand on issues involved with this topic? What words or phrases in the draft indicate the values the writer holds with regard to this topic? How does the writer identify her cause with the interests (or different values) of her audience?

7. <u>The Supporting Points</u>. List the main points, in order. Number them in order of interest to *you*. Which of them could be explained or supported more fully? What evidence, examples, or details might do the trick? Which of the supporting points could be de-emphasized or eliminated? If the writer has used outside research, is it incorporated well and documented correctly?

8. <u>The Paragraphs</u>. Which paragraphs are clearest? best developed? Which paragraphs need further development? What kinds of information might help?

9. <u>The Organization</u>. How is the draft organized — chronologically, spatially, emphatically, or in some other way? Given the organizational pattern, could the main points be presented in a more effective way? What suggestions can you make for transitions between paragraphs that would make connections clearer and easier to follow?

10. <u>The Format/Design</u>. If the writer has used visuals, are they effective? Why, or why not? Are the sources for the visuals correctly cited? How effective is the writer's choice of font, typeface, and other visual elements?

11. <u>The Sentences</u>. Choose three sentences you consider the most interesting or best written — stylistically effective, entertaining, or otherwise memorable. Then choose three sentences you see as weak — confusing, awkward, or uninspiring. Advise your peer on how to revise those three weak sentences.

12. <u>The Words</u>. Circle the words that are particularly effective; underline those that are weak, vague, or unclear. Do any words need to be defined or replaced? Are there any potentially offensive words in the draft?

13. <u>The Tone</u>. What dominant impression does the draft create — serious, humorous, satiric, persuasive, argumentative, or objective? Is the tone appropriate to the topic and audience? Is it consistent? Mark specific places where the writer's voice comes through most clearly. Ask the writer if this is the intended tone — and if he finds your comments surprising.

14. <u>The Conclusion</u>. Does the draft conclude in a memorable way? Does it end abruptly? trail off? restate the introduction? How else might this draft end? If you like the conclusion, give two reasons why.

15. <u>Final Thoughts</u>. What are the main strengths of this draft? weaknesses? What surprised you — and why? What do you want to know more about? What is the writer's single most important comment or point?

Responses to workshop questions like those in Example 3.4 are more useful when they are written down and clipped to the original draft than if they are just discussed. When the questions are used as a worksheet to elicit written answers, students may initially take twenty-five or thirty minutes to work through them while reviewing an essay. But as the term progresses, they will work more quickly.

Online and Electronic Peer Response

The questions listed in Example 3.4 can also serve as a guide for students responding to drafts electronically. If you're teaching in a computer-supported classroom, you might ask students to respond to each others' drafts online in class. If you've already worked in class on effective peer-response strategies (whether you teach in a computer-supported classroom or not), you might ask students to e-mail their drafts to each other or post their drafts to a course Web site and respond outside of class. Asking students to respond to each other's essays outside of class can save class time — but be sure to reserve some time for students to talk face-to-face in peer-response groups, so they can ask questions and make sure they understand the comments others have made on their work.

If you require electronic peer response, be sure students have the hardware and software necessary to complete the task. If you're teaching in a wired or wireless classroom, you likely will already have chosen the program you wish to use (see the section on multimodal learning technologies in Chapter 1), but if students do not have access to a common program designed for peer response, they are at least likely to all have access to Microsoft Word, in which they can utilize the Track Changes feature that allows them to suggest changes, insert comments, and highlight parts of the text. This feature also allows writers to accept and reject changes, deleting comments after they have addressed the issues raised. Whatever method you choose, be sure to provide a handout that explains how students should use the technology.

Evaluating Peer-Response Groups

After one or two sessions, during which students work in their writing groups on their own, try asking for a brief, written evaluation of the group's effectiveness:

1. What does your writing group do well?
2. What has helped you as a writer? What has helped you as a reader?
3. Suggest one thing your group could do differently to improve its effectiveness. Complete this statement: "Next time let's try _____."
4. What are you contributing to the group?
5. What would you like to do better?

Have students discuss their evaluations at a subsequent group meeting and implement some of their own suggestions. Later have them evaluate the groups again:

1. What has your group accomplished so far?
2. What has your group been most helpful with? What has it been least helpful with? Explain.
3. What has each group member contributed?
4. How can you help make your group more effective?

In this way—and especially when you use these questions as the basis of whole-class analysis and discussion—you can keep loose tabs on each group's work and reinforce the idea that students are responsible for the success of their groups. In addition, the groups will learn from the successes and trials of other groups as well as from the contributions of individual group members.

Understanding Cultural and Multilingual Differences in Peer-Response Groups

Asking students to evaluate their peer-response groups periodically will help you and them recognize differences in how and what group members contribute. Students—influenced by personality, gender, cultural differences, and a range of other kinds of differences—will adopt various roles, creating complex group dynamics. One student might be authoritarian, directly telling others how to change their work; another might ask questions, probing for more information; another might try to mediate suggestions, playing a collaborative role; yet another might be silent or resistant or simply unsure of what to contribute. Students' educational backgrounds, expectations, and preferences for the kinds of responses they find useful will further complicate the dynamics.

Students need to understand that communication is influenced by cultural context and that working in groups requires flexibility and openness to others and their ideas. In their article "Variation in EFL-ESL Peer Response," Adina Levine, Brenda Oded, Ulla Connor, and Iveta Asons assert that "students may use culturally diverse rules for how much and what kind of criticism should be expressed" (2). Drawing on earlier studies of ESL peer response, they also observe, more specifically, "While both Chinese and Spanish-speaking students preferred critical comments to help them improve their drafts, and both preferred teacher feedback to student feedback, they differed on the amount and kind of talk that was needed to identify problems" (2). Given such variation, it's imprudent to make sweeping generalizations about how students' cultural backgrounds affect peer response, but Levine's study, which examines "the nature of peer response in the foreign language and second language writing of student populations in two different learning settings: Israel and the U.S." (8), and other similar studies provide a starting point for addressing and working with such differences.

Ilona Leki, in "Meaning and Development of Academic Literacy in a Second Language" (included in Part III of this book), takes a broader view of cultural differences, not simply as they relate to peer response but, rather, to the larger realm of academic literacy. At the end of her article, she writes, "Given how complex literacy issues in second, third, or fourth languages can become, perhaps the only reasonable stance to take, at least initially, is one of modest flexibility and willingness to learn from others, one in which 'you do a lot of observing and then you think about it'" (p. 436). Such observation can take place when students evaluate their own peer-response groups, pointing to their own strengths and to areas they wish to improve.

STUDENT CONFERENCES

Another way to mediate cultural differences and respond directly to the needs of individuals is through student conferences. The student-teacher conference has a number of functions, but the primary ones have to do with getting to know your students better as writers, intervening more directly in their composing processes, and letting them know you care about how they are doing. The student conference gives you the opportunity to explain writing strategies, discuss the strengths and weaknesses of a student's work, plan and examine future work, and in general establish the kind of relationship that will foster strong teacher-student interaction. Most important, though, the conference allows the student to talk about his or her writing, ideas, and plans.

Unfortunately, in spite of all these desirable goals and possibilities, you usually can't rely solely on your office hours for fostering contact with your students, especially if you teach at an institution where many students are balancing responsibilities of work, school, family, and home. Probably the best way to ensure personal contact and effect useful help with revisions, then, is by instituting a system of conferences held in the office, in the classroom, or electronically. Mandatory conferences need to be specified as such from the beginning of the course, preferably on the syllabus. You will need to check with your WPA to learn whether it is acceptable to use occasional class time for individual conferences. For instance, you may be permitted to assign writing groups a task that they will accomplish outside of class and use class time to meet individually with class members whose schedules do not permit meeting at other times. The number of conferences you schedule with your students is up to you. Some teachers specify only one or two conferences per term; others ask their students to meet with them weekly or biweekly.

Conferences work best when they have one of the following purposes:

- Discussion of a plan or draft for a new assignment.
- Discussion of the content or structural revisions of a draft in progress.
- Discussion of the progress of any long-term, ongoing project (a research essay, for instance).
- Discussion of a process, particularly changes in a student's writing process, and the sharing of anecdotes about writing (since you, the teacher, are a writer, too, with your own blocks, ruts, successes).
- Discussion of activities meant to deal with specific and identified patterns of formal problems: syntactic errors, verb endings, and the like.

Usually the conversation focuses on a draft the student has submitted. Each conference should draw on past work and past discussions in order to support and stimulate the student's future work. Student-teacher conferences, then, are always conversations about writing — and about moving forward. Through one-on-one discussion of students' work (previous, in hand, or planned), you get to know your students, demonstrate your interest in their work, and provide a responsive audience and individualized instruction. The students, meanwhile, get to talk about their intentions and their work to an interested and expert mentor. Getting students to take an active part in conferences, however, is not always easy. Many of them are more than willing to let the teacher dominate any discussion, particularly during a one-on-one conference. Others may be intimidated by the very idea of meeting alone with the teacher or of having the teacher's complete attention. To students used to blending into the crowd of the classroom, the potential for miscommunication or misjudgment may seem high. But as soon as they realize that the direction of the conference belongs to them, rather than to you, they will be more comfortable meeting and talking about their work.

Therefore, in addition to the very real advantage of helping students "own" their learning and writing, conferences provide a safe space to discuss ongoing problems or issues of concern. For instance, if a student has been absent or tardy often, you can show your concern: "I've noticed you've missed three classes already this term. Is there some problem or issue I should know about?" Or if a student is especially quiet in class, you can ask how you can help provide a space for her to speak: "I've noticed that you're very quiet in class. I'm sure you have a lot to say. Would it be helpful if I called on you?" Problems in the classroom often stem from issues outside class, and you can guide students to the appropriate resources for help, such as the counseling center or disability services office. Conferences also provide a good time to learn about how your classroom practices are working. You might ask, "How's your writing group going?" or "What kinds of classroom activities have been most or least helpful to you in your writing?" Students' answers to such questions will help you modify classroom practices before the end-of-the-term evaluations come back and it's too late to make changes.

Using a regular conference system means your teaching will be more inter-active than presentational, and your students' learning will be more collabor-ative and active. If students view writing as a complex, long-term, interactive process of prewriting, drafting, receiving feedback, and revising, they will seek responses from you and from their peers. Regularly scheduled conferences are simply an extension of this process: Writers talk themselves through their drafts, over the rough spots, and into new territories, while you, as the reader-teacher, provide a knowledgeable, supportive audience. Students (all writers, for that matter) are encouraged when they know somebody cares enough to read, respond to, and talk about what they write.

However you decide to structure conferences for your course, let your students know your reasons for doing so, and establish a schedule as early in the term as possible so students will know what kind of feedback to expect and when. They should understand that yours is not the only word and that feedback from their peers — individually, in writing groups, in whole-class workshops — and from writing center tutors is useful as well. Using all of these methods of feed-back will give students a variety of responses to their work, emphasizing a broader audience for that work (and keeping you from carrying the total weight of being the only respondent).

Scripting the Conference

In a conference, it is a good idea to assume the writer knows the work better than you do. The student wrote the essay and knows the kind of effort that went into it, what was hard and what was easy. The writer may also have thought about purpose, audience, and possibilities for revision. Your questions and responses will help the student see the draft in a fresh or less subjective way. In conferences, then, you use your experience as a reader to teach students how to read their own work.

Successful conferences are usually based on a script. Whether you stick to or diverge from that script depends on the conference, but having a script means you have a plan. When you open a conference with such scripted questions as "How can I help you?" and "What is your purpose in this piece of writing?" you set the direction for the conference yet allow the student to steer. Other open-ended, scripted questions that can help students get going include the following:

- What are the stronger sections? the weaker? Why?
- Who is your audience?
- What are you pleased with? What are you not so happy with?
- What did you learn in writing this?
- Is this finished? If not, what would you like to change?

- What surprised you in this essay?
- What did you discover while writing this?
- What is the key line or passage? Why is it so important?

If you can teach the student to use the conference as a chance to communicate with a supportive, informed reader, you will both relax a little and become two writers, or perhaps a writer and a writing coach, working together to push a draft forward and, ultimately, to improve the student's overall writing and reading skills. Often it is helpful to let the student know exactly what you understand from the reading. Tell the student what you think she is getting at in the essay so that she can compare your reading and understanding with what she hoped readers would understand. If you missed the point, the student will see the need for appropriate revision.

Student investment in a conference also ensures student "ownership" of the essay under discussion. It is all too easy for teachers to appropriate students' work by being too much the director, by revising for students instead of helping them choose the course of the revision. The issue here is one of responsibility, and responsibility depends entirely on the nature of the discussion and the spirit in which advice is given and received. For example, a student who questions the introduction to his essay does so because he suspects there is a better place to begin. And with his question, he opens the door for you to point to one or more spots that might work as a better beginning. You might give a mini-lesson on audience, tension, tone, even argumentation—depending on the nature of the assignment—as you discuss introductions and what they can do. It is always left to the students to evaluate your advice, to weigh what they have learned in the conference and to consider their own instincts before deciding what to do in the next draft. A discussion initiated by the student about possible leads differs considerably from one initiated by the teacher saying that the introduction should be replaced by the third paragraph. In the latter case, the student's responsibility (and initiative) for the assignment is lost. When an essay improves as the result of a revision, the student should "own" the improvement.

A successful conference should end with at least one concrete assignment, one that shows you and the student agree on your expectations for the next stage of work. In addition, both you and the student should come away with a clear sense of what has been accomplished. You should know what expectations have been raised, what task comes next, and why.

Student-teacher conferences about drafts may be demanding, but they are a much more efficient way to help students understand content and questions of organization than just marking up their essays. For these conferences to be useful, they must be dialogic—meetings in which students can ask you questions, explain themselves, react to suggestions. In these ways the bond between writer and reader becomes real and personal. The more conferences you hold with your students, the better they will come to understand the concept of an audience and the responsibilities of a writer.

EVERYBODY'S ISSUES

Absenteeism and Tardiness

In writing courses, the most common classroom-management problem has nothing to do with classroom order or activities — it is absenteeism. The temptation to skip classes can be great for FY students, who may for the first time in their lives be in a situation in which no one is forcing them to go to school. In dealing with absenteeism, teachers must first consider that this is college and they have no way to compel attendance.

Even before the term begins, you should be familiar with your school's policy on class attendance and should work with it as best you can. In general, unless your department has a specific written policy, teachers may be forbidden or discouraged from using grades to compel attendance in writing courses. Some schools will not allow you to fail a student who never comes to class but writes the assigned essays. Still, you have options. You can, of course, make class participation and writing-group work a part of the final grade so that the grades of those students who do not attend class will suffer. In addition, brief in-class writing assignments and group projects will encourage steady attendance.

Often the best way to deal with absenteeism is to plan the course so as to discourage it. Try this: Give information about graded assignments on one class day, hold editing workshops on another class day, have graded essays due on yet another class day. In other words, fill up the week with requests for specific actions, and provide meaningful progress toward a goal. If a student misses a class, the goal becomes harder to attain and the tasks at hand become more difficult. If a student skips a writing-group session and then receives a poor grade on an essay because the support for his thesis is vague, and if he realizes his writing group would have pointed out this shortcoming, he will quickly become aware of the concrete advantages of attending class.

Whatever your policy on absenteeism may be, you should spell it out clearly in the syllabus so that when problems do occur you can point to the written policy. If a student misses two or more classes in a row, you may wish to call or send an e-mail, showing your concern. Students often have valid reasons for missing classes (illness or family emergency), but if the problem persists, it is best to know about the situation early enough to advise students of their options (including withdrawing from the course). You will also need to decide whether you want to — or if your institution requires you to — distinguish between excused and unexcused absences.

You may also encounter students who consistently show up for class five, ten, even fifteen minutes late. Here again, your school may have a policy, but usually this matter is best settled privately. Speak to the student after class or in conference, and find out whether there is a valid reason for the lateness. Surprisingly often, students do have good excuses — a long walk across campus between classes, an inconsiderate teacher running late in a previous class, personal responsibilities of different sorts — but just as often the lateness is a result of late rising, poor planning, or careless habits.

If the student's reasons for lateness do not seem valid, state politely but seriously that students who are late will be marked as absent. If you take attendance at the start of each class, students will quickly realize that latecomers are marked as absent. Treating students as responsible adults and showing an interest in them can have a good effect: Tardy students often begin appearing in class on time.

Late Essays

Late essays — written assignments handed in (often slipped surreptitiously under your office door or into your office mailbox) after their due date — can be another problem, but only if you allow them to be. State in your syllabus that you will not accept late essays: "No late assignments. Period." Or, if your composition program allows it, make the consequences for late assignments clear in the syllabus: "Grades will be reduced by one-half of a letter grade for each day an assignment is late." When the inevitable requests for extensions appear or when the late essays show up, you can adjust the policy as seems fit and fair. It is often better to announce an unyielding policy initially and then adjust it than to announce a liberal policy, see it abused, and then try to establish a harder line. If you do receive a late essay that has not been explained in advance, one common way of dealing with it is to note the time and date it reached you, write "late essay" on it, and lower the grade. You can also give it credit without reading it, which will keep the student from being penalized for not turning in the essay but will not add to the student's grade average. You can, of course, choose instead not to accept it.

Class Cancellations

No matter how carefully you construct your syllabus and plan your classes, sometimes events beyond your control intervene. A hurricane blows through, two feet of snow fall overnight, or you wake with the stomach flu. If your school cancels classes for a weather emergency, for example, you have a few options. You can try to compress two days of learning/readings into one day, you may cut readings or assignments to stay on schedule, or you can provide opportunities for students to do work outside the classroom. If you have an online discussion board set up, you can conduct some of the work online.

If you're ill or cannot make it to class for some other legitimate reason, be sure to follow the procedure that your school has set up for reporting absences. It might involve contacting your department chair or WPA. If there is no policy for what to do when you cannot be in class, have alternate plans at your disposal. You might, for example, ask students to do an extra assignment (respond to the reading, complete a prewriting activity, or attend a campus event and write a review of that event) and e-mail it to you or post it to your course-management site. Or you might ask students to meet in peer-response groups outside of class. If you have a colleague who teaches on a different schedule than you, you can agree ahead of time to substitute for one another should a personal emergency arise. If you choose this last option, be sure to provide your colleague with an attendance sheet and the materials your students have read for the day.

Use of Personal Technology in the Classroom

You'll need to set policies early in the term—ideally on the syllabus—about the use of personal technology in the classroom. Will you allow your students to use laptops or other portable electronic devices in class? Why, or why not? Students may write more quickly on laptops and find them useful for in-class writings and note-taking, but some will also be tempted to check e-mail or surf the Web in class. Cell phones might be useful for quickly looking up a fact to supplement classroom conversation, but the rings and buzzes can be frustrating, and students with mobile phones in class are often tempted to text. As useful as technology is, it can also be a distraction. Weigh the pros and cons of using certain technologies in the classroom, and make your policies and parameters clear from the beginning.

Disruptive Students

Rare is the problem with classroom order that cannot be solved by talking to the right person—in private. College students are anxious to prove their maturity and usually will not continue behavior that they have been made to understand is undesirable, particularly if they realize that their peers also disapprove. If one or two students continually skip or disrupt class, speak to them after class separately—or ask them to stop by during your office hours. In one-on-one conversation, you can stress the importance of participation and get a better sense of the reasons for the student's behavior. In most cases—and particularly if they don't feel humiliated—FY students are willing to act as productive members of the class. If you provide such students with a series of classroom opportunities to demonstrate their improved attitude, they will nearly always help you and the rest of the class out by becoming more cooperative.

You may find, however, that some students do not respond to subtlety or to the personal approach. Occasionally, a student will test a teacher's authority, often in cases when a teacher is less experienced, female, and/or young. Differences in race, sexual orientation, or physical ability—depending on the backgrounds and expectations of the students—can also affect classroom interactions. While on most days, all will go well, in cases of serious classroom disruptions, you should make yourself aware of what sorts of backup you have from your department and university. Some students have become accustomed to acting out, have learned to deflect reprimands, and show little respect for others. Find out from your WPA, if necessary, how your program wishes you to handle such disruptive students. You may need to ask the student to speak to the WPA directly, or you may simply need to tell the student to leave the class. If you choose to talk with a disruptive student in private, be sure to leave your office door open and, whenever possible, have a trusted colleague within listening distance. Your safety is important. It is also important that such disciplinary issues not disrupt your class any more than is necessary. If a student is resistant or becomes confrontational in class, it's best to dismiss the whole class for that day and go directly to your WPA for help. It is very rare for student defiance to reach such a level, but if it does, don't try to handle it alone. If necessary, call campus security. In less severe cases, seek immediate assistance from your program or department head, and if the disruptive behavior continues, get the student out of your class. You owe it to the other students in the class—as well as to yourself.

Disabilities and Learning Differences

Teachers and students alike come to class with various disabilities and learning differences—some visible, others invisible. Some disabilities and differences require making specific accommodations and working with disability services or other campus offices; all require some element of understanding and perhaps further research. *Disability and the Teaching of Writing*, edited by Cynthia Lewiecki-Wilson and Brenda Jo Brueggemann, "introduces writing instructors to the many ways that disability—as topic, theory, identity, and a presence in our classrooms—calls for new practices in the teaching of writing" (v). This resource, which includes opportunities for reflecting on your teaching and suggestions for student activities, provides a good starting point for learning more about creating an inclusive classroom.

Although no hard and fast rules exist for dealing with every disability or learning difference, some general principles can help you create a pedagogy that is sensitive to difference. First, make sure you include a statement about disability accommodations in your syllabus. Often your school will have a template for such statements (one that provides contact information for the office of disability services as well as information about student responsibilities in terms of documentation and accommodation). Make sure your syllabus is available in print and in electronic form. If the syllabus is in electronic form, students who have visual impairments can make the text larger or use a screen reader. On the first day of class, show your openness to working with all students; invite those who need accommodations to talk with you after class.

When students do talk with you, listen to their concerns and understand that their needs often go beyond a list of accommodations. For example, if you have a student with a stutter or disfluency, that student may sometimes wish someone would offer the word she cannot say at a particular moment, but at other times she may simply want others to be patient as she finishes her sentence—no matter how long it takes. Recognize, too, that learning differences are not necessarily documented disabilities but your attention to differences can make your classroom more accessible. Present information in more than one mode to accommodate various learning styles. For example, show visuals, read them aloud, and then create activities (individual and group activities) that help reinforce what you want students to learn. Also provide opportunities throughout the term for students to give you feedback; ask students what activities and aspects of the classroom experience contribute to their learning, ask what can be improved, and take their suggestions seriously.

Plagiarism, Intellectual Property, and Academic Integrity

All of us go to books, teachers, friends, experts, movies, and Web sites for information and ideas that we then use in our decision making, thinking, and writing. If we have strong opinions about the superiority of foreign-made over U.S.-made cars, for example, chances are we came to those opinions through conversations and reading. Yet we often neglect to mention the sources for our opinions and focus instead on the ideas themselves. We're so used to taking the credit for our opinions that we rarely name our sources; doing so seems unnecessary. Sometimes we want to take all the credit for what we think are our own unique thoughts; at other times, we don't really consider where our thoughts or opinions came from. In some cultures, it's considered impolite or even disrespectful to note your sources; indeed, our concept of plagiarism doesn't exist in some cultures, and it has changed over time even in our own.

Writing students in North America, however, don't enjoy the luxury of eliding their sources. When students present the work or thinking of others as their own, it's called plagiarism, whether their intention was to compensate for academic-performance anxiety, steal someone else's ideas and get away with it, or take full credit in all innocence for what became their ultimate opinion. Plagiarism can range from downloading an entire essay from the Web and submitting it for a grade to lifting the opening paragraph from a recent *Time* article. It can be as obvious as a beautifully written passage from Terry Tempest Williams amid a jumble of otherwise impenetrable prose, or it can be as subtle as an artfully worked-in argument from a sociology text. Most important, it can be deliberate or accidental; students can plagiarize with anything from full knowledge of the consequences to none at all. The range of attitudes can be based on experience, knowledge, or cultural background. However, whatever the reasons for or degree of plagiarism, it spells a problem that you'll want to approach quickly and efficiently.

Defining the Terms Given the current academic climate's insistence on a responsible use of sources, it's important that you and your students have a clear understanding of academic integrity, plagiarism, and intellectual property (one's ideas and work). Plagiarism — the use of someone else's words, ideas, or, images without giving credit to the source — can result in serious consequences. At some colleges, students who plagiarize fail the course automatically; at others, they are expelled. In academic circles, plagiarism is a serious offense: Professors who plagiarized, even inadvertently, have had their degrees revoked or their books withdrawn from publication. Outside academic life, eminent political, business, and scientific leaders have been stripped of candidacies, positions, and awards because of plagiarism. Therefore, you'll want your students to be able to acknowledge directly and credit specifically the intellectual property of others. They must be able to give credit where credit is due.

Example 3.5 shows Penn State's guide to plagiarism, which is provided to incoming students so they won't *un*knowingly commit plagiarism.

However, students and teachers are often confused by what exactly constitutes plagiarism—in other words, exactly when and where *is* credit due? It's important that you teach students which types of sources to acknowledge. Information that is well known or that you gather yourself does not need to be cited. But what exactly can be considered "well known"? In Chapter 18 of *The Everyday Writer*, Fifth Edition, Andrea Lunsford offers the following list of materials that do not require acknowledgment:

> *Common knowledge*
> *Facts available in a wide variety of sources*
> *Your own findings from field research* (217)

Lunsford also offers the following list of materials that must be cited and included in a bibliography or works-cited list:

> *Quotations, paraphrases, and summaries*
> *Facts that aren't widely known or claims that are arguable*
> *Visuals from any source*
> *Help provided by others* (217–18)

Example 3.5   PENN STATE'S GUIDE TO UNDERSTANDING PLAGIARISM

The Source

> The U.S. has only lost approximately 30 percent of its original forest area, most of this in the nineteenth century. The loss has not been higher mainly because population pressure has never been as great there as in Europe. The doubling of U.S. farmland from 1880 to 1920 happened almost without affecting the total forest area as most was converted from grasslands.
>
> –Bjorn Lomborg, *The Skeptical Environmentalist*

Word-for-Word Plagiarism

In the following example, the writer tacks on a new opening part of the first sentence in the hope that the reader won't notice that the rest of the paragraph is simply copied from the source. The plagiarized words are italicized.

> Despite the outcry from environmentalist groups like Earth First! and the Sierra Club, it is important to note that *the U.S. has only lost approximately 30 percent of its original forest area, most of this in the nineteenth century. The loss has not been higher mainly because population pressure has never been as great there as in Europe. The doubling of U.S. farmland from 1880 to 1920 happened almost without affecting the total forest area as most was converted from grasslands.*

Quotation marks around all the copied text, followed by a parenthetical citation, would avoid plagiarism in this case. But even if that were done, a reader might wonder why so much was quoted from Lomborg in the first place. Beyond that, a reader might wonder why you chose to use a quote here instead of paraphrase this passage, which as a whole is not very quotable, especially with the odd reference to Europe. Using exact quotes should be reserved for situations where the original author has stated the idea in a better way than any paraphrase you might come up with. In the above case, the information could be summed up and simply paraphrased, with a proper citation, because the idea, even in your words, belongs to someone else. Furthermore, a paper consisting largely of quoted passages and little original writing would be relatively worthless.

Plagiarizing by Paraphrase

In the following case, the exact ideas in the source are followed very closely — too closely — simply by substituting your own words and sentences for those of the original.

Original	*Paraphrase*
The United States has only lost approximately 30 percent of its original forest area, most of this in the nineteenth century.	Only 30 percent of the original forest area in the United States has been lost.
The loss has not been higher mainly because population pressure has never been as great there as in Europe.	Europe has fared slightly worse due to greater population pressure.

The doubling of U.S. farmland from 1880 to 1920 happened almost without affecting the total forest area as most was converted from grasslands.	Even though U.S. farmland doubled from 1880 to 1920, little forest area was affected since the farms appeared on grasslands.

The ideas in the right column appear to be original. Obviously, they are just Lomborg's ideas presented in different words without any acknowledgment. Plagiarism can be avoided easily here by introducing the paraphrased section with an attribution to Lomborg and then following up with a parenthetical citation. Such an introduction is underlined here:

> Bjorn Lomborg points out that despite environmentalists' outcries . . . (page number).

Properly used, paraphrase is a valuable rhetorical technique. You should use it to simplify or summarize so that others' ideas or information, properly attributed in the introduction and documented in a parenthetical citation, may be woven into the pattern of your own ideas. You should not use paraphrase simply to avoid quotation; you should use it to express another's important ideas in your own words when those ideas are not expressed in a way that is useful to quote directly.

Mosaic Plagiarism

This is a more sophisticated kind of plagiarism wherein phrases and terms are lifted from the source and sprinkled in among your own prose. Words and phrases lifted verbatim or with only slight changes are italicized:

> Environmentalist groups have long bemoaned the loss of U.S. forests, particularly in this age of population growth and urbanization. Yet, *the U.S. has only lost approximately 30 percent of its original forest area, and most of this in the nineteenth century.* There are a few main reasons for this. First, *population pressure has never been as great* in this country *as in Europe.* Second, the explosion of *U.S. farmland, when it doubled from 1880 to 1920, happened almost without affecting the total forest area as most was converted from grasslands.*

Mosaic plagiarism may be caused by sloppy note-taking, but it always looks thoroughly dishonest and intentional and will be judged as such. In the above example, just adding an introduction and a parenthetical citation will not solve the plagiarism problem since no quotation marks are used where required. But adding them would raise the question of why those short phrases and basic statements of fact and opinion are worth quoting word for word. The best solution is to paraphrase everything: Rewrite the plagiarized parts in your own words, introduce the passage properly, and add a parenthetical citation.

Summary

Using quotation marks around someone else's words avoids the charge of plagiarism, but when overdone, makes for a patchwork paper with little flow to it. When most of what you want to say comes from a single source, either quote directly or paraphrase. In both cases, introduce your borrowed words or ideas by attributing them to the author and then follow them with a parenthetical citation.

The secret of using sources productively is to make them work for you to support and amplify your ideas. If you find, as you work at paraphrasing, quoting, and citing, that you are only pasting sources together with a few of your own words and ideas thrown in — that too much of your paper comes from your sources and not enough from your own mind — then go back and start over. Try rewriting the paper without looking at your sources, just using your own ideas; after you have completed a draft entirely of your own, add the specific words and ideas from your sources to support what you want to say.

If you have any doubts about the way you are using sources, talk to your instructor as soon as you can.

Source: http://english.la.psu.edu/undergraduate/plagiarism-policy

---

Specific Department Plagiarism Policy Some departments have official plagiarism policies that you must explain to the class early on in the term, adhere to, and enforce. It's important to include a copy of the plagiarism statement with your syllabus, so students can refer to it at any time. The English Department at

Penn State, for example, has a detailed plagiarism policy that is summarized in the following statement: "The Department of English insists on strict standards of academic honesty in all courses. Therefore, plagiarism, the act of passing off someone else's words or ideas as your own, will be penalized severely."

Teaching toward the Prevention of Plagiarism   Of course, the best policy for dealing with plagiarism is to avoid inviting it in the first place. Successful teachers avoid writing assignments that lend themselves to easy answers found in readily available sources, those that populate various online paper mills and for-hire essay-writing sites, and those that have been around the department for years. Another way to prevent plagiarism is to suggest essay topics that must be personalized in some way. And if you make certain that all students' essays have gone through several revisions and that all early drafts are turned in with the typed final versions, you can be pretty sure your students have written their own essays. When assigning research projects, you might ask your students to keep and submit research portfolios, which include notes on their sources as well as multiple drafts of their papers. These portfolios can provide a forum for the teacher to intervene early and prevent any plagiarism-related issues. Good assignment planning and classroom management can make plagiarism difficult — sometimes more difficult, in fact, than writing the essay.

When you've taught your students how to acknowledge the work of others responsibly, explained your university's plagiarism policy, and designed writing assignments and policies that discourage plagiarism, you've done just about all you can. Even teachers who take the time to explain the many good reasons for citing sources receive plagiarized essays. You can stress that by crediting their sources, students not only demonstrate the extra research they've conducted; they also place their own intellectual endeavor in the context of the conversation that has come before. By crediting their sources, students thank those whose work they've built on. In short, crediting sources provides a means of establishing the student's ethos as a writer. Failure to credit sources corrupts the textual conversation, misleads readers, and destroys the credibility of the writer and the work. By raising these issues, you'll provide a forum for discussing the ethical and cultural dimensions of citing, paraphrasing, and quoting sources; concepts of intellectual property; and academic integrity.

Internet Plagiarism   Even the best teachers sometimes have to deal with intentional plagiarism, and given the ease of downloading papers from the Internet, it's no surprise. There are more than 250 different term-paper sites on the Web, each one allowing college essays to be downloaded, tweaked to provide some seeming evidence of originality, and passed off as the student's own. Some sites, such as www.termpapersites.com, list several member sites, advertising free essays or ones that can be custom ordered. Taken together, term-paper sites represent a genuine threat to the integrity of teaching writing in the United States. The Kimbel Library of Coastal Carolina University offers an online list of active Internet paper mills, compiled in conjunction with a teaching effectiveness seminar; the list is updated every six months. (For more information, see the Web site listed at the end of this chapter.)

Confronting Plagiarism One of the most uncomfortable issues teachers face is suspecting a student of plagiarizing, but there isn't an experienced teacher among us who hasn't had to deal with the issue. Before the widespread use of computers, teachers went to the library to try to locate the original source — the "smoking gun" — before they could confront, let alone punish, a student suspected of plagiarism. Today, many schools use Web plagiarism trackers and plagiarism-detection software (such as www.turnitin.com, www.plagiarism.com, and www.canexus.com) as a means of identifying plagiarized or purchased research papers as well as the plagiarized source. Many teachers, however, have raised concerns about the unauthorized archiving of students' work and the climate of suspicion plagiarism trackers create. Your judgment as a teacher will likely be better than any plagiarism tracker; after all, if you didn't think it was plagiarized in the first place, why would you submit it to the Web site for identification as a plagiarized essay? If you suspect that a student has downloaded an essay from the Internet, you can simply type a phrase from that essay into a search engine such as Google, which checks the results against most paper mills.

If you do find indisputable evidence of plagiarism, you need to determine how to proceed. Consider whether the student intended dishonesty or whether the uncited material is a result of ignorance, carelessness, or turpitude. Most teachers would rather not set the wheels of institutional punishment going unless they are sure the student intended dishonesty. Instead, they will try to deal with the student's failure in the context of the class, by asking the student to rewrite the essay or by giving that one essay a failing grade. Pressing plagiarism cases publicly is time-consuming and unpleasant, and only where the intent to deceive is clear and the case is obvious and provable is it common for a teacher to invoke the full majesty of the academic code against a plagiarist.

As in other areas, however, you need to know your institution's policy on reporting plagiarism. (For scholarly discussions of plagiarism, see Curzan and Damour, pp. 176–82; Haswell and Lu; and Lunsford, Chapter 14 of *The St. Martin's Handbook,* Seventh Edition. See also the Web site **bcs.bedfordstmartins.com /rewriting**, which offers, among a wealth of other writing resources, an interactive tutorial on avoiding plagiarism; also available through *Re:Writing* are helpful research tools for teachers and students, such as *ModelDoc Central, The Bedford Bibliographer,* and *The Bedford Research Room.*

WORKS CITED

Brookfield, Stephen D., and Stephen Preskill. *Discussion as a Way of Teaching: Tools and Techniques for Democratic Classrooms.* 2nd ed. San Francisco: Jossey-Bass, 2005. Print.

Curzan, Anne, and Lisa Damour. *First Day to Final Grade: A Graduate Student's Guide to Teaching.* 3rd ed. Ann Arbor: U of Michigan P, 2011. Print.

Elbow, Peter, and Pat Belanoff. *Sharing and Responding.* New York: Random, 1989. Print.

Eldred, Janet M. "Pedagogy in the Computer-Networked Classroom." *Computers and Composition* 8.2 (1991): 47–61. Rpt. in *Computers in the Composition Classroom: A Critical Sourcebook.* Ed. Michelle Sidler, Richard Morris, and Elizabeth Overman Smith. Boston: Bedford 2008. 239–50. Print.

Haswell, Richard H., and Min-Zhan Lu. *CompTales.* New York: Longman, 2007. Print.

Levine, Adina, Brenda Oded, Ulla Connor, and Iveta Asons. "Variation in EFL-ESL Peer Response." *TESL-EJ* 6.3 (2002): 1–18. Print.

Lewiecki-Wilson, Cynthia, and Brenda Jo Brueggemann, eds. *Disability and the Teaching of Writing: A Critical Sourcebook.* Boston: Bedford, 2008. Print.

Lunsford, Andrea. *The Everyday Writer.* 5th ed. Boston: Bedford, 2013. Print.

——. *The St. Martin's Handbook.* 7th ed. Boston: Bedford, 2011. Print.

Polanyi, Michael. *Personal Knowledge: Towards a Post-Critical Philosophy.* New York: Harper, 1964. Print.

Weaver, Richard. *Language Is Sermonic.* Ed. Richard L. Johannesen, Rennard Strickland, and Ralph T. Eubanks. Baton Rouge: Louisiana State UP, 1970. Print.

Wysocki, Anne Frances, Johndan Johnson-Eilola, Cynthia L. Selfe, and Geoffrey Sirc. *Writing New Media: Theory and Applications for Expanding the Teaching of Composition.* Logan: Utah State UP, 2004. Print.

Useful Web Sites

Bedford Researcher
bedfordresearcher.com

Bedford/St. Martin's Model Documents Gallery
bedfordstmartins.com/modeldocs

Bedford/St. Martin's Plagiarism Workshop
bedfordstmartins.com/plagiarism

Eve 2.4 Essays Verification Engine
www.canexus.com

Kimbel Library: Internet Paper Mills
www.coastal.edu/library/presentations/mills2.html

Penn State's Plagiarism Policy
english.la.psu.edu/undergraduate/plagiarism-policy

Plagiarism.com
www.plagiarism.com

***The St. Martin's Handbook,* Seventh Edition Site**
bedfordstmartins.com/smhandbook

Turnitin.com
www.turnitin.com

CHAPTER

4

Successful Writing Assignments

> *To me, creating a successful assignment involves both responding to a rhetorical situation — that my students need to write something — and creating rhetorical situations for my students. Thus, it's important to provide information to students about their purpose, available means of persuasion and constraints (including genre, medium, length), and potential audiences. This also means considering the rhetorical canons for the occasion. For example, as I'm inventing the assignment, what are my resources and constraints? And how might I deliver this assignment to my students effectively so that the assignment is clear and specific and supports them in approaching a situation with complexity and awareness?*

> —MICHAEL J. FARIS

ASSIGNMENTS

Initiating student writing and designing and evaluating writing assignments are at the heart of a composition teacher's job. The life of a writing teacher has often been described as a perpetual search for effective topics, writing prompts, and assignments. No matter how polished their courses seem, all good writing teachers remain on the lookout for more fruitful ways to help students develop as writers as they identify reasons to write, find topics they care about, and write for audiences they know.

There's no best way to run a writing program, let alone design a writing course, but there are basic issues to take into consideration as you think about your course and assignments. Even if your composition program has provided you with textbooks and a syllabus, you'll still need to take two basic issues into consideration as you plan your course. What genres will you ask your students to write? Will your students have a free choice of topics? Some FY writing teachers (and programs) specify every feature of every writing assignment, from topic and genre to deadline and format, while others encourage students to make their own choices. There are advantages to both course designs as well as to many of the designs that fall somewhere in between. Some students thrive in a tightly designed writing course, finding security in established boundaries even though others might feel that they're simply doing what the teacher wants, writing artificial essays about uninteresting subjects. In a course offering more freedom and options in terms of choosing, topics, genres, and modes of delivery, some students blossom. They experiment with different forms and genres and feel emotionally invested in their writing, more so than if they had to respond to a teacher's specifications; nevertheless, other students in that same class might feel as though they've been set adrift. The benefits for teachers also vary. Some teachers feel more comfortable evaluating essays that are all alike in terms of format, length, and genre, whereas others are invigorated by responding to student projects on a variety of topics, some in innovative forms, such as radio essays, hypertext essays with audio clips and images, and braided essays that incorporate personal narrative, research, and textual analysis.

In *Genre and Writing,* Wendy Bishop and Hans Ostrom encourage teachers "to be aware of the power of discourses and genres that we have claimed for ourselves," arguing that "we need to return this power to our students, encouraging alternate understandings of genre as form *and* as social practice" (1). That is, the assignments teachers give (as well as the kinds of scholarly work they do) can help create, break, or reinforce conventions (such as whether a writer should use "I" in academic writing, whether a thesis statement must be explicit or the argument can be implied, and whether students are encouraged to write more formally or conversationally). Bishop and Ostrom, as well as other composition scholars, want teachers to consider the potential effects of the choices they make in giving assignments. The assignments you give will help shape the way your students view writing and its purposes — and they will also shape you.

For a first-time teacher, following a preset syllabus and series of writing assignments designed by experienced, successful teachers can be a good idea. Whether these carefully developed and sequenced assignments come from your composition program or from a good textbook doesn't matter as long as they are assignments that you can use with confidence. Depending on whether the textbook is a rhetoric, rhetorically arranged reader, thematic reader, or handbook, you'll find a wide variety of assignments that reflect different philosophies of teaching, learning, and writing. Just a glance at the textbooks shelved in your composition office will reveal a range of writing assignments: basic rhetorical methods of development; arguments; personal essays; Web site construction and other multimodal assignments; literacy studies, including narratives and autobiographies; institutional and political critiques; traditional rhetorical exercises, including imitation; and research projects, including collaborative research and ethnographies. Some assignments encourage writing to learn; others present writing as a way to communicate something the writer has already learned.

The assignments in textbooks have been developed by experienced teachers; often, they've been tested by a number of teachers across the nation who have helped refine and improve them. Therefore, if the pedagogical theories supported by the textbook you're using are close to your own, chances are the book's assignments will work well for you, too. As you create assignments for your classes, carefully consider what you want students to learn and what kinds of writing you want to read — and then choose, refine, or design writing assignments that will help you achieve these goals. If you're using a textbook as a starting place, remember that you can adjust the topics and specifications to suit your purposes and your class. The following discussion offers guidelines and examples to help you create writing assignments and to guide students as they respond to the assignments.

Defining Good Assignments

What a Good Assignment Is Not   Before we turn to defining good assignments, we want to spend a little time talking about what a good assignment is *not* — and the reasons why it is not. A good assignment is not one that can be answered with a simple true/false or yes/no answer: "Do the SAT exams have too much power over students' lives?" Such assignments do not offer a writer enough purpose or give enough direction, and students are often at a loss for a place to go after they have formulated their simple answers. A good assignment is not one that leads to unfocused or too-short answers. For example, "How do you feel about the ozone layer?" does not give students enough direction.

A good assignment is also not one that assumes too much student knowledge. "What are the good and bad points of U.S. foreign policy?" or "Is America decaying as the Roman Empire did?" would be far too broad, and even a minimal answer would require students to do a considerable amount of reading and research. Nor is a good assignment one that poses too many questions in its attempt to elicit a specific response:

> In the reality television show *Survivor,* what do producers wish to suggest about society? What do the competitions, the injunction to "outwit, outplay, outlast," and the fact that there can only be one "survivor" at the end suggest about human relationships — and their relationship to nature? What image does the show provide of different cultures? of group dynamics? of moral leadership? What ethical message does the show give its viewers?

This sort of assignment means to help students by supplying them with many possibilities, but it can provoke panic as inexperienced writers scramble to deal with each question separately.

Finally, a good assignment is not one that asks students for a too-personal answer: "Has there ever been a time in your life when you felt you just couldn't go on?" or "What was the most exciting thing that ever happened to you?" Though you might sometimes get compelling writing in response to such visceral topics, some students will be put off and not wish to answer them, while others will revel in the chance to advertise their angst or detail their road trip to Daytona Beach — or worse. Either way, you are likely to get some bad writing, replete with evasions, clichés, or experiences so troublesome that you cannot think of any way to respond.

What Is a Good Assignment?   If good assignments are not any of these things, then what are they? Foremost, a good assignment has to have a purpose. If you ask students to write a meaningless exercise, that is what you will get. (If, on the other hand, the assignment is meant as exercise or practice, then simply be honest with yourself as well as your students about your pedagogical purpose.)

An assignment such as "Describe your dorm room in specific detail" has no purpose but to make students write; the response to such an assignment is meaningless as communication (except, of course, if you simply want them to get practice in noticing and writing about details). If the assignment is extended, though, to "Describe your dorm room, and explain how various details in it reflect your personality and habits," it becomes a rhetorical problem. The answer to the assignment now has a purpose.

A good assignment is also meaningful within students' experience. *Meaningful* here does not necessarily mean "completely personal," but if students can tap into some of their experiences, then they might have a starting place for accessing the world of opinion or fact. Though you can perhaps talk coherently about the recession during the Reagan era or the English-only movement of the 1990s, many seventeen- and eighteen-year-olds might consider these subjects to be topics for historical research. The subjects that students can be expected to write about well without doing research are those that fall within their own range of experience — the economy as it relates to their own neighborhood or circle of family and friends, or the English-only issue as it relates to their high school experiences.

A good assignment asks for writing about specific and immediate situations rather than abstract and theoretical ones. When you pose a hypothetical situation in an assignment, make certain it is one students can conceptualize. "If you had been Abraham Lincoln in 1861 . . ." is the sort of assignment that will only invite wearying and uninformed fantasy, whereas "Write a letter to the board of trustees explaining why it should reconsider its decision to raise tuition by $1,000 per year" is a hypothetical situation (or perhaps it is not) that students can approach in an informed and realistic manner.

A good assignment should suggest a single major question to which the thesis statement of the essay is the answer. "Is smoking tobacco harmful, and should the tobacco laws be changed?" asks for several different, though related, theses. It is better to stay with a single question whose ramifications can then be explored: "Discuss why tobacco should or should not be legal, supporting your argument with details from your own experience or the experiences of people you know."

The written assignment itself should be neither too long nor too short. It should generally be no longer than two or three paragraphs, unless you're providing step-by-step guidelines; for example, you may need to provide directions for an assignment that requires students to use technology in a specific way. Too long and too complex an assignment will frustrate and confuse students. Too short an assignment, on the other hand, will fail to give sufficient guidance.

A good assignment, then, must be many things. Ideally, it should help students practice specific stylistic and organizational skills. (If you want your students to format their essays in a particular way, specify the format that you want to read. See "Creating a Syllabus" in Chapter 1.) A good assignment should furnish enough data (from format and page length to rhetorical method or genres and topic limits) to give students an idea of where to start. A good assignment should both encourage students to do their best writing and give the teacher his or her best chance to help them do just that.

Assignment Sequences

Sequenced writing assignments have been used in composition classes for decades. Most teachers are familiar with sequences based on the work of nineteenth-century Scottish logician Alexander Bain. The Bain sequence divides writing into four "modes of discourse": narration, description, exposition, and argumentation (118–21). The first two modes, which are the most concrete, can serve as the bases for initial course assignments; they allow students to draw on their own experiences and observations for subject matter, seldom forcing any higher-level generalizations or deductions. The second two modes, which are the most abstract, are reserved for later assignments, when students will presumably be better able to manipulate nonpersonal ideas and concepts in an expository or a persuasive fashion.

Increasingly, however, teachers have chosen sequences of assignments that are not based so much on distinct rhetorical methods of development (or what many have called "modes of discourse") as on encouraging students to examine their own experiences and beliefs (and how those beliefs have developed), consider the viewpoints of others (through research and analysis), and then— with an awareness of audience and attention to options for delivery— present their work to others. Note, for example, the sequence of assignments created by Jessica Enoch (see Sample Syllabus 1 in Chapter 1). The first assignment asks students to identify five pressing issues they might write about— and to explain their personal interest in each topic. The major assignments then ask students to do research (annotated bibliography), to define an issue (report), to take a position (position argument), to propose a solution (proposal), and finally to create a multimodal essay that will engage and capture the interest of a particular audience.

As you consider your own sequence of assignments, make sure that each one is connected to the others and that your students expand their repertoire. In creating the sequence, you must first consider the skills you wish students to develop and how they can best learn those skills through a series of related tasks. If you want students, for example, to recognize effective uses of research to support an argument, you could:

1. Assign readings that incorporate outside sources effectively.
2. Ask students to write a one-paragraph summary of the argument of one of those readings, for homework or as an in-class writing exercise.
3. Ask students to write a two-page *analysis* of how the writer incorporates the sources to support or complicate the argument.
4. Ask students to write a two-page *assessment* of how effective the sources are in supporting the argument.

After students work through the process of analyzing and assessing another author's argument and use of sources, you can then build on this competency by teaching students how to create their own arguments and how to incorporate outside sources into their work. The next step would be to provide sources for students, perhaps by giving them a packet of readings on a topic on which you want them to write. In doing so, you can focus your attention on teaching students to create their own arguments and to support those arguments without giving them the added responsibility of finding their own sources (that will come later).

5. Ask students to write an introductory paragraph that includes a clear thesis.
6. Ask them to locate ten to twelve quotations from the packet of readings that support or help complicate their argument.
7. Ask them to write a two-page assessment of which quotations will be most useful and to reflect on how they will incorporate those sources into their paper.

Students will then be ready to begin drafting. Once they have completed their drafts, they can work in peer-response groups to summarize their classmates' arguments, analyze how the outside sources are incorporated, and assess the efficacy of the argument and support. Such an arrangement of assignments creates a logical progression in which the assignments inform each other.

Later in the term, you can ask students to locate their own sources, adding lessons in electronic and library research. In any sequence of assignments, try to connect each assignment both to skills that have been practiced previously and to skills that will follow.

Research Assignments

Even though a large percentage of college writing programs specifically require research assignments, most teachers and students continue to be stymied by them. Why? Because we all seem to forget that we're already researchers. Every one of us does research every day. Whether we're searching the yellow pages to find a doctor, reading music reviews in *Rolling Stone* to decide which music to download, or checking out a political candidate's Web site, we're researching. We conduct research in order to make informed decisions, come to an opinion, learn how to do something, make sense of the world or the people around us.

If your program requires a research assignment, then you'll want to begin talking to your students early in the term about the amount of research they conduct on a regular basis. You'll also want to find time to ask them about the reasons they research, their methods and sources, and the amount of time successful research can take. We think you'll be surprised at how lively your class can become when your students begin tapping into their own expertise. Furthermore, these early talks can help guide your students toward a topic or critical question that interests them, even if the general topic itself is teacher-generated.

The research assignment is often weighted more than other writing assignments for several reasons. First, it's usually a longer assignment, an extended essay of *at least* fifteen hundred words (or six typed pages). Second, besides asking students to demonstrate the usual essay-writing skills, the research assignment demands that they demonstrate their mastery of library and Internet research skills and of careful, thorough documentation. This assignment offers students the chance to read widely and deeply on a particular subject, to use outside sources and voices to prove or support their argument, and to think critically about an issue to the point that they arrive at an informed, well-supported opinion. It's much more (and much more interesting) than merely stringing together quotations; the research assignment gives students an opportunity to weave together and balance their own voice and opinions with those of their outside sources. In other words, this assignment provides students a forum for entering an intellectual conversation. Finally, because the overall assignment is usually composed of a series of smaller assignments (from an initial list of ten sources and an annotated bibliography to a tentative thesis statement and a first-draft opening paragraph), it can take from several weeks to an entire term to fulfill.

Even though the assignment may hover over them for a month or more, when students have a personal connection to their topic, then their research, analysis, synthesis, and interpretation can be intellectually invigorating for them. Following their progress can be just as interesting for their teacher. Thus, the research assignment can be the most important and most interesting assignment in the writing course, building powerfully on everything that came before it (particularly if it's not presented as a separate writing entity or genre).

The research assignment provides the teacher with the chance to take on a form that students may think inviolable and to demonstrate that the shape of every piece of writing is determined by the writer's purpose. This assignment can also show students that finding information from outside sources (home, library, Internet, observation) is not a specialized activity but something all writers do to find out what they want or need to know — something they themselves do every day. The research assignment even promises students as great a chance for personal discovery and creativity as any piece of personal writing they've done during the term. In addition, it provides an opportunity to introduce students to the quickly changing world of academic research, which will undergird all the other work they do in college.

There are many useful texts and handbooks that can help guide you and your students through the research process. One especially helpful source is Wendy Bishop and Pavel Zemliansky's *The Subject Is Research,* which includes essays on many aspects of writing research essays (such as "Finding the Voices of Others without Losing Your Own," "The Internet Can Be a Wonderful Place, But . . . ," and "Interviewing"); prompts for sharing ideas at the end of each section; and "Hint Sheets," which are practical assignments and guides for both teachers and students. The essays and sample assignments are very accessible, written with FY writing students in mind, and help demystify the research process.

To begin, a short introductory lecture or classroom discussion should help students understand what a college research essay is *not*. For one thing, it is not a research report or an extended summary of what is known about a topic. It also is not a recycled encyclopedia entry. Like any other type of essay students have written for your class, the research essay must have a purpose, and part of the challenge of writing a research essay is discovering that purpose. To discover the purpose, students must look beyond their own experiences, find out what they want to know, and explore their interests openly. Their reactions to this process are as important to the research essay as they were to the personal essays they may have written at the beginning of the course.

Though it is important that students learn to document sources and build all their essays around a controlling idea or thesis, they should be given some freedom in choosing the form in which to express what they discover. They may want to use first-person pronouns and include personal experiences and observations. In the future, whenever students are asked to write a formal research essay, they will be expected to follow the specific conventions of the discipline in which they are working. They will conduct research in the discipline and write scholarly essays for those best equipped to guide them: the faculty members in their discipline. The best that the teacher of an FY writing course can do is give students a feel for the excitement of research, impress upon them the ethics of honest reporting, and stress the importance of following discipline-specific guidelines.

What must drive the research assignment, then, is not a desire to "get it right" formally but the student's curiosity and desire to explore. This motivation is best served by an open, or at least democratically structured, choice of topics. As early as the first few weeks of the semester, challenge students to think about how their own experiences raise questions that research can help answer. Some of the best research topics (and essay topics, too) grow out of the writer's experiences. For example, one of our students survived an abusive relationship with her boyfriend and wondered why she had stayed with him as long as she did. She wrote an essay that focused on a paradox—that many victims of abuse feel dependent on their abusers. Another student visited graveyards on Cape Cod, searching for the headstone of an ancestor. He noticed certain recurring designs on the older headstones and wondered about their significance.

Sometimes, too, research topics grow out of essay topics that were discarded because they seemed to demand more background than could be handled in a short work. Other topics may stem from class discussion, newspaper articles or editorials, lectures by visiting speakers, late-night conversations, or even a reference work's subject index, as when a student looks up a general area of interest (advertising) and then focuses on narrower subject headings (advertising—effects on children).

Example 4.1 provides a brainstorming exercise that can help get your students thinking about what makes them curious—and, therefore, what they wish to research further.

Example 4.1 **SEARCHING THE STOREHOUSE OF IDEAS:
AN INVENTION EXERCISE**

1. Brainstorm for five minutes to generate a list of things about which you know something but would like to know more. Make the list as long as you can. Whenever possible, be specific, and don't censor yourself.
2. Brainstorm for another five minutes, making a list of things about which you don't know much but would like to learn more. Write down whatever comes to mind.
3. Look at both lists and circle the one item that piques your curiosity more than any other item does.
4. Now take another five minutes and build a list of questions about the item you chose. If that topic goes nowhere — that is, if you can't come up with a strong list of questions about the topic that you'd like to learn the answers to — try another topic from your brainstormed list.

Students who have the freedom to act on their own curiosity can't dismiss an unsuccessful essay with the excuse that the assigned topic was boring. More important, such freedom fosters conditions that can make research genuinely rewarding — for example, late-night moments browsing the Web or in the library when students stumble on a source that suddenly opens a door to their topic. In doing research, students can experience, often for the first time, the joy of discovery. The key is that they are in command of the journey.

The rewards of allowing students to choose their topics can be great. When allowed to find out for themselves whether a topic is fruitful or fruitless, most students overcome their alienation from research and come to approach all research essays with more confidence. They also come to see that what they think does indeed matter and that, through research, they can become authorities capable of interpreting and analyzing information.

A Model Five-Week Research Assignment   Although there are many variations on the research essay, typically it is an eight- to ten-page documented piece, researched and written in just over a month. By providing a structure within the course that supports students' activities, you can facilitate the tasks of conducting research and writing an essay based on that research.

While teachers agree that procrastination is the enemy of good research writing, many students have never researched and written an essay more than

twenty-four hours before it was due. The following five-week model incorporates short weekly assignments that allow you to supervise students' progression toward the completion of interesting research essays.

Week 1: Invention

At the beginning of the term, encourage students to begin collecting possible
topics for research. Ask, for example, "What have you seen, experienced, or
read that raises questions that research might help answer?" Students might
want to know about the major areas of study that lead to the best chances of
employment and to the most lucrative job offers, the effects of stepfamilies on
student achievement, or whether the United States should require genetically
modified foods to be labeled before being sold. The key is to stress the extent
to which the success of the project depends on the student's curiosity about
the topic; in fact, you may want to provide students with opportunities to discuss their potential topics in their writing groups.

Despite your emphasis on curiosity, many students will continue to hold
some stale assumptions about research and research essays being only form
and facts. Therefore, begin the week by bringing these assumptions into the
open. Ask students to complete the following freewriting exercise:

1. Write *Research and Research Essays* at the top of a page in your notebook,
   and spend five minutes freewriting about any initial thoughts, preconceived notions, or prejudices that come to mind when you focus on
   these words.
2. Skip a few lines, and freewrite for another five minutes, this time focusing on people, anecdotes, situations, and specific experiences that come
   to mind when you think of these words.
3. Now spend five minutes making a list of sayings, clichés, rules, principles, and ideas about research and research essays that you've heard,
   including those you believe to be untrue.

This exercise can serve as the means for launching a class discussion about
how the research assignment may differ from other writing assignments students have done in the past. In writing a research essay, the point is not simply
to collect and document information on a topic but to do something with the
information. Usually a controlling question will inform and guide the research
and writing.

Students must also be helped to discover that research, in the hands of a good
writer, is lively as well as informative. You may want to provide the class with
copies of a strong research-based essay or article that challenges the assumption
that facts "kill" writing. Popular magazines that value good writing — *New Yorker,
Harper's, New Republic, Rolling Stone,* and *Sports Illustrated* — are good sources. Or
look to the work of some of the best essayists who also happen to be first-rate
researchers: Sandra Steingraber, Barry Lopez, Joan Didion, Lewis Thomas, Terry
Tempest Williams, and John McPhee. A successful student research essay, either

from your files or a real student's work in a textbook such as Lunsford's *The St. Martin's Handbook,* will work as well. Any research-based essay, student or professional, that features lively writing and an engaging treatment will challenge the prejudice that writing based on research is boring. Suggest that students read the essay looking for literary devices that hold their interest, and follow up with a discussion about what a research-based essay shares with any other essay type: a distinct voice and point of view, concrete information, a discrete focus, and perhaps even the telling of a story. Most important, though, help students see that the writer of the research essay has the same motivation as the writer of the personal essay: the desire to make sense of something. Both writers share their discoveries with their readers.

This first week you'll need to confront one final problem: library-phobia. Some students will wish to retreat to the false security of Web-only searches in the privacy of their dorms. To help them learn about the range of resources available, a library tour is the best option. Most university libraries offer orientation programs, ranging from tours to in-class presentations, but we have found it useful to accompany our classes to the library by devoting a large part of one class to a library tour. When students are ready to begin their research, they're ready to learn about appropriate sources and they are often more comfortable asking their teacher specific questions than they are asking a reference librarian, whom they do not know. For many students, this tour may be the first introduction to the world of the college library, with its online resources, bound volumes of journals, books, and staff of librarians.

Most colleges offer access to electronic databases that can be indispensable to researchers. Students will need help accessing the electronic journals, indexes, and other helpful resources. They will also need an introduction to the kinds of databases most useful for the research they wish to carry out. You might wish to create a handout with essential information, including the Web site students should use to access the library databases, provided by the college; the ones you think will be most helpful to students; and the appropriate username and password if they wish to access such databases off campus.

Week 2: Focusing Topics

When your students come to class with their tentative topics, be prepared for generality. Many students will begin with the big picture: "My topic is advertising," or "I want to write about whales." These general topics are not necessarily bad places to begin. They give researchers plenty of room in which to roam until they discover what they are really interested in. But a lack of focus plagues college research essays (and most other essays), and the sooner students narrow their topics, the better. Among other things, a narrower focus makes the research process more efficient; instead of being compelled to glance at forty articles on the depletion of rain forests, a student can choose the five articles that deal with its impact on native peoples. A narrow focus also means that the writer is more likely to reveal less obvious aspects of the subject. At this point, your job is to help students narrow their focus to the point where they are making a specific comment or asking a "focusing" question about their chosen topic.

In an in-class writing activity, ask students to answer the following question: "What do I need to find out in order to answer my focusing question?" For example, if the student's focusing question is "Why do many college students abuse alcohol?" that student would then need to research the consumption patterns among college students: Do they differ from those in the general population? Do drinking patterns vary by gender? How frequently do college students seek treatment? How often does abuse end in tragedy? Have efforts by colleges to curtail abuse succeeded anywhere? Why, or why not?

If the exercise is successful, students will leave the class with a clear sense of the direction they want their research to take. In conferences, help the undecided students settle on a tentative focus (or two). They can change their minds later, but for now they need a discrete trail to follow.

A follow-up class discussion about sources would also be useful. Ask students where they ran into problems with their research and what references proved to be indispensable. Spend some time discussing how to evaluate sources. Most students will be unfamiliar with college-level indexes. Their favorite sources for high school research essays were probably online encyclopedias and general Web search engines. They should be pushed to dig more deeply and to turn to more authoritative sources. Encourage them to find more specific and reliable information — the kind of information found in peer-reviewed journals and books.

Week 3: Research

Begin the week with a discussion of note-taking. This skill has unfortunately suffered from the wide availability of photocopiers, scanners, and the copy and paste commands on computers. The student reasons, "Why do any writing from a source when I can make a copy and bring it home or simply copy from a Web page and paste into a word-processing program?" The answer is simple: By taking the time to write about sources as they research, students are in effect starting to write their essays. Note-taking is thus a kind of prewriting. In addition, taking good notes helps the student-researcher internalize and personalize the information, lessening the chances of unintentionally plagiarizing by copying and pasting and then losing track of the original source.

Students struggle with their research material to gain control of it. When students are swamped with information, their voices may get lost in the chorus of experts. But by paraphrasing, summarizing, and analyzing sources, students begin to establish authority over their own essays.

Despite their experience, many students aren't sure what distinguishes a paraphrase from a summary or even what constitutes plagiarism. Some students have never used notes to synthesize or analyze source material — let alone to support their opinions. In class, hand out a page containing passages from a Web site or print source. Then show two paraphrases of a passage, one of which is plagiarized. Use these two examples as a basis for discussing the improper use of a source. Then ask each student to paraphrase a different passage from the source and to work in pairs to check each other's work for plagiarism. Their questions can be the basis for further discussion. (For additional information on plagiarism, see Penn State's Guide to Understanding Plagiarism in Chapter 3.)

Ask students to summarize in their own words the source's central idea. Then talk about what seems worth quoting from the sample passage and what constitutes a strong quotation. Finally, introduce another type of note-taking—analysis or commentary, in which the writer reflects on what the source says and how it relates to the purpose of the research essay. This kind of writing is probably most important of all because it encourages students to make active use of the information, shaving it and shaping it.

The discussion about note-taking inevitably segues into another about documentation conventions. At this point, you can review the basics of formats for documenting sources. Students inevitably worry about the formal aspects of citing their sources, especially Internet sources, so point them to the appropriate sources for the documentation format you expect them to use.

Keep pressing students to narrow the focus of their subjects even if they are not sure they can find enough information. Encourage them to deepen their searches by checking more specialized journals and to broaden the scope of their hunt by considering nonlibrary sources — interviews, informal surveys, campus lectures, films, and so forth. Though some students may have started their research with a clear thesis in mind, most others will not yet be sure what they want to write about. Challenge these students to consider some tentative ideas, articulate a trial thesis, or pose a controlling question.

Week 4: Beginning Drafts

Some students will feel ready to attempt a draft at this point; others will be immersed in collecting information; and still others may decide to abandon their topic altogether. Here is where you can help move the process along. Because research, like writing, is a recursive process, you'll want to use assignments and discussion during Week 4 to prod your students to complete a first draft.

Try beginning the week with the following in-class exercise on voice. Students often think research essays are supposed to sound, as one student wrote, as though they were "generated by individuals who can facilitate and implement effective word usage at a level that far surpasses themselves" — in other words, as if they weren't written by human beings. With the following exercise, you can inspire a critical discussion of the reasons — good and bad — that scholarly writing often adopts an impersonal, detached voice, as well as why these reasons may not apply to less formal research essays. At the very least, students should understand that the voice for their essays should be appropriate to their purpose, subject, and audience — and, most important, express who they are.

1. Assume that you're a fashion-conscious person with imported leather shoes and exquisitely tasteful designer clothes. Today, as you were getting out of a taxicab, another taxi whizzed by you, splashing you with

a wave of muddy water. Spend ten minutes composing a letter to a friend, describing the incident.

2. Now assume that you're the driver of the first taxicab. Spend ten minutes composing a story to tell your friends over lunch, describing the same incident.

After listening to several examples of each version read aloud in class, students may recognize that they can write effectively in more than one voice. You might point out the voices they have used — in their college admission essays, in letters to their parents, and especially in their research essays. Reinforce the point that no single voice is appropriate to research writing; as with any piece of writing, the writer of a research essay assumes a voice that best serves the writer's purpose. Urge students not to abandon the "real" voices they discovered in their personal essays but to adapt that voice to the new rhetorical situation, for then their ideas will be more memorable to readers.

You might follow up this discussion with an assignment that asks students to write three distinctly different one- or two-paragraph leads for their essays, paying special attention to voice. Consider providing examples of published or student work, with different kinds of introductions — for example, introductions that use a scene, a quotation, a description, an anecdote, a profile, a question, a case study, or a comparison. Ask your students to share their three introductions with the class, and ask the readers to mark the lead that most encourages them to read on and to explain why it does. Beginnings have an enormous influence over the direction of a piece of writing; working on three different ways to start an essay may point students in a useful direction. This exercise also reintroduces the idea of writing for an audience: Each lead may well be aimed at a different audience.

As students begin their drafts, they should try to nail down the controlling idea around which they will build the essay. Doing so is not easy. Swamped with expert information, much of it contradictory, they may be unsure of what they think — let alone what they want to argue. Careful note-taking should have helped them overcome the feeling that they are in over their heads. Just as important, however, is for them to tune out the voices of their sources and take some time to listen to their own voice. Assign the following freewriting exercise to help students reflect on the purpose of their essays and perhaps come up with a thesis statement:

An Exercise for Formulating a Thesis

1. Quickly read over your notes and review your most important sources. Your head may be swimming with information. Now open a blank document on your computer. Begin freewriting a narrative of how your thinking about your topic has developed since you began working on your research essay. What did you think when you started? What did you discover? What did you think then? What do you think now? Write quickly for ten minutes.

2. Press enter a few times, and then freewrite for another ten minutes, focusing on specific stories, anecdotes, people, case studies, and observations that stand out in your mind when you reflect on what you've learned. Describe them in as much detail as you can.

3. Spend another ten minutes writing a dialogue between yourself and someone you imagine you are talking to about your topic (your instructor, roommate, or friend, for example). Begin by trying to answer the question you think that person would be most likely to ask about your topic, and go on from there.

4. Finally, spend five minutes composing a one- or two-sentence answer to this question about your topic: "So what?"

When this exercise works, several things happen. First, when students have drowned out the chorus of experts and can write in their own voice, they establish their authority over the material. Second, through freewriting they produce writing that they can use in their drafts. The dialogue in Step 3 can help them determine how to structure the essay, whereas the final question challenges them to state their point succinctly.

Week 5: Completing the Draft

The drafts are due at the end of this week. With the five-week approach, any revisions are made subsequently. But students have probably never revised a research essay, and they have probably put an enormous effort into producing a strong first draft. No matter how curious they are about the topic, they are looking forward to being done with it.

You may want to provide exercises and class discussions this week that will assist students with their writing. You might showcase some research essays from previous terms that demonstrate inventive approaches. You can also introduce the conventional ways of structuring an essay: by posing a question and proposing an answer; by describing cause and effect or effect and cause; by narrating events chronologically; by posing a problem and proposing a solution; by comparing and contrasting; by treating the known and then the unknown; by discussing the simple and then the complex, the specific and then the general, or the general and then the specific. You might show how successful essays often effectively mix two or more of these conventions.

You'll undoubtedly also need to discuss in some detail the format of the essay, especially that of the works-cited section. In addition, address how visual devices make an essay more readable: block quotations, bulleted lists, subheadings or subtitles, photographs, and diagrams. Briefly discuss methods of weaving quotations into the text, and reiterate the importance of attribution.

Also remind students of the devices writers use to make a work memorable. It might be helpful to list some of these methods on the board:

People on the page. Ultimately, what makes a subject interesting is its effect on people. Demonstrate this effect by pointing to profiles, case studies, or quotations from interviews. People love stories: They bring a point to life, and they arouse a reader's curiosity about what will happen next. Research essays can make use of anecdotes or can even tell the story of what the writer learned, serving as a kind of narrative of thought.

Strong openings and conclusions. Students should recognize strong openings and conclusions and how they improve a paper.

Tone. Discuss what the tone of a work reveals about the writer's relationship to the subject.

Active voice. Remind students to avoid passive-voice constructions, a bane of research writing. Find examples, and discuss the reasons the passive voice is so often lifeless.

Detail. The meat of strong writing is specific, concrete information. In a research essay, details aren't just sensory; they can be statistics, unusual facts, strong quotations — any sort of memorable, convincing point.

Surprise. Readers like to be surprised. Ask students to consider what they can tell their audience that might be surprising. Ask what surprised them from their research and whether they can use a surprise to hook their readers early on in the essay.

At the end of the week, when your students print out their essays and bring them to class, they will feel as if they are finished. Having labored over their essays for five weeks, they are likely to find the prospect of revision difficult to face. Because they may have difficulty seeing the possibilities for further development, you may want to end the week with an exercise in essay resuscitation. Ask students to bring to class another copy of their draft, scissors, and tape.

An Exercise in Revision

1. Cut out each paragraph from your essay, and shuffle the pieces.
2. Go through the paragraphs, and look for the core paragraph, the one that most clearly reveals the purpose of your essay. It may be the paragraph that contains the thesis. Set it aside.
3. Go through the remaining stack of paragraphs and make two piles: paragraphs that are relevant to the core in some way, and those that seem to have little to do with it. You may find that part of a paragraph seems unimportant and the rest is useful. Cut away what is unimportant, and set it aside.
4. Working with the pile of relevant paragraphs and your core paragraph, rebuild your essay. Try new beginnings, new conclusions, and new middles. Don't worry about transitions; you can add those later. Look especially for gaps, places where you should add information. Splice in your ideas for new material. Tape the pieces of paper together when you have an order that seems promising, even if it is the same one you started with.

Discuss what the cut-and-paste exercise suggests about where to go next. This exercise is most useful in helping students conduct a "purpose test" on their drafts, encouraging them to ask, "Is every piece of information contributing to a convincing thesis?" They should not consider it a setback that their work ended up in pieces but as a chance to take another, fresher look.

Additional Research Assignments   The five-week schedule described in the preceding section helps students produce eight- to ten-page essays that rely heavily on research. It can be adapted for the production of shorter or even longer essays. An alternative to the five-week schedule is the three-part research assignment (see Example 4.2), which students work on for much of the term. This assignment is course-related, allowing students to delve more deeply into some aspect of the course that interests them. If you included a list of suggested readings with your syllabus, students will have a head start on the research process and a model of the kinds of texts they will find most helpful. Though less detailed than the five-week assignment, the three-part assignment encourages in-depth research and scholarly inquiry and allows students to consider their own personal investment in their research topic.

Other approaches are based on the notion that the writer's curiosity should drive the process. The collaborative research project, in which students work in small groups on subjects of shared interest, each finding his or her own angle, is an example of one such approach. In some cases, students even collaborate on writing the essay and then present their findings to the class.

Example 4.2   THREE-PART RESEARCH ASSIGNMENT

Part 1: Essay on Course-Related Issues

In this three- to four-page, double-spaced essay, you will begin exploring your final research paper by working on a course-related issue early on. You may want to write about a particular topic we've discussed (such as the relationship between visual and word-based rhetoric) or about the rhetorical methods you'd like to explore further (such as whether narrative or description can also be a form of argument). Whatever you choose to write about, you'll want to demonstrate that you've been keeping up with the reading, in-class writing, and discussion. Do your best to convince your reader that this topic is important to you, either personally or academically.

You need a title, an introductory paragraph, a compelling thesis statement (or controlling idea), well-developed paragraphs that illustrate or explore your topic, and a tentative list of bibliographic materials/sources. Your research must investigate some facet of writing or reading or a rhetorical concept.

Part 2: Overview of Research-Based Assignment

Please map out an overview of your ongoing research-based assignment. (Although length is negotiable, five to six double-spaced pages should be enough.) The purpose of this assignment is to lead you into the thick of your topic and force you to get organized and focused! By this time in the term, though, you're probably already feeling somewhat knowledgeable — if not also opinionated — about your topic. Broken into full sections, each with a heading, this overview should include the following items:

1. The significance of your topic (why you're writing about it, why it's a worthy topic for investigation for this course)
2. Your conception and definition of your topic (how you're thinking about your topic and defining your terms)
3. The relation of this topic to your intellectual, academic, literate, cultural, or emotional development (and, if you're collaborating with a writing partner, an explanation of how the two of you are working together)
4. The way you are entering the ongoing intellectual (and perhaps emotional) conversations surrounding this topic (who the leading researchers on this topic are, their opinions, the main currents of thought, how you are joining the conversation)
5. Your research method (how you are conducting your research — at the library; on the Web; through interviews, ethnographic studies, personal experience)
6. Your plan of work (the time line for the work you have left to do)
7. Your updated bibliography

This assignment will help you become more fluent in your topic and will strongly inform your final research project. You will not, however, be able to paste large passages of this assignment into your final project. If you're not already working collaboratively, you'll need to work on this assignment in your writing group.

Part 3: Putting Together the Term-Long, Research-Based Project

Your paper will be long enough to merit headings. Here are some provisional headings for you to consider:

Title.

Introduction. (You may want to keep this heading as is.) Here's where you provide an overview and, perhaps, a very brief look at what some of your sources say about your topic. Eventually you come to the critical question that fuels your research.

Background of the Problem or Critical Question. (You may want to keep this heading — or change it to something that works better for your essay.) In this section you provide the history or background of your problem or critical question. It's also a place for you to show off your reading and knowledge.

Response to the Problem or Critical Question. (Again, experiment with this heading.) I mean "response" loosely: Here you move from the background of the problem or question to your so-called response or solution, which will feature your thesis statement. The background and response parts of your essay might end up as one section rather than two.

Body of the Text. (This section will be the longest part of your research essay. You will need to think of appropriate headings and subheadings for this section.) You want to introduce the sections/features of your argument, the basic assertions that support your thesis statement. For each major assertion/development, you may want a separate subheading. Many of the readings in our textbook use subheadings, so you have examples of how this is done.

Conclusion. After doing so much research, you may have difficulty coming up with your own conclusion. One successful way to work on your conclusion is to think about it in three subsections (which rarely merit separate subheadings): (1) the clear-cut or obvious conclusions you can draw from your research; (2) the inferences you can make (though not obvious, given your knowledge of the subject, you feel confident making them); and (3) the implications of your research for others — that is, where someone else might pick up where you've left off.

Works Cited. This list begins a new page at the end of the essay and should follow MLA style.

Web Assignments

Increasingly, writing teachers comfortable with technology are moving beyond traditional writing assignments and asking their students to work on Web projects. Writing for the Web, of course, is different from writing traditional academic essays. Paragraphs tend to be much shorter, and the visual aspect is nearly as important as the words. If you and your students already have some experience creating Web sites and if you're discussing visual literacy in your class, you may wish to have your students create Web sites. You can work on one site as an entire class, have students work in small groups or pairs, or have students create their own individual sites. Whatever formation you choose, the sites should somehow be related to the class. For example, students could create a site introducing others to the work and focus of the class, or they could present their research findings in a way that's accessible to a broad audience. You should make your expectations clear—explaining how students' work will be assessed and evaluated—because the skills and competencies they'll need for Web projects differ somewhat from those associated with more traditional writing assignments.

Here are some general guidelines for assigning Web design projects:

1. Familiarize yourself with the Web-authoring programs to which your students have access.
2. Check into whether students will have access to school Web space or if they'll need to go through a commercial server. Many commercial servers provide "free" Web space, but such space does come with a price: pop-up advertisements over which neither the author of the Web site nor the viewer has much control.
3. Look at and evaluate several existing Web sites together as a class before asking students to create their own sites. Discussing what is or is not effective on other sites will help your students get ideas for their own sites. For examples of what not to do, take your students to "Vincent Flanders' Web Pages That Suck" (listed at the end of this chapter). Through viewing and discussing both positive and negative examples, students will gain a better understanding of content and design issues, including the significance of organizational structure, design consistency, color, images, and navigational ease.
4. Discuss with students the purpose of and audience for the Web sites they'll be creating. Such concerns will help determine the text, images, and design for their sites. If you foreground such issues, students will better know what to include and what to leave out.
5. Provide step-by-step handouts for your students and addresses of helpful Web sites. In order to write step-by-step instructions for your

students, you will likely have to create a Web site of your own and track the process you went through. Alternately (or in addition), you can provide students with Web sites that provide clear guidelines, such as *PC World*'s article, "Instant Web Sites" (listed at the end of this chapter). This article provides directions as well as links to templates for billboard sites, galleries, and interactive blogs. Also make a list of sites from which students can get free images and graphics, starting with CoolArchive (listed at the end of this chapter) to point students to additional resources. In your list of resources, discuss copyright and intellectual property issues, reminding students both to ask permission for using images and to cite their sources.

6. Give students a series of deadlines for completing different parts of the project. Just as you would have drafts, peer response, and conferences for traditional papers, you can do the same for Web projects.

7. If possible, schedule some office hours in a computer lab or in a space where you and your students have access to a computer so you can view and work on the Web project in conference sessions. Once students complete their Web sites, provide some time and space for them to showcase their work.

Assignments Delivered Orally

If you ask students to do presentations or to create texts that are meant to be spoken (a radio essay, for example), you will need to teach the different components of texts meant to be read silently and those meant to be delivered orally. Sentence structures that appear simple — even choppy — on the page are often quite effective when spoken. Repeated phrases that seem redundant on the page become clear — even powerful — when read aloud. Furthermore, the bulleted lists, white space, and bracketed cues that would be odd in formal essays translate well into oral texts.

As you create your assignment, there are several elements of the rhetorical situation you will need to consider:

1. What is the purpose of the assignment? to inform, persuade, entertain?

2. What will the content or topic be? How will this assignment build on earlier assignments? (Will students rewrite an essay they have already written to make it suitable for oral delivery? Will they present on a topic they have already researched but not yet written about?)

3. Who is the audience? (Should students see you, their classmates, or someone else as the primary audience?)

4. When students present what they have written, what format should they use? (Should they read from the text, speak from notes, or memorize the text?)

5. What visuals will they use? Will you require handouts? a PowerPoint? some other use of visuals?
6. How much time will they have to speak/read? (Do students need to reserve time for questions and comments — or time to pass out handouts?)

In addition to these considerations, students will need to know how the presentations will be evaluated. Will you evaluate students primarily on the written product (whether the piece is written in such a way that it could be delivered effectively), their oral delivery (clarity of voice, eye contact, gestures), or some mix of both?

Because you may be combining two assignments (an assignment for writing or revising a text for oral delivery, as well as an assignment to make an oral presentation), your written assignment to students might be longer than usual. Example 4.3 provides such an assignment. (For further discussion of oral delivery and its relationship to writing, see Chapter 10.)

Example 4.3   **SAMPLE ASSIGNMENT: REVISING A TEXT
                  TO DELIVER IT ORALLY**

Having, as a class, attended two creative nonfiction readings and discussed both how the writers created memorable prose and how their delivery enhanced the effective elements already in the text, you will turn to one of your own creative nonfiction essays, revise it for oral delivery, and do a reading of a selection from your piece for the class. The purpose of this assignment is twofold: First, you will gain experience revising a text written originally for silent reading, turning it into a text for oral delivery; second, you will gain practice presenting your work in front of an audience. Your classmates and I will be your audience, so you should choose a selection that illustrates effective elements of the genre: consideration of tone, attention to detail, character development, and so on.

Although you will be reading your text, you should practice enough that you can look up often, making eye contact with your audience. You will read for ten minutes and reserve an additional two minutes for questions from your classmates. Be prepared in the question/answer time to discuss the ways in which you revised your initial essay. When you hand in the revised text, also staple a copy of your original essay to the back.

Assignments That Call for the Use of Visual Components

Any assignment — print text, digital, or oral — can make use of visuals, such as photographs, graphics, drawings, even videos. Visuals can be both a primary vehicle of and an aid to communication. That is, a carefully organized montage of pictures can communicate without words, but for the purpose of this text, we assume that you will be asking students to use visuals to support and further an argument or effect they have already worked to develop in writing.

Like other assignments, those that call for the use of visuals should be sequenced carefully, providing students an opportunity (1) to reflect on their own visual literacy — what they already know and can bring to the assignment — both in writing and in class discussions; (2) to analyze and evaluate various uses of images in texts; and (3) to use visuals effectively in their own texts, incorporating them appropriately and documenting sources properly. (For additional discussion of visual literacy and specific assignments, see Chapter 10. See also Cynthia Selfe's "Toward New Media Texts: Taking Up the Challenges of Visual Literacy" in Part III of this book.)

One popular assignment in composition classes is a literacy narrative, asking students to reflect on their own memories of reading and writing or to tell a story about their own acquisition of new literacy. Visuals can work especially well in a literacy narrative assignment. In "Toward New Media Texts" (p. 481), Cynthia Selfe provides an assignment for a visual essay, one that, in a section for teachers, details goals, time required, a sequence of assignments, and a useful vocabulary (including definitions for "visual impact," "visual coherence," "visual salience," and "visual organization"). For students, her assignment provides objectives, tasks, suggested format, information on documenting images from online sources, and information on creating and documenting images for poster board essays (pp. 488–91). Additionally, she provides guides for composer/designer reflection as well as reader/reviewer reflection (pp. 492–93). Although Selfe provides a more detailed assignment in her article, Example 4.4 offers a shortened version of Selfe's assignment.

Example 4.4   **VISUAL ESSAY ASSIGNMENT**

"Compose a visual essay that represents and reflects on

1. the range of different literacy practices, values, and understandings you have developed over your lifetime (from birth to now)

2. how you have developed these literacies (where, how, who helped)

3. your feelings about these literacies" (p. 490).

Your essay "should demonstrate a high degree of visual impact" and "overall coherence," and it "should identify 2–4 major points as particularly important (using strategies to make these points prominent and stand out from other elements: size, color, contrast, placement, etc.)" (p. 490).

Multimodal Assignments

Although we've presented the sections on assignment sequences, research assignments, Web assignments, assignments that call for oral delivery, and assignments that call for the use of visuals separately, most teachers will likely draw from all of these sections when developing assignments. That is, you might create a sequence of assignments that requires students to do textual analysis, to interview others, and to create an argument that they present orally in a multimedia presentation that includes images, a sound clip, and a video clip. Or perhaps you will require students to create a blog that they update weekly, one that includes their writing, images, and links to video clips and other Web pages.

Blogs   In their online article "Moving to the Public: Weblogs in the Writing Classroom," Charles Lowe and Terra Williams provide helpful information for those interested in assigning students to write blogs. Their students do a range of writing, using their blogs as places to post reading responses, articles about writing, research responses, personal writing, and links to other blogs. Lowe and Williams consider the issues of public and private writing, stating, "Moving journal writing to the Web using Weblogs where Internet surfers can read and link to student writing potentially opens our students' texts to the unknown outside of the classroom, but our experience with student blogging has shown that 'less private writing' may equally help writers to compose their lives, albeit in a social, more public way."

If you ask students to create and keep a blog, you'll need to decide whether the blogs should be set up in less public spaces (such as on Blackboard, Moodle, or Angel, which are password protected and meant to be read only by other students and the teacher) or on a public site such as Blogger.com, which provides privacy settings that students can control but allows for a public audience.

Some teachers ask students to use blogs to comment on each other's work in progress, so students might explore topics for an assignment, ask for recommendations for sources, and post drafts — seeking comments from classmates in the process. If you choose to have students use blogs for peer response, be sure that they are updating their blogs regularly — sharing ideas and creating community throughout the process, not just posting a rough draft a few times during the term. (For more information on assigning blogs, see the full text of Lowe and Williams's article, available online and cited at the end of this chapter.)

Creating Assignments and Explaining Them to Students

After you decide on the length, number, and sequence of assignments, you can get down to the business of creating each one. Be sure to include the task (what the student is to do or learn how to do), the stance (the author's position in terms of audience and purpose), the process (Will you require rough drafts? group work?), the format (How long should the essay be? How should it be delivered?), and the criteria for evaluation. You will want to write down all assignments beforehand and pass out copies of them to your students — and, if possible, post them online—rather than writing them on the board or reading them aloud. Providing written assignments allows you to be as specific as you wish to be — to put into words exactly what you want your students to do and learn — and helps prevent misunderstandings by the students.

When you hand out an assignment, take some time to go over the wording and explain how to read writing prompts in general. Students need to know, for all their classes, that words such as *analyze, describe,* and *explain* tell them the strategy, even the rhetorical method of development, to use and often determine the form of their response. Example 4.5, from *Making Sense* by Cheryl Glenn, provides an activity that will help students consider their own understanding of important words in assignments.

Example 4.5   **MAKING SENSE OF COLLEGE-LEVEL WRITING ASSIGNMENTS**

In preparation for making sense of your college-level writing assignments, take a minute to write out what each of the following terms means to you:

inform	describe	entertain	analyze	define
persuade	prove	compare	argue	explore
convince	evaluate	propose	formulate	classify
observe	report	explain		

Working with one or two classmates, compare your answers. Discuss your group's response with the rest of the class. You may be surprised by the range of definitions you and your classmates give these important academic terms. (Glenn 17)

Discussing strategy words with students (and providing them the actual definitions for these words) is a good way to begin your larger discussion of the criteria that will be used to evaluate their drafts and essays. In a sense, criteria for the evaluation of essays are the theoretical heart of any course in rhetoric or writing, but you need to boil them all down to specifics for each new assignment. For each type of assignment, a slightly different kind of invention works best and a slightly different group of forms or genres is appropriate, as are different levels of descriptive detail or narration and different methods of logical development. In a new assignment to a class, you need to describe thoroughly what you want to see, from specific thesis statements to levels of support, formal structure, use of personal pronouns, use of dialogue, various conventions, and so forth. Some of these criteria will be spelled out in the wording of the assignment, but some you should present and discuss in class. As you continue teaching, it is a good idea to ask students whose essays are particularly effective whether you can make photocopies of their work for use in subsequent semesters. Such models of successful responses to assignments can help students immensely by letting them see concretely what your necessarily abstract criteria can produce.

REVISION

As the sample syllabi in Chapter 1 suggest, the revision of students' drafts before the essays are submitted for a grade is an important element of college writing courses. Including a revision option is, of course, up to you (unless your department has a policy requiring or forbidding one), but most successful writing teachers are committed supporters of revision. Their experience has shown them that the reasons for allowing revision seem to outweigh by far any inconveniences. In many writing classes, in fact, revision isn't just an option: It's structured into the course schedule with first, second, and final drafts due on particular days. Sometimes the teacher reads all the drafts; at other times the teacher reads the first and final drafts, asking students to work on other drafts in their peer-response groups. If your writing course uses portfolios, your students may be writing new essays even as they revise their earlier pieces throughout the term.

Using revision in a composition course can transform the relationship between the teacher and the student: Instead of serving as the judge and jury, the teacher joins the student in improving that student's writing. The teacher is released from the burden of putting a grade on every piece of writing at the same time that the student is released from the pressure of always writing toward a grade. In other words, allowing for revision provides a less-judgmental relationship between teacher and student. Furthermore, it invites students into the editing process, a process that is difficult to understand if all their written work is graded and then filed away without their having any chance to reexamine or change it. Research into the composing process has revealed that far too many students sit down at the keyboard and write out their essay, submitting it with little or no editing or revision. Far too many students still see writing as a one-shot, make-it-or-break-it event. Because the very idea of revision (let alone large-scale revision) is alien to these students, requiring revision allows them to approach the task of editing as an authentic "re-seeing" of their writing. All students deserve to learn that self-evaluation and self-correction are elements crucial to successful writing.

Revision can work in several different ways, but all of them involve the same general idea: Someone responds to and/or evaluates a student's essay and then returns it to the writer, who then revises it. Sometimes it's the teacher who collects, reads, and responds to all the essays; at other times it's a member of the writing group who considers the draft. The mechanics of turning in and responding to essays differ from system to system (some teachers grade drafts; others simply provide comments to aid in revision), but all have in common a focus on rewriting.

Revisions are usually the focus of conferences and peer-response group or workshop sessions, but you needn't use either of these systems. Another system using a revision routine might work as follows: Students must turn in Essay 1 on the day it is due. They will either mark the essay DRAFT, which indicates that the writer wants the essay evaluated but not graded, or they will leave it unmarked, which indicates that the essay is to be evaluated and graded. You evaluate all the essays but grade only those considered final efforts. On the drafts your task is to provide guidance in revising, not merely in editing. You are looking not for a neater or more "correct" copy of an essay but for a re-envisioned essay. Thus your terminal or closing comments will contain far more specific suggestions and criticisms than will those on a graded essay. The terminal comments on a preliminary draft must serve as blueprints or suggestions for revision, whereas those on a final essay must, by the nature of the grading process, be more concerned with justifying the grade and giving closure to the assignment.

The next week, you return the students' essays and give those students who had turned in drafts a week to ten days in which to revise their drafts, which must then be turned in for a final grade. If a draft is very good, as occasionally one is, the student may return it unchanged; most students, however, rewrite their essays. When the final versions are handed in, ask that the original draft be clipped to the revision so that the changes will be evident. Also ask that any comments from workshop members be attached as well. On this second sweep through Essay 1, you will read the essay, write comments in the margins, note any remaining formal errors, write a short comment on the success of the revision and the general quality of the essay, and return it to the writer for the last time.

In the week before the final drafts of Essay 1 are due, rough drafts of the next assignment, Essay 2, will have come in and perhaps a few early revisions of Essay 1 will have arrived as well. By the time you get all the final versions of Essay 1, you will be seeing the rough drafts of Essay 3. During any given week, therefore, you may be evaluating or grading as many as three assignments. It is not as confusing as it sounds. Here is a diagram:

Week 2

Monday   *Friday*
Drafts of Essay 1 due

Week 3

Monday   *Friday*
Drafts of Essay 1 returned   Drafts of Essay 2 due
Some final drafts of Essay 1
turned in this week

Week 4

Monday   *Friday*
Final drafts of Essay 1 due   Drafts of Essay 3 due
Drafts of Essay 2 returned
Some final drafts of Essay 2
turned in this week

Week 5

Monday   *Friday*
Final drafts of Essay 1 returned
Final drafts of Essay 2 due
Drafts of Essay 3 returned
Some final drafts of Essay 3
turned in this week

Other permutations of the revision system work better for some teachers. For example, you may permit students to submit multiple versions of an essay, especially if the class is working in peer-response groups. Other teachers may allow only one or two revisions during the term. Still others allow students to submit their revisions during a "revision week" at the end of the term. This option allows students more time in which to revise, but it also results in a great influx of essays — in various states of revision — to be read and graded during that final, hectic week. Teachers who grade all essays as they come in and then regrade those that students choose to revise give students a clear idea of how they are doing in terms of grades. In such a system, however, the grading process is burdensome for the teacher because the terminal comment on a graded essay is expected to justify the letter grade rather than provide suggestions for revision.

The most common objection to requiring revision is that it creates more work for the teacher. And in some ways, it does. In a class of twenty-four students that demands six graded essays from each student, the teacher must read and evaluate 144 essays. If revision is allowed, the number of essays to be evaluated naturally increases — whether it's the writing group or the teacher who does the evaluation. But there is not as much extra work for the teacher as there might seem to be at first. The revision option places more of the added responsibility on the student. Reading for evaluation takes less time than the combined effort of reading for evaluation, assigning a grade, and justifying the grade; and the final reading and grading of the revision take less time than reading for evaluation and justifying the grade. Grading the revised version takes less time because you already know the writer's purpose. In neither reading should you give small, formal errors the amount of attention that you would give such errors in a single reading. In the first reading, in fact, you mark no errors at all, although you may mention serious error patterns in your terminal comment. In the second reading, errors get only a checkmark. The act of revision generally means that the final essay will have fewer formal problems.

This paean to revision should not obscure the problems it can present. The most obvious one is the students' temptation to use the teacher only as an editor. If you mark all the formal errors on each rough draft, you will lead your students to believe that their revision need be no more than a simple reprinting of the essay with the formal errors corrected. If you want to mark errors in drafts, do so with a simple checkmark over the error, which the writer must then identify and correct. Encourage students to rely on one another as editors and proofreaders before submitting drafts; if you can develop peer-response groups, your pedagogical life can be better. Don't hesitate to say, "This draft isn't ready for me."

The second problem that revision presents is psychological: Students tend to believe that an essay that has been revised in a formal process will automatically receive a higher grade than one the teacher sees only once — the A-for-effort misconception. If a draft merits a D and the revision raises the grade to a C, the student often has a hard time understanding why, with all the changes he made, the essay is not worth an A or a B. Students may see any essay without serious formal errors as worthy of an A or a B, not realizing that its content is vacuous or its organization incoherent. (See Chapter 5, "Evaluating Student Essays," for a sample rubric for grading.) Such issues make for useful classroom discussion and exploration. After an assignment has been graded, the class can analyze the criteria for evaluation and grading. Some students, used to grade inflation, simply cannot get used to receiving Cs and even lower grades, especially if the work is formally perfect or they received high grades in high school. One way around this expectation is to assign an essay no grade at all until after at least one revision has been submitted or until you can declare the essay "acceptable" (usually the equivalent of a passing grade or a C).

As you evaluate the merits of a revision option, keep in mind that revision of written work is immensely useful to students. No longer is an essay a one-shot deal, submitted in fear or resignation because it must soar or crash on its maiden voyage. The opportunity for revision can foster commitment to the assignment and real intellectual growth. By allowing students to reflect on and improve their writing, a teacher allows them to see writing for what it is: a process of re-seeing a subject, a process that isn't completed until the writer is ready to say, "I can do no more."

WORKS CITED

Bain, Alexander. *English Composition and Rhetoric.* London: Longmans, 1877. Print.

Bishop, Wendy, and Hans Ostrom, eds. *Genre and Writing: Issues, Arguments, Alternatives.* Portsmouth: Boynton/Cook, 1997. Print.

——, and Pavel Zemliansky, eds. *The Subject Is Research.* Portsmouth: Boynton/Cook, 2001. Print.

Glenn, Cheryl. *Making Sense: A Real-World Rhetorical Reader.* 3rd ed. Boston: Bedford, 2010. Print.

Lowe, Charles, and Terra Williams. "Moving to the Public: Weblogs in the Writing Classroom." *Into the Blogosphere.* University of Minnesota, n.d. Web. 24 May 2012.

Lunsford, Andrea. *The St. Martin's Handbook.* 7th ed. Boston: Bedford, 2011. Print.

Wysocki, Anne Frances, Johndan Johnson-Eilola, Cynthia L. Selfe, and Geoffrey Sirc. *Writing New Media: Theory and Applications for Expanding the Teaching of Composition.* Logan: Utah State UP, 2004. Print.

Useful Web Sites

CoolArchive
  www.coolarchive.com

Instant Web Sites
  www.pcworld.about.com/magazine/2201p123id113447.htm

Moving to the Public: Weblogs in the Writing Classroom
  blog.lib.umn.edu/blogosphere/moving_to_the_public.html

Vincent Flanders' Web Pages That Suck
  www.webpagesthatsuck.com

5

Evaluating Student Essays

> *Grading can be intimidating, but I've found that it can also be a rewarding experience where I actually do most of my "real teaching." In my experience, grading four or so papers at a time, then taking a break, helps alleviate some of that intimidation. A mentor once told me that all students want in the grading process is clearness, fairness, and consistency, and grading in smaller batches helps me maintain those three qualities.*
>
> –JOHN BELK

In a sense, it is unfortunate that we have to grade student essays at all; far too often a grade halts further work on and thought about a piece of writing. If we could limit our responses to advice for revision and evaluation of progress, we could create a supportive, rather than a competitive or judgmental, atmosphere in our classrooms. As Peter Elbow proposes in "Embracing Contraries," teachers can learn to be allies or coaches for students — not simply gatekeepers and judges (337). Since most colleges and universities require us to grade student essays, we need to concentrate on specific ways to make our evaluations useful and meaningful. If approached cautiously and thoughtfully, evaluating and marking our students' work can serve as an encouraging record of student progress — but only if we supply students with useful information.

Unless your department favors a holistic grading system in which a group of teachers collaboratively creates a set of standards and grades student papers as a group, you will be using the more common method of grading: individual evaluation. (For more on holistic grading, see "Holistic Grading" on the CSTW Web site, cited at the end of this chapter.) In preparing to grade and evaluate your first stack of essays, you must consider some questions. First, are you expected to enforce departmental grading standards? If your department or writing program has such standards, you must be prepared to grade accordingly, for in all probability the standards were instituted in a serious attempt to reduce grade inflation and standardize grades within the composition program. (For more information on grading, see Curzan and Damour; Davis; and Zak and Weaver, cited at the end of this chapter.) Regardless of whether you have to follow departmental guidelines, the issue of grading criteria usually comes down to practical questions you will have to answer for yourself: Will you assume that every essay can be, or must be, revised to meet a higher standard? Will you assume that every essay starts out as a potential A and, with each flaw, discredits itself, gradually becoming a B, a C, and so on? Or will you assume that each essay begins as a C — an average or competent essay — and then rises above or falls below that middle ground? To a great degree, the answers to these questions will depend on the ethos of the program in which you're teaching, your teaching experience, and your own experience as a student receiving grades.

Teachers who begin the work of evaluation with the assumption that all essays should be A's tend to see only what is wrong with the essays that don't meet that standard. Those teachers who start from the position that most FY essays are average—or C's—are perhaps grudging with their A's. Whichever position you start from, you will have to reach some decision about one other question: Will improvement—presumably the goal of your writing course—be taken into consideration during final grading? What about students who start out writing C-level essays and work up to B-level work—should they be given a B even if their grade average is only a C-plus? This question can be answered in the following two ways, assuming you want to make improvement a consideration.

One method of treating improvement is to set up your schedule of written assignments so that later assignments are worth a larger percentage of the grade for the course, thus weighting the final grade in favor of improvement late in the course (the syllabi at the end of Chapter 1 do this). The second method is to use the concept of "degree of difficulty," assigning more cognitively demanding topics as the course progresses, with the most difficult writing assignment earning the highest grade percentage. Thus an essay creditable in the second week would seem simplistic in the eighth week. The first method often works better for newer teachers since the second method, establishing degrees of assignment difficulty, is learned only with experience.

You'll also want to think carefully about how to address your students. Some teachers talk directly with their students about the kinds of comments they find helpful—which ones make them feel like revising, which ones make them feel like quitting. Nancy Sommers, for example, interviewed fifty students, asking them about teachers' comments on their work; she then created a DVD—*Beyond the Red Ink: Students Talk about Teachers' Comments*—that features seven students talking about teacher comments and providing advice to teachers. The students value encouraging comments, ones that, in student Jorge García's words, "*begin* conversations, not *end* them" (Sommers, *Beyond*). The written comments you make on a student's essay will often be the basis of your relationship with that student. It is important that you consider this relationship as you comment and grade and that your responses to students' writing be part of a respectful conversation.

We expect students to respect our knowledge of the subject and our good intentions toward them; in return, we must respect their attempts to fulfill our expectations and to move forward in their learning. Pamela Gay, in "Dialogizing Response in the Writing Classroom: Students Answer Back," encourages teachers to provide opportunities for students to respond to comments on their texts. Peter Elbow offers similar advice, encouraging teachers to take five minutes after handing back essays to have students write a note to the

don't mind this

teacher in response (359). Such interaction will help you see more clearly how students are interpreting (and sometimes misinterpreting) the comments you make. Since you're likely to encounter a wide range of abilities and motivations as you evaluate your students' essays, you'll need to consider each student's work separately because comparisons are inherently invidious. Allowing students to respond in writing to your comments on their work is one way of reminding yourself that each student is an individual — and that each will respond differently to the kinds of comments you make.

Your students may constitute a diverse group in terms of age, background, ability, culture, and ethnicity. To all of them, however, you represent — though you may not always feel comfortable with it — the academic community; many will see you as a sort of gatekeeper of discourse and opportunity. Although some of them may hesitate to join in the conversation of what they see as your community, you should assume and respect their desire to be a part of it, and you should take responsibility for helping them become a part of it. As you write your comments and suggestions, remember that some of your students' backgrounds may be far different from your own and that of the academic community. You will want, therefore, to represent academic conventions to them with a sympathetic, as well as a judicious, eye. *sympathetic and judicious*

STANDARDS AND EVALUATION

Formal Standards

As all experienced writing teachers know, formal errors in standardized English are by far the easiest to mark, recognize, and correct. You mark a spelling error here, a sentence fragment there. There is a natural feeling after having marked formal errors that you have done a solid, creditable job of reading a student's essay, when you may not have responded to content issues at all.

That false sense of having completed a job makes formal evaluation seductive. Because of it, teachers are often tempted to base most of their grade on the formal qualities of the essay and not enough on the content. One can easily see why: Formal evaluation is concrete and quantitative; it demands few complex judgment calls and ignores content evaluation. When teachers fill a student essay with red marks, they may think they've done a thorough reading of it — so why do more? Justifying a D on the basis of three fragments and nine misspelled words is easier than dealing with the complex, sometimes arbitrary world of content: thesis statements, patterns of development, assertions, and support. A piece of writing consists of far more than its grammar and punctuation, however. In reading to "correct" rather than to respond to the fullness of a piece of writing, we lose the pleasure of reading our students' work and too often overlook what the student has done well. If we stress nothing but formal grading, we quickly become pedants, obsessed with correctness to the detriment of meaning. We do have a responsibility to evaluate formal errors, for as Mina

Shaughnessy says, they are "unintentional and unprofitable intrusions upon the consciousness of the reader" that "demand energy without giving any return" (12). We must mark them, but we should not give them more than their due.

In 2006, to update the research done in 1988 by Connors and Lunsford (see "Frequency of Formal Errors in Current College Writing," cited at the end of this chapter; see also "'Mistakes Are a Part of Life': A National Comparative Study" in Part III of this book), Andrea A. Lunsford and Karen J. Lunsford surveyed nearly nine hundred student essays and identified the twenty errors most often made by students, who now almost uniformly compose on computers. Here, in order of occurrence, is the new list of the twenty most common error patterns (Lunsford, *Easy Writer*, 2):

1. Wrong word
2. Missing comma after an introductory element
3. Incomplete or missing documentation
4. Vague pronoun reference
5. Spelling (including homonyms)
6. Mechanical error with a quotation
7. Unnecessary comma
8. Unnecessary or missing capitalization
9. Missing word
10. Faulty sentence structure
11. Missing comma with a nonrestrictive element
12. Unnecessary shift in verb tense
13. Missing comma in a compound sentence
14. Unnecessary or missing apostrophe (including *its/it's*)
15. Fused (run-on) sentence
16. Comma splice
17. Lack of pronoun-antecedent agreement
18. Poorly integrated quotation
19. Unnecessary or missing hyphen
20. Sentence fragment

You will need to determine, of course, how much emphasis you want to give to each kind of formal error. Within any group of serious errors, many teachers distinguish between *sentence-level* or *syntactic errors* (sentence fragments, fused sentences, comma splices) and *word-level errors* (spelling, verb forms, agreement). Syntactic errors are considered much more serious than word-level errors because these more global errors often present the reader with a situation in which it is impossible to know what the writer meant. When teachers quantitatively count errors, they nearly always count syntactic errors and word-level errors separately.

Another issue to consider when responding to formal elements in student writing is the extent to which deviations from standardized English may be the result of differences in dialects, languages, and cultures. There are many sources that provide guidance for considering and respecting a variety of language uses; such sources can help you gain a better understanding of important differences among students and their language practices. (See Elbow's chapter "Inviting the Mother Tongue: Beyond 'Mistakes,' 'Bad English,' and 'Wrong Language'" in *Everyone Can Write,* and Chapters 33–37 in Lunsford's *EasyWriter,* cited at the end of this chapter.)

Once again, looking at an essay in terms of its formal and mechanical problems is an important part of your task but only a small part of it. Read your students' writing with an eye to discerning their error patterns and note the most important patterns in your end comment, citing a few specific examples. If you find that several students struggle with the same issues, spend some time in class going over the formal and mechanical errors most frequently made by students in your class. By seeing patterns rather than individual mistakes, students can work on breaking those patterns one at a time, concentrating on a series of single goals in a way that does not overwhelm them.

Standards of Content

Unlike formal correctness, in which conventions are generally agreed upon (a comma splice is, after all, a comma splice), content is a much more abstract business. And despite the fact that content is every bit as important as form, writing teachers are less confident about their ability to judge ideas and organization and therefore may be tempted to give these aspects of composition less than their due when grading.

In response to content, teachers must make serious judgments that inform the evaluation and the final grade of an essay. Usually grades for content are assigned on the basis of the success of the essay in four specific areas, which Paul Diederich calls *ideas, organization, wording,* and *flavor* (55–57).

Connors and Lunsford's "Teachers' Rhetorical Comments on Student Papers" shows that more teachers comment on *ideas* than on any other single area. More than 56 percent of the essays they examined contained teachers' comments on ideas and their support (208). In general, comments on ideas are based on the following questions:

1. How well does the essay respond to the assignment?
2. How novel, original, or well presented is the thesis of the essay?
3. Are the arguments or main points of the essay well supported by explanatory or exemplary material?
4. Is the thesis carried to its logical conclusion?

Connors and Lunsford's study reveals that, after comments on supporting evidence and examples, teachers are most likely to comment on an essay's *organization.* Comments on organization are based on questions such as the following:

1. Does the essay have a coherent plan?
2. Is the plan followed out completely and logically?
3. Is the plan balanced, and does it serve the purpose of the essay?
4. Are the paragraphs within the essay well developed?

Issues of *wording* can impinge on the formal standards of a work; but with respect to content, comments on wording are more concerned with word choice than with grammatical correctness. Addressed are such questions as the following:

1. Does the essay use words precisely?
2. Does the essay use words in any delightful or original fashion?

Finally, there is the level of *flavor*, the term Diederich uses for what others might call *style*. More than 33 percent of the essays analyzed by Connors and Lunsford contained comments on issues of flavor or style in response to the following questions:

1. Is the writing pleasing to the reader?
2. Does the writer come across as someone the reader might like and trust?
3. Does the writer sound intelligent and knowledgeable?
4. Are the sentence structures effective?

Although these guidelines can help you grade content, it is ultimately you who must decide whether an essay says something significant, has a strong central idea, adheres to standards of logic in development, and supports its contentions with facts. All teachers know the uncomfortable sense of final responsibility that goes with the territory of teaching, so don't hesitate to share your problems, solutions, and evaluation questions with your colleagues.

Evaluating Formal Standards and Standards of Content When Responding to ESL Student Writing

In many ways, responding to and evaluating ESL student writing isn't any different from providing feedback to students for whom English is their first language. That is, you should always first make positive comments, acknowledging what a student has done well — complimenting good ideas, logical organization, or effective details and examples.

Once you have found elements that work well, you can consider those content elements that still need work. For example, you can comment on the clarity of one idea and ask the student to bring that same clarity to another, showing the student how to build upon successes.

Although content should be your primary focus, when responding to ESL student writing, sentence-level issues often seem more pressing because it can be difficult to get to the ideas when idioms, sentence structure, verb forms and tenses, prepositions, articles, and punctuation press against the conventions of standardized English. If the number of formal errors seems overwhelming, look for patterns of error, those errors that appear several times and that interfere with understanding, instead of marking each one. You will likely find that you can categorize the areas on which the student still needs to work. For example, you might find six instances of confusing word order, twelve sentences in which the subject and verb do not agree, eighteen missing or misused articles, and eleven places where the student has used the wrong form of a word. Instead of ranking these errors numerically, however, your next step is to consider which errors most interfere with understanding. Some errors—such as using the wrong part of speech or an incorrect preposition—will often confuse readers, preventing them from understanding the writer's point; other errors, though, such as a missing article, will simply irritate or amuse readers without preventing communication. You will want to give more attention to the errors that interfere with the writer's message. OK, good advice → Should grade her paper wir?

You can then make a list of the most serious errors and sit down with the student after class or during a scheduled conference to go over the areas that require the most attention in revision (or if you're dealing with a final draft, you can provide a list of goals for the student to work toward for the next assignment). When you talk with the student, point first to the places where the student does something well—in terms of content as well as punctuation and grammar. If there are six places where the student has used a preposition correctly, draw attention to those areas and then ask the student which preposition would work in the places where you recognize preposition errors. Show the student that you have read his or her work carefully, that you appreciate what is working well, and that you want to work with the student to build on the knowledge and skills already evidenced in the essay.

A handbook provides another helpful resource for ESL students, who often know the rules of grammar and punctuation even better than native speakers. If the handbook you are using includes a verb tense chart or a section on parts of speech, you can talk through those sections in reference to the student's paper. At other times, though, no rule exists for what you want the student to know, and you simply have to act as an informant, perhaps explaining an idiom or acknowledging an exception to a rule the student has put into practice.

Marking patterns of error rather than every mistake (regardless of its level of seriousness) and praising the effective elements of the essay will give both you and the student perspective on the writing. Instead of seeing an essay with forty-seven errors, you and the student can see a well-organized essay that includes appropriate details and examples—and also needs work in three or four specific areas. As you evaluate and grade the essay, that perspective will be important, and as the student considers the assignments to come, she will have specific areas on which to focus.

GENERAL ROUTINES FOR EVALUATION

If you are not using the multidraft evaluation process discussed in Chapter 4 (pp. 120–23), you might consider another efficient procedure for handling essays, one suggested decades ago by Richard Larson (152–55). First, read over the essay quickly, making no marks but trying to get a sense of the organization and the general nature of the work. Try to decide during this initial reading what you like about the essay and what elements need work. Next, reread the essay more slowly, marking it for errors and writing marginal comments. You may read it paragraph by paragraph this time, thinking less about overall organization. Finally, reread the essay quickly, this time taking into consideration its overall purpose, its good and bad features, the number of formal errors, and your marginal notes and comments. After this reading, write your terminal comment and grade the essay.

Next, make a note of the essay in your student file. Compare its successes and failures with those of the student's past essays, and note any improvement or decline. You might at this point add to your terminal comment a sentence or two concerning the essay's success compared with previous efforts. Finally, you can put the essay in your outbox and take up another one.

There are other evaluation procedures, of course. Some teachers use evaluation sheets detailing areas of content, organization, and style. The teacher fills out a sheet for each essay and clips it to the essay instead of making comments directly on the student's work. The evaluation sheets can be formatted so that each student submits the same sheet for all assignments, providing an easy way for both student and teacher to track progress, particularly with regard to trouble spots.

Other teachers respond electronically, using the Track Changes and Insert Comment features of Microsoft Word or providing a secure Web site (usually through a course-management system) to which students can upload their papers. If you respond electronically, you can keep copies of your comments, allowing you to track student progress. Whether you have students e-mail their papers to you or upload them to a course-management site or some other secure site, you will need to teach students the technology they are expected to use. If you have students send their papers by e-mail, be sure your virus protection software is up to date.

The final task, of course, is to return students' essays. You should return student work as quickly as possible — no doubt you can remember the anxiety of waiting for your own teachers to get essays back to you. If you are commenting electronically, you can return papers quickly by e-mail or have students log on to the site you're using. Although responding electronically can allow you to return papers as quickly as you're able to read and respond to them, it also invites quick responses — sometimes reactions from students. Be prepared for e-mail responses and questions or ask students to wait a day or two before responding. Likewise, if you're returning papers in class, some students may rush to your desk, asking to speak with you immediately about their grades. You may want to ask them to look carefully at their essays and your comments and to set up a meeting during your office hours if they have questions and concerns. Time and reflection help diffuse immediate emotional reactions to a grade and allow a student to prepare for a more productive meeting with you.

[handwritten margin note: This is a good idea for me.]

MARGINAL COMMENTS

A good number of the marks you make on students' essays will be marginal comments about specific words, sentences, and paragraphs. Making marginal comments allows you to be specific in your praise or questioning—you can call attention to strengths or weaknesses where they occur. Marginal comments may deal with substantive matters, arrangement, tone, support, and style. (For detailed discussions of both marginal and terminal comments, see Elbow; S. Smith; and Straub and Lunsford, cited at the end of this chapter.)

In writing marginal comments, you want to balance advice and criticism with praise. Try to avoid the temptation to comment only on form or to point out only errors. You can use conventional editing symbols (if you explain to students what they mean), but do not let them be your only marginal effort. Nor should you use a mere question mark if you do not understand a section; instead, spell out your question. If reasoning is faulty, do not merely write "logic" or "coh?"; let the student know what is wrong, and try to provide some direction for revision. Teacher shorthand can be very confusing to students, leaving them perplexed, as the following humorous example illustrates. In his poem "Amphibians Have Feelings Too," Gerald Locklin recounts the story of a teacher who "kept scrawling / FRAG in the margin" of a student's papers until

> The last day of the semesters rolled around
> and after everyone else had left
> this student came up to the desk and said,
> 'Mr. Odin, there's just one thing I'd like to ask you.'
> 'Sure. What is it?'
> 'Why have you been writing FROG on my paper all semester?' (107)

To limit such confusions, it is more useful to write comments as if you are having a conversation with the text. Elbow reminds teachers to make "comments on students' writing sound like they come from a human reader rather than from an impersonal machine or a magisterial, all-knowing God source" (359). For example, according to Elbow, instead of writing "awk" in the margin, you might write, "I stumbled here" (359), thereby helping your students see that their writing has an effect on real readers.

What other sorts of marginal comments are effective? Remember that praise is always welcome. If students write something impressive or make stylistic choices that seem effective or appealing, do not hesitate to tell them. A simple "Good!" or "Yes!" next to the sentence can mean a great deal to a struggling writer, as you may recall from responses to your own work. In addition, a simple question such as "Evidence?" or "Does this follow?" or "Proof of this?" or "How did you make this move?" or "Seems obvious. Is it true?" can lead students to question their assertions more effectively than will a page of rhetorical injunctions.

Mary Beaven mentions three sorts of marginal comments that she has found particularly helpful:

1. Asking for more information on a point that the student has made.
2. Mirroring, reflecting, or rephrasing the student's ideas, perceptions, or feelings in a nonjudgmental way.
3. Sharing personal information about times when you, the teacher, have felt or thought similarly. (139)

All of these sorts of comments are text-specific; they thus make students feel as if the teacher is genuinely interested in what they have written. Note also that the kinds of marginal comments *you* use will likely be the kinds of marginal comments students themselves use in their peer-response groups, so try to model the use of helpful comments.

Marginal comments are nearly always short—single sentences or phrases. As Nancy Sommers points out in "Responding to Student Writing" (included in Part III), marginal comments tend to "freeze" students in the current draft, whereas terminal comments often invite a new draft (p. 333). It is best, therefore, to limit your marginal comments when evaluating first drafts. If you write a response to every feature of an essay (from punctuation and usage to logic and style), you will put in a tremendous amount of work and your students are likely to be put off. For many good reasons, students tend to believe that the more a teacher comments on their work (even when the commentary is in the form of praise), the worse the work is. So consider three or four marginal comments per page an upper limit, at least for substantive comments. Anne Curzan and Lisa Damour remind teachers that

> the key to writing good comments on students' work is striking the balance between too little and too much. Bear in mind how frustrated you have been over the years when you have put time into an assignment only to get it back with a grade and nothing else on the last page. Of equal importance, remember that students can absorb only so much constructive criticism in one shot. Focus your comments on one or two major problems and perhaps one minor one (e.g., the style of the conclusion) and accept the fact that you cannot cover all the bases in your response to one assignment. (133)

Purely formal marginal or interlinear comments on errors are another area entirely. You must decide for yourself on a system for noting such errors, and you must explain that system to students. (See the section on "Formal Standards" earlier in this chapter.) Much will depend on your philosophy.

Two teachers are likely to see the same page of student writing in two completely different ways. One might mark a fragment, a comma splice, and three misspellings, whereas the other might mark those errors plus four misuses of the comma, three awkward phrasings, a misplaced modifier, and five questionable word choices. A great deal depends on the stage of the composing process the student is concentrating on. ESL and BW teachers, for instance, tend to concentrate on global errors that obstruct meaning before pointing out errors that violate conventions of standardized English. (For more on the variation among teacher responses, see Straub and Lunsford, cited at the end of this chapter.)

Members of the minimalist school of marking errors leave minor faults alone unless they are the only errors in an essay. In "Minimal Marking," Richard

Haswell explains this method: "All surface mistakes in a student's paper are left totally unmarked within the text. These are unquestionable errors in spelling, punctuation, capitalization, and grammar. . . . Each of these mistakes is indicated only with a check in the margin by the line in which it occurs" (601). Haswell's method may seem radical, but the sight of an essay whose margins are completely filled with criticism can make any writer despair.

Certainly after the term has run for a few weeks and students have become aware of their individual error patterns, you may find that simply placing a checkmark over an error is effective. This system asks students to discover for themselves the cause of and solution for their errors and saves you from having to continue as editor. Because checkmarks are also considerably faster to apply, you can devote more time to an attentive rhetorical reading of the essay and thus to providing substantive comments.

TERMINAL COMMENTS

Terminal, or general, comments are probably the most important message you give students about their essays, even more important than the grades you assign. (We are calling all general comments *terminal* comments because Connors and Lunsford's research indicates that 84 percent of all teachers place their longer comments at the end of a student paper rather than at the beginning.) Students turn first to their grades and then to your comments, which they interpret as a justification of the grade. Therefore, terminal comments must do a great deal in a short space: They must document the strengths and weaknesses of an essay, let the student know whether she responded well to your assignment, help create a psychological environment in which the student is willing to revise or write again, encourage and discourage specific writing behaviors, and set specific goals that you think the student can meet.

The type of terminal comment you make will depend on your purpose — on whether, for example, you are justifying an irrevocable grade or making suggestions for revision. The task of justifying a grade often forces a teacher to focus the terminal comment in a closed way on the successes and problems of the essay. It is a kind of autopsy report on a moribund essay, one that will not see further development. Advice on revision, however, can focus on the future and build on an analysis of error patterns and the student's ongoing writing experience. Both sorts of terminal comments share certain components, though, and more than anything else the difference between them is a matter of the percentages of these components that each contains.

Extensive research by Connors and Lunsford indicates that the most common kind of terminal comment that composition teachers make on a student essay — 42 percent of all terminal comments — opens with praise for some aspect of the essay and then makes suggestions for other areas of the essay that need work (207). In addition, terminal comments most commonly begin with larger-scale issues — content, organization, general effectiveness — and then discuss the smaller-scale issues of form and mechanics; thus, teachers often move from global to local concerns. More than 75 percent of terminal comments deal with the large-scale rhetorical issues in student essays (207). The average length of terminal comments, according to the sample studied, is about thirty-one words, but the most effective comments are somewhat longer (211).

After analyzing the most effective comments, Connors and Lunsford derived several characteristics of a good terminal comment. First, every terminal comment should focus on general qualities, presenting the teacher's impression of the essay as a whole. Second, a good terminal comment devotes a large part of its content to an evaluation of the essay's thesis and how well the thesis is supported, answering the question, "How well does the thesis respond to the assignment?" If a thesis is thought of as a promise of what the essay will include, the terminal comment should evaluate how well the essay keeps this promise. The evaluation must take in content, organization, and style, concentrating all of this information in a short space.

In addition, Connors and Lunsford write that the teacher should maintain a serious yet interested tone — not risking humor at the writer's expense unless the essay has earned an A. The teacher's comment should include praise for the effective elements of the essay as well as mention of the elements that need work. It should point out improvements made since previous efforts and encourage revision. Except perhaps to mention one or two of the most important error patterns, the teacher need not spend time pointing out formal errors or summarizing material covered in the marginal comments. In general, a terminal comment need not ever contain more than 200 words and seldom more than 150.

Meeting these goals is not as difficult as you might think. After an entire afternoon of grading, you will have gained a sense of your class as a continuum of writing abilities. Even when fatigue sets in and your critical apparatus gets creaky, you will see how each essay compares with the ones that came before and with those of the rest of the class this time. But if you are still uncertain about your ability to write good comments or want to look at examples of comments that good teachers make, your colleagues are a natural resource. Inquire about teachers in the department who are highly respected, and ask them whether they would be willing to check your annotations and show you theirs. Colleagues constantly help one another with revisions of their own scholarly writing, so it is natural to seek help in the same way when you want to improve your writing of terminal comments. Also consider the most worthwhile and helpful comments you have received on your own essays.

Researchers in the field of composition studies agree that teachers would do well to avoid two extremes: harsh or disrespectful comments that usurp student control over the text ("You have no idea what you're talking about"; "This is a zero draft; start over"), and minimal or generic comments that seem disengaged from the text and offer little real response or help ("Logic?" or just a question mark; "Rewrite"). As Elbow observes, "Most students benefit when they feel that writing is a transaction with human beings rather than an 'exercise in getting something right or wrong'" (359). Somewhere between the two extremes of taking over a student's writing and being disengaged from it is where we try to be: reading carefully and offering genuine commentary from the continuum of generic knowledge that we do, after all, possess. Both aggressive willingness to take over and direct students' work and coy withdrawal from sharing our valuable evaluative opinions serve students badly. As Richard Straub puts it, "The best responding styles will create us on the page in ways that fit in with our classroom purposes, allow us to take advantage of our strengths as teachers, and enable us to interact as productively as we can with our students. Ultimately, they will allow us to make comments that are ways of teaching" (248). Your terminal comments should show students that you have read their work carefully, that you care about helping them improve their writing, and that you know enough about the subject to be able to help them effectively. As in all features of teaching, your terminal comments will be useful to students only if they demonstrate humanity and competence. (For more on how students respond to teacher comments, see Nancy Sommers's DVD, *Beyond the Red Ink*, cited at the end of this chapter.)

THE GRADE

The comments you make in the margins and at the end of an essay are the truly important responses that the student gets from you about his writing, but the grade remains the first thing the student looks for. Although grading can be difficult, it can be made easier for you and for all new teachers if you can organize or attend a departmental grading seminar. Such a seminar will bring together new and experienced teachers to discuss and practice grading. This group need not meet more than once or twice and need not be large, but in one afternoon, experienced teachers can share many of their techniques and standards with new teachers — and everyone can learn from one another.

The grading seminar works best when the participants bring copies of several unmarked essays, enough so that every teacher present receives a copy. Each teacher should mark and grade his or her copy of the essay separately and contribute to the discussion following the marking session. Out of this discussion of the problems and strengths of each essay will come a stronger sense of context and unity for both new and experienced teachers.

Though they can be difficult to organize, such seminars are extremely useful in giving new teachers a sense of how to grade essays. They also introduce teachers to the philosophy and practice of holistic grading, which involves a group evaluation by trained "raters." These kinds of seminars can be linked to formal assessments of student writing, a practice increasingly called for by administrators. If your department is undertaking an assessment of student writing, you might ask to participate. (For additional information on formal assessment, see Huot and O'Neill's *Assessing Writing*, cited at the end of this chapter.)

If you have to proceed alone, however, make certain that your grading system corresponds to that used by your school, lest you find out at the end of the term that you must adapt your system to some other one. Before you grade your first essay, find out whether your school uses a four-point system or a five-point

A= Great
B= Above Av, But Not great
C= Average
D= Below average
F= Unacceptable

system and whether you can give plus/minus grades. If your department, your program, or even those with whom you share an office have devised standards of grading that you agree to follow, you can avoid many anxieties about grading.

As you grade, be on the alert for the B fallacy: the temptation to overuse the B. This grade does, after all, seem like a nice compromise: An essay is not A quality, but a C is so . . . average. To many teachers, new and experienced alike, a C seems like a condemnation. Why not a B? If you think you are assigning too many B's and are vaguely dissatisfied with and confused by this practice, try to get back on track by asking yourself what elements in the essay deserve that grade. What, in short, makes this essay better than average? Is it word choice? organization? expression of ideas? If you can honestly point to a specific area in which the essay is better than most others you've seen, it may deserve the B. If you can find no specific area in which the essay excels, you can be fairly certain it is indeed average.

METHODS AND CRITERIA FOR GRADING

Course-Based Grading Criteria

Many teachers using the professional evaluation method have found that a system of course-based (or individual class-based) grading criteria works to involve their students in the evaluation process. Course-based evaluation does not put all grading responsibility into students' hands, of course, but by involving all the members of your class in important decisions — about what they want to learn and have you evaluate — you make grading seem less arbitrary.

To work with your students to develop course-based evaluation, you should plan one or two sessions on grading criteria early in the term. Let students know that these sessions are important and that the weightings and criteria that result from them will be in use for the rest of the course. Begin the sessions by asking each student to list on paper the writing skills and issues that seem most important for the class to cover and emphasize. Then assemble students into groups of three and ask them to compare lists and be prepared to present the group's choices of important issues to the class. After the groups have met for ten minutes or so, ask each group to elect a person to place its list on the board. This will produce seven or eight such lists ranging from "understand assignments" and "use the Web for research" to "correct comma use" and "document sources properly." There will be a tremendous amount of overlap, of course, so you will need to point out and erase repetitive categories. You will still be left with as many as thirty possible issues or criteria. Number them on the board.

Next, ask each student to vote for a weighting on the criteria that are listed — from five points for most heavily weighted criteria to one point for least important criteria. From this initial tally, which you can write on the board, the larger number of issues can be whittled down to a smaller number, usually around five to ten. At this point the class needs to discuss the weighting of these criteria: which are to be more important and which less, the standards to be used in judging, and the ways in which you will apply these standards. Usually the outcome of these discussions will be a sheet of criteria that you draw up on the basis of the class determination. Everyone in the class receives a copy of these criteria, and you use the weighted criterion issues in both your evaluations and final grading. Here is an example of an evaluation-criteria sheet produced by one of our FY classes:

Evaluation Criteria — English 101, Section 22

1. Final essays will have a clear central idea that is supported by examples.
2. Paragraphs and sentences will have good transitions linking them so as to allow smooth reading.
3. Introductions will catch the reader's attention in some interesting way.
4. Sentences will have different lengths and types.
5. All sentences will have proper grammatical construction.
6. Research materials will be properly introduced, quoted, and cited.
7. Essays will show attention to and knowledge of the conventions of the genre used.

Although the criteria your class comes up with may not align exactly with either the criteria you might apply or with the weighting you would give, you will find that students usually have a remarkably accurate idea of what sorts of standards might be usefully applied to their writing. Moreover, the discussion of what is central and what is less important to their writing makes them participants in the process rather than mere pawns of other powers. Most students appreciate the opportunity to be involved in the process, though some might prefer that the teacher establish the grading criteria.

Rubrics

How, though?

One way of establishing grading criteria is to create your own rubric, one that makes your expectations explicit and allows students to set goals for themselves. Because people often disagree about what constitutes good writing, it's important to clarify your expectations — for yourself and for your students. When used as guidelines, rubrics can be helpful in communicating with students and in ensuring that your evaluation process is as fair and consistent as possible. The disadvantages of some rubrics, however, are that they can become too systematic and replace individual comments, especially when you assign numerical values to the constitutive parts of each essay and use the rubric only in the context of grading. Rubrics that assign numerical values to each part of an essay (clear and graceful transitions = 7 points, functional transitions = 5 points) cause students to think more about what they "got points 'off' for" than how they can become better writers overall.

Rubrics can take many shapes and be used in a variety of ways. Sometimes, they take the form of a checklist, detailing what you expect from a particular assignment. Other times, teachers structure them according to grades: what an A essay looks like, what a B essay looks like, and so on. Another structure for rubrics is a prioritized list; you put the most important components of the essay higher on the list (thesis, support, organization, and so on), creating a kind of hierarchy of concerns on which to focus. The shape of the rubric you use (if you use one) will likely depend on your purpose: Will you use it as a way of defining your expectations for the kind of writing students will do? as a way of structuring your course? as peer-response guidelines? as a self-checklist for students before essays are due? as a guide for responding to students' essays? as a scoring device?

Example 5.1, from the Penn State University composition department, shows a rubric that establishes criteria for evaluation and describes how such criteria translate into particular grades. Examples of other rubrics are available from the University Writing Program at Virginia Polytechnic Institute Web site, listed at the end of this chapter. The Web site also offers paragraph descriptions of what a teacher might expect from essays earning particular grades and a writing assessment checklist, including a list of criteria in the form of questions ("Do the introduction and conclusion focus clearly on the main point?" for example), boxes to check (excellent, fair, poor), a space for comments, and an area to record strengths of the work and suggestions for change.

While the paragraph descriptions work well in helping teachers discuss expectations for a successful essay and as a reminder of grading criteria for completed essays, the writing assessment checklist works well when attached to a draft or as a point of discussion in conferences, providing guidance for revision. In any case, rubrics — though helpful in making expectations explicit — should not replace marginal and terminal comments on students' essays. If you do use a rubric, remember to emphasize to students that the process of writing and response is complex. Strong writing is more than its constituent parts, and there are aspects of both the writing and reading process for which rubrics cannot account. Likewise, responding well to a student's writing requires more than placing checkmarks and circles on a rubric.

Example 5.1 PENN STATE UNIVERSITY'S FIRST-YEAR WRITING GRADING STANDARDS

These grading standards establish four major criteria for evaluation at each grade level: purpose, reasoning and content, organization, and expression. Obviously, every essay will not fit neatly into one grade category; some essays may, for instance, have some characteristics of B and some of C. The final grade the essay receives depends on the weight the instructor gives each criterion and whether the essay was received on time.

The A Essay

1. The A essay fulfills the assignment—and does so in a fresh and mature manner, using purposeful language that leads to knowledge making. The essay effectively meets the needs of the rhetorical situation in terms of establishing the writer's stance, attention to audience, purpose for writing, and sensitivity to context. Furthermore, the writer demonstrates expertise in employing the artistic appeals of ethos, logos, and pathos appropriately.

2. The topic itself is clearly defined, focused, and supported. The essay has a clear thesis that is supported with specific (and appropriate) evidence, examples, and details. Any outside sources of information are used carefully and cited appropriately. The valid reasoning within the essay demonstrates good judgment and an awareness of the topic's complexities.

3. The organization—chronological, spatial, or emphatic—is appropriate for the purpose and subject of the essay. The introduction establishes a context, purpose, and audience for writing and contains a focused thesis statement. The following paragraphs are controlled by (explicit or implicit) topic sentences; they are well developed; and they progress logically from what precedes them. (If appropriate, headings and subheadings are used.) The conclusion moves beyond a mere restatement of the introduction, offering implications for or the significance of the topic.

4. The prose is clear, readable, and sometimes memorable. It contains few surface errors, none of which seriously undermines the overall effectiveness of the paper for educated readers. It demonstrates fluency in stylistic flourishes (subordination, variation of sentence and paragraph lengths, interesting vocabulary).

The B Essay

1. The assignment has been followed and fulfilled. The essay establishes the writer's stance and demonstrates a clear sense of audience, purpose, and context.

2. The topic is fairly well defined, focused, and supported. The thesis statement is adequate (but could be sharpened), especially for the quality of supporting evidence the writer has used. The reasoning and support are thorough and more than adequate. The writer demonstrates a thoughtful awareness of complexity and other points of view.

3. The B essay has an effective introduction and conclusion. The order of information is logical, and the reader can follow it because of well-chosen transitions and (explicit or implicit) topic sentences. Paragraph divisions are logical, and the paragraphs use enough specific detail to satisfy the reader.

4. The prose expression is clear and readable. Sentence structure is appropriate for educated readers, including the appropriate use of subordination, emphasis, varied sentences, and modifiers. Few sentence-level errors (comma splices, fragments, or fused sentences) appear. Vocabulary is precise and appropriate; punctuation, usage, and spelling conform to the conventions of standardized English discussed in class.

The C Essay

1. The assignment has been followed, and the essay demonstrates a measure of response to the rhetorical situation, insofar as the essay demonstrates some sense of audience and purpose.

2. The topic is defined only generally; the thesis statement is also general. The supporting evidence, gathered honestly and used responsibly, is, nevertheless, often obvious and easily accessible. The writer demonstrates little awareness of the topic's complexity or other points of view; therefore, the C essay usually exhibits minor imperfections or inconsistencies in development, organization, and reasoning.

3. The organization is fairly clear. The reader could outline the presentation, despite the occasional lack of topic sentences. Paragraphs have

adequate development and are divided appropriately. Transitions may be mechanical, but they foster coherence.

4. The expression is competent. Sentence structure is relatively simple, relying on simple and compound sentences. The essay contains some sentence-level errors; word choice is correct though limited. The essay contains errors in spelling, usage, and punctuation that reveal a lack of familiarity with the conventions of standardized English discussed in class.

The D Essay

1. The D essay attempts to follow the assignment but demonstrates little awareness of the rhetorical situation in terms of the writer's stance, audience, purpose, and context. For example, the essay might over- or underestimate (or ignore) the audience's prior knowledge, assumptions, or beliefs. The writer may have little sense of purpose.

2. The essay may not have any thesis statement, or, at best, a flawed one. Obvious evidence may be missing, and irrelevant evidence may be present. Whatever the status of the evidence, it is inadequately interpreted and rests on an insufficient understanding of the rhetorical situation. Or it may rely too heavily on evidence from published sources without adding original analysis.

3. Organization is simply deficient: Introductions or conclusions are not clearly marked or functional; paragraphs are neither coherently developed nor arranged; topic sentences are consistently missing, murky, or inappropriate; transitions are missing or flawed.

4. The D essay may have numerous and consistent errors in spelling, usage, and punctuation that reveal unfamiliarity with the conventions of standardized English discussed in class (or a lack of careful proofreading).

The F Essay

1. The F essay is inappropriate in terms of the purpose of the assignment and the rhetorical situation. If the essay relates vaguely to the assignment, it has no clear purpose or direction.

2. The essay falls seriously short of the minimum length requirements; therefore, it is insufficiently developed and does not go beyond the obvious.

3. The F essay is plagued by more than one of the organizational deficiencies of a D essay.

4. Numerous and consistent errors of spelling, usage, and punctuation hinder communication.

5. It may be plagiarized: Either it is someone else's essay, or this essay has used sources improperly and/or without documentation.

Contract Grading

Contract grading is a related but different system, and it may be best left in the hands of experienced FY writing teachers. It involves working out a specific individual contract with each student about how much work he or she will do, what kinds of work will be done, and what standards will be applied. Students' grades are based on the degree to which their work meets the criteria of the contract, and they can each contract for different grades. One student might contract, for instance, for an A if he completed seven 5-page essays of at least two drafts per essay, twenty journal entries of at least a page each, and classwork contributions each day. A B-range grade would be for less achievement, and so on. Some students choose to contract for B's or even for C's.

In an appendix to *Everyone Can Write,* Peter Elbow includes examples of contracts that he uses in writing courses. He begins with a letter to his FY students, one that explains the contract-grading system, offers sample contracts for a B and an A, and then spells out his goals as a teacher in the "Final Thoughts" section. Example 5.2 shows his contract for a B. You'll want to consult Elbow's text for the full versions of his sample contracts. While the details of your contract might differ from the specifics of Elbow's, reflecting your own values and expectations, his contract provides a starting place — an example of what teachers might expect in terms of students' behavior in class and in terms of their approach to assignments.

Finally, although contract grading can be a useful technique, in order for teachers to use it successfully, some experience with standard grading techniques is necessary. While for now, at least, it would probably be wise to wait before using contract grading, when and if you are ready to do so, be sure to talk with other teachers who have used this method successfully and ask for examples of their contracts. (For more information on contract grading, see Elbow; see also John A. Smith's "Contracting English Composition," which describes a system of contract grading in an introductory college composition course; both are cited at the end of this chapter.)

Example 5.2   **PETER ELBOW'S EXAMPLE OF A CONTRACT FOR A GRADE OF B**   *This is like Religion.*

You are guaranteed a B for the final grade if you meet the following conditions:

1. Don't miss more than one week's worth of classes.
2. Don't be habitually late. (If you are late or miss a class, you are responsible for finding out any assignments that were made.)
3. Don't have more than one late major assignment and one late smaller assignment.
4. Keep up your journal assignments.
5. Work cooperatively in groups. Be willing to share some of your writing, listen supportively to the writing of others and, when they want it, give full and thoughtful responses.
6. Major assignments need to meet the following conditions:

   - Include a process letter, all previous notes and drafts, and all feedback you have received.
   - *Revisions.* When the assignment is to revise, make it more than just a correcting or fixing. Your revision needs to reshape or extend or complicate or substantially clarify your ideas — or relate your ideas to new things. Revisions don't have to be better but they must be different — not just touched up but changed in some genuine way.
   - *Mechanics, copyediting.* When the assignment is for a *final draft,* it must be well copyedited — that is, free from virtually all mistakes in spelling and grammar. It's fine to get help in copyediting. I don't ask for careful copyediting on early and midprocess drafts, but it's crucial for final drafts.
   - *Effort.* Your papers need to show solid effort. This doesn't mean that you have to suffer; it's fine to have fun and even fool around with assignments. It just means that I need to see solid work.
   - *Perplexity.* For every paper, you need to find some genuine question or perplexity. That is, don't just tell four obvious reasons why

dishonesty is bad or why democracy is good. Root your paper in a felt *question* about honesty or democracy — a problem or an itch that itches *you*. (By the way, this is a crucial skill to learn for success in college: how to *find* a question that interests you — even in a boring assignment.)

- *Thinking.* Having found a perplexity, then use your paper to do some *figuring out*. Make some intellectual gears turn. Thus your paper needs to *move* or *go somewhere* — needs to have a line of thinking.

- Please don't panic because of these last three conditions. I recognize that if you emphasize effort, perplexity, and thinking, you will have a harder time making your papers intellectually tidy and structurally well organized. It's okay if your essays have some loose ends, some signs of struggle — especially in early drafts. But this lack of unity or neatness needs to be a sign of *effort,* not lack of effort.

Your final grade will fall rapidly below a B if you don't meet these conditions. (417–18)

Portfolio Grading

The last twenty-five years have seen a great deal of interest in moving from the evaluation of individual student essays to a larger consideration of the student's overall writing ability. In practical terms, this means considering a portfolio of the student's writing. The term *portfolio* comes from Latin words meaning "to carry" and "sheets, or leaves, of paper," and until recently the word was usually associated with the large, flat cases in which artists carry samples of their work. Writing teachers have begun to use the term in a similar way, to indicate a folder, case, or notebook in which the whole range of writing a student does during a term is stored. (Yancey and Weiser's edited collection, *Situating Portfolios: Four Perspectives,* cited at the end of this chapter, is a particularly helpful guide to theories and models of portfolio assessment; see also Belanoff and Dickson; Black et al.; Calfree and Perfumo; Murphy; and Yancey.)

Increasingly, students are saving their work electronically in e-portfolios, a format that increases a student's rhetorical choices in presenting and organizing writing and makes it possible to share that writing more widely. You can encourage students to organize, save, and reflect on their work, not only in first-year writing but in their other classes as well. Such collections of work can even be edited and shared with potential employers or graduate programs years later. Although e-portfolios provide exciting opportunities for students to organize, save, and share their work, they also provide unique challenges. If you decide to have your students create e-portfolios, be sure to provide them with guidance on effective design options, the kinds of hardware and software they should use, and whether their work — if it's posted online — should be password protected or available publicly. (For a step-by-step guide to creating e-portfolios using Microsoft Word and Excel, see the link under "Useful Web Sites" at the end of this chapter.)

Much of the conversation surrounding portfolio evaluation has to do with using the process in whole writing programs, either to determine a student's placement in the program or to determine exit standards from basic writing courses. (For information on portfolio assessment in whole programs, see Belanoff and Elbow; Hamp-Lyons and Condon; and Roemer, Schultz, and Durst, cited at the end of this chapter.) Your program may indeed use some version of portfolio assessment, in which case you will be trained in the appropriate methods. In this section, however, we discuss how individual teachers can use portfolios to work with students and evaluate their work.

Why should you consider using portfolios? Many teachers use them because they have been dissatisfied with the system of evaluating individual essays. Grading essays separately provides snapshots of what students are doing on particular topics in a given week, but the aggregate may not be a coherent picture of the students' progress or abilities. Assigning a grade each week moves the course along in a linear way, but the teacher often has difficulty envisioning progress because he or she remembers each assignment largely in the form of a letter in a grade book. Teachers are left with thin data to go on when summing up their students' abilities at the end of the term.

Portfolios, on the other hand, provide a physical record of where students begin, how they progress during the term, and where their writing abilities seem to be heading as the course ends. Rather than showing a series of letter-grade snapshots, a portfolio demonstrates the kind of progress a student has made, the ways in which the student used successive drafts to work through the writing process, the student's strengths and weaknesses in choosing topics and working on different types of assignments, and the themes in the student's work. The portfolio serves students and teachers as a continual source of material for conversation, documenting where things have been and where they are going in their editorial relationship. For teachers, portfolios encourage what Bonnie Sunstein and Joseph Potts call "reflexive theorizing" about their teaching and expectations in a writing course (9).

Finally, the portfolio gives students exactly what it has always given artists: a place to store, and from which to show, their best work. Some teachers require students to keep in their portfolio everything they write for the class, including in-class writings, journals, notes, prewriting, drafts and final essays, and other exercises and assignments. Others, though, allow students more freedom in selecting and ordering their material, asking students to choose their strongest pieces and to order them in a way that best represents their growth and strength as a writer. E-porfolios provide an especially interesting forum for students to make choices in organizing and presenting their work, allowing them to provide hyperlinks to commentary, sources, earlier drafts, images, and more. Whether you ask your students to create traditional or electronic portfolio, to keep everything or to pick and choose, portfolios usually contain examples of several different kinds of writing, and they often contain different drafts of each assignment.

Usually, students are asked to write either a cover letter describing each assignment in their portfolios or an opening reflective essay in which they introduce the work they've chosen to include. In their descriptions or reflective introduction, they discuss the rhetorical techniques and moves they made in each essay, the strengths and weaknesses, and how each piece relates to the readings in the course. They also have the opportunity to consider the progress they've made and what specific elements they want to continue working on in their writing.

Reflective cover letters benefit both students and teachers. Through this process of putting the portfolio together and reflecting on their writing, students often come to better understand how various components of the course fit together. Students also have the opportunity to explain their revision choices and contextualize their work, providing teachers more information with which to determine a final grade. If students effectively use their cover letters to explain their rationale for revision and if they can clearly articulate both their strengths and weaknesses, teachers can more efficiently see the progress students have made.

Example 5.3 provides a portfolio assignment that gives students guidance on assembling the portfolio.

Example 5.3 **PORTFOLIO ASSIGNMENT** Poetry?

The final portfolio, as you know, will count for a large percentage of your grade in our class. As a result, you will probably want to work on your portfolio from now to the end of term. Here are some issues you should consider:

What to Include

You must include the final, revised draft of your research-based argument (along with earlier drafts) and at least four other assignments, also with drafts; but you may also decide to include all of the work you have done for our course as part of your portfolio. That means that you might wish to submit some thoughtful and well-written listserv postings, substantive responses you have made to a group member's work, or your study notes as well as drafts and final revisions of all your assignments.

How to Prepare the Cover Letter

A very important part of this assignment concerns the cover letter you write to us. The job of the cover letter, which is crucial to your success, is to

- introduce your portfolio;
- describe the contents of your portfolio, using specific details and explaining the rationale for your choices;
- comment on specific, concrete strengths and weaknesses in your writing, particularly noting areas of improvement you can identify from first draft to revision;
- evaluate the overall effectiveness of the portfolio and suggest the grade you believe it has earned;
- reflect on what you have learned about writing, and about improving writing, during this term's work; and
- discuss your future plans for developing your writing abilities.

It probably goes without saying by now that we will be looking carefully at the kind of claims, warrants, reasons, backing, and qualifiers you use; at how well you deploy ethical, emotional, and logical proofs; and at the stylistic qualities of your prose. Polish, polish, polish!

How to Format the Portfolio

The choice here is yours, but be sure to save time for thinking carefully about format: How do you intend to display your work? Will you present an e-portfolio? What kind of cover or binder will you prepare? What will you put in your table of contents? Do you want to add an "acknowledgments" page? How will you use color, graphics, and so on? In short, think about the concrete object here — and how you want it to represent you.

What We'll Be Responding To

When we sit down to read, study, and evaluate your portfolios — a process we really look forward to and enjoy — we will be looking very carefully at several key elements:

- Imaginative presentation of the portfolio. Here we want to see how you decide to put the portfolio together, literally how it looks as a material or electronic object, what its parts are, how it is presented as a "final" product.

- Quality and effectiveness of the cover letter. Here we want to see your mind at work, detailing your choices, explaining them, making a compelling rationale for those choices — and then analyzing the pieces in the portfolio, showing in what ways your writing has changed, progressed, and so forth. Finally, we will be looking for evidence here that you have read and understood the textbooks in the course, that you know some things about the rhetorical canons of invention, arrangement, style, and so on that you can put to good use in your analysis.
- Quality of the revisions you have done on pieces in your portfolio. Of special importance, of course, will be the final revision of your research-based argument. In this final draft, we will be looking for
  1. a clearly articulated claim supported by strong evidence and good reasons;
  2. effective appeals to audience;
  3. a clear structure, with logical connections among parts;
  4. sophisticated interweaving of sources throughout your essay;
  5. use of vivid and memorable language;
  6. effective sentence variety;
  7. effective use of visuals, images, and so on;
  8. a powerful opening and closing; and
  9. flawless editing.

Handout created by Andrea Lunsford

As Lunsford's handout shows, it's important to guide students in preparing their portfolios. As you create your own handout and decide how you will evaluate the portfolios, consider these questions posed by Nedra Reynolds and Rich Rice in *Portfolio Teaching: A Guide for Instructors*:

- Do the reflective elements provide reasons for students' choices and identify the changes they have made to essays or projects in preparing the portfolio?
- Are the entries focused, developed, organized, or do they reflect the qualities of good writing your course has emphasized?
- Is the arrangement and/or navigation scheme effective? (49)

These questions will help you begin to assess student portfolios, but as Reynolds and Rice show, you'll also need to decide how much revision is enough, how much the writing process should count, and how much improvement should count (50–51).

There are several ways in which you can use portfolios in your course, and you should check with your WPA for advice on which ones are appropriate for your program. The least elaborate writing portfolio is a simple folder for storing assignments. This use of the portfolio should not be confused with portfolio grading, however, since teachers use a more traditional grading method, even as they require students to keep all of their work. As each assignment is graded and completed, the student adds it to the portfolio, along with notes, drafts, and workshop comments. The teacher continues to keep a grade book — but at the end of the term calls for each student's portfolio. The portfolio, then, is evidence the teacher can examine for information about the student's development during the semester, perhaps using it to determine part of the final grade.

Even such a simple use of portfolios has advantages, especially if the course involves student-teacher conferences. The portfolio is brought to every conference and provides the basis for a discussion of the student's progress. Such longitudinal conferences are greatly enhanced by the inclusion of a table of contents that shows exactly what the folder contains. Notes, drafts, and final versions are marked with number-letter designations, keyed to the table of contents, and placed in the portfolio in sequential order. See Example 5.4 for the opening of a typical table of contents.

Example 5.4 **SAMPLE BASIC PORTFOLIO TABLE OF CONTENTS**

This folder contains important material. If found, please return to

Owner   _____

Address _____

Phone   _____

E-mail   _____

<u>Assignment 1</u>

Topic:

    1a. First draft; length and date:

    1b. Workshop evaluations; names of readers and date(s):

    1c. Conference(s); notes and date(s):

    1d. Final draft; length and date:

Final grade:

Student's comment on grade and teacher's evaluation:

A more comprehensive portfolio plays a central role in determining the final grade, though it does not completely leave the evaluation of essays until the end of the course. In this system, students keep a portfolio like the one described previously, but instead of assigning each essay a final grade within a few weeks of its submission, the teacher reads work submitted during the semester for acceptability. Acceptability, which may correspond to a grade of C or lower, merely indicates that a draft is finished enough to be left for a time while the student goes on to new work. The drafts and notes go into the portfolio, and the student drafts the next essay. The table of contents for this sort of portfolio uses slightly different notations (see Example 5.5). At the end of the semester, the teacher asks students to choose a specified number of accepted drafts for final revision and grading. These are placed in a separate portfolio, which is due at the end of the term; each essay within it is graded separately.

Example 5.5   **SAMPLE COMPREHENSIVE PORTFOLIO**
            TABLE OF CONTENTS

Assignment 1

Topic:

    1a. First draft; length and date:

    1b. Workshop evaluations; names of readers and dates:

    1c. Conference(s); notes and date(s):

    1d. Second draft; length and date:

    1e. Third draft; length and date (if needed):

Date of Acceptability:

Student's comment on accepted draft:

Revision intention:

In addition to acting as a physical storage system, the portfolio acts as a mental "cold storage" system. As all writers know, revising work too soon after drafting it is not easy; writers have a hard time getting emotional distance from something just created. So by storing "acceptable" essays in a portfolio, students are assured of having basically workable drafts and the time and distance that make final revisions fruitful.

The final system using portfolios is the most comprehensive. In it, the portfolio itself, rather than individual essays, is the focus of the course. In this system, no essay is ever graded individually. Students continue to work on assignments or topics until they wish to move on to the next one, and they may be asked to write evaluations of their essays or reflections on how their work is developing.

The teacher may or may not use this system in conjunction with some version of the acceptability system. At the end of the semester, the teacher looks through the entire portfolio, usually in conference with the student, and grades it as a whole, taking into consideration effort, progress, the work of peers, the quality of each piece of writing, the organization and presentation of the material, and the student's reflection on the writing. This is a significant departure from the standard methods involved in student evaluation, and you should make certain your program allows it before you institute this most thorough of portfolio systems.

Most teachers who use portfolios assign a large percentage of the final grade to the portfolio, often as much as 50–70 percent. You may wish to assign grades to some assignments early in the term so that students are aware of your grading style and criteria. Some students believe that if they revise multiple times, they are guaranteed an A on their portfolio at the end of the term. Even if you're not assigning grades on individual essays or assignments, be prepared to let students know how they're doing in the course at any point during the term. One of the advantages of using portfolios is that you don't have to grade every assignment. You can comment on students' work, expecting that they will revise before the end of the term. If a student's work, however, is particularly weak — and especially if a student is in danger of failing the course — you need to let that student know his or her standing in the class and how it might be improved. Some teachers institute a policy of telling students if their work is below average. Even some of your strong writers, though, are likely to feel anxious if they're not receiving grades regularly. To calm grade anxiety, tell students that even though you're not formally grading each assignment, you are willing to talk with them during conferences or office hours about where they stand in the course. You may wish to assign tentative grades at specific times in the term or give students a written midterm evaluation that includes a tentative grade.

HANDLING THE PAPER LOAD

No matter what method of grading/evaluation you choose, it's normal to feel overwhelmed by a stack of papers demanding your attention. You might even be tempted to procrastinate, which will only cause more anxiety as the paper pile continues to grow higher. Talk with experienced teachers in your program about how they handle the pressures of grading. Here are some strategies we've found effective:

- Carefully design your writing assignments and evaluation criteria so students understand what is expected from them. If you provide time for questions and explanations up front, you'll spend less time correcting misunderstandings on each essay.
- If you're teaching more than one class, consider staggering assignments, having them due on different days.
- Consider your own schedule as you create your syllabus, recognizing the other responsibilities you have.
- Use whole-class workshops to remind students of your expectations. Instead of reading every draft, for some assignments, you can ask for two or three students to volunteer to have their papers workshopped. You will carefully read and comment on these drafts and discuss with the class what works and what needs improvement. (See Chapter 3 for guidance on conducting whole-class workshops.)
- Have group conferences instead of individual conferences. You can quickly read the papers before the conference, making notes for yourself of things to say and have students read the papers of those in their groups to provide additional feedback for the writer.
- As you're grading, make a list of comments you find yourself making a lot. Go back to your assignment and revise it to make it clearer for future classes. Go over your list with the class on the day you hand back the papers, making sure students understand your expectations.
- Provide opportunities for ungraded assignments or those you mark with a check, check plus, or check minus. Journals, Web-based discussion entries, and in-class writings give students experience writing, but they don't need to be graded and commented on individually.

If you have difficulty focusing when grading, consider finding a fellow teacher with whom you can do parallel grading. Meet at a coffee shop, and agree to grade for a couple hours before having lunch together or going for a walk. If someone else is grading with you, you'll be less likely to get up to do something else. Also remember that with experience you will learn your own strategies and become more efficient.

THE END OF THE TERM

Final Grades

That final grade next to a student's name represents your ultimate judgment on that student, usually the only judgment carried away from your class. It is both a difficult task and a relief, a closure, to mark down that letter. You have, of course, since before the first day been preparing a system that would allow you to judge each student's performance. In front of you are the following factors:

1. Grades for each written essay
2. Weight of each assignment (by percentage)
3. Test grades, if any
4. Amount of class participation
5. Faithfulness of homework and journal, if required
6. Amount of perceived improvement in writing ability

Of these six factors, the first three are easily amenable to a mathematical solution, and many teachers have devised ways to quantify the last three as well. To arrive at a mathematical "raw score" for a student is a bit time-consuming but not difficult. If each essay and test is weighted alike, you need only convert the letter grade to its numerical equivalent, add the numbers, divide by the number of assignments, and then convert the result back to a letter grade. Consider the example of student X, whose grades are B−, C, B+, D, C+, C+, B−, and C−. The following example assumes a four-point system:

Conversion Chart							
A	4.0	B+	3.3	C+	2.3	D+	1.3
A−	3.7	B	3.0	C	2.0	D	1.0
		B−	2.7	C−	1.7	F	0.0

Belmont → you need to learn the European system

The student's grades thus convert to:

$$2.7 + 2.0 + 3.3 + 1.0 + 2.3 + 2.3 + 2.7 + 1.7 = 18.0$$

The next step is to divide the sum by the number of assignments:

$$18 \div 8 = 2.25$$

The result can be converted back into a grade or left in the form of a grade-point average. If you convert to a grade, you must establish your own cutoff points. In this case, a 2.25 GPA is closer to a C+ than to a C. The grade becomes more difficult to decide when the GPA is 2.5 or 2.85. In such cases, you must apply other criteria in deciding whether to lower the grade or raise it.

If your assignments are not all weighted the same, working out the raw score is a more complex process. Let's assume, for instance, that you are considering nine grades, which are weighted as follows (percentages refer to the percentage of the raw score):

Assignment 1	5%
Assignment 2	10
Assignment 3	15
Assignment 4	5
Assignment 5	10
Assignment 6	10
Assignment 7	15
Assignment 8	10
Assignment 9	20
Total	100%

Do a break down of each assignment?

The following table can help you figure the weighting of each assignment:

	5%	10%	15%	20%	25%	30%	40%
A	5.00	10.00	15.00	20.00	25.00	30.00	40.00
A−	4.75	9.50	14.25	19.00	23.75	28.50	38.00
B+	4.50	9.00	13.50	18.00	22.50	27.00	36.00
B	4.25	8.50	12.75	17.00	21.25	25.50	34.00
B−	4.10	8.20	12.30	16.40	20.50	24.60	32.80
C+	3.90	7.80	11.70	15.60	19.50	23.40	31.20
C	3.75	7.50	11.25	15.00	18.75	22.50	30.00
C−	3.60	7.20	10.80	14.40	18.00	21.60	28.80
D+	3.40	6.80	10.20	13.60	17.00	20.40	27.20
D	3.25	6.50	9.75	13.00	16.25	19.50	26.00
D−	3.10	6.20	9.30	12.40	15.50	18.60	24.80
F	2.50	5.00	7.50	10.00	12.50	15.00	20.00

Using the table is not difficult. Simply find the value of each grade indicated at the left according to the percentage value indicated at the top of each column, and add up the values for all assignments. The score for assignments that are all A's would be 100 and that are all F's, 50. If you wish to convert the final numerical score to a grade, you can use this chart:

A = 96–100		C = 75–77	
A− = 92–95		C− = 72–74	
B+ = 88–91		D+ = 68–71	
B = 85–87		D = 65–67	
B− = 82–84		D− = 62–64	
C+ = 78–81		F = 50–61	

To give an example of this system in action, let us evaluate student Y's nine grades. They are, respectively, C+, D+, B−, A−, C−, C−, B, C+, and C−. Given the weighting of the grades previously mentioned, student Y's grades would be as follows:

Assignment 1 (5%) C+ = 3.90
Assignment 2 (10%) D+= 6.80
Assignment 3 (15%) B− = 12.30
Assignment 4 (5%) A− = 4.75
Assignment 5 (10%) C− = 7.20

Assignment 6 (10%) C− = 7.20
Assignment 7 (15%) B = 12.75
Assignment 8 (10%) C+ = 7.80
Assignment 9 (20%) C− = 14.40
Total Score: 77.10

The score of 77.1 equals either a C or a C+ on the grade scale. Once again, you will have to establish your own cutoff points. To simplify, you might move scores of half a point and greater to the next higher number and scores of less than half a point to the next lower number. Thus a rating of 77.1 would mean a raw score of C.

A spreadsheet can also help you calculate grades. To create a grading spreadsheet, start by entering the column headings in the columns of row one. You will need columns for the student name last and first), two columns for each assignment (one for the raw score and one for the weighted score), and a column for the final grade.

	A	B	C	D	E	F	G	H	I
1	Last Name	First name	Assign. 1	5%	Assign. 2	10%	Assign. 3	85%	Final Grade

Next enter formulas to calculate each weighted score, a formula that will multiply the raw score by the decimal equivalent of the percentage. For example, in cell D2 enter the formula = C2*.05. This formula will multiply the raw score you enter into column C by the weight of the assignment, 5% or .05.

	A	B	C	D	E	F	G	H	I
1	Last Name	First Name	Assign. 1 Raw Score	5%	Assign. 2 Raw Score	10%	Assign. 3 Raw Score	85%	Final Grade
2	Inu	Art		= C2*.05		= E2*.1		= G2*.85	

In the final grade column, enter a formula that adds all of the weighted scores. For this example, enter = D2 + F2 + H2. To check the accuracy of your formulas, enter test data for which you know the answer. For example, if you are planning on using a 4-point scale, enter a 4.0 in each raw score. If the final grade comes up to 4.0, you'll know that you have entered the formulas correctly.

Things get more complicated for those wishing to record raw scores as a letter grade rather than a numeric value. For those interested, the VLOOKUP function in Microsoft Excel is the best way to convert letter grades to a numeric value. Consult the Excel Help function or the Internet for help in using the VLOOKUP function.

Mathematical systems can aid us in figuring a final grade, but they are not all that goes into it. The raw score based on the graded assignments will certainly be the most important element in determining a final grade, but if we haven't already made allowances for them, we must add in our judgments of many subtle qualities that fall under the heading "class participation." Did the student attend classes and conferences faithfully? How serious was the student about making revisions? How hard did the student try? How willing was the student to help others in workshops and peer response? How much time did the student give to journal entries? These and other considerations must eventually go into the process of turning the raw mathematical score into a final grade. And ultimately, as with grades on individual papers, this decision is one that you, the teacher, must make alone.

The question of failing a student is painful, especially if you know the student has been trying hard to pass — it is less difficult to write down the F for a student who has given up coming to class or who has not written many assignments. But that desperate, struggling one is hard to fail.

No one wants to fail such students. If a student is in danger of failing, you may want to recommend dropping the course, seeking outside help, and picking it up again at a later time. Most students in this position will drop a class if they see there is no hope, but sometimes no amount of advice helps; the student cannot or does not drop out, and you are left with no alternative but writing down that damning F.

STUDENT EVALUATIONS OF COURSE AND TEACHER

Teachers have to make final judgments about their students in the form of grades, but students' judgments about the teacher and the course, important as they are, are often optional. Not all departments demand that teachers ask their students to fill out teacher- or course-evaluation forms. Even if yours does not, however, you will learn a great deal about your course and your teaching by developing an evaluation form or using a departmental or school form and asking students to complete it. Evaluation forms should be filled out anonymously, either as homework or during one of the last days of classes. You may want to seal them — unread — in an envelope and ask one of your students to keep them until after you have turned in your grades.

If you don't have a departmental form to work from, you may want to use or adapt the following questions.

An Evaluation Form (Be sure to space questions to leave room for students' responses.)

1. How would you improve the content of the course?
2. What was the most useful assignment in the course? Explain.
3. What was the least useful assignment? Explain.
4. In what particular way was/were the textbook(s) helpful? for which assignment? What are the weaknesses of the textbook(s)? Do you recommend that it/they be used again?
5. What responses to and comments on your written work seemed helpful and encouraging or useless or discouraging? What specific advice do you have for the instructor?
6. How has the revision policy affected the way you do your writing? Do you have any suggestions that might improve this policy?
7. Do you believe the course requirements are fair? Why, or why not?
8. Did the peer-response sessions help you improve your work? How might the group structure be improved?
9. Did you know what the instructor's objectives for the course were? If so, did the instructor accomplish these objectives?
10. How might the instructor make in-class presentations more effective?
11. How did the grading policy compare to those in other courses in terms of clarity and fairness?
12. How helpful were the conferences? Would more or fewer be better?
13. What general comments do you have?

After you have turned in your grades, you can take some time to read these evaluations. We have found that they are more easily understood and applied if you let a few days or even several weeks go by before reading them. As you do, note in writing any elements that surprised you and any changes you plan to make on the basis of the evaluations. Sometimes you will be transported by your evaluations; sometimes you will be chagrined. But they are always important input for your teaching life, and they are worth your attention.

AFTERWORD

Your evaluations have been read and digested; your grade sheets have been marked, signed, and turned in. Nothing remains but the stack of students' theme folders (or portfolios) and your faithful grade book, filled with red and black hieroglyphics where previously only blank squares existed. Your first writing course is a memory; you are now a seasoned veteran, a resource for the nervous new teachers of next year. You will be able to help them by telling them what helped you and to welcome them to the conversation that is always going on among teachers of writing.

WORKS CITED

Beaven, Mary H. "Individualized Goal Setting, Self-Evaluation, and Peer Evaluation." *Evaluating Writing: Describing, Measuring, Judging.* Ed. Charles R. Cooper and Lee Odell. Urbana: NCTE, 1977. 135–56. Print.

Belanoff, Pat, and Marcia Dickson. *Portfolios: Process and Product.* Portsmouth: Boynton/Cook, 1991. Print.

Belanoff, Pat, and Peter Elbow. "Using Portfolios to Increase Collaboration and Community in a Writing Program." *Journal of Writing Program Administration* 9.3 (1986): 27–39. Print.

Black, Laurel, et al., eds. *New Directions in Portfolio Assessment: Reflective Practice, Critical Theory, and Large-Scale Scoring.* Portsmouth: Boynton/Cook, 1994. Print.

Calfree, Robert, and Pam Perfumo, eds. *Writing Portfolios in the Classroom: Policy and Practice, Promise and Peril.* Hillsdale: Lawrence Erlbaum, 1996. Print.

Connors, Robert J., and Andrea A. Lunsford. "Frequency of Formal Errors in Current College Writing, or Ma and Pa Kettle Do Research." *CCC* 39.4 (1988): 395–409. Print.

———. "Teachers' Rhetorical Comments on Student Papers." *CCC* 44.2 (1993): 200–23. Print.

Curzan, Anne, and Lisa Damour. *First Day to Final Grade.* 3rd ed. Ann Arbor: U of Michigan P, 2011. Print.

Davis, B. G. *Tools for Teaching.* San Francisco: Jossey-Bass, 1993. Print.

Diederich, Paul B. *Measuring Growth in English.* Urbana: NCTE, 1974. Print.

Elbow, Peter. "Embracing Contraries in the Teaching Process." *College English* 45.4 (1983): 327–39. Print.

———. *Everyone Can Write: Essays toward a Hopeful Theory of Writing and Teaching Writing.* New York: Oxford UP, 2000. Print.

Gay, Pamela. "Dialogizing Response in the Writing Classroom: Students Answer Back." *Journal of Basic Writing* 17.1 (1998): 3–17. Print.

Hamp-Lyons, Liz, and William Condon. "Questioning Assumptions about Portfolio-Based Assessment." *CCC* 44.2 (1993): 176–90. Print.

Haswell, Richard. "Minimal Marking." *CE* 45.6 (1983): 600–604. Print.

Huot, Brian, and Peggy O'Neill. *Assessing Writing: A Critical Sourcebook*. Boston: Bedford, 2009. Print.

Larson, Richard. "Training New Teachers of Composition in the Writing of Comments on Themes." *CCC* 17.3 (1966): 152–55. Print.

Locklin, Gerald. "Amphibians Have Feelings Too." *In Praise of Pedagogy*. Ed. Wendy Bishop and David Starkey. Portland: Calendar Island P, 2000. 107. Print.

Lunsford, Andrea A. *EasyWriter*. 4th ed. Boston: Bedford, 2010. Print.

——. *The St. Martin's Handbook*. 7th ed. Boston: Bedford, 2011. Print.

Lunsford, Andrea A, and Karen Lunsford. "'Mistakes Are a Fact of Life': A National Comparative Study." *CCC* 59.4 (2008): 781–806. Print.

Murphy, Sandra. "Assessing Portfolios." *Evaluating Writing: The Role of Teachers' Knowledge about Text, Learning, and Culture*. Eds. Charles Cooper and Lee Odell. Urbana: NCTE, 1999. 114–35. Print.

Reynolds, Nedra, and Rich Rice. *Portfolio Teaching: A Guide for Instructors*. 2nd ed. Boston: Bedford, 2006. Print.

Roemer, Marjorie, Lucille M. Schultz, and Russel K. Durst. "Portfolios and the Process of Change." *CCC* 42.4 (1991): 455–69. Print.

Shaughnessy, Mina P. *Errors and Expectations: A Guide for the Teacher of Basic Writing*. New York: Oxford UP, 1977. Print.

Smith, John A. "Contracting English Composition: It Only Sounds like an Illness." *Teaching English in the Two-Year College* 26.4 (1999): 427–30. Print.

Smith, Summer. "The Genre of the End Comment: Conventions in Teacher Responses to Student Writing." *CCC* 48.2 (1997): 249–68. Print.

Sommers, Nancy. *Beyond the Red Ink: Students Talk about Teachers' Comments*. Boston: Bedford, 2012. DVD.

——. "Responding to Student Writing." *CCC* 33.2 (1982): 148–56. Print.

Straub, Richard. "The Concept of Control in Teacher Response: Defining the Varieties of 'Directive' and 'Facilitative' Commentary." *CCC* 47.2 (1996): 223–51. Print.

Straub, Richard, and Ronald F. Lunsford. *Twelve Readers Reading: Responding to College Student Writing*. Cresskill: Hampton, 1995. Print.

Sunstein, Bonnie S., and Joseph P. Potts. "Teachers' Portfolios: A Cultural Site for Literacy." *Council Chronicle* 4.1 (1993): 9. Print.

White, Edward M., William D. Lutz, and Sandra Kamusikiri. *Assessment of Writing: Politics, Policies, Practices*. New York: MLA, 1995. Print.

Yancey, Kathleen Blake. *Portfolios in the Writing Classroom*. Urbana: NCTE, 1992. Print.

Yancey, Kathleen Blake, and Irwin Weiser, eds. *Situating Portfolios: Four Perspectives*. Logan: Utah State UP, 1997. Print.

Zak, Frances, and Christopher C. Weaver, eds. *The Theory and Practice of Grading Writing*. Albany: State U of New York P, 1998. Print.

Useful Web Sites

Center for the Study and Teaching of Writing: Holistic Grading
cstw.osu.edu/handbook/responding/holistic

Creating Electronic Portfolios Using Microsoft Word and Excel
electronicportfolios.com/portfolios/howto/WordPortfolios.pdf

II

Rhetorical Practices

6

Teaching Invention

When students express doubt or frustration about generating a paper topic, it's often the case that what they've come up with seems to them not "serious" or "intellectual" or "academic" enough for a college assignment. In situations like this, I'll try to remind students that the measure of success in a writing course is first and foremost the quality of the writing itself—prose style, organization, voice, etc. This reminder in fact makes the choice of a topic more rather than less crucial to a paper's success, but it does so by altering a student's sense of what constitutes the "right" topic. Students can then begin to see that it's less important that what they write about be timely or weighty than that it be something—big, small, or in between—which enlivens them, because that will in turn enliven their prose.

–Nathan Redman

Invention, the central, indispensable canon of rhetoric, traditionally means a systematic search for arguments. In composition classes, it has taken on a much broader meaning: a writer's search for all the kinds of material — both in the writer's memory and in external sources — that can shape and determine what can be presented and even known. When they write arguments and analyses, invention strategies help students discover the *thesis,* or the central claim or assertion of a piece of writing, and all the *supporting* material that illustrates, exemplifies, or proves the validity of the thesis. For personal and lyric essays, narratives, and descriptive writing, invention techniques help writers draw from their memory and observations for the kinds of details that will add depth to their essays (for more on the connection between memory and invention, see Chapter 9; see also Ede, Glenn, and Lunsford, cited at the end of this chapter). No matter what forms and genres you ask your students to write, without content there can be no effective communication, and invention is the process that supplies writers and speakers with content.

Invention is particularly important in college writing courses because it helps students *generate* and *select from* material they will write about (Lauer, *Invention* 3). They'll generate far more material than they can use and then go through the process of selecting the material that best fits with their purpose and audience. This process is often difficult, especially for students who have had little practice with it. When faced with a writing assignment, many students are troubled not by the lack of a subject or topic (often one is supplied) but by a seeming lack of anything important or coherent to write about it. Invention comes into play here, providing processes by which students can draw from their own knowledge and experience and supplement what they already know with research.

who teaches this?

with what you know

troppo importante

The systems of invention discussed in this chapter will provide this assistance. Most FY students have had little opportunity to practice serious, extended, coherent writing, and few of them have read even two books in the past year. Clearly, many of our students are in need of training in invention; without some introduction to the techniques of discovering subject matter and arguments, they might flounder all term in a morass of vague assertions and unsupported, ill-thought-out essays. They need a system that will buoy them until they can swim by themselves.

BRINGING THE RHETORICAL CANON OF INVENTION INTO THE WRITING CLASSROOM

In their introduction to *Landmark Essays: Rhetorical Invention in Writing,* Richard E. Young and Yameng Liu discuss the study of invention as both theoretically sophisticated and rooted in pedagogical practices. The essays in their collection span forty years and explore various issues related to the process of composing, such as "the nature of invention as an art, the role of rhetorical invention in the creation of knowledge, [and] the possibility for teaching invention" (xiii). Each of these issues is important not only to theoretical debates but also to classroom practices. Yet rather than sketching the debates about invention that have taken place in composition studies over the past fifty years, in this chapter we provide exercises and strategies that you can use to teach invention in your own classroom, helping students tap their own experience and observations, even as they use research to supplement what they already know.

Composition scholars Richard Young and Janice Lauer advocate the classroom use of heuristic procedures or systematic strategies that will aid students in discovering and generating ideas about which they might write. Such strategies may be as simple as asking students about a subject: *who? what? when? where? why?* and *how?* — the traditional journalistic formula. Or they can be as complex as the matrix presented in Young, Becker, and Pike's *Rhetoric: Discovery and Change.* Essentially, this heuristic asks the student to look at any subject from different perspectives. A student writing about a campus demonstration, for example, might look at it as a "happening" frozen in time and space, as the result of a complex set of causes, as a cause of certain effects, or as one tiny part of a larger economic pattern. Looking at a subject in different ways loosens up the mind and jogs the writer out of a one-dimensional, or tunnel-vision, view of a subject.

Another classroom use of invention is characterized most notably by the work of Ken Macrorie and, more pervasively, Peter Elbow. Interested in how writers establish "voice" in writing and realize individual selves in discourse, Elbow's work with students presents dramatic evidence of such activity. In a series of influential books (*Writing without Teachers, Writing with Power, Embracing Contraries,* and *Everyone Can Write*), Elbow focuses on how writers come to know themselves and then share those selves with others. In "What Is Voice in Writing?" he deals with a question related to invention that has perplexed theorists and teachers of rhetoric for thousands of years — "Is ethos real virtue

[handwritten margin notes: "journaling within the curric for extra practice?" and "think abt class with Clara"]

or the appearance of virtue?"—and links this question to the modern debate about the relationship between voice and identity (*Everyone Can Write* 188, 192). Elbow recognizes that voice and its relation to self and text are controversial issues, yet in the midst of controversy he works to make theories of voice and invention practical for teachers of writing, advocating invention strategies such as freewriting and journaling, which we discuss later in this chapter.

A third approach to invention in the writing classroom can be drawn from Gregory Ulmer's highly theoretical work *Heuristics: The Logic of Invention*, which he describes as "a project of invention . . . applying to academic discourse the lessons arising out of a matrix crossing French poststructuralist theory, avant-garde art experiments, and electronic media in the context of schooling" (xi). Although Ulmer's work is marked more by critical theory than practical class-room application, he provides important insights about the ways in which available technology not only shapes invention but also processes of thinking, writing, reading, and learning. He encourages play, curiosity, experimentation, looking for patterns, and associational thinking rather than linear thinking. Ulmer's work is particularly applicable to the creation of hypertext and other multimodal projects, yet some more traditional invention techniques, such as clustering, fit well with the playful, associational invention Ulmer advocates. If your students are working with images, you might have them create visual collages, drawing from a range of images that inform their topic.

Ulmer's work is also applicable to the process of selection that invention ultimately entails. Instead of narrowing one's research in order to exclude mate-rials that do not fit neatly with a particular argument, Ulmer suggests that the job of a writer (especially in producing electronic texts) is to compose or choreograph a great deal of information; he writes, "The user of a database . . . encounters in principle the full paradigm of possibilities through which a mul-titude of paths may be traced. Argument provided one path and suppressed everything else." Ulmer continues, "In hypermedia, a composer constructs an information environment, and the user chooses the path or line through the place provided" (38). As is clear from this quotation, Ulmer links the process of invention with the qualities of the writing produced—and the kind of reader such writing invites.

The invention strategies that work best for your class will depend on the genres you're asking students to produce and the purpose of that composing. In this chapter, the term *invention* deals generally with strategies for helping students access materials that will guide and strengthen their writing, no matter what forms and genres they're working with. Some of the forms of invention we consider relate to the development and expansion of three different but closely related elements: the *thesis statement,* a declarative sentence that serves as the backbone of an essay; the *subject matter,* which fills out, expands, and ampli-fies the thesis; and the *argument,* a specialized form of subject matter consisting of persuasive demonstrations of points that the writer wants to prove. Some of the techniques discussed here will work best for one or two of these elements, whereas others work for all three. You will easily see the characteristics of each

questioning = heuristic

technique, and you can choose those you wish to adapt according to what you want your students to learn. We also consider the process of invention as it relates to more personal forms of writing and to multimodal projects — forms of writing that don't necessitate a thesis statement or linear argument.

HEURISTIC SYSTEMS OF INVENTION

Nearly all the systems of invention covered in this chapter can be called *heuristic*, or questioning, systems. (The Greek word *heurisis* means "finding" and is related to Archimedes' cry of *"Eureka!* I have found it!") In her foundational study of invention, contemporary rhetorical theorist Janice Lauer defines heuristic procedure as

> a conscious and non-rigorous search model which explores a creative problem for seminal elements of a solution. The exploratory function of the procedure includes generative and evaluative powers: the model generously proposes solutions but also efficiently evaluates these solutions so that a decision can be made. Heuristic procedures must be distinguished from trial-and-error methods which are non-systematic and, hence, inefficient, and from rule-governed procedures which are rigorous and exhaustive processes involving a finite number of steps which infallibly produce the right solution. (*Invention* 4)

Although the systems described here differ widely in their approaches, with few exceptions they fit Lauer's definition. (For more recent work on invention, see Atwill and Lauer, cited at the end of this chapter.)

Using Heuristic Strategies in the Classroom

In judging the heuristic procedures discussed in this chapter, you can run each one through Lauer's questions for testing heuristics (see Example 6.1). The three necessary characteristics of effective heuristic procedures, according to Lauer, are *transcendency, flexible order,* and *generative capacity.*

Example 6.1   **LAUER'S TEST FOR HEURISTIC MODELS**

1. Can writers transfer this model's questions or operations from one subject to another?

2. Does this model offer writers a direction of movement which is flexible and sensitive to the rhetorical situation?

3. Does this model engage writers in diverse kinds of heuristic procedures? ("Toward a Methodology" 269)

Each system described in this chapter is discrete. You can choose one and ignore the others, or you can use several concurrently or at different times. Because invention is a central skill in composition, you will want to introduce at least one system early in the course; otherwise, you may not have a coherent framework on which to hang the other elements of the writing process. Your students can practice some of these methods (for example, prewriting, freewriting, and brainstorming) with you in class. They can use the other methods at home, after you introduce them in classroom exercises. Ideally, your students will gradually assimilate these systems of invention into their subconscious, recalling them when needed.

The goal, then, is to make these artificial systems of discovery so much a part of the way students think about problems that the systems become second nature. Truly efficient writing is almost always done intuitively and then, at the revision stage, checked against models for completeness and correctness. You should not expect the process of subconscious assimilation to complete itself within ten or fifteen weeks. However, when a system of invention is conscientiously taught and practiced for that period of time, it will become a useful tool for students and, eventually, may become part of their thought processes.

CLASSICAL TOPICAL INVENTION

The tradition of classical rhetoric, as it developed from Aristotle and Cicero and then was codified by Quintilian, is the only complete system that we will deal with in this book; it remains one of the most definitive methodologies ever evolved by the Western mind. The rhetoric of the Renaissance was largely informed by it. Even the epistemological rhetoric of the eighteenth century is far less coherent as a system than is classical rhetoric in its finished form. In contrast to classical rhetoric, contemporary rhetoric is in its infancy, with many workable techniques but no fixed structure. Many books have been devoted to analyzing and explaining the structure and usefulness of the classical rhetorical tradition, but for our purposes, only a few techniques drawn from classical theory are useful.

The classical technique that we will concentrate on as an aid to invention is that of the *topics,* or seats of argument. The *topics* can be used to conceptualize and formulate the single-sentence declarative thesis that usually constitutes the backbone of an FY essay, as well as to invent subject matter and arguments. Remember, though, that all classical techniques were originally devoted to the creation of persuasive discourse and that classical invention works most naturally in an argumentative mode; it should not be expected to work as well for nonexpository prose.

Aristotle is responsible for our first introduction to the *topics* or "seats of argument," but his doctrine was continued and amplified by the other classical rhetoricians. The *topics* were conceived of as actual mental "places" (the term itself comes from geography) to which the rhetorician could go to find arguments.

The system of *topics* described here is a modern arrangement of classical topical invention adapted from the work of Edward P. J. Corbett and Robert Connors; Richard P. Hughes and P. Albert Duhamel; and other teachers at the University of Chicago (including Bilsky et al.). These *topics* are not so much places to go for ready-made arguments as they are ways of probing one's subject in order to find the means to develop that subject. The four common *topics* that are most useful to students are *definition, analogy, consequence,* and *testimony.*

1. **Definition** The *topic* of definition involves the creation of a thesis by taking a fact or an idea and expanding on it by precisely identifying its nature. The subject can be referred to its class, or genus, and the argument made that whatever is true of the genus is true of the species: "A single-payer national health plan is a socialist policy—and should therefore be classed with other socialist policies." A far less powerful and less sophisticated form of definition is "the argument from the word"—the use of dictionary or etymological meanings to define things or ideas.

2. **Analogy** The *topic* of analogy is concerned with discovering resemblances or differences between two or more things, proceeding from known to unknown. It should always be kept in mind that no analogy is perfect and that all analogies deal in probabilities. Nonetheless, analogy is a useful tool for investigating comparisons and contrasts: "The first week of college is like the first week of boot camp." Another type of analogical reasoning is the argument from contraries, or negative analogy: "The marijuana laws are unlike Prohibition." Although analogy is often thought of only as a figure of speech, it is an important tool of demonstration as well.

3. **Consequence** The *topic* of consequence investigates phenomena in a cause-to-effect or effect-to-cause pattern. The best use of consequence is in the prediction of probabilities from patterns that have previously occurred: "Coal-burning power plants, automobiles, and other human-made sources of carbon dioxide pollution have led to global warming, which—if not curbed—can have serious negative effects on the environment." The *topic* of consequence is prone to two fallacies. The first is the fallacy of *post hoc, ergo propter hoc,* "after this, therefore because of this." Just because one element precedes another element does not mean that the former is the cause of the latter. An extreme example of this fallacy is, "The Louisiana Purchase led to global warming." The second fallacy, *a priori,* claims but does not demonstrate a cause-effect relationship between two phenomena. To support the first cause-effect relationship claimed above, the writer would need to cite scientific studies that link these sources of carbon dioxide pollution to global warming and to provide evidence that global warming can have negative effects on the environment.

4. ***Testimony*** The *topic* of testimony relies on appeals to an authority, some external source of argumentation. For example, the authority could be an expert opinion, statistics, or the law. This *topic* is not as useful today as it once was: Our controversial age has produced so many authorities whose views are in conflict with one another that all too often they cancel one another out, and celebrities often give paid — and therefore untrustworthy — testimony in the form of advertising. Still, testimony can be a good starting place for an argument, especially when students have a familiarity with, and an understanding of, the source of the testimony.

Using Classical Topical Invention in the Classroom

When using classical topical invention in your classes, you'll need first to teach the use of the *topics* in general and then familiarize students with their use in generating theses, subject matter, and arguments. Classical invention takes just a short time to teach because it is elegantly simple. Students are often impressed when they learn the background of the technique — at last, a high-level classical skill! — and use it with enthusiasm once they have learned to apply the different terms.

Ultimately, a thesis or an argument must say something about the real world. Teaching the *topics* requires using examples, and good examples are to be had by applying each *topic* to a definite subject and coming up with several thesis statements. You may want to pass out examples for students to have in front of them as they begin to create their own theses. You won't find that drawing theses from the *topic* is difficult for you. In the following discussion of vaccination, run through the topical-thesis mechanism.

Definition Definition always answers the question "What is/was it?" in a variety of contexts. The subject can be defined in its immediate context, in a larger context, in different settings, in space, in time, or in a moral continuum. Here are a couple of examples:

- A vaccine is a weakened or killed pathogen that stimulates immunity against the pathogen.
- A vaccine controversy is a disagreement regarding the efficacy, ethics, or safety of vaccination.

Analogy Analogy always asks the question "What is it like or unlike?" and the subject of the analogy usually answers the question by explaining a lesser-known element in the context of a better-known element. Many analogies are expressed in the form of metaphors.

- Vaccines are important weapons in the war against disease.
- Mandatory vaccination is like other ethically questionable programs formerly sponsored by the government: forced sterilization and internment camps.

Consequence   Consequence always answers the question "What caused/causes/ will cause it?" or "What did it cause/is it causing/will it cause?" It is not a *topic* to be taken lightly because, even in a thesis statement, it demands that the writer trace the chains of consequence to the end. Consequence can be either explanatory or predictive.

- Mandatory vaccination prevents parents from having full control over their children's health care.
- Some vaccinations may trigger autoimmune or other disorders.
- In many cases, an exemption from mandatory vaccination requires a doctor's signature; requiring a doctor's signature takes control over children's health decisions away from parents.
- Children under the age of fourteen are more likely to suffer adverse effects from the hepatitis B vaccine than to contract the disease without being vaccinated.

Testimony   Testimony always answers the question "What does an authority say about it?" Authorities can range from experts and statistics to eyewitnesses and accepted wisdom.

- The Association of American Physicians and Surgeons does not support vaccination mandates.
- The World Health Organization recommends that the hepatitis B vaccination be a part of universal childhood vaccination programs.
- According to the Advisory Committee on Immunization Practices, the measles, mumps, rubella vaccine should not be administered to those with a compromised immune system.

These are just a few available statements for each topic. Using the *topics* to create theses demands some immediate knowledge of the subject, but students will derive theses and argumentative lines that are very specific. You can also see that some *topics* will be more fruitful than others. The *topics* of definition, analogy, and consequence are the most useful for creating theses, whereas testimony is most naturally suited to the buttressing of already created theses.

The *topics* are not magic formulas that can make something out of nothing, but they are useful in organizing masses of information. Students need not have more than a layperson's knowledge of vaccination to come up with some of the preceding statements, but after having created these, they will have a clearer understanding of what they do and do not know. They will also have a much better idea of where they need to go to look up information they do not have at hand. As you work through the *topics* in class, spend enough time on each of the first three (testimony is more specialized) to allow your students to digest the examples you provide and to see the process by which you arrive at the statements under each topic. You may want to pass out a photocopied sheet with the examples of the *topics* in action on a particular subject. After you explain the examples and show how they derive from the *topics*, assign a few subjects and ask students to use the topical system to come up with at least three theses for each topic (perhaps nine theses in all). After this assignment has been written, either in class or as homework, ask students to volunteer to read their theses aloud in class. The next step is to ask students to come up with ideas for an essay on a subject relevant to another class they are currently enrolled in and to apply classical topical invention to that subject. At this point, students should be comfortable enough with the system — perhaps even openly pleased with it — to be able to reel off theses for other subjects without much trouble.

Once students have successfully used the *topics* to produce theses, they will readily see how they can use them to generate supporting subject matter. After they have chosen their thesis from among the myriad possibilities that the topical system offers, they are left with many other statements that are at least indicators of other informational lodes. Very often after choosing a thesis, students can structure their essays around other statements that they need to change only slightly to make them subordinate to the main purpose of their essays.

If you have the time in class, ask your students to put together a rough topic outline of a projected essay by arranging as many of the theses they have generated as possible in an order that could be used to structure an essay (remind them that often they may have to change the direction of the theses slightly to subordinate them to the main thesis). Here is an example of such a rough outline using some of the statements generated about vaccination:

Main thesis: Mandatory vaccination prevents parents from having full control over their children's health care.

Subordinate thesis 1: Parents should be allowed to make informed decisions about their children's health care without interference from the state.

   Minor thesis: Many parents object to certain vaccinations for safety reasons.

   Minor thesis: Some vaccinations may trigger autoimmune and other disorders.

   Minor thesis: Although the World Health Organization argues that the hepatitis B vaccine should be a part of childhood immunization, children under fourteen are more likely to suffer adverse effects from the vaccine than to contract the disease without vaccination.

Subordinate thesis 2: Even though most states allow some exceptions from mandatory vaccination, parents often face difficulties when trying to get an exemption.

   Minor thesis: In most cases, a doctor must sign the exemption, which takes the decision-making power out of the hands of parents.

   Minor thesis: Some doctors refuse to sign the exemption or to treat patients who are not vaccinated.

Subordinate thesis 3: Certain vaccinations can protect the public from life-threatening diseases, but states should not mandate vaccines; instead, parents should be allowed to make choices on a vaccine-by-vaccine basis.

Although this list is more structured than those that many students will come up with, it exemplifies how such a topic list can be constructed.

The preceding description shows a deductive use of the *topics*, in which the thesis statement is decided on and then subject matter is arranged according to the perceived needs of the thesis. The *topics* can, of course, also be used inductively, to explore the subject and gather a mass of potential material, with the student creating a thesis only after the subject material has been grouped or categorized. With this inductive use of the *topics*, it is necessary for students to leave the whole area of thesis creation until after they have used the topical system to gather subject matter. You may well find that students often cannot wait to begin to arrange the material under a thesis and so greet the stage of thesis creation with enthusiasm.

Classical invention, in its simplified form, can be satisfying to teach. You use a tradition of education that is as old as any in Western culture. And since it is easy enough for students to memorize, they can carry it with them for use in other classes. It is neither the simplest nor the most complex heuristic system, but it has a charm and a comprehensiveness that make it one of the most attractive.

JOURNAL WRITING

Over the last thirty years, journal writing has become an intrinsic part of many English classes. Journals serve as a repository of material and concepts that can lead to more formal essays; journal writing does not impose systematic techniques of invention and thus can have a salutary effect on students' feelings about writing (Gannett). Journal writing can take many forms. Some forms are more structured than others, while all forms are used for different pedagogical purposes:

- *Writing logs:* The writing log helps students reflect on their writing processes, providing a place for them to keep track of their thoughts about writing and particular assignments—both while they are working on the assignment and after they've completed it. Reading a writing log that they have kept over a period of time can help students identify their own strengths and weaknesses as writers. The writing log can also be used as a place to record ideas for future writing assignments.

- *Reading journals:* The reading journal helps students make sense of and reflect on their reading assignments; in it, students can wrestle with ideas, note correspondences with and differences between the reading and their own experience, and prepare for class discussions. One effective format for the reading journal is the double-entry notebook, in which students write facts or quotations from their reading on one side of the page and personal responses or observations on the other side. The reading journal works well in the literature-based composition class—or in any class requiring a substantial amount of reading.

think alot
this; annotation
will be import.

a C2 class would require both, right?

- *Commonplace books:* Used by many writers, the commonplace book is a journal where students record not only experiences, ideas, observations, and images but also quotations from their reading. The commonplace book, when used well and often, becomes a rich source for informal essays, often containing powerful details as well as the voices of others. It is especially helpful to writers of creative nonfiction.
- *Research journals:* A research journal helps students keep track of their research process and the development of their ideas on a particular topic; like the reading journal and commonplace book, it can also include quotations and the student's thoughts or responses to the ideas of others. When combined with a research project, the research journal helps ensure students are thinking regularly about their project, provides a record of their development of ideas, allows students to respond informally to their reading, and may encourage more personal investment in the research process.
- *"Everyday" journals:* Many students already keep personal "everyday journals." Some teachers assign journals simply because they want students to write every day. Teachers might provide general prompts if students get stuck (such as, "What book or movie has affected your thinking?" or "What person do you most admire? Explain."), but the topics for everyday journal writing are generally chosen by students themselves. In addition to encouraging students to write daily, these journals often become repositories of ideas for formal essays.
- *Blogs:* Blogs function as a more public, online journal for students, providing a place to showcase writing and images throughout the term. Blogs also allow students to receive feedback on their writing.

Using Journals in the Classroom

For students to get the most from journal writing, it is necessary to introduce them to the art of keeping a journal. First, acquaint your students with the definition of *journal* — a record of reactions, not actions. A journal is not a diary, nor is it a record of events. If you fail to be specific about this, students may end up writing diary entries — "Got up at 7:30, went to the Commons for breakfast, saw Diane." Students need to be shown, and then convinced, that a journal is a record of a mind and its thoughts, rather than a record of a body and its movements. (For an essay on journal writing written for students, see Anson and Beach, cited at the end of this chapter.) One good way of demonstrating this difference is by showing students excerpts from the journals of established writers — such as Plath, Thoreau, Pepys, Woolf, and Hawthorne — or from student writing submitted in previous classes. Compared to keeping a journal, keeping a diary will soon seem to most of your students like a lame activity.

Along with familiarizing students with good examples of journal writing, you may want to provide particular prompts that will help get them started. Example 6.2 offers journal prompts that could be used for either writing logs or everyday journals. Provide just enough prompts so that students will occasionally have to grope for a sense of their own will to write something; too many questions and suggestions can be a crutch. Encourage students to move beyond each prompt to more self-directed writing.

One potential problem with journal writing for FY students is their tendency to rely on ready-made opinions, premanufactured wisdom, and clichés. Because some students have not yet begun to question their parents' or their friends' norms, they sometimes repeat the most appalling prejudices as if they had invented them. A ready-made challenge to such secondhand thought is the requirement that students be as concrete in their entries as possible. Discourage generalizing and opining unless the opinion can be tied to some actual experience in the student's life. (This is, after all, good argumentation — no assertions should be made without concrete support.) Macrorie suggests that students write journal entries on the same topic over a period of time, from "different and developing viewpoints" (*Telling Writing* 137). Such writing gives students the distance they need to reflect on, deepen, and enrich their perceptions and thus make their stories more moving and effective. But most important, Macrorie tells us, journals are the best starting place and the best storehouse for ideas: "A journal is a place for confusion and certainty, for the half-formed and the completed" (*Telling Writing* 141). love amot this

---

Example 6.2   **JOURNAL PROMPTS**

Journal Statements

You will submit ten *single-spaced* journal statements of one page each throughout the term: no more than one each Wednesday (you get to pick the Wednesdays). The purpose of the journal statements is twofold: (1) to help you think strategically about your writing assignments; and (2) to help you both examine yourself as a writer and imagine yourself as a writer who sets goals and develops specific, effective steps to achieve them.

The subject of each of your journal statements should be different. The following options — some on writing in general, others specifically about this course — should help get you started on the weekly journal assignment.

Journal 1: What are two of your strengths as a writer? What are two of your writing weaknesses? Specifically, how would you like to improve as a writer? What could you do or learn to make such improvements?

Good introduction to the course journal

Journal 2: What expectations do you have for the course? What is your feeling toward first-year college writing? What has been your experience in a writing classroom? What did you like or dislike?

Journal 3: Informational process analyses should provide a specific audience with information it needs to replicate a process. Use this journal entry to describe possible topics for your process analysis essay, considering the following questions: What sorts of directions or instructions could students on campus, incoming students, or people in your community benefit from? Why?

Journal 4: Look at two editorials from this week's campus newspaper. What are the writers' goals? What kinds of appeals do the writers make? Explain the (in)appropriateness of each writer's use of rhetorical appeals.

Journal 5: Spend several minutes freewriting about particular difficulties that you have encountered thus far when drafting your process analysis. Specifically, what strategies have you used to work through these problems? What special concerns about your first draft would you like your peer reviewer to address during this week's draft workshop?

Journal 6: How do you define literacy? How can you measure it? How might your definition differ from that of your classmates?

Journal 7: Write for several minutes about the pressures you feel as a college student. *someone learning english?*

Journal 8: How do you respond to any writing assignment? In other words, is your reaction always the same, or does it vary, depending on the course, the teacher, or the level of instructional detail or freedom?

Journal 9: What specific revision strategies that we have discussed could you use to revise your process analysis assignment? Why will these strategies help you to create a more effective essay?

Journal 10: Do you ever get frustrated while driving or shopping? Why? What kinds of incidents, events, or situations can lead to your frustration?

Journal 11: Think for a minute about a special problem or talent you have. Maybe you're shy, behind in your classwork, overly committed, out of shape, or out of money; maybe you're highly motivated, popular, or particularly witty. Make a list of both the causes and consequences of your problem or gift. Which list provides you with more information about your problem or talent?

Journal 12: Write about the specific parts of the composing process that are most difficult for you. What particularly pressing concerns do you have when drafting your essays? What presents you with the most trouble? Why?

Journal 13: What are your feelings about the role of technology in education?

Journal 14: Reflect on your writing progress during the course of this semester. Consider the following questions as you write: How did you envision your writing at the beginning of the semester? How do you "see" your writing now? What improvements or discoveries have you made? What setbacks or successes have you experienced?

Elbow also recommends having students keep a journal, what he calls a "free-writing diary." He warns that it is "not a complete account of your day; just a brief mind sample from each day" (*Writing without Teachers* 9). Like Macrorie, Elbow sees the "freewriting diary" as the mother lode of ideas for essays. Elbow writes that "freewriting helps you to think of topics to write about. Just keep writing," he tells his readers; "follow threads where they lead and you will get the ideas, experiences, feelings, or people that are just asking to be written about" (*Writing with Power* 15). If your students like the idea of a freewriting diary but need a bit of structure and encouragement, the Web site 750words.com encourages participants to write 750 words each day and gives points and badges (small rewards) to those who write three pages a day.

Many students already keep a shorter version of Elbow's "freewriting diary" by sending tweets or writing status updates on social media sites. Students can be encouraged to extend such short updates into daily journal entries, providing the contextual details surrounding the short statement they make publicly. If they have difficulty thinking of things to write, they can review their status updates, seeing which ones provoked response, which ones raised questions, and which needed more information to make sense to a larger audience.

Like postings on social media sites, blogs also provide a public forum for student writing, one that encourages reader response. If you're teaching a themed course, you might have students choose an aspect of the theme that interests them and create a blog that reflects that interest. For a theme-based composition class on food, for example, one student might create a blog on cheese, another on fast food; one might do reviews of local student-friendly places to eat, another on living with celiac disease. Keeping a blog in preparation for a more in-depth assignment (such as a research paper) allows students to write about their experiences and to do research for each post, which keeps students from procrastinating if they're required to post each week.

Whether you ask students to keep a private journal or create a public blog, you, too, should join your students in the journal-keeping practice, perhaps by keeping a teaching journal — or a blog related to writing or teaching. (For some examples of teaching blogs, see Nancy Sommers's "Between the Drafts" and *Bits*, Bedford/St. Martin's blog forum for composition teachers, cited in the Useful Web Sites section at the end of the chapter.)

Nancy Comley, when she was director of FY writing at Queens College, City University of New York, encouraged her teaching assistants to keep their own journals. Comley writes that

> through the journal one comes to know oneself better as a teacher, and in the discipline of keeping a journal the teacher can experience what students experience when they are told to write and do not really feel like it. As part of the journal, I suggest that each teacher keep a folder of the progress (or lack of it) of two of his or her students, noting the students' interaction with the class and the teacher as well as evaluating their written work. Such data can form the basis for a seminar paper presenting these case histories, augmenting journal observations with student conferences and with research done into special problems or strengths the students had as writers. (55–56)

Encouraging teachers to keep a journal is in keeping with Comley's sage pedagogical advice: Never give an assignment you have not tried yourself.

especially a book; read it and then read it with them

Evaluating Journals

The issue of whether to evaluate journals is simple to answer: don't. Instead, read the entries to ensure that the student has made a sincere effort and assign a grade based on the number of pages a student turns in; four a week for ten weeks might earn an A; three a week, a B; and so on. Students are expected to write for themselves, yet they know that the instructor will see everything in the journal. While some teachers put no marks on journals except for a date after the last entry, others initiate a written conversation with the students, and still others write on separate sheets of paper that they insert into the journals. At times, you may find an entry directed to you — an invitation to reply.

Journals, then, shouldn't be judged by the standards you might bring to a student essay. The fact that students' journals do have an audience, however —

namely, the teacher—means that they "do not speak privately," as Ken Macrorie puts it in *Telling Writing* (130). Macrorie insists that journals

> can be read with profit by other persons than the writer. They may be personal or even intimate, but if the writer wants an entry to be seen by others, it will be such that they can understand, enjoy, be moved by [it]. (131)

Helping students distinguish between what is personal and what is private is an important task for teachers who assign and read student journals. Emphasizing that you won't be grading the journals but that you will be reading them should help students work toward balancing the different demands of writing for themselves versus writing for others.

The issue of writing for oneself versus writing for others, however, becomes more complex if you're asking students to keep public blogs, which might be about their personal experiences and thoughts but should also be created with an audience in mind. Since many students have experience with online writing—whether through keeping a blog or using social media sites—they should be prepared to talk about the choices they make when posting their writing online.

BRAINSTORMING

Using Brainstorming in the Classroom

Brainstorming is the invention method used by most professional and academic writers. The technique of brainstorming is simple: The writer decides on a subject, sits down in a quiet place with pen and paper or computer, and writes down everything that comes to mind about the subject. Alex Osborne codified the main rules of brainstorming in the late 1950s:

1. Don't criticize or evaluate any ideas during the session. Simply write down every idea that emerges. Save the criticism and evaluation until later.
2. Use your imagination for "free wheeling." The wilder the idea the better, because it might lead to some valuable insights later.
3. Strive for quantity. The more ideas, the better chance for a winner to emerge.
4. Combine and improve ideas as you proceed. (84)

The writer, in other words, free-associates, writing down as many ideas as possible. After doing so, the writer either tries to structure the information in some way—by recopying it in a different order or by numbering the items, crossing some out, adding to others—or finds the list suggestive enough as it stands and begins to work.

Brainstorming is extremely simple—and effective. The most widely used inventive technique, brainstorming moves in naturally to fill the void if no structured method is ever taught. Research suggests that if an inventive system is not internalized by around age twenty, brainstorming is adopted, probably because it represents the natural way the mind grapples with the storage and retrieval of information. Most professional and academic writers were never taught systematic invention and therefore turned to brainstorming.

Sometimes, young, self-conscious writers who have little specialized educational experience are initially stymied by brainstorming, for their stores of knowledge and general intellectual resources aren't as developed as those of experienced writers. Hence, they go dry when confronted with the task of listing ideas about an abstract topic. You may want to walk such writers through the brainstorming system by doing a sample exercise on the board or in small groups before you turn them loose with their own ideas. Brainstorming works well as a collaborative exercise, allowing students to feed off each other's ideas and draw from and extend each other's knowledge.

CLUSTERING

In *Writing the Natural Way,* Gabriele Lusser Rico describes clustering. Based on theories of the brain's hemispheric specialization, Rico's creative search process taps the right hemisphere of the brain, the hemisphere sensitive "to wholeness, image, and the unforced rhythms of language" (12). Usually, Rico tells us, beginning writers rely solely on the left hemisphere, the hemisphere of reason, linearity, and logic. By clustering, they can learn to tap the other hemisphere as well and produce writings that demonstrate

> a coherence, unity, and sense of wholeness; a recurrence of words and phrases, ideas, or images that [reflect] a pattern sensitivity; an awareness of the nuances of language rhythms; a significant and natural use of images and metaphors; and a powerful "creative tension." Another by-product of clustering seem[s] to be a significant drop in errors of punctuation, awkward phrasing, even spelling. (11)

Using Clustering in the Classroom

Clustering is an easy-to-use invention activity because there is no right or wrong way to cluster. Rico guarantees that the words will come and that writing eventually takes over. Students' clusters — and your own — are likely to be messy, drawing on both memory and association and displaying a mix of images, experiences and ideas. Here are Rico's simple directions for clustering, using the word *afraid* as an example:

1. Write the word *afraid* in the upper third of the page, leaving the lower two-thirds of the page for writing, and circle it. We'll start with this word because even the most hesitant of us will discover many associations triggered by it.
2. Now get comfortable with the process of clustering by letting your playful, creative . . . mind make connections. Keep the childlike attitude of newness and wonder and spill whatever associations come to you onto paper. What comes to mind when you think of the word? Avoid judging or choosing. Simply let go and write. Let the words or phrases radiate outward from the nucleus word, and draw a circle around each of them. Connect those associations that seem related with lines. Add arrows to indicate direction, if you wish, but don't think too long or analyze. There is an "unthinking" quality to this process that suspends time.
3. Continue jotting down associations and ideas triggered by the word *afraid* for a minute or two, immersing yourself in the process. Since there is no *one* way to let the cluster spill onto the page, let yourself be guided by the patterning . . . [abilities of your] mind, connecting each association as you see fit without

worrying about it. Let clustering happen naturally. It will, if you don't inhibit it with objections from your censoring . . . mind. If you reach a plateau where nothing spills out, "doodle" a bit by putting arrows on your existing cluster.

4. You will know when to stop clustering through a sudden, strong urge to write, usually after one or two minutes, when you feel a shift that says "Aha! I think I know what I want to say." If it doesn't happen suddenly, this awareness of a direction will creep up on you more gradually, as though someone were slowly unveiling a sculpture. . . . Just know you will experience a mental shift charac- terized by the certain, satisfying feeling that you have something to write about.

5. You're ready to write. Scan [your] clustered perceptions and insights. . . . Something therein will suggest your first sentence to you, and you're off. Students rarely, if ever, report difficulty writing that first sentence; on the contrary, they report it as being effortless. Should you feel stuck, however, write about anything from the cluster to get you started. The next thing and the next thing after that will come because your [right hemisphere] has already perceived a pattern of meaning. Trust it. (36–37)

Like brainstorming, clustering works best when it's done very quickly, when students don't have time to edit or overthink their responses. Remind them that it's good if their clusters are messy, if they go off on tangents. When a clus- ter works well, students are surprised by how much material they were able to develop and the connections that their minds naturally made — even without conscious thought. If students wish to edit and organize their handwritten clus- ters as part of the selection and ordering process, there are Web sites that allow for mapping and clustering. One especially useful site, bubbl.us, allows users to choose colors, insert hyperlinks, and edit. It's best, though, for students to begin their clusters with pen and paper, and to save editing and organization until they've produced a lot of material.

When you model clustering for your students, allow a volunteer to suggest the starting place, the center word that you will work from. Don't try to explain the process as you're clustering; wait until after you're done and then take them through the process of your own clustering, explaining the associations you made and where you might go from there if you were to write about something that came up in your cluster. Students can practice clustering in pairs, too, choos- ing the same center word and then comparing their clusters. Such an activity allows students both to recognize their own individual ideas and associations and to see how much knowledge is communally constructed.

FREEWRITING

Unlike the heuristic-type invention techniques discussed in this chapter, free- writing is not a device through which experience can be consciously processed, nor do freewriting exercises (in their pure form) provide theses, arguments, or subject matter. Rather, freewriting — like clustering — is a ritual that can elicit possible subjects to which the conscious mind may not have easy access. What freewriting does best is loosen the inhibitions of the inexperienced writer. Thus, while freewriting differs strikingly from some of the other techniques discussed in this chapter, it follows well from both brainstorming and clustering. Once students have scanned their brainstorming lists or cluster diagrams and have an idea for a topic or first line, they are ready to freewrite — to begin putting the ideas suggested by their lists or cluster into prose, even as they hold out the possibility of discovering even more new material.

Freewriting, of course, does not need to follow another invention activity such as brainstorming or clustering. Freewriting itself can be a good starting place for invention. A number of writers over the past sixty years have developed freewriting exercises as methods of getting potential writers used to the idea of writing. Perhaps the first mention of freewriting-type exercises is in Dorothea Brande's 1934 book *Becoming a Writer,* in which the author suggests freewriting as a way for young would-be novelists to get in touch with their subconscious selves. Brande advocates writing "when the unconscious is in the ascendent":

> The best way to do this is to rise half an hour, or a full hour, earlier than you customarily rise. Just as soon as you can — and without talking, without reading — begin to write. Write anything that comes to your head. Write any sort of early morning revery, rapidly and uncritically. The excellence or ultimate worth of what you write is of no importance yet. Forget that you have any critical faculty at all. (50–51)

Brande's technique, the ancestor of freewriting, was largely ignored by teachers of expository writing until the 1950s, when Ken Macrorie, who had read *Becoming a Writer,* began to use an updated version of it in his composition classes. He modified Brande's directions for use in general composition and told his students to "go home and write anything that comes to your mind. Don't stop. Write for ten minutes or till you've filled a full page." This exercise produced writing that was often incoherent but that was also often striking in its transcendence of the dullness and clichéd thought teachers too often come to expect in English papers (*Uptaught* 20). Macrorie popularized the freewriting technique with his books *Uptaught* and *Telling Writing,* but it was Peter Elbow who developed and refined freewriting, making it a well-known tool. In his *Writing without Teachers* (which every writing teacher should read for the author's opinions on how to teach and learn writing), Elbow presents the most carefully wrought freewriting plan published thus far.

Using Freewriting in the Classroom

Freewriting is a kind of structured brainstorming, a method of exploring a topic by writing about it — or whatever else it brings to mind — for a certain number of minutes without stopping. It consists of a series of exercises, conducted either in class or at home, during which students start with a blank piece of paper or a blank word-processing document, think about their topic, and then simply let their minds wander while they write. For as long as their time limit, they write or type everything that occurs to them (in complete sentences as much as possible). They must not stop for anything. If they can't think of what to write next, they can write "I can't think of what to write next" over and over until something else occurs to them. When their time is up, they can look at what they've written. (If freewriting on a computer, students can try turning off their monitor or dimming their laptop screen while they type to prevent self-censorship as they write.) Students may find much that is unusable, irrelevant, or nonsensical. But they may also find important insights and ideas that they didn't know they had; freewriting has a way of jogging loose such ideas. As soon as a word or an idea appears on paper, it often triggers others.

The point of freewriting is to concentrate on writing, taking no time to worry about what others might think of it. When writers struggle to keep words — any words — flowing, they overload their "academic superego," which is usually concerned with content, criticism, spelling, grammar, and any of the other formal or content-based issues of correctness that so easily turn into writing blocks. In other words, they are writing — for five, ten, or fifteen minutes. Here are Elbow's directions for freewriting:

> Don't stop for anything. Go quickly without rushing. Never stop to look back, to cross something out, to wonder how to spell something, to wonder what word or thought to use, to think about what you are doing. If you can't think of a word or a spelling, just use a squiggle or else write, "I can't think of it." Just put down something. The easiest thing is just to put down whatever is in your mind. If you get stuck, it's fine to write, "I can't think what to say" as many times as you want, or repeat the last word you wrote over and over again, or anything else. The only requirement is that you never stop. (*Writing without Teachers* 3)

The requirement that the student never stop writing is matched by an equally powerful mandate to the teacher: Never grade or evaluate freewriting exercises in any way. You can collect and read them — they are often fascinating illustrations of the working of the mind — but they must not be judged. To judge or grade freewriting would obviate the purpose of the exercise; this writing is free, not to be held accountable in the same way as other, more structured kinds of writing. Be sure to tell students that you will not be grading their freewriting. The value of freewriting lies in its capacity to release students from the often self-imposed halter of societal expectations. If you grade or judge such creations, you will convey the message that this writing is not free.

Most teachers who use pure freewriting use it at the opening of each class, every day for at least four or five weeks of the term. A session or two of freewriting, though interesting, is insufficient. For long-term gains, students must freewrite frequently and regularly. Only then will the act of writing stop being the unnatural exercise that some students see it as and start being a part of a writer's habit. Regular freewriting in class has two particularly worthwhile effects, says William Irmscher: "It creates the expectation that writing classes are places where people come to write, and it makes writing habitual" (82–83). Students can also freewrite outside of class. You can assign freewriting as homework, grading it only according to whether or not it is done.

Combined with brainstorming and clustering, freewriting can be used as an aid to writing longer pieces. But you won't want to try this combination of techniques until students are comfortable with each one individually. Combining techniques is most fruitful when students use them at home, since they require an extended period of time. Example 6.3 provides an exercise that helps students combine the brainstorming, clustering, and freewriting invention techniques.

The Benefits of Freewriting

Pure freewriting does not provide the neatness of the heuristic systems nor even the coherent processes of some other invention techniques, but as long as you explain its purpose and make certain that students don't see it as busywork, freewriting can accomplish two important goals.

First, it can familiarize beginning writers with the physical act of writing. Mina Shaughnessy suggests that it is hard for some teachers to understand exactly how little experience many FY students have had in writing (14–15). Their handwriting may be immature, and their command of sentence structure may suffer because they cannot match their writing process with their thought process. Freewriting forces them to produce, without the conscious editorial mechanism making the writing process harder than it is. A full five or six weeks of directed freewriting can make a difference.

Second, freewriting demystifies the writing process. After simply pouring out their thoughts in a freewriting exercise, students can no longer view the ability to write as a divine gift that has been denied them. They soon come to realize the difference between writing and editing, a difference crucial to their willingness and their ability to write. Freewriting primes the pump for more structured writing by demonstrating that a writer normally cannot, and need not, produce a perfectly finished essay on the first try, that the process has many steps, and that even the most seemingly unpromising gibberish can yield valuable material.

Example 6.3   **COMBINING INVENTION TECHNIQUES**

Give students a subject to write about and then suggest the following pattern:

1. Brainstorm for ten minutes.
2. Choose one item from your brainstorming list.
3. Cluster that word or idea for five minutes.
4. Set a timer or an alarm clock for twenty minutes, and freewrite for the entire time. Don't stop, and use only the brainstormed list and cluster as a basis for ideas.

Although students may grow tired while writing and may discard much of what they write, this piece of writing (or maybe the next one) will be the first draft of an essay that they can edit and you can grade. This technique works best when you assign the topics a week or so before the essays are due. Successful topics range from "censorship" to "social media sites" — topics even teenage students have lived with for many years.

WORKS CITED

Anson, Chris M., and Richard Beach. "Journeys in Journaling." *The Subject Is Writing.* Ed. Wendy Bishop. 2nd ed. Portsmouth: Boynton/Cook, 1999. 20–29. Print.

Atwill, Janet, and Janice M. Lauer, eds. *Perspectives on Rhetorical Invention.* Knoxville: U of Tennessee P, 2003. Print.

Bilsky, Manuel, et al. "Looking for an Argument." *CE* 14.4 (1953): 210–16. Print.

Brande, Dorothea. *Becoming a Writer.* 1934. New York: Harcourt, 1970. Print.

Comley, Nancy R. "The Teaching Seminar: Writing Isn't Just Rhetoric." *Training the New Teacher of College Composition.* Ed. Charles W. Bridges. Urbana: NCTE, 1986. 47–58. Print.

Corbett, Edward P. J., and Robert J. Connors. *Classical Rhetoric for the Modern Student.* 4th ed. New York: Oxford UP, 1998. Print.

Ede, Lisa, Cheryl Glenn, and Andrea Lunsford. "Border Crossings: Intersections of Rhetoric and Feminism." *Rhetorica* 13.4 (1995): 401–41. Print.

Elbow, Peter. *Embracing Contraries.* New York: Oxford UP, 1986. Print.

——. *Everyone Can Write.* New York: Oxford UP, 2000. Print.

——. *Writing without Teachers.* New York: Oxford UP, 1973. Print.

——. *Writing with Power.* New York: Oxford UP, 1981. Print.

Gannett, Cinthia. *Gender and the Journal.* Albany: State U of New York, 1990. Print.

Hughes, Richard P., and P. Albert Duhamel. *Rhetoric: Principles and Usage.* Englewood Cliffs: Prentice, 1967. Print.

Irmscher, William F. *Teaching Expository Writing.* New York: Holt, 1979. Print.

Kinneavy, James. *A Theory of Discourse.* 1971. New York: Norton, 1980. Print.

Lauer, Janice. "Heuristics and Composition." *CCC* 21.5 (1970): 396–404. Print.

——. *Invention in Contemporary Rhetoric: Heuristic Procedures.* Diss. U of Michigan, 1970. Print.

——. "Toward a Methodology of Heuristic Procedures." *CCC* 30.3 (1979): 268–69.

Lauer, Janice, Janet Emig, and Andrea A. Lunsford. *Four Worlds of Writing.* 4th ed. New York: HarperCollins, 1995. Print.

Macrorie, Ken. *Telling Writing.* Rochelle Park: Hayden, 1970. Print.

——. *Uptaught.* Rochelle Park: Hayden, 1970. Print.

Odell, Lee. "Assessing Thinking: Glimpsing a Mind at Work." *Evaluating Writing.* Ed. Charles R. Cooper and Lee Odell. Urbana: NCTE, 1999. Print.

——. "Piaget, Problem-Solving, and Freshman Composition." *CCC* 24.1 (1973): 36–42. Print.

Osborne, Alex F. *Applied Imagination.* New York: Scribner, 1957. Print.

Rico, Gabriele Lusser. *Writing the Natural Way.* Los Angeles: Tarcher, 1983. Print.

Shaughnessy, Mina. *Errors and Expectations: A Guide for the Teacher of Basic Writing.* New York: Oxford UP, 1977. Print.

Ulmer, Gregory L. *Heuristics: The Logic of Invention.* Baltimore: John Hopkins UP, 1994. Print.

Young, Richard E. "Invention: A Topographical Survey." *Teaching Composition: Ten Bibliographic Essays.* Ed. Gary Tate. Fort Worth: Texas Christian UP, 1976, 1-44. Print.

Young, Richard E., Alton L. Becker, and Kenneth L. Pike. *Rhetoric: Discovery and Change.* New York: Harcourt, 1970. Print.

Young, Richard E., and Yameng Liu, eds. *Landmark Essays: Rhetorical Invention in Writing.* Davis: Hermagoras, 1994. Print.

Useful Web Sites

Between the Drafts: Nancy Sommers's Teaching Journal
blogs.bedfordstmartins.com/hackerhandbooks

Bits: Ideas for Teaching Composition
blogs.bedfordstmartins.com/bits

Online Clustering/Mapping Site
bubbl.us

A Site That Provides Space for Students to Keep a Freewriting Journal
750words.com

7

Teaching Arrangement and Form

*"What do you want?" "How long does this have to be?" "Should this be five
paragraphs?" are some of the questions teacher-pleasing students often ask us.
While prescriptive arrangements can help answer those questions, my aim is to teach
students to recognize the flexibility of rhetoric.*

—JESSICA O'HARA

One of the continuing criticisms of classical rhetoric is its seemingly arbitrary
canonical divisions: Is there any essential reason for assuming that the process
of generating discourse should be divided into the restrictive classifications of
invention, arrangement, style, memory, and delivery? And if these divisions are
arbitrary, having no real connection to the composing process, why use them
in a book like this?

Controversial though they may be, the divisions of rhetoric are useful conventions. Were we to try to describe the composing process as the seamless interaction of form and content that it apparently is, our discussion would have to
be considerably deeper and more theoretical than space allows here. Separating
invention and arrangement is a convenient tool for discussing certain features
of process composing, even though the two operations are deeply interrelated
and, except in certain invention techniques such as freewriting and brainstorming, rarely carried out separately by practiced writers. Experienced writers know
that invention, arrangement, and style are inextricably intertwined, that no
approach to one can ever ignore the others.

Because of this intimate relationship between form and content, Richard
Larson writes that "form in complete essays has not been the subject of much
theoretical investigation" (45). Invention, with its many open-ended systems,
has received much more recent attention, reflecting a move away from formal
requirements in general and a move toward self-ordered expression. Still, no one
can claim that expectations about the characteristics of the different genres
do not exist. Therefore, the demands of arrangement remain an integral part
of rhetoric.

The arrangement of material in any writing grows out of a complex blend of
the author's purpose and knowledge of the subject, as well as the formal expectations of the audience and the parameters shaped by the medium used. In the
course of ten or fifteen weeks, few teachers can present, and even fewer students
can grasp, all of the intricacies in the marriage of form and content, let alone
all of the techniques used by experienced writers. Students can, however, begin
to appreciate these intricacies in the material that is familiar to them. For example,

you might ask students to examine the patterns of arrangement in articles and essays written by academics in other fields of study and to deduce the writers' conventional formats wherever possible. You can also introduce students to both the conventional and creative forms of arrangement covered here, which include simple and short formats that can be adapted to nearly any subject matter, longer and more complex ones used specifically in argumentation, and options for arranging creative essays and writing for the Web. You can demonstrate and assign one, two, or all of these patterns of arrangement. You and your students should remember, however, that these patterns are not absolutes; they must be seen as convenient devices, not as rigid structures.

RHETORICAL FORM

Specific internal arrangement of elements creates rhetorical form, which may also be called genre, mode, or organization. Some teachers argue that preconceived arrangement (or formal structure) is artificial, that all organization should grow naturally out of the writer's purpose. Others see readily identifiable organization and form as the first step toward successful communication. Each teacher must gradually develop a conception of form and learn to strike a balance between form and content. This chapter can only suggest the various available alternatives that have long been used in the teaching of rhetoric.

sort of agree

Forms and arrangements can sometimes be assigned and used artificially; therefore, when we discuss form with our students, we must remind them (and ourselves) of the relationships between structure and content: that purpose, the needs of the audience, and the subject should dictate arrangement — not vice versa. We cannot, then, merely offer our students one or two prefabricated, all-purpose arrangements. Instead, we must regularly ask students to recognize the interconnections between form and content and between genre and intention, and we must work to assist them in the subtle task of creating forms that fit their ideas and emphases.

Whatever methods of arrangement or form you choose to teach, you want your students to realize that the conventions can be adapted and changed according to the needs of a particular subject and a particular audience. Methods of arrangement can provide a rough framework on which to build an essay, but they should neither limit the development of an essay nor demand sections that are clearly unnecessary.

Prescriptive forms of arrangement, however, can be helpful for multilingual writers, especially those for whom English is not a first — or strong — language. Analyzing the typical structure and arrangement of genres common in academic writing can help make formal expectations clear. As you discuss the genres you want students to write, point out common features, showing students that although arrangement is not always set, there are features that readers expect to see in particular genres.

The prescriptive forms discussed in this chapter should be thought of and taught as stepping-stones only, not as ends in themselves. You will want to teach your students to transcend them as well as to use them. Kenneth Burke conveys an immensely important message in telling us that "form is an arousing and fulfillment of desires, . . . correct in so far as it gratifies the needs . . . it creates" (124). Form must grow from the human desires for both the familiar and the novel. If the prescriptive forms we give our students can help them realize this primary purpose, then we can offer the forms with the certainty that they will provide scaffolding only until the students can dismantle them and build on their own.

CLASSICALLY DESCENDED ARRANGEMENTS

The first theorists to propose generic forms for rhetoric were the Greeks, whose ideas were then rendered more formally and more technically by Roman rhetoricians. The first arrangement we have record of is from Aristotle, who may have been responding to the complicated, "improved" methods of arrangement detailed by his sophistic competition when he wrote, "A speech has two parts. You must state your case, and you must prove it. . . . The current division is absurd" (*Rhetoric* 1414b). With the exception of the three-part essay, which has been generalized and modernized, all classical arrangements descend from Aristotle, and all are essentially argumentative in nature—like classical rhetoric itself. These arrangements, organized formally rather than according to content, rarely suit narrative, descriptive, or expository writing and can confuse students who try to use them for nonargumentative purposes. In the fourth edition of *Classical Rhetoric for the Modern Student,* Edward P. J. Corbett and Robert Connors point out that, instead of being topically organized, classical arrangements are "determined by the *functions* of the various parts of a discourse" (259).

The elements discussed as parts of each method of arrangement have no necessary correlation with paragraphs. Some students are tempted to think of a six-part essay as a six-paragraph essay, but except for some minor and very prescriptive forms, such as the five-paragraph theme, each element in a discourse scheme consists of a minimum of a single paragraph. Therefore, a four-part essay might consist of a single paragraph for the introduction, three paragraphs for the statement of fact, four paragraphs for the argument, and a single paragraph for the conclusion. Since each element can theoretically consist of an unlimited number of paragraphs, you should beware of letting your students fall into the habit of perceiving each element as a single paragraph.

The Three-Part Arrangement

"A whole," says Aristotle, "is that which has a beginning, a middle, and an end" (*Poetics* 24). Aristotle's observation—original, true, and now obvious—is the starting place for the most widely accepted method of rhetorical arrangement, the three-part arrangement. Like the dramatic works Aristotle was describing, a complete discourse, such as a successful essay, has three parts: an introduction, a body of some length, and a conclusion. From the simplest single-paragraph exercise to a forty-page research essay, every writing assignment is expected to contain these three parts.

The simplicity of this arrangement has positive and negative aspects. On the one hand, it is easy to teach and demonstrate, it is not overly structured, and it is the one truly universal pattern of arrangement, workable for exposition and argumentation alike. On the other hand, it provides little actual guidance in structuring an essay, especially if the assignment calls for a response longer than five hundred words. With such longer essays, students often find that although they are able to shape their introductions and conclusions, the bodies of their essays are amorphous. Nothing in the three-part essay provides interior structure to guide beginning writers in constructing the body of their essays, nearly always the longest part. The three-part arrangement, then, is most suitable for assignments of under five hundred words. Each of the three parts can be taught separately.

The Introduction   "The Introduction," writes Aristotle, "is the beginning of a speech, . . . paving the way . . . for what is to follow. . . . The writer should . . . begin with what best takes his fancy, and then strike up his theme and lead into it" (*Rhetoric* 1414b). In the three-part essay, the introduction has two main tasks. First, it must catch and hold the reader's attention with an opening "hook" — an introductory section that does not announce the thesis of the essay but instead begins to relate the as-yet-unannounced thesis in some brief, attention-catching way. The introduction can open with an anecdote, an aphorism, an argumentative observation, or a quotation. Donald Hall calls such an opening strategy a "quiet zinger, . . . something exciting or intriguing and at the same time relevant to the material that follows" (38).

Second, the introduction must quickly focus the attention of the reader on the thesis. This central informing principle of the essay is determined by the writer's purpose, subject, and audience. It is usually found in the form of a single-sentence declarative statement near the end of the introduction. The thesis statement represents the essay-length equivalent of the topic sentence of a paragraph; it is general enough to announce what the essay plans to do yet specific enough to suggest what the essay will not do. Sheridan Baker makes the controversial suggestion that the thesis statement is always the most specific sentence in the opening paragraph and should always come at the end of that paragraph. Although this is an easy-to-teach truism that may help students structure their introductions, critics have disputed how accurately it reflects the practice of experienced and published writers.

The Body of the Essay   According to Aristotle, the body of the essay is a middle. In truth, little more can be said of the middle in terms of the theory of the three-part essay, but in practice, writers can choose from many organizational plans. Some teachers trail off into generalities when they discuss the body of the essay, talking about "shaping purpose," "order of development," and "correct use of transitions" — necessary considerations but of little help to students adrift between their first and last paragraphs.

The body of the three-part essay can take many shapes: Writers can develop their essays according to the physical aspects, chronology, or logic or association of the subject matter; or by illustrating points, defining terms, dividing and classifying, comparing and contrasting, analyzing causes and effects, or considering problems and solutions. Whatever organizational plan writers choose, they want to be sure that the main points of the body relate not only to the thesis but to one another. Box 7.1 shows the four general principles of organization offered by Andrea A. Lunsford in *The St. Martin's Handbook*.

The Conclusion   Like the introduction, the conclusion presents special challenges, for it should indicate that a full discussion has taken place. Often the conclusion begins with a restatement of the thesis and ends with more general statements that grow out of it, reversing the common general-to-specific pattern of the introduction. This restatement is usually somewhat more complex than the original thesis statement, since now the writer assumes that readers can marshal all of the facts of the situation as they have been presented in the body of the essay. A typical, if obvious, example of the opening of a conclusion might be "Thus, as we have seen," followed by the reworded thesis.

In addition to reiterating the consequence and import of the thesis, however, the conclusion should include a graceful or memorable rhetorical note. Writers can draw on a number of techniques to conclude effectively and give their text a sense of ending: a provocative question, a quotation, a vivid image, a call for action, or a warning. Baker writes that a successful conclusion satisfies the reader because it "conveys a sense of assurance and repose, of business completed" (22). William Zinsser, however, in *On Writing Well*, insists that

> the perfect ending should take the reader slightly by surprise and yet seem exactly right to him. He didn't expect the [piece] to end so soon, or so abruptly, or to say what it said. But he knows it when he sees it. (78–79)

Zinsser goes on to tell writers of nonfiction that when they are ready to stop, they should stop: "If you have presented all the facts and made the point that you want to make, look for the nearest exit" (79). Often, however, the best conclusions are those that answer the "so what?" of the thesis statement and overall argument.

real world implications? implications for literature and so on?

Box 7.1 PRINCIPLES OF ORGANIZATION

Space — *where* bits of information occur within a setting

Time — *when* bits of information occur, usually chronologically

Logic — *how* bits of information are related logically

Association — *how* bits of information are related in terms of images, motifs, personal memories, and so on (Lunsford 55–60)

Using the Three-Part Arrangement in the Classroom

Although it is applicable to many modes of discourse, the classical three-part arrangement simply does not provide enough internal structure to help students put together the middle sections of their essays. The three-part form is useful mainly as an introduction to the conventions of introductions and conclusions. The easiest way to consider the body of an essay is to teach patterns of other, more fully developed arrangements.

After introducing the basic three-part structure, you can discuss the importance of introductions and conclusions. Try to choose examples that put special emphasis on the structures of these parts and ask students to respond to your examples. You might assign a series of short, in-class essays on topics your students have chosen. So that students concentrate on recognizable introductions and conclusions, you might allow them to dispense with the writing of the body of each essay and to submit instead a rough outline or list of components.

An Exercise for Small Groups

This exercise is especially useful when students work in writing groups: After each short essay assignment is written in class, ask students to work with their group to evaluate the introductions and conclusions. They might answer specific questions, such as those listed in Example 7.1. You might display the most effective introductions and conclusions so that they are visible to the entire class or ask some students to read their introductions or conclusions aloud. After students have conferred and improved one another's work and after the introductions and conclusions have been hammered into a final form, allow those students who have become intrigued by the ideas they've been working with to complete the essay for a grade. Several days of this kind of practice can give students competence in beginning and ending their essays.

Example 7.1 **QUESTIONS FOR SMALL GROUPS**

- What does the opening of this essay accomplish?
- How does it "hook" the reader?
- How can you help the writer improve the opening?
- Does the essay end in a memorable way? Or does it seem to trail off into vagueness or end abruptly?
- If you like the conclusion, what about it do you like?
- Can you help the writer improve the conclusion?

The Four-Part Arrangement

After blasting the hair-splitting pedagogues of his day and declaring that an oration has only two parts, Aristotle relented and admitted that as speakers actually practice rhetoric, a discourse generally has four parts: the *proem* or *introduction,* the *statement of fact,* the *confirmation* or *argument,* and the *epilogue* or *conclusion* (*Rhetoric* 200). Specifically an argumentative form, this four-part arrangement does not adapt well to narrative, description, or exposition.

The Introduction   Called the *proem* (from the Greek word *proemium,* meaning "before the song") by Aristotle and the *exordium* (from the Latin weaving term for "beginning a web") by the author of the Roman handbook *Rhetorica ad her-renium,* the introduction to the four-part essay has two functions, one major and one minor. The major task is to inform the audience of the purpose or object of the essay; the minor task is to create a rapport, or relationship of trust, with the audience. The introduction to the four-part essay, then, performs functions similar to that of the introduction to the three-part essay. It draws readers into the discourse with the promise of interesting information and informs them of the main purpose while rendering them well-disposed toward the writer and the subject.

"The most essential function and distinctive property of the introduction," writes Aristotle, "[is] to show what the aim of the speech is" (*Rhetoric* 202). Corbett and Connors tell us that the introduction serves two important audience-centered functions: It orients the audience within the subject, and even more importantly, it seeks to convince readers that what is being introduced is worthy of their attention (260). In a fashion similar to the "quiet zinger" that opens the three-part essay, the four-part essay can catch readers' attention by using different devices. Richard Whately describes five different types of introductions that can arouse the reader's interest (see Box 7.2). The usefulness of these types of introductions is not limited to the four-part essay, though they do complement argumentative subject matter. The various introductions can accomplish the major task of acquainting the audience with the subject as well as the minor task of rendering the reader attentive to and well-disposed toward the writer.

In rendering an audience benevolent, writers must be aware of certain elements concerning the rhetorical situation in which they find themselves. In the third edition of *Classical Rhetoric for the Modern Student,* Corbett offers five questions that writers must ask themselves with regard to their rhetorical situation before they can be certain of the conditions for their discourse:

1. What do I have to say?
2. To or before whom is it being said?
3. Under what circumstances?
4. What are the predispositions of the audience?
5. How much time or space do I have? (290)

The introduction is the best place to establish "bridges" between writer and reader by pointing to shared beliefs and attitudes—that is, by creating what

---

Box 7.2 **WHATELY'S TYPES OF INTRODUCTIONS**

Inquisitive introductions show that the subject in question is "important, curious, or otherwise interesting."

Paradoxical introductions dwell on characteristics of the subject that seem improbable but are nonetheless real. This form of introduction searches for strange and curious perspectives on the subject.

Corrective introductions show that the subject has been "neglected, misunderstood, or misrepresented by others." As Whately says, this immediately removes the danger that the subject will be thought trite or hackneyed.

Preparatory introductions explain peculiarities in the way the subject will be handled, warn against misconceptions about the subject, or apologize for some deficiency in the presentation.

Narrative introductions lead to the subject by narrating a story or anecdote. (Whateley 189–92)

Kenneth Burke calls identification of the writer with the audience and the audience with the writer.

The Statement of Fact   The Romans called the statement of fact the *narratio,* and it is sometimes today referred to as the *narration or background*. But Corbett's term *statement of fact* works well, especially since we now use *narration* to signify dramatized activities. This section of a discourse also presents more than just background. The statement of fact is a nonargumentative, expository presentation of the objective facts concerning the situation or problem—the subject—under discussion.

The statement of fact may contain circumstances, details, summaries, even narrative in the modern sense. It sets forth the background of the problem and very often explains the central point as well. Perhaps the best general advice remains that of Quintilian, who in the first century CE, recommended that the statement of fact be *lucid, brief,* and *plausible*. Writers can order a statement of fact in a number of different ways: in chronological order, from general situation to specific details, from specific to general, or according to topics. The tone of the statement of fact should be neutral, calm, and matter-of-fact, free of overt stylistic mannerisms and obvious bias. Writers are best served by understatement, for readers will readily trust a writer they deem to be striving for fairness.

The Confirmation   Also called the *argument*, the confirmation is central to the four-part essay and is often the longest section. Corbett tells us that the confirmation is easily used in expository as well as argumentative prose; historically, it has been used mainly in argumentation. Simply put, the confirmation is used to prove the writer's case. With the audience rendered attentive by the introduction and informed by the statement of fact, the writer is ready to show the reasons why her position concerning the facts should be accepted and believed.

Most of the argumentative material discovered in the invention process is used in this section.

Aristotle theorizes that argumentative discourse deals with two different sorts of questions: Deliberative (or political) oratory is always concerned with the future, and forensic (or judicial) oratory is always concerned with the past. If the question is about events in the past, the confirmation will try to prove the following:

1. Whether an act was committed
2. Whether an act committed did harm
3. Whether the harm of the act is less or more than alleged
4. Whether a harmful act was justified

If the question is about a course for the future, the confirmation will try to prove that

1. A certain thing can or cannot be done. If it can be done, then the confirmation tries to prove that
2. It is just or unjust
3. It will do harm or good
4. It has not the importance the opposition attaches to it

After deciding on a question and a position, the writer can move into the argument, choosing from definitions, demonstrations of cause or effect, analogies, authoritative testimony, maxims, personal experiences — evidence of all sorts — in order to prove a point.

The writer can build an argument in different ways, but classical rhetoricians offer a rough plan. If there are, for instance, three specific lines of argument available to the writer — one strong, one moderately convincing, and one weak — they should be grouped thus: the moderate argument first, the weak argument second, and the strong argument last. This arrangement begins and ends the confirmation on notes of relative strength and prevents the writer's position from appearing initially weak or finally anticlimactic.

The Conclusion   Called the *epilogue* by the Greeks and the *peroration* by the Romans (from *per-oratio*, a "finishing off of the oration"), the conclusion, according to Aristotle's *Rhetoric*, has four possible tasks:

1. It renders the audience once again well-disposed toward the writer and ill-disposed toward the writer's opponent.
2. It magnifies the writer's points and minimizes those of the opposition.
3. It puts the audience in the proper mood.
4. It refreshes the memory of the audience by summarizing the main points of the argument.

Most conclusions do recapitulate the main points, or at least the central thesis, of the discourse. The other three possible tasks are less concrete. Although the conclusion tends to be the most obviously emotional of all the sections, the use of *pathos* (emotional appeal) in written assignments is a dangerous technique for beginners, in whose hands it can all too easily degenerate into *bathos* (laughable emotional appeal). The best conclusions restate or expand their main points and then sign off gracefully with a stylistic flourish that signals the end of the discourse.

Using the Four-Part Arrangement in the Classroom

Although the four-part arrangement gives more direction to an essay than does the three-part arrangement, it is not as adaptable to different sorts of discourse. The four-part pattern generally demands subject-directed, nonpersonal writing that can support an argumentative thesis. For an essay with such an arrangement, students usually need several days in which to conceptualize and investigate their subjects. They will also need to apply techniques of invention or conduct research on their subjects before writing their first drafts. Some teachers prefer to provide the subjects on which their students are to write four-part essays, at least in the beginning, because this arrangement works best when applied to rigidly defined questions.

You may want to assign subjects that support several different argumentative theses. You can decide whether to begin with a question involving actions in the past (a forensic question) or one involving future policy (a deliberative question). Here are some possible forensic and deliberative topics:

Forensic Topics

- The 2012 Department of Justice decision to no longer defend Section 3 of DOMA (the Defense of Marriage Act, signed into law by President Clinton in 1996, defining marriage as the legal union between a man and woman)
- Law schools' objections to military recruiters on campus
- The role of school soda and candy vending machines in the increased rate of childhood obesity

Deliberative Topics

- Should the federal government institute a national identification-card system?
- Is mandatory recycling good for the state?
- Should all undergraduates be required to have proficiency in a foreign language?

Obviously, deliberative topics change as the issues of the day change. Current campus controversies make excellent topics.

While students can certainly master the forms in a week, that amount of time does not allow for a topic to be thoroughly researched. You may want to overlook the generalizations and the abstract, vague arguments your students make while they learn to apply the four parts of the arrangement. You can also give them some peer-response group work that reinforces what they are learning about arrangement.

After your students complete their first drafts of the four-part essay assignment, ask them to join their peer-response groups and read one another's drafts. Have them evaluate each other's drafts by asking the questions listed in Example 7.2. Many teachers like to drift among the peer-response groups as they work and remind students that any form must be adapted to its content. To help students adapt form to content, you may want to talk with students individually while the groups are meeting.

Example 7.2   **PEER-RESPONSE QUESTIONS FOR THE FIRST DRAFT OF A FOUR-PART ESSAY**

Introduction

- Do the first several sentences attract my interest?
- Is the subject clearly defined in the introduction?
- Is the introduction too long?
- Who is the audience?
- Do I want to know more, to keep reading? Why or why not?

Statement of Fact

- Does this section clearly explain the nature of the problem or situation?
- Is there anything not told that I need to know?
- Does the problem or situation continue to interest me?

Confirmation

- Is the argument convincing?
- Does the order of presentation seem reasonable?
- Has any obvious argument been left out?
- Has the opposing position been competently refuted?

Conclusion

- Has the case been summarized well?
- Do I feel well-disposed toward the writer? Why or why not?
- Does the ending seem graceful?

After the groups complete their discussions and evaluations of the draft essays, ask the students to submit typed copies of their essays. You may want to distribute copies of the essays (without the student writers' names) and review with the class the strengths and weaknesses of each argument. Often students will volunteer drafts of their essays for class review if they know they can remain anonymous.

The more that students know about the formal qualities of the four-part form and what is successful in argument, the easier it will be for them to write their next essays.

The Six-Part Arrangement

The classical oration form used by Cicero and Quintilian was a four-part form, but the Latin rhetoricians went on to divide the second part into narration (otherwise known as statement of facts) and division (or partition). They also divided the third part, the confirmation, into confirmation and refutation. Cicero said that "the aim of confirmation is to prove our own case and that of refutation (*reprehensio*) is to refute the case of our opponents" (337). Thus, one version of classical oration looks like this:

1. *Exordium,* or introduction
2. *Narratio,* or statement of facts
3. *Divisio,* or partition or division
4. *Confirmatio,* or proof of the case
5. *Reprehensio,* or refutation of opposing arguments
6. *Peroratio* (or *conclusio*), or conclusion

whereas my writer's Reviewers?

Setting off the refutation in its own section is not a meaningful change from the four-part arrangement, since the confirmation of the four-part essay can also be refutative. Still, a separate section of refutation makes the task of dealing with opposing arguments mandatory; hence, it can provide more structure for an essay. This section also provides an opportunity for the writer or speaker to consider opposing arguments and to make a concession or two. Although the refutation does not always present the writer's own positive arguments, it usually does—that is, unless the opposing arguments are so powerful or so well accepted that the audience would not listen to an opposing confirmation without first being prepared by the refutation.

Corbett tells us that refutation is based on *appeals to reason, emotional appeals, ethical or personal appeals* of the writer, or *wit.* Refutation can usually be accomplished in one of two ways: (1) the writer denies the truth of one of the premises on which the opposing argument is built; or (2) the writer objects to the inferences drawn by the opposition from premises that cannot be broken down.

Hugh Blair, in his influential book *Lectures on Rhetoric and Belles-Lettres,* published in 1783, offers a slightly different version of the six-part arrangement. Blair's arrangement was largely influenced by the classical theorists, but Blair was also a practitioner of pulpit oratory. Hence, his arrangement shows both classical and sermonic elements. His discourse model is composed of these six elements:

1. exordium, or introduction
2. statement and division of the subject
3. narration, or explication
4. reasoning, or arguments
5. pathetic or emotional part
6. conclusion (341)

In this breakdown, the introduction captures the attention of the audience, renders the reader benevolent, and so on. Like some of the classical theorists, Blair distinguishes two sorts of introductions: the *principium,* a direct opening addressed to well-disposed audiences, and the *insinuatio,* a subtler method that prepares a hostile audience for arguments counter to its opinions.

The *insinuatio* generally opens by first admitting the most powerful points made by the opposition, by showing how the writer holds the same views as the audience on general philosophical questions, or by dealing with ingrained audience prejudices. The *principium* can proceed with the knowledge that the audience is sympathetic, going directly to the task of rendering readers attentive.

In Blair's arrangement, as in the three-part arrangement, the thesis is clearly stated at the end of the introduction, but here the thesis is immediately followed by the "division," or announcement of the plan of the essay, which is Blair's first large departure from the four-part essay. Both the statement and the division should be short and succinct. According to Blair, the division should avoid "unnecessary multiplication of heads" (Golden and Corbett 114). In other words, it should contain as simple an outline as possible, presented in a natural, non-mechanistic fashion.

The next two sections, "narration" and "reasoning," correspond to the statement of fact and the confirmation in the four-part essay. However, Blair's model then proposes that a new division of arrangement, termed the pathetic part, follow the argumentation section. The word *pathetic* in this case refers to the emotional appeal of classical rhetoric. Thus, after presenting an argument, the writer would appeal to the audience's feelings; in addition, the writer would begin to draw the discourse to a close.

Following the pathetic part of this six-part form is the conclusion, which is similar to the conclusion presented in the less-detailed arrangements discussed earlier in the chapter.

Using the Six-Part Arrangement in the Classroom

For the advanced or honors student, this more detailed form is profitable and is best taught as an extension of the four-part essay. Teachers who provide advanced students with a more complex arrangement often find that the students are unwilling to go back to the less-detailed structure and its larger burden of decision. Often teachers present the six-part arrangement, spending time on the four-part structure and then progressing to the classical oration and Blair's arrangement. Each successive structure subsumes those that precede it.

Because your students will probably need more time to think through and develop their argumentative essays than they will need for any other type of discourse, your choice for this assignment is paramount. Even when they understand the argumentative arrangement, students cannot assemble their essays overnight. The forensic and deliberative topics mentioned earlier can be profitably applied to these arrangements. But by the time you have reached the stage of teaching these forms, it is often close to the end of the term, and students will be able to choose their own topics. Having been led through the four-part form, they know which topics can be well argued and which will present problems. Sometimes, however, the class will need to work together, coming up with and developing topics for stumped classmates.

To familiarize your students with the soon-to-be-assigned form, you may want to hand out a model of the form. You will want to exemplify as well as introduce each element in a new argument. Some teachers elicit an argumentative subject from the class and then, with the class, outline the course of that argument on the board. Students often have strong ideas of how one specific form of arrangement best suits a particular argument. Working together in this way is the best practice you can give your students.

OTHER PATTERNS OF ARRANGEMENT

Arrangements for Rhetorical Methods

In the 1970s, rhetorical theorist Frank J. D'Angelo, in *A Conceptual Theory of Rhetoric*, isolated what he considered to be the ten most common patterns of arrangement: narration, process analysis, cause-effect, description, definition, analysis, classification, exemplification, comparison, and analogy. He then presented each in the form of a model or fixed outline that students could use as a plan for essays of their own. Other rhetoricians, too, have listed and dealt with some of these patterns of arrangement — indeed, insofar as they recapitulate the classical topics, they can be said to go back to Aristotle. Many textbooks, in fact, are organized according to "patterns of exposition," "modes," or "rhetorical methods." In her rhetorically arranged textbook, *Making Sense,* Cheryl Glenn explores in depth the "nine rhetorical methods everyone uses to make sense of the world" and argues that we use these methods as powerful tools for understanding and creating the kinds of texts and images we encounter every day (iii). Instead of prescribing fixed outlines for arrangement, Glenn offers guidance for organizing texts that make use of such rhetorical methods as narration, description, exemplification, classification and division, comparison and contrast, process analysis, cause-and-effect analysis, definition, and argument. What follows is a condensed version of the principles of arrangement that Glenn details, including guidance for helping writers achieve their purposes, even as they anticipate their readers' needs. These patterns of arrangement can be used both for paragraphs and whole essays.

Arrangement for Narrative   Glenn notes that most narratives follow a chronological order, often building to a climax and then making or reaffirming a point or lesson (61). Yet she also discusses variations to strict chronological order in writing narratives, such as using flashbacks, "a glimpse of the past that illuminates the present," or flashforwards, "a technique that takes readers to future events" (62). She also reaffirms the importance of guiding readers through the use of transitional words and phrases — such as *first, then,* and *next* — and appropriate verb tense (63).

Arrangement for Description   Three methods for arranging descriptive essays include a "spatial organizational pattern, with the details arranged according to their location," a chronological pattern, and an emphatic pattern, in which details are arranged in order of importance (Glenn 137–38). Because sensory details are central to description, point of view — what Glenn defines as "the assumed eye and mind of the writer" — is important to both spatial and chronological order. Glenn also suggests that students keep their audiences in mind as they write descriptions, considering "an order that reflects the audience's physical or mental point of view" rather than their own, moving from most familiar (to the reader) to least familiar, from most remote (from the reader) to closest, from least persuasive (to the reader) to most persuasive (138). You can also remind students that photographs and other kinds of images can help suggest an organizational format, guiding the writer and visually grounding the reader.

Arrangement for Exemplification   In exemplification, each paragraph must be related to the thesis or generalization, and examples must be organized in a purposeful order (emphatically or chronologically, for example), an order that makes the connections both between each example and in relation to the thesis clear (Glenn 220).

Arrangement for Classification and Division   When classifying and dividing, the purpose and thesis statement determine arrangement. The organization might be chronological, emphatic ("starting with the least important category or part and ending with the most important — which could be the largest, the most complex, the most entertaining, or the most persuasive"), or logical (Glenn 285). In any case, students should use details to provide balance, topic sentences and transitional words to provide clarity, and a strong conclusion to explain the importance of the classification and division (285).

Arrangement for Comparison and Contrast   Writers doing comparisons and contrasts usually organize their texts in one of two ways: either by making "a point-by-point case" for each subject individually or by comparing and contrasting each corresponding point of each subject (one point rather than one subject at a time) (Glenn 353).

Arrangement for Process Analysis   As Glenn observes, "a process analysis is presented as a chronological sequence of actions or steps," usually in a fixed order, in which the steps and the results are consistent (415). Generally, the writer includes every step in the process, unless readers already know — or don't need to know — particular steps. As in other rhetorical methods, necessary details and transitions are significant in a process analysis.

Arrangement for Cause-and-Effect Analysis   One possibility for opening a cause-and-effect essay is to begin "with a description of the event or situation" to be analyzed and then to introduce the thesis, which should explain whether the writer will focus on causes, consequences, or both (Glenn 478). After the introduction, there are various options for arrangement: narrating the causes and effects in chronological or reverse chronological order — or, alternately, ordering "the causes emphatically, from least to most important" (479). Depending on the material students are working with, either of these arrangements can be effective, so long as the order remains consistent and the conclusion is strong, perhaps revealing the larger or long-term implications.

Arrangement for Definition   While there is no fixed organization for writing definitions, like that in any other essay the arrangement must be tied to the writer's purpose — in this case either informing or persuading. The writer must first establish a "definition for the term or concept and then support [that] definition by using examples, descriptions, comparisons and contrasts, narratives, or another method of development" (Glenn 580). Finally, the writer must conclude in a way that will help readers decide what to do with the information the writer has offered.

Arrangement for Argument   Much of the information presented so far in this chapter has been geared toward writing effective arguments. Whether using a three-part arrangement or a more detailed format, students should make a clear and supportable claim; balance appeals to reason, character, and emotion; and avoid logical fallacies. What Glenn adds to these traditional expectations is the potential power of images to enhance logical, ethical, and pathetic appeals. The placement of such images — and how they are introduced and explained — can provide strong support for a well-developed argument.

   As you teach arrangements for the rhetorical methods, note that many of the arrangement strategies overlap and that, although neither the methods for developing nor the ways of organizing texts are discrete, they still remain useful.

Arrangements for Creative Nonfiction Essays

If you're asking students to write personal or lyric essays, there are many patterns of arrangement available to them. Narration, description, and comparison-contrast are all common rhetorical methods of developing creative nonfiction, and their patterns of arrangement provide useful starting places. But just as writers of creative nonfiction can rarely depend on one method of development, neither can they depend on one discrete pattern of arrangement to fulfill their writing purposes. One method or pattern is simply too restrictive for the more amorphous essay form. Thus, many of the very best creative nonfiction essays draw from several patterns.

Though many students will have experience writing traditional narratives in which the narration follows a chronological arrangement, they often need to learn additional techniques in order to imagine new ways of structuring their material to achieve a particular effect. Lyric essays, for example — although they may contain narrative sections — almost always move away from a strict chronological arrangement. An arrangement common to both lyric and narrative essays is association. As Lunsford notes in *The St. Martin's Handbook*, "associational organization is common in personal narrative, where writers can use a chain of associations to render an experience vividly for readers" (60). Personal narrative, too, comes in many forms — each with various options for arrangement.

In "Collage, Montage, Mosaic, Vignette, Episode, Segment," Robert L. Root Jr. introduces teachers to some of the terminology related to various forms of personal essays and options for arrangement in creative nonfiction. He acknowledges that the terminology is not fixed: What Root refers to as the "segmented essay" (a piece written in loosely connected sections, rather than chronological narrative) is what Peter Elbow calls a "collage essay." Root points to additional terms and adjectives suggested by contemporary authors: Rebecca Blevins Faery uses the adjectives "fragmented" and "polyphonic" to describe a similar form, and Carl Klaus suggests the term "disjunctive" (362). Still another option is "mosaics," Mark Rudman's term for patterned essays (363). Mosaics — like Elbow's collage — suggest a visual metaphor, which might help students imagine a form that creates a larger picture or effect by using many smaller parts or sections. (For examples and further discussion of these types of essays, see DePeter; Elbow's "Your Cheatin' Art: A Collage" in *Everyone Can Write*; and Fontaine and Quaas, cited at the end of this chapter.)

Using Arrangements for Creative Nonfiction Essays in the Classroom

One advantage to teaching segmented essays is that choosing an arrangement that differs from a traditional linear form can help students think about — and even understand — their experiences in a new way. Just as a collage or mosaic is organized according to patterns of color and shape to create an overall effect, so too can an essay be organized by the emotional color or shape of a series of related experiences. The essay can also be shaped around an idea or abstraction (fear or comfort, for instance), an object or image related to an idea (such as Susan Griffin's "Red Shoes"), or a memory and reflection on one's telling of the story (Patricia Hampl's "Memory and Imagination" provides a fitting example).

Such essays provide interesting opportunities for revision as well. If you can move students away from an attachment to linear narrative (the too familiar

"This is how it happened, so I can't change it"), they will begin to see and talk about the important effects of arrangement. Students can literally cut up (disassemble) their essays and move the various sections around to create different movements.

A danger of such forms is that, if they're not done well or if the audience for such essays has expectations for a more traditionally arranged piece, they can lose readers. The connections between sections are often intuitive and associational, and providing clues for readers can sometimes be difficult for less experienced writers. There are, however, certain patterns of arrangement with which many readers will be familiar. In a slightly different format, Root offers the strategies for arrangement listed in Box 7.3.

An additional means of helping students imagine alternate ways of arranging essays is to lead a discussion on the organization of their favorite movies or television shows. Although these shows are now in syndication, many students will be familiar with *Seinfeld* and *Friends,* for example, sitcoms that often have two or three seemingly independent stories in each episode but then tie the stories together (often through irony and humor) in a final scene. Or they might be familiar with more recent shows such as *Lost,* which makes use of nonlinear narratives by including more than one story line set in different times, or *Damages,* which uses flashforwards by beginning with a crime scene and then going back in time. Students will also be able to recall movies that use flashbacks or ones that show the same scene or situation from several different perspectives. For instance, in *Dead Man Walking,* viewers watch Susan Sarandon's character (Sister Helen Prejean) try to make sense of a crime through a series of flashbacks, and each flashback is revised as she learns more of what really

---

Box 7.3 **ARRANGEMENT STRATEGIES FOR CREATIVE NONFICTION ESSAYS**

Juxtaposition — arranging one item alongside another item so that they comment back and forth on one another

Parallelism — alternating or intertwining one continuous strand with another (present/past tense)

Patterning — choosing an extraliterary design and arranging literary segments accordingly (Root uses Nancy Willard's "The Friendship Tarot," in which Willard uses tarot cards as an organizational guide, as an example)

Accumulation — arranging a series of segments or scenes or episodes so that they add or enrich or alter meaning with each addition

Journaling — writing in episodes or reconstructing the journal experience in drafts (Root 367)

happened. _Memento_ employs reverse chronology in order to show the perspective of a man suffering from short-term memory loss. _Eternal Sunshine of the Spotless Mind_ and _Pulp Fiction_ also make use of nonlinear narrative; students will be able to provide many other examples. Though you and your students may not have seen all the same films or television shows, through discussion you can come up with specific patterns of arrangement that are repeatedly used in popular culture. And students can use similar patterns of arrangement in their own essays.

An Exercise for Linking Invention and Arrangement

The following exercise will help students recognize important connections between invention and arrangement strategies. Since the arrangement of creative nonfiction prose is often — though not always — associational, clustering is an effective invention technique (see Chapter 6 for more on clustering). Ask students to create a cluster from a word that might call up physical, metaphorical, experiential, and visual associations. The word _cold,_ for instance, might work well. Depending on their experiences and associations, clusters might include any of the following: _snow, ice, steel, sneeze, stare, chill, shiver, goosebumps, frost._ The cluster might also include places or people. Have students choose five of the words from their clusters that are most suggestive to them; they may choose one branch of the cluster or words from several different branches.

Next, ask students to use each of the five words as a different section heading, using white space to separate each segment, and to write a short vignette under each word. One vignette might be a memory, another might be a character sketch of an especially "cold" person, another might be a philosophical reflection on ice, and still another might be a description of goosebumps. The sense of coldness will provide overall coherence to the essay, and the associations students make through repeating imagery of coldness will enhance cohesion.

After writing this piece, students will have created a segmented essay. They can now try a word of their own choosing as the center word for their cluster and the organizational center of their essay. They can include as many sections as they desire in their next piece, and they can experiment with different patterns of arrangement in organizing their material.

Arrangement and Multimodal Writing

Like creative nonfiction essays, many other forms of writing — especially writing for the Web — require nonlinear forms of arrangement, or even if the arrangement appears to be linear, readers may be invited by the use of hyperlinks to read in a nonlinear fashion. Collin Gifford Brooke, in _Lingua Fracta: Toward a Rhetoric of New Media,_ sees arrangement as _pattern_ rather than _sequence_ (92). Most writing for the Web — from blog entries to social media updates to articles that embed hyperlinks — depends on more than the sequence of ideas. Such writing also depends on images, color, headings, subheadings, key words, spacing, repetition, links to sources, and an organization in which key information can be taken in quickly, since many readers scan information online rather than reading slowly and carefully. (For more on the ways in which "computer technologies heighten our awareness of the visuality of texts" (59), see Anne Frances Wysocki's "awaywithwords: On the Possibilities in Unavailable Designs" in Part III of this text.)

Considering Arrangement for New Media in the Classroom

One way of helping students consider arrangement for new media in the classroom is to show them three or four examples of Web pages — ones that are arranged effectively and ones that are not. (If you prefer, ask students to suggest examples.) As a class, analyze the examples, having students list what makes a page effective or ineffective in terms of arrangement. For example, perhaps an ineffective page has no headings, subheadings, or images and requires a lot of scrolling. As your students analyze particular pages, be sure to remind them to consider such rhetorical concerns as audience, purpose, and topic — and how these concerns affect arrangement.

TECHNIQUES OF EDITING AND PLANNING

Much of this chapter addresses methods of arrangement that are "transcendent"; that is, they prefigure the essays patterned on them. Some rhetoricians call these arrangements generative, on the theory that form can help generate content. Some of the prescriptive arrangements we have seen are fairly flexible, but many teachers distrust the idea of prescriptive or transcendent arrangements. Rather than using preexisting arrangements, such teachers subscribe to the organic model of composition, one in which invention, arrangement, and style are informed by writers' perceptions of their subject, purpose, and audience. Most mature writers do compose organically, but it can be argued that they do so because they have completely internalized prescriptive forms. In any case, many teachers continue to offer students section-by-section prescriptive arrangements; otherwise, they may feel they have little more to offer than vague maxims: "organize your points clearly," "strive for unity, order, and coherence," and "don't ramble or digress."

As a teacher, you *can* offer students sound advice without being prescriptive. Following are some techniques for editing and rearranging sections.

Using the Outline in the Classroom

Outlines can be used successfully as an editorial or revision technique rather than as a tool for generating and arranging material initially. After all, writing is an epistemological tool, and composition researchers are proving that writing is a way of knowing. As the famous E. M. Forster quotation goes, "How can I know what I think until I see what I say?"

Many successful writers draw up an ordered list of topics before they write, but the list is more note-taking for possibilities than it is any kind of set plan. Many teachers, therefore, suggest that their students turn to ordering lists or brainstorming lists for the generative part of the composing process, and then use outlines in the editing stage of composition.

The two most useful sorts of outlines for composition are the *topic outline* and its more complex sibling, the *topic-sentence outline*. The topic outline, as its name suggests, is a listing of the sections of the proposed essay, its topics and their subtopics, with a key word or a short clause attached to each letter or number as a designation of content. For the topic-sentence outline, the writer creates a topic sentence for each paragraph in the proposed essay and orders these topic sentences as the topics and subtopics of the essay; thus the major and minor ideas of the essay can be ranked according to their importance or the writer's purpose.

As you may imagine, this second sort of outline is extremely difficult to create beforehand. Yet both these outlines can be turned around and written after the first draft of the essay has been completed. What were once devices for creating frustration can become easily usable and illuminating tools for editing. If your students have initial difficulties coming up with outlines for their own work, you can ask them to create an outline from a text written by someone else. A possible topic outline to use as an example could be extrapolated from William Zinsser's "College Pressures," which uses methods of classification and division and cause and effect. For the purpose of this example, we focus mainly on classification, though cause and effect will become evident in the expansion of the topic outline:

- Introduction — four kinds of pressures
- Classification 1: economic pressure
- Classification 2: parental pressure
- Classification 3: peer pressure
- Classification 4: self-induced pressure
- Conclusion — four kinds of pressures

From this simple topic outline, each idea can be expanded into a topic sentence:

- There are four types of pressures that university students face.
- Because of economic pressures, students pursue safe subjects and high grades rather than intellectual curiosity.
- Parental pressures often lead students to pursue careers that offer prestige and money rather than personal fulfillment.
- Competition with classmates raises the bar, and students feel compelled to do more.
- As a result of heightened competition, students put too much pressure on themselves.
- All these pressures combined can cause students a great deal of anxiety.

Though both the simple topic outline and the expanded sentence outline are based on a reading of Zinsser's essay, after working through the process, students will be ready to create outlines of their own essays. Example 7.3 will walk you through the steps.

Example 7.3 **HELPING STUDENTS CREATE AN OUTLINE OF A DRAFT ESSAY**

After your students complete their first drafts using one of the forms of arrangement (either one covered in this chapter or one proceeding intuitively), ask them to draw up an outline of the paragraphs in their drafts. Do not insist on sets and subsets at this point; merely suggest a numbered list, each number representing a paragraph. After each number, the student should write a short sentence summarizing the paragraph.

After each paragraph has been thus represented and charted, each student will have what is in essence a map of the argument of the essay. At this point, have students meet in peer-response groups to exchange lists and discuss them for ten minutes or so. Questions to be asked about each list include the following:

1. Are there any paragraphs or topics that don't seem to relate well to the development of the subject?
2. Is there anything that should be cut?
3. Might one or several paragraphs work better in another position in the essay?
4. Is there any important part of the essay that seems to be missing?

After writing and discussing their outlines, students will have a much clearer idea of what changes need to be made in the paragraph arrangement of a rough draft. Generally, adding a few paragraphs and cutting or rearranging a few others will be the result, yielding a much more conscientiously organized final draft. The practice that the students will get in paragraph-level transitions is an extra bonus.

The same sort of after-the-fact outlining can also be done using the simpler topic outline, but the sentence outline produces clearer realizations about what the writer is saying as the argument proceeds.

Using Winterowd's "Grammar of Coherence" Technique in the Classroom

In "The Grammar of Coherence," W. Ross Winterowd argues that beyond the sentence level—that is, at the level of paragraphs and essay-units (what Willis Pitkin calls "discourse blocs")—*transitions* control coherence (830). Form and coherence, says Winterowd, are synonymous at the paragraph and discourse-bloc level, and we perceive coherence as consistent relationships among transitions. Thus, recognizing and controlling these transitional relationships are important skills for students, and the editorial technique that can promote them is implicit in Winterowd's discussion.

Winterowd identifies seven transitional relationships among parts of an essay (see Box 7.4). The application of knowledge of these seven relationships can help students order the parts of their essays. Winterowd suggests that this list of transitional relationships can be used for many generative and analytic purposes, but here we examine it as a tool for maintaining coherence among the parts of an essay.

To use this list for maintaining coherence, first introduce your students to the transitional concepts, using illustrative handouts. Winterowd suggests that these concepts are much more easily illustrated than defined or explained, especially for beginning writers. A look through any readily available anthology of essays will usually provide good material for examples. Choose blocks of two or three paragraphs—the shorter the better. After talking for a few minutes about the transitional relationships in the examples, ask students to do a short imitation exercise, copying the transitional form of several of the examples while substituting their own content. The next step is to go directly to the anthology and work orally on the transitional links between paragraphs. By this time, students should be able to manipulate the terms fairly confidently.

After the imitation exercise has been completed, ask students to bring to class one of the essays they have already written and had evaluated. Then ask them to go over the essay, marking each paragraph as it relates to the previous one. Each paragraph will be marked *alternativity, causativity,* and so forth. After

---

Box 7.4 **WINTEROWD'S SEVEN TRANSITIONAL RELATIONSHIPS**

Coordination: expressed by the terms *and, furthermore, too, in addition, also, again*

Obversativity: expressed by *but, yet, however, on the other hand*

Causativity: expressed by *for, because, as a result*

Conclusativity: expressed by *so, therefore, thus, for this reason*

Alternativity: expressed by *or*

Inclusativity: expressed by a colon

Sequentiality: expressed by *first . . . second . . . third, earlier . . . later, and so forth*

the imitation practice, this task is not as hard as it sounds; most students will see the transitional relationships fairly easily. There will, of course, be the occasional mystery paragraph, which students can discuss with a friend or with the entire class. This exercise provides students with an immediate method for analyzing their essays for coherence and for learning to strike or regroup selected paragraphs that have no observable relation to the surrounding paragraphs.

After having practiced this exercise on finished essays, your students should be ready to use the method on rough drafts of in-progress essays. Winterowd's system works well for checking arrangements already generated. You may want to ask your students to work in writing groups to check one another's essays for transitional relationships between paragraphs. Although essays with clear transitions between paragraphs and between blocks of discourse may have other problems, they will generally be coherent. Continually using this method in c ass will help students gain an intuitive grasp of transitions that will prove benef ial in the drafting process.

WORKS CITED

Aristotle. *Poetics.* Trans. S. H. Butcher. *Criticism: The Major Texts.* Ed. W. J. Bate. New York: Harcourt, 1970. Print.

——. *Rhetoric.* Trans. Rhys Roberts. New York: Modern Library, 1954. Print.

Baker, Sheridan. *The Practical Stylist.* 3rd ed. New York: Crowell, 1969. Print.

Blair, Hugh. *Lectures on Rhetoric and Belles-Lettres.* 1783. Philadelphia: Zell, 1866. Print.

Brooke, Collin Gifford. *Lingua Fracta: Toward a Rhetoric of New Media.* New York: Hampton P, 2009. Print.

Burke, Kenneth. *Counter-Statement.* Los Altos: Hermes, 1953. Print.

Cicero. *De Partitione Oratoria.* Trans. H. Rackham. London: Heinemann, 1960. Print.

Corbett, Edward P. J. *Classical Rhetoric for the Modern Student.* 3rd ed. New York: Oxford UP, 1990. Print.

Corbett, Edward P. J., and Robert J. Connors. *Classical Rhetoric for the Modern Student.* 4th ed. New York: Oxford UP, 1999. Print.

D'Angelo, Frank J. *A Conceptual Theory of Rhetoric.* Cambridge: Winthrop, 1975. Print.

——. *Process and Thought in Composition.* Cambridge: Winthrop, 1977. Print.

DePeter, Ronald A. "Fractured Narratives: Explorations in Style." *Elements of Alternate Style.* Ed. Wendy Bishop. Portsmouth: Boynton/Cook, 1997. 26–34. Print.

Elbow, Peter. *Everyone Can Write.* New York: Oxford UP, 2000. Print.

Faery, Rebecca Blevins. "Text and Context: The Essay and the Politics of Disjunctive Form." *What Do I Know? Reading, Writing, and Teaching the Essay.* Ed. Janis Forman. Portsmouth: Boynton/Cook, 1996. 55–68. Print.

Fontaine, Sheryl I., and Francie Quaas. "Transforming Connections and Building Bridges: Assigning Reading, and Evaluating the Collage Essay." *Teaching Writing Creatively.* Ed. David Starkey. Portsmouth: Boynton/Cook, 1998. 111–25. Print.

Glenn, Cheryl. *Making Sense.* 3rd ed. Boston: Bedford, 2010. Print.

Golden, James, and Edward P. J. Corbett. *The Rhetoric of Blair, Campbell, and Whately.* Carbondale: Southern Illinois UP, 1990. Print.

Griffin, Susan. *The Eros of Everyday Life.* New York: Doubleday, 1995. Print.

Hall, Donald. *Writing Well.* 2nd ed. Boston: Little, 1976. Print.

Hampl, Patricia. "Memory and Imagination." *The Fourth Genre.* Ed. Robert L. Root Jr. and Michael Steinberg. Boston: Allyn, 1999. 297–305. Print.

Klaus, Carl. "Excursions of the Mind: Toward a Poetics of Uncertainty in the Disjunctive Essay." *What Do I Know? Reading, Writing, and Teaching the Essay.* Ed. Janis Forman. Portsmouth: Boynton/Cook, 1996. 39–53. Print.

Larson, Richard. "Structure and Form in Non-Fiction Prose." *Teaching Composition: Twelve Bibliographic Essays.* Ed. Gary Tate. 2nd ed. Fort Worth: Texas Christian UP, 1987. 45–72. Print.

Lunsford, Andrea A. *The St. Martin's Handbook.* 7th ed. Boston: Bedford, 2011. Print.

Pitkin, Willis. "Discourse Blocs." *CCC* 20.2 (1969): 138–48. Print.

Root, Robert L., Jr. "Collage, Montage, Mosaic, Vignette, Episode, Segment." *The Fourth Genre.* Ed. Robert L. Root Jr. and Michael Steinberg. Boston: Allyn, 1999. 358–68. Print.

Rudman, Mark. "Mosaic on Walking." *The Best American Essays 1991.* Ed. Joyce Carol Oates. Boston: Ticknor and Fields, 1991. 138–53. Print.

Whately, Richard. *Elements of Rhetoric.* 6th ed. London: Fellowes, 1841. Print.

Willard, Nancy. "The Friendship Tarot." *Between Friends.* Ed. Mickey Pearlman. Boston: Houghton, 1994. 195–203. Print.

Winterowd, W. Ross. "The Grammar of Coherence." *CE* 31.8 (1970): 828–35. Print.

Wysocki, Anne Frances. "awaywithwords: On the Possibilities in Unavailable Designs." *Computers and Composition* 22.1 (2005): 55–62. Print.

Zinsser, William. "College Pressures." *Blair and Ketchum's Country Journal* 6.4 (1979): n. pag. Print.

——. *On Writing Well.* 3rd ed. New York: Harper, 1985. Print.

8

Teaching Style

> One thing I try to convey to students about style, beyond discussions of grammar
> and usage, is that style is formed through clarity and attitude. One must be willing
> to take and convey a stance through language choices, tone, punctuation, references,
> subtlety, etc., because to convey a stance responsibly is to explore the possibilities of
> language — known and unknown — available within and across current systems of
> expression. To do this in a way that is comprehensible to others is the epitome of
> style, or as rap artists might say dopeness.
>
> —DAVID F. GREEN JR.

Once considered little more than the study of schemes, tropes, and rhetorical
flourishes, style has become one of the most important canons of rhetoric — at
least, Edward P. J. Corbett tells us, if success is measured by the sheer number
of works published ("Approaches" 83). Besides Corbett, who has written a classic
work on stylistic analysis, other scholars have taken the study of style into the
realms of poetry, creative nonfiction, and other forms of literary writing. Style
also lurks behind much contemporary deconstructive and reader-response literary criticism, and cultural critics have considered the socioeconomic ramifications of style and revision, deepening our understanding of the connections
among style, substance, and meaning along historical as well as contemporary
continua. Lisa Ede, Cheryl Glenn, and Andrea Lunsford, in an article that explores
connections between feminism and rhetoric, define style as "the material embodiment of the relationships among self, text, and world" (423). One goal of teaching style in your writing classes is to help students explore these relationships
through writing.

Style, in other words, is not just "style." All composition teachers can benefit
from a background in stylistics, and one of the easiest ways to obtain such a
background is to borrow the duality that W. Ross Winterowd creates in *Contemporary Rhetoric*. Winterowd divides the study of style into two areas: *theoretical
stylistics*, concerned primarily with the nature and existence of style, the application of stylistic criteria to literary studies, and the linguistic attributes of
different styles; and *pedagogic stylistics*, which deals with the problem of teaching
students to recognize and develop styles in their own writing (252). This chapter
deals almost completely with works on pedagogic stylistics, which are far fewer
in number than works in the fascinating — but not always classroom-practical —
field of theoretical stylistics. (For more on the history of style, see Chapter 1,
"The History of an Idea," in Ben Yagoda's *The Sound on the Page*, cited at the end of
this chapter.)

STYLE: THEORY AND PEDAGOGIC PRACTICE

Milic's Three Theories of Style

Perhaps the central theoretical problem presented by the study of style is the question of whether style as an entity really exists. Is it, as Chatman and Levin claim, "the totality of impressions which a literary work produces," or is it merely "sundry and ornamental linguistic devices" tacked on to a given content-meaning (*Literary Style* 337–38)? There is no agreement at all on this question among the foremost theorists of style in our time, yet all writing teachers must answer this question for themselves before they can decide on a teaching method.

Three distinct views of the nature of style have emerged, says the eminent theorist Louis T. Milic, who identifies and describes these views in "Theories of Style and Their Implications for the Teaching of Composition" (126). Milic's first theory, given the daunting name *Crocean aesthetic monism,* is based on the critical theories of twentieth-century Italian philosopher Benedetto Croce. Milic writes that Crocean aesthetic monism, the most modern theory of style,

> is an organic view which denies the possibility of any separation between content and form. Any discussion of style in Croce's view is useless and irrelevant, for the work or art (the composition) is a unified whole, with no seam between meaning and style. ("Theories" 67)

In Crocean theory, then, the sentences *John gave me the book* and *The book was given to me by John* have different semantic meanings as well as different syntactic forms. *passive v. active*

The second theory is what Milic calls *individualist* or *psychological monism* and is best summed up by the famous aphorism of the French naturalist Georges de Buffon, *"Le style c'est l'homme même,"* usually translated as "Style is the man." Psychological monism holds that a writer cannot help writing the way he does for that is the dynamic expression of his personality. This theory claims that no writer can truly imitate another's style, for no two life experiences are the same; it further holds that the main formative influences on writers are their education and their reading ("Typology of Styles" 442). Both the psychological and the Crocean theories are monisms in that they perceive style and content as a unity, inseparable from each other, either because different locutions say different things or because an individual's style is her habitual and consistent selection from the expressive resources available in language, which is not consciously amendable to any great degree.

The third theory of style, and the one most applicable to teaching, is what Milic calls the *theory of ornate form,* or *rhetorical dualism.* The assumption behind rhetorical dualism is that "ideas exist wordlessly and can be dressed in a variety of outfits depending on the need or the occasion" ("Theories" 67). As the critic Michael Riffaterre puts it, "Style is understood as an emphasis (expressive, affective, or aesthetic) added to the information conveyed by the linguistic structure, without alteration of meaning." In other words, "language expresses and style stresses" (443).

Milic points out that the two monisms make the teaching of style a rather hopeless enterprise, since for the Croceans there is no "style," form and content being one, and for the individualists style is an expression of personality, and we cannot expect writers to change their personality. These monisms render all of the resources of rhetoric useless ("Theories" 69). In order to retain options, then, teachers must be dualists, at least to some degree. Although dualistic theory cannot be proved true empirically, it still seems to be the only approach we have to improving students' writing style. If we cannot tell a student that the struggle to find the best words to express an idea is a real struggle, then we cannot teach style at all.

A confessed individualist himself, Milic is aware that dualism must be adopted at least conditionally if we are to teach style. In an important essay, "Rhetorical Choice and Stylistic Option," he tries to resolve the division between his beliefs and the pedagogic options offered by dualism. He argues that most of what we call style is actually the production of a huge unconscious element that he terms the *language-generating mechanism*. This mechanism, processing subconscious choices and operating at a speed that the conscious mind cannot possibly match, creates most of what we call style. After these decisions have been made, an editing process takes over that can make any stylistic changes the author consciously desires.

Milic distinguishes between *stylistic options,* decisions made unconsciously while the language-generating mechanism is proceeding, and *rhetorical choices,* decisions made consciously while the mechanism is at rest. Rhetorical choices, in other words, are an evaluation of what has been intuitively created by the language-generating mechanism, an editorial element that can be practiced consciously and thus something we can teach our students. Of course, certain rhetorical choices can become habits of mind and thus stylistic options. The process of adding to the repertoire of the language-generating mechanism is what we hope to accomplish. Milic thus seems to integrate successfully his roles as theorist and teacher.

In this chapter, then, we focus on rhetorical choices because they are the only elements of style that can be handled consciously. In the realm of pedagogic stylistics, we must keep our discussion at a considerably lower level of abstraction than is characteristic of most of the works mentioned by Corbett in his bibliographic essay "Approaches to the Study of Style." The possibilities of our changing a student's style in ten or fifteen weeks are limited; Milic tells us that the process of learning to write takes a dozen years and must begin much earlier than age eighteen. Style is the hardest canon to teach, linked as it is to reading. Only avid and accomplished readers can generate and perceive style, recognizing it in a contextual continuum. The more models and styles a writer knows or is aware of, the more raw data there are to feed the language-generating mechanism and the more informed are the choices that can be made both intuitively and consciously.

A Pedagogic Focus on Rhetorical Choices

So, how do we teach style? In "Teaching Style: A Possible Anatomy," Winston Weathers mentions several obligatory tasks for those who aim to teach style at the college level. The first task is "making the teaching of style significant and relevant for our students" (144). Many beginning writers view the concept of style with suspicion, as if it were something that only effete snobs should be interested in. Thus, Weathers tells us, it is our task to justify the study of style on the grounds of better communication and as a proof of individuality. Style can be taught as a gesture of personal freedom or as a rebellion against rigid systems of conformist language, rather than as dainty humanism or mere aesthetic luxury.

Students convinced that style is indeed a gesture of personal freedom will invest maximum effort in stylistic concerns. Bill Roorbach, in *Writing Life Stories,* wants students to learn about style by "forgetting about style." He writes:

> In this exercise you are to throw a fit. . . . Break the bass drum of your punctuation with the pedal of your adjectives. Ram your stout verb sticks through your adverbial tom-toms. Nix prolixity. Fling symbols out the windows; listen to the crash. (140)

Of course, this exercise does anything but convince students to forget about style. Rather, it helps students to play with language and interrogate their own preconceived notions of what "style" means.

The second task Weathers mentions is that of revealing style as a measurable and viable subject matter. Style seems vague and mysterious to many beginning writers because they have mostly been exposed to the metaphysical approach to style, in which arbitrarily chosen adjectives are used to identify different styles — the "abrupt," the "tense," the "fast-moving," the "leisurely," and the popular "flowing" styles. As a result of hearing styles described in these nebulous terms, students cannot see how such an amorphous entity might be approached or changed. Therefore, they need to be exposed to the actual components, the nuts and bolts, of style — words, phrases, clauses, sentences, paragraphs — and to the methods of analyzing them before they can begin to use them to control their rhetorical options.

For example, in writing the preceding exercise, Roorbach does not forget about style at all, for the assignment itself is ripe for stylistic analysis. You might ask students first to identify Roorbach's tone (colloquial in most parts; angry or violent, perhaps) and then to consider how he achieves that tone through the rhetorical choices he makes: using short imperative and declarative sentences; starting sentences with monosyllabic, active (not to mention violent) verbs; incorporating metaphors; being attentive to sound (such as the onomatopoeia of "crash" and the near rhyme of "fling symbols out the windows"). Students will quickly see that "getting mad" on the page involves many stylistic choices. As teachers, we have important tools for explaining these stylistic features.

In "A Primer for Teaching Style," Richard Graves tells us that the following four explanatory methods are primary:

1. We can identify the technical name of a particular stylistic feature or concept.
2. We can give a definition or description of the feature.
3. We can provide a schematic description of the feature.
4. We can provide an example or illustration of the feature. (187)

The goals of these methods are recognition and then gradual mastery of the different features. Explanations such as this one can be used in both stylistic analyses and exercises in imitation, the central practical activities described in this chapter. In addition to demonstrating discrete skills, though, every essay a student writes must be informed by certain questions of style. Like the other canons of rhetoric, style must be approached philosophically as well as practically.

Choosing a Rhetorical Stance

The study of style needs to be prefaced by a careful discussion of both the purpose of each piece of writing a student does and the interrelationships among author, subject (work), universe, and audience. M. H. Abrams presents a useful diagram of these elements in *The Mirror and the Lamp* (8).

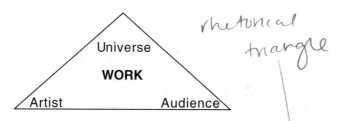

These four elements, based on the rhetorical theory of Aristotle, form a central construct in modern communication theory. Composition teachers use a version of this construct called the *communication triangle* to help students formulate their concepts of the whole rhetorical situation in which they find themselves.

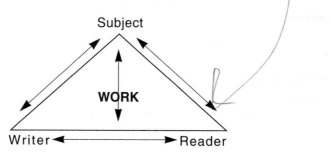

Each of these elements suggests a question that writers must face every time they sit down to write, and a significant factor in each question must necessarily be style. No one factor can predominate in a successful piece of writing, however, and Wayne Booth's famous essay, "The Rhetorical Stance," offers a well-expressed overview of this complexity. The "rhetorical stance" he discusses

> depends on discovering and maintaining in any writing situation a proper balance among the three elements that are at work in any communicative effort: the available arguments about the subject itself, the interests and peculiarities of the audience, and voice, the implied character of the speaker. (74)

A "corruption" of the rhetorical stance, according to Booth, overemphasizes any one of the three elements of the communication triangle of author-audience-subject. Students' compositions are prone to all three sorts of corruptions or imbalances.

One type of imbalance, the *pedant's stance*, occurs when the writer concentrates only on the subject while ignoring the author-audience relationship. This reliance on nothing but subject-based discourse makes the pedant's stance dry and uninteresting. It makes no concessions to a personal voice or to the reader's interest. It is the sort of depersonalized prose that students often think their teachers want to hear. Ken Macrorie's famous term for it is *Engfish,* and it is found in its purest form at a relatively high academic level—as "dissertation style."

> Example: One may observe an attempt at the pedant's stance in this sentence; note how the formal tone distances the reader.

Another sort of imbalance is the *advertiser's stance*, which concentrates on impressing the audience and underplays the subject. This imbalance is not so frequent as the pedant's stance, mainly because only experienced writers will attempt it. Booth tells us that the "advertiser" overvalues pure effect. Student "advertisers" are likely to write directly to the teacher, attempting to charm by using candor, humor, or personal attention—often a novel experience for the teacher.

> Example: Have you ever wondered what the advertiser's stance might look like in a sentence? Sure you have. We all have; haven't we?

Related to the advertiser's stance is the *entertainer's stance,* which "sacrifices substance to personality and charm" (78). An imbalance in favor of the speaker's ethical appeal, this stance is the rarest corruption of the rhetorical stance found in students' essays. Most students are unaware of the methods used by writers to generate ethical appeal; hence, their imbalances are likely to tilt in other directions. Many FY writers were taught in high school never to use *I* in their writing—the key word of the entertainer's stance.

> Example: I want so much to show you what it means to write from an entertainer's stance, but I feel it's far more important to be true to my own voice, my own style.

Booth's questions of rhetorical balance are essential to an understanding of the methods available for the manipulation of stylistic choices. The question

of the relationship between writer and subject is important, but more central
to students' understanding of style will be the question of their relationships as
writers to their audience — an audience that, in the final analysis, will usually
be composed only of you, their teacher. Obviously, students will attempt to
choose a style that will suit their identified readership, and the voice they choose
for a letter to a close friend will be very different from the one they choose for
an essay to be read by their English teacher. But the danger of artificiality in
the voice chosen for the essay is all too real.

[handwritten: voice should feel natural; natural voice establishes trust?]

Considering the Audience for Student Essays

Teachers and scholars have explored the problem of the teacher as the final
audience for student-written texts by trying to create other plausible audiences,
with the most obvious sorts of such assignments being letters to the editor of
a local newspaper, letters to the president of the United States, or letters to the
university or college president. Some assignments have been created that specify
a complex writing situation, complete with subject and audience; one example
is an assignment that asks students to define and give examples of "conventional
diction" to a group of ninth-grade French students who know basic English but
who need more information about how Americans really use it.

The problem with these plausible or created audiences (not including the
ethical problems some teachers have with the artificial aspect of hypothetical
audiences) stems from the fact that the students are always aware that behind the
"editor" or the "French students" stands the teacher, who ultimately wields
the power of the grade. This awareness makes the assignment even more complex. The student knows that in reality she is writing the way the teacher thinks
the student should write to the editor or for ninth graders, not the way the
student really would write to them. In other words, a student must try to write
for another person's concept of a fictional audience. It is no wonder that students
often freeze solidly into take-no-chances dullness in such assignments.

The alternative, to specify no audience at all, leaves the student in a simpler —
but no less difficult — situation. Most FY students, accustomed to the rich contextual responses of oral communication, find it difficult to conceptualize the
abstract, fictionalized "universal audience" that the Belgian rhetorician Chaim
Perelman says is the ultimate audience for written discourse (402).

FY students also have trouble adjusting their styles, which may be sharp and
skillful at the oral level, to what seem to them the difficult conventions of non-
contextual written discourse. As a result, they tend to write pedantically, on
the assumptions that stressing the subject is the safest thing to do and that as
college students they need to sound "grown-up." They cannot create a fictional
audience easily, so they tend to write into the void.

The problem of audience is not easily solved, since both overspecification and
underspecification of audience can have unfortunate consequences. One compromise is to admit that the teacher is the audience and to attempt to work
accordingly. However, if you choose to specify an audience other than yourself,
you'll need to imaginatively place yourself in the position of that audience,

considering the various factors that would influence how that audience would likely receive the writer's text. A related option, especially if you allow students to choose their own topics and forms, is to have students identify their own audience. Students can be asked to carefully weigh all the elements of the rhetorical situation (including, among other factors, style and audience) and to report on their attention to these elements by providing answers to the questions in Example 8.1 with their final drafts. Your task as teacher would thus be to evaluate the extent to which the piece of writing works, given the rhetorical situation the student has imagined.

Example 8.1   **REPORTING ON THE RHETORICAL SITUATION**

1. What is your subject?
2. What audience are you addressing?
3. What exigence are you responding to? (the "so what?" question)
4. What is your purpose?
5. What genre or form have you chosen to deliver your message?
6. What specific rhetorical strategies (including stylistic features) will help you achieve your purpose?

LEVELS OF STYLE

Intimately related to the question of audience is the concept of different levels of style. Cicero mentions the high, middle, and low styles of oratory and suggests that each has its place and purpose. In the early days of teaching composition, however, this sort of liberalism was supplanted by prescriptive judgments about the different levels of style. Style was either right or wrong, correct or incorrect, and in general only an attempt to write in a high, "literary" style was acceptable. Gradually, this dichotomy between good and bad gave way to the three hierarchical levels of style that many of us were raised on: formal or literary style; informal or colloquial style; and vulgar or illiterate style. Of the three, only formal style was considered proper for writing; the other two instead reflected the way people talk or the style of letters to friends. (The vulgar style was how *they* talked, not how *we* talk.) Toward the middle of the twentieth century, this hierarchy was liberalized, becoming a continuum from which any stylistic form could be chosen (Marckwardt viii).

Certain levels of stylistic formality *do* correspond better than others to the needs and perceptions of readers of particular genres. Contemporary writers of the personal essay, for example, tend to choose a style somewhere between colloquial and formal. And those writing articles or academic arguments tend to choose a more formal style. For this reason, we can — depending on the form and context — teach a particular level of style not as more correct but as more appropriate for specific rhetorical situations, knowing that the level of style will change depending on the writer's purpose, the reader's expectations, the demands of the form, and the context. See Example 8.2 for an exercise designed to help you discuss the nature and effects of different levels of style.

Example 8.2 **STYLE TRANSLATIONS**

1. Bring in samples of various kinds of discourse: a business letter, an e-mail from a friend, the transcript from an online chat, responses to a status update on a social media site, the most recent State of the Union Address, and excerpts from personal essays and theoretical articles.

2. Read and discuss your samples in small groups, seeking to name the level of style each writer uses.

3. Now, translate one or two passages into a style different from the one in which it was originally written. If the piece was formal, for example, translate it into more colloquial language.

4. Read your translations to the class.

5. Discuss the challenges you faced with your translations, including how meaning changed (or didn't change) depending on the level of style.

In *Style: An Anti-Textbook,* Richard Lanham condemns the utilitarian prose and the "plain style" most commonly taught in FY writing classes, asserting that language as play should be the key concept in composition classes. "Style," says Lanham, "must be taught for and as what it is — a pleasure, a grace, a joy, a delight" (28). Given the limitations under which most writing teachers labor, you may not get that far. Students cannot learn to control style in three or four months, but if you provide them with good models and classroom exercises, they will become aware of style as a concrete entity. And perhaps they'll take a step further toward Lanham's goal: taking "a self-consious pleasure in words" (27).

EXERCISES FOR DEVELOPING STYLE

Most FY students declare that they have no writing style — that mysterious "extra" quality that only professional writers possess. It's no wonder they feel this way: Even if they have been introduced to style, the introduction was probably to literary style, a vague quality described by their teacher as "vigorous" or "curt" or "smooth" that can be found only in the writing of Hawthorne or Baldwin or Woolf. Style, nebulous and qualitative, is not to be found in students' writing — so they think.

As Winston Weathers points out, though, "improvement in student style comes not by osmosis, but through exercises" ("Teaching Style" 146). Classroom practice helps reinforce the notion that no writer, not even a student writer, is a prisoner of unchangeable ways of writing. By introducing students to the exercises included here, you can begin to make style understandable to your students and demonstrate that they, too, can develop their own style. (For detailed information on conducting stylistic analyses of both student and professional writing, see Corbett and Connors, cited at the end of this chapter.)

IMITATION

Hans Ostrom, in "'Carom Shots': Reconceptualizing Imitation and Its Uses in Creative Writing Courses," discusses the ideological and pedagogical reservations many teachers of writing and literature have about imitation. Some teachers want to empower students by helping them find "their own voices" rather than imitating others' writing; others want to venerate "great authors" and keep students from messing with supposed perfection. Many teachers value "originality" and find imitation exercises suspect. While we don't advocate asking students to imitate someone else's work to the point that they begin to write and sound exclusively like their favorite author, we do recognize the value of imitation for helping students expand their own stylistic repertoires.

Different imitation techniques, whether they consist of direct copying, composition based on models, or controlled mutation of sentence structures, all have one thing in common: They lead students to internalize the structures of the piece being imitated. With those structures internalized, a student is free to make the informed choices that are the wellspring of creativity. William Gruber puts it succinctly when he suggests that imitation does not affect creativity but assists in design:

> Standing behind imitation as a teaching method is the simple assumption that an inability to write is an inability to design — an inability to shape effectively the thought of a sentence, a paragraph, or an essay. (493–94)

Imitation exercises provide students with practice in that "ability to design" that is the basis of a mature prose style.

Using Imitation Exercises in the Classroom

Ostrom emphasizes that the imitation assignments he gives students are "different from an 'apprentice's' modeling of a 'master's' work" (167). His method of imitation is "more of a carom shot, one text playing off another" (167). He illustrates it by explaining his combined use of imitation and micronarration in a fiction writing course: After students read Gertrude Stein, for example, they write micro-stories (short fictions of one or two pages) that "jazz around with language in some way, not necessarily Stein's way" (167). He discusses how this exercise encourages students to see texts as invitations "to manipulate language in a similar way" (168). Combined with Corbett and Connors's methods for analyzing a text's stylistic features in *Classical Rhetoric for the Modern Student,* Ostrom's method of imitation can help students first learn to articulate what is going on stylistically in another person's text and then to work on style in their own writing.

Such exercises in imitation can also help students begin to understand the context in which they create writing. Without knowledge of what has been done by others, there can be no profound originality. Speaking of his own instruction through the use of imitation, Winston Churchill said, "Thus I got into my bones the essential structure of the ordinary British sentence — which is a noble thing." If you can help your students get the structure of ordinary sentences "into their bones," the time and effort you devote to imitation exercises will be worthwhile.

There are many ways to introduce imitation exercises into a FY class, and you can decide how you wish to approach them based on the amount of time you have available. Some kinds of imitation can be done as homework, but others require the sort of encouragement that you can provide only in a classroom. One important point applies to all sorts of imitation, however: If you choose to use this technique, be prepared to work with it throughout the entire term to gain benefits from it. Donna Gorrell's *Copy/Write,* Winston Weathers's *An Alternate Style,* David Starkey's collection *Teaching Writing Creatively,* and Wendy Bishop's collection *Elements of Alternate Style* provide additional ideas and exercises. Also, Frank Farmer, in his chapter "Sounding the Other Who Speaks in Me: Toward a Dialogic Understanding of Imitation" in *Saying and Silence,* draws on Bakhtin's work to offer an outline for dialogic imitation.

You may encounter some resistance in teaching imitation. Some students are initially suspicious of the method, seeing it as a block to their originality. They may balk at the rigidity of some of the exercises. Higher-level students sometimes see it as beneath their capacities (and obviously, for some students, it will be). Other students, however, delight in what imitation has to offer: a chance to write differently, to break tired habits of writing they may have fallen into. While some students will struggle, others will flourish. To help those who struggle with imitation, ask for volunteers to read both original passages and their imitations aloud in class.

In teaching imitation, you will have to keep reminding your students of the two criteria for success: (1) the more removed the new content is from that of the original, the better the imitation will be; and (2) the structure of an imitation should coincide perfectly with the given rhetorical model. Asking students to revise something they've already written will almost always guarantee that the content differs between the imitation and the piece being imitated. In Example 8.3 students are asked to produce distinctive imitations.

Example 8.3   **AN EXERCISE IN IMITATION, REVISION, AND REFLECTION**

- Choose a passage (two paragraphs or so) from a favorite prose writer's work.
- Copy the passage by hand, paying particular attention to sentence patterns.
- Now choose a passage from an essay you have written.
- Rewrite your own passage using the exact same sentence structures (and order) used by your favorite author in the passage you copied.
- Then write a paragraph reflecting on the choices and changes you made in revising your work in terms of another writer's sentence patterns. What did you add? What did you cut? Did this exercise make you think about your own style in a different way?

LANGUAGE VARIETY

In her often anthologized essay "Mother Tongue," Chinese American writer Amy Tan writes, "Language is the tool of my trade. And I use them all — all the Englishes I grew up with" (147). Later in the essay, she lists some of the Englishes she uses in her novel *The Joy Luck Club:*

> . . . the English I spoke to my mother, which for lack of a better term might be described as "simple"; the English she used with me, which for lack of a better term might be described as "broken"; my translation of her Chinese, which could certainly be described as "watered down"; and what I imagined to be her translation of her Chinese if she could speak in perfect English, her internal language, and for that I sought to preserve the essence, but neither an English nor a Chinese structure. (152)

Even if English is, for most of your students, their first language, they most likely speak — and possibly write — several varieties of English. Because students may not, at first, understand what you mean by "varieties of language," it's helpful to provide examples. There are many varieties of English, and your students will be able to brainstorm categories. As a starting place, consider asking students to think about the stylistic characteristics of particular regions of the United States, particular professions, and particular cultural or ethnic groups, perhaps providing examples like the following:

- In her essay "On a Hill Far Away," Annie Dillard writes of talking with a young boy in rural Virginia: "'Do you know how to catch a fish when you haven't got a rod, or a line, or a hook?'. He was smiling, warming up for a little dialect, being a kid in a book. He must read a lot. 'First, you get you a *stick*. . . .' He explained what sort of stick. 'Then you pull you a thread of honey-suckle . . . and if you need a *hook*. . . .' " (82).

- In "Testimony," a speech that the naturalist and writer Terry Tempest Williams delivered before a congressional subcommittee, students will recognize several occupational languages at work. In the following passage, Williams draws from medical and scientific vocabularies: "I can tell you that my mother, who had ovarian cancer, didn't know she had any more options after a radical hysterectomy, Cytoxan, cisplatin, Adriamycin treatments, and six weeks of radiation therapy had failed to offer her a cure. Pacific yew, *Taxus brevifolia,* taxol were not words in her vocabulary, or in her doctor's vocabulary for that matter" (126).
- Garrett Hongo, in "Kubota," writes about his Hawaiian-born Japanese grandfather and the stories "Kubota" (his grandfather) would tell, including a moral: " 'study *ha-ahd,*' he'd say with pidgin emphasis. 'Learn read good. Learn speak da kine *good* English.' The message is the familiar one taught to [m]any children of immigrants: succeed through education" (69).
- In *Talkin That Talk*, Geneva Smitherman provides an example of a preacher "exhorting his congregation to take care of themselves and their bodies"; she continues:

PREACHER: Y'all wanna stay here awhile?
CONGREGATION: Praise the Lord!
PREACHER: Well, y'all better quit all this drankin, smokin, and runnin 'round. Cause, see, for me, I got a home in Heaven, but I ain't homesick! (202)

In each of these examples, the writers intentionally shift among different varieties of English in order to achieve a particular effect. Utilizing such shifts is one way of affecting style. (It's also important to remember that the issues surrounding language variety are not limited to style; they affect many other aspects of teaching and learning. For more on language variety and diversity, see Ball; Ball and Lardner; Delpit and Dowdy; Gilyard; Jordan; Min-Zhan Lu; and Smitherman, *Talkin That Talk*, " 'The Blacker the Berry, the Sweeter the Juice': African American Student Writers," and "Toward a National Public Policy on Language," cited at the end of this chapter.)

Such shifts can sometimes be difficult for less experienced writers, and so your students will likely look to you for guidance. As Andrea A. Lunsford explains, "The key to shifting among varieties of English and among languages is appropriateness: you need to consider when such shifts will help you connect with your audience, get their attention, make a particular point, or represent the actual words of someone you are writing about" (518). In the writing your students will do in class, much will depend on the forms and genres you ask them to write. For example, if you ask them to write personal essays or other forms of creative nonfiction, it may be appropriate to shift varieties of language through dialogue, for doing so can reveal character. Shifts are also appropriate when students write the kinds of alternate-styled texts we discuss later in this chapter: Double-voiced texts, for example, require shifts — often from an academic to a more personal voice. However, if you assign traditional argumentative essays, students will need to know specifically what — if any — place shifting among varieties of English should have in their writing for your class.

In the "Hint Sheet" section of *The Subject Is Writing*, Wendy Bishop offers fifteen prompts to help students consider language communities. We've included several of these questions in Example 8.4 (for the full list, you'll want to consult Bishop's book). You can use these questions as prompts for in-class writing, as journal prompts, or — with some tinkering — even as prompts for fully developed essays.

Example 8.4 **BISHOP'S PROMPTS FOR WRITING ABOUT LANGUAGE COMMUNITIES**

love!

1. What languages do you speak? When do you speak them and to whom?

2. Under what circumstances does your dialect (register, vocabulary) change? Tell a story about this.

3. Do you have a peer group that uses a certain language? Give examples.

4. Do you or someone you know work in a profession with its own language? For instance, what is the language of school? What is the language of therapy? What is advertising language?

5. Have you lost a language? Where, how, why? (*Subject* 209–10)

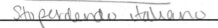 *Sto perdendo italiano*

Teaching an Awareness of Language Variety

Throughout "Mother Tongue," Amy Tan recalls times when she became aware of the particular variety of English she used at any given time. For instance, when her mother attended a talk Tan was giving to an academic audience, Tan became aware of the way "a speech filled with carefully wrought grammatical phrases" suddenly seemed burdened "with nominalized forms, past perfect tenses, conditional phrases, all the forms of standard English [she] had learned in school and through books, the forms of English [she] did not use at home" with her mother (147). Often, we become aware of the many languages we use only when others do not understand what we are trying to say. Example 8.5 lists some questions you can ask students to help them consider the variety of "Englishes" they use. Helping students gain an awareness of their own varieties of language in daily speech can help them use — or not use — such language patterns in their writing.

Example 8.5   THE "ENGLISHES" YOU SPEAK AND WRITE

- What words or phrases common in your own vocabulary have others questioned, laughed at, commented on, or not understood? (Examples might range from the regionally influenced "might could have" or "the plants need watered" to terms such as "totes" or "amazeballs," words that have meaning among friends but that may leave parents perplexed.)

- How would you classify these terms and phrases? Which ones are regionally influenced? family influenced? culturally influenced? learned from your peers?

- Which varieties of English do you use in your writing for school? Are there any you'd like to use in your writing that you don't use already? Are there any you use in writing that you'd rather not use?

In "Inviting the Mother Tongue: Beyond 'Mistakes,' 'Bad English,' and 'Wrong Language,'" (*Everyone Can Write*) Peter Elbow describes in personal terms the conflict many writing teachers feel: "On the one hand, I feel an obligation to invite all my students to use their own language and not make them conform to the language and culture of mainstream English" (323). "On the other hand," Elbow continues, "I feel an obligation to give all my students access to the written language of power and prestige" (323). Elbow goes on to observe—as has Geneva Smitherman and other scholars—that the choice does not entail an "either/or" decision. Smitherman argues that the "mother tongue language or dialect . . . can establish the firm foundation upon which to build and expand the learner's linguistic repertoire" ("National Public Policy" 172). The rhetorical and linguistic habits of various cultures and geographic regions are not only effective forms of communication but can also be stylistically powerful. We need only to look at the work of such writers as Gloria Anzaldúa, Alice Walker, Amy Tan, bell hooks, Zora Neale Hurston, Henry Louis Gates Jr., Geneva Smitherman, and Barbara Mellix, who have a command of both standard English and various dialects (additional "Englishes"), to understand the power of using more than one kind of English in writing. Many of these writers have published essays and books that reflect on the choices they make about language use in writing; these texts can help your students reflect on similar issues as well. (See, for example, Barbara Mellix's "From Outside, In," cited at the end of this chapter.)

You may be thinking, *Okay: I recognize the value of teaching standard English and of encouraging my students to use their home languages in writing, but how do I do both in a one-semester course?* Elbow suggests inviting "students to leave their exercises and low-stakes writing in the home dialect," and on major essays to "invite copy-editing into *two* final drafts: one into correct SWE [standard written English] and one into the best form of the student's home dialect" (342). Another solution is to teach a variety of forms: personal essays that lend themselves to a variety of diverse language uses as well as to the rhetorical/stylistic features of more traditional academic arguments. Alternate-styled texts — such as collage essays and double-voiced texts — allow for additional possibilities, giving students a recognizable form for intentionally shifting between voices or dialects in writing. In any case, the key is to emphasize intention, purpose, context, and audience. That is, whenever students switch among language varieties in their essays, they should have a reason for doing so and an awareness of how such switches might affect their audience.

Language Varieties and Varying Syntax

Related to an awareness of English language varieties is the important stylistic practice of varying syntax. While not all writing teachers want their students to draw from all the varieties of language they have at their disposal (some teachers focus more on teaching a particular kind of academic discourse), nearly all writing teachers look for syntactic variety. As Virginia Tufte writes in *Artful Sentences: Syntax as Style*, syntax "gives words the power to relate to each other in a sequence, to create rhythms and emphasis, to carry meaning — of whatever kind — as well as glow individually in just the right place" (9). You can tell students repeatedly to vary sentence structure, but unless they have models, unless they understand the real effects of rhythm in both speech and writing, they are not likely to understand what you mean — or how they can use certain language patterns to good effect *and* how to change patterns that are not effective. (For exercises in varying syntax and crafting sentences, see Nora Bacon's *The Well-Crafted Sentence: A Writer's Guide to Style*, cited at the end of this chapter.)

Language practices that are influenced by factors such as geographic region, ethnicity, or culture can also affect writing at the sentence level, producing a kind of rhythm — for good or ill. Just as rhythm is recognizable in patterns of speech, so it is in patterns of writing at the level of syntax. Bill Roorbach, in *Writing Life Stories,* helps students become more aware of language variety by asking them to be attentive to the rhythm of their writing:

> A sense of rhythm is a cultural sense, a sense of tradition. Do your sentences pick up the cadences of childhood rhymes? Of marching bands? Of biblical phrasing? Of television scripts? Of the squad room? Of a preacher's repetition? . . . Variety, as in all things, is key. (150)

In other words, rhythm in writing (which is influenced by the structure and length of sentences, word choice, repetition, and punctuation) is in many ways linked to culture and tradition — from what we've internalized from reading, from listening, and from simply living. Example 8.6 shows an exercise that Roorbach uses to help his students practice being attentive to rhythm in their reading and writing and work toward variety in their writing. (For additional exercises on structural variety and rhythm in written discourse, see Chapter 10 in Joe Glaser's *Understanding Style,* cited at the end of this chapter.)

Example 8.6 **ROORBACH'S "TAP YOUR FEET" EXERCISE**

Pull out the work of a favorite writer, and read it listening and feeling for rhythm and rhythms. Tap your feet as you read out loud. Look for repeated words or phrases that set up a beat. Listen for sentences that rise, for sentences that fall. Where does the prose stop? What kinds of words create pauses? . . . How do paragraph lengths fit into the music of the work? Is there a visual rhythm? Can you sing any lines?

Then pull out another author, and do it again. What accounts for the changes you hear in rhythm?

Finally, pull out your own draft, and read the same way. Are you satisfied? Can you get more music in there? more of a beat? more aural surprises? more variety?

I'll make your charge more concrete: Do you start most sentences with the subject? Do you always subordinate in the same way? Do you avoid alliteration, repetition? Does every paragraph end on a rising note, or falling? Does every sentence have about the same number of beats, every paragraph the same number of sentences?

Shake it up, baby! (152–53)

ALTERNATE STYLES: GRAMMAR B

Winston Weathers's *An Alternate Style: Options in Composition* is perhaps the most accessible text for students interested in expanding their repertoire of stylistic options. Weathers writes that

> one of our major tasks as teachers of composition is to identify compositional options and teach students the mastery of the options and the liberating use of them. We must identify options in all areas of vocabulary, usage, sentence forms, dictional levels, paragraph types, ways of organizing material into whole compositions: options in all that we mean by style. Without options, there can be no rhetoric, for there can be no adjustment to the diversity of communication occasions that confront us in our various lives. (5)

Thus, it ultimately rests with teachers to introduce students to their stylistic options. Once students stop viewing their styles as predestined and unchangeable and begin to perceive style as quantitative and plastic, they can begin to seek what Richard Lanham calls "grace" and "delight" in their writing as they learn how to control their rhetorical choices and stylistic options.

Weathers defines Grammar B as "a mature and alternate (*not* experimental) style used by competent writers and offering students of writing a well-tested set of options that, added to the traditional grammar of style, will give them a much greater opportunity to put into effective language all the things they have to say" (*Alternate Style* 8). Some elements of alternate style (see Weathers for others) include crots, or sections of sentences that work together but may be only loosely connected to the sentences that follow; labyrinthine sentences, which are long, winding sentences that may use embedded phrases, lists, multiple forms of punctuation, and explanations within explanations; sentence fragments; double voices that suggest two sides of a story or different attitudes toward the same subject; and lists. Weathers cites examples of how these stylistic features have been used by literary writers; if you're using a reader, you can point out examples from it to students.

Using Alternate Styles in the Classroom

Though still available in many university libraries and some used bookstores, Weathers's *An Alternate Style: Options in Composition* is out of print. However, a more recent book based on Weathers's work can help you introduce a range of styles to your composition class: *Elements of Alternate Style: Essays on Writing and Revision,* edited by Wendy Bishop, includes both essays and exercises meant to introduce students to elements of alternate style and to give them an opportunity to apply what they learn in writing new compositions and revising pieces they've already written. The essays are short, directed to student writers, and full of exercises and examples. In "'You Want Us to Do WHAT?' How to Get the Most Out of Unexpected Writing Assignments," for example, Ruth Mirtz includes an assignment sheet that explains Weathers's terms and offers guidelines for revising an essay previously written using Grammar A (traditional grammar) by using the techniques of Grammar B:

> Don't change topics/it's too late now.
> If you conceive of a Grammar B-like device that fits what you want to say (that is, breaks one rule of Grammar A to good effect), do it.
> Don't change font styles every other word or add obscure symbols and call it Grammar B. It won't B.
> Have fun. Play. Take a Chance. If it Fails because you tried something that didn't work, it didn't Fail. If it fails because you didn't try, it failed.
> Do as the handout describes, not as it does. This handout uses too many Grammar B techniques because it's trying to illustrate possibilities rather than make sense.
> The POINT of this assignment, which I place at the end of the handout instead of [at] the Grammar A position at the beginning of the handout, is to understand

better what Grammar A is all about by using Grammar B, to explore what Grammar A (and Grammar B, perhaps) fails to express, to be politically aware (instead of politically correct) of who gets to make rules like Grammar A and who doesn't, who gets to use Grammar B and why, what the rules of Grammar A accomplish in terms of communication, expression, meaning-making, to explore further the concept of revision by writing a radically different version of a paper and comparing the effect, and to imagine more possibilities and power in language than Grammar A (or our assumptions and ignorances about Grammar A) allow us. (107)

By carrying out such an assignment and then comparing their earlier drafts to their revisions, students potentially come to understand better how style can change not only how people read and respond to their work but also how they themselves think about and understand an experience or topic.

Alternate styles can be used for a variety of pedagogical purposes — to help students recognize stylistic options, to produce radical revisions, even to teach Grammar A. In asking students to attempt alternate styles, it is important to reiterate that one reason traditional rules of grammar exist is that they are effective in helping guide readers. Writers who use alternate styles also must keep their readers in mind. There are times when the teaching and practice of Grammar A and Grammar B can be mutually reinforcing.

Example 8.7 provides an assignment for a labyrinthine sentence. By giving students such an assignment, you provide an example of what is expected and can spend time in class analyzing the grammatical features that work well in labyrinthine sentences: lists, embedded clauses and phrases, resumptive modifiers, parentheticals, and so on. The assignment also provides an opportunity to discuss rules of punctuation, such as when it is appropriate to use semicolons or dashes. Thus, through analyzing and practicing this element of alternate style, students learn more about sentence variety and grammatical complexity — all while writing one long sentence.

Example 8.7 LABYRINTHINE SENTENCE ASSIGNMENT

Though I fully understand the great challenge — even the difficulty — of such a task, for your labyrinthine sentence assignment (of at least two hundred words), you need to construct a very long, circuitous sentence: one that leads and directs your readers, taking them through the labyrinthine with both grace and ease (and maybe even a pleasant surprise), never becoming overly repetitious or wordy (avoiding filler words or the overuse of adjectives and adverbs); one that is grammatically correct, showing careful attention to each word, clause, and phrase and how these elements (along with the various parts of speech) work together to create meaning; one that is correctly punctuated, using the full range of options available to you — including dashes, colons, commas, parentheses, semicolons, and some end punctuation; one that is coherent, demonstrating control and a command of language, syntactic structure, and subject matter; one that shows an attention to vocabulary, using words that are precise and appropriate in diction, sound, and sense; and one that is as interesting as it is complex; for in order to complete this assignment effectively and successfully, you will need to be patient, flexible, and creative — sensitive to almost every aspect of writing as you demonstrate the considerable effort involved in the craft of language.

In case you're wondering, the preceding sentence contains 210 words. It can be done.

Evaluating Alternate Styles

You may be wondering how to respond to, evaluate, even grade alternate styles. The labyrinthine sentence assignment in Example 8.7 can be evaluated according to Standardized English and the elements referred to in the assignment itself. For many other alternate style assignments, however, there are few established criteria against which to measure student responses. You might intuitively know what works and what doesn't, but how do you translate your gut-level responses into language that will help students further refine their writing? If the evaluation of traditional assignments seems subjective to students, the evaluation of alternate style assignments must seem even more so. And how do you evaluate an assignment when you've asked students to take risks?

Wendy Bishop, in the appendix to *Elements of Alternate Style*, gives guidance on how to respond to, evaluate, and grade alternate-style texts. She provides two sets of questions—questions students can ask about their own pieces and questions teachers and classmates can ask in response to their reading. The questions students can ask themselves include the following:

- Can I describe why this writing requires this style/format?
- Are there places in the writing that I covered up, patched, [or] ignored problems I was having [with] understanding my own writing goals or aims?
- If I recast this as a traditionally styled writing, what would I lose and what would I gain?
- In my final draft, am I paying attention to the reader? Have I done everything I can to "teach" the reader how to read my piece while still maintaining the integrity of my writing goals and ideas? (175)

Notice how these questions encourage students to balance the attention they give to each element of the communication triangle (subject, writer, reader, and work) discussed earlier in this chapter.

Bishop also provides guidance for teachers and classmates responding to alternate-style texts, including the following prompts:

- Here's how I read your text. Here's where I had trouble reading your text and why.
- Can you tell us what effects you were hoping for, where you achieved them and where you think you may have fallen short?
- What do you wish you had done (what would you still like to do) to push this text even f[u]rther? Why haven't you? How can you? (175–76)

These questions ask writers to consider reader response, to interrogate their own intentions and the extent to which they were able to carry out their purposes, and to keep working.

For grading alternate-style texts, Bishop suggests using process cover sheets (which are similar to the portfolio cover letters discussed in Chapter 5). Bishop provides a series of questions, directs writers to choose six out of eight of them to answer, and asks them to compose a letter that includes those answers. She also offers the following grading options:

1. Grade the letter as a traditional persuasive essay for the insights discussed and explored, and don't grade the project beyond done/not done.
2. Grade both the letter and the project as part of an entire class portfolio. This may mean allowing for more experimentation (even individually productive "failure") by evaluating this "slot" in the portfolio as done/not done (in good faith).
3. Grade the text on the basis of traditional criteria—a mixture of assignment goals and [the] teacher's estimate of the degree to which those goals were met, using the process cover sheet to add depth to this subjective evaluation.
4. Grade using a combination of these options. (177)

Whether you use instruction and practice in writing alternate styles as in-class exercises, as fully developed essays, as revision techniques, or to encourage students to consider the effects of stylistic differences in what they read and write, such instruction can be quite valuable in helping students expand their stylistic range.

WORKS CITED

Abrams, M. H. *The Mirror and the Lamp.* New York: Oxford UP, 1953. Print.

Bacon, Nora. *The Well-Crafted Sentence: A Writer's Guide to Style.* Boston: Bedford, 2009. Print.

Ball, Arnetha F. "Cultural Preference and the Expository Writing of African-American Adolescents." *Written Communication* 9.4 (1992): 501–32. Print.

Ball, Arnetha, and Ted Lardner. "Dispositions Toward Language: Teacher Constructs and the Ann Arbor Black English Case." *CCC* 48.4 (1997): 469–85. Print.

Bishop, Wendy, ed. *Elements of Alternate Style: Essays on Writing and Revision.* Portsmouth: Boynton/Cook, 1997. Print.

——. *The Subject Is Writing.* 2nd ed. Portsmouth: Boynton/Cook, 1999. Print.

Booth, Wayne. "The Rhetorical Stance." *Contemporary Rhetoric: Conceptual Background with Readings.* Ed. W. Ross Winterowd. New York: Harcourt, 1975. 71–79. Print.

Chatman, Seymour, and Samuel R. Levin, eds. *Literary Style: A Symposium*. London: Oxford UP, 1971. Print.

——. *Essays on the Language of Literature*. Boston: Houghton, 1967. Print.

Corbett, Edward P. J. "Approaches to the Study of Style." *Teaching Composition: Twelve Bibliographic Essays*. Ed. Gary Tate. 2nd ed. Fort Worth: Texas Christian UP, 1987. 83–130. Print.

——. *Rhetorical Analyses of Literary Works*. New York: Oxford UP, 1969. Print.

Corbett, Edward P. J., and Robert Connors. *Classical Rhetoric for the Modern Student*. 4th ed. New York: Oxford UP, 1999. Print.

Delpit, Lisa, and Joanne Kilgour Dowdy, eds. *The Skin That We Speak*. New York: Norton, 2002. Print.

Dillard, Annie. *Teaching a Stone to Talk*. New York: Harper, 1982. Print.

Ede, Lisa, Cheryl Glenn, and Andrea Lunsford. "Border Crossings: Intersections of Rhetoric and Feminism." *Rhetorica* 13.4 (1995): 410–41. Print.

Elbow, Peter. *Everyone Can Write*. New York: Oxford UP, 2000. Print.

Farmer, Frank. *Saying and Silence: Listening to Composition with Bakhtin*. Logan: Utah State UP, 2001. Print.

Gilyard, Keith. *Voices of the Self*. Detroit: Wayne State UP, 1991. Print.

Glaser, Joe. *Understanding Style: Practical Ways to Improve Your Writing*. New York: Oxford UP, 1999. Print.

Gorrell, Donna. *Copy/Write: Basic Writing through Controlled Composition*. Boston: Little, 1982. Print.

Graves, Richard. "A Primer for Teaching Style." *CCC* 25.2 (1974): 186–90. Print.

Gruber, William. " 'Servile Copying' and the Teaching of English." *CE* 39.4 (1977): 491–97. Print.

Hongo, Garrett. "Kubota." *The Best American Essays: College Edition*. Ed. Robert Atwan. Boston: Houghton, 1998. 64–76. Print.

Irmscher, William F. *Teaching Expository Writing*. New York: Holt, 1979. Print.

Joos, Martin. *The Five Clocks*. New York: Harcourt, 1961. Print.

Jordan, June. "Nobody Mean More to Me than You: And the Future Life of Willie Jordan." *City Kids, City Teachers: Reports from the Front Row*. Ed. William Ayers and Patricia Ford. New York: New, 1996. 176–93. Print.

Kiefer, Kathleen, and Charles R. Smith. "Improving Students' Revising and Editing: The Writer's Workbench." *The Computer in Composition Instruction: A Writer's Tool*. Ed. William Wresch. Urbana: NCTE, 1984. 65–82. Print.

Lanham, Richard. *Style: An Anti-Textbook*. 2nd ed. Philadelphia: Paul Dry, 2007. Print.

Lu, Min-Zhan. "Redefining the Legacy of Mina Shaughnessy: A Critique of the Politics of Linguistic Innocence." *Journal of Basic Writing* 10.1 (1991): 26–40. Print.

Lunsford, Andrea A. *The St. Martin's Handbook*. 7th ed. New York: Bedford, 2011. Print.

Macrorie, Ken. *Uptaught*. Rochelle Park: Hayden, 1970. Print.

Marckwardt, Albert H. Introduction. *The Five Clocks*. Martin Joos. New York: Harcourt, 1961. i–x. Print.

Mellix, Barbara. "From Outside, In." *The Fourth Genre*. Ed. Robert L. Root Jr. and Michael Steinberg. Boston: Allyn, 1999. 113–20. Print.

Milic, Louis T. "Against the Typology of Styles." *Literary Style: A Symposium*. Ed. Seymour Chatman and Samuel R. Levin. London: Oxford UP, 1971. 442–50. Print.

——. "Rhetorical Choice and Stylistic Option: The Conscious and Unconscious Poles." *Literary Style: A Symposium*. Ed. Seymour Chatman and Samuel R. Levin. London: Oxford UP, 1971. 77–88. Print.

——. "Theories of Style and Their Implications for the Teaching of Composition." *CCC* 16.2 (1965): 66–69, 126. Print.

Miller, Edmund. *Exercises in Style*. Normal: Illinois State UP, 1980. Print.

Mirtz, Ruth. "'You Want Us to Do WHAT?': How to Get the Most Out of Unexpected Writing Assignments." *Elements of Alternate Style: Essays on Writing and Revision*. Ed. Wendy Bishop. Portsmouth: Boynton/Cook, 1997. 105–15. Print.

Ostrom, Hans. "'Carom Shots': Reconceptualizing Imitation and Its Uses in Creative Writing Courses." *Teaching Writing Creatively*. Ed. David Starkey. Portsmouth: Boynton/Cook, 1998. 164–71. Print.

Perelman, Chaim. "The New Rhetoric: A Theory of Practical Reasoning." *The Rhetoric of Western Thought*. Ed. James L. Golden et al. Dubuque: Kendall-Hunt, 1983. 402–23. Print.

Riffaterre, Michael. "Criteria for Style Analysis." *Literary Style: A Symposium*. Ed. Seymour Chatman and Samuel R. Levin. London: Oxford UP, 1971. 442–50. Print.

Roorbach, Bill. *Writing Life Stories*. Cincinnati: Story, 1998. Print.

Smitherman, Geneva. "'The Blacker the Berry, the Sweeter the Juice': African American Student Writers." *The Need for Story: Cultural Diversity in the Classroom and Community*. Ed. Anne Haas Dyson and Celia Genishi. Urbana: NCTE, 1994. 80–101. Print.

——. *Talkin That Talk : Language, Culture, and Education in African America*. New York: Routledge, 2000. Print.

——. "Toward a National Public Policy on Language." *The Skin That We Speak*. Ed. Lisa Delpit and Joanne Kilgour Dowdy. New York: New, 2002. 163–78. Print.

Starkey, David, ed. *Teaching Writing Creatively*. Portsmouth: Boynton/Cook, 1998. Print.

Tan, Amy. "Mother Tongue." *The Best American Essays: College Edition*. Ed. Robert Atwan. Boston: Houghton, 1998. 146–53. Print.

Tate, Gary, ed. *Teaching Composition: Twelve Bibliographic Essays*. 2nd ed. Fort Worth: Texas Christian UP, 1987. Print.

Tufte, Virginia. *Artful Sentences: Syntax as Style*. Cheshire: Graphics P, 2006. Print.

Weathers, Winston. *An Alternate Style: Options in Composition*. Rochelle Park: Hayden, 1980. Print.

——. "Teaching Style: A Possible Anatomy." *CCC* 21.2 (1970): 114–49. Print.

Weaver, Richard. *Ideas Have Consequences*. Chicago: U of Chicago P, 1948. Print.

Williams, Terry Tempest. *An Unspoken Hunger*. New York: Pantheon, 1994. Print.

Winterowd, W. Ross, ed. *Contemporary Rhetoric: Conceptual Background with Readings*. New York: Harcourt, 1975. Print.

Yagoda, Ben. *The Sound on the Page: Style and Voice in Writing*. New York: Harper Resource, 2004. Print.

9

Teaching Memory

> I used to think memory was only about memorization, which seemed irrelevant
> to teaching writing. But the canon of memory is so much more. It refers to the
> storehouse of knowledge — personal and public — that a rhetor must pull from
> when composing. Remembering the smell of a friend's house, feelings from a first
> date, an image from a protest, or words someone said a long time ago can help
> writers connect to readers. I've also learned that memories (and the physical places
> that house memories, such as archives and memorials) are never complete. By
> recognizing the rhetorical richness of memory, students begin to question how
> memories include and exclude, while also considering the consequences of those
> selections.
>
> —Craig Rood

"Memory has been forgotten," asserts Kathleen Welch in a critique of writing textbooks that give no attention to the final two canons of rhetoric: memory and delivery (153). Much of this "forgetfulness" can be attributed to the common belief that rhetorical memory is concerned simply with memorizing speeches. Edward P. J. Corbett and Robert Connors, who do not include a section on memory in their influential text *Classical Rhetoric for the Modern Student,* explain, "The reason for the neglect of this aspect of rhetoric is probably that not much can be said, in a theoretical way, about the process of memorizing; and after rhetoric came to be concerned mainly with written discourse, there was no further need to deal with memorizing" (22). Although there may be little need to deal with memorizing in a book on teaching writing, we — like other scholars of rhetoric — are finding ways to remember memory and the role it can play in teaching writing, especially as it informs the teaching of personal writing and an analysis of the ways in which various media shape collective memory.

Winifred Bryan Horner, in her introduction to *Rhetorical Memory and Delivery,* calls for further attention to these two rhetorical practices, for — as she argues — all of the canons "are necessary for a full understanding of a communication act, whether it be written, spoken, electronic, or some combination of any or all of these" (ix). Gregory Ulmer gives particular attention to electronic rhetoric in his theorizing; he argues, "One of the profound changes of a hyperrhetoric designed for organizing audiovisual as well as print practices will be the necessary return of delivery and memory and their adaption to a new social machine" (38). Responding to the calls of Welch, Horner, Ulmer, and other scholars of rhetoric and composition, we devote this chapter to exploring the ways a fresh understanding of memory can invigorate the teaching of writing, and we give equal attention to delivery in Chapter 10.

Instead of seeing "memory" as linked exclusively to the memorization of speeches, we prefer Sharon Crowley's claim, in "Modern Rhetoric and Memory," that memory "is a heuristic, a way of stimulating selection, reworking, and amplification of *all* that writers know" (44). This expanded definition provides many useful entries into the study of memory and its uses for the teaching of writing.

MEMORY AND COMPOSITION STUDIES

Drawing on Patrick Mahony's 1969 study "McLuhan in the Light of Classical Rhetoric," John Frederick Reynolds argues for "four interrelated approaches to memory in modern composition studies: memory as mnemonics, memory as memorableness, memory as databases, and memory as psychology" (7). Developing these ideas further, Reynolds suggests that composition teachers can help students develop "sight mnemonics" or "visual sensibility" in relation to texts, allowing students to better retrieve or remember what they have read (8). Further, students can practice the rhetorical art of memory by making their own writing memorable to readers by writing about significant situations, including details, and using powerful language — all elements of contemporary memoir or creative nonfiction.

In figuring memory as databases, Reynolds points to Horner's important distinction between individual memory and cultural memory (which is stored in books, on computers, in databases, in recordings, even in public memorials) (11). Finally, in seeing memory as psychology, Reynolds quotes Mahony's idea of " 'a oneness of memory, electronic technology, and the human unconscious' " (qtd. in Reynolds 6). Welch, too, sees a connection between memory and psychology, arguing in *Electric Rhetoric* that the "idea of memory as shards of consciousness, or mentalité, and the connection of memory to psychology (cognitive and depth, to name two kinds) continues to be an important area in the historicizing and production of discourses" (153). A consideration of both individual memory and cultural memory can be particularly useful in teaching this rhetorical canon.

The study of memory has important implications for the many kinds of writing students do in composition courses — personal writing, research-based writing, and multimodal projects. These categories ("personal," "research-based," and "multimodal"), of course, are not mutually exclusive. Strong personal writing requires research, and research essays should be informed and driven by students' concerns and marked by a personal voice; both kinds of writing can be presented in a variety of ways. Effective writing requires attention to memory in at least four ways:

1. Through invention exercises: Both classical rhetoricians and contemporary scholars link the rhetorical canons of invention and memory, for without invention, it is impossible to draw upon and use stored knowledge — whether it is stored in a person's mind or externally in books, databases, or art.

2. Through research: Both an individual's memories and arguments often need to be supplemented, confirmed, challenged, or extended by research.
3. Through recognizing memory as communal: Both those who write from their own memories and those who use other texts as sources must recognize the communal nature of memory.
4. Through experiences, images, and ideas worth communicating — and communicating well: Writers often remember particular images and experiences for a reason, but they may need to work to make the idea behind those images and experiences not only communicable but also memorable to their audience.

REMEMBERING AND MAKING WRITING MEMORABLE: TEACHING MEMOIR AND PERSONAL WRITING

Nonfiction writer and novelist Bill Roorbach opens his chapter "Memory" in *Writing Life Stories* with an epigraph from E. L. Doctorow: "'When you use memories as a source, they're no different from any other source — the composition still has to be made'" (qtd. in Roorbach 18). This reminder — that memories are sources like any others — is important for students who are sometimes tempted to believe that writing from experience or about memories involves a simple transcription of what "really happened."

Writers, like psychologists, understand that memory is complicated, limited, and faulty. As Roorbach states, "What's remembered, recorded, is never the event, no matter how precise the measurement" (19). Roorbach claims, further, that readers come "to memoir understanding that memory is faulty, that the writer is going to challenge the limits of memory" (21). Challenging the limits of memory, students should be reminded, is not the same thing as making things up completely, as the critical response to James Frey's supposed memoir *A Million Little Pieces* illustrates. But the difference between "what really happened" and "what I remember, why I remember it, and *how I interpret it* in the context of my essay" is worth discussing in class. (One useful source for beginning such a discussion is Patricia Hampl's essay "Memory and Imagination" from *I Could Tell You Stories,* cited at the end of this chapter. In this essay, Hampl reflects on the complexity of truth and imagination, telling a story that contains literal inaccuracies and then reflecting on why she told the story as she did.)

Whether you're asking students to write a memoir, a personal essay, or some other autobiographical piece that requires attention to memory (such as a literacy narrative), the key elements of such essays are the same. Rise Axelrod and Charles Cooper, who include guidance for writing from personal memory in *The St. Martin's Guide to Writing,* identify such features as "a well-told story," "vivid description," and "autobiographical significance" (17). Such features come from memory as evoked through invention as well as through research that uses external aids to memory; such qualities, too, make writing memorable for readers.

Invention

As Crowley reminds us, memory "is associative, global; it privileges disquisition, repetition, digression, allusion, allegory" (43). Invention strategies such as brainstorming, clustering, and freewriting demonstrate and emphasize the associative power of memory (see Chapter 6 for detailed discussions of these invention techniques). Clustering, in particular, provides students a visual representation of the connections their minds naturally make between images and memories they may not have consciously related. Like a word-association game, one image or experience reminds them of another and then another, expanding connections from the center word or idea.

Invention exercises provide a perfect starting place for accessing memories. Example 9.1 provides a series of invention exercises for students beginning to write literacy narratives.

Example 9.1 REMEMBERING CHILDHOOD LITERACY

1. For five minutes, brainstorm a list of books you remember from childhood (they might be books your family owned, ones you borrowed from the library, ones you read in school, or books someone else read to you).

2. For three minutes, brainstorm a list of people who read to you or to whom you read (parents, grandparents, siblings, teachers, neighbors, and so on).

3. Pick an element from one of these lists (a book title or the name of a person) and use it as a central word for a cluster. Cluster for five minutes.

4. Look at your cluster. Are there any associations or experiences you wrote down that interest or surprise you? Freewrite for twenty minutes on the element that interests or surprises you the most.

5. Do an online search for the books you remember. Write down further details about the most significant books: what the covers look like, a description of major characters or plotlines. Look back at your freewriting, and mark places where you might add additional detail.

Note: Although this example uses books and reading as its focus, you can modify it to focus on writing.

After doing the invention exercises, students will likely be surprised by how much they remember about their childhood literacy. Equally interesting is how much their invention exercises will overlap with their classmates' work.

Memory as Communal

Crowley suggests in "Modern Rhetoric and Memory" that citizens are shaped by their knowledge of culture and history, which is "stored in memory" (36). Books, of course, are cultural artifacts, and for students who grew up in similar cultures, family and educational rituals of reading will likely have similarities (reading before bed, story time in school or at a public library, reading aloud one at a time in class, and so on). As an extension of the invention exercises, you can ask students to write on the board the name of one of the books they read (or that was read to them) as children. As students write the names of books on the board, you'll likely hear exclamations of "Oh, yeah! I remember that one!"

As students discuss what they have in common (for instance how many have read *Winnie the Pooh,* the *Chronicles of Narnia,* or Dr. Seuss?), they can become resources for each other, supplying details others might have forgotten. They can also recognize the ways particulars are, if not universal, at least culturally and historically formed — that writing about their memories communicates to others on some level because readers can identify with those memories.

Encourage your students to consider how their memories have been shaped not only by print texts but also by images — from television, the Internet, and other sources. Example 9.2 asks students to remember cultural and historical events — and whether and how their classmates remember those same events.

Example 9.2   **REMEMBERING CULTURAL AND HISTORICAL EVENTS**

Write about a cultural or historical event that you remember from childhood. How was this memory shaped? Did you see news coverage of the event on television? Did your parents or teachers talk about it?

In groups of four, discuss the events you wrote about. Does anyone else in your group remember the same event? What are the similarities and differences between what you remember?

Research

Personal writing can also be informed through research. External memory aids — such as memory books or scrapbooks; childhood memorabilia; photo albums; family videos; journals or diaries; old report cards (for those writing literacy narratives); and even information on childhood books, toys, and TV shows found online — are indispensable resources for including detail in personal writing. Example 9.3 will get students thinking about the kind of research they can do to inform and enhance their personal writing. (For more on research as it relates to personal writing, see Goldthwaite's "This, Too, Is Research" included in Bishop and Zemliansky, cited at the end of this chapter.)

Example 9.3 RESEARCH FOR DETAILS

Exchange a draft of your personal essay with a classmate. Ask your classmate to mark places where you could add additional detail. Then create a plan for the research you will do. Where will you find the information you need? Could you interview your parents or siblings? do an Internet search? look through old e-mails or text messages or photos?

Experience, Image, Idea

Crowley writes, "People who know nothing outside their own experience cannot compose discourse that anyone else cares about" (43). That is not to say that writing from experience produces vacant or worthless writing but that writers must consider the ideas that arise from and are suggested by their experiences or the images that stick in memory. Experience provides a source of knowledge, but as Doctorow reminds us, the composition must still be made. Students must relate experiences in engaging ways (through scene, dialogue, concrete detail, attention to language and form) and consider the "so what?" question important to any form of writing. In memoir and other forms of personal writing, the "so what?" question does not need to be answered explicitly through a thesis statement at the beginning or a moral tacked on at the end, but the writer should have a sense of purpose, and that purpose should suggest an idea — something readers can take from the piece.

Well-rendered experiences, those written with attention to image and detail, can make the idea of a piece memorable to readers. Eighteenth-century rhetorician George Campbell writes in *The Philosophy of Rhetoric* that "vivid ideas are not only more powerful than languid ideas in commanding and preserving attention, they are not only more efficacious in producing conviction, but they are also more easily retained" (925). One reason that people have told stories throughout generations and in every culture is that story helps make ideas memorable; teaching students the intricacies of powerful narrative and lyrical writing can help make their writing memorable, too. Example 9.4 provides an exercise to be dictated to your class and which will help students test how memorable their writing is to readers.

Example 9.4   **WHAT READERS REMEMBER—AND WHY:**
                A CLASSROOM EXERCISE

1. For this exercise, I'll read a short essay aloud in class. Listen carefully, and when I'm finished, I'll ask the class a series of questions.
2. What do you remember about the piece? What words or phrases stood out (strong verbs or metaphors and similes)? What characters do you remember (a well-developed major character or even a quirky minor character)? What idea did you take from the piece?
3. Why were these features or textual elements memorable to you?
4. In pairs, do this exercise with your essay draft.

Students can do this exercise in peer-response groups, reading their essays aloud and asking their peers to tell them what was memorable, but it's worth doing the exercise at least once as an entire class because sometimes what's memorable is what students need to revise away from: awkward phrasing; the use of a word that, although interesting, is not precise (sometimes, when you ask students to use memorable words, they'll consult a thesaurus and use words that sound good but don't necessarily fit in terms of meaning); a character who is stereotyped; and so on. The question of *why* some element stands out in memory remains important.

COLLECTIVE MEMORY

According to Gregory Ulmer, "changes in the equipment of memory involve changes in people and institutions as well" (36). Information is stored not just in minds and books but also in artwork, on computer hard drives and memory cards, on film, in public parks, and in multiple other places. Michael Bernard-Donals observes that "the visual—photographic and screen images, paintings and other plastic arts—provides a corrective to the language of narrative that can only go so far to account for multiple human experiences" (381). Images, he asserts, point not only to aspects of cultural or individual memory but also to "that which has dropped out of memory altogether, and which profoundly disturbs what we are able to write: as history, as personal narrative, or as an engagement with the world" (381–82). The power of visuals to inform and reshape collective memory; the power of media, historians, and families to mediate memory through both story and images; and the power of images to reveal what Bernard-Donals calls "collective amnesia" (384)—all of these aspects of memory provide a rich resource for analysis and representation in writing classes.

Considering Collective Memory in the Writing Classroom: A Multimodal Approach

In her course at Stanford University, "Why and How We Remember: The Rhetoric of Mediated Memory," Andrea A. Lunsford asks her students to explore a number of issues related to memory: "What do we choose to remember — and to forget? How are collective memories formed? How are memories revised and shaped by the media used to present them?" Her students carry out three major projects — both individual and collaborative, showing attention to many kinds of sources and modes of writing and presentation. Examples 9.5–9.7 guide students through these three projects on memory: an analysis of a memorial, an exploration of the ways time and media shape public memory, and a multimodal research-based memoir.

Example 9.5   **POPULAR ARTICLE ON A CAMPUS OR LOCAL MEMORIAL**

For this assignment, choose a memorial on campus, defining *memorial* loosely to include any of the artifacts, buildings, place names, etc. that are intended, partially or in whole, to remember a person or event. Visit the memorial when you have at least half an hour to observe, and take careful notes. Then, consider and record your answers to the following questions:

- What do your eyes take in first about the memorial?
- Where do your eyes move next, and what draws your attention? Why does it draw your attention?
- What seems most straightforward about the memorial's message? What is obscure, puzzling, confusing?

Once you've done an initial observation of the memorial itself, study its surroundings:

- What direction does it face?
- What does it look out toward?
- What is in its background?
- What is the immediate surrounding area like?

Then consider how the memorial speaks to its surroundings and is in turn shaped by them.

- What effect do the surrounding grounds, other objects, etc. have on the memorial and its message?
- Why do you think the memorial has this particular location and these particular surroundings?
- Finally, how does the memorial "write" or create the memory of its occasion in a particular way; just how does it tell the story of what it is remembering in a way that will be persuasive to future audiences?

You may want to take a photo of the memorial or to find a representation of it on the Web — especially since our course focuses on the effects of media on representation and memory. Take your notes, photos, etc. with you as you do a little digging into the history of the memorial. Check out books on Stanford in the bookstore and sources in Green Library. Find out as much as you can about the memorial.

Finally, write a brief (three- to five-page) article intended for a popular newspaper, magazine, or journal about this memorial and then prepare a four-minute class presentation, this time for our class as the intended audience. Please submit the text for the presentation, along with a memo reflecting on what you have learned about writing for (brief) oral performance.

(Lunsford, "Why and How").

Example 9.6   **EXPLORATION OF HOW A PERSON, EVENT,
                  OR OBJECT HAS BEEN REMEMBERED DIFFERENTLY
                  ACROSS A RANGE OF MEDIA AND/OR TIME**

For this collaborative project, you will work with two other class members to conduct research and prepare a presentation on a memory or set of memories. You might, for this assignment, decide to investigate the memory/memories of someone like Angela Davis who was arrested and tried for murder in 1970. At the time of the arrest and trial, the news accounts in magazines and newspapers "remembered" Davis in very different ways, and the disparity between predominantly white news media representations and those of predominantly black news media was profound. Pictures of Davis at the time could make her look like a hero — or a villain. In addition, at least one song was written about her, again "remembering" her in a distinct way. You might also choose to focus on something that you remember vividly — a famous sporting or musical event, perhaps, or an unforgettable person or even a particular product. For example, it might be interesting to take something like Dr. Pepper and see how that product gets remembered at different times and in different media. My guess is that early Dr. Pepper advertisements were notably different from those that later appeared on television — or than those that appear today on billboards.

Your goal in this assignment is to study the way something is represented and hence remembered — and to think hard about how the medium of expression influences and shapes that representation/remembering. We will take time in class to discuss ground rules for these group projects, set out time lines, and decide on how to share and evaluate the work of all members. Plan to present this exploration in writing (including illustrations of how the person, event, or object has been represented, since this seems like an assignment in which the writing will necessarily involve other media) and to present a brief collaborative overview of your findings in class. Finally, work with members of your group to write a reflective memo to me and the class about what you've learned about working with a small group to prepare a presentation, about moving from writing to oral presentation, and about the relationship between writing and speaking.

(Lunsford, "Why and How")

Example 9.7   **RESEARCH-BASED MULTIMEDIA MEMOIR:**
               A RADIO OR VIDEO ESSAY

This assignment may well grow out of either your first or second assignment, but this time you will be designing your essay specifically for listening and/or viewing. We will be hearing at least two radio essays in class, and others will be available to you on our Web site and in the media library; in addition, we'll take a look at one student-written video essay.

For this assignment to be effective, you will need to create a storyboard for the essay and then write the material for it and record it, using your own voice and other voices if necessary, and adding a sound track and (if you are working in video) visual images.

Before you begin work on this project, decide who your audience will be and where your essay would be "published": for example, on National Public Radio, on the Stanford radio network, or on a personal Web site.

We will develop the criteria for this assignment together, and our course will culminate in your formal presentation about this work. For this assignment, then, you will have two end products: the radio/video essay itself and a formal class presentation in which you talk about the work you did to create the essay, using clips from it to illustrate your points.

(Lunsford, "Why and How")

Although these three assignments form a sequence in a class devoted to the study of memory, you need not teach a themed course in order to adapt the assignments to your purposes. Example 9.5 asks students to do analysis and research and to write for a popular audience. Example 9.6 asks students to work collaboratively to explore the ways in which time and media affect memory and perception, and to present and reflect on their work together. Finally, Example 9.7 asks students to shape their work in a way that will likely be memorable to contemporary audiences, using available technologies to present their work to others. Together, these three assignments also provide students with opportunities to work with visuals — taking photos, analyzing visuals, and using images in their own presentations.

WORKS CITED

Axelrod, Rise B., and Charles R. Cooper. *The St. Martin's Guide to Writing*, 9th ed. New York: Bedford, 2010. Print.

Bernard-Donals, Michael. "Forgetful Memory and Images of the Holocaust." *College English* 64.4 (2004): 380–402. Print.

Berthoff, Ann E. *The Making of Meaning.* Portsmouth: Boynton/Cook, 1981. Print.

Bishop, Wendy, and Pavel Zemliansky, eds. *The Subject Is Research.* Portsmouth: Boynton/Cook, 2001. Print.

Campbell, George. "From *The Philosophy of Rhetoric.*" *The Rhetorical Tradition.* Ed. Patricia Bizzell and Bruce Herzberg. 2nd ed. Boston: Bedford, 2001. 902–46. Print.

Cicero. *On the Ideal Orator.* Trans. James M. May and Jakob Wisse. New York: Oxford UP, 2001. Print.

Corbett, Edward P. J., and Robert Connors. *Classical Rhetoric for the Modern Student.* 4th ed. New York: Oxford UP, 1999. Print.

Crowley, Sharon. "Modern Rhetoric and Memory." *Rhetorical Memory and Delivery: Classical Concepts for Contemporary Compositions and Communication.* Ed. John Frederick Reynolds. Hillsdale: Erlbaum, 1993. 31–44. Print.

Frey, James. *A Million Little Pieces.* New York: Doubleday, 2003. Print.

Goldthwaite, Melissa. "This, Too, Is Research." *The Subject Is Research.* Ed. Wendy Bishop and Pavel Zemliansky. Portsmouth: Boynton/Cook, 2001. 193–203. Print.

Hampl, Patricia. *I Could Tell You Stories: Sojourns in the Land of Memory.* New York: Norton, 1999. Print.

Horner, Winifred Bryan. "Introduction." *Rhetorical Memory and Delivery: Classical Concepts for Contemporary Compositions and Communication.* Ed. John Frederick Reynolds. Hillsdale: Erlbaum, 1993. ix–xii Print.

Lunsford, Andrea A. *The St. Martin's Handbook.* 7th ed. New York: Bedford, 2011. Print.

——. "Why and How We Remember: The Rhetoric of Mediated Memory (Course Syllabus). *CourseWork.* Stanford U, 2004. Web. 16 Nov. 2012.

Reynolds, John Frederick, ed. *Rhetorical Memory and Delivery: Classical Concepts for Contemporary Compositions and Communication.* Hillsdale: Erlbaum, 1993. Print.

Roorbach, Bill. *Writing Life Stories.* Cincinnati: Story, 1998. Print.

Ulmer, Gregory L. *Heuristics: The Logic of Invention.* Baltimore: Johns Hopkins UP, 1994. Print.

Welch, Kathleen. *Electric Rhetoric: Classical Rhetoric, Oralism, and New Literacy.* Cambridge: MIT P, 1999. Print.

Useful Web Site

Andrea A. Lunsford's Syllabi for Courses on Memory
www.stanford.edu/~lunsfor1/syllabus.html

10

Teaching Delivery

Considering delivery enriches the composition classroom in invaluable ways. I urge students to think about composition as an embodied, multimodal act. How do their thoughts exist as more than ideas — as words that are heard or seen by eyes or ears (of varying abilities)? As symbols that might appear on paper but might also appear on computer (or other) screens? As concepts that can be expressed with words, images, colors? Suddenly, composition is more than responding to a prompt or "thinking up ideas and writing them down"; instead, composition becomes a great problem-solving activity.

–Heather Adams

DELIVERING WRITING, DELIVERING PEDAGOGY

According to Cicero, delivery "must be regulated by the movement of the body, by gesture, by facial expression, voice, and movement" (61). Because of this association with oratory, delivery — like the rhetorical canon of memory — has long been neglected in rhetoric texts devoted to writing. However, in the past twenty years, prompted in large part by fast-paced changes in technology, scholars of rhetoric and composition have also been recognizing the significance of delivery in textual performance (especially since computers allow for the use of sounds, images, colors, icons, and interactivity — blurring the boundary between performance and text) and other kinds of multimedia performances in which writing plays a significant role, such as speeches written to be read or presentations supported by visual accompaniments that include both text and images. Because of these changes, contemporary scholars of rhetoric and composition teachers alike need to be more inclusive in their approach to delivery.

Of course, the technological conditions in which one writes and teaches have always had an effect on writing and pedagogy. (For more on the relationship between writing technologies and delivery, see Ben McCorkle's *Rhetorical Delivery as Technological Discourse: A Cross-Historical Study*, cited at the end of this chapter.) Quintilian, in his *Institutes of Oratory*, dealt not only with the kinds of oral delivery Cicero wrote about but also written delivery as it was influenced by the technology of his time. Quintilian observes that "we can write best on *waxen tablets*, from which there is the greatest facility for erasing" and encourages students to "take care to leave some pages blank, on which we may have free scope for making any additions; since want of room sometimes causes a reluctance to correct, or, at least, what was written first makes a confused mixture with what is inserted" (Book X, chapter III, 290). He further expresses his preference for waxen tablets over parchment paper because "the frequent movement of the hand

backwards and forwards, while dipping the pen in ink, causes delay, and interrupts the current of thought" (Book X, chapter III, 290). Such relationships
among theory, practice, and the technologies of writing call for continued
intensive study in our rapidly changing time.

As Kathleen Blake Yancey reminds us, the term *delivery* can be used not only
to refer to oratory and writing but also to pedagogy. Yancey and other scholars have been investigating the varied ways instruction in college composition
courses is "delivered" to differing populations and in various contexts. Yancey,
in *Delivering College Composition,* pinpoints some important questions and issues
related to delivering composition pedagogy when she asks, "What is composing?
How should it be delivered?" She encourages teachers and researchers to think
carefully "about what college composing is, how it is best learned, and what
that might mean for a curricular space that is affected and shaped by—indeed
in dialogue with—a corresponding physical space" (12). Consideration of these
questions and issues will inform both the arrangement and content of this
chapter on delivery: What is the nature of composition? What literacies do composing and the teaching of composition demand, utilize, invite? In what ways do
material conditions, including physical space, affect the work that composition
teachers and students do?

THE CHANGING NATURE OF WRITING, READING, AUDIENCE, AND CONTEXT

In the twenty-first century, how do teachers and scholars of writing define our
subject? It is almost a cliché today to say that the traditional rhetorical triangle
of writer, reader, and text has exploded out at every angle. Post-structuralist critiques have made discussion of a monolithic student writer problematic; while
work on double consciousness (following W. E. B. DuBois) and multiple voices
(Anzaldúa, hooks, Royster) has undermined the concept of a writer's singular
"voice" while highlighting the ways in which writing is collaborative (Lunsford
and Ede, "Collaborative Learning" and "Let Them Write"; and Ede and Lunsford,
Singular Texts).

And what of the concept of reader or audience? In his well-known article "The
Writer's Audience Is Always a Fiction," Walter Ong writes:

> A history of literature could be written in terms of the ways in which audiences
> have successfully been fictionalized from the time when writing broke away
> from oral performance, for, just as each genre grows out of what went before it,
> so each new role that readers are made to assume is related to previous roles. (12)

Readers, we know, both play and resist roles called for by written texts rather
than passively receiving the messages writers construct. Readers actively shape
(and are shaped by) the reading process by re-reading, writing in margins,
writing notes or other texts of their own in response, reading aloud, discussing
ideas, interpreting, misinterpreting, remembering, forgetting, dismissing, accepting, synthesizing, making connections, articulating objects, and playing a host

of other roles in addition (see Eberly; Ede and Lunsford; Park; Royster; and Selzer).

The notion of what constitutes a text has also expanded almost out of bounds; first of all, post-structuralists continue to argue that all the world is a text; and, second, what constitutes a text continues to shift with the emergence of new media and technologies.

New media and technology also blur the boundaries separating the traditional language arts: reading, writing, speaking, and listening. When we watch television, for example, we are reading as well as listening, and we may be talking back or even composing our own countertexts. When the president addresses the nation, he appears to be engaged in an oral presentation, when in fact, he is reading a written text. When a student sits at a computer studying a Web site rich with audio, images, and video, what are all the literate acts in which she is engaged?

These changing understandings of writing and literacy offer opportunities to create richly mediated texts that are exciting for teachers and students alike, but these opportunities also bring challenges, such as the pressing need for new and expanded definitions of writing and reading as well as writers and readers.

Establishing Goals — and Delivering on Them

As Marvin Diogenes and Andrea A. Lunsford observe in "Toward Delivering New Definitions of Writing," "For the present generation of college-aged students, reared and schooled in a culture of cable TV, computers, poetry slams, zines, the Internet, and the World Wide Web, writing is no longer a stable, black-and-white affair: writing is Technicolor, oral, and thoroughly integrated with visual and audio displays" (142). With an understanding not only of their student population at Stanford but also the exigencies of twenty-first-century communication, Diogenes and Lunsford describe the ways they and their colleagues in Stanford University's Program in Writing and Rhetoric have worked to "deliver an enlarged, enhanced definition of writing," one that includes attention to the teaching of "oral, visual, and multimedia rhetoric" (146).

In their article, they list the goals for a course that would work toward expanding the definition of writing. Such goals include, but are not limited to, the following:

- To identify, evaluate, and synthesize materials across a range of media and to explore how to present these materials effectively in support of the student's own arguments.
- To analyze the rhetoric of oral, visual, and multimedia documents with attention to how purpose, audience, and context help shape decisions about format, structure, and persuasive appeals.
- To learn to design appropriate and effective oral and multimedia texts.
- To reflect systematically on oral, visual, and multimedia rhetoric and writing. (Diogenes and Lunsford 147)

Their pedagogical strategy for achieving these goals was to design a sequence of assignments that led to a multimedia research-based argument. (For more on creating sequenced writing assignments, see Chapter 4.) The assignments included tasks such as "substantive writing, research, collaboration, and delivery of the argument in one or more media" as well as attention to the process of completing a large project — from proposal to research to drafting and revising to presenting findings publicly (148). Diogenes and Lunsford go on to describe the final assignment, "a reflective essay that essentially analyzed [students'] work in the course, noting how various media shaped their writing, how their rhetorical choices were affected by various media, and how they used a new medium effectively in the presentation of research" (148). Although in their article Diogenes and Lunsford do not describe the assignments in as much depth as they would to students actually carrying them out, their description does show how the sequence repeats certain activities such as research, rhetorical analysis, and presentation — providing students multiple opportunities to analyze and practice various forms of delivery.

Using Diogenes and Lunsford's goals and description as a guide, it is possible to design a sequence of your own. Example 10.1 provides a sample sequence.

Example 10.1   **AN ASSIGNMENT SEQUENCE FOR CREATING AND ANALYZING MULTIMEDIA RHETORIC**

Project proposal: Write a two-page proposal for your research-based argument that explains your topic, focus, and the potential significance of your argument. (5%)

Annotated bibliography: Provide an annotated bibliography that includes the six most important sources for your research-based argument. In addition to traditional print-based texts, your sources can also include visual, oral, or multimedia texts. (5%)

Comparative analysis: Choose three sources (from your list of six) that offer significant perspectives on the topic you have chosen for your research-based argument. Write a five-page comparative analysis of these three sources. Your analysis should indicate the strengths and weaknesses of each piece and also consider the rhetorical appeals each piece uses. (10%)

Research-based argument: Write an eight-page argumentative essay in which you draw on and integrate the sources you have used in your previous two assignments. (30%)

Rhetorical analysis 1: In a three-page essay, analyze the rhetorical strategies you used to make your research-based argument persuasive to an
academic audience (your instructor and classmates). How did your
purpose, audience, and context shape the choices you made? (10%)

Persuasive piece: Identify an audience outside of the university that
might be interested in your research, and choose a form that would best
convey your argument to that audience. You might write a magazine
article, prepare a pamphlet, create a commercial, or even write a song.
Your goal is to present your topic and research to a more general audience,
an audience that would be interested in your topic but might not have a
scholarly background in your research area. (20%)

Rhetorical analysis 2: In a three-page essay, analyze the rhetorical
strategies you used to make your argument persuasive to your chosen
audience. How did your purpose, audience, and context shape the choices
you made? (10%)

Multimedia presentation: I have reserved the last two weeks of class for
presentations. Prepare a twelve-minute presentation in which you discuss
your research experience and present your findings to the class. Be
prepared to discuss your research-based argument and to present your
persuasive piece, indicating its intended audience. (10%)

Other Options for Exploring Multiple Modes of Delivery

There are many textbooks that provide readings, assignments, and guidance
for analyzing and creating multimedia texts. Bedford/St. Martin's, for example,
offers texts such as *How to Write Anything, ReMix,* and *Seeing & Writing.* Christine Alfano and Alyssa O'Brien's *Envision: Writing and Researching Arguments*
links particularly well with the goals Diogenes and Lunsford describe in their
article. (Alfano and O'Brien are both lecturers in Stanford University's Program in Writing and Rhetoric.) *Envision* introduces students to visual rhetoric
and provides guidance for composing research arguments and multimedia
presentations.

   Even if you do not use a textbook that is explicitly devoted to the creation
and analysis of multimedia texts, most composition textbooks have interactive Web sites with materials for both teachers and students. Furthermore, we
are all bombarded with advertisements and e-mails that work in multimedia

ways to command attention and persuade to action. Through analyzing, creating, presenting, and evaluating such multifaceted texts, students will learn not only to better understand the many ways writing is deliverd but also to develop and practice the multiple literacy skills required to perform such tasks in rhetorically sophisticated and responsible ways. Example 10.2 provides an exercise in analysis. (Chapter 4, Successful Writing Assignments, provides practical advice for and additional assignments dealing with Web, oral, and visual texts.)

Example 10.2 **ANALYZING THE "SELVES" WE DELIVER ONLINE —
AN IN-CLASS EXERCISE**

Project a user profile from Google+, Tumblr, or Facebook for the whole class to view. (Given the sometimes explicit nature of such profiles, it's wise to choose one — preferably featuring various forms of writing, images, and sound — before you're standing in front of the class.) Provide students the following directions:

1. List the many genres and forms of writing used in the profile. (Many profiles have lists, poetry, song lyrics, blogs, e-mails, public bulletins, instant message logs, manifestos, reviews, narratives, comments from "friends," and a variety of other forms.)
2. List the potential audience(s), both intended and unintended, for the profile (close friends, acquaintances, strangers, stalkers, family members, law enforcement, employers, and so on).
3. Analyze the use of images and sounds in constructing the user's identity. What do viewers (think they) know about the individual by the pictures, icons, and other images used? What might the chosen sound and/or video clips say about the individual?
4. Analyze the "friends" linked to the person: How many friends does this person have? Why does the person have so many or so few? What do these friends look like? What does the user's choice of friends say about him or her? (A more in-depth approach would lead to analyzing each friend's profile, which can be very time-consuming.)

5. Consider the extent to which delivery is controlled by the layout of the program. What information is the user required to provide? What choices are left to the user in terms of layout, design, and information provided?

6. After analyzing such elements, consider the multiple ways — through various genres, images, sounds, and design — individuals compose and "deliver" selves (and are composed by audiences and influences beyond their control) in such interactive electronic spaces.

Often, students are savvier at using technology than they are at analyzing their use of technology (and the opposite is often true for teachers). In carrying out such an exercise collaboratively, students will quickly recognize the complicated rhetorical choices individuals make — sometimes consciously, other times unconsciously — and may also gain a better understanding of the potential effects of such choices.

UNDERSTANDING MULTIPLE LITERACIES AND THEIR EFFECTS ON DELIVERY

Closely related to the changing nature of writing and other rhetorical concerns is the issue of how first-year writing incorporates, interrogates, and expands students' multiple literacies — and helps them explore literacy within the context of their local communities. In addition to studying multiple literacies in school settings (Yagelski), teacher-researchers increasingly seek to learn more about student literacies at home (Heath, *Ways with Words* and *Words at Work*); in communities and other nonschool settings (Ball; Flower; Goldblatt, *Because We Live Here*, and *Writing Home*; Mahiri; Mathieu; Moss, *Literacy* and *Community Text*; Welch); and at work (Bazerman; Lovitt and Goswami; Odell and Goswami; Selzer). One important way to incorporate attention to delivery in the writing classroom is to examine how out-of-school literate behaviors interact with those demanded in school, exploring the full range of literacies students possess and then linking those literacies to the goals of both the teacher and students. Many teachers, too, provide opportunities for students to work with their communities on literacy projects. (For a home literacy autobiography written by a teacher-researcher, see Goldblatt's *Writing Home*, cited at the end of this chapter.)

One Approach to Considering Multiple Literacies: Defining Computer Literacies

In *Multiliteracies for a Digital Age*, Stuart A. Selber encourages readers to reimagine computer literacy, to focus — as Neil Postman has also urged — "on the conse-

quences and contexts of technology rather than merely on the technology itself"
(1). Selber details three vital forms of literacy that students need to acquire in
relation to computers: functional literacy, critical literacy, and rhetorical literacy. Tables 10.1, 10.2, and 10.3 display both visually and textually the parameters
Selber sets for such literacies.

TABLE 10.1 Selber's Parameters of a Functional Approach to
Computer Literacy

Parameters	Qualities of a Functionally Literate Student
Educational Goals	A functionally literate student uses computers effectively in achieving educational goals.
Social Conventions	A functionally literate student understands the social conventions that help determine computer use.
Specialized Discourses	A functionally literate student makes use of the specialized discourses associated with computers.
Management Activities	A functionally literate student effectively manages his or her online world.
Technological Impasses	A functionally literate student resolves technological impasses confidently and strategically.

Source: Selber 45.

TABLE 10.2 Selber's Parameters of a Critical Approach to
Computer Literacy

Parameters	Qualities of a Critically Literate Student
Design Cultures	A critically literate student scrutinizes the dominant perspectives that shape computer design cultures and their artifacts.
Use Contexts	A critically literate student sees use contexts as an inseparable aspect of computers that helps to contextualize and constitute them.
Institutional Forces	A critically literate student understands the institutional forces that shape computer use.
Popular Representations	A critically literate student scrutinizes representations of computers in the public imagination.

Source: Selber 96.

TABLE 10.3 Selber's Parameters of a Rhetorical Approach to
Computer Literacy

Parameters	Qualities of a Rhetorically Literate Student
Persuasion	A rhetorically literate student understands that persuasion permeates interface design contexts in both implicit and explicit ways and that it always involves larger structures and forces (e.g., use contexts, ideology).
Deliberation	A rhetorically literate student understands that interface design problems are ill-defined problems whose solutions are representational arguments that have been arrived at through various deliberative activities.
Reflection	A rhetorically literate student articulates his or her interface design knowledge at a conscious level and subjects [. . .] actions and practices to critical assessment.
Social Action	A rhetorically literate student sees interface design as a form of social versus technical action.

Source: Selber 147.

Using Selber's Approach in the Classroom

Selber's approach to computer literacy demonstrates the ways that a seemingly "singular" literacy can be broken up into constituent parts and understood in its complexity. That is, any literacy requires multiple literacies. With this understanding of complexity, Selber's ideas can be used in a number of ways in the composition classroom.

Using a digital projector, document camera, or handouts, provide students with Selber's tables and guide them through the following exercise.

1. What literacies do you need to understand the information in the tables? Are there concepts you don't understand? Are there words you need to have defined? Is important information or context missing? Where would you go to find the information you need in order to understand Selber's ideas? (Be sure to provide students the bibliographic information for Selber's book!)
2. Use the tables as a checklist, checking off the computer literacies you already have (and making notes on the extent to which you have those literacies, since specific literacies are often better measured on a continuum rather than understood as something a person has or doesn't have). What literacies do you wish to gain or strengthen? How might you go about doing so?

3. Think about another literacy— something other than computer literacy—
with which you feel comfortable (waiting tables, fixing cars, dancing,
carpentry, mastering a particular computer game, or any other skill or
competency). Now, make your own tables, demonstrating the multifaceted nature of your own chosen literacy. Do the terms *functional*,
critical, and *rhetorical* also apply to the literacy you've chosen? If not,
what different terms would you use? What supporting terms help
clarify your understanding of a chosen literacy? (This project can also
be carried out in groups.)

By carrying out one or all of these exercises, students can begin to understand
the complexity and multiplicity of any given literacy and will be better prepared
to consider the various ways literacies overlap and inform each other.

You can then move from a discussion of the literacies students use outside of
school to a discussion of the terms *functional, critical,* and *rhetorical* as they apply
to writing, reading, speaking, and listening—the very literacies first-year writing
seeks to improve. What does it mean to be functionally, critically, and rhetorically literate in these areas? In what ways do students practice those literacies
and adapt them for other settings—other courses they're taking, communication at home, participation in their communities?

Expanding Consideration of Multiple Literacies in the Classroom

One way to explore the questions asked above is to have students brainstorm
lists (a separate page for each list) of all the kinds of reading, writing, speaking,
and listening they do—and in what contexts they perform these acts. After
students have composed (either in groups or individually) their seemingly discrete lists, ask them to consider the places of overlap: For example, in writing
a paper for school, do they also read, speak, and listen? When they listen to a
lecture, do they also take notes, read the words on the chalkboard or projection
screen, and read the instructor's and their classmates' body language? Almost
every activity—inside or outside of school—requires some level of visual, aural,
and gestural literacy. Students must also be aware, however, of the difference
between a literacy of delivery (writing texts, sharing images, and speaking) and
a literacy of reception (reading, listening, observing). That is, knowing how to
read body language is not the same as having the skill to use body language
effectively in an oral presentation. Although learning to read body language is
important to learning to use it, it is possible to be functionally literate in one
skill and not the other. Examining this difference will help reinforce the multiple skills and knowledge sets required for functional, critical, and rhetorical
literacies.

This general discussion of multiple literacies can then be applied to a more
specific classroom activity, the analysis of an assignment, as described in
Example 10.3.

Example 10.3   **MULTIPLE LITERACIES FOR SPECIFIC ASSIGNMENTS**

1. Consider your next assignment. List the literacies required in order to fulfill the assignment. Will you need to do research? (Will such research require skill in using an online database, a search engine, or field research, or skill in incorporating and citing sources?) Will you be analyzing a text or a situation? (Will you need knowledge of a specific terminology or theory in order to do so?) What form or genre will you use? (What are the conventions you need to know?)

2. What tools and media will you use in your delivery of the final "product"? What format, typeface, and citation style will you use? If you're using visuals, how will you be attentive to attribution and fair use?

3. After you've considered the multiple literacies, media, and tools needed to fulfill the assignment, list the ones with which you feel most comfortable and least comfortable. What questions do you have?

Since different mediums and literacies require knowledge of different conventions, conventions that must be taught, spend some time in class answering students' questions and providing guidance, making sure they're prepared to carry out the assignment.

The need for skill in and knowledge of multiple and overlapping literacies is inescapable, but by analyzing the skills and competencies you want students to develop, you can help make the process of learning less overwhelming, less mysterious, and more exciting as students recognize the options they have. (For another assignment on considering multiple literacies, see the Visual Essay Assignment in Chapter 4; also, see Chapter 8 for information and exercises related to language variety.)

DELIVERING PEDAGOGY: EXTRATEXTUAL SPACES

We conclude this chapter by expanding the notion of delivery to include, as Yancey and her colleagues have done in *Delivering College Composition,* consideration of material conditions that affect the teaching and learning of composition. She and the colleagues who wrote essays for her edited collection use the lens of *delivery* to "look at college composition in diverse institutions and regions of the country," studying specific "classrooms, sites, and programs" from research universities, comprehensive universities, and liberal arts colleges to high schools and cyberclassrooms (ix). One facet of that exploration is a closer look at how material conditions, including physical space, affect the work composition teachers and students do. In Chapter 11, we encourage more study of these important issues.

One Approach to Delivery in Extratextual Spaces

In his essay "Design, Delivery, and Narcolepsy," Todd Taylor considers "the body language of instructors and students operating in the architectural space of a four-walled, institutional classroom" (128). Taylor's concern is why students often fall asleep in class — and what teachers can learn from such behavior. He considers teachers' and administrators' lack of attention to the "lives of students: what they think about, their priorities, what they want, who they are, how their minds and bodies operate" (138) and argues that attention to such elements might lead to profitable changes in matters ranging from classroom design to what time the school day begins to the genres taught and to what is discussed in class.

Using Taylor's Approach in the Classroom

Taylor encourages attention to the actual design of classroom spaces, what he calls "the ergonomics of delivery," and how such ergonomics "both reflect and reshape pedagogical design" (130). One example of how space can affect pedagogy is the difficulty of encouraging small group work in a room in which chairs are bolted to the floor. Your students will be able to find many more examples as they work through the questions and activities suggested in Example 10.4.

Example 10.4   ANALYZING DELIVERY IN CLASSROOM SPACES

1. List the methods of instruction and aids to learning used in your composition class (e.g., lecture, whole-class discussions, small-group work, peer response, reading aloud, reading silently, writing on the chalkboard, writing on paper, writing with the use of computers, etc.). In which of these activities are you actively involved? Which ones are carried out primarily by your teacher? Which ones aid most in your learning of the subject matter?

2. Write about the physical space of the classroom: its size; the presence or absence of climate control (a usable thermostat); the presence or absence of windows (and whether they open); the proximity of the classroom to other classrooms, hallways, buildings, offices, streets; the number of

chairs/desks, their arrangement (rows, circle, half-circle), their size, and whether there are any for left-handers; the presence, age, and arrangement of other equipment in the room (chalkboard or whiteboard, TV/DVD, projector, screen, document camera, computers, clock, and so on); whether any equipment is outdated, distracting, or seldom used; the location of doors; the kind and quality of lighting; the extent to which the room is accessible to those with disabilities (learning disabilities, mobility impairment, blindness, deafness).

3. Read your responses to questions one and two, and make a claim concerning the extent to which the physical space of the classroom shapes, interrupts, and/or aids your learning. What specific improvements might be made by you, your teacher, or those who have control over the physical space of the classroom?

In doing this classroom exercise, you might meet student resistance ("It's your job, not mine, to set up the classroom in a way conducive to learning") or excuses for poor performance ("I can't perform well on in-class writings because of bad lighting and hallway noise"), but even what at first can come across as excuses can provide useful information for teachers. Although you cannot unbolt the desks from the floor or eliminate all hallway noise, you can request a different classroom for the next term or make other changes. You may not even be aware, for example, of the ways your pedagogy works — or doesn't work — for those with particular disabilities. For example, projecting key points on a screen in large print, emphasizing those points verbally, and then providing an exercise that reinforces those points can help those with visual impairments, difficulty hearing, and different learning styles.

This exercise may make you aware of students' learning needs and how your use of classroom space and technology can help you address students' concerns. The immediate benefit of this exercise for students is that it can expand their understanding of delivery and help them recognize the ways that not only individuals but also objects and physical spaces influence communication. This exercise can also be used as a precursor for an assignment in which students analyze the other places in which they write — dorm rooms, libraries, coffee shops — perhaps prompting students to modify their own surroundings or to seek out other places more conducive to writing. Likewise, such exercises can help students consider other physical spaces that shape and affect both their communicative practices and opportunities for learning, reminding them there are concrete steps they can take to communicate and to learn more effectively. In engaging such thoughts and discussions, students will have a better sense of the multiple ways the study of writing—in its numerous forms—is "delivered" and how they can deliver their own texts to others in effective ways.

WORKS CITED

Alfano, Christine, and Alyssa O'Brien. *Envision: Writing and Researching Arguments.* 3rd ed. New York: Longman, 2011. Print.

Anzaldúa, Gloria. *Borderlands/La Frontera.* San Francisco: Lute, 1987. Print.

Ball, Arnetha. "Cultural Preference and the Expository Writing of African American Adolescents." *Written Communication* 9.4 (1992): 501–32. Print.

Bazerman, Charles. *Shaping Written Knowledge: The Genre and Activity of the Experimental Article in Science.* Madison: U of Wisconsin P, 1988. Print.

Cicero. *On the Ideal Orator.* Trans. James M. May and Jakob Wisse. New York: Oxford UP, 2001. Print.

Diogenes, Marvin, and Andrea A. Lunsford. "Toward Delivering New Definitions of Writing." *Delivering College Composition: The Fifth Canon.* Ed. Kathleen Blake Yancey. Portsmouth: Boynton/Cook, 2006. 141–54. Print.

DuBois, W. E. B. *The Souls of Black Folk: Essays and Sketches.* 1903. New York: Modern Library, 2003. Print.

Eberly, Rosa A. "From *Writers, Audiences, and Communities* to *Publics:* Writing Classrooms as Protopublic Spaces." *Rhetoric Review* 18.1 (1999): 165–78. Print.

Ede, Lisa, and Andrea A. Lunsford. *Singular Texts/Plural Authors: Perspectives on Collaborative Writing.* Carbondale: Southern Illinois UP, 1990. Print.

Flower, Linda. *Learning to Rival.* Mahwah: Erlbaum, 2000. Print.

Goldblatt, Eli. *Because We Live Here: Sponsoring Literacy beyond the College Curriculum.* New York: Hampton P, 2007. Print.

——. *Writing Home: A Literacy Autobiography.* Carbondale, Southern Illinois UP, 2012. Print.

Heath, Shirley Brice. *Ways with Words: Language, Life, and Work in Communities and Classrooms.* Cambridge: Cambridge UP, 1983. Print.

——. *Words at Work and Play: Three Decades in Family and Community Life.* Cambridge: Cambridge UP, 2012. Print.

hooks, bell. *Talking Back: Thinking Feminist, Thinking Black.* Boston: South End, 1989. Print.

Latterell, Catherine G. *ReMix: Reading and Composing Culture.* 2nd ed. Boston: Bedford, 2010. Print.

Lovitt, Carl, and Dixie Goswami. *Exploring the Rhetoric of International Professional Communication: An Agenda for Teachers and Researchers.* Amityville: Baywood, 1999. Print.

Lunsford, Andrea, and Lisa Ede. "Collaborative Learning: Lessons from the World of Work." *Writing Program Administration* 9 (1986): 17–27. Print.

——. "Let Them Write—Together." *English Quarterly* 18.4 (1985): 119–27. Print.

Lyon, Scott. "Rhetorical Sovereignty: What Do American Indians Want from Writing?" *CCC* 51.3 (2000): 447–68. Print.

Mahiri, Jabari, ed. *What They Don't Learn in School.* New York: Lang, 2002. Print.

Mathieu, Paula. *Tactics of Home: The Public Turn in English Composition.* Portsmouth: Boynton/Cook, 2005. Print.

McCorkle, Ben. *Rhetorical Delivery as Technological Discourse: A Cross-Historical Study.* Carbondale: Southern Illinois UP, 2012. Print.

McQuade, Donald, and Christine McQuade. *Seeing & Writing.* 4th ed. Boston: Bedford, 2010. Print.

Moss, Beverly. *Literacy across Communities.* Cresskill: Hampton, 1994. Print.

——. *A Community Text Arises.* Cresskill: Hampton, 2002. Print.

Odell, Lee, and Dixie Goswami. *Writing in Non-Academic Settings.* New York: Guilford, 1985. Print.

Ong, Walter. "The Writer's Audience Is Always a Fiction." *PMLA* 90.1 (1975): 9–21. Print.

Park, Douglas. "Analyzing Audiences." *CCC* 37.4 (1986): 478–88. Print.

Quintilian. *Institutes of Oratory.* Trans. John Shelby Watson. London: George Bell and Sons, 1891. Print.

Royster, Jacqueline Jones. "When the First Voice You Hear Is Not Your Own." *CCC* 47.1 (1996): 29–40. Print.

Ruszkiewicz, John, and Joy T. Dolmage. *How to Write Anything.* 2nd ed. Boston: Bedford, 2012. Print.

Selber, Stuart A. *Multiliteracies for a Digital Age.* Carbondale: Southern Illinois UP, 2004. Print.

Selzer, Jack. "The Composing Processes of an Engineer." *CCC* 34.2 (1983): 178–87. Print.

Taylor, Todd. "Design, Delivery, and Narcolepsy." *Delivering College Composition: The Fifth Canon.* Ed. Kathleen Blake Yancey. Portsmouth: Boynton/Cook, 2006. 127–40. Print.

Welch, Nancy. *Living Room: Teaching Public Writing in a Privatized World.* Portsmouth: Boynton/Cook, 2008. Print.

Yagelski, Robert. *Literacy Matters.* New York: Teachers College P, 2000. Print.

Yancey, Kathleen Blake, ed. *Delivering College Composition: The Fifth Canon.* Portsmouth: Boynton/Cook, 2006. Print.

11

Invitation to Further Study

During my first semester in graduate school, I took a seminar in the history and theory of composition studies. As one of two first year students and the only new teacher, I was initially intimidated by the experience of my peers. I felt like I was at a disadvantage when it came to understanding and contributing to the discussion because I had such little anecdotal evidence of my own to refer to. By the end of that semester, I realized that I had just as much of an entry into the conversation as any of my peers or professors. Learning to consider my successes and failures in the classroom (even with that first group of students) in light of the questions posed by composition scholars immediately grounded me as a teacher. Getting in the habit of looking to what is happening in the field has helped me build a foundation from which I am able to effectively learn from my own experiences.

–Laura Michael Brown

If theory is tested when we put it into practice, the reverse holds true as well: All our classroom practices need to be reexamined continually in the light of contemporary scholarly discussions. Beginning teachers are often interested in finding out why certain theories translate well into practice, whereas others that seem to have equal potential fail miserably. Even after a year in the classroom, during which they have experienced successes, teachers often cannot explain those successes in terms of their theoretical base. Fortunately for those interested in the theory and practice of composition, arenas in which to explore the complex relationship between theory and practice are easily found.

WAYS INTO THE SCHOLARLY AND PEDAGOGIC CONVERSATION

Professional organizations—such as the Conference on College Composition and Communication (CCCC), the Modern Language Association (MLA), the Rhetoric Society of America (RSA), the International Society for the History of Rhetoric (ISHR), the National Council of Teachers of English (NCTE), Teachers of English to Speakers of Other Languages (TESOL), Writing Program Administrators (WPA), the National Writing Centers Association (NWCA), the Conference on Computers and Composition, Language and Learning across the Curriculum (LALAC), and state and local organizations—offer a way to learn about the current concerns in this field as well as a wide arena for scholarly activity on writing and rhetoric. Many teachers and scholars of writing feel that attending one of these organizations' national or state meetings every year provides the excitement of learning and sharing that sustains them through their next year of hard work.

The NCTE is the most broad-based of these organizations, for its membership comprises teachers of language arts, literature, and writing from prekindergarten through college. For college-level writing teachers, perhaps the most stimulating and useful professional meeting is the CCCC, held annually, usually in March. Over a four-day period, the CCCC offers hundreds of sessions that attempt a balance among pedagogy, theory, and research in writing and rhetoric. Like most other organizations, it also offers graduate students special membership and conference rates.

Some professional organizations publish their own journals. *College Composition and Communication* (CCC), *College English* (CE), *English Journal* (EJ), *Teaching English in the Two-Year College* (TETYC), and *Research in the Teaching of English* (RTE) are all published by the NCTE, and subscriptions to some of these journals are automatic on joining the organization. Numerous journals are published by other organizations or institutions (including university and commercial presses): *Journal of Business and Technical Communication; Contemporary Issues in Technology and Teacher Education Journal; Across the Disciplines; TESOL Journal; Writing Program Administration* (WPA); *Rhetoric Society Quarterly* (RSQ); *Rhetorica; Composition Studies; JAC: A Journal of Advanced Composition; Computers and Composition; Journal of Basic Writing; Journal of Teaching Writing; Writing Center Journal; Written Communication; Kairos: A Journal of Rhetoric, Technology, and Pedagogy; Writing on the Edge*; and many others.

Many of the journals mentioned thus far are available online at the sponsoring organizations' Web sites, where visitors can check out the latest information on calls for papers, upcoming publications, conferences, and other events (see the list of Useful Web Sites at the end of this chapter). In addition, beginning teachers of writing may want to join one or more listservs in rhetoric and composition.

The last thirty years have seen a veritable explosion of publications in the field of composition and rhetoric. When the field emerged as its own discipline in the late 1960s, only three journals existed; today that number has expanded tenfold. Perhaps best of all for beginning teachers, almost all these journals welcome new voices in the profession, offering opportunities for publication that did not exist forty years ago.

Just as journals have proliferated in the field, so have book series. The major publisher of works in rhetoric and composition since the 1960s, Southern Illinois University Press, led the way with the *Landmarks in Rhetoric and Public Address* series, to which it has added other series, most notably *Studies in Rhetoric and Feminisms, Rhetorical Philosophy and Theory*, and *Rhetoric in the Modern Era*. NCTE also sponsors a monograph series, *Studies in Writing and Rhetoric*, intended to highlight the best current research in the field. Other publishers that sponsor important series in rhetoric and composition include the University of Pittsburgh Press, Southern Methodist University Press, University of Wisconsin Press, Utah State University Press, Boynton/Cook, Ablex, University of Michigan Press, Hampton Press, and State University of New York Press.

COMPOSITION/RHETORIC AND ITS CONCERNS

The proliferation of journals, book series, conferences, and graduate programs devoted to composition/rhetoric suggests that this field represents an umbrella under which many areas of study cluster together. Like other fields (English studies, for example, encompasses both British and American literature across all historical periods as well as critical theory, narrative theory, and often folk-lore, creative writing, and applied linguistics), composition/rhetoric (also known as writing studies) is a large endeavor. It brings together researchers and teachers interested in subjects as diverse as the history and theory of rhetoric; feminist writing pedagogies; the history, theory, and pedagogy of composition; composition and technology; literacy studies; disability studies; and specific areas of writing or groups of writers, such as writing across the curriculum, writing in the disciplines, basic writing, advanced composition, and multilingual writers. The field has been shaped, too, by cultural studies, and many scholars study writing in relation to class, sexuality, race, gender, and other aspects of identity. This array of subjects calls for a range of methodologies. Thus scholars of composition/rhetoric draw on historiography, rhetorical analysis, discourse analysis, feminist analysis, ethnography (and other forms of qualitative research), and social science methodology (such as quantitative analysis of survey data).

CENTRAL CONCERNS

Across this range of subfields and methods lie several central concerns, three of which seem particularly important to the work of writing teachers.

The Content of First-Year Writing and Transfer

The first pressing concern is the question of what should be the content of first-year writing and how — or if — that content will allow students to transfer the knowledge and skills they've gained to other settings both inside and outside the university. This general question prompts more specific inquiries, such as:

- What theories should shape the teaching of composition: process theory, rhetorical theory, cultural studies, feminist theory (Tate, Rupiper, and Schick)? Should first-year writing classes focus on the writing process (Tobin and Newkirk), or are post-process theories of writing of greater pedagogical importance (Kent)? Should first-year writing focus on broad academic discourse, or should it be an introduction to writing studies (Downs and Wardle; see Part III of this text)?
- What forms and genres should we teach students to write? personal narratives and other forms of creative nonfiction? research papers and other

forms of academic argument? Web sites and other electronic texts? letters
to the editor and other forms that prompt civic engagement? Which of
these genres will help students in the writing they do for other classes
and outside the classroom (Beaufort; Wardle)?

- What are the most important skills and concepts for students to learn in
  the writing classroom? the importance of drafting and revision? how to
  write and support an argument? close reading? rhetorical analysis? documentation of sources? critical thinking?
- How should readings be used in the writing classroom? Should teachers
  and students give equal attention to reading and writing? Should texts be
  used as models to develop better writing, as content for the discussion
  of ideas and politics, as sources for the development of critical reading
  strategies?

The ways in which composition scholars, textbook authors, writing program
administrators, and individual teachers answer these questions shape the field
of composition studies, writing programs, and particular classrooms.

Across the nation, composition programs are flourishing in wildly divergent
directions. Is there any foundation common to all of these programs? Should
there be?

Disciplinarity and Assessment

Closely related to the content of first-year writing is the second concern: Who
are we as a discipline? rhetoric and composition? writing studies? literacy studies? Where do we locate ourselves in the university? Are we housed in English
departments, writing studies departments, communications departments? From
whom do we receive our support? Are corporations supporting our research?
(If so, what is the influence of corporate interests?)

Who we are as a discipline and where we are housed and how we're supported
affect processes of assessment—of programs, of faculty, and of student learning
(Huot and O'Neill). Who are we testing, in the name of what standards, and for
whose purposes? Do assessments for accreditation purposes show us anything
about student learning? What type of assessment is most effective—and why?

While we as a nation seem completely devoted to assessing and testing, the reasons for doing so are far from clear. Even more troubling is the fact that current
theories of testing (like most of the tests themselves) rest on a questionable epistemology, one that views knowledge as quantitative, externalized, and statistically
verifiable. Although such a view has been under attack since the early twentieth
century in almost every field, it still underlies most testing efforts today.

Diversity and Difference

Another major concern of writing teachers and researchers is diversity. Once
composition scholars began to question the ways in which focusing on the
writing process led inevitably to essentializing students, the full impact of diver-

sity in writing classes became unavoidable. Even a supposedly homogeneous group of students will reveal wide diversity, and most of our classrooms are far from homogeneous. The same is true, too, of teachers and scholars. Growing recognition of the role that material and personal contexts — gender, sexual orientation, race, ethnicity, socioeconomic class, age, ability, religion, culture, and linguistic background — play in writing and teaching has led to a generation of exciting scholarship. We list many compelling studies, works that have added in deeply significant ways to our knowledge about diversity and difference, at the end of this chapter under the heading "Axes of Difference." For more on diversity, both in the field of rhetoric and composition and in the writing classroom, we invite you to read the articles in Part III of this text, especially Jacqueline Jones Royster's "When the First Voice You Hear Is Not Your Own," Stephanie L. Kerschbaum's "Avoiding the Difference Fixation: Identity Categories, Markers of Difference, and the Teaching of Writing," Ilona Leki's "Meaning and Development of Academic Literacy in a Second Language," Paul Kei Matsuda's "The Myth of Linguistic Homogeneity," Bruce Horner and his colleagues' "OPINION: Language Difference in Writing: Toward a Translingual Approach," and Cheryl Glenn's "Representing Ourselves."

It should not be surprising that one of the many lessons we learn from these scholarly works is a grammatical one, for structures of hierarchy and power are inscribed in our language as well as in the ways we talk about gender, race, class, and clan and in the ways we read, write, think, and respond. Unless we learn this lesson, we may listen to our very diverse students in class and read this important scholarship to little or no avail. The time has never been more ripe for all teachers to gain insights from studying important works such as those listed here as a central part of their pedagogy.

ANOTHER INVITATION TO FURTHER RESEARCH

These areas of concern represent only a few of the issues facing writing teachers today. In spite of five decades of intense scholarship and research, we have only begun to fill in the outlines of theories of language and learning that will shape the discourse of education in the twenty-first century. Unlike some other areas of English studies, which have been intensively examined for centuries, composition and rhetoric offer many areas in which the surface has hardly been scratched.

In short, exciting scholarly and pedagogic work awaits if you find yourself drawn to it. We hope that this book helps you settle into teaching writing with enthusiasm and confidence. We also hope it raises many questions you may want to pursue as teacher, scholar, and writer.

WORKS CITED

Anson, Chris. *Writing and Response: Theory, Practice, and Research.* Urbana: NCTE, 1989. Print.

Beaufort, Anne. *College Writing and Beyond: A New Framework for University Writing.*
   Logan: Utah State UP, 2007. Print.

Downs, Douglas, and Elizabeth Wardle. "Teaching about Writing, Righting Misconceptions: (Re)Envisioning 'First-Year Composition' as 'Introduction to Writing
   Studies.'" *CCC* 58.4 (2007): 552–84. Print.

Huot, Brian, and Peggy O'Neill. *Assessing Writing: A Critical Sourcebook.* Boston:
   Bedford, 2009. Print.

Kent, Thomas, ed. *Post-Process Theory: Beyond the Writing-Process Paradigm.* Carbondale:
   Southern Illinois UP, 1999. Print.

Tate, Gary, Amy Rupiper, and Kurt Schick, eds. *A Guide to Composition Pedagogies.* New
   York: Oxford UP, 2001. Print.

Tobin, Lad, and Thomas Newkirk. *Taking Stock: The Writing Process Movement in the '90s.*
   Portsmouth: Boynton/Cook, 1994. Print.

Wardle, Elizabeth. "'Mutt Genres' and the Goal of FYC: How Can We Help Students
   Write the Genres of the University?" *CCC* 60.4 (2009): 765–89. Print.

Useful Web Sites
Rhetoric and Composition Journals

CEA Forum
   journals.tdl.org/ceaforum/index

College Composition and Communication (CCC)
   http://www.ncte.org/cccc/ccc/

College English (CE)
   www.ncte.org/journals/ce

Composition Studies
   www.compositionstudies.uwinnipeg.ca

Computers and Composition
   www.bgsu.edu/cconline

Currents in Electronic Literacy
   currents.cwrl.utexas.edu

JAC: A Journal of Advanced Composition
   www.jaconlinejournal.com/home.html

Journal of Teaching Writing
   journals.iupui.edu/index.php/teachingwriting

Kairos: Rhetoric, Technology, and Pedagogy
   english.ttu.edu/kairos

Radical Teacher
   www.radicalteacher.org

Rhetoric Society Quarterly (RSQ)
   rhetoricsociety.org/aws/RSA/pt/sp/rsq

Teaching English in the Two-Year College (TETYC)
www.ncte.org/journals/tetyc

Writing on the Edge
woe.ucdavis.edu/

The Writing Instructor
www.writinginstructor.com

Writing Program Administration (WPA)
wpacouncil.org/journal/index.html

SUGGESTED READINGS FOR TEACHERS OF WRITING

Thirty years ago, a graduate student or new teacher interested in entering the field of composition/rhetoric could attempt to read all the major contributions to the field, including the canonical texts in the history of rhetoric. Today, thanks to the inspired work of many scholars noted in this chapter and especially to the work of people of color and women, who have opened up the canon and led the way in expanding the concept of literacy, no such attempt at "coverage" is possible. And we think that's a good thing: Knowledge production should be as free and varied as possible.

We conclude this invitation to further study, then, with a list of commonly used reference works and brief lists of books and articles in eight areas of study; please note, though, that some of these categories overlap. Reading these selected works will give you something more important than coverage: an entry into the conversations that animate the field.

Bibliographies and Other Reference Works

Enos, Theresa, ed. *The Encyclopedia of Rhetoric and Composition: Communication from Ancient Times to the Information Age.* New York: Routledge, 2010. Print.

Gurak, Laura, and Mary M. Lay. *Research in Technical Communication.* Westport: Preager, 2002. Print.

Moran, Michael G., and Martin J. Jacobi. *Research in Basic Writing: Bibliographic Sourcebook.* New York: Greenwood, 1990. Print.

Moran, Michael G., and Ronald F. Lunsford. *Research in Composition and Rhetoric: A Bibliographic Sourcebook.* Westport: Greenwood, 1984. Print.

Reynolds, Nedra, Jay Dolmage, Patricia Bizzell, and Bruce Herzberg. *The Bedford Bibliography for Teachers of Writing.* 7th ed. Boston: Bedford, 2012. Print.

Smagorinsky, Peter. *Research on Composition: Multiple Perspectives on Two Decades of Change.* New York: Teachers College P, 2006. Print.

Rhetorical History, Theory, and Practice

Beale, Walter. *A Pragmatic Theory of Rhetoric.* Carbondale: Southern Illinois UP, 1987. Print.

Bizzell, Patricia, ed. *Feminist Historiography in Rhetoric.* Spec. issue of *Rhetoric Society Quarterly* 32.1 (2002): 7–124. Print.

Bizzell, Patricia, and Bruce Herzberg, eds. *The Rhetorical Tradition.* 2nd ed. Boston: Bedford, 2001. Print.

Burke, Kenneth. *Language as Symbolic Action.* Berkeley: U of California P, 1966. Print.

Glenn, Cheryl. *Rhetoric Retold: Regendering the Tradition from Antiquity to the Renaissance.* Carbondale: Southern Illinois UP, 1997. Print.

——. *Unspoken: A Rhetoric of Silence.* Carbondale: Southern Illinois UP, 2004. Print.

Johnson, Nan. *Gender and Rhetorical Space in American Life, 1866–1910.* Carbondale: Southern Illinois UP, 2002. Print.

Kates, Susan. *Activist Rhetorics and American Higher Education, 1885–1937.* Carbondale: Southern Illinois UP, 2001. Print.

Logan, Shirley Wilson. *We Are Coming: The Persuasive Discourse of Nineteenth Century Black Women.* Carbondale: Southern Illinois UP, 1999. Print.

Lunsford, Andrea A., ed. *Reclaiming Rhetorica.* Pittsburgh: U of Pittsburgh P, 1995. Print.

Neel, Jasper. *Aristotle's Voice: Rhetoric, Theory, and Writing in America.* Carbondale: Southern Illinois UP, 1994. Print.

——. *Plato, Derrida, and Writing.* Carbondale: Southern Illinois UP, 1988. Print.

Poulakos, John, and Takis Poulakos. *Classical Rhetorical Theory.* Boston: Houghton, 1999. Print.

Ritchie, Joy, and Kate Ronald. *Available Means: An Anthology of Women's Rhetoric.* Pittsburgh: U of Pittsburgh P, 2001. Print.

Swearingen, C. Jan. *Rhetoric and Irony: Western Literacy and Western Lies.* New York: Oxford UP, 1991. Print.

Villanueva, Victor. *Bootstraps: From an American Academic of Color.* Urbana: NCTE, 1993. Print.

Vitanza, Victor J. *Negation, Subjectivity, and the History of Rhetoric.* Albany: State U of New York P, 1997. Print.

Welch, Kathleen. *The Contemporary Reception of Classical Rhetoric.* Hillsdale: Erlbaum, 1990. Print.

——. *Electric Rhetoric.* Cambridge: MIT P, 1999. Print.

Composition History and Theory

Adams, Katherine. *A Group of Their Own: College Writing Courses and American Women Writers, 1880–1940.* Albany: State U of New York P, 2001. Print.

Berlin, James. "Rhetoric and Ideology in the Writing Class." *CE* 50.5 (1988): 477–94. Print.

——. *Rhetoric and Reality: Writing Instruction in American Colleges, 1900–1985.* Carbondale: Southern Illinois UP, 1987. Print.

Brereton, John. *The Origins of Composition Studies in American Colleges, 1875–1925: A Documentary History.* Pittsburgh: U of Pittsburgh P, 1995. Print.

Brueggemann, Brenda. *Lend Me Your Ear: Rhetorical Constructions of Deafness.* Washington: Gallaudet UP, 1999. Print.

Connors, Robert. *Composition/Rhetoric: Backgrounds, Theory, and Pedagogy.* Pittsburgh: U of Pittsburgh P, 1997. Print.

Crowley, Sharon. *Composition in the University: Historical and Polemical Essays.* Pittsburgh: U of Pittsburgh P, 1998. Print.

Faigley, Lester. *Fragments of Rationality: Postmodernity and the Subject of Composition.* Pittsburgh: U of Pittsburgh P, 1992. Print.

Flower, Linda. *The Construction of Negotiated Meaning: A Social Cognitive Theory of Writing.* Carbondale: Southern Illinois UP, 1994. Print.

Gere, Anne Ruggles. *Intimate Practices: Literacy and Cultural Work in U.S. Women's Clubs, 1880–1920.* Urbana: U of Illinois P, 1997. Print.

Harris, Joseph. *A Teaching Subject: Composition since 1966.* Upper Saddle River: Prentice, 1997. Print.

Miller, Richard E. *As If Learning Mattered: Reforming Higher Education.* Ithaca: Cornell UP, 1998. Print.

Miller, Susan. *Textual Carnivals: The Politics of Composition.* Carbondale: Southern Illinois UP, 1991. Print.

Miller, Tom. *The Formation of College English.* Pittsburgh: U of Pittsburgh P, 1997. Print.

Olson, Gary A. *Rhetoric and Composition as Intellectual Work.* Carbondale: Southern Illinois UP, 2002. Print.

Vanderberg, Peter, Sue Hum, and Jennifer Clary-Lemon. *Relations, Locations, Positions: Composition Theory for Writing Teachers.* Urbana: NCTE, 2006. Print.

Composition Practice and Pedagogy

Bishop, Wendy. *Something Old, Something New: College Writing Teachers and Classroom Change.* Carbondale: Southern Illinois UP, 1990. Print.

——. *Teaching Lives: Essays and Stories.* Logan: Utah State UP, 1997. Print.

Bloom, Lynn Z. *Composition Studies as a Creative Art: Teaching, Writing, Scholarship, Administration.* Logan: Utah State UP, 1998. Print.

Brodkey, Linda. *Writing Permitted in Designated Areas Only.* Minneapolis: U of Minnesota P, 1996. Print.

Elbow, Peter. *Everyone Can Write.* New York: Oxford UP, 2000. Print.

Halasek, Kay. *A Pedagogy of Possibilities.* Carbondale: Southern Illinois UP, 1999. Print.

Harris, Joseph. *A Teaching Subject: Composition since 1966.* Upper Saddle River: Prentice, 1997. Print.

Hunter, Susan, and Ray Wallace. *The Place of Grammar in Writing Instruction.* Portsmouth: Boynton/Cook, 1995. Print.

North, Stephen. *The Making of Knowledge in Composition.* Portsmouth: Boynton/Cook, 1987. Print.

Rose, Mike. *Possible Lives.* Boston: Houghton, 1995. Print.

Sullivan, Patricia, and Donna Qualley, eds. *Pedagogy in the Age of Politics.* Urbana: NCTE, 1994. Print.

Wiley, Mark, Barbara Gleason, and Louise Phelps. *Composition in Four Keys.* Mountain View: Mayfield, 1996. Print.

Literacy Studies

Brandt, Deborah. *Literacy as Involvement: The Acts of Writers, Readers, and Texts.* Carbondale: Southern Illinois UP, 1990. Print.

Cushman, Ellen, et al. *Literacy: A Critical Sourcebook.* Boston: Bedford, 2001. Print.

Flower, Linda. *Learning to Rival.* Mahwah: Erlbaum, 2000. Print.

Gilyard, Keith. *Voices of the Self.* Detroit: Wayne State UP, 1991. Print.

Heath, Shirley Brice. *Ways with Words*. New York: Cambridge UP, 1983. Print.

Hobbs, Catherine, ed. *Nineteenth Century Women Learn to Write*. Charlottesville: U of Virginia P, 1995. Print.

Lindemann, Erika, ed. *Reading the Past, Writing the Future: A Century of American Literacy Education and the National Council of Teachers of English*. Urbana: NCTE, 2010. Print.

Mahiri, Jabari, ed. *What They Don't Learn in School*. New York: Lang, 2002. Print.

Moss, Beverly. *Literacy across Communities*. Cresskill: Hampton, 1994. Print.

Royster, Jacqueline Jones. *Traces of a Stream*. Pittsburgh: U of Pittsburgh P, 2000. Print.

Selfe, Cynthia, and Susan Hilligoss. *Literacy and Computers: The Complications of Teaching and Learning with Technology*. New York: MLA, 1994. Print.

Street, Brian. *Cross-Cultural Approaches to Literacy*. New York: Cambridge UP, 1993. Print.

Stuckey, J. Elspeth. *The Violence of Literacy*. Portsmouth: Boynton/Cook, 1991. Print.

Trimbur, John. *Popular Literacy: Studies in Cultural Practices and Politics*. Pittsburgh: U of Pittsburgh P, 2001. Print.

Tuman, Myron. *A Preface to Literacy: An Inquiry into Pedagogy, Practice, and Progress*. Tuscaloosa: U of Alabama P, 1987. Print.

Yagelski, Robert. *Literacy Matters*. New York: Teachers College P, 2000. Print.

Axes of Difference

Ball, Arnetha, and Ted Lardner. "Dispositions toward Language: Teacher Constructs of Knowledge and the Ann Arbor Black English Case." *CCC* 48.4 (1997): 469–85. Print.

Belcher, Diane, and Ulla Connor, eds. *Reflections on Multiliterate Lives*. Clevedon: Multilingual Matters, 2001. Print.

Brueggemann, Brenda Jo. *Lend Me Your Ear: Rhetorical Constructions of Deafness*. Washington: Gallaudet UP, 1999. Print.

Brueggemann, Brenda Jo, et al. "Becoming Visible: Lessons in Disability." *CCC* 52.3 (2001): 368–98. Print.

Cook, William W. "Writing in the Spaces Left." *CCC* 44.1 (1993): 9–25. Print.

Delpit, Lisa. *Other People's Children*. New York: New, 1995. Print.

Delpit, Lisa, and Joanne Dowdy, eds. *The Skin That We Speak: Thoughts on Language and Culture in the Classroom*. New York: Norton, 2002. Print.

Flynn, Elizabeth. *Feminism beyond Modernism*. Carbondale: Southern Illinois UP, 2002. Print.

Foster, David, and David Russell. *Writing and Learning in Cross-National Perspectives*. Urbana: NCTE, 2002. Print.

Fox, Helen. *Listening to the World: Cultural Issues in Academic Writing*. Urbana: NCTE, 1994. Print.

Gilyard, Keith, ed. *Race, Rhetoric, and Composition*. Portsmouth: Boynton/Cook, 1999. Print.

Glenn, Cheryl. "Representing Ourselves." *CCC* 60.2 (2008): 420–39. Print.

Goldstein, Lynn. "For Kyla: What Does the Research Say about Responding to ESL Writers?" *On Second Language Writing*. Ed. Tony Silva and Paul Kei Matsuda. Mahwah: Erlbaum, 2001. 73–89. Print.

hooks, bell. *Teaching to Transgress: Education and the Practice of Freedom*. New York: Routledge, 1994. Print.

Horner, Bruce, et al. "Opinion: Language Difference in Writing: Toward a Translingual Approach." *College English* 73.3 (2011): 303–21. Print.

Jarratt, Susan, and Lynn Worsham. *Feminism and Composition Studies: In Other Words*. New York: MLA, 1994. Print.

Jordan, Jay. *Redesigning Composition for Multilingual Realities*. Urbana: NCTE/CCC/SIUP, 2012. Print.

Kerschbaun, Stephanie L. "Avoiding the Difference Fixation: Identity Categories, Markers of Difference, and the Teaching of Writing." *CCC* 63.4 (2012): 616–44. Print.

Li, Xiao-Ming. *"Good Writing" in Cross-Cultural Context*. Albany: State U of New York P, 1996. Print.

Lu, Min-Zhan. *Shanghai Quartet: The Crossings of Four Women of China*. Pittsburgh: Duquesne UP, 2001. Print.

Lyons, Scott Richard. "Rhetorical Sovereignty: What Do American Indians Want from Writing?" *CCC* 51.3 (2000): 447–68. Print.

Malinowitz, Harriet. *Textual Orientations: Lesbian and Gay Students and the Making of Discourse Communities*. Portsmouth: Boynton/Cook, 1994. Print.

Matsuda, Paul Kei. "The Myth of Linguistic Homogeneity in U.S. College Composition." *College English* 68.6 (2006): 637–51. Print.

Moss, Beverly. *A Community Text Arises*. Cresskill: Hampton, 2002. Print.

Pough, Gwendolyn. "Empowering Rhetoric: Black Students Writing Black Panthers." *CCC* 53.3 (2002): 466–86. Print.

Richardson, Elaine. "'To Protect and Serve': African American Female Literacies." *CCC* 53.4 (2002): 675–704. Print.

Royster, Jacqueline Jones, and Jean Williams. "History in the Spaces Left: African American Presence and Narratives of Composition Studies." *CCC* 50.4 (1999): 563–84. Print.

Severeino, Carol, Juan Guerra, and Johnella Butler, eds. *Writing in Multicultural Settings*. New York: MLA, 1997. Print.

Silva, Tony, and Paul Kei Matsuda, eds. *On Second Language Writing*. Mahwah: Erlbaum, 2001. Print.

Sloane, Sarah. "Invisible Diversity: Gay and Lesbian Students Writing Our Way into the Academy." *Writing Ourselves into the Story*. Ed. Sheryl I. Fontaine and Susan Hunter. Carbondale: Southern Illinois UP, 1993. 29–39. Print.

Smitherman, Geneva. *Talkin and Testifyin*. Detroit: Wayne State UP, 1997. Print.

——. *Talkin That Talk: Language, Culture and Education in African America*. New York: Routledge, 2000. Print.

Walters, Keith, and Beverly Moss. "Axes of Difference in the Writing Classroom: Rethinking Diversity." *Theory and Practice in the Teaching of Writing*. Ed. Lee Odell. Carbondale: Southern Illinois UP, 1993. 132–85. Print.

Young, Morris. "Standard English and Student Bodies: Institutionalizing Race and Literacy in Hawaii." *CE* 64.4 (2002): 405–31. Print.

Computers, Technology, and New Media

Blair, Kristine, and Pamela Takayoshi, eds. *Feminist Cyberscapes: Mapping Gendered Academic Spaces*. Norwood: Ablex, 1999. Print.

DeWitt, Scott Lloyd. *Writing Inventions: Identities, Technologies, Pedagogies.* Albany: State U of New York P, 2001. Print.

Duffelmeyer, Barbara B. "Critical Computer Literacy: Computers in First-Year Composition as Topic and Environment." *Computers and Composition* 17.3 (2000): 289–307. Print.

Grabill, Jeff. "Utopic Visions, the Technopoor, and Public Access: Writing Technologies in a Community Literacy Program." *Computers and Composition* 15.3 (1998): 297–315. Print.

Grusin, Richard, and Jay David Bolter. *Remediation: Understanding the New Media.* Cambridge: MIT P, 1999. Print.

Gurak, Laura. *Cyberliteracy.* New Haven: Yale UP, 2001. Print.

Hawisher, Gail, et al. *Computers and the Teaching of Writing in American Higher Education, 1979–1994: A History.* Norwood: Ablex, 1996. Print.

Hawisher, Gail, and Cynthia Selfe, eds. *Literate Lives in the Information Age: Stories from the United States.* Mahwah: Erlbaum, 2004. Print.

——. *Passions, Pedagogies, and Twenty-First Century Technology.* Logan: Utah State UP, 1999. Print.

Johnson-Eilola, Johndan. *Nostalgic Angels: Rearticulating Hypertext Writing.* Norwood: Ablex, 1997. Print.

Johnson-Eilola, Johndan, and Stuart A. Selber. "Policing Ourselves: Defining the Boundaries of Appropriate Discussion in Online Forums." *Computers and Composition* 13.3 (1996): 269–91. Print.

Manovich, Lev. *The Language of New Media.* Cambridge: MIT P, 2002. Print.

Palmeri, Jason. *Remixing Composition: A History of Multimodal Writing Pedagogy.* Urbana: NCTE/CCC/SIUP, 2012. Print.

Palmquist, Mike, Katie Kiefer, James Hartvigensen, and Barbara Goodlew. *Transitions: Teaching in Computer Supported and Traditional Classrooms.* Greenwich, CT: Ablex, 1998. Print.

Porter, James. *Rhetorical Ethics and Internetworked Writing.* Greenwich, CT: Ablex, 1998. Print.

Regan, Alison E., and John D. Zuern. "Community Service Learning and Computer-Mediated Advanced Composition." *Computers and Composition* 17.2 (2000): 177–96. Print.

Reiss, Donna, Dickie Selfe, and Art Young, eds. *Electronic Communication across the Curriculum.* Urbana: NCTE, 1998. Print.

Selber, Stuart A. *Multiliteracies for a Digital Age.* Carbondale: Southern Illinois UP, 2004. Print.

Selfe, Cynthia. *Technology and Literacy in the Twenty-First Century: The Importance of Paying Attention.* Carbondale: Southern Illinois UP, 1999. Print.

Selfe, Richard. *Sustainable Computer Environments: Cultures of Support in English Studies and Language Arts.* Cresskill: Hampton P, 2004. Print.

Wysocki, Anne Frances. "awaywithwords: On the Possibilities in Unavailable Designs." *Computers and Composition* 22.1 (2005): 55–62. Print.

Wysocki, Anne Frances, Johndan Johnson-Eilola, and Cynthia L. Selfe. *Writing New Media: Theory and Applications for Expanding the Teaching of Composition.* Logan: Utah State UP, 2004. Print.

Yancey, Kathleen Blake. "Made Not Only in Words: Composition in a New Key." *CCC* 56.2 (2004): 297–328. Print.

FY Writing Programs: Models and Administrative Practices

Anson, Chris, et al. *Scenarios for Teaching Writing.* Urbana: NCTE, 1993. Print.

Bartholomae, David, and Anthony Petrosky. *Facts, Artifacts, Counterfacts.* Montclair: Boynton/Cook. 1986. Print.

Berlin, James. *Rhetorics, Poetics, Cultures: Refiguring English Studies.* Urbana: NCTE, 1996. Print.

Brereton, John, ed. *Traditions of Inquiry.* New York: Oxford UP, 1985. Print.

Carden, Patricia. "Designing a Course." *Teaching Prose: A Guide for Writing Instructors.* Ed. Fredric V. Bogel and Katherine K. Gottschalk. New York: Norton, 1988. 20–45. Print.

Coles, William. *The Plural I — and After.* Portsmouth: Boynton/Cook, 1988. Print.

Donovan, Timothy, and Benjamin McClelland, eds. *Eight Approaches to Teaching Composition.* Urbana: NCTE, 1980. Print.

Downs, Douglas, and Elizabeth Wardle. "Teaching about Writing, Righting Misconceptions: (Re)Envisioning 'First-Year Composition' as 'Introduction to Writing Studies.'" *CCC* 58.4 (2007): 552–84. Print.

Elbow, Peter, and Pat Belanoff. *A Community of Writers: A Workshop Course in Writing.* Boston: McGraw, 2002. Print.

Fahnestock, Jeanne, and Marie Secor. "Teaching Argument: A Theory of Types." *CCC* 34 (1983): 20–30. Print.

Foster, David. *A Primer for Writing Teachers: Theories, Theorists, Issues, Problems.* 2nd ed. Portsmouth: Boynton/Cook, 1993. Print.

Hartzog, Carol P. *Composition and the Academy: A Study of Writing Program Administration.* New York: MLA, 1996. Print.

Janangelo, Joseph, and Kristine Hansen. *Resituating Writing: Constructing and Administering Writing Programs.* Portsmouth: Boynton/Cook, 1995. Print.

Julier, Laura. "Community-Service Pedagogy." *A Guide to Composition Pedagogies.* Ed. Gary Tate, Amy Rupiper, and Kurt Schick. New York: Oxford UP, 2001. 132–48. Print.

Pytlik, Betty P., and Sarah Liggett, eds. *Preparing College Teachers of Writing: Histories, Theories, Programs, Practices.* New York: Oxford UP, 2001. Print.

Shor, Ira, and Caroline Pari. *Critical Literacy in Action.* Portsmouth: Boynton/Cook, 1999. Print.

Tate, Gary, Amy Rupiper, and Kurt Schick. *A Guide to Composition Pedagogies.* New York: Oxford UP, 2001. Print.

Tinberg, Howard B. *Border Talk: Writing and Knowledge in the Two-Year College.* Urbana: NCTE, 1997. Print.

Walvoord, Barbara. *Helping Students Write Well: A Guide for Teachers in All Disciplines.* 2nd ed. New York: MLA, 1986. Print.

Yancey, Kathleen Blake. *Portfolios in the Writing Classroom.* Urbana: NCTE, 1992. Print.

Yancey, Kathleen Blake, and Irwin Weiser, eds. *Situating Portfolios: Four Perspectives.* Logan: Utah State UP, 1997. Print.

Pedagogic Issues for College Teachers

Fishman, Stephen M., and Lucille McCarthy. *John Dewey and the Challenge of Classroom Practice.* New York: Teachers College P, 1998. Print.

hooks, bell. *Teaching to Transgress: Education and the Practice of Freedom.* New York: Routledge, 1994. Print.

Light, Richard. *Making the Most of College.* Cambridge: Harvard UP, 2001. Print.

Macedo, Donaldo. *Literacies of Power.* Boulder: Westview, 1994. Print.

Roen, Duane, Veronica Pantoja, Lauren Yena, Susan K. Miller, and Eric Waggoner, eds. *Strategies for Teaching First-Year Composition.* Urbana: NCTE, 2002. Print.

Salvatori, Mariolina. *Pedagogy: A Disturbing History, 1819–1929.* Pittsburgh: U of Pittsburgh P, 1996. Print.

Sternglass, Marilyn. *Time to Know Them: A Longitudinal Study of Writing and Learning at the College Level.* Mahwah: Erlbaum, 1997. Print.

Stock, Patricia Lambert, and Eileen Schell. *Moving a Mountain.* Urbana: NCTE, 2001. Print.

III

An Anthology of Essays

INTRODUCTION

We hope that the first two parts of this book have helped you organize, plan, and make choices about the writing course you teach. Our central purpose has been to focus on the practical concerns of real writing teachers in real classrooms, and we've tried to keep that purpose in sight. But we also realize that the concerns of teachers are often theoretical as well as practical.

Part III includes readings from composition studies that address both practical and theoretical concerns. Like the first two parts, this one is included to help you be the most effective and the most informed teacher you can be. In addition, we hope that this collection of essays (some of the best we know) will serve to reinforce our invitation to you to join the field of composition studies. We'd like you to become a reader of, as well as a contributor to, the ongoing conversation in the field. Teaching writing is the ground for almost everything else that goes on in composition studies, but in the last forty-five years, the field has become an established scholarly discipline as well — one that we hope will interest you.

The essays reprinted here consider composition theory and practice, particularly in terms of the social conditions that inform literacy practices and policies. These discussions serve as the basis for much of what we do in the classroom — the theories we choose to build on, the traditions and wisdom we challenge, and the speculations we deem most promising. These discussions also reflect current social and literate practices outside of the classroom. Parts I and II suggest that every teaching practice is theoretical as well as social. Part III demonstrates just how social exigencies shape the intimate relationship between theory and practice. Rhetorical theory, in its relation to pedagogy, is neither arcane nor archaic knowledge, nor is it merely desirable knowledge for a writing teacher to possess. Rhetorical theory is the very stuff that makes a writing teacher effective. A great deal of this theoretical background may be intuitive — learned through practice, simple listening, commonsense awareness of life, and social interactions. But sometimes rhetorical theory becomes more useful when it is foregrounded and contextualized, both pedagogically and socially. For this reason, we have chosen the essays that follow. To provide context, we have included original publication information in a footnote near the start of each essay.

Our theories — the ideas we evolve to explain what has happened and to predict on that basis what will happen — arise inside and outside our classrooms and are shared in hallway conversations, meetings, workshops, and journal articles. From there, they are carried back into the world of action — for those of us in composition studies—back to our classrooms through our teaching and the textbooks we write and use. The best textbook is simply the best teaching on a much larger scale — a repository of successful ideas and techniques available to other teachers and their students.

Our own research and the research available to us help keep us current in the ongoing discussion about writing and the teaching of writing. But this conversation is not a recent one: It has been going on in different forms for over twenty-five hundred years, and it will continue long after we are gone. The late Kenneth Burke, in one of his most famous passages, likens such ongoing conversation to a parlor that we all may visit for a while:

> Imagine you enter a parlor. You come late. When you arrive, others have long preceded you, and they are engaged in a heated discussion, a discussion too heated for them to pause and tell you exactly what it is about. In fact, the discussion had already begun long before any of them got there, so that no one present is qualified to retrace for you all the steps that had gone before. You listen for a while, until you decide that you have caught the tenor of the argument; then you put in your oar. Someone answers; you answer him; another comes to your defense; another aligns himself against you, to either the embarrassment or gratification of your opponent, depending upon the quality of your ally's assistance. However, the discussion is interminable. The hour grows late, you must depart. And you do depart, with the discussion still vigorously in progress. (110–11)

Of course, even some good teachers have never entered this conversation. But from our own experiences, we can testify to the excitement, usefulness, and inspiration that can come from joining a national community of people who are all working on the same questions and issues. Besides addressing the basic issues surrounding students' writing and teaching students to write, our conversation also addresses issues of working with students whose strongest language or dialect is not "Standardized" English, the dialect used in textbooks, on tests, and in many books. Even the notion that there is a "Standardized" English is arguable.

Therefore, the essays included here speak not only to the established concerns of basic writers, process writing, teachers' responses, and grammar, but also to the possibilities of exploring a range of literate practices as they play out in language variation, the relationship between reading and writing and personal identity. In considering these issues, we have chosen those articles that have been the most helpful to us, especially when we were looking to understand our own teaching. And that, for us, is the bottom line: The scholarship and theory collected here returns to our teaching and to our students' learning. Counter to popular thinking, we teachers do not live in an ivory tower. Every day, most of us are called back to the people and places that are truly important to us, our students and our writing classes.

WORK CITED

Burke, Kenneth. *The Philosophy of Literary Form*. Berkeley: U of California P, 1941.

Douglas Downs and Elizabeth Wardle

Teaching about Writing, Righting Misconceptions: (Re)Envisioning "First-Year Composition" as "Introduction to Writing Studies"

First-year composition (FYC) is usually asked to prepare students to write across the university; this request assumes the existence of a "universal educated discourse" (Russell, "Activity Theory") that can be transferred from one writing situation to another. Yet more than twenty years of research and theory have repeatedly demonstrated that such a unified academic discourse does not exist and have seriously questioned what students can and do transfer from one context to another (Ackerman, Berkenkotter and Huckin, Carter, Diller and Oates, Kaufer and Young, MacDonald, Petraglia, Russell "Activity Theory"). However, for all practical purposes, writing studies as a field has largely ignored the implications of this research and theory and continued to assure its publics (faculty, administrators, parents, industry) that FYC can do what nonspecialists have always assumed it can: teach, in one or two early courses, "college writing" as a set of basic, fundamental skills that will apply in other college courses and in business and public spheres after college.[1] In making these unsupportable assurances to stakeholders, our field reinforces cultural misconceptions of writing instead of attempting to educate students and publics out of those misconceptions. When we continue to pursue the goal of teaching students "how to write in college" in one or two semesters—despite the fact that our own scholarship extensively calls this possibility into question—we silently support the misconceptions that writing is not a real subject, that writing courses do not require expert instructors, and that rhetoric and composition are not genuine research areas or legitimate intellectual pursuits. We are, thus, complicit in reinforcing outsiders' views of writing studies as a trivial, skill-teaching nondiscipline.

Though we complain about public misconceptions of writing and of our discipline, our field has not seriously considered radically reimagining the mission of the very course where misconceptions are born and/or reinforced; we have not yet imagined moving first-year composition from teaching "how to write in college" to teaching *about writing*—from acting as if writing is a basic, universal skill to acting as if writing studies is a discipline with content knowledge

This article is reprinted from *College Composition and Communication*, 58.4 (June 2007): 552–85.

to which students should be introduced, thereby changing their understandings about writing and thus changing the ways they write. Here we champion such a radical move by proposing, theorizing, demonstrating, and reporting early results from an "Intro to Writing Studies" FYC pedagogy. This pedagogy explicitly recognizes the impossibility of teaching a universal academic discourse and rejects that as a goal for FYC. It seeks instead to improve students' understanding of writing, rhetoric, language, and literacy in a course that is topically oriented to reading and writing as scholarly inquiry and encouraging more realistic understandings of writing.

In this article, we explore and theorize the connection between writing studies' standing in the academy and what it teaches in the courses it accepts as its *raison d'être*, first-year composition. Despite the progress our field has made over the years at erasing theory/practice oppositions, it is still too easy to imagine pedagogy as "practice," removed from the realm of serious theory or research about the work or direction of writing studies as a discipline. Resisting the notion that talk about pedagogy is merely talk about "practice" is especially important to writing studies because our field is conceived — by those who fund it, those who experience it, and most of those who work in it — as primarily pedagogical. Part of our purpose here is to insist on the deep disciplinary implications of FYC pedagogy; a pedagogical move whose intention is to help resituate an entire field within the academy demonstrates that pedagogy has impact beyond the daily teaching to-do list. For example, reimagining FYC as Intro to Writing Studies might create more natural gateways to WAC and WID programs than FYC typically does now. Further, the Intro to Writing Studies course would be akin to the introductory courses offered in all other disciplines (i.e., Intro to Chemistry or Intro to Philosophy) and would potentially serve as a cornerstone course for writing studies majors beginning to take root across the country. (Having a major, of course, dramatically changes a field's standing in the academy.) While we use the bulk of this article to help readers envision the Intro to Writing Studies pedagogy, our concern is not simply to improve writing instruction but also to improve the position of writing studies in the academy and change common misconceptions about writing.

We begin by establishing the grounds on which we question the traditional "teaching college writing" goal of FYC and theorize a more pedagogically successful alternative. We examine several important misconceptions about writing and writing skills transfer that suffuse expectations for FYC: that academic writing is generally universal, that writing is a basic skill independent of content or context, and that writing abilities automatically transfer from FYC to other courses and contexts. We then describe the introductory pedagogy, report on our own and our students' experiences in pilot courses, and address the challenges to both teachers and students of a writing course whose content is writing theory and research. We conclude by addressing some critiques of the intro pedagogy, showing how they in fact reinforce the case for reimagining FYC both to improve writing instruction and to improve the standing of writing studies in the academy.

Systemic Misconception and Misdirection of Mainstream FYC

A number of assumptions inform the premise that academic writing is somehow universal: writing can be considered independent of content; writing consists primarily of syntactic and mechanical concerns; and academic writing skills can be taught in a one or two introductory general writing skills courses and transferred easily to other courses. These assumptions are reflected in public policy reports such as *Standards for Success* by the Center for Educational Policy Research, which focuses primarily on the need for grammar instruction — even sentence diagramming — in writing instruction. The "blue ribbon" National Commission on Writing in America's Schools and Colleges has produced two reports, *The Neglected R* and *Writing: A Ticket to Work . . . Or a Ticket Out*, both of which favor college professors' and business professionals' impressions of students' writing over actual data developed by writing studies scholarship. Not surprisingly, those impressions focus on syntactic and mechanical concerns and assume that "writing is writing," involving "learn-once/write-many" basic skills. The content-versus-form misconception — as old as FYC itself — appears in standardized testing, with the SAT "writing" test giving better scores to longer essays and completely discounting factual errors. It also finds its way into *New York Times* editorials, where no less a public intellectual than Stanley Fish argues that it is possible to, and therefore that FYC should, focus strictly on writing's grammatical forms and disavow interest in its content.

The field of writing studies has made part of its business for the last forty years testing these assumptions and articulating more complex, realistic, and useful ways of thinking about writing. We understand writing as inseparable from content (CCCC; Crowley; Reither) and as more than collections of grammatical and syntactical constructions (Broad; Diller and Oates; Haswell, *Gaining Ground*). Despite research demonstrating the complexity of writing, misconceptions persist and inform FYC courses around the country that attempt to teach "academic discourse." We next review several of the most intransigent problems that stem from misconceptions about writing.

Academic Discourse as a Category Mistake

The WPA Outcomes Statement adopted by the Council of Writing Program Administrators in April 2000 (http://wpacouncil.org/positions/outcomes.html) highlights four major outcomes for writing instruction: rhetorical knowledge; critical thinking, reading, and writing; processes; and knowledge of conventions. These outcomes, which reflect an ideology of access to the academy and a desire to prepare students for academic writing, are increasingly being adopted nationwide (Ericsson). But can FYC fulfill these expectations?

Studies suggest that students write for various communities within the university, each of which uses writing in specialized ways that mediate the activities of the people involved (Bazerman, "Life," *Shaping*; Bazerman and Paradis; Berkenkotter, et al.; Hyland; Miller; Russell, "Activity," "Rethinking"; Smit). While some general features of writing are shared across disciplines (e.g., a view of research writing as disciplinary conversation; writing strategies such as the "moves" made in most research introductions; specialized terminology and explicit citation — see Hyland or Swales, for example), these shared features are realized differently within different academic disciplines, courses, and even assignments (Howard; Hull; Russell, "Looking"; Shamoon). As a result, "academic writing" is constituted by and in the diversity of activities and genres that mediate a wide variety of activities within higher education; its use as an umbrella term is dangerously misleading. In this sense, positing "academic writing" as the object upon which first-year students and teachers can act creates what philosopher Gilbert Ryle labeled a category mistake, "committed when, in seeking to give an account of some concept, one says that it is of one logical type or category when in fact it is of another" (Lyons 44). Ryle's example is mistaking a single building on a university campus for the university itself (Lyons 44–45).

In a similar fashion, asking teachers to teach "academic writing" begs the question: *which* academic writing — what content, what genre, for what activity, context, and audience? FYC teachers are thus forced to define academic discourse for themselves (usually unconsciously) before they can teach it. FYC teachers trained in English studies and working in English departments realize academic writing as the genres and content mediating English studies — for example, literary and rhetorical analyses (MacDonald; Wardle, "Cross-Disciplinary" and "Mutt Genres"). These instructors are unlikely to be involved in, familiar with, or able to teach the specialized discourses used to mediate other activities within disciplinary systems across the university. In effect, the flavor of the purportedly universal academic discourse taught in FYC is typically humanities-based and more specifically English studies-based.

The Open Question of Transfer

Even when FYC courses do attempt to directly address the complexity of "academic discourse," they tend to operate on the assumption that writing instruction easily transfers to other writing situations — a deeply ingrained assumption with little empirical verification. Our field does not know what genres and tasks will help students in the myriad writing situations they will later find themselves. We do not know how writing in the major develops. We do not know if writing essays on biology in an English course helps students write lab reports in biology courses. We do not know which genres or rhetorical strategies truly are universal in the academy, nor how to help FYC students recognize such universality. According to David Smit's summary of what we know about transfer, assumptions of direct and automatic transfer from one writing situation to another are unfounded. With scant research-based information about how to best help students write successfully in other courses, FYC teachers do not know whether choosing genre A over genre B will be of service to students who must write genre B or genre C later on. In "academic discourse" FYC, then, instructors must hope that any writing instruction will help students in some way and/or limit their teaching to basic scribal and syntactic skills.[2] The limited research on writing transfer (e.g., Beaufort; McCarthy; Walvoord; Walvoord and McCarthy) mirrors the larger body of research on educational transfer (Perkins and Salomon, "Teaching" and "Transfer") in suggesting that neither choice may serve students adequately. We are not arguing that transfer of writing knowledge cannot happen; rather, we are arguing that "far transfer" is difficult (Perkins and Salomon, "Teaching" and "Transfer") and that most current incarnations of FYC do not teach for it as explicitly as is necessary.

Resisting Misconceptions

The range of theoretical and practical problems associated with teaching and transferring "universal educated discourse" (Russell, "Activity Theory") or "general writing skills instruction" (Petraglia, "Introduction" and "Writing") forces us to ask what FYC can actually do to prepare students for academic writing, particularly as it is currently constituted: taught in English departments mostly by adjuncts and graduate students and enrolling students from a variety of majors. By enacting the assumption of the larger academic culture that academic writing can be taught in one or two introductory writing skills courses, FYC effectively reinforces the misconceptions about the nature of writing on which that assumption is based.

If writing studies as a discipline is to have any authority over its own courses, our cornerstone course must resist conventional but inaccurate models of writing.[3] A reenvisioned FYC shifts the central goal from teaching "academic writing" to *teaching realistic and useful conceptions of writing*—perhaps the most significant of which would be that writing is neither basic nor universal but content- and context-contingent and irreducibly complex. Keith Hjortshoj's juxtaposition of two master narratives about writing illustrates this shift. A common narrative prescribes that "all good writing should have a thesis, clearly stated in the introduction. Following paragraphs should each present a point that supports this thesis, and the essay should end with a logical conclusion. Writing throughout the essay should be clear, concise, and correct" (33). A more realistic narrative recognizes that

> features of good writing vary from one situation to another. These variations depend, for example, on the *subject* of the writing, its *purpose*, and the *reader's expectations*. The *form* of writing used in a field of study often structures those expectations. As a consequence, the features of good writing in a literature course will differ greatly from the features of good writing in business or astronomy, and what seems clear to one audience might not be clear to another. (33)

By teaching the more realistic writing narrative *itself*, we have a theoretically greater chance of making students "better writers" than we do by assuming the one or two genres we can teach them will automatically transfer to other writing situations. Instead of teaching situational skills often incorrectly imagined to be generalizable, FYC could teach about the ways writing works in the world and how the "tool" of writing is used to mediate various activities.

WRITING ABOUT WRITING: RATIONALE AND DESCRIPTION

In light of what we know as a field about the subject of writing, we propose a radically reimagined FYC as an Introduction to Writing Studies — a course about how to understand and think about writing in school and society (Russell, "Activity Theory"). The course includes many of the same activities as current FYC courses: researching, reading, and writing arguments. However, the course content explores reading and writing: How does writing work? How do people use writing? What are problems related to writing and reading and how can they be solved? Students read writing research, conduct reading and writing auto-ethnographies, identify writing-related problems that interest them, write reviews of the existing literature on their chosen problems, and conduct their own primary research, which they report both orally and in writing. This course would serve as a gateway to WAC and WID programs better able to address issues of specialized discourse within specific academic disciplines.

Downs has taught writing-about-writing courses in second-semester composition classes at the University of Utah, a Research-I university, and at Utah Valley State College, a regional teaching college, both of approximately 25,000 students. Between spring 2003 and spring 2005, he taught the curriculum in three sections totaling about sixty students, and formally evaluated the course alongside a traditional "academic writing" version of an FYC course in a semester-length study involving forty students. Wardle has implemented a similar curriculum at the University of Dayton, a private liberal arts school of over 10,000. In the fall semesters of 2004 and 2005, she taught the curriculum in a first-year writing course of twenty-four honors and engineering students. At the end of each semester, the students evaluated the course both anonymously and in portfolio reflections.

Grounding Principles and Goals

Though there are a number of ways to institute an Intro to Writing Studies course, our iterations of the course were designed according to shared core beliefs and a desire to resist and alter students' misconceptions about writing. The first of our shared beliefs corresponds with James Reither's assertion that writing cannot be taught independent of content. It follows that the more an instructor can say about a writing's content, the more she can say about the writing itself; this is another way of saying that writing instructors should be expert readers. When the course content is writing studies, writing instructors are concretely enabled to fill that expert reader role. This change directly contravenes the typical assumption that first-year writing can be about anything, that somehow the content is irrelevant to an instructor's ability to respond to the writing.

Second, the course is forthcoming about what writing instruction can and cannot accomplish; it does not purport to "teach students to write" in general nor does it purport to do all that is necessary to prepare students to write in college. Rather, it promises to help students understand some activities related to written scholarly inquiry by demonstrating the conversational and subjective nature of scholarly texts. In this course, students are taught that writing is conventional and context-specific rather than governed by universal rules — thus they learn that within each new disciplinary course they will need to pay close attention to what counts as appropriate for that discourse community. Taking the research community of writing studies as our example not only allows writing instructors to bring their own expertise to the course, but also heightens students' awareness that writing itself is a subject of scholarly inquiry. Students leave the course with increased awareness of writing studies as a discipline, as well as a new outlook on writing as a researchable activity rather than a mysterious talent.

Third, the course respects students by refusing to create double standards or different rules for student writers than for expert writers. For example, students learn to recognize the need for expert opinion and cite it where necessary, but they also learn to claim their own situational expertise and write from it as expert writers do. This respect for students is in accord with the field's ethos, thus blending a pedagogical advantage with a disciplinary one. In addition, creating high expectations for students aligns well with current learning theory: students can accomplish far more than we typically give them credit for being able to, if only we will ask them to do it.

In sum, then, the course does not teach from principles that contravene writing studies research. Instead, it draws on research from the field and principles and ethics that shape the field to help students understand the nature of writing and to explore their own writing practices. Unlike pedagogies that are so detached from writing studies' specialized knowledge as to deny it, the Intro pedagogy emerges from that knowledge and ethos.

Readings

In the writing studies course, we use readings that report research about writing and theorize ways of thinking about writing to raise important questions and to provide examples of various textual moves related to scholarly writing based on primary research. The articles we assign vary, as do the ideas on which we focus; thus, we do not prescribe an "ideal" set of readings here. However, the common denominators among our readings are these:

- Material in readings is centered on issues with which students have first-hand experience — for example, problems students are prone to experience throughout the writing process, from conceptual questions of purpose, to procedural questions of drafting and revision, to issues surrounding critical reading.
- Data-driven, research-focused readings seem more useful than highly theoretical pieces. The former tend to be both more readable and more concrete, making them more accessible and relevant to students.

Studies by Berkenkotter, Sommers, Perl, Flower and Hayes, Murray, Swales, Dawkins, Beason, and Berkenkotter and Huckin encourage students' thinking about invention, introductions, drafting, revision, punctuation and mechanics, error, and conventions of science-reporting articles. Articles that focus on critical reading, notably Haas and Flower's "Rhetorical Reading Strategies" and Margaret Kantz's "Helping Students Use Textual Sources Persuasively," explicitly critique typical student reading strategies and compare them to more effective reading strategies. Readings from Lakoff and Johnson on metaphor and James Gee on cultural discourses explicitly explore situated, motivated discourse; critique notions such as "objective information" and "disembodied text"; and help students demystify the myth of the isolated, inspired writer.

While we are sensitive to concerns about writing courses based on readings, research writing generally entails thoughtful responses to other writing. If writing cannot be separated from content, then scholarly writing cannot be separated from reading. To center the course on student writing and avoid merely banking information, students discuss, write about, and test every reading in light of their own experiences; they discuss why they are reading a piece and how it might influence their understanding of writing. Rick Evans' "Learning Schooled Literacy," for example, helps students reflect on how their past reading and writing experiences shaped them, while Lucille McCarthy's "A Stranger in Strange Lands" explains why students might feel frustration about writing in new classrooms.

Reflective Assignments

Class time spent on readings focuses more on students' reactions to them than on the readings themselves; thus, our students write about issues raised by readings by responding to prompts such as, "How are your experiences with research writing like and unlike Shirlie's as Kantz describes them? What would you do differently if you could?" We find that students' responses initiate excellent class discussions, and that throughout the course students come back to ideas in the readings they write about to frame discussions about their writing experiences.

We also assign literacy narratives or auto-ethnographies in which students take stock of their literacy educations, experiences, and habits. We encourage students to think historically and to identify sources of their current attitudes and approaches to literacy, and we help students clarify their open questions, problems, and skepticisms regarding writing. What do they like and dislike about writing? What problems do they have with writing? What do they sense they do not know that they would like to? Recognizing dissonances and gaps from their own experiences helps students identify research questions for the course's research focus.

Research Assignments

The most noteworthy feature of the course is that students conduct primary research, however limited, on issues of interest to both themselves and the field of writing studies. Conducting primary research helps students shift their orientation to research from one of compiling facts to one of generating knowledge (e.g., Greene, "Mining;" Kantz; Nelson, "Constructing," "Research"; Spivey). Primary research projects also clarify for students the nature of scholarly writing processes that the course is tasked with teaching and empowers them to write with legitimate originality and conviction. Perhaps most importantly, conducting first-hand research on writing allows students to take control of problem areas in their own writing when they focus on those problems directly in their research projects. Consequently, the course about writing becomes a *writing* course in which students study writing to learn more about it and potentially improve their own.

The research project is tightly scaffolded. Students begin by conducting library research about the topics of their research questions and learn enough about primary research to suggest methods for studying their questions. They write formal research proposals that articulate their research questions and outline the methods they plan to use in their studies. The questions students develop can be fascinating indeed, as these examples from our courses illustrate:

- Do college freshmen and seniors use rhetorical strategies at all or in similar ways?
- How useful is Microsoft Word's grammar checker?
- What makes a classic literary work a "classic"?
- What makes an effective business plan?
- How does music (or lighting, or other environmental factors) affect writing and revision?
- How do literacy activities vary at high- and low-income day cares?
- What kinds of writing will a social work major encounter in his career?
- Is writing taught in medical school? Should it be, and if so, how?

We assign activities throughout the research project that help students become more proficient at writing with sources, including interpretive summaries in which students practice reading rhetorically and contributively by constructing arguments about what a given article says and what the author may mean by writing it. Annotated bibliographies help students organize their library research and negotiate with instructors about issues such as number of sources, which we teach is contingent, like so much else, on the project in question. A standalone literature review moves students toward understanding various studies and statements on an issue as positions in a three-dimensional space rather than as simple binaries. Developing a "community map" of opinion helps students envision research and argument as community inquiry and identify gaps that their primary research can address. Students' primary research methods include surveys and interviews, read aloud/think aloud protocols, close observations of actual writing processes, or discourse analyses of various documents. Through primary research, students begin to learn that careful observation and empirical data-gathering techniques bolster their authority and reduce their reliance on other experts' pronouncements.

It bears emphasizing that we maintain reasonable expectations for students. Circumstances — particularly the sixteen-week timetable to which no scholar is held — and limited knowledge and experience do not allow for highly ambitious and rigorous projects; students are practicing moves rather than acting as paragons. However, we find that students are able to accomplish discourse analysis of small corpuses, interviews and surveys of manageable numbers of subjects, and small-scale ethnographies and case studies that emphasize quality over quantity in sites, observations, field notes, and coding.

Presentation Assignments

One conception of writing we strive to help students shift is imagining "writing" essentially as merely drafting a paper. The course design helps us show students that most scholarly researched writing in fact begins with becoming curious and establishing a question and moves through research. What students traditionally imagine as writing is actually only the final move in a much larger series of events. However, in our courses, students do arrive at this final move, presenting their research in both a significant written report and an oral presentation.

The final three weeks of our course are devoted to presentations and revision workshops. Students prepare ten-minute presentations of their research and participate on panels organized to create conversation among panelists. Students tend to be genuinely interested in comparing findings and learning from each other the outcomes of their arduous but useful projects. We have rarely seen better student presentations in terms of generating student interest, discussion, and ideas for further research. In fact, throughout the course, as students exchange research tales, data, and questions, it is clear that the writing studies pedagogy answers Reither's and Kleine's calls for communities of inquiry.

THE WRITING ABOUT WRITING COURSE: STUDENT OUTCOMES

To demonstrate the flavor of the pedagogy, its strengths, and its weaknesses, we present two case studies. The first is about a struggling C student in Downs's course, doubtful about his own reading and writing abilities; the second is about a confident honors student in Wardle's course who found the course challenging but met all the goals. These contrasting cases demonstrate the flexibility and appropriateness of the curriculum for a variety of students.

Case Study 1: Trying to Change Jack's Disposition toward Writing

Jack and "English" (writing and reading) have never been friends, and they still are not after Jack waded through English 2020, "Intermediate Writing: The Science and Technology of How Writing Works," at Utah Valley State College (UVSC). But they have perhaps come to an understanding.

A twenty-nine-year-old chemistry major, Jack had tried college immediately after high school but decided that "the almighty dollar" looked better, so he worked as a state corrections officer before regaining the desire to return to college. Though articulate, thoughtful, and bright, Jack lacked self-confidence. His writing apprehension made his semester a long struggle to simply complete assignments. Although Jack earned only a C-, largely because of incomplete work, we include his story to illustrate how the course can work for less well-prepared students.

As his literacy narrative reveals, Jack's experiences with English (again, both writing and reading) in grade school, high school, and college convinced him that he could do nothing right on paper:

> I had very bad experiences that went back as far as I can remember. My mother, sisters, and father were all very good at English and could not understand how I was getting such bad grades in the classes. At one time, my father even said I was stupid. I guess I started to believe him and just kind of gave up. It got to the point that I just didn't care, and I almost didn't graduate from high school. It wasn't that I didn't care about everything, just those things I wasn't good at. I loved Chemistry and Physics and Math, I had taken AP classes in all of those subjects and did well. It was just the English thing. (Reflective Letter)

In high school, Jack was tracked into what he called "English for dummies" where "we sat around and looked at pictures." After a bad experience in a college technical writing class, Jack left college for ten years. Upon his return, he was placed in UVSC's lowest-level remedial writing course (089) but found the experience so distasteful that he retook a placement exam and earned a place in the first-semester writing course, English 1010. There he "had a teacher who thought of my writing what I had known all along, and that was I stink" (Reflective Letter). Not surprisingly, Jack "never really had the hope of doing well" in 2020 and took it only because he "had to take it to make it through school" (Reflective Letter). In an early thought piece responding to Stuart Greene's "Argument as Inquiry," he wrote:

> I feel as though I come into this class with a handicap. I am a student returning to school after 10 years on the job market. I spent everyday writing papers for my last job but never really took the time to think about what I was writing. When you write police reports over and over you just kind of report the facts. I have never put much thought into the papers that I have written. (Thought Piece 3)

Jack "never thought about my audience when writing and maybe that is my problem. Or maybe I am just a hopeless cause" (Thought Piece 3). Reading Flower and Hayes' "The Cognition of Discovery: Defining a Rhetorical Problem" gave Jack a clear and concrete comparison of how invention worked for more expert writers versus how he imagined the task of figuring out what to write. He thought of writing as focused on facts (from his police-report writing) and following rules: "I try to get the information in the paper and the length of the paper needed and make sure it is done properly" (Thought Piece 9). Though he took only the broadest, most accessible points from such readings, he understood those well and his reflective pieces were usually insightful in connecting the readings to his own experiences.

Throughout the course, Jack's engagement remained high, even when writing assignments came late, or not at all, because he'd been too worried about doing them wrong to even begin them. The day of the first draft-reading workshop, everyone but Jack provided drafts of their literacy narratives. In fact he *had* brought a draft but was unwilling to show it to anyone because he was convinced it was all wrong—and indeed it wasn't exactly right. Later in the course, he began to look forward to workshops: reading Nancy Sommers' "Revision Strategies of Student Writers and Experienced Adult Writers" and hearing that other writers, too, have extreme doubts about the quality or rightness of their work helped Jack accept that "not exactly right" is okay when it comes to writing. He had to learn that writing is a series of attempts toward an ideal that is probably never reached.

Only the most authoritarian direction pushed Jack into his semester research project. Since he expected "research" to mean finding and paraphrasing what other people had previously said, Jack was nearly paralyzed by the requirement to do first-hand research and report it in the context of existing research:

> When this assignment was first given I was a little scared about going out on a limb and committing myself to a research question. I mean what if I couldn't find anything on what I was researching? Or worse yet what if the teacher thought it was a dumb question to do research on? After talking to the professor and thinking about it I have decided that if I think about this too much and don't get it done I will get a zero and if I just do the best I can what is the worst that can happen to my score? (Research Proposal)

Because Jack was researching in a subject area with which Downs has more than passing familiarity, Downs was able to help him find resources and arrive at a researchable question much more effectively than if Jack had been researching stem cell research or the death penalty. But even more importantly, the course encouraged Jack to tap his own interests in and experiences relating to writing. So when Jack submitted a proposal nearly five weeks late—he spent those weeks vacillating among a number of questions and entertaining the option of dropping the course—his idea was anything but "dumb":

> I have decided to write about police reports and the way they act as a debriefing for the officer, at least they did for me. The problem with this is that a police report is supposed to report the facts and not become a biased statement or put opinion in it so the court can use it.
>
> The trick with me was I was trained to just write the facts and until this class that is what I always believed I did. Since this class I have seen that my old reports were biased and just my opinion of what I saw. I guess that no one really can write just the facts. . . . I intend to show that even though police officers are told to do one thing they are really trying to get us to use the report as a debrief. Which show a contradiction in the purpose of the report. . . . I think that a lot of officers whether they realize it or not they use the police report to accomplish something very emotional, and that is the debrief. (Research Proposal)

Jack's recognition that officers were encouraged to make reports serve a de facto cathartic purpose contrasts strikingly with his assertion near the beginning of the course that "when you write police reports over and over you kind of just report the facts" (Thought Piece 3). His final paper combined research on report writing and stress in police work with accounts and police reports from his own experience as a corrections officer. In the most astute section of the paper, Jack compares his report of an incident with another officer's report of the same incident, working through differences in style, account, perspectives, and tone to demonstrate how those differences could be read as emotive.

Most of the paper wasn't as strong—Jack got a late start on the project that left him no time for the extensive drafting and revision process designed into the course. But Jack's moves were more important than the paper itself—a value at the heart of the writing-about-writing pedagogy. As teachers of college composition and researchers of writing, we want—and are taking—license to decide that what students like Jack *know to do* in order to conduct critical, researched inquiry at the college level is more important than whether they master APA format or produce marginally more fluent writing. Jack may not measurably know better "how to write" if by that we mean greater felicity with punctuation or syntax or even the ability to produce a particular genre. But what Jack reports he did learn in the course represents a more important goal for FYC:

> I can say something did happen to me in this course and that was I really started to think for myself. Your class has also made me realize that I'm really not that bad of a writer. I also learned that writing a paper is not just all about the rules. I still don't think that I am that great a writer but I do know that a lot of people struggle with their writing and that makes it a little easier for me to write without fear of what people will think. I guess one thing that this course did for me was to open my mind and make me think that it all depends on who is reading my writing and that it isn't all me that stinks. (Reflective Letter)

It was the course's focus on how writing works and its constant drive to help students understand writing that helped Jack learn these key principles of writing. Had he been allowed to write about "intelligent design" rather than studying writing itself; had he been reading pieces about what makes good citizenship rather than reading research on writing; had class discussions focused on the news of the day rather than describing and grappling with writers' problems; had the course focused just on teaching Jack "how to" write a research paper rather than on the nature of writing; had the class simply enjoined Jack to "research scholarly articles" instead of relentlessly studying how scholarly articles do what they do; it seems unlikely that Jack would have made the progress he did. (If other writing pedagogies succeed in helping students better understand the game of writing and themselves as writers, we might ask why he hadn't learned these things in four previous college writing courses.) In 2020, Jack gained the ability to place himself—his background, abilities, processes, attitudes, and writing—in a broader context of what is known more generally about writers and writing. His case shows that even students potentially disadvantaged by an intense curriculum can benefit from it by changing the ways they understand themselves as writers and imagine the project of writing.

Case Study 2: How Stephanie Learned That Research Is Messy

Stephanie entered the University of Dayton (UD) in Fall 2004 as a biology major in the University Honors Program. Self-identifying as a reader who enjoyed her English classes and was confident in her reading and writing abilities, Stephanie received three credit hours toward FYC for her AP English score and enrolled in Wardle's English 114 Freshman Writing Seminar instead of the English 101/102 sequence taken by most UD students. She was not, then, typical of students at UD or at most universities across the country. However, she was fairly typical of most students in the Freshman Writing Seminar—motivated, prepared, and hardworking.

Despite Stephanie's preparation and experience with reading and writing, she found the course work challenging; the seminar about writers, writing, and discourse covered entirely new ground for her. In past English classes, everything she wrote "dealt with literature instead of composition" (Reflection 1). In high school, she "hardly ever felt it necessary to revise a paper" and her research consisted of "just looking up what other people wrote and rephrasing it" (Reflection 1). The seminar forced her to change her habits and understandings.

Stephanie consistently found ways to link class readings to her own personal experience, linkages that led to her course project. Whereas many students selected research topics related entirely to their own experience with little direct regard for the course readings, Stephanie's interest in reading led her to become fascinated by Haas and Flower's "Rhetorical Reading Strategies and the Construction of Meaning." She felt that her own experiences with reading disproved Haas and Flower's findings that "novice" readers do not use rhetorical reading strategies. Consequently, Stephanie spent the semester grappling with rhetorical reading—what it was, who studied it, and how *she* might go about studying it.

Finding and reading literature on the topic and writing a literature review proved important in Stephanie's development as a reader and researcher:

> I do not now think that lit reviews are merely paraphrasing things other people have said. In fact, [they are] a place to frame the whole argument in your research paper. Without the lit review to explain what has been said before you, what you have to say doesn't matter to anybody. It also helps to focus your main ideas within your conclusion, by pointing out major ideas and connecting them with each other: Lit reviews basically create the framework for what you're going to do, and how what you're doing will fit into the discourse community. (Reflection 4)

The notion of joining a discourse community or ongoing conversation was a central one for the course. Most students were fascinated by the notion that researchers are responding and writing to one another in an ongoing conversation. Stephanie pursued the notion further in her end of semester reflection:

> . . . I never before realized that every written text is part of an ongoing conversation with those who have discussed the topic before and those who will read your writing in the future and write their own texts in response to yours. I did not connect reading and writing so strongly in the past. . . . (Reflection 1)

When Stephanie felt she adequately understood the "conversation" about rhetorical reading, she designed her own study. Like studies conducted by professionals, hers was messy, complicated, surprising, and imperfect. She set out to discover "whether students read rhetorically in the first place, and if not, whether a push in the right direction aids in the use of rhetorical reading skills" (Final Paper 7). To conduct the research, she contacted five college students from three universities and asked them to complete a three-part reading exercise similar to the exercise given by Haas and Flower (171–172). Stephanie asked participants to complete "a list of questions designed to create a general profile of how these students felt about and approached the reading of a difficult text"; to read a passage from the introduction of Linda Flower's article, "Construction of Purpose in Writing and Reading"; and to write a short explanation of what this text meant. Stephanie did not provide participants with outside information in order to "ensure that whatever information they wrote came from the selected text and not from another place" (Final Paper 8). Finally, Stephanie asked participants to read a portion of the introduction to "Revision Strategies of Student Writers and Experienced Adult Writers" by Nancy Sommers, again with no information about the text or where it came from. "This time, however, before writing a response, the reader was asked a series of questions designed to stimulate rhetorical responses, or at least get the reader to start thinking of the writing in such a way as to induce the gathering of rhetorical information" (Final Paper 9).

Almost immediately, Stephanie confronted the difficulties of conducting primary research. She had allowed participants to complete the exercise individually and at their own pace; as a result, some of them were slow to complete the various pieces and Stephanie worried that she would not finish the study on time. She also found that her participants may not have clearly understood her directions (or perhaps chose not to follow them), and, since she was not with the participants when they completed the exercise, she could not clarify the directions. In her final paper, Stephanie addressed methodological shortcomings, explaining ways in which the study could be improved and pointing out the limitations of her findings, which were based on a small number of participants and therefore not generalizable. That students not only *could* but *should* acknowledge shortcomings in their research papers came as a surprise to all the students, including Stephanie. Before the course, they perceived that research must sound perfect and clear-cut. They learned in the seminar that research is never perfect or clear-cut, and that acknowledging shortcomings is essential in a paradigm where research is conversation and readers need to evaluate and perhaps replicate studies.

Stephanie was also confused and surprised by her research findings. Much to her dismay, her results confirmed Haas and Flower's study: the students in Stephanie's study were no more able to use rhetorical strategies than the students in the original study. Even when students were told to ask rhetorical questions about the text, those questions did not seem to help them. According to

Stephanie, "None of the first year college students in this study are able to make the transition between the rhetorical information they gather and the comprehension of the text, making this rhetorical information useless" (Final Paper 12). Stephanie found, however, that the only senior in her study did ask himself rhetorical questions and used them to better understand what he read. Interestingly, Stephanie also identified problems beyond those discussed by Haas and Flower. Not only did the first-year students in Stephanie's study fail to use rhetorical reading strategies, they simply failed to understand the content. In fact, the rhetorical questions they asked themselves led them to further misunderstand what they were reading. Stephanie ended her study with more questions than answers, as well as ideas about what she would change if she were to conduct the study again.

As a result of her experiences with real participants, research methodology, and primary data, Stephanie realized a truth about research: it's messy. Moreover, Stephanie's and her classmates' previously held misconceptions about research writing were beginning to dismantle. Their research writing experiences prior to the writing seminar taught them that the right answers to all questions exist "out there somewhere" and that their task is to locate and write up those answers in their own words. When the students became surprised and confused by the results of their own studies, they began to question how they read other people's research as well. They came to understand the contextual and conditional nature of research because their own experiences no longer supported the notion of research writing as objective and acontextual.

At the end of the semester, Stephanie reflected positively on her experiences in the course. Although she "hated it at times," she learned a great deal about the connection between reading and writing, expanded her own reading and writing skills, and developed knowledge about rhetorical reading from which others could benefit: "I would be willing to share everything I have learned with anybody. In fact, from the start of our class, I would try to explain to people how to become better readers and writers . . ." (Reflection 6).

While most students won't achieve Stephanie's level of success in the writing studies course, her story illustrates what is possible: students come to see writing as a conversation, research as historical and contextual, and research findings as messy, complicated, and inconclusive. These are truths about writing that Stephanie, and many other students in the English 114 Writing Seminar, walked away understanding.

Student Feedback

While Stephanie and Jack had radically different experiences, they and most of our other students shared a range of outcomes. Commonalities were apparent in students' end-of-semester reflections, the most prevalent being increased self-awareness about writing, improved reading skills, and a new understanding of research writing as conversation.

Increased Self-Awareness about Writing   Students suggested that they thought a lot about their own writing by the end of this course. For example, one student wrote that the course provided new opportunities to look at her writing: "It's been a real blessing to see more of who *I am* as a writer. . . . Being involved in so many discussions about writing really helped me to take my vision of how I write, and put it on the chopping block (next to Flower and Hayes and Murray)." Another realized, "I need to do more to get other people involved in my writing." A signature comment from Downs's class was, "I never knew that there was so much written about writing. It was extremely helpful to my writing to be able to study these techniques."

Improved Reading Abilities and Confidence   The course focus on reading makes students more aware of their own reading practices and sometimes stretches their abilities. One of Wardle's students commented

> In high school, I would skim the required reading and look for the main details, or if I was given questions to answer I would skim the reading and only look specifically for the answers. In college, I began to read things entirely, from the articles required in English and History to my Chemistry textbook, searching for the main points and occasionally taking notes on the readings if I was having trouble understanding the article.

Students also become much more likely to recognize texts not as information but as the words of real people. As such, they adopt more of the habits of experienced scholarly writers in thinking of and referring to their sources as people. In comparison to students in "academic writing" pedagogies, they are much more likely to introduce sources as people speaking (e.g., "Royar and Giles have studied this question at length . . ."), much less likely to blind quote, and more selective and precise in their use of descriptive attributive verbs such as *argues*, *claims*, *insists*, *questions*, *states*, and *believes* rather than "the book says." They also become more used to critical maneuvers with texts; as one student wrote, "[Readers must] look at the purpose of [a piece of] writing, find the motivation."

Raised Awareness of Research Writing as Conversation   Unlike students in other pedagogies we have used, students in the Introduction to Writing Studies course conceptualize research writing much more like expert scholarly researchers do, as turns in a conversation or contributions to addressing an open question. A student in Wardle's class saw that "One needs to gather the information already found by other researchers who have either joined or started this conversation, so that one knows what they are going to say in relation to what has already been said by others." Another student wrote,

> . . . I have learned that research is joining an ongoing conversation. In order to do a research project, I had to first learn what others had said in the past on gender and politeness before I even began doing my own research study. I had to become knowledgeable on the conversation that had taken place previously, before I jumped into the current conversation.

Students in the course experience something of how scholarly researchers take authority for themselves and state opinions, thus making their writing more "authentic." As one of Downs's students said, "You made me feel as if my opinion mattered."

These three outcomes were the most obvious ones achieved collectively by students in our courses; though there were others, we have little space to describe them here. Nearly all students reported newfound confidence in their abilities to complete "hard" work, commenting that "After finishing, I was utterly astonished" or noting they accomplished something they "still don't believe" they did. Many commented that they had learned about structuring large projects and completing primary research projects. A number noted that for the first time in an English course they found peer review not only useful but essential and asked for more in future courses — perhaps because all of the students were invested in their work and in the assignments.

Finally, it bears noting that the students in these courses left with an understanding of the field of writing studies. By the end of the term, students used the language of the field often (calling themselves "recursive writers," calling the data they collected "artifacts") and discussed questions that still need to be taken up by the discipline. Though few of these students, if any, will likely earn PhDs in rhetoric and composition, they move into their chosen disciplines with realistic and useful conceptions of writing and they know where to go for answers when confronted by writing-related problems.

CHALLENGES AND CRITIQUES

Despite our positive experiences and the positive feedback of most of our students, there are inevitable challenges inherent to this pedagogy. We also find that some of our colleagues resist this pedagogy, for a variety of reasons. Here we briefly outline the challenges we have experienced, as well as respond to additional critiques offered by some of our colleagues.

Challenges

No pedagogy offers perfect solutions, and ours is no exception. Our pedagogy is demanding, confusing to students early on, does not allow for "perfect" student work, and — most obviously — cannot be taught by someone not trained in writing studies. Rather than gloss these challenges, we feel they must be openly discussed if the pedagogy is to see widespread use.

The course is demanding and different. In high school, most of our students experienced English classes that revolved around literature and they often have similar expectations for FYC. By contrast, our course content is not only entirely new, but the readings and assignments are lengthy and complex. As a result, the first few weeks can be difficult as students adjust their expectations of the course and begin to understand its goals. Our classroom experience also suggests that because the writing studies pedagogy is demanding on several levels (engagement, reading, critical thinking), it inverts the traditional FYC bell curve with most students achieving exceptional success or failing and few students earning Cs. Underengaged students may be at greater risk of failing the course than their more invested counterparts.

We do not want to institute a course that can function as a "weed out" course for underprepared students; our goal remains to help students learn more about writing and become more successful writers in the university. The course may be easier for students over two semesters, rather than one; in this scenario, the first semester could be devoted to reading writing studies literature, choosing a research topic, and beginning library research and the second semester devoted to primary research.

Few appropriate resources exist for first-year students. Currently no textbooks exist[4] that provide surveys of our field's central principles and important works tailored for undergraduate students, perhaps in part because the field has not yet summoned enough of a center to agree on what those principles and works might be. While challenging, this approach does have benefits: students receive coaching about how to read scholarly articles (a literacy task too often ignored in courses that purport to teach "academic discourse"), and the texts serve as examples of principles such as how to cite sources and how to organize research reports.

Realistically, however, teaching a more widespread and easily implemented introductory course about writing studies will require a textbook like those in other fields summarizing writing studies research. Publisher interest in such a textbook hinges on projected sales, so the course must be taught in larger numbers before publishers will be convinced of the viability of such a textbook; in the meantime, instructors must accept and produce intermediary solutions like supplemental texts that condition publishers and the field to the idea of such textbooks.

Students will produce imperfect work. Given the limits of time and audience-appropriate resources, students often only grasp the most central concepts of highly nuanced and rich readings. Students' research plans, library research, primary methods, and results are limited because of short time, lack of funding, and inexperience. Fewer students produce "complete" and polished final papers in the writing studies course than in other FYC pedagogies. This difference might be problematic for instructors who believe that students should produce perfected and polished writing; only the very best students in the writing studies course will do so. However, we assert that accepting imperfect work recognizes important truths about all research writing: it takes a long time, is inevitably imperfect, and requires extensive revision. The rewards of accepting imperfection as part of a challenging research and writing curriculum outweigh the deficiencies of courses in which students produce more-polished but less-demanding and realistic writing assignments.

Instructors must be knowledgeable about writing studies. Finally, we acknowledge the elephant in the room: instructors must be educated in writing studies to teach the curriculum we suggest, and a significant portion of the national corps of college writing instructors do not have appropriate training to do so. In this sense, ours is a truth-telling course; it forefronts the field's current labor practices and requires that we ask how FYC students are currently being served by writing instructors who *couldn't* teach a writing studies pedagogy. Our field's current labor practices reinforce cultural misconceptions that anyone can teach writing because there is nothing special to know about it. By employing nonspecialists to teach a specialized body of knowledge, we undermine our own claims as to that specialization and make our detractors' argument in favor of general writing skills for them. As Debra Dew demonstrates, constructing curricula that require specialization goes a long way toward professionalizing the writing instruction workforce.

Critiques

In this section, we respond to two critiques leveled at this pedagogy by some of our colleagues: that this course may not improve student writing and that this pedagogy arises merely from a desire to teach topics that interest us. While we believe these critiques have little merit, both will likely arise again and therefore need to be addressed.

Teaching about writing may not improve student writing. As we noted in discussing the implications of Jack's experience, writing about writing may not result in measurable improvements in students' writing any more than other types of FYC courses. Assessments suggest that particular courses or time periods have not improved student writing (Benton & Slocombe; Curry & Hager; Graham; Scharton), have had no discernible effects on student writing (Jewell, et al.; Sanders), or have even worsened student writing (Scharton). Part of the reason may be that improvement in writing happens slowly and is unlikely to be evident in essays written for a particular course over the short run (Witte and Faigley). Studies do show that over a period of one to three years, college students' writing does improve (Hughes & Martin; Haswell, "Change," "Documenting"); however, it is difficult to attribute improvement to composition courses (Davis) or to any particular curriculum (e.g., Haswell, "Change"; Hurtgen; Vandament).

However, we are not arguing that FYC can have no effect on students' writing. Rather, we are positing different sorts of improvement as the primary focus of the course. Those who seek "general writing improvement" are bound to be disappointed in this pedagogy, but we would argue that the goal of "general writing improvement" ignores the necessity of defining what counts as "writing" and "improvement." Our experiences suggest that some of our criteria for student success in writing courses—such as recognizing the conversational nature of research writing or gaining confidence in and perspective on one's writing abilities and processes—are positively impacted by the writing studies pedagogy. The question is whether and for whom such gains will count as "improved writing."

The writing studies pedagogy is also consonant with current understandings of transfer. Proven means of facilitating transfer include self-reflection, explicit abstraction of principles, and alertness to one's context (Langer; Perkins and Salomon, "Teaching" and "Transfer"; Smit; Beaufort 186; Flower and Hayes). Teaching students what we know about writing and asking them to research their own writing and the writing of others encourages this self-reflection and mindfulness, thereby improving the possibility that students will maintain a stance of inquiry toward writing as they write in other disciplinary systems. Only with additional implementation of the pedagogy and longitudinal studies to assess students' later writing experiences will we be able to tell whether this theory bears out in practice.

The course simply represents the instructor's desire to teach about things she knows and enjoys. We believe this critique is rooted in the notion that graduate instructors specializing in literature often attempt to teach their own interests and expertise in composition courses at the expense of writing instruction. We submit that our curriculum is not remotely analogous. The case we make for a course *about* writing represents a bid to share our unique disciplinary expertise in a course of the same disciplinary designation; this is no more and no less than any other faculty member across the academy does.

While faculty in other disciplines are expected to teach the content and methods of their fields even in the most introductory courses, many (if not most) FYC classes throughout the country allow students to write on any range of topics, topics which often fall outside the writing teachers' specialization. Writing teachers and students alike are better served by focusing specifically on topics teachers know. To argue otherwise accepts and perpetuates the myth that content is separable from writing — that an FYC instructor *need not be* expert in the subject matter of a paper in order to evaluate the quality of writing in that paper, or need not be a subject expert on writing in order to teach writing. Such claims accept the premise that writing instruction can be limited to fluent English syntax, grammar, and mechanics. As a field, we would do well to ask what assumptions about writing in general and writing studies in particular would lead some to argue that teaching the content and methods of our field is inappropriate, unproductive, or harmful to students.

CONCLUSION

Those of us working in writing studies find ourselves today confronted by the fact that our own research and theory calls our cornerstone course — and the underlying assumptions upon which it is based — into question. Added to this difficulty is the fact that few outside our own discipline know we exist; if they do know we exist, they know little or nothing about what we do as writing scholars. Certainly, our own research and theory about the nature of writing has done little to influence public conceptions of writing. These two problems — teaching at odds with our research, and lack of public awareness — can be remedied together through a writing studies pedagogy. While this pedagogy has its drawbacks, we feel those are far outweighed by its benefits.

First, this pedagogy overcomes the problem of contradictory research and practice: rather than purporting to teach students "academic writing" and claiming to prepare them for writing in their disciplines, the course teaches students what we as a field have learned *about* writing as an object of study. Thus, the course acquires an attainable goal and a clear content while continuing to help students understand how writing works in the academy so that they can succeed there. Its content does not distract from writing (the perennial difficulty of writing-course content), since the content *is* writing.

Second, the pedagogy teaches potentially transferable conceptions of the activity of writing rather than "basic" writing skills that are in fact highly specialized and contextualized. This content and the overall project of the course create intellectual rigor and resist characterization of writing instruction as remedial, basic, or inexpert; in doing so, the course professionalizes writing instruction, as Dew demonstrates in a similar program at University of Colorado-Colorado Springs. In addition, this course tells our field's stories, conceptions, and questions by rendering its teaching, researching, and scholarly practices visible—thus serving as an introductory course to a potential writing studies major.

Finally, the course has the added benefit of educating first-year students, adjuncts, and graduate students about the existence and content of the writing studies field. Over time, as these groups move on to other disciplines, professions, and administrative positions, their knowledge about our field may be of assistance in creating more writing studies majors. At the very least, educating the public about our discipline in this way should result in a more widespread understanding and awareness of its existence, focus, and research findings.

As we teach such courses across the country, we will raise awareness not only about the existence of our discipline, but about what we do as a discipline—what we study and think about. Making this change, introducing first-year students to the knowledge of our discipline, will, we believe, lead us further toward full disciplinarity, a fulfillment marked by courses that come from our research and theory, pedagogy that emerges from our common knowledge, and a public awareness of what we do. This realization of disciplinary praxis is one that we look forward to with excitement and optimism.

ACKNOWLEDGMENTS

We appreciate the feedback and support of Donna Kain (East Carolina State), Steve Bernhardt (University of Delaware), and CCC editor Deborah Holdstein.

NOTES

1. We distinguish between what we take as "industry standard" in FYC and different but relatively rare pedagogies that approach FYC more effectively, such as gateway courses to WID programs. Our critique is of dominant "academic

discourse" and "cultural studies" pedagogies that teach writing apart from specific contexts.

2. It is often assumed that "skills" or moves such as taking a position, building arguments, developing paragraphs, and writing clear and forceful sentences are "general writing skills" that transfer across all situations. Such "static abstractions" (Connors) are meaningless in the absence of specific contexts and useless in the presence of such contexts. For example, even if all writing were about "taking a position," the ways of doing so vary radically across disciplines, and therefore can only meaningfully be taught within a discipline. What constitutes clarity or forcefulness for a scholar in English is simply different — in kind, not just degree — from what constitutes these qualities in engineering.

3. Other disciplines share the same struggle: To what extent will a misinformed public trump the specialized knowledge of the discipline? Usually, however, these battles take place in secondary education rather than college; higher education has not deemed it the public's right to determine the curriculum of any collegiate subject save the "basic" subject of writing, as Sharon Crowley observes. Letting nonspecialists dictate our pedagogy leaves us with no standing; our writing studies pedagogy addresses this problem.

4. Wendy Bishop's *The Subject Is . . .* series as well as the new book *Conversations about Writing* by Elizabeth Sargent and Cornelia Paraskevas are partial exceptions.

WORKS CITED

Ackerman, John M. "Reading, Writing, and Knowing: The Role of Disciplinary Knowledge in Comprehension and Composing." *Research in the Teaching of English* 25 (1991): 133–78.

Bazerman, Charles. *Shaping Written Knowledge: The Genre and Activity of the Experimental Article in Science.* Madison, WI: U of Wisconsin P, 1988.

——. "The Life of Genre, the Life in the Classroom." Ed. Wendy Bishop and Hans Ostrom. *Genre and Writing: Issues, Arguments, Alternatives.* Portsmouth, NH: Boynton/Cook, 1997. 19–26.

Bazerman, Charles, and James Paradis, eds. *Textual Dynamics of the Professions: Historical and Contemporary Studies of Writing in Professional Communities.* Madison, WI: U of Wisconsin P, 1991.

Beason, Larry. "Ethos and Error: How Business People React to Errors." *College Composition and Communication* 53 (2001): 33–64.

Beaufort, Anne. *Writing in the Real World: Making the Transition from School to Work.* New York: Columbia U Teachers College P, 1999.

Benton, Steve, and John Slocombe. *Status Report of the UGE Portfolio Assessment Committee.* Kansas State U, 2000.

Berkenkotter, Carol. "Decisions and Revisions: The Planning Strategies of a Publishing Writer." *College Composition and Communication* 34 (1983): 156–72.

Berkenkotter, Carol, and Thomas N. Huckin. *Genre Knowledge in Disciplinary Communication: Cognition/Culture/Power.* Hillsdale, NJ: Erlbaum, 1995.

Berkenkotter, Carol, Thomas Huckin, and John Ackerman. "Conventions, Conversations, and the Writer: Case Study of a Student in a Rhetoric Ph.D. Program." *Research in the Teaching of English* 22 (1988): 9–44.

Bishop, Wendy. *The Subject Is Writing: Essays by Teachers and Students.* 3rd ed. Portsmouth, NH: Boynton/Cook, 2003.

Bishop, Wendy, and Pavel Zemliansky, eds. *The Subject Is Research: Processes and Practices.* Portsmouth, NH: Boynton/Cook, 2001.

Broad, Bob. *What We Really Value: Beyond Rubrics in Teaching and Assessing Writing.* Logan, UT: Utah State UP, 2003.

Carter, Duncan. "Critical Thinking for Writers: Transferable Skills or Discipline-Specific Strategies?" *Composition Studies/Freshman English News* 21.1 (1993): 86–93.

CCCC Committee on Professional Standards. "A Progress Report from the CCCC Committee on Professional Standards." *College Composition and Communication* 42 (1991): 330–44.

Center for Educational Policy Research. "English." *Understanding University Success (A Project of the AAU and The Pew Charitable Trusts).* Eugene, OR: Center for Educational Policy Research, 2003. 16–27. 18 May 2005. http://s4s.org/under standing.php.

College Entrance Examination Board. National Commission on Writing in America's Schools and Colleges. *The Neglected "R": The Need for a Writing Revolution.* New York: College Entrance Examination Board, April 2003. 18 May 2005. http://www.writingcommission.org/prod_downloads/writingcom/neglectedr .pdf.

——. *Writing: A Ticket to Work . . . Or a Ticket Out. A Survey of Business Leaders.* New York: College Entrance Examination Board, Sept. 2004. 18 May 2005. http://www.writing commission.org/prod_downloads/writingcom/writing-ticket-to-work.pdf.

Connors, Robert J. *Composition-Rhetoric: Backgrounds, Theory, and Pedagogy.* Pittsburgh: U of Pittsburgh P, 1997.

Council of Writing Program Administrators. "WPA Outcomes Statement for First-Year Composition." *WPA: Writing Program Administration* 23.1/2 (1999): 59–66. 18 May 2005. http://wpacouncil.org/positions/outcomes.html.

Crowley, Sharon. *Composition in the University: Historical and Polemical Essays.* Pittsburgh: U of Pittsburgh P, 1998.

Curry, Wade, and Elizabeth Hager. "Assessing General Education: Trenton State College." *Student Outcomes Assessment: What Institutions Stand to Gain.* Ed. Diane F. Halpern. San Francisco: Jossey-Bass Publishers, 1987. 57–66.

Davis, Ken. "Significant Improvement in Freshman Composition as Measured by Impromptu Essays: A Large-scale Experiment." *Research in the Teaching of English* 13 (1979): 45–48.

Dawkins, John. "Teaching Punctuation as a Rhetorical Tool." *College Composition and Communication* 46 (1995): 533–48.

Dew, Debra Frank. "Language Matters: Rhetoric and Writing I as Content Course." *WPA: Writing Program Administration* 26.3 (2003): 87–104.

Diller, Christopher, and Scott F. Oates. "Infusing Disciplinary Rhetoric into Liberal Education: A Cautionary Tale. *Rhetoric Review* 21 (2002): 53–61.

Ericsson, Patricia. "Beyond the Laments, Beyond the Boundaries: Communicating about Composition." Diss. Michigan Technological U, 2003.

Evans, Rick. "Learning 'Schooled Literacy': The Literate Life Histories of Mainstream Student Readers and Writers." *Discourse Processes* 16 (1993): 317–40.

Fish, Stanley. "Devoid of Content." *New York Times.* May 31, 2005: A17.

Flower, Linda. "The Construction of Purpose in Writing and Reading." *College English* 50 (1988): 528–50.

Flower, Linda, and John R. Hayes. "The Cognition of Discovery: Defining a Rhetorical Problem." *College Composition and Communication* 31 (1980): 21–32.

Gee, James Paul. *An Introduction to Discourse Analysis: Theory and Method*. London: Routledge, 1999.

———. "Literacy, Discourse, and Linguistics: Introduction." *Journal of Education* 171 (1989): 5–17.

Graham, Janet Gorman. "A Comparison of the Writing of College Freshmen and College Seniors with a Focus on Indications of Cognitive Development." Diss. U of Maryland College Park, 1988.

Greene, Stuart. "Argument as Conversation: The Role of Inquiry in Writing a Researched Argument." *The Subject Is Research Processes and Practices*. Eds. Wendy Bishop and Pavel Zemliansky. Portsmouth, NH: Boynton/Cook-Heinemann, 2001. 145–56.

———. "Mining Texts in Reading to Write." *Journal of Advanced Composition* 12 (1992): 151–70.

Haas, Christina, and Linda Flower. "Rhetorical Reading Strategies and the Construction of Meaning." *College Composition and Communication* 39 (1988): 167–83.

Haswell, Richard. "Change in Undergraduate and Post-graduate Writing Performance (Part I): Quantified Findings." 1984. ERIC: ED 269780.

———. "Documenting Improvement in College Writing: A Longitudinal Approach." *Written Communication* 17 (2000): 307–52.

———. *Gaining Ground in College Writing: Tales of Development and Interpretation*. Dallas: Southern Methodist UP, 1991.

Hjortshoj, Keith. *The Transition to College Writing*. Boston: Bedford, 2001.

Howard, Rebecca Moore. "WPAs and/versus Administrators: Using Multimedia Rhetoric to Promote Shared Premises for Writing Instruction." *WPA: Writing Program Administration* 27.1–2 (2003): 9–22.

Hughes, Gail F., and Gerald R. Martin. "The Relationship between Instructional Writing Experience and the Quality of Student Writing: Results from a Longitudinal Study in the Minnesota Community College System." 1992. ERIC: ED 345276.

Hull, Glynda. "Hearing Other Voices: A Critical Assessment of Popular Views on Literacy and Work." *Changing Work, Changing Workers: Critical Perspectives on Language, Literacy, and Skills*. Ed. Glynda Hull. Albany: SUNY P, 1997. 3–39.

Hurtgen, James R. "Assessment of General Learning: State University of New York College at Fredonia." *The Campus-Level Impact of Assessment: Progress, Problems, and Possibilities*. Eds. Peter J. Gray and Trudy W. Banta. San Francisco: Jossey-Bass, 1987. 59–69.

Hyland, Ken. *Disciplinary Discourses: Social Interactions in Academic Writing*. 2004 Michigan classics ed. Ann Arbor: U of Michigan P, 2004.

Jewell, Ross M., John Cowley, Gerald Bisbey, and John H. Bushman. "The Effectiveness of College-Level Instruction in Freshman English. Final Report." U.S. Office of Education Project No. 2188, Amended. 1969. ERIC: ED 037476.

Kantz, Margaret. "Helping Students Use Textual Sources Persuasively." *College English* 52 (1990): 74–91.

Kaufer, David S., and Richard Young. "Writing in the Content Areas: Some Theoretical Complexities." *Theory and Practice in the Teaching of Writing: Rethinking the Discipline*. Ed. Lee Odell. Carbondale, IL: Southern Illinois UP, 1993. 71–104.

Kleine, Michael. "What Is It We Do When We Write Articles Like This One — And How Can We Get Students to Join Us?" *The Writing Instructor* 6 (1987): 151–61.

Lakoff, George, and Mark Johnson. *Metaphors We Live By*. Chicago: U of Chicago P, 1980.

Langer, Ellen J. *Mindfulness*. Reading, MA: Addison-Wesley, 1989.

Lyons, William. *Gilbert Ryle: An Introduction to His Philosophy*. Highlands, NJ: Humanities, 1980.

MacDonald, Susan Peck. "Problem Definition in Academic Writing." *College English* 49 (1987): 315–31.

McCarthy, Lucille. "A Stranger in Strange Lands: A College Student Writing Across the Curriculum." *Research in the Teaching of English* 21 (1987): 233–65.

Miller, Carolyn. "Genre as Social Action." *Quarterly Journal of Speech* 70 (1984): 151–67.

Murray, Donald. "All Writing Is Autobiography." *College Composition and Communication* 42 (1991): 66–74.

Nelson, Jennie. "Constructing a Research Paper: A Study of Students' Goals and Approaches." Technical Report No. 59. Berkeley: Center for the Study of Writing, 1992. ERIC: ED 342019.

——. "The Research Paper: A 'Rhetoric of Doing' or a 'Rhetoric of the Finished Word'?" *Composition Studies: Freshman English News* 22.2 (1994): 65–75.

Perkins, David N., and Gavriel Salomon. "Teaching for Transfer." *Educational Leadership* 46 (1988): 22–32.

——. "Transfer of Learning." *International Encyclopedia of Education, Second Edition.* Ed. T. Husén and T. N. Postlethwaite. Oxford: Pergamon, 1992. 18 May 2005. http://learnweb.harvard.edu/alps/thinking/docs/traencyn.htm.

Perl, Sondra. "The Composing Processes of Unskilled College Writers." *Research in the Teaching of English* 13 (1979): 317–36.

Petraglia, Joseph. "Introduction: General Writing Skills Instruction and Its Discontents." Petraglia xi–xvii.

——, ed. *Reconceiving Writing, Rethinking Writing Instruction.* Mahwah, NJ: Laurence Erlbaum, 1995.

——. "Writing as Unnatural Act." Petraglia 79–100.

Reither, James. "Writing and Knowing: Toward Redefining the Writing Process." *College English* 47 (1985): 620–28.

Russell, David R. "Activity Theory and Its Implications for Writing Instruction." Petraglia 51–77.

——. "Looking Beyond the Interface: Activity Theory and Distributed Learning." *Distributed Learning: Social and Cultural Approaches to Practice.* Eds. Mary R. Lea and Kathy Nicoll. London: Routledge, 2002. 64–82.

——. "Rethinking Genre in School and Society: An Activity Theory Analysis." *Written Communication* 14 (1997): 504–54.

——. *Writing in the Academic Disciplines: A Curricular History.* 2nd ed. Carbondale, IL: Southern Illinois UP, 2002.

Sanders, Sara Elise. "A Comparison of 'Aims' and 'Modes' Approaches to the Teaching of Junior College Freshman Composition Both with and without an Auxiliary Writing Lab." Diss. U of Texas-Austin, 1973.

Sargent, Elizabeth M., and Cornelia C. Paraskevas. *Conversations about Writing: Eavesdropping, Inkshedding, and Joining In.* Toronto, Canada: Thomson Nelson, 2005.

Scharton, Maurice. "Models of Competence: Responses to a Scenario Writing Assignment." *Research in the Teaching of English* 23 (1989). 163–80.

Shamoon, Linda. "Survival Tactics: Rethinking and Redesigning a Writing Program during the New Abolitionism." *Composition Chronicle* (May 1995): 4–7.

Smit, David. *The End of Composition Studies.* Carbondale, IL: Southern Illinois UP, 2004.

Sommers, Nancy. "Revision Strategies of Student Writers and Experienced Adult Writers." *College Composition and Communication* 31 (1980): 378–88.

Spivey, Nancy Nelson. "Transforming Texts: Constructive Processes in Reading and Writing." *Written Communication* 7 (1990): 256–87.

Staples, Brent. "The Fine Art of Getting It Down on Paper, Fast." *New York Times* 15 May 2005, late ed., sec 4: 13.

Swales, John M. *Genre Analysis: English in Academic and Research Settings.* New York: Cambridge UP, 1990.

Vandament, William E. "A State University Perspective on Student Outcomes Assessment." *Student Outcomes Assessment: What Institutions Stand to Gain.* Ed. Diane Halpern. San Francisco: Jossey-Bass, 1987. 25–28.

Walvoord, Barbara. "Freshman, 'Focus,' and Writing Across the Curriculum." *Freshman English News* 14.2 (1985): 13–17.

Walvoord, Barbara, and Lucille McCarthy. *Thinking and Writing in College: A Naturalistic Study of Students in Four Disciplines.* Urbana, IL: NCTE, 1990.

Wardle, Elizabeth. "Can Cross-Disciplinary Links Help Us Teach 'Academic Discourse' in FYC?" *Across the Disciplines* 1 (2004). http://wac.colostate.edu/atd/articles/wardle2004/.

———. "'Mutt Genres' and the Goal of FYC: How Can We Help Students Write the Genres of the University?" *College Composition and Communication* 60.4 (2009): 765–89.

Witte, Stephen, and Lester Faigley. *Evaluating College Writing Programs.* Carbondale, IL: Southern Illinois UP, 1983.

Donald M. Murray

The Teaching Craft:
Telling, Listening, Revealing

The mirror surprises. The gray beard has turned white. The apprentice teacher is asked to speak as a master. The amateur who came to teaching late teaches teachers, and what was chutzpah is confirmed by rank. I have fooled them all.

But not myself. I am still apprentice to two trades which can not be learned: writing and teaching. I am thankful for the anxiety of each blank page, the stagefright before each new class. yup

I spend my time looking ahead to what I have not tried, to what I have not learned. But when I am asked to look back over my shoulder I discover reason in what I had believed was accident. I seem to have done three kinds of teaching, each new stage building on the one before, as if my progress had been calculated, not the result of tossing away my notes after every class.

TEACHING BY TELLING

When we begin to teach we have to learn to teach standing up. When I came to teaching nineteen years ago I thought the classroom a casual place where we would converse. Of course, I would do most of the conversing. They would listen, and they would learn.

I found myself on a stage playing to an audience that did not particularly want to listen or to learn. I was expected to stimulate, motivate, entertain, perform.

I found I had two hands, enormous hands, and no place to put them. Sometimes my right hand got tied in the cord of the window blind and I was tied to the window on the right side of the classroom. I would dismiss the class and try to get untied before the next class arrived. One of my colleagues confessed he took home a lectern and practiced letting go. He had been frozen to the lectern for each entire class.

I found that I chewed on a right knuckle when I spoke. It did not clarify my mumble. At times I spoke so fast I could not even follow what I was saying myself, and at other times the silence rose in the room like an irreversible tide. I think it was at least a year that I only taught the upper lefthand corner of the ceiling, another year before I faced the blurred faces, a third year before they

---

This article was adapted by the author from his CEE Luncheon Address, November 21, 1981, at the NCTE Convention in Boston. He is a Pulitzer Prize winner who teaches at the University of New Hampshire.

This article is reprinted from *English Education* 14.1 (Feb. 1982): 56–60.

turned to people. It took me longer to have the courage to turn my back on the class and use the blackboard. I was certain if I turned away from them they'd leave — or attack.

I had to learn to pace the class. Remember that wonderful scene in the movie, *Starting Over*, when Burt Reynolds teaches for the first time, tells the class everything he knows about writing, and dismisses the class? Then a student raises his hand and says that only five minutes have gone by.

To teach well standing up we have to be able to see through the complexities of the subjects we have learned to the unifying simplicities. We have to learn to repeat without seeming to repeat, to hear the question asked instead of the question expected, to read the audience, to teach by telling.

In teaching teachers many of us, myself very much included, advocate inductive methods of teaching, forgetting that we had to learn to teach by telling first, to perform, to get attention and hold it, to command the classroom. Teaching standing up isn't easy; it's an art in itself. And we have colleagues who make a respectable career of teaching by telling. But after approximately five years of teaching standing up I was moved to a new classroom, and I found I had a new craft to learn.

TEACHING BY LISTENING

The chairs were not in rows, and there was no desk at the front of the room. There was a great rectangle of tables. I would have to learn to teach sitting down.

I couldn't do it at first. I had in the old classroom occasionally, toward the end of the semester, slid out from behind the lectern and leaned against the front of the desk trying to appear casual. And there had been moments when I had even perched on the desk, but I was still looking down at my students. I was not really teaching sitting down.

At first I brought a lectern into the classroom and used it at the head of the table. And then for a semester or two I hopped up and down, sometimes standing, sometimes sitting. I found it was an enormous challenge to teach sitting down.

When at last I found I could remain in my seat, sitting at the same level as my students, I listened in a different way, and perhaps they were able to speak in a different way when I was not looking down at them and they were not looking up at me.

I still needed to be able to teach by telling. I did not discard that discipline as much as I built on it. I knew my students would not leave or attack, even if they should. I knew how to pace and clarify. I knew how to read their faces. At last I could begin to listen to what they were saying. When I did listen I found that they were discovering in their writing and their reading what I had been telling them, and they found it before I told them. Somehow I had developed an environment in which we wrote writing and read writing and in which we were able to share what we were learning.

At times I was a bit worried, perhaps a bit hurt. I remember once when I was called out of the room, the discussion had not been going well, but when I came back in the discussion was going very well indeed. I slipped back into my seat; they didn't notice I was there. But after a while I was able to enter into the discussion and share what I was learning from the text and from them. I hadn't been excluded, just the opposite; when I was able to listen they were able to include me in their learning.

I had a new role to play. I could still teach by telling. My students seemed to appreciate the times I told, but I noticed they were much shorter lectures, hardly lectures at all. They would sometimes be opening remarks, the establishing of a topic to be discussed; or concluding remarks, the summing up of what had been discussed, an effort to put the discussion into context.

My preparation for class changed. It focused more on my own learning through my own reading and writing, so that I was able to enter into the discussion of what we were learning during the time of the course. My teaching was more fun, more spontaneous. I learned from my students, and they were excited that I was learning from them as they learned from me. I became quicker on my feet sitting down than standing up — the apparently contradictory metaphor was accurate. I learned to react quicker and better, to take advantage of the accidents that led to learning. And as my class gave me more time to learn I gave them more time to learn.

It took, me at least ten years to learn to teach sitting down. I felt I had at last learned teaching by listening when Tim said at the end of class, "That was the best class we've had." And I was able to answer, "I know. I didn't speak for the first fifty minutes."

TEACHING BY REVEALING

In the past few years I found that I am exploring a new form of teaching. It has seemed a natural evolution. I still at times teach by telling and I still, even more of the time, teach by listening. But I also realize that I have become comfortable enough to teach by revealing my own learning.

This is related to what Frank Smith calls "demonstrations." He has pointed out the importance of showing how something is done in a number of his articles and in his book, *Writing and the Writer* (New York, Holt Rinehart and Winston, 1982, 257 pages). But demonstration can and should be an effective way of telling. The teacher shows the student how to do a particular kind of writing, or demonstrates a particular method of reading. The focus is on showing how to do something properly.

The same connotation holds in the modeling by teachers that Richard Beach and others are interested in studying. It is important for the teachers of teachers, especially, to model the kind of teaching they advocate. Too many of our education courses are taught by methods and attitudes that contradict what is being taught.

I suppose that I am demonstrating and that I am modeling, but I feel that I am at least extending these activities as I am learning how to reveal myself learning.

More and more I teach by writing in public. I have even, when invited to do a "reading," responded by offering to do a "writing." This, in part, brings the beginner's terror back to my teaching and keeps me from being bored by the sound of my own voice. But I think it does something more than that. Both writing and reading are essentially private acts, but if we are to teach them we must find ways to make them public.

When I face the blackboard to write in public I do not know what I will hear myself say. I recreate the experience of the blank page. I write to find out what I will write. It does not matter whether I write badly or well. Mistakes can be more productive and instructive than writing without mistakes. On my page alone I often see a breakdown in syntax at the point of a breakthrough in meaning. I am not looking, however, for correctness or incorrectness; I am looking for what Maxine Kumin calls, "the informing material." I am listening for voice; I am seeking the hint of an order.

And then, another time, I am working in public to make a text come clear. I cut, I add, I reorder. I follow the conventions of language, or I ignore them, if that is what I have to do to make the meaning clear. My students share their search for meaning with me. We teach each other by learning.

We read a text together, following false scents, racing down trails that suddenly stop, losing our bearings, helping each other find meaning in the prose and sharing with the writer, who may be teacher or may be student, the many ways that meaning may be found in a text and made clear.

I no longer know what I will teach or what I will learn in a class, or from a class. I am never sure, in fact, what has been learned. But I do know that learning is taking place, for I am learning, and my students are learning, and we are revealing our learning to each other.

Wendy Bishop

Helping Peer Writing Groups Succeed

Imagine you are entering a freshman level composition classroom. It is the tenth week of a fifteen-week semester. The teacher sits to one side of the room, conferencing with a single student about the student's paper which rests on a table between them. The rest of the twenty-student class has been divided into peer writing groups of four to five students. The class is noisy, for each group is busy discussing a paper and students talk freely, offering revision suggestions. The writer and a group historian note these suggestions, and a group monitor moves the discussion on, seeing to it that the group reviews at least some of each member's writing before the one hour class is over.

After the teacher conferences with several students, she then moves for a time from group to group, offering additional suggestions and encouragement, and checking on work accomplished. A few minutes before the class ends, the groups briefly summarize their work and each discussion is transcribed into written notes by the group historian. Finally, the teacher checks to make sure that the class as a whole is clear about future class sessions and/or assignments.

I have just described an idealized but obtainable writing classroom, one in which students join together in collaborative work and develop their writing abilities in a non-threatening environment. The teacher is guide and assistant to the work at hand. This holistic approach to writing and the teaching of writing makes many new demands on both students and teachers who need to change their attitudes and expectations to participate in such a classroom. Because of these sometimes unexpected demands, teachers trying to introduce peer writing groups into their curriculum often feel let down by a method that has been presented in glowing terms yet can prove problematic in practice. Has group work been overrated? Have teachers been deceived? Or, have teachers become confused by the apparent simplicity of a rather complex teaching method?

I would like to explore these questions by reviewing research that discusses the use of peer writing groups, by profiling successful and unsuccessful peer writing groups and, finally, by offering a plan for preparing and training students for the method. Such a plan must also include guidelines for evaluating the effectiveness of peer writing groups in the composition classroom.

This article is Chapter 2 of Wendy Bishop, *Teaching Lives: Essays and Stories* (Logan: Utah State University Press, 1997), 14–24.

RESEARCH ON PEER WRITING GROUPS

The value of using peer writing groups as a teaching method, if not over-rated, has sometimes been oversimplified. A brief review of current research and practice shows this. In general, collaborative peer writing groups do benefit the student. The claims for the efficacy of the method are many and various. Mary Beaven, discussing peer evaluation, claims that the collaborative method allows students to develop audience awareness, to check their perceptions of reality, to strengthen their interpersonal skills, and to take risks; the entire process results in improvement in writing and students' ability to revise. Thom Hawkins agrees that students strengthen their interpersonal skills and risk-taking or creative abilities.

Kenneth Bruffee found that peer tutors and tutees at work in a collaborative environment deal with higher order concerns such as paper focus and development. Tutees feel comfortable enough with peers to bring up these concerns which go beyond the usage level, and the writing abilities of tutors also improves as a direct result of the collaborative writing act. Researchers like Francine Danis, who found that 75% of the students in her study correctly identified both major and minor writing problems, and Anne Gere, who felt that student responses (grades five to twelve) did deal with meaning, would seem to support Bruffee's contention that students in peer groups do more than simply act as proofreaders of each other's work. Other research by Anne Gere and Robert Abbott reaffirmed the power of peer writing groups to stay focused on discussions about writing. Their research also shows that group discussions where teachers are present are significantly different from those in which teachers are absent.

Drawbacks to the method must be noted. First, collaborative learning can be time consuming (see Beaven and Abercrombie), for those writing about this method agree that some training of group members is necessary. Mary Beaven also notes that some instructors are unable to allow students the freedom required (student- rather than teacher-centered, discussion rather than lecture dominated classrooms) and therefore end up doing double work, designing *and controlling*, directing *and correcting* the groups. This problem seems to be one of teacher awareness and training rather than an inherent flaw in the method.

A final criticism develops from close research observation of groups and from student evaluations. Francine Danis found that students are not always sure of their group role, aren't able to stand back from their own writing, don't know what they want to know, and have a reluctance to offer critical comments. Elizabeth Flynn felt students lacked critical ability and attributed this to students' tendencies to supply missing information in a paper in order to make sense out of what they were reading. Again, these are problems that can be somewhat alleviated by student and teacher preparation for the method. The fact that students do need to develop a critical vocabulary from which to discuss their works is supported in Kenneth Bruffee's articles concerning the importance of language communities. Clearly, there is a need to introduce writing students to the vocabulary and terminology of the composition community.[1]

PROFILES OF PEER WRITING GROUPS

Now let us enter another freshman composition classroom. Again, it is the tenth week of a fifteen-week semester. Again, the teacher is conferencing with one student and four or five peer writing groups are in session. We will observe three of the groups.

In Group A, students form a tightly knit circle. Members are discussing organizational changes that would benefit a group member's paper. The writer of the paper listens and makes notes as does the group secretary. Soon, the group monitor reminds the group that other papers remain to be discussed. The transition to the next paper is made smoothly. If the teacher were to come over to the group, she could slip into a nearby seat and participate; talk would continue, although it would be altered somewhat by the group's awareness of her presence.

If you asked members of Group A how the group method was working, members would most likely be enthusiastic, pointing out changes they have made in papers as a result of the discussion, showing how every member of the group helps by offering suggestions, explaining that they appreciate the teacher's comments but also enjoy developing their writing skills together. Group A is a successful, fully developed peer writing group.

Here is an evaluation from a member of such a group:

> This is the first time I've had an English class where groups were formed. I found that I had an easier time talking in the groups then in class discussion. So I must say that it has value in letting me get my ideas across to other people in class, with much less apprehension.

Group B looks a lot like Group A. Most of the members are concentrating on a single paper. However, comments on this paper are tentative. The group gets stalled on a grammar point that no one is really interested in discussing nor competent to decide. When this happens, the writer of the paper starts to explain what she meant to do in the paper and other group members look bored. They've heard her talk like this before. Still, the members are polite and wait until the writer stops talking before moving on to another point: they find several misspellings in the paper. When the class ends, this group has only discussed two of four papers as the monitor forgot to move them on. The historian suggests that the group forgo the end of session summary and no one cares. When the teacher moves toward the group, discussion wanes and dies awkwardly. When asked how the group is doing, members can't articulate their group's progress, but insist that everything is okay. Talk picks up slowly as the teacher moves away.

Group B is finding the group method only mildly successful, for members are never really sure if they are talking about writing "in the right way." They don't feel that other members give them truly honest evaluation of their work and don't trust the evaluations they do receive. They are confused when they get teacher-graded papers returned that have low grades. They wonder why group members didn't catch more of the problems the teacher marked. They feel comfortable with each other but are sometimes lazy and unsure of their own abilities to discuss or change their writing. They accept working in groups but are constantly waiting for something to happen. Group B is an under-developed peer writing group.

Here is an evaluation from a member of such a group:

> I do like the idea of the groups. But could you please float around & insert "starter" statements for some groups if need be? Sometimes our group doesn't go very far under the analysis that we write in our journals.

Group C looks different than either Group A or Group B and looks different every time members try to start working together. Members of this group often don't come to class or come late and try to leave early. Some members are easily distracted; they look through their own bags or papers or watch other groups covertly. When this group does have more than one or two members, a single student may dominate the talk. No one has volunteered or been elected for the positions of historian and monitor. Often the group drifts, finishing work too quickly or not moving along at all. When the teacher comes to join this group, a single member enters into a private dialogue with her. Other group members may try to avoid contact with the teacher, both in and out of class.

Group C is sure the group method is useless. No one in the group knows what is going on and the class is boring. The dominant member is resentful, feeling he is doing too much work, and the other members feel they are in the grip of yet another un-elected teacher–dictator. Group members feel unsure of their own writing and do not see how they can teach each other. They have strong suspicions that the teacher is holding back something or is too lazy to really teach them. Group C is not simply underdeveloped; it is really not a peer writing group at all.

Here is an evaluation from a member of such a group:

> Individuals a little lax in group to have assignments read (including myself). We don't know what to write about, probably because we don't know what you want and don't know how to find it in the stories.
>   What are we looking for?

The observer of this writing class and the teacher might agree: when peer groups are fully developed (Group A), the method is exciting and rewarding for students and teacher alike, but when peer group interactions are under-developed (Group B) or break down (Group C), the method is discouraging and group work all too often feels like a matter of luck.

Obviously, these profiles are only useful in that they give a teacher a way to begin to sort out group interaction patterns. Each teacher will vary in the way she labels her groups. For instance, I evaluate group success on a continuum between fully developed and under-developed groups as distinct from non-cohering groups. Diana George in her article "Writing with Peer Groups in Composition" distinguishes between task-oriented, leaderless, and dysfunctional groups. In both cases, in-class observations have taken place and serious consideration has been given to groups in order for a teacher to improve future group work. By profiling her own writing groups, a teacher can learn how writing peer groups can become useless and sometimes lifeless. If even one of several important problems is present in a group, such a problem can quickly move the group from success to failure. Therefore, teachers need to be aware of the attributes of successful groups and learn what can be done to move groups from failure to success and doing so will enable composition teachers to feel more comfortable using peer writing groups.

The following list shows ways groups can fail or succeed and notes the names of researchers or writers who touch on these concerns when discussing peer writing groups. I have developed my profiles of group weaknesses and strengths after reading these writers and observing composition and literature classes which I conducted by group method at the University of Alaska, Fairbanks campus, from fall 1985 to spring 1987.

Ways Peer Writing Groups Fail

1. Too much or too little leadership (Hawkins; Elbow 1977; George).
2. Poor attendance or participation or preparation of some students leading to resentment between members (Hawkins; Flynn 1982).
3. Unclear group goals; group doesn't value work or works too quickly (Johnson and Johnson; Hawkins; George).
4. Group doesn't feel confident of group members' expertise or members are afraid to offer criticism (Lagana; Danis; Flynn).
5. Group doesn't understand new role of instructor (Ziv).
6. Group never develops adequate vocabulary for discussing writing (Danis; Bruffee).
7. Group fails to record suggestions or to make changes based on members' suggestions (George).

Ways Peer Writing Groups Succeed

1. Group successfully involves all members (Johnson and Johnson; Hawkins; Elbow).
2. Group works to clarify goals and assignments (Johnson and Johnson; Elbow 1977; Danis).
3. Group develops a common vocabulary for discussing writing (Beaven; Bruffee; Danis).
4. Group learns to identify major writing problems such as organization, tone, and focus, as well as minor writing problems such as spelling errors, and so on (Bruffee; Danis; Gere; Gere and Abbot).
5. Group learns to value group work and to see instructor as a resource which the group can call on freely (Rogers; Danis; Flynn).

Most writers are in agreement, students and teachers need preparation and training for successful peer group work. Those teachers who divide students into groups merely to provide momentary relief from the lecture classroom will develop failures similar to those listed above.

PREPARING FOR PEER WRITING GROUPS

Although the peer writing groups profiled in this paper show students critiquing each other's drafts, groups can serve a broader variety of purposes. Students can work together to discuss readings, to complete exercises, to explore writing invention strategies, and to help members with forming very early drafts. Additionally, the peer group method can be adapted to classes at the primary and secondary level, to advanced or creative writing classes, and to diverse academic disciplines.

Teachers who want to use peer writing groups in their classroom should plan ahead. They need to realize that the group method rests on a theory of collaborative learning and they will be more successful if they read widely in this area. While reading, a teacher should ask several questions:

1. Do I understand the theory behind peer writing groups?
2. Do I have a clear use for this method in my classroom?
3. What are my goals for students when using this method?

Additionally, because group work is based on a theory of learning that students may be unfamiliar with or resistant to, the well prepared teacher will acquaint students with concepts of collaborative learning through prepared handouts, class discussion, and continual monitoring of group work. After gaining a deeper understanding through reading, teachers need to visualize the place of peer writing groups in their entire curriculum. Students need to develop a group identity and participate in a new writing community. To function well, group members must be present, which requires a class attendance policy. A teacher might decide to use groups for a certain percentage of class time. I have found using groups 50 to 75% of my available class periods most effective. This percentage allows my students to develop a group identity yet regroup into a class on a regular basis in order to maintain a class identity also.

Classroom communities are formed by the school registrar, academic departments, and the enrolling student. How should peer group communities be formed? To start, teachers may divide a class into sets of four to five students or students may start working collaboratively in pairs and then pairs may be joined. Although many criteria could be presented for forming such groups, nothing in the peer group literature supports any one in particular. First week diagnostic writings may be used to organize groups with a balance of strong and weak writers. Students may rate themselves on matters such as ability to lead, to help, to take risks, and so on, and groups may be balanced with a member strong in each area. In addition, I try to balance groups by gender and by age.

Once groups are formed, there is no certain number of sessions needed to develop a strong sense of group community. Some groups develop rapport immediately and some take much longer. Groups can develop a radical (sometimes disruptive) streak and also a conservative (and equally disruptive) bent. Groups work best when they are balanced, focused, and comfortable. Depending on my course goals, I try to let groups work together for at least four sessions, and I rarely leave a group together for an entire semester.

The more groups are used, the more adept a teacher becomes in divining group personalities. Sometimes a teacher needs to intervene and change group membership (placing an overly dominant member in another, more challenging group, and so on), but often it is wiser to let the group itself solve group problems. Ideally, groups that stay together over a long period develop a strong group identity and sense of shared community. Equally, groups that change membership, partially or wholly, are often revitalized and ready to undertake new course challenges with greater enthusiasm.

Because groups develop as real writing communities, choosing a group name can help members identify with their new community. Ordering and clarifying group members' roles such as monitor and historian and general member also assures that group work will be carried on in an orderly manner. Groups are formed to work together, so group projects should be clearly articulated in handout form or as directions on the chalkboard, and group work should be real work, contributing to each member's writing development.

Time should be allowed for groups to share their work, conclusions, and progress with the whole class in order to support the class as a larger community and to keep groups from becoming too isolated. Reporting on what the group accomplished each session, in the form of historian's notes in a group folder, provides useful artifacts for group self-evaluation and teacher evaluation of the group session. To review, when forming groups for the first time, I ask the members to give themselves a name and to chose a monitor (timekeeper) and historian (secretary). Each group is given a folder for saving work and recording discussions.

TRAINING PEER WRITING GROUPS

To work well together, peer writing groups need training in two areas in particular: group roles and writing response. It is not enough to ask the groups to elect a monitor and a historian, but those individuals should have clear directions as to their roles. If a monitor does not act as the group caretaker, making sure each member gets time to respond to writing and time to have writing discussed and making sure the group performs the group tasks in time to share with the whole class, then the group will risk failure. If the historian does not record group discussions, there will be little continuity from session to session and no product to show the group and the teacher where the group has been and what it has done. When groups are first formed, handouts to elected members, as well as a handout detailing the responsibilities of a member in general — attendance, support, sharing, and so on — can speed the training in this area.

Even more important, group members will be teaching each other to talk about writing. This talk can be initiated by the teacher, reinforced by the class text, and nurtured by whole class discussion, but it will be brought to fruition in the group itself as members learn to improve their writing. In this effort, the teacher functions as the conduit linking the class to the academic community. She may begin by teaching the class necessary terminology (concerning writing process and writing analysis) and by training writers and readers to work together through role playing, reviewing sample essays, and so on. In their initial critique sessions, groups can work to answer set questions or can learn to develop their own critical concerns for papers. If composition terms such as prewriting, drafting, revising, focus, organization, and tone are introduced in class discussion, show up on group handouts, are reinforced in peer writing group discussions, and recorded in group minutes, such terms will soon become part of the peer group's working vocabulary.

MONITORING PEER WRITING GROUPS

During group work, the teacher is extremely busy, although not necessarily appearing so, for she is the group and class facilitator, deciding when to intervene in groups and when to reconvene the groups into a class to share results, review strategies, or speed up information dissemination. Sometimes the best thing a teacher can do is to listen and watch her groups quietly and unobtrusively; sometimes she must participate in groups to insure that each group is working efficiently, but there is no single right way to help groups succeed.

A teacher needs to experiment, but she should do so carefully. She should keep records of her groups (a personal journal is a good place to start), for she learns from each one of them. She can monitor groups by sight (regularly noting what is happening in each by direct observation); by sound (listening to tape recordings of groups at a later date); by direct contact (visits to and participation in groups); and by reviewing group or individual artifacts (learning logs, group weekly reports, group self-evaluations, questionnaires). It is important to remember that the teacher should be actively involved with the groups on a class by class basis.

EVALUATING PEER WRITING GROUPS

A teacher can evaluate the effectiveness of her peer writing groups, although few methods for doing so are quantifiable. Good evaluation results from good planning and from sensitive and careful review throughout and at the end of each course.

Teachers can determine if students are attaining [. . .] goals she set for group work. Group folders when examined tell a story of good attendance, completed work, and enlarged understanding. Self-evaluation on the part of students and teacher can chronicle success with the method and pinpoint areas for future work and improvement. And, most important, gains in individual student writing can be assessed.

In brief, a teacher can use any of the monitoring documents (group folders, tapes of group work, group self-evaluations, and so on) as well as her own journal of group work to develop a fairly clear profile of how successful each group was.

Measurements of student growth in collaborative learning techniques and writing in general can be accomplished with pre and post testing in the following areas:

1. pre and post written descriptions of what students feel can be accomplished in writing groups,
2. pre and post written descriptions of students' writing process,
3. pre and post writing apprehension tests,
4. pre and post essay samples.

Teachers would hope to find that post written descriptions of the group method show a greater understanding of and enjoyment of the method. Post descriptions of students' writing process should show a greater awareness of the writing process in general and as it relates to an individual student. Post writing apprehension tests should show a decline in writing apprehension. And post essay samples should show an improvement in writing when holistically evaluated (Bishop "Qualitative").

A teacher who hopes to use peer writing groups in her classroom should prepare for success. She needs to understand her writing groups will not always be completely effective but can be made more effective if she is willing to train herself and her students. In a sense, a teacher using peer writing groups must become a researcher in her own classroom. She plans for her class, trains group members, monitors and evaluates them, and, the next semester, begins the process again, refining and developing her talents as a group facilitator based on her own observations. This teacher will be willing to experiment, to redefine group failures as steps in a larger process that leads to success, and to have realistic expectations for this holistic teaching method. Before long, those expectations will be met and, hopefully, surpassed.

NOTE

1. This review of research into writing peer groups was completed in 1986, and significant amounts of work have been done on this subject since that time. I'd send readers to *Small Groups in Writing Workshops: Invitations to a Writer's Life* (Robert Brooke, Ruth Mirtz, and Rick Evans) for recent scholarship and bibliographic references.

Muriel Harris

Talking in the Middle: Why Writers Need Writing Tutors

The work of a writing center is as varied as the students who stream in and out the doors. A writing center encourages and facilitates writing emphasis in courses in addition to those in an English department's composition program; it serves as a resource room for writing-related materials; it offers opportunities for faculty development through workshops and consultations; and it develops tutors' own writing, interpersonal skills, and teaching abilities. Moreover, writing centers, by offering a haven for students where individual needs are met, are also integral to retention efforts, are good recruiting tools, provide a setting for computer facilities that integrate word processing with tutoring, are rich sites for research, and by their flexibility and ability to work outside of institutionalized programs are free to spawn new services and explore new writing environments. But these aspects of the work of a writing center do not define its core, its primary responsibility — to work one-to-one with writers. In doing so, writing centers do not duplicate, usurp, or supplement writing or writing-across-the-curriculum classrooms. Writing centers do not and should not repeat the classroom experience and are not there to compensate for poor teaching, overcrowded classrooms, or lack of time for overburdened instructors to confer adequately with their students. Instead, writing centers provide another, very crucial aspect of what writers need — tutorial interaction. When meeting with tutors, writers gain kinds of knowledge about their writing and about themselves that are not possible in other institutionalized settings, and it is this uniqueness of the tutorial setting that I will focus on here.

Tutorial instruction is very different from traditional classroom learning because it introduces into the educational setting a middle person, the tutor, who inhabits a world somewhere between student and teacher. Because the tutor sits below the teacher on the academic ladder, the tutor can work effectively with students in ways that teachers can not. Tutors don't need to take attendance, make assignments, set deadlines, deliver negative comments, give tests, or issue grades. Students readily view a tutor as someone to help them surmount the hurdles others have set up for them, and as a result students respond differently to tutors than to teachers, a phenomenon readily noticed by tutors who end a stint of writing center tutoring and then go off to teach their

---

This article is reprinted from *College English* 57.1 (Jan. 1995): 27–42.

own classes. Dave Healy, who both tutors and teaches, aptly describes this scenario:

> In the center, writers may try to invest me with authority, but I can resist their efforts. In the classroom, I can try to resist, but as long as I'm going to be assigning my students grades, my nonauthoritative pose is simply that: a pose. In the classroom, I can't get away from making assignments, and as long as I make them, no matter how enlightened or open-ended they may be, they're still mine. I can never adopt the kind of stance in relation to one of my assignments that I can in relation to an assignment that a writer brings to the center. And increasingly that stance feels crucial to the kind of work I want to do with writers.

Most students come to writing centers because they are required to (Bishop, Clark), but even so, students leave feeling that the tutorial has been a beneficial experience. Why is this so? The relationship with a tutor is likely to begin with questions like "How can I help you?" or "What would you like to work on today?" A truly reluctant student knows that she doesn't have to do anything, won't be graded, and in a worst-case scenario, can silently count the cracks in the ceiling while the tutor talks. But the vast majority of students start on a more positive note. Here's someone who might just help them, maybe even show them what's wrong, what to fix, or what the writing assignment is about. As the conversation progresses, they begin to talk more freely and more honestly because they are not in the confines of a teacher/student relationship where there are penalties for asking what they perceive as "dumb" questions (the penalty being that the teacher will find out how little they know or how inept they are in formulating their questions). Moreover, students realize that they don't have to listen passively and accept what is "told" to them by an authoritative speaker.

In addition to student attitudes toward tutors, another powerful component of the tutorial has to do with how tutors acquire needed information. Whereas teachers get information about students from conferences and from students' contributions to classroom interaction, much of what's needed comes from the written products students turn in. And those products are often analyzed when teachers are sitting alone at their desks, away from the students. By contrast, in the interaction between tutor and student, the tutor picks up clues from watching and listening to the student. Tutors' questions can lead students to offer information they didn't know was needed and to clarify their answers through further questioning. Students can also offer other useful information they would be less willing to give teachers. Sitting with a student for a half-hour or an hour, a tutor is able to work primarily with the writer as a person, even when the paper is there on the table between them. Tutors use talk and questioning and all the cues they can pick up in the face-to-face interaction. The conversation is free to roam in whatever direction the student and tutor see as useful. That is, the tutor can ask about writing habits and processes, can listen to the student's responses to various questions, and can use them as cues for further questions; and the student can express concerns not visible in the product. Moreover, either one is free to bring up some potentially relevant concern that takes them off in a different, more fruitful direction. The flexibility and interaction of a tutorial permits a close look at the individual student, something that Jim, a peer tutor in our Writing Lab, has noted. Jim spends one day a week in the classroom and then works with those students every week in tutorials. He notes that in the classroom his students are a sea of "hands, faces, and comments," but when these same students come to the Writing Lab, they become very different individuals with distinct personalities, needs, and ways of learning. Linda Flower views teachers' "product-based inferences" as a limitation that may radically underestimate students' knowledge, problem-solving efforts, and unresolved dilemmas. When that happens, notes Flower, teachers "may be trying to diagnose and teach a thinking process in the dark" ("Studying Cognition" 21). The face-to-face interaction of tutor and student permits some light to enter.

The power of the tutor's position outside the evaluative setting is also apparent in student evaluations that acknowledge tutors' expertise. There are always impressively high ratings, positive comments, and effusive notes of appreciation, far beyond what any of us who also teach in classrooms will get when we switch to wearing our grade-giving-instructor hats. As tutors, we are there to help reduce the stress, to overcome the hurdles set up by others, and to know more about writing than a roommate or friend, maybe even as much as their teachers. Students may not have come willingly and may (as is often the case) have come with inappropriate expectations that the tutor will fix the paper or show them what to do. Accordingly, they may initially be irritated or unhappy that the tutor's role is not to proofread the paper for them or tell them how to get a higher grade. But given a few minutes of tutorial conversation, students begin to see that the tutor can help them learn how to proofread or how to fix their papers. Every tutor has tales of students who turn sullen, morose, or even hostile when they learn that the tutor isn't a free editor, but who eventually calm down and join in the conversation about strategies they can use. At the end of such a tutorial, as they are packing up, such students are apt to offer a "Hey, thanks a lot. That helped." Just as frequently, students who come in nervous, apprehensive, defeated, or eager to get any help they can emerge from their sessions feeling more positive, more in control of their own writing. The enormous power of these positive responses to tutors cannot be overemphasized. Students may ignore the existence of the center until required to come in, they may come with all the wrong expectations, and their attitudes toward writing may vary from anger to anxiety about grades to eagerness to produce the best paper they are capable of, but the vast majority emerge feeling that the experience was positive. A number of useful consequences account for how tutors and students can work together and why tutorial collaboration is different in kind from the way students interact with their teachers.

To illustrate this collaboration as well as to shine some light on what goes on in a tutorial, I will use not only language we are familiar with as teachers and scholars but also the language of students — who constitute a different though not entirely separate discourse community. The student comments are typical of the hundreds made each semester on evaluation forms that students attending our Writing Lab are asked to fill out anonymously.

ENCOURAGING INDEPENDENCE IN COLLABORATIVE TALK

- *I felt very comfortable with Pam. She helped me by making me do the work. She let me think my problems through instead of telling me what to do to correct my problems.*
- *Richard is a great tutor. He helps you understand more what you're doing by having you do it yourself.*
- *He let me decide everything instead of telling me what to change or do.*
- *He made me think and realize more than in our class without telling me exactly how to write.*
- *These people know their stuff! But she didn't just give me answers. She got me thinking.*
- *Colleen's tutorial style challenges you to think and re-think your material.*
- *He made me teach myself. He didn't tell me anything.*
- *She knows how to help without giving answers. She makes me think.*
- *The help at the Writing Lab allows you to think on your own. He did not critique my paper, but he asked me questions that made me see how to critique and think about my own paper.*
- *I like how she wanted answers from me. She didn't just tell me what to do to make something right.*

A number of common threads tie these comments together. Students insist that they prefer to do their own work, come to their own conclusions, write what was in their own heads: these students do not want to be told what to do. Cynics and new tutors-in-training may assume that most writers, when faced with turning in a paper, would probably be happiest if given directions for action. But this is not the case, as studies by Allen and by Walker and Elias have shown. Students were asked to rate how satisfied they were with tutorials in which the tutor either assumed control and explained what had to be done or used questioning that permitted the student to think through the process and reach her own conclusions. From the students' perspectives, the more highly satisfactory tutorials were those in which the students were active participants in finding their own criteria and solutions. Among the hundreds of completed forms that I read every semester, I can remember only one student complaint about this approach: "All she did was ask me questions." Given the student perception of a tutor as other than a teacher, we can see why students feel free from the classroom constraint of having to listen to the teacher and to do as they are told. Even non-directive, student-centered teachers who see their advice and suggestions as open-ended possibilities their students can freely reject should recognize that such suggestions are often not taken precisely as they are intended. Students feel freer to develop their own ideas in settings other than teacher/student conversations (and, of course, teacher comments on papers) and welcome the opportunity to have someone help them sort through and formulate conceptual frameworks for drafts of their papers. Peer response groups may help, but a tutor who is trained to ask probing questions and who focuses her attention on the writer offers a more effective environment for the writer during the generative stages of writing (Harris, "Collaboration"). It appears that writers both need and want discussion that engages them actively with their ideas through talk and permits them to stay in control.

A second strand in these comments, the reiteration of the word "think," indicates that tutorial conversation differs from classroom discussion. As Douglas Barnes explains, tutorial or "exploratory" talk encourages thinking and discovery:

> Exploratory talk often occurs when peers collaborate in a task, when they wish to talk it over in a tentative manner, considering and rearranging their ideas. The talk is often but not always hesitant, containing uncompleted or inexplicit utterances as the students try to formulate new understandings; exploratory talk enables students to represent to themselves what they currently understand and then if necessary to criticize and change it. . . . Presentational talk performs a different and more public role. When students are called on in class, when they feel to be under *evaluation*, they seldom risk exploration, but prefer to provide an acceptable performance, a "right" answer. (50)

I have italicized the word "evaluation" because it highlights the limitations of classroom discussion and teacher-student conferences. When talking with a teacher, most students will feel pressure to perform, to look as if they're knowledgeable — in other words, to use presentational talk. Tossing around ideas to see how they play out is more easily accomplished in a tutorial than in a teacher's conference, and as Cynthia Onore points out, exploratory language, though less controlled and controlling, has more power to generate confident assertions and make connections than does presentational language. Tutors adept at the kind of collaboration that encourages useful exploratory talk may guide the conversation, but they do not inhibit the student. In students' perceptions, the person sitting next to them is merely a tutor, someone to "help you bring out your ideas." In light of current theories of collaboration and social construction of knowledge — that, as Kenneth Bruffee states, "knowledge is an artifact created by a community of knowledgeable peers and that learning is a social process not an individual one" (11) — we are less inclined to see the resulting paper as containing only the student's ideas, but that is not the issue here. Getting the student engaged — truly and actively engaged — is. Long before "empowerment" became a coin of the composition realm, tutors basked in the glow of hearing students leave a tutorial saying, "OK, so now I know what I want to write. It was there in my head, but I just couldn't get it out."

ASSISTING WITH ACQUISITION OF STRATEGIC KNOWLEDGE

- *She made me think, didn't tell me what to do, just how to do it.*
- *She helped me look at my paper from a different point of view. That helped a lot, and I know how to do that now.*
- *I learned how to bring out ideas by asking questions and what to do to develop them.*
- *The Writing Lab helped me see how to solve a problem instead of just telling me what's wrong.*

- *I learned how to organize my paper. It was hard to see how to do that with all the notes I collected from my library searching.*
- *I learned to discuss what I want to say and how to go about doing that.*
- *I explained my organizational problems, and she was able to help me revise my paper without doing it for me, giving me skills to connect with other papers I may write.*
- *This makes me focus on how I write.*
- *I wanted to structure my paper but I didn't get exactly how I could do this. She helped me see how, and now I know I can write the paper I am capable of writing.*
- *I didn't see how I was causing myself problems with my writing. She really helped me see how to do it better for the way that I write.*

Writers need several types of knowledge, some more easily gained in the classroom and others more appropriately acquired in the one-to-one setting of a tutorial. If Barnes shows us *why* tutorial talk encourages knowing, Louise Phelps tells us *what* kinds of knowledge are needed: propositional and procedural. One kind of knowledge, that which she identifies as propositional knowledge, is theoretical. It consists of knowing about a set of possibilities for action but does not help us know *how* to act, for as Phelps says, "theory can never tell people directly what to do" because theoretical knowledge does not embed within itself rules for how to apply it (863). Such knowledge is general and not tied to the individual. Phelps explains that much of what is given in textbooks and lectures is formal knowledge in which knowing is learning to name concepts and to articulate their relationships (870). By contrast, practical knowing — the knowledge of the practitioner — arises out of the individual's recognition of a set of possibilities for actions, internalized images, descriptions, and prescriptions. Textbooks and classroom discussions can build this kind of practical knowledge but not the second kind of practical knowledge that Phelps identifies. This second kind of practical knowledge is knowing from personal experience *how* to act, in the sense of possessing a habit or skill for performing an activity. For example, students may think they know how to brainstorm an idea or argument, but only when sitting with a student can a tutor help the student see *how* it feels to turn off that internal editor, which rejects avenues of thought before they are fully explored, or *how* to take brainstorming notes before an idea evaporates from memory or *how* to let threads of an argument or analogy continue to play themselves out in various directions. A student who began a tutorial complaining that he doesn't know what else to add to a paper that's too short is likely to progress from answering a tutor's questions to offering some suggestions to grabbing a sheet of paper and forgetting that there is a tutor sitting next to him as he works through a more extended reason for supporting (or rejecting) election campaign reform. The student begins to learn "how it feels" to do this. An even more concrete example is the student who learns how to proofread for spelling, missing words, or typos. Such a student may have come to the writing center knowing in some general sense what proofreading is but not knowing what it feels like to pace oneself very slowly or to focus on words one by one.

Helping students get the "feel" of some aspects of writing is part of what a tutor can do as she sits next to the student, talking, modeling, and offering suggestions, even though writing is a more sophisticated activity than any of these. Tutors can help students learn *how* to proofread, *how* to let go and brainstorm, *how* to capture a flood of ideas in the planning stage, *how* to take all those scraps of paper and note cards and organize them, *how* to insert revisions into a text, *how* to draw back and figure out if the organizational structure is appropriate, or *how* to check on paragraph development. If needed, a tutor can model a process or can watch the student as she goes through a process herself (Harris, "Modeling"), looking for what is working appropriately and what might be done more effectively in a different way. Or a tutor can suggest a few possible strategies, any one of which might be more appropriate for this particular writer who writes in his or her particular way. This may seem obvious because it is what tutors often do in a tutorial, but it can startle a student as he suddenly "sees" what he's supposed to do in order to achieve whatever it was he was trying to achieve.

This recognition of possible strategies is part of what Linda Flower includes in the kinds of knowledge writers need. Such knowledge, she explains, "involves reading a situation and setting appropriate *goals,* having the *knowledge* and *strategies* to meet one's own goals, and finally, having the metaknowledge of *awareness* to reflect on both goals and strategies. Strategic knowledge is a contextualized form of knowing; it develops over time and out of experience" ("Studying Cognition" 23). Similarly, Alred and Thelen recognize the need for strategic knowledge: "We know intuitively that teaching students to write requires much more than teaching a canon of rules; it requires that we enable students to rehearse a variety of strategies" (471). The rehearsal by some students may go well on their own, but it may not for others. That rehearsal enacted with a tutor watching and offering feedback and advice is a particularly effective tutorial practice. Strategies are easy to learn in an environment where the person next to the writer can answer questions as the writer proceeds and can offer some midstream correction or encouragement when something is not going well. Flower's strategic knowledge is that form of procedural knowledge, or knowing *how,* that Phelps describes, and Flower also notes that writers should have optional strategies in their repertoire for different tasks and different purposes ("Negotiating Academic Discourse" 245). When knowing-in-action, as Phelps calls it (873), bogs down and doesn't work, the writer needs what Phelps calls "reflection-in-action" and what Flower points to when she insists on the writer's need for metacognitive awareness of the acts of setting goals and invoking strategies ("Negotiating Academic Discourse" 222). Learning how to view what has been done, gaining the high ground, is yet another task the tutor can assist with. In the tutorial conversation the tutor helps the student recognize what's going on and how to talk about it as well as how to act. Although tutors often help with propositional knowledge — for example, knowledge of various academic genres of writing, knowledge of rhetorical structures, or knowledge of cultural variations in rhetorical values that perplex international students — the art of the tutor is to collaborate with students as they acquire the practical knowledge they need.

ASSISTING WITH AFFECTIVE CONCERNS

- *I learned my paper wasn't as bad as I thought it was. It's easier to do a good job when you don't think your writing's terrible.*
- *I like the atmosphere. I can ask my questions here, and I learned some techniques to overcome writing anxiety.*
- *They treat you as equals. It is not like teachers helping students. This makes the student feel more at ease.*
- *If you have a block, as I did on how to write a paper, the tutor will help you remember what you have learned in the past.*
- *She talked to me with an accepting attitude even though my paper was shaky. She worked with me, and not like she was over me.*
- *I'm trying to overcome my fear of writing, and this is the place to be.*
- *He helped me sort through my lack of confidence.*
- *I am less stressed about my paper because I actually know what I am trying to say now.*
- *She was easy to talk to. I could ask questions without feeling stupid.*
- *She was patient and gave me confidence. I needed to be convinced that I was approaching my paper correctly.*

No one doubts that student writers too often lack confidence in their skills or that they find writing to be an anxiety-producing task, but the classroom teacher cannot attend to the variety of worries that inhibit some student writers. Those fears range from evaluation anxiety to long-standing reluctance to have a teacher "bleed all over" their papers, from writing blocks of various levels of intensity to defeatist convictions that they are not good writers. In tutorials students often unburden themselves and find a sympathetic ear as well as some suggestions for getting past their affective concerns. As I read evaluations every semester, it appears that tutorial assistance gives students confidence about themselves and their writing. The word "confidence" repeats itself so often that I have asked students to talk about why they feel more confident after talking with a tutor. Typically the response is that a student initially feels unsure that a paper meets an assignment or is well written. When a tutor helps the writer set up criteria to use for her own assessment, the writer gains confidence in deciding whether the paper is ready to be turned in. Or the tutor can give the writer some reader response that helps her see what needs more clarification. Tutors can also help when students worry that their mental representation of what they wanted to write does not sufficiently overlap the product that actually appears on paper. Helping writers match intention or plan with the written result is often a useful exercise, particularly since tutors often find that the writer's mental representation is far richer than the less impressive draft. Asking the writer some questions or requesting more details often results in the writer's seeing what else he should have included or where (or how) the paper drifted away from the intended goal. After such sessions, students talk about "feeling better" about their papers or knowing what else they want to do when they revise. It appears from some evaluations that their newly found confidence also results in stronger motivation. While the role of motivation in language learning has not been a major topic of composition research, tutors recognize that dealing with affective concerns and offering encouragement result in increased motivation to continue expending effort on a paper.

Another affective concern reflected in student comments is that it is stressful for them to talk about their writing with someone whom they perceive as having some institutional authority over them. Such students view themselves as being treated as inferiors, talked down to, demeaned in some way when talking with teachers, but not with tutors. The collaborative atmosphere of the tutorial, the sense of being with someone who does not assume any authoritative posture, seems to relieve that strain or eliminate the fear. It is undoubtedly true that some teachers do reinforce the stereotypical authoritarian stance or aren't as adept as they might be in using language that their students understand. But it would be worth investigating whether students' perceptions of teachers' roles in some way create in some students the belief that they have been reduced to an inferior stance or treated as a lower form of life. Though teachers may well seek the same collegial tone as tutors, some students cannot see the similarity because they expect their teachers to perceive them as inferiors. The power structure of academia may remain intact in part because some students perpetuate it in their own minds. There may also be a language issue here, the issue of different discourse communities, as discussed below.

INTERPRETING THE MEANING OF ACADEMIC LANGUAGE

- *He helped me understand my prof's meaning.*
- *She explained what needed to be done in language that I understood.*
- *I got in-depth explanations of handouts given in class. I didn't understand in class with just the teacher's explanations.*
- *You do a fantastic job with helping students understand what to do with an assignment. I had interpreted it in a way that was not correct.*
- *Now I know how to write an expressive paper. I was off course before.*
- *I was having a problem seeing what continuity was.*
- *We worked on what is a letter to an editor. This is not something I learned to do in my country.*
- *Thanks. You helped me see what my teacher wants me to do when I revise.*
- *She answered all my questions about what response writing is. I got the help I needed.*
- *The prof couldn't explain what I needed to know, but thanks to Linda, I understand now.*

A cursory reading of these student comments would be that they are praising tutors for being able to explain better than teachers, but a more appropriate analysis might be that these students are reporting that the tutor interpreted teacher language by translating it into their language, that is, gave meaning to terms they had heard and read and not understood. Just as Phelps points out that practitioner teachers cannot easily translate their problems into the critical discourse of theory (863), student writers cannot easily translate their problems into the discourse of composition or make meaning of the language about writing. When students recognize problems, they normally do not have the meta-knowledge that Flower says is needed or the necessary metalanguage to locate the appropriate section of a textbook, ask a teacher, or tell a tutor. Students coming to a writing center do not — most often cannot — say they want to work on invention strategies or sharpen their focus or improve the coherence of a paper. They come in saying that they "need help" or that the paper "doesn't flow." It is even more likely that they give the paper to the tutor, hoping the tutor can give names to their internal sense that something is needed. Student language is not the language we use. Mary Louise Pratt observes that students and teachers inhabit separate communities, though she acknowledges that there is hardly total homogeneity in either the teacher community or student community. Pratt's interest is in getting us to move away from viewing groups as existing separately, a view that gives rise to a linguistics that seeks to capture the identity but not the relationality of social differentiation. But, she explains, dominant and dominated groups are not comprehensible apart from each other, for their speech practices are organized to enact these differences and their hierarchy. Any dominated group is required simultaneously to identify with and disassociate itself from the dominant group.

Students' discourse consequently is both distinct from and permeated by that of teachers, the dominant group. Pratt offers the interesting suggestion that there be a "linguistics of contact" (60), which studies the operation of language across lines of differentiation, focusing on the nodes and zones of contact between groups. Since tutors live in this contact zone somewhere between teachers and students, tutorial talk may be a particularly fruitful area in which to research what those nodes and zones are.

That teachers view themselves as set apart and different from their students is apparent from Cheryl Towns's study of how members of the composition profession refer to students when writing articles in the pages of *College Composition and Communication*. In the nineteen articles she analyzed, Towns found that students were referred to often, over 345 times, with the highest frequency characterizing them as "mere fledglings," new and inexperienced, novices, learners. Much of the language was about relationships between teachers and students, and the most prevalent category was "teacher as teacher" and "student as student," despite comments in the same articles which deplored this traditional relationship. The metaphors used were often of seeing, getting students "to see," "to observe," and teachers were perceived as givers with students as receivers or teachers as leaders and students as followers. Towns concluded that "though we may be beginning to see the need to move beyond the traditional power structure of the classroom, we are still deeply entrenched in it" (97).

Tutors are thus other than teachers in that they inhabit a middle ground where their role is that of translator or interpreter, turning teacher language into student language. "Focus," "coherence," and "development" are not terms as readily understood by students as teachers think. As a result, a common tutorial task is helping the student understand the comments a teacher has made on a paper, thus confirming the results of a study by Mary Hayes and Donald Daiker which vividly demonstrates how little of what teachers write in the margins of papers is understood in any useful way. Similarly, Jill Burkland and Nancy Grimm note: "Through our experiences as tutors in our university's Writing Center and through years in the composition classroom, we were aware that teachers' intentions are often unrealized, that written communication on papers is often misunderstood or misinterpreted by students" (237–38). Other studies report similar conclusions in tones of defeat and discouragement. As Knoblauch and Brannon note, "The depressing trouble is, we have scarcely a shred of empirical evidence to show that students typically even comprehend our responses to their writing, let alone use them purposefully to modify their practice" (1). Similarly, in a large-scale study that looked at teacher comments, Robert Connors and Andrea Lunsford found a portrait of teachers having little time and less faith that their comments would be understood.

Students' difficulties in understanding teacher comments are partly this difference in vocabulary, but there is also the problem of students' perception of teacher intent behind the comments. When a paper is returned with numerous teacher responses, some students may read the marginalia and end comments; most don't. They skip down to the grade and wander into the writing center assuming that the teacher didn't like their writing. For too many students, the intent of a teacher's comments is "to rip my writing," "to bleed all over my paper," or "to cut me to shreds." Suggestions, notes of encouragement, and even praise are not always noted by student writers. A large number of comments "means" (from the student's perception) that the teacher didn't like the paper, and so another tutorial task is to help students read and interpret teacher response in a different light, not entirely as criticism but as including well-meaning suggestions. For example, a student who came to our Writing Lab had a paper with the following comment: "What is the thread of connection here to your explanation on page 7 — that such cultural practices provoke inter-family rivalry?" While the teacher was suggesting some potentially interesting connections for the writer to explore, the writer read that as a comment on her failure to see the connection herself. She needed a tutor to help interpret the intent of that message just as other students need tutors to help them understand the meaning of other kinds of teacher language. It is certainly not the case that all written response fails or that all students draw a complete blank when seeking to comprehend the import of those comments. Some response gets through, but instead of beating our breasts and assuming guilt by failure or taking such findings as indictments of teachers, we need to recognize the reality of language users in different groups straining across chasms to hear each other. If we accept differences in language communities as realities, then we can view the writing center as the institutionalized mechanism to facilitate the flow of otherwise impeded communication.

It follows from this problem of different languages that students often don't understand their assignments (which are, after all, written by teachers, not students). Misunderstanding the assignment happens with such astonishing regularity that we ought more properly to view it as part of the educational process — learning the language of academic communities, learning how to understand that language, and learning how to act on that understanding. John Ackerman, using restraint in reporting on the findings of an extensive research project, notes that "in many cases the assignment given by an instructor and the assignment taken by a student are not a reciprocal fit" (96). Because students often need help in learning how to interpret these writing assignments, it is a frequent topic of tutorial collaboration. An assignment to "interpret" a passage in a literary work is as confusing to some students as an assignment to "interpret" readings in current health care economics is to other students. Other students are overwhelmed by "analyze and compare" assignments or unable to figure out how to respond to what Louise Z. Smith calls a "bewildering array of heuristics" in complex assignments with multiple prompts (465). In composition courses as well as writing-across-the-curriculum courses, students may be unable to plunge in, stymied by an inability to figure out what the assignment is asking for. "We worked on improving his understanding of the assignment" is perhaps one of the most common summaries of tutorial sessions in writing centers. Some students recognize their difficulties with this and come to the center asking that the tutor read the paper to see if it meets the assignment; others come with a draft asking, "Am I on the right track?" Such students are neither stupid nor lazy — they are being honest in acknowledging that they don't have a clear idea of what the assignment is or whether they have managed to write a paper that lands somewhere in the right ballpark. The tutor's task is to help the student see how her long, impassioned narrative of the emotional stresses and strains on her family during a divorce does not meet the assignment to "take a stance on a current societal issue and defend it." Flower sees the frequent tendency to misunderstand or misinterpret assignments in terms of the individual differences students bring to the classroom:

> Students hold some significantly different, tacit representations of supposedly common academic tasks. Because these multifaceted mental representations are constructed from prior experience, from inferences about the social and rhetorical context, and from writers' own values and desires, students may approach a common reading-to-write assignment with meaningfully different sets of goals, strategies, and criteria. . . . These differences can cause problems. Because these representations are often tacit, students and teachers may be in unspoken disagreement about what constitutes an "appropriate" representation. ("Studying Cognition" 21)

Yet despite these differences, says Flower, classroom syllabi assume a homogeneity that doesn't exist, a "one size fits all" situation ("Studying Cognition" 22). Individual differences as well as language confusions must have an appropriate setting in which they can be tended to when the need arises, and the writing center is that place.

To compound the problem of the need for individualized attention to differences in student representations of task assignments, we have to be aware that students are also not always well versed in the shifting conventions in various kinds of academic discourse. An engineering student may need help in understanding why his nuclear engineering report was graded down ("lacks conciseness") for having the kind of extended introductory paragraph that earned A's in his freshman composition course. The student who wrote objective problem statements in her research reports for computer science classes doesn't understand the need for some subjectivity in writing the problem identification section of a research report on a controversial environmental policy in which she has to defend or refute an issue. One instructor may view a nursing student's clinical knowledge as acceptable support; another may require the writer to support that knowledge by citing published research. In the writing center this means helping the writer articulate what the problem is. The tutor may assist in identifying which conventions and rules the writer is working with and when the writer has to return to the content teacher for clarification. Occasionally students appear with personal sets of half-understood suggestions that have become rigid and inappropriate rules (Harris, "Contradictory Perceptions"; Rose); at other times, as Terese Thonus has shown us, students learning English as a second language need particular help threading their way through the multiple messages, different criteria, and differing standards they encounter in academia.

When Gerald Alred and Erik Thelen note that writing "is bound up with creativity, cognition, language formation, personality, and social interaction" (471), their list nicely captures the sense of a mix of internal variations among writers as well as the outside forces that play upon writers and their texts. Situated as they are to work one-to-one with each writer and his or her needs, tutors can attend to individual differences. Equally important, as students repeatedly tell us in their evaluation comments, tutors work with them in ways that enable and encourage independent thinking and that help them see how to put their theoretical knowledge into practice as they write. Moreover, tutorial interaction helps writers gain confidence in themselves as writers by attending to their affective concerns and assists them in learning what academic language about writing means. Writing centers may still have to contend with a diminishing minority who view them as unnecessary frills, sucking up funds, space, and personnel to duplicate what goes on in the classroom or to coddle remedial students who shouldn't have been admitted in the first place, but as we turn our attention to the work of the tutor, we become increasingly aware that writing instruction without a writing center is only a partial program, lacking essential activities students need in order to grow and mature as writers.

WORKS CITED

Ackerman, John. "Students' Self-Analysis and Judges' Perceptions: Where Do They Agree?" In *Reading-to-Write: Exploring a Cognitive and Social Process.* Ed. Linda Flower et al. 96–111.

Allen, Nancy. "Developing an Effective Tutorial Style." *Writing Lab Newsletter* 15.3 (November 1990): 1–4.

Alred, Gerald, and Erik Thelen. "Are Textbooks Contributions to Scholarship?" *College Composition and Communication* 44.4 (December 1993): 466–77.

Barnes, Douglas. "Oral Language and Learning." In *Perspectives on Talk and Learning.* Ed. Susan Hynds and Donald Rubin. 41–54.

Bishop, Wendy. "Bringing Writers to the Center: Some Survey Results, Surmises, and Suggestions." *Writing Center Journal* 10.2 (Spring/Summer 1990): 31–44.

Bruffee, Kenneth. "Peer Tutoring and the 'Conversation of Mankind.'" In *Writing Centers: Theory and Administration.* Ed. Gary Olson. Urbana: NCTE, 1984. 3–15.

Burkland, Jill, and Nancy Grimm. "Motivating through Responding." *Journal of Teaching Writing* 5 (1986): 237–47.

Clark, Irene. "Leading the Horse: The Writing Center and Required Visits." *Writing Center Journal* 5.2/6.1 (Spring/Summer 1985; Fall/Winter 1985): 31–34.

Connors, Robert, and Andrea Lunsford. "Teachers' Rhetorical Comments on Student Papers." *College Composition and Communication* 44.2 (May 1993): 200–23.

Flower, Linda. "Negotiating Academic Discourse." In *Reading-to-Write: Exploring a Cognitive and Social Process.* Ed. Linda Flower et al. 221–52.

——. "Studying Cognition in Context." In *Reading-to-Write: Exploring a Cognitive and Social Process.* Ed. Linda Flower et al. 3–32.

Flower, Linda, et al. *Reading-to-Write: Exploring a Cognitive and Social Process.* New York: Oxford UP, 1990.

Harris, Muriel. "Collaboration Is Not Collaboration Is Not Collaboration." *College Composition and Communication* 43.1 (February 1992): 369–83.

——. "Contradictory Perceptions of Rules of Writing." *College Composition and Communication* 30.2 (May 1979): 218–20.

——. "Modeling: A Process Method of Teaching." *College English* 45.1 (January 1983): 74–84.

Hayes, Mary H., and Donald Daiker. "Using Protocol Analysis in Evaluating Responses to Student Writing." *Freshman English News* 13.2 (Fall 1984): 1–4, 10.

Healy, Dave, "late night talk." Posting to the WCenter electronic bulletin board, 13 May 1993.

Hynds, Susan, and Donald Rubin, eds. *Perspectives on Talk and Learning.* Urbana: NCTE, 1990.

Knoblauch, C. H., and Lil Brannon. "Teacher Commentary on Student Writing." *Freshman English News* 10 (1981): 1–4.

Onore, Cynthia. "Negotiation, Language, and Inquiry: Building Knowledge Collaboratively in the Classroom." In *Perspectives on Talk and Learning.* Ed. Susan Hynds and Donald Rubin. 57–72.

Phelps, Louise Wetherbee. "Practical Wisdom and the Geography of Knowledge in Composition." *College English* 53.8 (December 1991): 863–85.

Pratt, Mary Louise. "Linguistic Utopias." In *Linguistics of Writing: Arguments between Language and Literature.* Ed. Nigel Fabb. New York: Methuen, 1987. 48–66.

Rose, Mike. "Rigid Rules, Inflexible Plans, and the Stifling of Language: A Cognitivist Analysis of Writer's Block." *College Composition and Communication* 31.4 (December 1980): 389–401.

Smith, Louise Z. "Composing Composition Courses." *College English* 46.5 (September 1984): 460–69.

Thonus, Terese. "Tutors as Teachers: Assisting ESL/EFL Students in the Writing Center." *Writing Center Journal* 13.2 (Spring 1993): 13–26.

Towns, Cheryl Hofstetter. "Dumbo or Colleague? Our Professional Perceptions of Students." *Composition Studies/Freshman English News* 21.1 (Spring 1993): 94–103.

Walker, Carolyn, and David Elias. "Writing Conference Talk: Factors Associated for High- and Low-Rated Writing Conferences." *Research in the Teaching of English* 21.3 (1987): 226–85.

Nancy Sommers

Responding to Student Writing

More than any other enterprise in the teaching of writing, responding to and commenting on student writing consumes the largest proportion of our time. Most teachers estimate that it takes them at least 20 to 40 minutes to comment on an individual student paper, and those 20 to 40 minutes times 20 students per class, times 8 papers, more or less, during the course of a semester add up to an enormous amount of time. With so much time and energy directed to a single activity, it is important for us to understand the nature of the enterprise. For it seems, paradoxically enough, that although commenting on student writing is the most widely used method for responding to student writing, it is the least understood. We do not know in any definitive way what constitutes thoughtful commentary or what effect, if any, our comments have on helping our students become more effective writers.

Theoretically, at least, we know that we comment on our students' writing for the same reasons professional editors comment on the work of professional writers or for the same reasons we ask our colleagues to read and respond to our own writing. As writers we need and want thoughtful commentary to show us when we have communicated our ideas and when not, raising questions from a reader's point of view that may not have occurred to us as writers. We want to know if our writing has communicated our intended meaning and, if not, what questions or discrepancies our reader sees that we, as writers, are blind to.

In commenting on our students' writing, however, we have an additional pedagogical purpose. As teachers, we know that most students find it difficult to imagine a reader's response in advance, and to use such responses as a guide in composing. Thus, we comment on student writing to dramatize the presence of a reader, to help our students to become that questioning reader themselves, because, ultimately, we believe that becoming such a reader will help them to evaluate what they have written and develop control over their writing.[1]

Even more specifically, however, we comment on student writing because we believe that it is necessary for us to offer assistance to student writers when they are in the process of composing a text, rather than after the text has been completed. Comments create the motive for doing something different in the next draft; thoughtful comments create the motive for revising. Without comments from their teachers or from their peers, student writers will revise in a consistently narrow and predictable way. Without comments from readers, students assume that their writing has communicated their meaning and perceive no need for revising the substance of their text.[2] yup!

This article is reprinted from *College Composition and Communication* 33 (May 1982): 148–56.

Yet as much as we as informed professionals believe in the soundness of this approach to responding to student writing, we also realize that we don't know how our theory squares with teachers' actual practice—do teachers comment and students revise as the theory predicts they should? For the past year my colleagues Lil Brannon, Cyril Knoblauch, and I have been researching this problem, attempting to discover not only what messages teachers give their students through their comments, but also what determines which of these comments the students choose to use or to ignore when revising. Our research has been entirely focused on comments teachers write to motivate revisions. We have studied the commenting styles of thirty-five teachers at New York University and the University of Oklahoma, studying the comments these teachers wrote on first and second drafts, and interviewing a representative number of these teachers and their students. All teachers also commented on the same set of three student essays. As an additional reference point one of the student essays was typed into the computer that had been programmed with the "Writer's Workbench," a package of twenty-three programs developed by Bell Laboratories to help computers and writers work together to improve a text rapidly. Within a few minutes, the computer delivered editorial comments on the student's text, identifying all spelling and punctuation errors, isolating problems with wordy or misused phrases, and suggesting alternatives, offering stylistic analysis of sentence types, sentence beginnings, and sentence lengths, and finally, giving our freshman essay a Kincaid readability score of eighth-grade which, as the computer program informed us, "is a low score for this type of document." The sharp contrast between the teachers' comments and those of the computer highlighted how arbitrary and idiosyncratic most of our teachers' comments are. Besides, the calm, reasonable language of the computer provided quite a contrast to the hostility and mean-spiritedness of most of the teachers' comments.

The first finding from our research on styles of commenting is that _teachers' comments can take students' attention away from their own purposes in writing a particular text and focus that attention on the teachers' purpose in commenting_. The teacher appropriates the text from the student by confusing the student's purpose in writing the text with her own purpose in commenting. Students make the changes the teacher wants rather than those that the student perceives are necessary, since the teachers' concerns imposed on the text create the reasons for the subsequent changes. We have all heard our perplexed students say to us when confused by our comments: "I don't understand how you want me to change this" or "Tell me what you want me to do." In the beginning of the process there was the writer, her words, and her desire to communicate her ideas. But after the comments of the teacher are imposed on the first or second draft, the student's attention dramatically shifts from "This is what I want to say" to "This is what _you_ the teacher are asking me to do."

This appropriation of the text by the teacher happens particularly when teachers identify errors in usage, diction, and style in a first draft and ask students to correct these errors when they revise; such comments give the student an impression of the importance of these errors that is all out of proportion to how they should view these errors at this point in the process. The comments create the concern that these "accidents of discourse" need to be attended to before the meaning of the text is attended to.

It would not be so bad if students were only commanded to correct errors, but, more often than not, students are given contradictory messages; they are commanded to edit a sentence to avoid an error or to condense a sentence to achieve greater brevity of style, and then told in the margins that the particular paragraph needs to be more specific or to be developed more. An example of this problem can be seen in the following student paragraph:

> *wordy – be precise*   *which Sunday?*   *comma needed*
> Every year [on one Sunday in the middle of January]
> *word choice*
> tens of millions of people cancel all events, plans
> or work to watch the Super Bowl. This audience in-
> *wordy*
> cludes [little boys and girls, old people, and house-
> *Be specific – what reasons?*
> wives and men.] Many reasons have been given to ex-
> *and why*
> plain why the Super Bowl has become so popular that
> *what spots?*
> commercial spots/cost up to $100,000.00. One explana-
> *awkward*
> tion is that people like to take sides and root for a
> *another what?*   *spelling*
> team. Another is that some people like the pagentry
> and excitement of the event. These reasons alone,
> *too*
> *colloquial*
> however, do not explain a happening as big as the
> Super Bowl.

You need to do more research.

This paragraph needs to be expanded in order to be more interesting to the reader.

In commenting on this draft, the teacher has shown the student how to edit the sentences, but then commands the student to expand the paragraph in order to make it more interesting to a reader. The interlinear comments and the marginal comments represent two separate tasks for this student; the interlinear comments encourage the student to see the text as a fixed piece, frozen in time, that just needs some editing. The marginal comments, however, suggest that the meaning of the text is not fixed, but rather that the student still needs to develop the meaning by doing some more research. Students are commanded to edit and develop at the same time; the remarkable contradiction of developing

interlinear comments
marginal comments } *too much?*

a paragraph after editing the sentences in it represents the confusion we encountered in our teachers' commenting styles. These different signals given to students, to edit and develop, to condense and elaborate, represent also the failure of teachers' comments to direct genuine revision of a text as a whole.

Moreover, the comments are worded in such a way that it is difficult for students to know what is the most important problem in the text and what problems are of lesser importance. No scale of concerns is offered to a student with the result that a comment about spelling or a comment about an awkward sentence is given weight equal to a comment about organization or logic. The comment that seemed to represent this problem best was one teacher's command to his student: "Check your commas and semicolons and think more about what you are thinking about." The language of the comments makes it difficult for a student to sort out and decide what is most important and what is least important.

When the teacher appropriates the text for the student in this way, students are encouraged to see their writing as a series of parts — words, sentences, paragraphs — and not as a whole discourse. The comments encourage the students to believe that their first drafts are finished drafts, not invention drafts, and that all they need to do is patch and polish their writing. That is, teachers' comments do not provide their students with an inherent reason for revising the structure and meaning of their texts, since the comments suggest to students that the meaning of their text is already there, finished, produced, and all that is necessary is a better word or phrase. The processes of revising, editing, and proofreading are collapsed and reduced to a single trivial activity, and the students' misunderstanding of the revision process as a rewording activity is reinforced by their teachers' comments.

It is possible, and it quite often happens, that students follow every comment and fix their texts appropriately as requested, but their texts are not improved substantially, or, even worse, their revised drafts are inferior to their previous drafts. Since the teachers' comments take the students' attention away from their own original purposes, students concentrate more, as I have noted, on what the teachers commanded them to do than on what they are trying to say. Sometimes students do not understand the purpose behind their teachers' comments and take these comments very literally. At other times students understand the comments, but the teacher has misread the text and the comments, unfortunately, are not applicable. For instance, we repeatedly saw comments in which teachers commanded students to reduce and condense what was written, when in fact what the text really needed at this stage was to be expanded in conception and scope.

The process of revising always involves a risk. But, too often revision becomes a balancing act for students in which they make the changes that are requested but do not take the risk of changing anything that was not commented on, even if the students sense that other changes are needed. A more effective text does not often evolve from such changes alone, yet the student does not want to take the chance of reducing a finished, albeit inadequate, paragraph to chaos — to fragments — in order to rebuild it, if such changes have not been requested by the teacher.

The second finding from our study is that *most teachers' comments are not text-specific and could be interchanged, rubber-stamped, from text to text.* The comments are not anchored in the particulars of the students' texts, but rather are a series of vague directives that are not text-specific. Students are commanded to "think more about [their] audience, avoid colloquial language, avoid the passive, avoid prepositions at the end of sentences or conjunctions at the beginning of sentences, be clear, be specific, be precise, but above all, think more about what [they] are thinking about." The comments on the following student paragraph illustrate this problem:

> *Begin by telling your reader what you are going to write about*
> In the sixties it was drugs, in the seventies it was
> *avoid "one of the"*
> rock and roll. Now in the eighties, one of the most
>
> controversial subjects is nuclear power. The United
> *elaborate*
> States is in great need of its own source of power.
>
> Because of environmentalists, coal is not an accept-
>
> able source of energy. [Solar and wind power have not
> *be specific*
> yet received the technology necessary to use them.] It
> *avoid "it seems"*
> seems that nuclear power is the only feasible means
>
> right now for obtaining self-sufficient power. How-
>
> ever, too large a percentage of the population are
>
> against nuclear power claiming it is unsafe. With as
> *be precise*
> many problems as the United States is having concern-
>
> ing energy, it seems a shame that the public is so
>
> quick to "can" a very feasible means of power. Nuclear
>
> energy should not be given up on, but rather, more
>
> nuclear plants should be built.

(margin annotations: "think more about your reader"; "Thesis sentence needed.")

One could easily remove all the comments from this paragraph and rubber-stamp them on another student text, and they would make as much or as little sense on the second text as they do here.

We have observed an overwhelming similarity in the generalities and abstract commands given to students. There seems to be among teachers an accepted, albeit unwritten canon for commenting on student texts. This uniform code of commands, requests, and pleadings demonstrates that the teacher holds a license for vagueness while the student is commanded to be specific. The students we interviewed admitted to having a great difficulty with these vague directives. The students stated that when a teacher writes in the margins or as an end comment, "choose precise language," or "think more about your audience," revising becomes a guessing game. In effect, the teacher is saying to the student, "Somewhere in this paper is imprecise language or lack of awareness of an audience and you must find it." The problem presented by these vague commands is compounded for the students when they are not offered any strategies for carrying out these commands. Students are told that they have done something wrong and that there is something in their text that needs to be fixed before the text is acceptable. But to tell students that they have done something wrong is not to tell them what to do about it. In order to offer a useful revision strategy to a student, the teacher must anchor that strategy in the specifics of the student's text. For instance, to tell our student, the author of the above paragraph, "to be specific," or "to elaborate," does not show our student what questions the reader has about the meaning of the text, or what breaks in the logic exist, that could be resolved if the writer supplied information; nor is the student shown how to achieve the desired specificity.

Instead of offering strategies, the teachers offer what is interpreted by students as rules for composing; the comments suggest to students that writing is just a matter of following rules. Indeed, the teachers seem to impose a series of abstract rules about written products even when some of them are not appropriate for the specific text the student is creating.[3] For instance, the student author of our sample paragraph presented above is commanded to follow the conventional rules for writing a five-paragraph essay — to begin the introductory paragraph by telling his reader what he is going to say and to end the paragraph with a thesis sentence. Somehow these abstract rules about what five-paragraph products should look like do not seem applicable to the problems this student must confront when revising, nor are the rules specific strategies he could use when revising. There are many inchoate ideas ready to be exploited in this paragraph, but the rules do not help the student to take stock of his (or her) ideas and use the opportunity he has, during revision, to develop those ideas.

The problem here is a confusion of process and product; what one has to say about the process is different from what one has to say about the product. Teachers who use this method of commenting are formulating their comments as if these drafts were finished drafts and were not going to be revised. Their commenting vocabularies have not been adapted to revision and they comment on first drafts as if they were justifying a grade or as if the first draft were the final draft.

Our summary finding, therefore, from this research on styles of commenting is that the news from the classroom is not good. For the most part, teachers do not respond to student writing with the kind of thoughtful commentary which will help students to engage with the issues they are writing about or which will help them think about their purposes and goals in writing a specific text. In defense of our teachers, however, they told us that responding to student writing was rarely stressed in their teacher-training or in writing workshops; they had been trained in various prewriting techniques, in constructing assignments, and in evaluating papers for grades, but rarely in the process of reading a student text for meaning or in offering commentary to motivate revision. The problem is that most of us as teachers of writing have been trained to read and interpret literary texts for meaning, but, unfortunately, we have not been trained to act upon the same set of assumptions in reading student texts as we follow in reading literary texts.[4] Thus, we read student texts with biases about what the writer should have said or about what he or she should have written, and our biases determine how we will comprehend the text. We read with our preconceptions and preoccupations, expecting to find errors, and the result is that we find errors and misread our students' texts.[5] We find what we look for; instead of reading and responding to the meaning of a text, we correct our students' writing. We need to reverse this approach. Instead of finding errors or showing students how to patch up parts of their texts, we need to sabotage our students' conviction that the drafts they have written are complete and coherent. Our comments need to offer student revision tasks of a different order of complexity and sophistication from the ones that they themselves identify, by forcing students back into the chaos, back to the point where they are shaping and restructuring their meaning.[6]

For if the content of a text is lacking in substance and meaning, if the order of the parts must be rearranged significantly in the next draft, if paragraphs must be restructured for logic and clarity, then many sentences are likely to be changed or deleted anyway. There seems to be no point in having students correct usage errors or condense sentences that are likely to disappear before the next draft is completed. In fact, to identify such problems in a text at this early first draft stage, when such problems are likely to abound, can give a student a disproportionate sense of their importance at this stage in the writing process.[7] In responding to our students' writing, we should be guided by the recognition that it is not spelling or usage problems that we as writers first worry about when drafting and revising our texts.

We need to develop an appropriate level of response for commenting on a first draft, and to differentiate that from the level suitable to a second or third draft. Our comments need to be suited to the draft we are reading. In a first or second draft, we need to respond as any reader would, registering questions, reflecting befuddlement, and noting places where we are puzzled about the meaning of the text. Comments should point to breaks in logic, disruptions in meaning, or missing information. Our goal in commenting on early drafts should be to engage students with the issues they are considering and help them clarify their purposes and reasons in writing their specific text.

For instance, the major rhetorical problem of the essay written by the student who wrote the [second] paragraph (the paragraph on nuclear power) [p. 337] . . . was that the student had two principal arguments running through his text, each of which brought the other into question. On the one hand, he argued that we must use nuclear power, unpleasant as it is, because we have nothing else to use; though nuclear energy is a problematic source of energy, it is the best of a bad lot. On the other hand, he also argued that nuclear energy is really quite safe and therefore should be our primary resource. Comments on this student's first draft need to point out this break in logic and show the student that if we accept his first argument, then his second argument sounds fishy. But if we accept his second argument, his first argument sounds contradictory. The teacher's comments need to engage this student writer with this basic rhetorical and conceptual problem in his first draft rather than impose a series of abstract commands and rules upon his text.

Written comments need to be viewed not as an end in themselves — a way for teachers to satisfy themselves that they have done their jobs — but rather as a means for helping students to become more effective writers. As a means for helping students, they have limitations; they are, in fact, disembodied remarks—one absent writer responding to another absent writer. The key to successful commenting is to have what is said in the comments and what is done in the classroom mutually reinforce and enrich each other. Commenting on papers assists the writing course in achieving its purpose; classroom activities and the comments we write to our students need to be connected. Written comments need to be an extension of the teacher's voice — an extension of the teacher as reader. Exercises in such activities as revising a whole text or individual paragraphs together in class, noting how the sense of the whole dictates the smaller changes, looking at options, evaluating actual choices, and then discussing the effect of these changes on revised drafts — such exercises need to be designed to take students through the cycles of revising and to help them overcome their anxiety about revising: that anxiety we all feel at reducing what looks like a finished draft into fragments and chaos.

The challenge we face as teachers is to develop comments which will provide an inherent reason for students to revise; it is a sense of revision as discovery, as a repeated process of beginning again, as starting out new, that our students have not learned. We need to show our students how to seek, in the possibility of revision, the dissonances of discovery — to show them through our comments why new choices would positively change their texts, and thus to show them the potential for development implicit in their own writing.

NOTES

1. C. H. Knoblauch and Lil Brannon, "Teacher Commentary on Student Writing: The State of the Art," *Freshman English News,* 10 (Fall 1981), 1–3.

2. For an extended discussion of revision strategies of student writers see Nancy Sommers, "Revision Strategies of Student Writers and Experienced Adult Writers," *College Composition and Communication,* 31 (December 1980), 378–88.

3. Nancy Sommers and Ronald Schleifer, "Means and Ends: Some Assumptions of Student Writers," *Composition and Teaching*, 2 (December 1980), 69–76.

4. Janet Emig and Robert P. Parker, Jr., "Responding to Student Writing: Building a Theory of the Evaluating Process," unpublished paper, Rutgers University.

5. For an extended discussion of this problem see Joseph Williams, "The Phenomenology of Error," *College Composition and Communication*, 32 (May 1981), 152–68.

6. Ann Berthoff. *The Making of Meaning* (Montclair, NJ: Boynton/Cook Publishers, 1981).

7. W. U. McDonald, "The Revising Process and the Marking of Student Papers," *College Composition and Communication*, 24 (May 1978), 167–70.

Andrea A. Lunsford and Karen J. Lunsford

"Mistakes Are a Fact of Life": A National Comparative Study

> *Mistakes are a fact of life. It is the response to the error that counts.*
> — Nikki Giovanni, *Black Feeling, Black Talk, Black Judgment*

Perhaps it is the seemingly endless string of what have come to be called "Bushisms" ("We shouldn't fear a world that is more interacted") and the complex response to them from both right and left. Perhaps it is the hype over Instant Messaging lingo cropping up in formal writing and the debate among teachers over how to respond (Farmer 48). Perhaps it is the long series of attempts to loosen the grip of "standard" English on the public imagination, from the 1974 special issue of *College Composition and Communication (Students' Right to Their Own Language)* to a 2006 special issue of *College English* devoted to *Cross-Language Relations in Composition*. Or perhaps it is the number of recent reports, many of them commissioned by the government, that have bemoaned the state of student literacy and focused attention on what they deem significant failures at the college level (see especially the recent reports from the Spellings Commission and Derek Bok's *Our Underachieving Colleges*).

Whatever the reasons, and they are surely complex and multilayered, forms of language use have been much in the news, with charges of what student writers can and cannot (or should and should not) do all around us. The times seemed ripe, then, for taking a close look at a national sample of student writing to see what it might tell us about the current state of affairs. With that goal in mind, we drew up plans to conduct a national study of first-year college student writing and to compare our findings to those of a similar study conducted over twenty years ago.

"THE FREQUENCY OF FORMAL ERRORS," OR REMEMBERING MA AND PA KETTLE

But we are getting a bit ahead of ourselves here. For now, flash back to the mid-1980s. Some readers may remember receiving a letter from Robert Connors and Andrea Lunsford asking them to participate in a national study of student writing by submitting a set of marked student papers from a first-year composition course. That call brought in well over 21,000 papers from 300 teachers around the country, and in fairly short order Andrea and Bob drew a random sample of 3,000 student papers stratified to be representative in terms of region of the country, size of institution, and type of institution.[1] While they later analyzed patterns of teacher response to the essays as well as the particular spelling patterns that emerged (in that study, spelling was the most frequent student mistake by some

This article is reprinted from *College Composition and Communication* 59.4 (June 2008): 781–806.

342

300 percent), they turned first to an analysis of which formal errors (other than spelling) were most common in this sample of student writing.

Why the focus on error in the Lunsford and Connors study? Bob and Andrea's historical research had led each of them to caches of student papers with teacher comments focusing on errors that sometimes seemed very out of date if not downright odd ("stringy" syntax, for example, or obsessive comments on how to distinguish between the use of "shall" and "will"), and they wondered what teachers in the 1980s would focus on instead. In addition, the 1938–39 research into student patterns of formal error carried out by John C. Hodges, author of the *Harbrace Handbook of English*, piqued their curiosity — and led to a review of earlier studies. As Connors and Lunsford put it:

> Beginning around 1910 . . . teachers and educational researchers began trying to taxonomize errors and chart their frequency. The great heyday of error-frequency seems to have occurred between 1915 and 1935. . . . Our historical research indicates that the last large-scale research into student patterns of formal error was conducted in 1938–39 by John C. Hodges. . . . Hodges collected 20,000 student papers, . . . using his findings to inform the 34-part organization of his *Harbrace Handbook*. (39)

As Connors and Lunsford noted, Hodges did not publish any results of his study in contemporary journals, though in a footnote to the preface of the first edition of his *Handbook,* he did list the top ten errors he found. Connors and Lunsford's research turned up two other "top ten" lists, one by Roy Ivan Johnson in 1917, the other by Paul Witty and Roberta Green in 1930. The three lists are presented in Table 1.[2]

TABLE 1 Historical Top Ten Errors Lists

Johnson (1917) 198 Papers	Witty & Green (1930) 170 Timed Papers	Hodges (late 1930s) 20,000 Papers
Spelling	Faulty connectives	Comma
Capitalization	Vague pronoun reference	Spelling
Punctuation (mostly comma errors)	Use of "would" for simple past tense forms	Exactness
Careless omission or repetition	Confusion of forms from similarity of sound or meaning	Agreement
Apostrophe errors	Misplaced modifiers	Superfluous commas
Pronoun agreement	Pronoun agreement	Reference of pronouns
Verb tense errors and agreement	Fragments	Apostrophe
Ungrammatical sentence structure (fragments and run-ons)	Unclassified errors	Omission of words
Mistakes in the use of adjectives and adverbs	Dangling modifiers	Wordiness
Mistakes in the use of prepositions and conjunctions	Wrong tense	Good use

Increasingly intrigued to see how formal error patterns might have shifted in the sixty-odd years since these earlier research reports, Connors and Lunsford set out to discover the most common patterns of student errors characteristic of the mid-1980s and which of those patterns were marked most consistently by teachers. Table 2 presents their findings.[3]

TABLE 2 Connors and Lunsford List of Most Frequent Formal Errors

Error or Error Pattern	# found in 3000 papers	% of total errors	# found marked by teacher	% marked by teacher	rank by # of errors marked by teacher
1. No comma after introductory element	3,299	11.5%	995	30%	2
2. Vague pronoun reference	2,809	9.8%	892	32%	4
3. No comma in compound sentence	2,446	8.6%	719	29%	7
4. Wrong word	2,217	7.8%	1,114	50%	1
5. No comma in non-restrictive element	1,864	6.5%	580	31%	10
6. Wrong/missing inflected endings	1,679	5.9%	857	51%	5
7. Wrong or missing preposition	1,580	5.5%	679	43%	8
8. Comma splice	1,565	5.5%	850	54%	6
9. Possessive apostrophe error	1,458	5.1%	906	62%	3
10. Tense shift	1,453	5.1%	484	33%	12
11. Unnecessary shift in person	1,347	4.7%	410	30%	14
12. Sentence fragment	1,217	4.2%	671	55%	9
13. Wrong tense or verb form	952	3.3%	465	49%	13
14. Subject-verb agreement	909	3.2%	534	58%	11
15. Lack of comma in series	781	2.7%	184	24%	19
16. Pronoun agreement error	752	2.6%	365	48%	15
17. Unnecessary comma with restrictive element	693	2.4%	239	34%	17
18. Run-on or fused sentence	681	2.4%	308	45%	16
19. Dangling or misplaced modifier	577	2.0%	167	29%	20
20. Its/it's error	292	1.0%	188	64%	18

As noted above, Table 2 omits spelling errors, which constituted such a large number of the formal errors that Andrea and Bob decided to study them separately (see "Exercising Demonolatry"). In analyzing the other most frequent patterns of formal error and teacher marking of them, Bob and Andrea drew some intriguing conclusions: First, teachers vary widely in their thinking about what constitutes a "markable" error. Second, teachers do not mark as many errors as the popular stereotype might have us believe, perhaps because of the difficulty of explaining the error or because the teacher is focusing on only a few errors at any one time. Finally, they concluded that error patterns had indeed shifted since the time of Hodges's *Harbrace Handbook*, especially in terms of a "proliferation of error patterns that seem to suggest declining familiarity with the visual look of a written page" (406).

While Andrea and Bob found errors aplenty in the 3,000 papers from 1984, they also found reason for optimism:

> One very telling fact emerging from our research is our realization that college students are not making more formal errors in writing than they used to. The numbers of errors made by students in earlier studies and the numbers we found in the 1980s agree remarkably. (406)

Table 3 presents their comparison of the findings of the three studies.

TABLE 3 Comparison of Three Studies' Findings

Study	Year	Average Length	Errors per Paper	Errors per 100 Words
Johnson	1917	162 words	3.42	2.11
Witty & Green	1930	231 words	5.18	2.24
Connors & Lunsford	1986	422 words	9.52	2.26

Given the consistency of these numbers, Connors and Lunsford concluded that "although the length of the average paper demanded in freshman composition has been steadily rising, the formal skills of students have not declined precipitously" (406).

ERROR STUDIES, 1986–2006

During the two ensuing decades, researchers have continued to study error patterns. Most notable, perhaps, is Gary Sloan's 1990 "Frequency of Errors in Essays by College Freshmen and by Professional Writers," which found that "[t]he distribution of errors in the students' writing is consistent with figures from previous studies. . . . Connors and Lunsford found 9.52 errors per essay or 2.26 errors per 100 words; my figures for the same are 9.60 and 2.04" (302). Sloan also found that professional writers were prone to making errors, though the errors they made often differed significantly from those of the first-year writers.

During these two decades, researchers also worked to put error study in context. In a 1987 update to Mina Shaughnessy's bibliographical essay on basic writing, Andrea Lunsford reviewed work aimed at reconceiving error as "an active part of learning" (213). And in 1988, Richard Haswell reported on a study of eight error patterns in student writing across the college years and beyond. Haswell's detailed and carefully nuanced analysis, which studies eight error patterns (formation of possessives, faulty predication, pronoun reference, syntactic parallelism, punctuation of final free modification, end punctuation, punctuation of compound sentences, and orthography) deserves to be read in its entirety. For the purposes of this essay, however, we note that he stresses the need to view all of the categories of error he studies in as rich a context as possible since "the causality of student error is very complex" (495). His own findings suggest that "raw number of errors . . . seems to be growing during college" although, paradoxically, student writers "simultaneously are making measurable growth . . . toward mature competence" (494–95). Thus, Haswell concludes, "To treat surface error as source rather than symptom may still be premature with college age writers" (495). Haswell's findings bear out Lunsford and Connors's analysis of teacher response and marking patterns, which suggests that teachers often mark errors in terms of their relationship to a complex context.

More recently, Christy Desmet and Ron Balthazor are using <emma>, an electronic markup and management application, to conduct what they describe as "a local ethnography of error marking" (6). In a look at errors in "478 essays drawn from ten sections with different instructors," they report "comma errors, development, diction, awkward phrasing, and spelling" as the five most frequent errors.[4] Studying error in the context of a complex range of factors — or in local contexts, as Desmet and Balthazor are doing — seems a very promising approach to us, and we hope to see more such studies in the coming years. To date, however, such studies are few, and those that have been done repeatedly point to the hurdles researchers faced in bringing them to completion.

A NEW STUDY OF STUDENT WRITING: THOSE IRB BLUES

With this review of error studies as well as the ongoing debate over what constitutes "good" college writing in mind, we set out to replicate the Connors and Lunsford study.[5] We began the study assuming that the last two decades have ushered in huge changes in writing. To take only the most obvious example, when Bob and Andrea conducted their study, almost all students were writing by hand. Today, students not only use basic word processing but have available many other tools — from color and font type to images and sound — in composing texts. While they write, spell checkers and grammar checkers give them incessant advice. In short, the digital revolution has brought with it opportunities and challenges for writing that students and teachers twenty-two years ago could scarcely imagine. What we had not expected, however, was the degree to which institutional practices have also changed in twenty-two years. In short, we simply could not have imagined how changes to institutional review board (IRB) policies and procedures would impact our research.

What we quickly learned was that researchers conducting the kind of multi-institutional nationwide research we were attempting must negotiate with the IRB at every single research site involved. Twenty-two years ago, Bob and Andrea's consent forms and other materials easily gained approval from their home institution IRBs—and that approval covered all requirements for institutional review. As a result, their study proceeded apace. For our research, however, while the process of gaining approval from the Stanford and UCSB IRBs was straightforward enough, we found ourselves mired in red tape as we sought volunteers interested in participating in the study; only then could we contact their IRB (if any) asking for permission to proceed. First, we sent out 800 invitations by email, then 2,500 invitations by email, and then 10,000 letters on Stanford University letterhead, and then we appealed to the WPA-L email discussion list—all asking for volunteers to participate and to provide accurate contact information for individual campus IRBs. Upon receiving notices of interest, we began communicating with the local IRB officials. To our surprise, instead of exempting or expediting local approval in light of the Stanford and UCSB approvals, many officials then asked us to go through their own *full review process*. Thus began the tedious, the time-consuming, the mind-numbing task of filling out dozens upon dozens of IRB forms, each with slightly different emphases and questions, and then waiting, sometimes for months, for a response.[6]

Compared to Andrea and Bob's experience, the effects of this expanded and noncollaborative IRB system were chilling. The data collection two decades ago took about three months. For this study, the data collection took six times as long—a full eighteen months. Two decades ago, a much larger number of campuses participated; for this study, we were limited to those that were willing and able to issue approvals in a timely manner.[7] Two decades ago, each teacher's packet of submitted papers represented nearly the full class;[8] for this study, the packets typically represented half the number of students. We do not know how many potential teacher participants we lost in this process, although we did hear from some volunteers who found themselves simply overwhelmed when they attempted to sponsor our project on their campuses. Ultimately, our project required literally countless hours of researcher time to submit the same IRB protocol over and over; it unexpectedly required us to trouble several colleagues to become local co-principal investigators; and it was reviewed and approved of by more IRB committees than ever touch a typical medical study—all so that we can tell you now that in a random stratified sample of 877 (of 1,826 total) anonymous student papers, we found 645 comma splices.

MORE ON METHODOLOGY: PREPARING THE PAPERS FOR CODING

But before we could count even one comma splice, before we could pull a random stratified sample, we had to prepare the papers carefully. As the packets
arrived, each paper was assigned a unique number that also indicated the region
and the type and size of its school in order to yield a stratified sample for analysis (see Appendix 1). As a research assistant marked the sample for stratification,
he also removed student names and all other identifying information from all
papers.[9]

Although the total paper archive we gathered is—regrettably—smaller
than the one in Bob and Andrea's previous study, it still represents a wide
range of papers. Our call for a set of papers from as close to the end of term as
possible and one that included teacher comments brought in papers from all
types of first-year writing courses (basic, regular, advanced, and specialty
courses). And because the data collection lasted eighteen months, we received
papers from all college terms, including some summer courses. In the previous study, Lunsford and Connors chose to remove papers that contained formal markers that suggested they were written by students for whom English
was a second language, because there were so few of them. For the current
study, determining which papers represented ESL writers seemed a harder
task, and in any event, we very much wanted to include papers written by
multilingual students in our study. The last twenty-two years have seen ESL
students more thoroughly integrated into mainstream writing classrooms,
and Generation 1.5 students are now recognized as a new group. This decision also helped to broaden the range of papers we could examine. And,
finally, many papers came in with their grades on them, and all possible
grades from A to F were well represented, again broadening the range of the
sample we could study.

Once the papers were rendered anonymous, and once we had a sense of the
overall total, we were able to pull our random stratified sample. We used an
initial small sample to create the coding rubric and then added to that a large
sample to be coded by volunteers. As paper packets continued to arrive and to
be processed during the coding phase of the project, we increased the sample
size to match the overall stratification.

DEVELOPING THE CODING RUBRIC

In attempting to replicate the previous study's development of a coding rubric,
we used a procedure employed in the earlier study: Andrea pulled a small, random stratified sample of 25 papers and marked every formal error that she could
find. A week or so later, she took another 25 papers and repeated the procedure,
marking every formal error. Her results are summarized in Table 4.

TABLE 4 Formal Errors in a 50-Paper Sample

Error or Error Pattern	# in 50 Papers
Wrong word	79
Comma splice	61
Missing comma after intro word or phrase	55
Possessive apostrophe error	48
Subject-verb agreement error	41
Missing internal citation with page number, etc.	35
Homonym error	32
Missing word	31
Pronoun / antecedent agreement error	28
Fragment	26
Unnecessary comma before coordinating conjunction joining compounds	24
Capitalization (missing or unnecessary)	24
Hyphen (missing or unnecessary)	21
Faulty sentence structure	21
Problems in tense sequence or shift, etc.	20
Pronoun reference error	20
Missing comma or comma needed for restrictive/nonrestrictive elements	17
Spelling error	17
Parallelism error	17
Unnecessary comma before quotation	15
Article error	15
Fused (run-on) sentence	15
Quotation marks inappropriately used for emphasis	13
Colon unnecessary before series or quotation (7) / missing (4)	11
Quotation not introduced or commented on	10
Shift or error in number	9
Wrong or missing preposition	8
Adjective/adverb confusion	8
Shift in person	8
Missing comma before verbal	7
Missing or extraneous comma in a series	7
Unnecessary comma around prepositional or other phrase	7
Missing quotation marks at beginning or end of quotation or both	7
Quotation not integrated into sentence	7
Dangling or misplaced modifier	7
Missing comma at one or the other end of a phrase	6
Unnecessary comma between verb and object	4
Missing comma with appositive	4
Missing comma before coordinating conjunction joining clauses	4
Missing comma around conjunctive adverbs	3
Unnecessary comma between subject and verb	3
Pronoun case error	3
Idiom error	3
Unnecessary semicolon	3
Split infinitive	2
A/an confusion	2
Comparative adjective error	2

From Andrea's initial list, we pulled the top 25 errors to include in the rubric. One early and clear result of this procedure: it sifted out a group of errors that did not show up at all on Bob and Andrea's earlier top twenty list, an issue we address below.

However, we were also curious about the fate of some of those earlier top twenty errors, and we knew that we needed to compensate for our smaller sample size. As a result, we added to our rubric the errors from the previous study that did not turn up in our initial sample. Additionally, the new rubric asked coders to identify the type of paper, to indicate whether the student or teacher employed technology beyond simple word processing, and to indicate whether the paper was part of a larger portfolio (either multiple drafts of the paper or one element of a whole term's worth of work). If the paper was an item in a portfolio, then the coder was instructed to select the final draft or last assignment to code, as indicated by dates. Again following the methods of the Connors and Lunsford study, our coders tallied both the errors they saw and those that the teacher had marked. To help explain the rubric, we also devised a listing of Error Examples in which we illustrated each error with real student examples pulled from our mini-sample of 50 papers.[10]

CODING THE PAPERS AND COLLATING THE RESULTS

Now that we had devised and tested a coding rubric of some 40 possible errors, we were ready for the coders. In the previous study, Bob and Andrea trained 50 coders in one afternoon and then, the next day, they worked together to mark 3,000 papers. We estimated that 30 coders would suffice to read 850 papers, and we invited volunteers from among teaching assistants, instructors, and professors in the UCSB programs in writing, education, and ESL/linguistics to help us do so. They arrived at 8:30 a.m. on a chilly Saturday in January 2006. By 10:00, we had all the volunteers trained on using the rubric. As in the original study, although the coders could consult with the researchers about how to classify something they saw in a paper, they were given much autonomy in deciding what constituted an error and how to categorize it. As a result, the judgment calls about specific items were distributed among the group. Armed with stacks of coding rubrics, most coders worked in two large classrooms we had reserved; some retreated to their nearby offices; all read at a diligent pace. Occasionally they returned to the conference room, where fresh papers awaited them along with a smorgasbord of snacks, lunch, and the soothing, continuous burble of two Mr. Coffees and one rescued-from-an-attic Mrs. Tea.

The coders worked feverishly all day, most until 9:30 that night. And it was at that point that we had our first inkling of one of this study's findings: these papers were much longer than those submitted two decades ago. Just how much longer we were to calculate later, after a coder had counted up the pages of body text. That Saturday evening, we quickly reassured our bleary-eyed coders that the 675 papers they had gotten through represented a remarkable achievement.

Then we asked twenty of the volunteers back for Round 2, held two weeks later. In the meantime, more packets of student papers had arrived, so we were able to increase our random stratified sample by 27 papers (for the total 877 papers). Based on feedback from the first reading, we expanded the coding rubric to allow coders to specify more types of comma errors, to list the actual missing and wrong words, and to record semicolon errors separately. Round 2 started at noon on a Friday in early February and went to 8:00 that evening. The remaining 15 papers from that coding session were coded by experienced volunteers over the next workweek. That week, we realized that the tallies for missing commas in the expanded coding rubric suggested that a specific comma error, the missing comma in a compound sentence (MCICS), represented a large proportion of those errors. To determine a better count for those, we asked a coder to go back through all of the papers again to count just that error.

Once the hurdle of coding all of the papers was behind us, we were faced with the task of adding up all of the error totals. At the end of each coding session, the coders had added their tallies for the set of papers they had marked. (The calculator key chains they used became the study's souvenir.) This gave us a rough estimate of the various totals. We turned then to the task of capturing more accurate totals. Our research assistants gently reminded us that computers were made for more than word processing, and so we decided to enter all of the tally marks into Excel spreadsheets.[11] A band of data-entry assistants went to work for three weeks, and our resident expert in Excel compiled all entries into a single spreadsheet. We spent the next few weeks double-checking the entries, then devised a way to extrapolate the totals for the top missing comma error (MCICS), and finally compiled our new top twenty list.[12]

WHAT WE FOUND: TWO MAJOR SHIFTS

Before we turn to a discussion of the particular formal errors in these essays, we want to note two major shifts that have taken place during the last two decades. First, we found that our sense that these papers were quite a bit longer than those in the Connors and Lunsford study was accurate: in fact, these papers turned out to be, on average, over two-and-a-half times longer than those in the previous study. In a further analysis, we found that papers in our sample ranged from a scant 1.5 pages to a densely written 23 pages, and we calculated from the total pages that the average length was 4.15 pages. Assuming the standard 250 words per full page, we calculated that the average number of words was 1,038 per paper. Thus, as Table 5 indicates, research across the decades demonstrates that college student essays have grown longer and longer with time.

TABLE 5 Comparison of Average Length of Student Essays, 1917–2006

Year	Average Paper Length
1917	162 words
1930	231 words
1986	422 words
2006	1038 words

The second trend we noted is a sea change in the types of papers teachers are asking students to write in first-year writing classes. Although the first study included some reports and a fair number of readings of (mostly) literary texts, the majority of the papers were personal narratives. When we analyzed the kinds of papers represented in this study, we found a range of paper types, as indicated in Table 6.

TABLE 6 Types of Papers Submitted in 2006

Type of Paper	Number Found in 877 Papers
Researched argument or report	287
Argument with very few or no sources	186
Close reading or analysis	141
Compare/contrast	78
Personal narrative	76
Definition	21
Description	18
Rhetorical analysis	16
Proposal	11
Process analysis	10
Reflective cover letter	3
Other*	30

*The "other" category included fiction, letters to aliens, an in-class essay, a news article, several I-searches, a play, several interviews, a biographical sketch, a book report, and several letters.

These results strongly suggest that emphasis on personal narrative has been replaced by an emphasis on argument and research. This finding is supported by Richard Fulkerson's recent map of our discipline, which points to the tremendous growth of argumentation-based textbooks in the last twenty years, despite wide differences in approaches to composition courses (672). Likewise, these results confirm a finding offered by Kathi Yancey and her colleagues: in a national survey of writing programs, an "overwhelming" majority of teachers indicated that they focus on argument- and research-based writing. Together, the two shifts we have identified suggest that student writers today are tackling the kind of issues that require inquiry and investigation as well as reflection and that students are writing more than ever before.

WHAT WE OBSERVED ABOUT TEACHER COMMENTS

We plan to address teacher comments on the papers in our study more thoroughly in a future analysis. At first blush, though, we are struck by how little some things have changed in terms of teacher comments. As they did twenty-two years ago, teachers in this study varied widely in what they decided to mark, and they often focused their marks on just a few specific patterns of error in any one paper. In addition, the vast majority of teachers in this sample (as in the Connors and Lunsford study) marked their papers by hand, employing a variety of inks and pencils and seeming to reserve red ink to signal that students should pay special attention. This time around, many teachers once again chose to mark most often the highly visible and easy-to-circle mistakes, such as apostrophe and spelling errors. Finally, as before, they frequently marked errors that confused a sentence's meaning, such as wrong words.

Generally, the teachers in this study marked slightly fewer of the overall errors than did teachers in the previous study. Two decades ago, the teachers marked 43 percent of the errors the coders found, whereas in this study they marked 38 percent. However, the current teachers were reading papers that were on average two-and-a-half times longer than those in the previous study. In many cases, too, there were references to previous drafts and peer review sessions, and we received 101 papers that were part of portfolios (and in many cases, we received the entire portfolio, too). The comments suggested that many students had already received more extensive feedback on earlier drafts, on which we did not focus in this study. Again, our results support claims by Richard Fulkerson and by Kathi Yancey's team that writing teachers—although they may differ strongly in their theoretical approaches to and aims for first-year composition courses—have nonetheless widely integrated an understanding of writing as a process, along with peer review and reiterative drafting, into their pedagogies.

One surprising finding for us: we received few examples of teachers using specialized computer technologies to comment on student papers. To be sure, we received many examples in which teachers had typed their final comments, and we saw several fairly extensive grading rubrics. What we had expected to collect, though, were examples of teachers using programs such as ConnectWeb, Comment, Daedalus, wikis, blogs, and so on for commenting. Our instructions had explicitly encouraged teachers who use technologies to participate in the study, and we had arranged for technical support. Yet only 56 of the 877 papers had comments that were made via technologies beyond the typed final comment; most typically, they employed Microsoft Word's commenting or highlighting features. It is possible that potential participants were put off by the extra steps it would have taken to copy or print

the files to submit to us. However, teachers who did submit texts clearly preferred pens and pencils as their commenting technologies. For many teachers,
it seems, the electronic commenting tools are still not accessible or convenient
enough, or still not pedagogically justified enough, to encourage their use.

WHAT WE ALSO FOUND: THE MOST COMMON FORMAL ERRORS IN 2006

After nearly two years of data gathering and analysis, we finally have a new list
of common formal errors, along with percentages marked by the teachers and by
our team of coders, as shown in Table 7. [See p. 355.] Two items on this list
instantly leapt out at us. First, while spelling errors out-numbered all others in
the Connors and Lunsford study by three to one, spelling errors in our study
came in at number 5, accounting for only 6.5 percent of all errors found. Second, "wrong word" in our study was by far the most frequent formal error,
accounting for nearly 14 percent of the errors. These findings are dramatic and,
it seems to us, related in interesting ways. Since almost every one of our 877
papers was word processed (a very few were handwritten on loose-leaf paper), we
assume that the spell-check function took care of many potential spelling problems. Indeed, a great number of the spelling errors in our study are homonyms
and proper nouns, mistakes that spell-checkers understandably do not flag.

But every blessing brings its own curse. In this case, many of the wrong word
errors appear to be the result of spell-checker suggestions. A student trying to
spell "frantic," for example, apparently accepted the spell-checker's suggestion
of "fanatic." Wrong word for sure. In addition, some students appear to be using
a thesaurus feature without also using a dictionary to understand the nuances
of meaning for various words — "artistic," for example, when "aesthetic" is the
appropriate choice. Still other wrong word mistakes seem to result from choosing a word that has a somewhat similar sound: "concur" rather than "conclude"
or "analyses" rather than "analyzes." Finally, many wrong words seem to come
from the simple failure to proofread: writing "begging" for "beginning" is no
doubt such a case in point.

A second category of mistakes also surfaced early on. Andrea's preliminary
analysis of 50 papers had turned up a number of problems with sources and
attributions. Indeed, these errors came to the fore in our coding, ranking numbers 3, 6, and 18 in our list of top twenty formal errors.[13] The shift to research-
based and argumentative writing clearly accounts for many of these mistakes:
as we read the 877 papers, we noted students struggling with the use of sources
on every front, from omitting citations completely to documenting them in
idiosyncratic if not downright bizarre ways. Such struggles seem to us a natural and necessary part of the practice that students must do to become familiar
with, much less master, any one documentation style: after all, entering the
conversation in a field, showing that you know the issues and have something
to contribute to them, choosing among a huge range of possible sources, and

TABLE 7 Most Common Formal Errors in 2006

Error or Error Pattern	# found in 877 papers	% of total errors	# found marked by teacher	% found marked by teacher	rank by # of errors marked by teacher
1. Wrong word	3,080	13.7	1,463	48	1
2. Missing comma after an introductory element	2,150	9.6	602	28	5
3. Incomplete or missing documentation	1,586	7.1	722	46	3
4. Vague pronoun reference	1,495	6.7	405	27	8
5. Spelling error (including homonyms)	1,450	6.5	788	54	2
6. Mechanical error with a quotation	1,444	6.4	674	47	4
7. Unnecessary comma	1,175	5.2	346	29	10
8. Unnecessary or missing capitalization	1,168	5.2	490	42	7
9. Missing word	1,024	4.6	491	48	6
10. Faulty sentence structure	996	4.4	297	30	13
11. Missing comma with a nonrestrictive element	850	3.8	229	27	16
12. Unnecessary shift in verb tense	847	3.8	304	36	11
13. Missing comma in a compound sentence	814	3.6	300	37	12
14. Unnecessary or missing apostrophe (including *its/it's*)	693	3.1	372	54	9
15. Fused (run-on) sentence	668	3.0	189	28	18
16. Comma splice	645	2.9	257	40	14
17. Lack of pronoun-antecedent agreement	612	2.7	253	41	15
18. Poorly integrated quotation	612	2.7	154	25	19
19. Unnecessary or missing hyphen	562	2.5	152	27	20
20. Sentence fragment	531	2.4	223	42	17

using them to document the work related to any particular topic are not easy skills to develop, especially for novice writers. In any case, teachers spent a lot of energy on correcting such errors, marking half of all missing or incomplete documentation mistakes, for example. It stands to reason that instructors would be attentive to such problems in research-based essays and arguments: after all, using sources appropriately and citing them clearly are major parts of such an assignment.[14]

Other mistakes—especially the number of capitalization and hyphenation errors—initially puzzled us, though a little reflection suggested a number of possible explanations. Some capitalization errors, for example, appear to result from Word automatically capitalizing a word that follows a period (such as a period used with an abbreviation). In these cases, the student had not corrected the error, even though it could have been caught with careful proof-reading. In still other cases, students seemed inclined to use capitals for the subject terms of their research papers, words that for them seemed to take on a certain significance. For instance, a student capitalized every occurrence of "basketball," as well as the names of other sports, in a paper that began, "Basketball, America's other pastime, is the third most popular sport in the USA after Baseball and Football." Alternatively, in other cases students seemed to be treating objects as proper nouns. For example, in this excerpt, the student visually equates the GED with a high school diploma through capitals: "One common belief is that a person with a GED education is less educated than a person who has achieved a High School Diploma"—implying that a diploma would be an "HSD." Surely the internal caps in names like eBay or iPod may add to student confusion—such seemingly random capitalization cannot help students who are trying to figure out why some words are capitalized in formal writing and others are not. Yet the most prominent uses of initial caps are advertising and headlines, and perhaps these kinds of texts may be contributing to the increase in capitalization errors. For many students, headlines and slogans may be very common reading—a big part of the nonrequired reading they do.

Hyphens also seemed to be causing a good bit of confusion. A number of hyphen mistakes apparently come from students hyphenating two-part verbs—"put-up," "log-in," "shut-down." Students seem more puzzled than ever by the fact that "sign-up sheet" is hyphenated but "sign up here" is not. In general, however, the trend seems to be moving more toward one unhyphenated word—firewall, laptop, email. To be sure, conventions regarding "email" are still very much in flux, with some reference works stipulating the hyphen and others, increasingly, rejecting it. This trend toward loss of hyphenation also seems apparent in formerly hyphenated prefixes ("supermarket," "overeat") and with compound adjectives. Our dictionaries list hundreds of "anti"-compounds, and the only hyphenated ones involve proper nouns ("anti-Russian") and words that start with "i" ("anti-immigration"). Could we have a "great hyphenation migration" on our hands? No wonder students are confused.

Of all the errors we noted, those we termed "faulty sentence structure" intrigued us most. Some of these errors seem to arise when students cut and paste passages from one sentence to another, or when they draft a sentence and then delete part of it to correct a mistake — but do not delete enough. But we found many more "faulty sentence structure" errors than these reasons could account for, so much so that we speculate that a number of them may result from students attempting to address complex topics in complex ways. Perhaps the rise in the number of these errors signals the cognitive difficulty associated with argument- and research-based writing, as might be expected to accompany a shift from personal narrative to argument and research.

In any case, faulty sentence structures certainly caused our readers to pause and say "What?!?" These errors tended to attract both teachers' and coders' attention because they so often confounded meaning. Critics of current educational practices point to sentences such as these as signs that today's digital texts are undermining clear thought and that high schools are failing to sharpen syntactic skills. But let's think again. Consider, for instance, the sentence that served as one of the examples of faulty sentence structure for the coders in our study: "However, Marlow had put caps in the gun, proving that Carmen became infuriated because she was rejected by Regan, as Marlow had also done, and killed Rusty." Faulty sentence structure, yes. But it is worth reflecting on what may lie behind errors such as these, which may actually signal syntactic growth. This sentence, for instance, is attempting to do some hard work: to signal the temporal and causal relationships among different scenes from *The Big Sleep*. It comes from a thoughtful analysis of that novel,[15] and even though this sentence is overwhelmed by the many incidents that occur, it is trying to sum up a very complex narrative. "It's the response to error that counts," as Nikki Giovanni reminds us: when we find examples of such fractured syntax, then, it seems especially important to respond in an open and exploratory way, searching with the student writer for the intended meaning.

HOW OUR FINDINGS DIFFER FROM THE CONNORS AND LUNSFORD STUDY

Seven student errors from Andrea and Bob's study dropped off in ours (though they do appear farther down in our list, as runners-up to the top twenty): wrong or missing verb ending; wrong or missing preposition; unnecessary shift in pronoun; wrong tense or verb form; lack of subject-verb agreement; missing comma in a series; and dangling modifier.[16] Somewhat surprising to us were the small number of dangling modifiers we found, and while it is conceivable that a few of these were counted as "faulty sentence structure," we believe it will take a more fine-grained analysis than the one we have done here to discover what changes in sentence length and syntax might be related to this admittedly small shift — dangling modifiers ranked number 19 in the Connors and Lunsford study. A few of the other errors that dropped out — wrong verb forms, missing verb endings, and subject-verb agreement — are sometimes flagged by grammar checkers, but again we doubt that these checkers alone can be responsible for the reduction in the number of such errors. When we looked at the wrong or missing prepositions in our study, we found that a number of these were counted as "wrong words," which would account for this change. Finally, the missing comma error suggests to us that students are still struggling with commas, though they are doing so with slightly different patterns than turned up twenty-two years ago.

WHAT WE DID NOT FIND

At the opening of this essay, we noted the many hard-core worriers who see a precipitous decline in student writing ability and who often relate that decline to the creeping influence of IM and other digital lingo as well as to sliding standards. Our findings do not support such fears. In fact, we found almost no instances of IM terms ("gtg," "imho") or even smilies in students' formal prose, although they sometimes appeared in notes to teachers or in the peers' comments. The students in this sample seemed aware of the ancient principle of *kairos* and wrote with a sense of what is appropriate for formal college writing. More surprising was the little evidence of what has come to be called — perhaps in homage to Winston Weathers's charming and important *An Alternate Style* — alternate or alternative discourse. With the exception of a handful of funny and often imaginative letters to aliens, all from the same class, as well as some fiction, the papers we examined stuck resolutely to what Weathers dubbed Grammar A: traditional usage, organization, and style. We had imagined, given our field's lively and intense discussion of alternate styles in the last decade, that we would see more evidence of such experimentation in student writing today.

We also found very little use of the many tools available to student writers today. To be sure, two of the essays were dressed to the nines with superimposed images, clip art, and wildly colored fonts — and a few included tables, charts, or figures. But only 25 papers used images at all, and only 5 more used colored fonts, hyperlinks, or blog-style entries. For the most part (847 of 877, to be exact), these student writers were not illustrating their texts, nor were they making use of different type sizes, fonts, color, and so on, much less making use of sound or video. No Web texts were submitted to our study. This finding may suggest that teachers' assignments do not yet encourage the use of such tools, or that teachers and students do not have ready access to the technologies that would support their use in writing. We suspect, however, that student writers simply do not yet associate such tools with formal school writing. In any event, for all the attention we give to multimedia forms of writing in our own teaching, and for all the advances the field of writing and rhetoric has made in teaching writing with technology, student writers in these first-year college classes continue to produce traditional print-based texts.

ONE MORE WORD ON ERROR

As we noted earlier, studies of error across the last ninety years yield remarkably similar findings. This conclusion holds true for our study as well, as shown in Table 8.

TABLE 8 Comparison of Error Rates per 100 Words

Study	Year	Errors per 100 Words
Johnson	1917	2.11
Witty & Green	1930	2.24
Connors & Lunsford	1986	2.26
Lunsford & Lunsford	2006	2.45

In comparing these numbers, we note that the Connors and Lunsford study did not include spelling errors, since they were the subject of another study. Our study did include spelling errors: if those are excluded, then the rate of error per 100 words (i.e., 2.299) remains almost exactly the same as it has been during the last century, though types of error vary considerably.

In looking at the rate of error in our and other studies, we are reminded of Joseph Williams's essay "The Phenomenology of Error." In its published form, that article contained 100 deliberate formal errors. Most readers, however, were not aware of them until the final sentence—which dramatically announced their presence. Noticing errors depends, then, on the reader's context. As Williams argues, if the piece of writing is professional prose, and if it is cognitively challenging and interesting, then readers do not notice error. The rate of error in our study, then, should also be seen as rate of *attention* to error. When readers look for errors, they will find them. For the current study, our coders were looking for 40 different types of errors, and they found an awful lot of them. Even so, the rate of error in this study remains consistent with results across nearly 100 years. Those who believe that we ought to be able to eliminate errors from student writing may need to realize that "mistakes are a fact of life" and, we would add, a necessary accompaniment to learning and to improving writing.

CONCLUSION

We offer these findings with caution, for the total number of papers we received—despite the extraordinary effort and generosity of our volunteers—was much smaller than we had hoped. Yet the study does reveal several important trends, such as the dramatic increase in length of student writing and the shift in the kinds of assignments instructors are giving, assignments that lead to concomitant shifts in errors. Perhaps most important, contrary to what the doomsayers would have us believe, this study confirms that the rate of student error is not increasing precipitously but, in fact, has stayed stable for nearly one hundred years. Nor, really, does it make sense to expect that today's students ought to make fewer mistakes as they learn to write than did their predecessors. The last two decades have seen massive changes in student enrollments, revolutions in writing technologies, and a nationwide shift in first-year writing courses to genres that demand particular cognitive and rhetorical strategies. In the face of these changes, student errors are not more prevalent — they are only *different*.

Our task now is to understand and document those differences better — to continue to work toward a more nuanced and context-based definition of error; to see whether similar large-scale studies produce similar top twenty lists; to identify any significant differences across regions, various groups, or disciplines; to ask how we might adapt our technologies to reduce certain errors and how we might adapt our pedagogies to address the errors to which technologies contribute; to analyze whether our focus on academic discourse is paying off in WAC issues and to compare writing teacher markings with those of teachers in other disciplines. One study cannot provide the documentation needed to convince administrators of the worth of college writing courses, or to demonstrate to colleagues the need to look beyond their own anecdotal accounts of student error, or to make visible the very interesting shifts that occur in each generation of college writers. Rather, we need a coordinated agenda.

Whether we can coordinate efforts in ways that allow us to meet IRB requirements seems a huge question arising from this study. Instead of two researchers attempting to conduct a centralized nationwide study, we might turn to a process used in many scientific fields. In this process, local researchers conduct experiments and then deposit the results into a central database, which in turn aggregates and creates models or visual representations of the data. We imagine a nationwide effort in which local writing program administrators (WPAs) could be principal investigators (PIs) for their own campuses, conduct a local version of this study, and then submit the anonymous results to a central location (perhaps sponsored by CCCC?). Or perhaps a consortium of WPAs could conduct a comparative study regionally, the better to make the data anonymous. Perhaps those campuses that already have large archives of student papers — often digital archives — could lead the way. In addition, if PIs could gain permission, as we did, to deposit collected student papers into a national archive (e.g., University of New Hampshire's), our field could build an important historical record.

Whether our field can move to adopt any of these suggestions or not, this study reaffirms our belief that student writers and the work they produce are worth such efforts — and more. As a group, the 877 papers we read were attempting to address serious issues in serious, if still maturing, ways; they radiated good humor and found amusement in things large and small; they wrestled with difficult sources and with textual conventions of all kinds; and they documented a range of contemporary values as well as hopes and dreams. And yes, they made mistakes — some real whoppers, others only tiny missteps, but all of them asking for our careful response.

Appendix 1: Stratification of All Student Papers

Region	1	2	3	4	5	6	7	Total
Total number of papers	316	292	317	296	158	118	329	1826
Total number of packets	24	20	18	18	12	8	19	119
Total number of 4–year schools*	16 (238)	15 (217)	13 (249)	9 (126)	7 (106)	5 (52)	10 (151)	75 (1139)
Total number of 2–year schools	8 (78)	5 (75)	5 (68)	9 (170)	5 (52)	3 (66)	9 (178)	44 (687)
Total number of state schools	17 (195)	11 (153)	13 (231)	12 (210)	8 (84)	6 (90)	15 (275)	82 (1238)
Total number of private schools	7 (121)	9 (139)	4 (68)	6 (86)	4 (74)	2 (28)	4 (54)	36 (570)
Total number of proprietary schools	0 (0)	0 (0)	1 (18)	0 (0)	0 (0)	0 (0)	0 (0)	1 (18)
Number of schools with total enrollments under 1,000	0 (0)	2 (30)	1 (1)	2 (37)	0 (0)	0 (0)	2 (27)	7 (95)
Enrollment 1,000–3,000	4 (46)	5 (86)	1 (15)	4 (42)	3 (37)	3 (37)	2 (26)	22 (289)
Enrollment 3,000–5,000	6 (74)	7 (82)	3 (60)	1 (16)	3 (62)	3 (27)	3 (69)	26 (390)
Enrollment 5,000–10,000	6 (102)	4 (59)	6 (103)	3 (54)	2 (20)	1 (46)	4 (64)	26 (448)
Enrollment 10,000–20,000	4 (42)	1 (24)	4 (59)	3 (44)	3 (26)	1 (8)	3 (50)	19 (253)
Enrollment over 20,000	4 (52)	1 (11)	3 (79)	5 (103)	1 (13)	0 (0)	5 (93)	19 (351)

*Note that the first number refers to the number of packets of papers received; the number in parentheses indicates the number of papers.

NOTES

1. Connors and Lunsford published several essays resulting from this study, including "Frequency of Formal Errors in Current College Writing, or Ma and Pa Kettle Do Research." This essay, which attempted a bit of humor — a try at what is now called "alternative discourse" — was huge fun to write. The loss of Bob Connors in a motorcycle accident in the summer of 2000 has left the field of what he termed composition-rhetoric without one of its best (and often funniest) spokespersons. We dedicate this essay to his memory.

2. The lists are quoted in Connors and Lunsford (405). The terms have been updated where possible.

3. The sample of papers Connors and Lunsford analyzed appeared to be written by native speakers. As a result, they pulled out of the sample any essays that were characterized by obvious ESL markers — though there were very few of these.

4. Desmet and Balthazor found the following errors: Comma errors, Development, Diction, Awkward, Spelling, Documentation, Other punctuation, Wordy, Apostrophe, Paragraph coherence, Tense, Transition, Comma splice, Expletive construction, Agreement pronoun-antecedent, Coherence, Paragraph unity, Vague pronoun reference, Agreement subject-verb, Fragment, Passive voice, Wrong preposition, Organization, and Logical fallacy — in decreasing order of frequency.

5. We are grateful to Bedford/St. Martin's for sponsoring both the previous and the current study. In particular, we thank editors Carolyn Lengel and Stephanie Butler for their patience, hard work, and pragmatic advice throughout this project.

6. Many thanks to James Ford for his help in this phase of the research.

7. Throughout the data collection, too, we were reminded several times that a natural disaster is a national disaster, with rippling effects on our research that we did not anticipate. When hurricanes Ivan (2004), Katrina (2005), and Rita (2005) destroyed communities, they put an enormous strain on nearby academic institutions that welcomed people who were displaced. With regret, some colleagues were forced to put aside their participation in our study, either because their own schools were flooded or because their programs suddenly doubled in size. Some of the student papers we did receive likewise attest to the trauma that these experiences evoked.

8. For the earlier study, teachers also sent multiple classes' worth of graded papers. In the current study, sometimes teachers from the same school sent their papers in the same packet.

9. We had collected papers with names on them so that we could allow students and teachers a window of time in which to withdraw from the study, should they wish; this procedure was a safeguard against coercion. The most common type of "other identifying information" removed was the phone number, especially as students informed teachers and peer group members how to reach them.

10. Many thanks to Alison Bright, who helped identify these examples and, at this point, became the project coordinator.

11. Many thanks to Elizabeth Freudenthal, who patiently led the data-entry and fact-checking, and to Paul Rogers, who contributed his Excel expertise.

12. The *missing comma in a compound sentence errors* (MCICS) came to be fondly known as the McIcks by our research team. Here is how the extrapolation was devised: We knew from the Round 2 rubric what proportions of all missing comma errors the MCICS constituted for both coders and teachers. We applied those percentages to the total missing comma errors on the Round 1 rubric, and we extrapolated

totals for both coders and teachers for the Round 1 MCICS. Then we added the Round 1 extrapolation to the count from Round 2.

We decided to use this extrapolation rather than the actual count that the single coder found because, when the coder focused on just one error instead of 40 possible errors, she found an even higher percentage of MCICS than our regular coders or the teachers did.

13. Note, too, that we did not count the errors on the Works Cited pages; had we done so, the number would have been much, much higher.

14. Of the papers that cited resources, 440 used MLA style; 42, APA style; and 29, another style that, if it was recognizable, was usually CSE.

15. Although we might guess that the student had also seen the film, the paper analyzes the novel.

16. In addition, we note that *its/it's* would have dropped off the list if we hadn't combined it with unnecessary or missing apostrophes. It was a separate error in the Connors and Lunsford study, coming in at number 20.

WORKS CITED

Bok, Derek. *Our Underachieving Colleges: A Candid Look at How Much Students Learn and Why They Should Be Learning More.* Princeton, NJ: Princeton UP, 2005.

Bush, George W. Presidential address. Washington, DC, June 27, 2006.

Connors, Robert, and Andrea A. Lunsford. "Frequency of Formal Error in Current College Writing, or Ma and Pa Kettle Do Research." *College Composition and Communication,* 39.4 (1988): 395–409.

Cross-Language Relations in Composition. Spec. issue of *College English* 68.6 (2006).

Desmet, Christy, and Ron Balthazor. "Finding Patterns in Textual Corpora: Data Mining, Research, and Assessment in First-year Composition." Paper presented at Computers and Writing 2006, Lubbock, Texas, May 25–29, 2006.

Farmer, Robert. "IM Online. RU?" *Educause Review,* 40.6 (2005): 48–63.

Fulkerson, Richard. "Composition at the Turn of the Twenty-First Century." *College Composition and Communication,* 56.4 (2005): 654–87.

Giovanni, Nikki. *Black Feeling, Black Talk, Black Judgment.* New York: W. Morrow, 1970.

Haswell, Richard. "Error and Change in College Student Writing." *Written Communication* 5 (1988): 470–99.

Hodges, John C. *Harbrace Handbook of English.* New York: Harcourt, 1941.

Johnson, Roy Ivan. "The Persistency of Error in English Composition." *School Review* 25 (October 1917): 555–80.

Lunsford, Andrea. "Basic Writing Update." *Teaching Composition: Twelve Bibliographical Essays.* Ed. Gary Tate. Texas Christian UP, 1987: 207–27.

Lunsford, Andrea, and Robert J. Connors. "Exercising Demonolatry: Spelling Patterns and Pedagogies in College Writing." *Written Communication* 9 (1992): 404–28.

Sloan, Gary. "Frequency of Errors in Essays by College Freshmen and by Professional Writers." *College Composition and Communication* 41.3 (1990): 299–308.

Students' Right to Their Own Language. Spec. issue of *College Composition and Communication* 25 (1974).

United States. Dept. of Education. Spellings Commission. *Commission Report: A National Dialogue: The Secretary of Education's Commission on the Future of Higher Education.* August 9, 2006 draft. 13 Sept. 2006. <http://www.ed.gov/about/bdscomm/list/hiedfuture /reports.html>.

Weathers, Winston. *An Alternate Style: Options in Composition*. Rochelle Park, NJ: Hayden, 1980.

Williams, Joseph. "The Phenomenology of Error." *College Composition and Communication* 32.2 (1981): 152–68.

Witty, Paul A., and Roberta La Brant Green. "Composition Errors of College Students." *English Journal* 19 (May 1930): 388–93.

Yancey, Kathleen Blake, Teddi Fishman, Morgan Gresham, Michael Neal, and Summer Smith Taylor. "Portraits of Composition: How Composition Gets Taught in the Twenty-first Century." (forthcoming)

Amy J. Devitt, Anis Bawarshi, and Mary Jo Reiff

Materiality and Genre in the Study of Discourse Communities

Over the past two decades the concept of discourse community has been one of the most hotly contested notions in the field, subject to the range of by now well-known critiques that claim it is too utopian, hegemonic, stable, and abstract.[1] Abstracted from real social situations, discourse communities may appear stable to advocates and critics assuming an imaginary consensus and a shared purpose that do not reflect real experience within communities. The concept of discourse community as stable and utopian has been, to some, so seductive that it both conceals the language and the social practices that take place within it and distracts researchers from examining how its internal workings may be recognized and studied. As a result, the concept of discourse community remains of limited pedagogical value.

To make communities tangible and their discourse actions palpable to students, writing teachers have begun to use ethnographic research, which, while valuable in locating the study of discourse within the behaviors of real communities, can be difficult to implement in the classroom. According to Beverly Moss, "When ethnographers study a community as outsiders, they must spend a significant amount of time gaining access to the community and learning the rules of the community well enough to gather and eventually analyze the data" (161). The process of sifting through the massive quantities of information gathered and attempting to stake out some analytical claims can present a major hurdle, particularly for student ethnographers. How do ethnographers connect what community members know and do with what they say and how they say it — their language practices? Genre analysis has been responsive to such questions and links patterns of language use to patterns of social behavior, reflecting the composition researcher's "narrower concern with communicative behavior or the interactions of language and culture" (Moss 156). Genre study allows students and researchers to recognize how "lived textuality" plays a role in the lived experience of a group. Teaching students how to analyze genres can provide discipline and focus to the study of discourse communities.

During the last half-century, genre theory has been reconceived by literary and rhetorical theorists as, among other things, "sites of social and ideological action" (Schryer 208) — as parts of all social environments. Language genres in these contexts become less transparent and more constitutive, less the means of classifying texts and more the sites at which language's social character can

---

This article is reprinted from *College English* 65.5 (May 2003): 541–58.

be understood. In this sense language and its genres are as material as the people using them. As sites of social action, genres identify the linguistic ecology of discourse communities, making the notion of community more tangible for teachers and students.

In the three connected essays that follow, we use the idea of genre to study discourse communities.[2] We examine several contexts of language exchange in which the use of genre theory may yield insight into teaching, research, and social interaction: legal practice, medical practice, and classrooms. Illustrating how genres can sometimes restrict access to communities, Amy Devitt examines jury instructions as a genre, considering how the genre affects the interactions of jurors in ways that inhibit the successful execution of their duties. Anis Bawarshi suggests how a specific textual genre, the patient medical-history form, works in and provides critical access into doctors' offices. Mary Jo Reiff discusses how the combination of ethnography and genre analysis can give teachers, researchers, and students clearer ways to understand their classrooms.

Together, the essays suggest how genre analysis contributes to the use of ethnomethodology as a research technique that focuses on language and society and that is especially eligible to contribute to the pedagogy of text-dependent subject matters. Whether we are studying academic, professional, or public communities, genres, considered as material entities, enable us to enrich the idea of a discourse community by giving discipline and focus to the study of the unities of language and society.

AMY J. DEVITT, "WHERE COMMUNITIES COLLIDE: EXPLORING A LEGAL GENRE"

Contemporary genre analysis focuses on the actual uses of texts, in all their messiness and with all their potential consequences. Genre analysis also ties that use to actual language, to the smaller bits of language that alert analysts to underlying ideas, values, and beliefs. Such analysis often reveals the conflicts between communities that use a genre, conflicts often invisible to analysis that looks at discourse in terms of its communities alone. This essay analyzes some genres, particularly jury instructions, that are created within one professional community to be used by nonmembers of that community. While their purposes seem to be inclusive, to give nonmembers access to the community's knowledge, genre analysis strongly suggests that the specialist and nonspecialist users have different beliefs, interests, and purposes as well as levels of knowledge. The consequences for both the professional communities and the larger society are significant, potentially drawing the boundaries around professional communities even more tightly. In order to keep from substituting one abstracted concept for another, to keep from idealizing and homogenizing the realities of genres, students should also see the messiness and especially the exclusiveness of genres.

Because genres represent their communities, they effect and make conse-

quential the communities' interests. But it is when genres encompass participants beyond a narrow community that the effects of those interests become
most troublesome. Surprisingly, many genres are designed within one specialist community for functions to be filled by nonmembers of that community.
Tax forms are designed by the IRS, but they are supposedly meant to be used
by people who may know little of tax regulations. The fact that so many people
hire specialists to complete their tax forms merely confirms the difficulty of
the task of translating specialists' knowledge into laypersons' actions. An
especially significant recent example is the ballot, both the propositions on it
and the physical construction of it. Ballots are created by politicians but are
completed by citizens. Ballots contain propositions that voters vote on, but
the propositions are written by lawyers and knowledgeable proponents of an
issue. To have our votes count, as we learned in the United States so vividly so
recently, we must not only feel informed enough to be willing to walk into the
voting booth (not always an easy task as the issues become ever more complicated and our politicians' explanations ever more simplified into sound bites);
we must also be able to understand the ballot once we are in the booth. The
genre of the ballot question makes it difficult to understand what is at issue.
Typical ballot questions combine explanatory statements with legislative amend-
ments, but the explanatory statements can rarely explain enough to enable the
voter to understand the amendment. Even the physical layout of the ballot, we
have learned, entails specialized but unstated knowledge, and good citizens
must decipher where to punch, mark, and pull, and with what definiteness and
strength. To mark a ballot seems a simple thing, but the community of election
commissioners actually brings specialist knowledge to the interpretation of
those ballots — knowledge not explained in the ballot genre. The specialists know
what a chad is, for one thing, and understand what the machines will and will
not count, how much must be punched for a vote to register. The specialists
know that drawing a line through one candidate's name will render that ballot
invalid, while the good citizen might know only that drawing such a line is a
known way to register displeasure. Even without getting into the language of
provisions, often unintelligible to even the most educated voters, the ballot as
a genre includes complications and presumptions that serve the interests of
the specialist creators but not of the nonspecialist users.

In fact, much of our civic lives involves genres that come out of a community
of specialists, whether lawyers, legislators, or government employees. Doing our
civic duty depends as much on our ability to understand and use genres accurately as it does on our willingness to be good citizens. Yet the difficulty remains
of community-embedded genres producing action by nonmembers of that
community. Although the borders of communities are more permeable and fluid
than the community metaphor suggests, clashes of knowledge and perspective
still result when specialists and nonspecialists meet, clashes that have consequences in terms of how participants interact, perform their actions, and produce certain effects in the world.

The inclusion of nonspecialists is vital to the U.S. judicial system, with the usually final decisions made not by all-knowing judges but by everyday citizens. Instructions to juries are designed to explain enough of the law so that a jury of peers can render an appropriate verdict. But jury instructions are written by lawyers, with their details hammered out by lawyers and the judge arguing privately, away from the ears of the jurors who must use them. By the time the judge gives a jury instructions, those instructions contain presumptions, implications, specifications known well by the law community but unknown to the unsuspecting jury members. The genre thus has a significance for the legal community that it does not have for the jurors. As a result, juries do not and cannot interpret the genre the way its creators intended, as lawyers would, and cannot render verdicts that follow those instructions fully and accurately, thus resulting in significant consequences, particularly for defendants.

One recent example turned on a single word (see Mathis). Michael Sharp was convicted of child endangerment in 1999 after he held on to his three-week-old daughter while police were trying to arrest him on an outstanding warrant. His girlfriend and a police officer testified that he seemed to be holding the baby carefully. Before long, Sharp handed the child to officers. At his trial, the judge in the case instructed the jury to find Sharp guilty if they found he had put the girl in a situation where her "body or health might be injured or endangered." The jury rendered a verdict of guilty. The problem, according to Sharp's lawyer and an appeals court, is that the word "might" has a different meaning in law than in common usage. The word has a different weight to each party; it is material in different ways. Courts define "might" as saying an action was probable, not merely possible. Since the jury instructions did not explain the court's meaning of "might," the appeals court overturned the verdict and ordered a new trial. As the appeals court judge wrote in his decision, "There is a very real possibility, especially under the facts of this case, that the jury would have returned a different verdict had the term 'might' been properly defined" (qtd. in Mathis). With the community of lawyers defining "might" differently than do nonmembers, can instructions to a jury ever specify the law sufficiently to let the jury do its job according to that law? The genre of jury instructions has a perhaps insurmountable task in needing to tell citizens unaware of legal technicalities how to follow the relevant law in making their decision, a task of making community members out of nonmembers, of getting nonmembers to enact and reproduce the agendas of a specialist community.

This difficulty is especially troubling in the particular jury instructions I have examined in detail, the instructions to a jury in the sentencing phase of a capital case — instructions to a jury deciding whether to sentence a defendant to death. Originally called in to examine potential bias in the pattern of instructions (a set of approved jury instructions that judges commonly use), I eventually worked to rewrite those instructions in order to make them clearer to an ordinary jury. What I discovered is that no matter how much I elaborated, no matter how many assumptions I made explicit, I could not capture in those instructions all the information that the lawyers considered relevant to the jury's task. Clarifying for the jury's purposes clashed with adhering to legal purposes. What seemed a reasonably straightforward genre when I began proved to be a genre mired in its specialized community's expectations and potentially misleading to its nonspecialized users. What was material to me and to juries was not material to lawyers and judges, and vice versa.

Part of the difficulty when specialized communities write to nonspecialist users lies in technical language, a difficulty commonly recognized and often addressed through defining key terms, but most of the difficulty comes from differences of interest and value that definitions cannot control. In capital cases, two key terms are "aggravating" and "mitigating," for juries must weigh aggravating and mitigating circumstances. These terms are so central to the law as well as to the task at hand that no definition or rewording could capture the full technical meaning of these terms to the courts. In addition, each potential juror may have a private sense of the value of these terms. But even greater difficulties arise from the use of common terms to serve specialist interests. The list of aggravating circumstances from the *Pattern Instructions* for the state of Kansas (a set of instructions modeled on existing instructions from other states) itemizes eight possible aggravating circumstances. Some of those circumstances appear to be matters of fact, though surely still contestable: that the defendant authorized someone else to commit the crime, that the defendant was imprisoned for a felony at the time, or that the defendant committed the crime for money, to avoid arrest, or to silence a witness. Other possible aggravating circumstances, though, require jurors to assess not only whether facts were proven but also the degree of seriousness of the crime: that the defendant previously "inflicted great bodily harm, disfigurement, dismemberment, or death on another," that the defendant knowingly "created a great risk of death to more than one person," or that the defendant "committed the crime in an especially heinous, atrocious or cruel manner." "The term 'heinous,'" the instructions continue, "means extremely wicked or shockingly evil; 'atrocious' means outrageously wicked and vile; and 'cruel' means pitiless or designed to inflict a high degree of pain, utter indifference to, or enjoyment of the sufferings of others." The list of aggravating circumstances is full of gradable words with no standard of comparison: "great" bodily harm and risk of death, "serious" mental anguish or physical abuse. Mitigating circumstances similarly depend on judgments of "significant" histories, "extreme" disturbances or distress, "relatively minor" participation, or "substantial" domination and impairment. When I asked about providing some standard or clarifying what is legally defensible, I was told that there is no legally tested standard and so none could be provided.

In fact, the greatness or seriousness of the crime is precisely what the jury is being asked to evaluate. Yet nowhere do the instructions say that. Rather, the jury instructions follow the legal community's need for events to be based in fact rather than value, so circumstances are treated as either existing or not existing. That perspective appears explicitly in the next instruction about burden of proof: the State must prove "that there are one or more aggravating circumstances and that they are not outweighed by any mitigating circumstances." In fact, however, to decide whether an aggravating circumstance exists requires deciding whether the action was great, serious, or, in perhaps the most notorious language, "heinous." For a jury to decide that a crime was "especially heinous" and thus that an aggravating circumstance exists, the jury is told to define "heinous" as "extremely wicked or shockingly evil." Here in the courtroom, in the setting of this specialized community based in logic and reasoning, a jury of peers is told to "determine" and "consider" "evidence" that will allow them to decide "beyond a reasonable doubt" that a crime was "extremely wicked or shockingly evil." The clash of specialized standards with common values produces a very confused genre, not to mention jury. The material language of the genre produces material consequences, for the defendant as well as for the jury's actions and the legal community's use of those actions.

One final example from these jury instructions reveals the subtle form this clash between members and nonmembers of specialist communities can take and how it materializes in actual practices, languages exchanges, and relations. In the instruction just examined, the jury is to decide that "there are one or more aggravating circumstances and that they are not outweighed by any mitigating circumstances." The jury is not told how to weigh these circumstances but rather how not to weigh them:

> In making the determination whether aggravating circumstances exist that are not outweighed by any mitigating circumstances, you should keep in mind that your decision should not be determined by the number of aggravating or mitigating circumstances that are shown to exist. (*Pattern* 56.00-F)

The negatives in these several instructions and the ones that follow compound, to a point that I believe most jurors would have difficulty interpreting: their decision rests on doubting (but not by counting) that some circumstances are not outweighed by others so that the defendant will not be sentenced to death. When I tried to rewrite these instructions to clarify and simplify them, though, I found that those negatives contained vital specialist presumptions. At one point, I suggested the wording, "In determining whether mitigating circumstances outweigh aggravating circumstances, you should not decide by counting the number of mitigating or aggravating circumstances that you believe exist." That revision failed to capture several legal details. Of course, it is not a matter of the jurors believing circumstances exist; they have to be shown to exist, though elsewhere jurors can be persuaded that they exist. (Note again the insistence on circumstances simply existing or not, without acknowledging that the jury must evaluate the severity of the act.) Most seriously of all, the lawyers told me, I had changed the burden of proof. The prosecutors must show that aggravating circumstances exist, first of all, and second that they are not outweighed by mitigating circumstances. The defense does not have to prove that mitigating circumstances outweigh aggravating circumstances. To serve their own purposes, jurors might well begin deliberations by weighing mitigating against aggravating (being careful now not to count), without realizing that they were shifting the burden of proof. Because the materiality of any language depends on how different communities are invested in it, language is considered to be transparent both by jurors and by judges and lawyers. Written by lawyers, the language of jury instructions assumes that the jurors will, like the lawyers, know what is important and know what to do, that the genre will enable nonmembers to behave as members would.

No amount of explication, definition, or simplification can capture the specialized legal knowledge required for a just and fair decision, as defined by the court system. The legal community — and our society — needs these distinctions, established by law and precedent, to be maintained. The genre of jury instructions is meant to guide jurors in following that law. Yet the complexity of the law, the technical nature of its precedents, and, in short, the embeddedness of the genre in its community make it impossible for nonspecialists to understand fully as a specialist would, no matter how well-written, detailed, or rhetorically sophisticated the jury instructions.

Leading to the linguistic and technical complexity of jury instructions is the rhetorical complexity of the situation. Lawyers and judges are in the position of maintaining the law while needing to achieve their goals through the actions of others, the relatively ignorant jurors. Jurors are in the position of deciding another human being's fate based on society's values, while being told to disregard their instincts unless they conform to the law, a law they do not fully understand. The genre of jury instructions attempts to enact those behaviors, but, like all genres, its effects depend on the actions of politically and morally interested people. Jurors must somehow address or respond to the jury instructions, giving those instructions material consequence, but jurors can respond by acting against those instructions. This reality is revealed most explicitly in the concept of jury nullification, in which individual jurors vote not according to the evidence and the law but according to their beliefs about the rightness of the law, the oppression of the defendant's group, or other beliefs and values not represented in the jury instructions or the facts of the case. Even without such explicit political motivation or deliberateness, jurors often decide in ways that may or may not match even the jurors' understanding of the instructions they received. The most immediately significant genre in a capital case is the verdict, a genre with real consequences. Jury instructions try to influence that verdict, but their effectiveness depends not just on the legal community's ability to convey important specialist information but also on the jury's ability and willingness to conform to their expected role. Jury instructions also try to influence future legal actions, whether appeals of this particular case or future similar cases. The material effects of the genre for the legal community cannot be captured in the jury's actions or the verdict alone. Although designed to transcend the narrow interests of the legal community, jury instructions also return to that community, becoming another potential precedent and more specialist knowledge.

Tax forms, ballot questions, jury instructions — all genres designed precisely to bring specialist and nonspecialist communities together — all function in complex linguistic, informational, and rhetorical situations. All genres exist through and depend on human action, so these community-spanning genres, too, depend on the cooperation of participants from multiple communities, on people accepting the roles the genres assign to them and on being able to carry out the tasks expected of them. Since people in fact often have conflicting interests and motivations, the effects of such genres may be unpredictable. Lawyers and judges, for example, surely want a fair and just verdict, but their community's values also emphasize winning, not being overturned on appeal, and building reputations as well as bank accounts. The general populace from which jurors come also wants a fair and just verdict, but that desire interacts with popular notions of fairness and rightness and with individual moral differences, ideas about social injustices, and experiences with the legal system, as well as with concerns for a speedy return to jurors' regular lives and paychecks.

The communal agendas of those who create genres may conflict with the interests of those who use them—users who would ideally reproduce the ideologies and agendas of the legal community, but who do not. To say that the genre of jury instructions—and other similar genres—simply cross community borders is to simplify the complex interaction of individuals and groups, motives and agendas, and to ignore the conflicting consequences of one genre serving different groups. To understand more fully these genres is to understand more fully how the generic materialities are their uses-in-contexts, with serious effects on people's lives.

ANIS BAWARSHI, "USING GENRE TO ACCESS COMMUNITY: THE PERSONAL MEDICAL HISTORY GENRE AS 'FORM OF LIFE'"

As Bruce Herzberg describes it, the concept of discourse community is based on the assumption that "language use in a group is a form of social behavior, that discourse is a means of maintaining and extending the group's knowledge and of initiating new members into the group, and that discourse is epistemic or constitutive of the group's knowledge" (qtd. in Swales 21). Hence the idea of discourse community is built on the premise that what we know and do is connected to the language we use. Such an understanding acknowledges the materiality of language, but does not necessarily give us access and insight into the complex motives, relations, commitments, and consequences that accompany the use of language to get things done in specific situations, as Devitt's examination of jury instructions describes.

Analyzing genres within their lived contexts reveals to students, teachers, and researchers the material strength of those communities and their power over members and nonmembers alike. Whether examining legal, medical, or pedagogical genres, genre study gives us specific access to the sites of language use that make up communities, in all their complexity. When we use genre analysis as ethnomethodological technique, we not only gain access into communities, but also begin to recognize how "lived textualities" interact with and transform "lived experiences." Such recognition becomes especially significant when we are teaching students how to use language to participate more knowledgeably and critically in various sites of language use. Using the genre of the

Patient Medical History Form as an example, I demonstrate how genre analysis gives access to the workings of discourse communities in a way that renders the idea of a discourse community a more tangible, helpful concept for teachers, students, and researchers.

Attention to the Patient Medical History Form (PMHF), a commonly used medical genre, suggests how focusing on a specific textual genre helps us to identify a discourse community by relating it to a specific site of interpersonal activity that most of us have experienced. The PMHF is a good way to understand something about how doctors function and how they treat us as patients. At the same time, it also serves to show that the community is not just a backdrop to language behavior, but a growing, moving environment that includes texts and speech as its constituents, just as people are its members. We compose our discourse communities as we write and speak within them. And genre is a key part of this process.

The idea of genre, despite the work of scholars in literary and rhetorical studies over the last few decades, is still more often than not understood as a transparent lens or conduit for classifying texts. The word *genre*, borrowed from French, means "sort" or "kind," and to study sorts or kinds of things is not thought to be as substantial as to study the things themselves. Genres appear to be transparent when they are understood as ways of classifying texts. But recent scholarship in genre theory has tried to dispel this view by stipulating genres to be language forms that have identifiable and changing roles in interpersonal relations and in larger collective contexts. One of the roots of the word genre is the Latin cognate *gener*, meaning to generate. This etymology suggests that genres *sort* and *generate*. Genres organize and generate the exchanges of language that characterize what we are referring to in this essay as discourse communities.

Carolyn R. Miller has defined genres as typified rhetorical ways of acting in recurring situations (159). Following Miller, Charles Bazerman defines genres as social actions. He writes:

> Genres are not just forms. Genres are forms of life, ways of being. They are frames for social action[, . . .] locations within which meaning is constructed. Genres shape the thoughts we form and the communications by which we interact. Genres are the familiar places we go to create intelligible communicative action with each other and the guideposts we use to explore the unfamiliar. (19)

To claim that genres are environments within which familiar social actions are rhetorically enacted is to understand them as language practices. David Russell calls them *"operationalized* social action[s]" (512) within which communicants come to know specific situations as they enact them in language practices. The extent to which genres organize and generate discourse communities appears vividly in the example of the physician's office. A physician's office might be considered a local discourse community and part of a wider one insofar as its members share language practices and have comparable purposes. These purposes are enacted in social relations that are partly marked by the PMHF, a genre that within the medical profession is one of its Wittgensteinian "forms of life." As patients we recognize this form on our first visit to a physician as one that solicits information regarding our physical data (sex, age, height, weight, and so on) as well as medical history, including prior and recurring physical conditions, past treatments, and a description of current physical symptoms. Included in the genre is also a request for insurance carrier information and then a consent-to-treat statement and a legal release statement, which patients must sign. The form is at once a patient record, a legal document, and an element in a bureaucracy, helping the doctor treat the patient and presumably protecting the doctor from potential lawsuits.

But these are not the genre's only functions. The PMHF also helps organize and generate the social and rhetorical environments within which patients and doctors speak to one another. For example, the fact that the genre is mainly concerned with a patient's physical symptoms suggests that one can isolate physical symptoms and treat them with little to no reference to the patient's state of mind and the effect that state of mind might have on these symptoms. This genre assumes that body and mind are separate and also helps to perpetuate this belief. In so doing, the PMHF reflects Western notions of medicine, notions that are rhetorically naturalized and reproduced by the genre and that are in turn embodied in the way the doctor recognizes, interacts with, and treats the patient as a synecdoche of his or her physical symptoms. For example, it is not uncommon for doctors and nurses to say "I treated a knee injury today" or "The ear infection is in room 3" when referring to patients. The PMHF is at work on the individual, urging the conversion of a person into a patient (an embodied self) prior to his or her meeting with the doctor at the same time as it is at work on the doctor, preparing him or her to meet the individual as an embodied "patient." In this way, the genre is a site for the exchange of language within which participants influence one another and identify their discourse communities. The mental state of patients may not be considered *material* to the injury or illness; conversely, the form tends to discourage patients' reporting of mental or emotional circumstances of injury and illness, with the result that they may be incompletely or inaccurately treated.

The PMHF is one of several related genres that constitute a community one could call "the physician's office." Each of these genres — which could include greetings, oral symptom descriptions, prescriptions, referrals, physical gestures, and explanatory metaphors — is a form of life that is part of other social practices (relations between doctors and patients, nurses and doctors, doctors and other doctors, doctors and pharmacists, and so on), all of which add up to what Amy Devitt has called "genre sets." As such a set, the physician's office is a multigenre community constituted by several interconnected genres, some of which may represent conditions of social conflict. Members of this community "play" various language games: they have multiple ways of identifying themselves and relating to others within the community. In this way genres help counter the idealized view of discourse communities as discursive utopias constituted by homogeneity and consensus. As Bazerman notes, "[G]enres, as perceived and used by individuals, become part of their regularized social relations, communicative landscape, and cognitive organization" (22). These social relations, communicative landscapes, and cognitive organizations, however, are always shifting, always multiple, as they are enacted by individuals within different genres. We can think of genres as the operational sites of discourse communities.

Teachers, students, and researchers gain ethnomethodological access to discourse communities through genre analysis, which enables them to observe how and why individuals use language in specific settings to make specific practices possible. Recognizing the presence of genres helps us to recognize the palpability and complexity of our discourse communities, to reduce their abstract, symbolic status, thereby making discourse communities more visible and accessible to ethnographic inquiry.

The following example, from the research of Anthony Paré, suggests the materialization of genre and its value for ethnographic inquiry. Paré records a portion of a conversation between a social work student, Michael, and his supervisor. The supervisor is responding to Michael's draft of an assessment report, a typical social work genre:

> That's right. So you wrote here, "I contacted." You want to see it's coming from the worker, not you as Michael, but you as the worker. So when I'm sometimes in Intake and [working] as the screener, I write in my Intake Notes "the screener inquired about." . . . So it becomes less personal. You begin to put yourself in the role of the worker, not "I, Michael." [I]t's a headset; it's a beginning. And even in your evaluations . . . the same thing: as opposed to "I," it's "worker," and when we do a CTMSP for placement for long-term care, "the worker." So it positions us, I think. It's not me, it's my role; and I'm in the role of professional doing this job. (67)

In this example, we notice the extent to which the genre becomes the site for the exchange of language and social interaction. The student, Michael, is learning to "play a language game," the genre of the "assessment report." This exchange between social work student and supervisor takes place within the genre, a genre that constitutes the social roles and material relations of social workers — roles as impersonal observers and "professionals" — thus constituting, in part, the community of social work.

It is in the sum of exchanges such as this one, exchanges constituted by the various and sometimes conflicting genres used in different settings, that individuals compose in and compose discourse communities.

MARY JO REIFF, "ACCESSING COMMUNITIES THROUGH THE GENRE OF ETHNOGRAPHY: EXPLORING A PEDAGOGICAL GENRE"

In "The Life of Genre, the Life in the Classroom," Charles Bazerman describes genres as the "road maps" that student writers consult as they navigate "the symbolic landscape" (19). As typical responses to repeated social situations, genres are rhetorical maps that chart familiar or frequently traveled communicative paths and provide guideposts as writers adapt to unfamiliar academic terrain and study parts of society beyond the classroom. Thus understood, genre analysis is well suited for use in ethnographic approaches to writing pedagogy. Exploring the implications of genre for rhetorical instruction, Carolyn R. Miller observes, "For the student, genres serve as keys to understanding how to participate in the actions of a community" (165). Since genres embed and enact a group's purposes, values, and assumptions, they can illuminate a community's discursive behaviors; however, the question of how students gain entrance to and participate in this discursive landscape remains a source of debate.

Taking up the issue of genre analysis in writing instruction, Aviva Freedman poses the following question: "Can the complex web of social, cultural and rhetorical features to which genres respond be explicated at all, or in such a way that can be useful to learners?" (225). Freedman objects to studying genres outside the contexts in which they are found, abstracting them from living situations. Her concern is shared by David Bleich, who argues that genres — like all language use — are not eligible for study once they are considered to be independent of their contexts of use: "[T]he process of study lies always *within* the language-using society. There is no sense in which the language one tries to understand can be thought of as located outside the living situation in which the thinker (who is all the while using the language) is working" (122). Studying genres within the actual contexts of their use — within real human groups — requires "insider" research (Freedman 234), a type of research that can be carried out through the use of ethnography. With its emphasis on participant/observation and on hands-on attention to communities, ethnography enables students to examine communicative actions within living situations and to see first-hand how communities use genres to carry out social actions and agendas.

To understand genres as situated actions, Miller has advocated an ethnomethodological approach, one that "seeks to explicate the knowledge that practice creates" (155) — knowledge rooted in the materiality of circumstances and conditions of actual use of genres. Similarly, Bazerman has argued that "[b]y forging closer links with the related [enterprise] of [. . .] ethnomethodology, genre analysis can play" a major role in investigating communication within social organizations (23). I consider how ethnomethodology as an academic research method and ethnography as a genre of writing that is particularly useful in writing pedagogy can provide more authentic language tasks in classrooms and can give students better access to contexts of language use beyond the classroom.

Certainly ethnography has become an increasing presence in composition as a research method and a pedagogy. However, Wendy Bishop and others distinguish between the general research method of ethnography and the more focused ethnographic writing research, which usually explores particular sites of literacy or particular literacy practices. Clarifying this distinction, Beverly Moss notes, "While ethnography in general is concerned with describing and analyzing a culture, ethnography in composition studies is [. . .] concerned more narrowly with communicative behavior or the interrelationship of language and culture" (156). Ethnography in composition, particularly as a pedagogical approach, is concerned with the general as well as the particular: with the lived experience or behavior of a culture (as in anthropology or sociology) and with the way in which this behavior manifests itself rhetorically.

If ethnographies are understood as studies of communities and their social actions and genres taken to be rhetorical manifestations or maps of a community's actions, then genre analysis is an especially helpful path in ethnographic methodology. In order to investigate a community's social motives and actions, student ethnographers can examine the uses of language associated with these actions (the group's spoken and written genres) by gathering samples of the genre and analyzing what the rhetorical patterns reveal about the community — its purposes, its participants, and its values, beliefs, and ideologies. Ethnography is both a genre (a research narrative) and a mode of genre analysis — a research methodology used to grasp cultural beliefs and behaviors, often through the examination of genres, which are "frames for social action" (Bazerman 19). In "Observing Genres in Action: Towards a Research Methodology," Anthony Paré and Graham Smart propose how ethnographic inquiry and genre analysis work together. Understanding genre as "a rhetorical strategy enacted within a community," they say that "a full appreciation of the part that [social] roles play in the production and use of generic texts can only be gained by observing an organization's drama of interaction, the interpersonal dynamics that surround and support certain texts" (149). Ethnographic observation of a community that foregrounds genre analysis allows researchers to explore more fully the complexity of the group's social roles and actions, actions that constitute the community's repeated rhetorical strategies, or genres.

While students don't have extended periods to carry out ethnographic studies, they can carry out what Bishop has labeled "mini-ethnographies," smaller-scale studies that explore particular literacy events or local phenomena in a community. Marilyn Chapman, in an essay on the role of genre in writing instruction, lists three main teaching interests with regard to genre: "*learning genres*, or widening students' genre repertoires; *learning about genres*, or fostering awareness [. . .] and *learning through genres*, or using genres as tools for thinking and learning in particular situations" (473). Using ethnography in the classroom would address these goals and would have students learn one research genre (ethnography), while they simultaneously use ethnographic techniques to learn about and through other genres. As a result, incorporating ethnography into the classroom ensures that all three of the above interrelated goals are met, giving students access to the material practices of both the classroom community and communities beyond the classroom.

With regard to the first goal, when students are assigned ethnographies, they learn a new genre to add to their repertoire, a research genre that carries with it particular purposes, participants, and agendas. According to Moss, the main purpose of this genre is "to gain a comprehensive view of the social interactions, behaviors, and beliefs of a community or a social group" (155). This purpose casts student researchers, as users of the genre, into dual roles as both participants in the community and observers of the community's interactions. Moss compares the ethnographer to a photographer who both "takes pictures of the community" and is "in the picture at the same time" (154). The process of inquiry and firsthand participant-observation entailed by this genre requires that students engage in several rhetorical strategies: critical and reflective thinking (when deciding upon what actions and artifacts to capture through pictures); what Clifford Geertz called "thick description" (when developing the pictures so that the details are vibrant and the images come to life); an awareness of the multiple audiences who will view the pictures; and, as someone who is also "in the picture," development of an ethos as an expert or producer of knowledge. These rhetorical strategies related to purpose, audience, and persona give rise to a number of rhetorical features and conventions. In order to address an audience and create a credible ethos, writers might include a description of the data-collection methods, an explanation of the data, and a discussion of their implications. To create a representation of lived experience, students might incorporate details, dialogue, and direct quotations from community participants. Students learn a new genre as they employ patternings of language and rhetorical strategies to create an empirically grounded representation of social realities.

The second goal, learning about genres and fostering genre awareness, is also accomplished through the use of ethnography. Since the main goal of an ethnographer, according to Moss, is to gain "increased insight into the ways in which language communities work" (170), it follows that the oral and written genres of groups will play a central role in the investigation of the social context of language use. Geertz defines ethnographies as "interpretations of interpretations" (9), meaning that students must study the genres that community members use to interpret their contexts in order to fully understand and themselves interpret the community.

For example, Susan, a pre-law student in my advanced composition class, carried out a mini-ethnography on the law community. In order to find out how novice members of the community become socialized to the values, beliefs, and knowledge of the community, Susan considered genres such as opinions, wills, deeds, and contracts; she focused her study on the genre of case briefs. She collected samples of constitutional law briefs, which, she recognized, "illustrated the legal community's shared value of commitment to tradition, as well as the need for a standard and convenient form of communicating important and complex legal concepts." While Susan also conducted interviews and observed lawyers in a small local firm, the genre analysis was the focus of her study, which helped to teach others about the habits and traditions of the law community. She learned about the generic features of case briefs, such as the technical terminology, rigid format, and formal style, and she became more aware of how these formal practices reflected and reinscribed the goals of the community. Recognizing that all the briefs follow the same format of presenting sections labeled "case information," "facts of the case," "procedural history," "issue," "holding," and "court reasoning," she surmised that "[e]ven the rigid structure of the format can help with our analysis by suggesting the community's emphasis on logic and order, which are two esteemed values of the profession." For students like Susan, using genre as a site for ethnographic inquiry cultivates a consciousness of the rhetorical strategies that characterize the daily work of a specific kind of professional community. By learning a community's language through its genres, students then have a more realistic sense of what it is to be a member of the community.

The third genre-related teaching interest is learning through genres, using genres to think about and understand particular situations. Ethnography gives students experience with genre analysis and with how research processes change received genres of reporting knowledge. As ethnographers seek to describe a community, they use various genres for research. Before beginning the study, students may write letters to seek permission to observe groups, or they might write proposals for their research or research plans and agendas. During the research, they use several genres such as field notes, journals or activity logs, project chronologies or summaries, progress reports, interview transcripts, even maps. When the research is completed, they may try to write in other genres that the situation warrants, like thank-you notes, self-assessments, peer assessments, or abstracts. Class time might be spent discussing the genre of the interview or the different purposes of descriptive versus analytic field notes. These genres are resources for supporting or extending thinking. Students learn a research genre that depends on genre analysis; they also learn to use, adapt, and possibly change a variety of genres during the different processes of inquiry.

When students carry out ethnographies, they become researchers who are also active social figures participating in and observing how people integrate their language genres with their wider collective purposes. Shifting the usual teacher/student relationship, students assume the role of investigators who are learning to speak from their own authority as researchers. As a result, classrooms become, in part, research sites at which all members are investigating, teaching, and learning. The research genre of ethnography creates a culture of inquiry, with language and genre the foci that lead to combined knowledge of rhetoric, collective values, and the broader purposes of different communities.

Students in these classrooms also help to create their own community while observing "meaningful discourse in authentic contexts," thus accomplishing what Freedman defines as the necessary criteria for learning genres: "exposure to written discourse" combined with "immersion in the relevant contexts" (247). Student ethnographers are able to study the uses of language and genre within real contexts, situations in which "speakers are alive, functioning, changing and interacting" (Bleich 120). Because ethnography is both a research genre (which functions for academic communities) and an approach to genre analysis (which explores communicative actions in groups outside the classroom), ethnographic work in class enables students to compose communities while composing in communities.

NOTES

1. See, for example, John Trimbur's call for a rhetoric of dissensus — a view of community based in "collective explanations of how people differ, where their differences come from, and whether they can live and work together with these differences" (610). See also Bizzell, Harris, Kent, and Leverenz.

2. We thank the many participants in a lively exchange at the 2001 Conference on College Composition and Communication, whose comments on our initial presentation have helped us clarify and elaborate our arguments.

WORKS CITED

Bazerman, Charles. "The Life of Genre, the Life in the Classroom." *Genre and Writing: Issues, Arguments, Alternatives*. Ed. Wendy Bishop and Hans Ostrom. Portsmouth, NH: Boynton, 1997. 19–26.

Bishop, Wendy. *Ethnographic Writing Research: Writing It Down, Writing It Up, and Reading It*. Portsmouth, NH: Boynton, 1999.

Bizzell, Patricia. *Academic Discourse and Critical Consciousness*. Pittsburgh: U of Pittsburgh P, 1992.

Bleich, David. "The Materiality of Language and the Pedagogy of Exchange." *Pedagogy* 1 (2001): 117–41.

Chapman, Marilyn L. "Situated, Social, Active: Rewriting Genre in the Elementary Classroom." *Written Communication* (1999): 469–90.

Devitt, Amy J. "Intertextuality in Tax Accounting: Generic, Referential, and Functional." *Textual Dynamics of the Professions: Historical and Contemporary Studies of Writing in Professional Communities*. Ed. Charles Bazerman and James Paradis. Madison: U of Wisconsin P, 1991. 335–57.

Freedman, Aviva. "Show and Tell? The Role of Explicit Teaching in the Learning of New Genres." *Research in the Teaching of English* 27 (1993): 222–51.

Geertz, Clifford. *The Interpretation of Cultures*. New York: Basic, 1973.

Harris, Joseph. *A Teaching Subject: Composition since 1966*. Englewood Cliffs, NJ: Prentice, 1997.

Kent, Thomas. "On the Very Idea of a Discourse Community." *CCC* 42 (1991): 425–45.

Leverenz, Carrie Shively. "Peer Response in the Multicultural Composition Classroom: Dissensus — A Dream (Deferred)." *JAC* 14 (1994): 167–86.

Mathis, Joel. "Appeal Brings Defining Moment." *Lawrence Journal-World* 4 Nov. 2000: B1.

Miller, Carolyn R. "Genre as Social Action." *Quarterly Journal of Speech* 70 (1984): 151–67. Rpt. in *Genre and the New Rhetoric*. Ed. Aviva Freedman and Peter Medway. London: Taylor, 1994. 23–42.

Moss, Beverly. "Ethnography and Composition: Studying Language at Home." *Methods and Methodologies in Composition Research*. Ed. Gesa Kirsch and Patricia Sullivan. Carbondale: Southern Illinois UP, 1992. 153–71.

Paré, Anthony. "Genre and Identity: Individuals, Institutions, Ideology." *The Rhetoric and Ideology of Genre: Strategies for Stability and Change*. Ed. Richard M. Coe, Lorelei Lingard, and Tatiana Teslenko. Cresskill, NJ: Hampton, 2002. 57–71.

Paré, Anthony, and Graham Smart. "Observing Genres in Action: Towards a Research Methodology." *Genre and the New Rhetoric*. Ed. Aviva Freedman and Peter Medway. Bristol: Taylor, 1994. 146–54.

Pattern Instructions for Kansas — Criminal 3d. Sect. 56.00-B-H. 2000.

Russell, David R. "Rethinking Genre in School and Society: An Activity Theory Analysis." *Written Communication* 14 (1997): 504–54.

Schryer, Catherine. "Records as Genre." *Written Communication* 10 (1993): 200–34.

Swales, John. *Genre Analysis: English in Academic and Research Settings*. Cambridge: Cambridge UP, 1990.

Trimbur, John. "Consensus and Difference in Collaborative Learning." *College English* 51 (1989): 602–16.

Mike Rose

The Language of Exclusion:
Writing Instruction at the University

> *"How many 'minor errors' are acceptable?"*
>   *"We must try to isolate and define those further skills in composition . . ."*
>   *". . . we should provide a short remedial course to patch up any deficiencies."*
>   *"Perhaps the most striking feature of this campus' siege against illiteracy . . ."*
>   *"One might hope that, after a number of years, standards might be set in the*
> high schools which would allow us to abandon our own defensive program."*

These snippets come from University of California and California state legislative memos, reports, and position papers and from documents produced during
a recent debate in UCLA's Academic Senate over whether a course in our freshman writing sequence was remedial. Though these quotations—and a half dozen
others I will use in this essay—are local, they represent a kind of institutional
language about writing instruction in American higher education. There are
five ideas about writing implicit in these comments: Writing ability is judged
in terms of the presence of error and can thus be quantified. Writing is a skill
or a tool rather than a discipline. A number of our students lack this skill and
must be remediated. In fact, some percentage of our students are, for all intents
and purposes, illiterate. Our remedial efforts, while currently necessary, can be
phased out once the literacy crisis is solved in other segments of the educational
system.

This kind of thinking and talking is so common that we often fail to notice
that it reveals a reductive, fundamentally behaviorist model of the development
and use of written language, a problematic definition of writing, and an inaccurate assessment of student ability and need. This way of talking about writing
abilities and instruction is woven throughout discussions of program and curriculum development, course credit, instructional evaluation, and resource allo-
cation. And, in various ways, it keeps writing instruction at the periphery of the
curriculum.

It is certainly true that many faculty and administrators would take issue
with one or more of the above notions. And those of us in writing would bring
current thinking in rhetoric and composition studies into the conversation.
(Though we often—perhaps uncomfortably—rely on terms like "skill" and "remediation.") Sometimes we successfully challenge this language or set up sensible
programs in spite of it. But all too often we can do neither. The language represented in the headnotes of this essay reveals deeply held beliefs. It has a tradition

---

This article is reprinted from *College English* 47.4 (Apr. 1985): 341–59.

381

and a style, and it plays off the fundamental tension between the general education and the research missions of the American university. The more I think about this language and recall the contexts in which I've heard it used, the more I realize how caught up we all are in a political-semantic web that restricts the way we think about the place of writing in the academy. The opinions I have been describing are certainly not the only ones to be heard. But they are strong. Influential. Rhetorically effective. And profoundly exclusionary. Until we seriously rethink it, we will misrepresent the nature of writing, misjudge our students' problems, and miss any chance to effect a true curricular change that will situate writing firmly in the undergraduate curriculum.

Let us consider the college writing course for a moment. Freshman composition originated in 1874 as a Harvard response to the poor writing of *upper-*classmen, spread rapidly, and became and remained the most consistently required course in the American curriculum. Upper division writing courses have a briefer and much less expansive history, but they are currently receiving a good deal of institutional energy and support. It would be hard to think of an ability more desired than the ability to write. Yet, though writing courses are highly valued, even enjoying a boom, they are also viewed with curious eyes. Administrators fund them — often generously — but academic senates worry that the boundaries between high school and college are eroding, and worry as well that the considerable investment of resources in such courses will drain money from the research enterprise. They deny some of the courses curricular status by tagging them remedial, and their members secretly or not-so-secretly wish the courses could be moved to community colleges. Scientists and social scientists underscore the importance of effective writing, yet find it difficult — if not impossible — to restructure their own courses of study to encourage and support writing. More than a few humanists express such difficulty as well. English departments hold onto writing courses but consider the work intellectually second-class. The people who teach writing are more often than not temporary hires; their courses are robbed of curricular continuity and of the status that comes with tenured faculty involvement. And the instructors? Well, they're just robbed.

The writing course holds a very strange position in the American curriculum. It is within this setting that composition specialists must debate and defend and interminably evaluate what they do. And how untenable such activity becomes if the very terms of the defense undercut both the nature of writing and the teaching of writing, and exclude it in various metaphorical ways from the curriculum. We end up arguing with words that sabotage our argument. The first step in resolving such a mess is to consider the language institutions use when they discuss writing. What I want to do in this essay is to look at each of the five notions presented earlier, examine briefly the conditions that shaped their use, and speculate on how it is that they misrepresent and exclude. I will conclude by entertaining a less reductive and exclusionary way to think — and talk — about writing in the academy.

BEHAVIORISM, QUANTIFICATION, AND WRITING

A great deal of current work in fields as diverse as rhetoric, composition studies, psycholinguistics, and cognitive development has underscored the importance of engaging young writers in rich, natural language use. And the movements of the last four decades that have most influenced the teaching of writing — life adjustment, liberal studies, and writing as process — have each, in their very different ways, placed writing pedagogy in the context of broad concerns: personal development and adjustment, a rhetorical-literary tradition, the psychology of composing. It is somewhat curious, then, that a behaviorist approach to writing, one that took its fullest shape in the 1930s and has been variously and severely challenged by the movements that followed it, remains with us as vigorously as it does. It is atomistic, focusing on isolated bits of discourse, error centered, and linguistically reductive. It has a style and a series of techniques that influence pedagogy, assessment, and evaluation. We currently see its influence in workbooks, programmed instruction, and many formulations of behavioral objectives, and it gets most of its airplay in remedial courses. It has staying power. Perhaps we can better understand its resilience if we briefly survey the history that gives it its current shape.

When turn-of-the-century educational psychologists like E. L. Thorndike began to study the teaching of writing, they found a Latin and Greek influenced school grammar that was primarily a set of prescriptions for conducting socially acceptable discourse, a list of the arcane dos and don'ts of usage for the ever-increasing numbers of children — many from lower classes and immigrant groups — entering the educational system. Thorndike and his colleagues also found reports like those issuing from the Harvard faculty in the 1890s which called attention to the presence of errors in handwriting, spelling, and grammar in the writing of the university's entering freshmen. The twentieth-century writing curriculum, then, was focused on the particulars of usage, grammar, and mechanics. Correctness became, in James Berlin's words, the era's "most significant measure of accomplished prose" (*Writing Instruction in Nineteenth-Century American Colleges* [Carbondale: Southern Illinois University Press, 1984], p. 73).

Such particulars suited educational psychology's model of language quite well: a mechanistic paradigm that studied language by reducing it to discrete behaviors and that defined language growth as the accretion of these particulars. The stress, of course, was on quantification and measurement. ("Whatever exists at all exists in some amount," proclaimed Thorndike.[1]) The focus on error — which is eminently measurable — found justification in a model of mind that was ascending in American academic psychology. Educators embraced the late Victorian faith in science.

Thorndike and company would champion individualized instruction and insist on language practice rather than the rote memorization of rules of grammar that characterized nineteenth-century pedagogy. But they conducted their work within a model of language that was tremendously limited, and this model was further supported and advanced by what Raymond Callahan has called "the cult of efficiency," a strong push to apply to education the principles of industrial scientific management (*Education and the Cult of Efficiency* [Chicago: University of Chicago Press, 1962]). Educational gains were defined as products, and the output of products could be measured. Pedagogical effectiveness—which meant cost-effectiveness—could be determined with "scientific" accuracy. This was the era of the educational efficiency expert. (NCTE even had a Committee on Economy of Time in English.) The combination of positivism, efficiency, and skittishness about correct grammar would have a profound influence on pedagogy and research.

This was the time when workbooks and "practice pads" first became big business. Their success could at least partly be attributed to the fact that they were supported by scientific reasoning. Educational psychologists had demonstrated that simply memorizing rules of grammar and usage had no discernible effect on the quality of student writing. What was needed was application of those rules through practice provided by drills and exercises. The theoretical underpinning was expressed in terms of "habit formation" and "habit strength," the behaviorist equivalent of learning—the resilience of an "acquired response" being dependent on the power and number of reinforcements. The logic was neat: specify a desired linguistic behavior as precisely as possible (e.g., the proper use of the pronouns "he" and "him") and construct opportunities to practice it. The more practice, the more the linguistic habit will take hold. Textbooks as well as workbooks shared this penchant for precision. One textbook for teachers presented a unit on the colon.[2] A text for students devoted seven pages to the use of a capital letter to indicate a proper noun.[3] This was also the time when objective tests—which had been around since 1890—enjoyed a sudden rebirth as "new type" tests. And they, of course, were precision incarnate. The tests generated great enthusiasm among educators who saw in them a scientific means accurately and fairly to assess student achievement in language arts as well as in social studies and mathematics. Ellwood Cubberley, the dean of the School of Education at Stanford, called the development of these "new type" tests "one of the most significant movements in all our educational history."[4] Cubberley and his colleagues felt they were on the threshold of a new era.

Research too focused on the particulars of language, especially on listing and tabulating error. One rarely finds consideration of the social context of error, or of its cognitive-developmental meaning—that is, no interpretation of its significance in the growth of the writer. Instead one finds W. S. Guiler tallying the percentages of 350 students who, in misspelling "mortgage," erred by omitting the "t" vs. those who dropped the initial "g."[5] And one reads Grace Ransom's study of students' "vocabularies of errors"—a popular notion that any given student has a more or less stable set of errors he or she commits. Ransom showed that with drill and practice, students ceased making many of the errors that appeared on pretests (though, unfortunately for the theory, a large number of new errors appeared in their posttests).[6] One also reads Luella Cole Pressey's assertion that "everything needed for about 90 per cent of the writing students do . . . appears to involve only some 44 different rules of English composition." And therefore, if mastery of the rules is divided up and allocated to grades 2 through 12, "there is an average of 4.4 rules to be mastered per year."[7]

Such research and pedagogy was enacted to good purpose, a purpose stated well by H. J. Arnold, Director of Special Schools at Wittenberg College:

> [Students'] disabilities are specific. The more exactly they can be located, the more promptly they can be removed. . . . It seems reasonably safe to predict that the elimination of the above mentioned disabilities through adequate remedial drill will do much to remove students' handicaps in certain college courses. ("Diagnostic and Remedial Techniques for College Freshmen," *Association of American Colleges Bulletin,* 16 [1930], pp. 271–272).

The trouble, of course, is that such work is built on a set of highly questionable assumptions: that a writer has a relatively fixed repository of linguistic blunders that can be pinpointed and then corrected through drill, that repetitive drill on specific linguistic features represented in isolated sentences will result in mastery of linguistic (or stylistic or rhetorical) principles, that bits of discourse bereft of rhetorical or conceptual context can form the basis of curriculum and assessment, that good writing is correct writing, and that correctness has to do with pronoun choice, verb forms, and the like.

Despite the fact that such assumptions began to be challenged by the late 30s,[8] the paraphernalia and the approach of the scientific era were destined to remain with us. I think this trend has the staying power it does for a number of reasons, the ones we saw illustrated in our brief historical overview. It gives a method—a putatively objective one—to the strong desire of our society to maintain correct language use. It is very American in its seeming efficiency. And it offers a simple, understandable view of complex linguistic problems. The trend seems to reemerge with most potency in times of crisis: when budgets crunch and accountability looms or, particularly, when "nontraditional" students flood our institutions.[9] A reduction of complexity has great appeal in institutional decision making, especially in difficult times: a scientific-atomistic approach to language, with its attendant tallies and charts, nicely fits an economic/political decision-making model. When in doubt or when scared or when pressed, count.

And something else happens. When student writing is viewed in this particularistic, pseudo-scientific way, it gets defined in very limited terms as a narrow band of inadequate behavior separate from the vastly complex composing that faculty members engage in for a living and delve into for work and for play. And such perception yields what it intends: a behavior that is stripped of its rich cognitive and rhetorical complexity. A behavior that, in fact, looks and feels basic, fundamental, atomistic. A behavior that certainly does not belong in the university.

ENGLISH AS A SKILL

As English, a relatively new course of study, moved into the second and third decades of this century, it was challenged by efficiency-obsessed administrators and legislators. Since the teaching of writing required tremendous resources, English teachers had to defend their work in utilitarian terms. One very successful defense was their characterization of English as a "skill" or "tool subject" that all students had to master in order to achieve in almost any subject and to function as productive citizens. The defense worked, and the utility of English in schooling and in adult life was confirmed for the era.

The way this defense played itself out, however, had interesting ramifications. Though a utilitarian defense of English included for many the rhetorical/conceptual as well as the mechanical/grammatical dimensions of language, the overwhelming focus of discussion in the committee reports and the journals of the 1920s and 1930s was on grammatical and mechanical error. The narrow focus was made even more narrow by a fetish for "scientific" tabulation. One could measure the degree to which students mastered their writing skill by tallying their mistakes.

We no longer use the phrase "tool subject," and we have gone a long way in the last three decades from error tabulation toward revitalizing the rhetorical dimension of writing. But the notion of writing as a skill is still central to our discussions and our defenses: we have writing skills hierarchies, writing skills assessments, and writing skills centers: And necessary as such a notion may seem to be, I think it carries with it a tremendous liability. Perhaps the problem is nowhere more clearly illustrated than in this excerpt from the UCLA academic senate's definition of a university course:

> A university course should set forth an integrated body of knowledge with primary emphasis on presenting principles and theories rather than on developing skills and techniques.

If "skills and techniques" are included, they must be taught "primarily as a means to learning, analyzing, and criticizing theories and principles." There is a lot to question in this definition, but for now let us limit ourselves to the distinction it establishes between a skill and a body of knowledge. The distinction highlights a fundamental tension in the American university: between what Laurence Veysey labels the practical-utilitarian dimension (applied, vocational, educationalist) and both the liberal culture and the research dimensions — the latter two, each in different ways, elevating appreciation and pure inquiry over application (*The Emergence of the American University* [Chicago: University of Chicago Press, 1965]). To discuss writing as a skill, then, is to place it in the realm of the technical, and in the current, research-ascendant American university, that is a kiss of death.

Now it is true that we commonly use the word *skill* in ways that suggest a complex interweaving of sophisticated activity and rich knowledge. We praise the interpretive skills of the literary critic, the diagnostic skills of the physician, the interpersonal skills of the clinical psychologist. Applied, yes, but implying a kind of competence that is more in line with obsolete definitions that equate skill with reason and understanding than with this more common definition (that of the *American Heritage Dictionary*): "An art, trade, or technique, particularly one requiring use of the hands or body." A skill, particularly in the university setting, is, well, a tool, something one develops and refines and completes in order to take on the higher-order demands of purer thought. Everyone may acknowledge the value of the skill (our senate praised our course to the skies as it removed its credit), but it is valuable as the ability to multiply or titrate a solution or use an index or draw a map is valuable. It is absolutely necessary but remains second-class. It is not "an integrated body of knowledge" but a technique, something acquired differently from the way one acquires knowledge — from drill, from practice, from procedures that conjure up the hand and the eye but not the mind. Skills are discussed as separable, distinct, circumscribable activities; thus we talk of subskills, levels of skills, sets of skills. Again writing is defined by abilities one can quantify and connect as opposed to the dynamism and organic vitality one associates with thought.

Because skills are fundamental tools, basic procedures, there is the strong expectation that they be mastered at various preparatory junctures in one's educational career and in the places where such tools are properly crafted. In the case of writing, the skills should be mastered before one enters college and takes on higher-order endeavors. And the place for such instruction — before or after entering college — is the English class. Yes, the skill can be refined, but its fundamental development is over, completed via a series of elementary and secondary school courses and perhaps one or two college courses, often designated remedial. Thus it is that so many faculty consider upper-division and especially graduate-level writing courses as de jure remedial. To view writing as a skill in the university context reduces the possibility of perceiving it as a complex ability that is continually developing as one engages in new tasks with new materials for new audiences.

If the foregoing seems a bit extreme, consider this passage from our Academic Senate's review of UCLA Writing Programs:

> ... it seems difficult to see how *composition* — whose distinctive aspect seems to be the transformation of language from thought or speech to hard copy — represents a distinct further step in shaping cogitation. There don't seem to be persuasive grounds for abandoning the view that composition is still a *skill* attendant to the attainment of overall linguistic competence.

The author of the report, a chemist, was reacting to some of our faculty's assertions about the interweaving of thinking and writing; writing for him is more or less a transcription skill.

So to reduce writing to second-class intellectual status is to influence the way faculty, students, and society view the teaching of writing. This is a bitter pill, but we in writing may have little choice but to swallow it. For, after all, is not writing simply different from "integrated bodies of knowledge" like sociology or biology? Is it? Well, yes and no. There are aspects of writing that would fit a skills model (the graphemic aspects especially). But much current theory and research are moving us to see that writing is not simply a transcribing skill mastered in early development. Writing seems central to the shaping and directing of certain modes of cognition, is integrally involved in learning, is a means of defining the self and defining reality, is a means of representing and contextu-alizing information (which has enormous political as well as conceptual and archival importance), and is an activity that develops over one's lifetime. Indeed it is worth pondering whether many of the "integrated bodies of knowledge" we study, the disciplines we practice, would have ever developed in the way they did and reveal the knowledge they do if writing did not exist. Would history or philosophy or economics exist as we know them? It is not simply that the work of such disciplines is recorded in writing, but that writing is intimately involved in the nature of their inquiry. Writing is not just a skill with which one can pre-sent or analyze knowledge. It is essential to the very existence of certain kinds of knowledge.

REMEDIATION

Since the middle of the last century, American colleges have been establishing various kinds of preparatory programs and classes within their halls to main-tain enrollments while bringing their entering students up to curricular par.[10] One fairly modern incarnation of this activity is the "remedial class," a desig-nation that appears frequently in the education and language arts journals of the 1920s.[11] Since that time remedial courses have remained very much with us: we have remedial programs, remedial sections, remedial textbooks, and, of course, remedial students. Other terms with different twists (like "developmen-tal" and "compensatory") come and go, but "remedial" has staying power. Exactly what the adjective "remedial" means, however, has never quite been clear. To reme-diate seems to mean to correct errors or fill in gaps in a person's knowledge. The implication is that the material being studied should have been learned during prior education but was not. Now the reasons why it was not could vary tremendously: they could rest with the student (physical impairment, motiva-tional problems, intelligence), the family (socio-economic status, stability, the support of reading-writing activities), the school (location, sophistication of the curriculum, adequacy of elementary or secondary instruction), the culture or subculture (priority of schooling, competing expectations and demands), or some combination of such factors. What "remedial" means in terms of curric-ulum and pedagogy is not clear either. What is remedial for a school like UCLA might well be standard for other state or community colleges, and what is con-sidered standard during one era might well be tagged remedial in the next.

It is hard to define such a term. The best definition of remedial I can arrive at is a highly dynamic, contextual one: The function of labelling certain mate-rial remedial in higher education is to keep in place the hard fought for, if historically and conceptually problematic and highly fluid, distinction between college and secondary work. "Remedial" gains its meaning, then, in a political more than a pedagogical universe.

And the political dimension is powerful — to be remedial is to be substandard, inadequate, and, because of the origins of the term, the inadequacy is metaphorically connected to disease and mental defect. It has been difficult to trace the educational etymology of the word "remedial," but what I have uncovered suggests this: Its origins are in law and medicine, and by the late nineteenth century the term fell pretty much in the medical domain and was soon applied to education. "Remedial" quickly generalized beyond the description of students who might have had neurological problems to those with broader, though special, educational problems and then to those normal learners who are not up to a particular set of standards in a particular era at particular institutions. Here is some history.

Most of the enlightened work in the nineteenth century with the training of special populations (the deaf, the blind, the mentally retarded) was conducted by medical people, often in medical settings. And when young people who could hear and see and were of normal intelligence but had unusual — though perhaps not devastating — difficulties began to seek help, they too were examined within a medical framework. Their difficulties had to do with reading and writing — though mostly reading — and would today be classified as learning disabilities. One of the first such difficulties to be studied was dyslexia, then labelled "congenital word blindness."

In 1896 a physician named Morgan reported in the pages of *The British Medical Journal* the case of a "bright and intelligent boy" who was having great difficulty learning to read. Though he knew the alphabet, he would spell some words in pretty unusual ways. He would reverse letters or drop them or write odd combinations of consonants and vowels. Dr. Morgan examined the boy and had him read and write. The only diagnosis that made sense was one he had to borrow and analogize from the cases of stroke victims, "word blindness," but since the child had no history of cerebral trauma, Morgan labelled his condition "*congenital* word blindness" (W. Pringle Morgan, "A Case of Congenital Word Blindness," *The British Medical Journal*, 6, Part 2 [1896], 1378). Within the next two decades a number of such cases surfaced; in fact another English physician, James Hinshelwood, published several books on congenital word blindness.[12] The explanations were for the most part strictly medical, and, it should be noted, were analogized from detectable cerebral pathology in adults to conditions with no detectable pathology in children.

In the 1920s other medical men began to advance explanations a bit different from Morgan's and Hinshelwood's. Dr. Samuel Orton, an American physician, posed what he called a "cerebral physiological" theory that directed thinking away from trauma analogues and toward functional explanations. Certain areas of the brain were not defective but underdeveloped and could be corrected through "remedial effort." But though he posed a basically educational model for dyslexia, Dr. Orton's language should not be overlooked. He spoke of "brain habit" and the "handicap" of his "physiological deviates."[13] Though his theory was different from that of his forerunners, his language, significantly, was still medical.

As increasing access to education brought more and more children into the schools, they were met by progressive teachers and testing experts interested in assessing and responding to individual differences. Other sorts of reading and writing problems, not just dyslexia, were surfacing, and increasing numbers of teachers, not just medical people, were working with the special students. But the medical vocabulary — with its implied medical model — remained dominant. People tried to *diagnose* various *disabilities, defects, deficits, deficiencies,* and *handicaps,* and then tried to *remedy* them.[14] So one starts to see all sorts of reading/writing problems clustered together and addressed with this language. For example, William S. Gray's important monograph, *Remedial Cases in Reading: Their Diagnosis and Treatment* (Chicago: University of Chicago Press, 1922), listed as "specific causes of failure in reading" inferior learning capacity, congenital word blindness, poor auditory memory, defective vision, a narrow span of recognition, ineffective eye movements, inadequate training in phonetics, inadequate attention to the content, an inadequate speaking vocabulary, a small meaning vocabulary, speech defects, lack of interest, and timidity. The remedial paradigm was beginning to include those who had troubles as varied as bad eyes, second language interference, and shyness.[15]

It is likely that the appeal of medical-remedial language had much to do with its associations with scientific objectivity and accuracy — powerful currency in the efficiency-minded 1920s and 30s. A nice illustration of this interaction of influences appeared in Albert Lang's 1930 textbook, *Modern Methods in Written Examinations* (Boston: Houghton Mifflin, 1930). The medical model is quite explicit:

> teaching bears a resemblance to the practice of medicine. Like a successful physician, the good teacher must be something of a diagnostician. The physician by means of a general examination singles out the individuals whose physical defects require a more thorough testing. He critically scrutinizes the special cases until he recognizes the specific troubles. After a careful diagnosis he is able to prescribe intelligently the best remedial or corrective measures. (p. 38)

By the 1930s the language of remediation could be found throughout the pages of publications like *English Journal,* applied now to writing (as well as reading and mathematics) and to high school and college students who had in fact learned to write but were doing so with a degree of error thought unacceptable. These were students — large numbers of them — who were not unlike the students who currently populate our "remedial" courses: students from backgrounds that did not provide optimal environmental and educational opportunities, students who erred as they tried to write the prose they thought the academy required, second-language students. The semantic net of "remedial" was expanding and expanding.

There was much to applaud in this focus on writing. It came from a progressive era desire to help *all* students progress through the educational system. But the theoretical and pedagogical model that was available for "corrective teaching" led educators to view writing problems within a medical-remedial paradigm. Thus they set out to diagnose as precisely as possible the errors (defects) in a student's paper — which they saw as symptomatic of equally isolable defects in the student's linguistic capacity — and devise drills and exercises to remedy them. (One of the 1930s nicknames for remedial sections was "sick sections." During the next decade they would be tagged "hospital sections.") Such corrective teaching was, in the words of H. J. Arnold, "the most logical as well as the most scientific method" ("Diagnostic and Remedial Techniques for College Freshmen," p. 276).

These then are the origins of the term, remediation. And though we have, over the last fifty years, moved very far away from the conditions of its origins and have developed a richer understanding of reading and writing difficulties, the term is still with us. A recent letter from the senate of a local liberal arts college is sitting on my desk. It discusses a "program in remedial writing for . . . [those] entering freshmen suffering from severe writing handicaps." We seem entrapped by this language, this view of students and learning. Dr. Morgan has long since left his office, but we still talk of writers as suffering from specifiable, locatable defects, deficits, and handicaps that can be localized, circumscribed, and remedied. Such talk reveals an atomistic, mechanistic-medical model of language that few contemporary students of the use of language, from educators to literary theorists, would support. Furthermore, the notion of remediation, carrying with it as it does the etymological wisps and traces of disease, serves to exclude from the academic community those who are so labelled. They sit in scholastic quarantine until their disease can be diagnosed and remedied.

ILLITERACY

In a recent meeting on graduation requirements, a UCLA dean referred to students in remedial English as "the truly illiterate among us." Another administrator, in a memorandum on the potential benefits of increasing the number of composition offerings, concluded sadly that the increase "would not provide any assurance of universal literacy at UCLA." This sort of talk about illiteracy is common. We hear it from college presidents, educational foundations, pop grammarians, and scores of college professors like the one who cried to me after a recent senate meeting, "All I want is a student who can write a simple declarative sentence!" We in the academy like to talk this way.[16] It is dramatic and urgent, and, given the current concerns about illiteracy in the United States, it is topical. The trouble is, it is wrong. Perhaps we can better understand the problems with such labelling if we leave our colleagues momentarily and consider what it is that literacy means.

To be literate means to be acquainted with letters or writings. But exactly how such acquaintance translates into behavior varies a good deal over time and place. During the last century this country's Census Bureau defined as literate anyone who could write his or her name. These days the government requires that one be able to read and write at a sixth-grade level to be *functionally* literate: that is, to be able to meet — to a minimal degree — society's reading and writing demands. Things get a bit more complex if we consider the other meanings "literacy" has acquired. There are some specialized uses of the term, all fairly new: computer literacy, mathematical literacy, visual literacy, and so on. Literacy here refers to an acquaintance with the "letters" or elements of a particular field or domain. And there are also some very general uses of the term. Cultural literacy, another new construction, is hard to define because it is so broad and so variously used, but it most often refers to an acquaintance with the humanistic, scientific, and social scientific achievements of one's dominant culture. Another general use of the term, a more traditional one, refers to the attainment of a liberal education, particularly in belles-lettres. Such literacy, of course, is quite advanced and involves not only an acquaintance with a literary tradition but interpretive sophistication as well.

Going back over these definitions, we can begin by dismissing the newer, specialized uses of "literacy." Computer literacy and other such literacies are usually not the focus of the general outcries we have been considering. How about the fundamental definition as it is currently established? This does not seem applicable either, for though many of the students entering American universities write prose that is grammatically and organizationally flawed, with very few exceptions they can read and write at a sixth-grade level. A sixth-grade proficiency is, of course, absurdly inadequate to do the work of higher education, but the definition still stands. By the most common measure the vast majority of students in college are literate. When academics talk about illiteracy they are saying that our students are "without letters" and cannot "write a simple declarative sentence." And such talk, for most students in most segments of higher education, is inaccurate and misleading.

One could argue that though our students are literate by common definition, a significant percentage of them might not be if we shift to the cultural and belletristic definitions of literacy or to a truly functional-contextual definition: that is, given the sophisticated, specialized reading and writing demands of the university — and the general knowledge they require — then it might be appropriate to talk of a kind of cultural illiteracy among some percentage of the student body. These students lack knowledge of the achievements of a tradition and are not at home with the ways we academics write about them. Perhaps this use of illiteracy is more warranted than the earlier talk about simple declarative sentences, but I would still advise caution. It is my experience that American college students tend to have learned more about western culture through their twelve years of schooling than their papers or pressured classroom responses demonstrate. (And, of course, our immigrant students bring with them a different cultural knowledge that we might not tap at all.) The problem is that the knowledge these students possess is often incomplete and fragmented and is not organized in ways that they can readily use in academic writing situations. But to say this is not to say that their minds are cultural blank slates.

There is another reason to be concerned about inappropriate claims of illiteracy. The term illiteracy comes to us with a good deal of semantic baggage, so that while an appropriately modified use of the term may accurately denote, it can still misrepresent by what it suggests, by the traces it carries from earlier eras. The social historian and anthropologist Shirley Brice Heath points out that from the mid-nineteenth century on, American school-based literacy was identified with "character, intellect, morality, and good taste . . . literacy skills co-occurred with moral patriotic character."[17] To be literate is to be honorable and intelligent. Tag some group illiterate, and you've gone beyond letters; you've judged their morals and their minds.

Please understand, it is not my purpose here to whitewash the very real limitations a disheartening number of our students bring with them. I dearly wish that more of them were more at home with composing and could write critically better than they do. I wish they enjoyed struggling for graceful written language more than many seem to. I wish they possessed more knowledge about humanities and the sciences so they could write with more authority than they usually do. And I wish to God that more of them read novels and poems for pleasure. But it is simply wrong to leap from these unrequited desires to claims of illiteracy. Reading and writing, as any ethnographic study would show, are woven throughout our students' lives. They write letters; some keep diaries. They read about what interests them, and those interests range from rock and roll to computer graphics to black holes. Reading, for many, is part of religious observation. They carry out a number of reading and writing acts in their jobs and in their interactions with various segments of society. Their college preparatory curriculum in high school, admittedly, to widely varying degrees, is built on reading, and even the most beleaguered schools require some kind of writing. And many of these students read and even write in languages other than English. No, these students are not illiterate, by common definition, and if the more sophisticated definitions apply, they sacrifice their accuracy by all they imply.

Illiteracy is a problematic term. I suppose that academics use it because it is rhetorically effective (evoking the specter of illiteracy to an audience of peers, legislators, or taxpayers can be awfully persuasive) or because it is emotionally satisfying. It gives expression to the frustration and disappointment in teaching students who do not share one's passions. As well, it affirms the faculty's membership in the society of the literate. One reader of this essay suggested to me that academics realize the hyperbole in their illiteracy talk, do not really mean it to be taken, well, literally. Were this invariably true, I would still voice concern over such exaggeration, for, as with any emotionally propelled utterance, it might well be revealing deeply held attitudes and beliefs, perhaps not unlike those discussed by Heath. And, deeply felt or not, such talk in certain political and decision-making settings can dramatically influence the outcomes of deliberation.

The fact remains that cries of illiteracy substitute a fast quip for careful analysis. Definitional accuracy here is important, for if our students are in fact adult illiterates, then a particular, very special curriculum is needed. If they are literate but do not read much for pleasure, or lack general knowledge that is central to academic inquiry, or need to write more than they do and pay more attention to it than they are inclined to, well, then these are very different problems. They bring with them quite different institutional commitments and pedagogies, and they locate the student in a very different place in the social-political makeup of the academy. Determining that place is crucial, for where but in the academy would being "without letters" be so stigmatizing?

THE MYTH OF TRANSIENCE

I have before me a report from the California Postsecondary Education Commission called *Promises to Keep*. It is a comprehensive and fair-minded assessment of remedial instruction in the three segments of California's public college and university system. As all such reports do, *Promises to Keep* presents data on instruction and expenses, discusses the implications of the data, and calls for reform. What makes the report unusual is its inclusion of an historical overview of preparatory instruction in the United States. It acknowledges the fact that such instruction in some guise has always been with us. In spite of its acknowledgment, the report ends on a note of optimism characteristic of similar documents with less historical wisdom. It calls for all three segments of the higher education system to "implement . . . plans to reduce remediation" within five years and voices the hope that if secondary education can be improved, "within a very few years, the state and its institutions should be rewarded by . . . lower costs for remediation as the need for remediation declines." This optimism in the face of a disconfirming historical survey attests to the power of what I will call the myth of transience. Despite the accretion of crisis reports, the belief persists in the American university that if we can just do x or y, the problem will be solved — in five years, ten years, or a generation — and higher education will be able to return to its real work. But entertain with me the possibility that such peaceful reform is a chimera.

Each generation of academicians facing the characteristic American shifts in demographics and accessibility sees the problem anew, laments it in the terms of the era, and optimistically notes its impermanence. No one seems to say that this scenario has gone on for so long that it might not be temporary. That, in fact, there will probably *always* be a significant percentage of students who do not meet some standard. (It was in 1841, not 1985 that the president of Brown complained, "Students frequently enter college almost wholly unacquainted with English grammar . . ." [Frederick Rudolph, *Curriculum: A History of the American Undergraduate Course of Study* (San Francisco: Jossey-Bass, 1978), p. 88].) The American higher educational system is constantly under pressure to expand, to redefine its boundaries, admitting, in turn, the sons of the middle class, and later the daughters, and then the American poor, the immigrant poor, veterans, the racially segregated, the disenfranchised. Because of the social and educational conditions these groups experienced, their preparation for college will, of course, be varied. Add to this the fact that disciplines change and society's needs change, and the ways society determines what it means to be educated change.

All this works itself rather slowly into the pre-collegiate curriculum. Thus there will always be a percentage of students who will be tagged substandard. And though many insist that this continued opening of doors will sacrifice excellence in the name of democracy, there are too many economic, political, and ethical drives in American culture to restrict higher education to a select minority. (And, make no mistake, the history of the American college and university from the early nineteenth century on could also be read as a history of changes in admissions, curriculum, and public image in order to keep enrollments high and institutions solvent.[18] The research institution as we know it is made possible by robust undergraduate enrollments.) Like it or not, the story of American education has been and will in all likelihood continue to be a story of increasing access. University of Nashville President Philip Lindsley's 1825 call echoes back and forth across our history: "The farmer, the mechanic, the manufacturer, the merchant, the sailor, the soldier . . . must be educated" (Frederick Rudolph, *The American College and University: A History* [New York: Vintage, 1962] p. 117).

Why begrudge academics their transience myth? After all, each generation's problems are new to those who face them, and people faced with a problem need some sense that they can solve it. Fair enough. But it seems to me that this myth brings with it a powerful liability. It blinds faculty members to historical reality and to the dynamic and fluid nature of the educational system that employs them. Like any golden age or utopian myth, the myth of transience assures its believers that the past was better or that the future will be.[19] The turmoil they are currently in will pass. The source of the problem is elsewhere; thus it can be ignored or temporarily dealt with until the tutors or academies or grammar schools or high schools or families make the changes they must make. The myth, then, serves to keep certain fundamental recognitions and thus certain fundamental changes at bay. It is ultimately a conservative gesture, a way of preserving administrative and curricular status quo.

And the myth plays itself out against complex social-political dynamics. One force in these dynamics is the ongoing struggle to establish admissions requirements that would protect the college curriculum, that would, in fact, define its difference from the high school course of study. Another is the related struggle to influence, even determine, the nature of the high school curriculum, "academize" it, shape it to the needs of the college (and the converse struggle of the high school to declare its multiplicity of purposes, college preparation being only one of its mandates). Yet another is the tension between the undergraduate, general education function of the university vs. its graduate, research function. To challenge the myth is to vibrate these complex dynamics; thus it is that it is so hard to dispel. But I would suggest that it must be challenged, for though some temporary "remedial" measures are excellent and generously funded, the presence of the myth does not allow them to be thought through in terms of the whole curriculum and does not allow the information they reveal to reciprocally influence the curriculum. Basic modifications in educational philosophy, institutional purpose, and professional training are rarely considered. They do not need to be if the problem is temporary. The myth allows the final exclusionary gesture: The problem is not ours in any fundamental way; we can embrace it if we must, but with surgical gloves on our hands.

There may be little anyone can do to change the fundamental tension in the American university between the general educational mission and the research mission, or to remove the stigma attached to application. But there is something those of us involved in writing can do about the language that has formed the field on which institutional discussions of writing and its teaching take place.

We can begin by affirming a rich model of written language development and production. The model we advance must honor the cognitive and emotional and situational dimensions of language, be psycholinguistic as well as literary and rhetorical in its focus, and aid us in understanding what we can observe as well as what we can only infer. When discussions and debates reveal a more reductive model of language, we must call time out and reestablish the terms of the argument. But we must also rigorously examine our own teaching and see what model of language lies beneath it. What linguistic assumptions are cued when we face freshman writers? Are they compatible with the assumptions that are cued when we think about our own writing or the writing of those we read for pleasure? Do we too operate with the bifurcated mind that for too long characterized the teaching of "remedial" students and that is still reflected in the language of our institutions?

Remediation. It is time to abandon this troublesome metaphor. To do so will not blind us to the fact that many entering students are not adequately prepared to take on the demands of university work. In fact, it will help us perceive these young people and the work they do in ways that foster appropriate notions about language development and use, that establish a framework for more rigorous and comprehensive analysis of their difficulties, and that do not perpetuate the raree [sic] show of allowing them entrance to the academy while, in various symbolic ways, denying them full participation.

Mina Shaughnessy got us to see that even the most error-ridden prose arises from the confrontation of inexperienced student writers with the complex linguistic and rhetorical expectations of the academy. She reminded us that to properly teach writing to such students is to understand "the intelligence of their mistakes."[20] She told us to interpret errors rather than circle them, and to guide these students, gradually and with wisdom, to be more capable participants within the world of these conventions. If we fully appreciate her message, we see how inadequate and limiting the remedial model is. Instead we need to define our work as transitional or as initiatory, orienting, or socializing to what David Bartholomae and Patricia Bizzell call the academic discourse community.[21] This redefinition is not just semantic sleight-of-hand. If truly adopted, it would require us to reject a medical deficit model of language, to acknowledge the rightful place of all freshmen in the academy, and once and for all to replace loose talk about illiteracy with more precise and pedagogically fruitful analysis. We would move from a mechanistic focus on error toward a demanding curriculum that encourages the full play of language activity and that opens out onto the academic community rather than sequestering students from it.

A much harder issue to address is the common designation of writing as a skill. We might begin by considering more fitting terms. Jerome Bruner's "enabling discipline" comes to mind. It does not separate skill from discipline and implies something more than a "tool subject" in that to enable means to make possible. But such changes in diction might be little more than cosmetic.

If the skills designation proves to be resistant to change, then we must insist that writing is a very unique skill, not really a tool but an ability fundamental to academic inquiry, an ability whose development is not fixed but ongoing. If it is possible to go beyond the skills model, we could see a contesting of the fundamental academic distinction between integrated bodies of knowledge and skills and techniques. While that distinction makes sense in many cases, it may blur where writing is concerned. Do students really *know* history when they learn a "body" of facts, even theories, or when they act like historians, thinking in certain ways with those facts and theories? Most historians would say the latter. And the academic historian (vs. the chronicler or the balladeer) conducts inquiry through writing; it is not just an implement but is part of the very way of doing history.

It is in this context that we should ponder the myth of transience. The myth's liability is that it limits the faculty's ability to consider the writing problems of their students in dynamic and historical terms. Each academic generation considers standards and assesses the preparation of its students but seems to do this in ways that do not call the nature of the curriculum of the time into question. The problem ultimately lies outside the academy. But might not these difficulties with writing suggest the need for possible far-ranging changes within the curriculum as well, changes that *are* the proper concern of the university? One of the things I think the myth of transience currently does is to keep faculty from seeing the multiple possibilities that exist for incorporating writing throughout their courses of study. Profound reform could occur in the much-criticized lower-division curriculum if writing were not seen as only a technique and the teaching of it as by and large a remedial enterprise.

The transmission of a discipline, especially on the lower-division level, has become very much a matter of comprehending information, committing it to memory, recalling it, and displaying it in various kinds of "objective" or short-answer tests. When essay exams are required, the prose all too often becomes nothing more than a net in which the catch of individual bits of knowledge lie. Graders pick through the essay and tally up the presence of key phrases. Such activity trivializes a discipline; it reduces its methodology, grounds it in a limited theory of knowledge, and encourages students to operate with a restricted range of their cognitive abilities. Writing, on the other hand, assumes a richer epistemology and demands fuller participation. It requires a complete, active, struggling engagement with the facts and principles of a discipline, an encounter with the discipline's texts and the incorporation of them into one's own work, the framing of one's knowledge within the myriad conventions that help define a discipline, the persuading of other investigators that one's knowledge is legitimate. So to consider the relationship between writing and disciplinary inquiry may help us decide what is central to a discipline and how best to teach it. The university's research and educational missions would intersect.

Such reform will be difficult. True, there is growing interest in writing adjuncts and discipline-specific writing courses, and those involved in writing-across-the-curriculum are continually encouraging faculty members to evaluate the place of writing in their individual curricula. But wide-ranging change will occur only if the academy redefines writing for itself, changes the terms of the argument, sees instruction in writing as one of its central concerns.

Academic senates often defend the labelling of a writing course as remedial by saying that they are defending the integrity of the baccalaureate, and they are sending a message to the high schools. The schools, of course, are so beleaguered that they can barely hear those few units ping into the bucket. Consider, though, the message that would be sent to the schools and to the society at large if the university embraced — not just financially but conceptually — the teaching of writing: if we gave it full status, championed its rich relationship with inquiry, insisted on the importance of craft and grace, incorporated it into the heart of our curriculum. What an extraordinary message that would be. It would affect the teaching of writing as no other message could.

Author's note: I wish to thank Arthur Applebee, Robert Connors, Carol Hartzog, and William Schaefer for reading and generously commenting on an earlier version of this essay. Connors and Hartzog also helped me revise that version. Bill Richey provided research assistance of remarkably high caliber, and Tom Bean, Kenyon Chan, Patricia Donahue, Jack Kolb, and Bob Schwegler offered advice and encouragement. Finally, a word of thanks to Richard Lanham for urging me to think of our current problem in broader contexts.

NOTES

1. Quoted in Lawrence A. Cremin, *The Transformation of the School: Progressivism in American Education* (New York: Alfred A. Knopf, 1961), p. 185.

2. Arthur N. Applebee, *Tradition and Reform in the Teaching of English: A History* (Urbana. Ill.: National Council of Teachers of English, 1974), pp. 93–94.

3. P. C. Perrin, "The Remedial Racket," *English Journal*, 22 (1993), 383.

4. From Cubberley's introduction to Albert R. Lang, *Modern Methods in Written Examinations* (Boston: Houghton Mifflin, 1930), p. vii.

5. "Background Deficiencies," *Journal of Higher Education*, 3 (1932), 371.

6. "Remedial Methods in English Composition," *English Journal*, 22 (1933), 749–75.

7. "Freshmen Needs in Written English," *English Journal*, 19 (1930), 706.

8. I would mislead if I did not point out that there were cautionary voices being raised all along, though until the late 1930s they were very much in the minority. For two early appraisals, see R. L. Lyman, *Summary of Investigations Relating to Grammar, Language, 2nd Composition* (Chicago: University of Chicago Press, 1924), and especially P. C. Perrin, "The Remedial Racket," *English Journal*, 22 (1933), 382–388.

9. Two quotations. The first offers the sort of humanist battle cry that often accompanies reductive drill, and the second documents the results of such an approach. Both from NCTE publications.

"I think . . . that the chief objective of freshman English (at least for the first semester and low or middle — but not high — sections) should be ceaseless, brutal drill on mechanics with exercises and themes. Never mind imagination, the soul, literature, for at least one semester, but pray for literacy and fight for it" (A University of Nebraska professor quoted with approval in Oscar James Campbell, *The Teaching of College English* [New York: Appleton Century, 1934], pp. 36–37).

"Members of the Task Force saw in many classes extensive work in traditional schoolroom grammar and traditional formal English usage. They commonly found students with poor reading skills being taught the difference between *shall* and *will* or pupils with serious difficulties in speech diagramming sentences. Interestingly, observations by the Task Force reveal far more extensive teaching of traditional grammar in this study of language programs for the disadvantaged than observers saw in the National Study of High School English Programs, a survey of comprehensive high schools known to be achieving important results in English with college-bound students able to comprehend the abstractions of such grammar" (Richard Corbin and Muriel Crosby, *Language Programs for the Disadvantaged* [Urbana Ill.: NCTE, 1965], pp. 121–122).

10. In 1894, for example, over 40% of entering freshmen came from the preparatory divisions of the institutions that enrolled them. And as late as 1915 — a time when the quantity and quality of secondary schools had risen sufficiently to make preparatory divisions less necessary — 350 American colleges still maintained their programs. See John S. Brubacher and Willis Rudy, *Higher Education in Transition: A History of American Colleges and Universities, 1636–1976*, 3rd ed. (New York: Harper and Row, 1976), pp. 241 ff., and Arthur Levine, *Handbook on Undergraduate Curriculum* (San Francisco: Jossey-Bass, 1981), pp. 54 ff.

11. Several writers point to a study habits course initiated at Wellesley in 1894 as the first modern remedial course in higher education (K. Patricia Cross, *Accent on Learning* [San Francisco: Jossey-Bass, 1979], and Arthur Levine, *Handbook on Undergraduate Curriculum*). In fact, the word "remedial" did not appear in the course's title and the course was different in kind from the courses actually designated "remedial" that would emerge in the 1920s and 30s. (See Cross, pp. 24–25, for a brief discussion of early study skills courses.) The first use of the term "remedial" in the context I am discussing was most likely in a 1916 article on the use of reading tests to plan "remedial work" (Nila Banton Smith, *American Reading Instruction* [Newark, Delaware: International Reading Association, 1965]. p. 191). The first elementary and secondary level remedial courses in reading were offered in the early 1920s; remedial courses in college would not appear until the late 20s.

12. *Letter, Word, and Mind-Blindness* (London: Lewis, 1902); *Congenital Word Blindness* (London: Lewis, 1917).

13. "The 'Sight Reading' Method of Teaching Reading, as a Source of Reading Disability," *Journal of Educational Psychology*, 20 (1929), 135–143.

14. There were, of course, some theorists and practitioners who questioned medical-physiological models, Arthur Gates of Columbia Teacher's College foremost among them. But even those who questioned such models — with the exception of Gates — tended to retain medical language.

15. There is another layer to this terminological and conceptual confusion. At the same time that remediation language was being used ever more broadly by some educators, it maintained its strictly medical usage in other educational fields. For example, Annie Dolman Inskeep has only one discussion of "remedial work" in her book *Teaching Dull and Retarded Children* (New York: Macmillan, 1926), and that discussion has to do with treatment for children needing health care: "Children who have poor teeth, who do not hear well, or who hold a book when reading nearer than eight inches to the eyes or further away than sixteen. . . . Nervous children, those showing continuous fatigue symptoms, those under weight, and those who are making no apparent bodily growth" (p. 271).

16. For a sometimes humorous but more often distressing catalogue of such outcries, see Harvey A. Daniels, *Famous Last Words* (Carbondale: Southern Illinois University Press, 1983), especially pp. 31–58.

17. "Toward an Ethnohistory of Writing in American Education," in Marcia Farr Whiteman, ed., *Writing: The Nature, Development, and Teaching of Written Communication,* Vol. 1 (Hillsdale, N.J.: Erlbaum, 1981), 35–36.

18. Of turn-of-the-century institutions, Laurence Veysey writes: "Everywhere the size of enrollments was closely tied to admission standards. In order to assure themselves of enough students to make a notable "splash," new institutions often opened with a welcome to nearly all corners, no matter how ill prepared; this occurred at Cornell, Stanford, and (to a lesser degree) at Chicago" (*The Emergence of the American University,* p. 357).

19. An appropriate observation here comes from Daniel P. and Lauren B. Resnick's critical survey of reading instruction and standards of literacy: "there is little to go back to in terms of pedagogical method, curriculum, or school organization. The old tried and true approaches, which nostalgia prompts us to believe might solve current problems, were designed neither to achieve the literacy standard sought today nor to assure successful literacy for everyone . . . there is no simple past to which we can return" ("The Nature of Literacy: An Historical Exploration," *Harvard Educational Review,* 47 [1977], 385).

20. *Errors and Expectations* (New York: Oxford University Press, 1977), p. 11.

21. David Bartholomae, "Inventing the University," in Mike Rose, ed., *When a Writer Can't Write: Studies in Writer's Block and Other Composing Process Problems* (New York: Guilford, 1985); Patricia Bizzell, "College Composition: Initiation into the Academic Discourse Community," *Curriculum Inquiry,* 12 (1982), 191–207.

Jacqueline Jones Royster

When the First Voice
You Hear Is Not Your Own

This essay emerged from my desire to examine closely moments of personal challenge that seem to have import for cross-boundary discourse. These types of moments have constituted an ongoing source of curiosity for me in terms of my own need to understand human difference as a complex reality, a reality that I have found most intriguing within the context of the academic world. From a collectivity of such moments over the years, I have concluded that the most salient point to acknowledge is that "subject" position really is everything.

Using subject position as a terministic screen in cross-boundary discourse permits analysis to operate kaleidoscopically, thereby permitting interpretation to be richly informed by the converging of dialectical perspectives. Subjectivity as a defining value pays attention dynamically to context, ways of knowing, language abilities, and experience, and by doing so it has a consequent potential to deepen, broaden, and enrich our interpretive views in dynamic ways as well. Analytical lenses include the process, results, and impact of negotiating identity, establishing authority, developing strategies for action, carrying forth intent with a particular type of agency, and being compelled by external factors and internal sensibilities to adjust belief and action (or not). In a fundamental way, this enterprise supports the sense of rhetoric, composition, and literacy studies as a field of study that embraces the imperative to understand truths and consequences of language use more fully. This enterprise supports also the imperative to reconsider the beliefs and values which inevitably permit our attitudes and actions in discourse communities (including colleges, universities, and classrooms) to be systematic, even systemic.

Adopting subjectivity as a defining value, therefore, is instructive. However, the multidimensionality of the instruction also reveals the need for a shift in paradigms, a need that I find especially evident with regard to the notion of "voice," as a central manifestation of subjectivity. My task in this essay, therefore, is threefold. First, I present three scenes which serve as my personal testimony as "subject." These scenes are singular in terms of their being my own stories, but I believe that they are also plural, constituting experiential data that I share with many. My sense of things is that individual stories placed one against another against another build credibility and offer, as in this case, a litany of evidence from which a call for transformation in theory and practice might rightfully begin. My intent is to suggest that my stories in the company of others demand thoughtful response.

This article is reprinted from *College Composition and Communication* 47.1 (Feb. 1996): 29–40.

[Second,] I draw from these scenes a specific direction for transformation, suggesting dimensions of the nature of voicing that remain problematic. My intent is to demonstrate that our critical approaches to voice, again as a central manifestation of subjectivity, are currently skewed toward voice as a spoken or written phenomenon. This intent merges the second task with the third in that I proceed to suggest that theories and practices should be transformed. The call for action in cross-boundary exchange is to refine theory and practice so that they include voicing as a phenomenon that is constructed and expressed visually and orally, *and* as a phenomenon that has import also in being a *thing* heard, perceived, and reconstructed.

SCENE ONE

I have been compelled on too many occasions to count to sit as a well-mannered Other, silently, in a state of tolerance that requires me to be as expressionless as I can manage, while colleagues who occupy a place of entitlement different from my own talk about the history and achievements of people from my ethnic group, or even about their perceptions of our struggles. I have been compelled to listen as they have comfortably claimed the authority to engage in the construction of knowledge and meaning about me and mine, without paying even a passing nod to the fact that sometimes a substantive version of that knowledge might already exist, or to how it might have already been constructed, or to the meanings that might have already been assigned that might make me quite impatient with gaps in their understanding of my community, or to the fact that I, or somebody within my ethnic group, might have an opinion about what they are doing. I have been compelled to listen to speakers, well-meaning though they may think they are, who signal to me rather clearly that subject position is everything. I have come to recognize, however, that when the subject matter is me and the voice is not mine, my sense of order and rightness is disrupted. In metaphoric fashion, these "authorities" let me know, once again, that Columbus has discovered America and claims it now, claims it still for a European crown.

Such scenes bring me to the very edge of a principle that I value deeply as a teacher and a scholar, the principle of the right to inquiry and discovery. When the discovering hits so close to home, however, my response is visceral, not just intellectual, and I am made to look over a precipice. I have found it extremely difficult to allow the voices and experiences of people that I care about deeply to be taken and handled so carelessly and without accountability by strangers.

At the extreme, the African American community, as my personal example, has seen and continues to see its contributions and achievements called into question in grossly negative ways, as in the case of *The Bell Curve*. Such interpretations of who we are as a people open to general interrogation, once again, the innate capacities of "the race" as a whole. As has been the case throughout our history in this country, we are put in jeopardy and on trial in a way that should not exist but does. We are compelled to respond to a rendering of our potential that demands, not that we account for attitudes, actions, and conditions, but that we defend ourselves as human beings. Such interpretations of human potential create a type of discourse that serves as a distraction, as noise that drains off energy and sabotages the work of identifying substantive problems within and across cultural boundaries and the work also of finding solutions that have import, not simply for "a race," but for human beings whose living conditions, values, and preferences vary.

All such close encounters, the extraordinarily insidious ones and the ordinary ones, are definable through the lens of subjectivity, particularly in terms of the power and authority to speak and to make meaning. An analysis of subject position reveals that these interpretations by those outside of the community are not random acts of unkindness. Instead, they embody ways of seeing, knowing, being, and acting that probably suggest as much about the speaker and the context as they do about the targeted subject matter. The advantage with this type of analysis, of course, is that we see the obvious need to contextualize the stranger's perspective among other interpretations and to recognize that an interpretive view is just that—interpretive. A second advantage is that we also see that in our nation's practices these types of interpretations, regardless of how superficial or libelous they may actually be within the context of a more comprehensive view, tend to have considerable consequence in the lives of the targeted group, people in this case whose own voices and perspectives remain still largely under considered and uncredited.

Essentially, though, having a mechanism to see the under considered helps us see the extent to which we add continually to the pile of evidence in this country of cross-cultural misconduct. These types of close encounters that disregard dialectical views are a type of free touching of the powerless by the power-full. This analytical perspective encourages us to acknowledge that marginalized communities are not in a good position to ward off the intrusion of those authorized in mainstream communities to engage in willful action. Historically, such actions have included everything from the displacement of native people from their homelands, to the use of unknowing human subjects in dangerous experiments, to the appropriation and misappropriation of cultural artifacts—art, literature, music, and so on. An insight using the lens of subjectivity, however, is a recognition of the ways in which these moments are indeed moments of violation, perhaps even ultimate violation.

This record of misconduct means that for people like me, on an instinctive level, all outsiders are rightly perceived as suspect. I suspect the genuineness of their interest, the altruism of their actions, and the probability that whatever is being said or done is not to the ultimate benefit and understanding of the people who are subject matter but not subjects. People in the neighborhood where I grew up would say, "Where is their home training?" Imbedded in the question is the idea that when you visit other people's "home places," especially when you have not been invited, you simply cannot go tramping around the house like you own the place, no matter how smart you are, or how much imagination you can muster, or how much authority and entitlement outside that home you may be privileged to hold. And you certainly cannot go around name calling, saying things like, "You people are intellectually inferior and have a limited capacity to achieve," without taking into account who the family is, what its living has been like, and what its history and achievement have been about.

The concept of "home training" underscores the reality that point of view matters and that we must be trained to respect points of view other than our own. It acknowledges that when we are away from home, we need to know that what we think we see in places that we do not really know very well may not actually be what is there at all. So often, it really is a matter of time, place, resources, and our ability to perceive. Coming to judgment too quickly, drawing on information too narrowly, and saying hurtful, discrediting, dehumanizing things without undisputed proof are not appropriate. Such behavior is not good manners. What comes to mind for me is another saying that I heard constantly when I was growing up, "Do unto others as you would have them do unto you." In this case, we would be implored to draw conclusions about others with care and, when we do draw conclusions, to use the same type of sense and sensibility that we would ideally like for others to use in drawing conclusions about us.

This scene convinces me that what we need in a pressing way in this country and in our very own field is to articulate codes of behavior that can sustain more concretely notions of honor, respect, and good manners across boundaries, with cultural boundaries embodying the need most vividly. Turning the light back onto myself, though, at the same time that my sense of violation may indeed be real, there is the compelling reality that many communities in our nation need to be taken seriously. We all deserve to be taken seriously, which means that critical inquiry and discovery are absolutely necessary. Those of us who love our own communities, we think, most deeply, most uncompromisingly, without reservation for what they are and also are not, must set aside our misgivings about strangers in the interest of the possibility of deeper understanding (and for the more idealistic among us, the possibility of global peace). Those of us who hold these communities close to our hearts, protect them, and embrace them; those who want to preserve the goodness of the minds and souls in them; those who want to preserve consciously, critically, and also lovingly the record of good work within them must take high risk and give over the exclusivity of our rights to know.

It seems to me that the agreement for inquiry and discovery needs to be deliberately reciprocal. All of us, strangers and community members, need to find ways to sustain productivity in what Pratt calls contact zones, areas of engagement that in all likelihood will remain contentious. We need to get over our tendencies to be too possessive and to resist locking ourselves into the tunnels of our own visions and direct experience. As community members, we must learn to have new faith in the advantage of sharing. As strangers, we must learn to treat the loved people and places of Others with care and to understand that, when we do not act respectfully and responsibly, we leave ourselves rightly open to wrath. The challenge is not to work with a fear of abuse or a fear of retaliation, however. The challenge is to teach, to engage in research, to write, and to speak with Others with the determination to operate not only with professional and personal integrity, but also with the specific knowledge that communities and their ancestors are watching. If we can set aside our rights to exclusivity in our own home cultures, if we can set aside the tendencies that we all have to think too narrowly, we actually leave open an important possibility. In our nation, we have little idea of the potential that a variety of subjectivities — operating with honor, respect, and reasonable codes of conduct — can bring to critical inquiry or critical problems. What might happen if we treated differences in subject position as critical pieces of the whole, vital to thorough understanding, and central to both problem-finding and problem-solving? This society has not, as yet, really allowed that privilege in a substantial way.

SCENE TWO

As indicated in Scene One, I tend to be enraged at what Tillie Olsen has called the "trespass vision," a vision that comes from intellect and imagination (62), but typically not from lived experience, and sometimes not from the serious study of the subject matter. However, like W. E. B. Du Bois, I've chosen not to be distracted or consumed by my rage at voyeurs, tourists, and trespassers, but to look at what I can do. I see the critical importance of the role of negotiator, someone who can cross boundaries and serve as guide and translator for Others.

In 1903, Du Bois demonstrated this role in *The Souls of Black Folk*. In the "Forethought" of that book, he says: "Leaving, then, the world of the white man, I have stepped within the Veil, raising it that you may view faintly its deeper recesses — the meaning of its religion, the passion of its human sorrow, and the struggle of its greater souls" (1). He sets his rhetorical purpose to be to cross, or at least to straddle boundaries with the intent of shedding light, a light that has the potential of being useful to people on both sides of the veil. Like Du Bois, I've accepted the idea that what I call my "home place" is a cultural community that exists still quite significantly beyond the confines of a well-insulated community that we call the "mainstream," and that between this world and the one that I call home, systems of insulation impede the vision and narrow the ability to recognize human potential and to understand human history both microscopically and telescopically.

Like Du Bois, I've dedicated myself to raising this veil, to overriding these systems of insulation by raising another voice, my voice in the interest of clarity and accuracy. What I have found too often, however, is that, unlike those who have been entitled to talk about me and mine, when I talk about my own, I face what I call the power and function of deep disbelief, and what Du Bois described as, "the sense of always looking at one's self through the eyes of others, of measuring one's soul by the tape of a world that looks on in amused contempt and pity" (5).

An example comes to mind. When I talk about African-American women, especially those who were writing non-fiction prose in the nineteenth century, I can expect, even today after so much contemporary scholarship on such writers, to see people who are quite flabbergasted by anything that I share. Reflected on their faces and in their questions and comments, if anyone can manage to speak back to me, is a depth of surprise that is always discomforting. I sense that the surprise, or the silence, if there is little response, does not come from the simple ignorance of unfortunate souls who just happen not to know what I have spent years coming to know. What I suspect is that this type of surprise rather "naturally" emerges in a society that so obviously has the habit of expecting nothing of value, nothing of consequence, nothing of importance, nothing at all positive from its Others, so that anything is a surprise; everything is an exception; and nothing of substance can really be claimed as a result.

In identifying this phenomenon, Chandra Talpade Mohanty speaks powerfully about the ways in which this culture coopts, dissipates, and displaces voices. As demonstrated by my example, one method of absorption that has worked quite well has been essentially rhetorical. In discussing nineteenth century African American women's work, I bring tales of difference and adventure. I bring cultural proofs and instructive examples, all of which invariably must serve as rites of passage to credibility. I also bring the power of story telling. These tales of adventure in odd places are the transitions by which to historicize and theorize anew with these writers re-inscribed in a rightful place. Such a process respects long-standing practices in African-based cultures of theorizing in narrative form. As Barbara Christian says, we theorize "in the stories we create, in riddles and proverbs, in the play with language, since dynamic rather than fixed ideas seem more to our liking" (336).

The problem is that in order to construct new histories and theories such stories must be perceived not just as "simple stories" to delight and entertain, but as vital layers of a transformative process. A reference point is Langston Hughes and his Simple stories, stories that are a model example of how apparent simplicity has the capacity to unmask truths in ways that are remarkably accessible—through metaphor, analogy, parable, and symbol. However, the problem of articulating new paradigms through stories becomes intractable, if those who are empowered to define impact and consequence decide that the stories are simply stories and that the record of achievement is perceived, as Audre Lorde has said, as "the random droppings of birds" (Foreword xi).

If I take my cue from the life of Ida Wells, and I am bold enough and defiant enough to go beyond the presentation of my stories as juicy tidbits for the delectation of audiences, to actually shift or even subvert a paradigm, I'm much more likely to receive a wide-eyed stare and to have the value and validity of my conceptual position held at a distance, in doubt, and wonderfully absorbed in the silence of appreciation. Through the systems of deep disbelief I become a storyteller, a performer. With such absorptive ability in the systems of interpretation, I have greater difficulty being perceived as a person who theorizes without the mediating voices of those from the inner sanctum, or as a person who might name myself a philosopher, a theorist, a historian who creates paradigms that allow the experiences and the insights of people like me to belong.

What I am compelled to ask when veils seem more like walls is who has the privilege of speaking first? How do we negotiate the privilege of interpretation? When I have tried to fulfill my role as negotiator, I have often walked away knowing that I have spoken, but also knowing, as Anna Julia Cooper knew in 1892, that my voice, like her voice, is still a muted one. I speak, but I can not be heard. Worse, I am heard but I am not believed. Worse yet, I speak but I am not deemed believable. These moments of deep disbelief have helped me to understand much more clearly the wisdom of Audre Lorde when she said: "I have come to believe over and over again that what is most important to me must be spoken, made verbal and shared, even at the risk of having it bruised or misunderstood" (*Sister* 40). Lorde teaches me that, despite whatever frustration and vulnerability I might feel, despite my fear that no one is listening to me or is curious enough to try to understand my voice, it is still better to speak (*Black* 31). I set aside the distractions and permeating noise outside of myself, and I listen, as Howard Thurman recommended, to the sound of the genuine within. I go to a place inside myself and, as Opal Palmer Adisa explains, I listen and learn to "speak without clenching my teeth" (56).

SCENE THREE

There have been occasions when I have indeed been heard and positively received. Even at these times, however, I sometimes can not escape responses that make me most weary. One case in point occurred after a presentation in which I had glossed a scene in a novel that required cultural understanding. When the characters spoke in the scene, I rendered their voices, speaking and explaining, speaking and explaining, trying to translate the experience, to share the sounds of my historical place and to connect those sounds with systems of belief so that deeper understanding of the scene might emerge, and so that those outside of the immediacy of my home culture, the one represented in the novel, might see and understand more and be able to make more useful connections to their own worlds and experiences.

One, very well-intentioned response to what I did that day was, "How wonderful it was that you were willing to share with us your 'authentic' voice!" I said, "My 'authentic' voice?" She said, "Oh yes! I've never heard you talk like that, you know, so relaxed. I mean, you're usually great, but this was really great! You weren't so formal. You didn't have to speak in an appropriated academic language. You sounded 'natural.' It was nice to hear you be yourself." I said, "Oh, I see. Yes, I do have a range of voices, and I take quite a bit of pleasure actually in being able to use any of them at will." Not understanding the point that I was trying to make gently, she said, "But this time, it was really you. Thank you."

The conversation continued, but I stopped paying attention. What I didn't feel like saying in a more direct way, a response that my friend surely would have perceived as angry, was that all my voices are authentic, and like bell hooks, I find it "a necessary aspect of self-affirmation not to feel compelled to choose one voice over another, not to claim one as more authentic, but rather to construct social realities that celebrate, acknowledge, and affirm differences, variety" (12). Like hooks, I claim all my voices as my own very much authentic voices, even when it's difficult for others to imagine a person like me having the capacity to do that.

From moments of challenge like this one, I realize that we do not have a paradigm that really allows for what scholars in cultural and postcolonial studies (Anzuldua, Spivak, Mohanty, Bhaba) have called hybrid people — people who either have the capacity by right of history and development, or who might have created the capacity by right of history and development, to move with dexterity across cultural boundaries, to make themselves comfortable, and to make sense amid the chaos of difference.

As Cornel West points out, most African Americans, for example, dream in English, not in Yoruba, or Hausa, or Wolof. Hybrid people, as demonstrated by the history of Africans in the Western hemisphere, manage a fusion process that allows for survival, certainly. However, it also allows for the development of a peculiar expertise that extends one's range of abilities well beyond ordinary limits, and it supports the opportunity for the development of new and remarkable creative expression, like spirituals, jazz, blues, and what I suspect is happening also with the essay as genre in the hands of African American women. West notes that somebody gave Charlie Parker a saxophone, Miles Davis a trumpet, Hubert Laws a flute, and Les McCann a piano. I suggest that somebody also gave Maria Stewart, Gertrude Mossell, Frances Harper, Alice Walker, Audre Lorde, Toni Morrison, Patricia Williams, June Jordan, bell hooks, Angela Davis and a cadre of other African American women a pencil, a pen, a computer keyboard. In both instances, genius emerges from hybridity, from Africans who, over the course of time and circumstance, have come to dream in English, and I venture to say that all of their voices are authentic.

In sharing these three scenes, I emphasize that there is a pressing need to construct paradigms that permit us to engage in better practices in cross-boundary discourse, whether we are teaching, researching, writing, or talking with Others, whoever those Others happen to be. I would like to emphasize, again, that we look again at "voice" and situate it within a world of symbols, sound, and sense, recognizing that this world operates symphonically. Although the systems of voice production are indeed highly integrated and appear to have singularity in the ways that we come to sound, voicing actually sets in motion multiple systems[;] prominent among them are systems for speaking but present also are the systems for hearing. We speak within systems that we know significantly through our abilities to negotiate noise and to construct within that noise sense and sensibility.

Several questions come to mind. How can we teach, engage in research, write about, and talk across boundaries *with* others, instead of for, about, and around them? My experiences tell me that we need to do more than just talk and talk back. I believe that in this model we miss a critical moment. We need to talk, yes, and to talk back, yes, but when do we listen? How do we listen? How do we demonstrate that we honor and respect the person talking and what that person is saying, or what the person might say if we valued someone other than ourselves having a turn to speak? How do we translate listening into language and action, into the creation of an appropriate response? How do we really "talk back" rather than talk also? The goal is not, "You talk, I talk." The goal is better practices so that we can exchange perspectives, negotiate meaning, and create understanding with the intent of being in a good position to cooperate, when, like now, cooperation is absolutely necessary.

When I think about this goal, what stands out most is that these questions apply in so much of academic life right now. They certainly apply as we go into classrooms and insist that our students trust us and what we contend is in their best interest. In light of a record in classrooms that seriously questions the range of our abilities to recognize potential, or to appreciate students as non-generic human beings, or to appreciate that they bring with them, always, knowledge, we ask a lot when we ask them to trust. Too often, still, institutionalized equations for placement, positive matriculation, progress, and achievement name, categorize, rank, and file, while our true-to-life students fall between the cracks. I look again to Opal Palmer Adisa for an instructive example. She says:

> Presently, many academics advocate theories which, rather than illuminating the works under scrutiny, obfuscate and problematize these works so that students are rendered speechless. Consequently, the students constantly question what they know, and often, unfortunately, they conclude that they know nothing. (54)

Students may find what we do to be alienating and disheartening. Even when our intentions are quite honorable, silence can descend. Their experiences are not seen, and their voices are not heard. We can find ourselves participating, sometimes consciously, sometimes not, in what Patricia Williams calls "spirit murder" (55). I am reminded in a disconcerting way of a troubling scene from Alex Haley's *Roots*. We engage in practices that say quite insistently to a variety of students in a variety of ways, "Your name is Toby." Why wouldn't students wonder: Who can I trust here? Under what kinds of conditions? When? Why?

In addition to better practices in our classrooms, however, we can also question our ability to talk convincingly with deans, presidents, legislators, and the general public about what we do, how we do it, and why. We have not been conscientious about keeping lines of communication open, and we are now experiencing the consequences of talking primarily to ourselves as we watch funds being cut, programs being eliminated, and national agencies that are vital to our interests being bandied about as if they are post-it notes, randomly stuck on by some ill-informed spendthrift. We must learn to raise a politically active voice with a socially responsible mandate to make a rightful place for education in a country that seems always ready to place the needs of quality education on a sideboard instead of on the table. Seemingly, we have been forever content to let voices other than our own speak authoritatively about our areas of expertise and about us. It is time to speak for ourselves, in our own interests, in the interest of our work, and in the interest of our students.

Better practices are not limited, though, even to these concerns. Of more immediate concern to me this year, given my role as Chair of CCCC, is how to talk across boundaries within our own organization as teachers of English among other teachers of English and Language Arts from kindergarten through university with interests as varied as those implied by the sections, conferences, and committees of our parent organization, the National Council of Teachers of English (NCTE). Each of the groups within NCTE has its own set of needs, expectations, and concerns, multiplied across the amazing variety of institutional sites across which we work. In times of limited resources and a full slate of critical problems, we must find reasonable ways to negotiate so that we can all thrive reasonably well in the same place.

In our own case, for years, now, CCCC has recognized changes in our relationships with NCTE. Since the mid-1980s we have grown exponentially. The field of rhetoric and composition has blossomed and diversified. The climate for higher education has increasingly degenerated, and we have struggled in the midst of change to forge a more satisfying identity and a more positive and productive working relationship with others in NCTE who are facing crises of their own. After 50 years in NCTE, we have grown up, and we have to figure out a new way of being and doing in making sure that we can face our challenges well. We are now in the second year of a concerted effort to engage in a multi-leveled conversation that we hope will leave CCCC well-positioned to face a new century and ongoing challenges. Much, however, depends on the ways in which we talk and listen and talk again in crossing boundaries and creating, or not, the common ground of engagement.

As I look at the lay of this land, I endorse Henry David Thoreau's statement when he said, "Only that day dawns to which we are awake" (267). So my appeal is to urge us all to be awake, awake and listening, awake and operating deliberately on codes of better conduct in the interest of keeping our boundaries fluid, our discourse invigorated with multiple perspectives, and our policies and practices well-tuned toward a clearer respect for human potential and achievement from whatever their source and a clearer understanding that voicing at its best is not just well-spoken but also well-heard.

WORKS CITED

Adisa, Opal Palmer. "I Must Write What I Know So I'll Know That I've Known It All Along." *Sage: A Scholarly Journal on Black Women* 9.2 (1995): 54–57.

Anzaldua, Gloria. *Borderlands/La Frontera*. San Francisco: Aunt Lute. 1987.

Bhabha, Homi K. *The Location of Culture*. London: Routledge, 1994.

Christian, Barbara. "The Race for Theory." *Cultural Critique* 6 (1987): 335–45.

Cooper, Anna Julia. *A Voice from the South*. New York: Oxford UP, 1988.

Du Bois, W. E. B. *The Souls of Black Folk*. New York: Grammercy, 1994.

Haley, Alex. *Roots*. Garden City: Doubleday, 1976.

Hernstein, Richard J., and Charles Murray. *The Bell Curve: Intelligence and Class Structure in American Life*. New York: Free, 1994.

hooks, bell. *Talking Back: Thinking Feminist, Thinking Black*. Boston: South End, 1989.

Lorde, Audre, *The Black Unicorn*. New York: Norton, 1978.

——. Foreword. *Wild Women in the Whirlwind*. Ed. Joanne M. Braxton and Andree Nicola McLaughlin. New Brunswick: Rutgers UP. 1990. xi–xiii.

——. *Sister Outsider*. Freedom: The Crossing Press, 1984.

Mohanty, Chandra Talpade. "On Race and Voice: Challenges for Liberal Education in the 1990s." *Cultural Critique* 14 (Winter 1989–90): 179–208.

——. "Decolonizing Education: Feminisms and the Politics of Multiculturalism in the 'New' World Order." Ohio State University. Columbus, April 1994.

Olsen, Tillie, *Silences*. New York: Delta, 1978.

Pratt, Mary Louise. "Arts of the Contact Zone." *Profession* 91 (1991): 33–40.

Spivak, Gayatri Chakravorty. *In Other Worlds: Essays in Cultural Politics*. New York: Routledge, 1988.

Thoreau, Henry David. *Walden*. New York: Vintage, 1991.

Thurman, Howard. "The Sound of the Genuine." Spelman College, Atlanta, April 1981.

West, Cornel. "Race Matters." Ohio State U, Columbus, OH, February 1995.

Williams, Patricia. *The Alchemy of Race and Rights*. Cambridge: Harvard UP, 1991.

Stephanie L. Kerschbaum   2012

Avoiding the Difference Fixation: Identity Categories, Markers of Difference, and the Teaching of Writing

When I was about a year old, my parents noticed that I did not react to loud noises, so they sat me in my high chair, stood behind me, and banged on some pots and pans. I didn't so much as flinch. In that moment, their interpretation of me as "a really laid-back baby" became "She's deaf, and that's why she doesn't get upset when Johnny yells or the dog barks." That re-categorization created new ways for them to make sense of my behavior: it is not that my parents didn't connect with me prior to learning that I have a profound hearing loss in both ears, but that the frame through which they made sense of me changed. Similarly, my own relationship to my disability has shifted, and continues to shift, over time and across contexts. Deafness does not exist for me as some concrete fact of my life with an absolute meaning that I can readily define for readers here and now in this article. Deafness takes on different meanings in a variety of institutional and social contexts, mediated through human relationships and technologies of all kinds. My deafness is very different from my friend Tom's deafness, and the two of us experience deafness very differently than does my grandmother. Yet even these comparisons are flawed because none of the three of us has an entirely stable "sort" of deafness whose meaning transcends the particular interactional contexts in which we find ourselves. Although I can describe to *College Composition and Communication* readers my deafness, explain ways that Tom, myself, and my grandmother embody different kinds of deafness, and portray some of the ways that each of us addresses our deafness in our daily lives, such explanations are only partial and passing because deafness, like any other identity category, is to be understood both through the contexts in which we communicate and act *and* by our embodiments of it.

This discussion of deafness illustrates a conundrum that exists across studies of difference in writing research: even as scholars of difference frame identity as, in Helen Fox's words, "multiple, or layered, or ever changing" (256), there is little understanding of how such understandings are constructed and negotiated on a moment-by-moment basis. In other words, how is knowledge about groups (e.g., deaf people) brought to bear on interactions with individual

---

This article is reprinted from *College Composition and Communication* 63.4 (June 2012): 616–44.

412

people affiliated with those groups (such as myself, Tom, or my grandmother)? Or, considered from another direction, how does knowledge gleaned through interaction with me, Tom, or my grandmother contribute to a collective awareness about deaf people? These questions point to concerns about essentialism and determinism as well as about how individual identities intersect with broader cultural categories. As Fox notes, descriptions of cultural groups are often seen as "'traditional' or unchanging, rather than as systems that blend and shift in response to pressures from the environment and their own members' ingenuity" (259). Such framing of cultural groups in relatively static terms highlights one of the challenges faced by contemporary writing studies scholars: that of using discourses about difference to attend simultaneously to broad group characteristics and to instability within categories. To address this issue, many writing researchers have described their own complex relationships to language, identity, and knowledge (e.g., hooks; Okawa; Villanueva; Young). However, writing teachers — particularly those new to teaching — frequently express anxiety about how to bring this nuance and richness into their classroom practices. In order to more fully respond to questions about how awareness of broad categories of identity matter when someone stands in front of a classroom or talks one-on-one with a student or responds to an email, what is needed is a flexible means for examining and re-examining the interplay between identity categories and the communicative performances in which those categories become meaningful.

These questions have long been central to examinations of difference and diversity and their implications for writing pedagogy. This work ranges broadly, as some researchers perform close studies of individual writers or groups of writers in order to help teachers understand the work these writers are doing (e.g., Cushman; Dunn; Lieber; Morris; Sohn) while other scholars build intersectional analyses of how particular category memberships are complexly articulated within writers' lives and discourses (e.g., Alexander; Fernheimer; LeCourt, *Identity* and "Performing"; Royster). In yet another vein of research, scholars examine the means by which individuals communicate across linguistic and cultural differences inside and outside of the classroom (e.g., Flower; Flower, Long, and Higgins; Glazier; Lyons). Taken together, this research on writers, populations, groups, and discourses offers sensitive, nuanced, and detailed portraits of difference. However, despite the many contributions made by this body of scholarship, it still presents some difficulties for teachers working to develop classroom environments sensitive to the ever-changing terrain of difference. The scholarship on difference described here urges teachers to develop deep knowledge bases about the writers they are likely to encounter in two primary ways: by becoming more aware of differences that have received little attention and by developing new insights on familiar differences. But at the same time that this research focuses teachers' attention in particular ways, new points of analysis and inquiry are always emerging as significant. How is attention to new points of difference cultivated against a backdrop of traditional identity categories? Discourses of difference that fix individual writers or groups of writers in

time and space can frustrate, rather than enable, the development of pedagogical resources that attend simultaneously to broad conceptual categories
and to the highly individual encounters that occur within writing classrooms
on a daily basis.

In this essay, my aim is to show how a specific focus on interactionally emergent and rhetorically negotiated elements of a communicative situation can
enrich the study of difference in composition research. I develop this argument
by first identifying two strategies used by writing researchers when forwarding new understandings of difference. I then demonstrate that these strategies
take categories as a central unit of analysis and interpretation. This overem-
phasis on categories, I argue, leads to the problem of fixing difference in order
to study it. Thus, the phrase *fixing difference* here refers both to the process of
treating difference as a stable thing or property that can be identified and
fixed in place as well as to attempts to fix, that is, improve, the way difference
is understood. To move away from this difference fixation, I build on writing
scholarship that takes as a central focus the articulation of change and argue
that teachers and researchers should orient to difference as rhetorically negotiated through a process named here as *marking difference*. When marking difference
rhetors and audiences alike display and respond to markers of difference, those
rhetorical cues that signal the presence of difference between two or more participants. To illustrate this perspective on difference, I then analyze a brief
encounter between two students performing peer review in a first-year writing
classroom, showing that even in the smallest moments of communication markers of difference make visible the dynamism, relationality, and emergence of
difference. Attention to marking in conjunction with more familiar and often
unconscious categorization processes can help teachers and researchers mediate between broad conceptual tools for talking about difference and the unique
qualities of individual moments of interaction.

Perspectives on difference that focus on categories as a means for identifying
and unpacking difference exhibit an impulse toward fixity that can constrain
their usefulness for negotiating the shifting terrain of difference in writing
classrooms. This fixity is visible in two strategies for addressing difference and
diversity: taxonomizing difference and redefining categories. In taxonomizing difference, writing researchers seek to develop more precise language for
identifying types of writers and students. Through these careful classification
schemes, scholars work to avoid over-simplistic portrayals of students by attending to intersections among various identity categories both within individuals
(e.g., De and Gregory) and between groups (e.g., Gonsalves) or by offering more
precise definitions of the categories used to identify writers (e.g., Valdes; Harklau,
Losey, and Siegal). Scholarship in this vein urges teachers to attend to a con-
stellation of details about a student in order to consider that student not solely
as, say, white, or German American, or deaf, but as the embodiment of a complex set of identifications that must be considered together, rather than independent from one another. The strength of such approaches is that they broaden
the range of interpretive possibilities. Rather than allowing any given classifi-

cation to determine a teacher's assessment of a student, the rich confluence of multiple factors holds open more potential directions for an interaction. However, in its emphasis on categorical means for identifying students, taxonomizing difference focuses teachers' attention from the outset on particular identity categories, and this focusing can make it difficult for teachers to identify other relevant, but not-already-taxonomized, factors that influence a communicative situation.

A second strategy reflected in writing studies research alongside considerations of intersecting categories is that of redefining categories. Within this approach, scholars complicate traditional understandings of categorical identifications such as race, ethnicity, gender, socioeconomic class, disability, and religion, as well as of categories developed within writing studies (e.g., ESL writers, basic writers). The categorical redefinitions performed by this scholarship, such as in Christina Ortmeier-Hooper's "English May Be My Second Language, but I'm not 'ESL,'" have helped us resist essentialism by showing the nuance and variety within any given grouping of writers. Yet, the central means offered to instructors for developing their own teaching and being responsive to their students is that of performing such categorical redefinition themselves by identifying categories of students and drawing on research and personal experience to continually reshape them. It is important for teachers to avoid reifying categories of students, but practices of categorical redefinition can also have the unfortunate consequence of maintaining attention to categories that may or may not be central to a given classroom interaction. The challenge lies in the inability of a stable set of fixed labels circulating within composition studies to adequately account for and describe the changes that are always occurring.

Both taxonomizing difference and redefining categories have enhanced teaching with and across differences, but they tend toward fixity by freezing particular subjects, details, and interpretations within the research literature. Yet, this scholarship, which creates a more precise language for difference and offers nuanced portrayals of various identity categories, is not motivated by a desire to freeze differences in time and space, but instead, by a desire to open up new interpretive ground and broaden the range of potential meanings available within categorical frames. Indeed, writing researchers have taken numerous approaches to documenting ongoing transformations of meaning, in many cases influenced by ethnographic research methods and methodologies (Lillis) and an explosion of writing research looking at writing in context (Juzwik et al.). Key to these efforts is increased attention to flexibility and change. In *Rhetorical Listening*, for example, Krista Ratcliffe challenges the logic of whiteness, which she defines as "a trope that fosters stasis by resisting and denying differences" (114), by urging readers to employ a variety of means of rhetorical listening to resist such fixity. Such listening is always situational, she notes, always in the moment. This emphasis on situatedness is also evident in performance-based analyses that focus on how individuals artfully use particular resources at particular times for particular audiences in order to create specific identities

(Gonçalves). Other writing scholars use revision as a trope for understanding the creation and recreation of identity through writing (Herrington and Curtis; Jung; Lee; Young). In literacy studies, researchers such as Suzanne Rumsey and Gail Hawisher and Cynthia Selfe have examined how multimodal forms of literacy (quilting and online social networks) reveal identity building and literacy transmission as unpredictable and dynamic processes. Finally, some scholars have begun to incorporate *time* as a dimension for interpreting classroom activity in order to describe identity construction as an ongoing process occurring across different time scales (see Lemke) in classrooms and through writing (Wortham, *Learning*; Burgess and Ivanič).

Despite the acknowledgments made within this research about continual change, resistance, and transformation through language, there remains a gap in writing studies with regard to the resources made available for writing teachers wishing to address difference. What means does the scholarship offer for doing this work without reducing unique, individual interactions to a broad category or a particular representation in the research literature? These reductions happen in spite of teachers' best efforts and are in many ways part of human behavior and sense making. As sociologist and gender theorist Cecilia Ridgeway explains in *Framed by Gender*, "social relations are situations in which people form a sense of who they are in the situation and, therefore, how they should behave, by considering themselves in relation to whom they assume others are in that situation" (6–7). But what details people notice, and consequently use, to define themselves and others are affected by a wide variety of factors, from personal and professional experiences to academic learning. This perspective is reinforced by anthropologist Renato Rosaldo as he notes that "[a]ll interpretations are provisional; they are made by positioned subjects *who are prepared to know certain things and not others*" (8, emphasis added). A few examples from our scholarly literature can help illustrate the danger of presuming understanding as well as the challenges of keeping meaning indeterminate. In *Authoring*, Janis and Richard Haswell describe the results of a study in which they asked sixty-four readers to respond to two student texts, provide suggestions for revision, and discuss their impressions of the students' gender. They found that the respondents drew upon broad gender stereotypes to interpret these texts and offer suggestions for revision. Haswell and Haswell's results dovetail with Ridgeway's work on the persistence of gender inequality. Ridgeway shows how individuals negotiate new situations by framing them with cultural beliefs—that is, stereotypes—about gender that consequently reinforce these beliefs and maintain gender inequality.

Identifying categories and using shared cultural beliefs to interpret those categories is not the only way student writing and experiences are fixed in time and space, however. A second problematic strategy is that of over-identification. Educational researchers Mary Louise Gomez, Anne Burda Walker, and Michelle L. Page describe processes of over-identification that occurred between student teachers and their students. The student teachers articulated connections between themselves and their students, but in making these connections they also ignored significant differences between themselves and their students. Recognizing a similar phenomenon in her own work with working-class students, Donna LeCourt acknowledges how hard it is to avoid assuming or presuming to "know" her students ("Performing"), a question Julie Lindquist takes up at length in "What's the Trouble with Knowing Students? Only Time Will Tell." These are key challenges faced by teachers and researchers who pay close attention to difference.

The current focus on difference in writing studies has prepared teachers to attend to particular details and has reinforced the need to continually become aware of new ones — that is, to hold open interpretations rather than presume understanding — but it has not yet fully articulated *how* such new interpretations might be built. The remainder of this article, then, suggests a new approach to difference in which teachers and researchers can practice a kind of attention to difference that cultivates awareness of new details, provides opportunity to interpret and re-interpret those details, and contextualizes them within specific moments of writing, teaching, and learning. This perspective complements processes of category identification and offers a means for mediating between category recognition and individual interaction.

FROM FIXING TO MARKING: READING DIFFERENCE INTERACTIONALLY

Categorical identification is integral to the human sense-making processes, but recognizing any given identity category (or categories) does not necessarily enable an understanding of what that identification means. In some cases, categorical recognition can constrain individuals' openness to various interpretive possibilities. In other words, identifying that I am deaf, am female, grew up in suburban Ohio, and wear glasses does not translate neatly into a pedagogical or interactional course of action. Moreover, knowledge about what it means to be deaf, for example, is frequently challenged by people who simultaneously fit and do not fit stereotypical or broadly circulating notions of deafness. To address this gap between categorical knowledge and interactional processes, composition studies needs a way of considering difference in the classroom that enables attention to the ways that differences take shape within and through the interactions that surround writing. From such a perspective, difference, rather than being presentable through categories and remaining relatively inert across time and space, is dynamic, relational, and emergent. Composition research cannot approach the study of difference by cataloguing or even predicting all the potential differences that might affect any given situation or set of writers and audiences. So we must learn to act — to listen, as Katherine Schultz and Krista Ratcliffe have argued — as difference itself takes shape when people learn and write in a wide variety of social contexts.

To demonstrate how such an orientation to difference might be built, I perform two closely related theoretical and empirical analyses. First, I draw on the ethical scholarship of Mikhail Bakhtin to articulate an orientation to difference as dynamic, emergent, and relational — three qualities that are not always well represented in talk about difference in writing research. Within that theoretical lens, I develop the concept of markers of difference, contextually embedded rhetorical cues that signal the presence of difference between one or more interlocutors, and suggest that markers of difference can bridge the conceptual gap between knowledge about difference and interactional involvement with difference. Second, I analyze a brief conversation between two students performing peer review in a first-year writing classroom to demonstrate markers of difference in action. A marker-based orientation to difference is crucial for contemporary writing research because when we write and read, we wrestle with not just texts, but with selves. To read and respond to others involves making sense of the locations individuals occupy in relation to others, and doing such work requires a way of asking and answering questions about how people are different from one another and what those differences mean.

In contrast to understanding difference as a thing or object that can be named or described, I define difference as a relation between two individuals that is predicated upon their separateness from one another, or what Bakhtin refers to as noncoincidence in being. This relation is signaled by the display and uptake of markers of difference. Difference-as-relation drives communicative efforts because it is part of a continual interplay between identification and differentiation. This interplay reveals the lived experience of difference as highly dynamic. Categories rarely capture that dynamism because categorical coherence lies in the ability to move across contexts. In addition, categories tend to suppress attention to the agency expressed by individual actors as they display and respond to difference. Thus, I want to shift some emphasis away from the categories and move toward understanding how categories take on meaning within interactions. Marking difference is a rhetorical lens — rhetorical because it emphasizes the relationship between speaker/writer and audience as well as the situated nature of all communicative activity — that acknowledges the important role that identity categories play in interaction. At the same time, markers of difference underscore attention to difference as it is performed during the moment-to-moment vicissitudes of communication.

Because they foreground individual responsibility and the uniqueness of each act of communication, Bakhtin's early ethical writings in *Toward a Philosophy of the Act* and *Art and Answerability* are important to this understanding of difference. What Bakhtin calls the "once-occurrent event of Being" (*Toward* 2) can be understood in terms of the singularity of each rhetorical situation. No two individuals will ever have the same relation to one another as they do to any other individual, and no situation will be exactly like any other current, past, or future situation. Bakhtin's work also foregrounds individual activity, which he describes as "participatory" and "responsible." Individuals have a responsibility, he argues, to make the most of every moment. To accept this responsibility is to maintain an openness to the Other, to keep possibilities open rather than to close them off.

Bakhtin's conceptions of "the once-occurrent event of being" and of responsibility to the Other in communication highlight difference as dynamic, relational, and emergent. Difference is dynamic because meanings shift from moment to moment and are continually evolving. To return to the example of my deafness, when I encounter a student who doesn't realize I'm deaf and asks me about my accent, I am positioned very differently than I am by a student who does realize that I'm deaf and who asks me if I know sign language. In both cases it may be the sound of my voice that marks me as different to these students, but each one takes up that marker in different ways and puts me in a different position to respond. In turn, as the conversations progress, the first student comes to realize that I'm not a foreigner and that I am deaf (shifting the meaning of the different-sounding voice), and the second student comes to realize that I may embody qualities that differentiate me from their expectations about deaf people. I, in my turn, choose to display particular cues in response—explaining that I'm deaf to the first student and saying aloud, "Yes, I do," to the second while not signing anything—in an attempt to assert to them my own identity claims. In interaction, then, what any one marker means for individual identity and interactional possibility is always shifting. Markers point to that dynamism by highlighting how individuals can deploy different markers to challenge or modify previous ones.

While it is true that categorical definitions and associations change over time, the categories themselves do not reflect the subtle moment-by-moment changes in individuals' impressions of one another that occur in interaction. This is what Bakhtin describes as the "unfinishedness" of being. He writes, "I have to be, for myself, someone who is axiologically yet-to-be, someone who does not coincide with his already existing makeup" (*Art* 13). Every semester when I meet students for the first time, even though this situation is a very familiar one, at the same time, no one semester beginning is identical to other semesters. I confess to once upon a time feeling a secret thrill when students would comment that at first they didn't even realize I was deaf. Now, however, I always assert my deafness. I have learned—from repeated encounters of this sort—my preferred way of managing the situation. I am not the same person I was when I felt that excitement at "passing," and I never seem to answer questions about my deafness the same way twice. I am always yet-to-be, always moving toward a new position or awareness, using different tools and resources for managing my identity in these situations.

In being yet-to-be, individuals are never coincident even with themselves. They do not remain in the same place, they do not carry or display the same differences, and what those differences are and what they mean is always shifting. Part of the reason differences are always shifting is because difference is relational. No two individuals have the same relation to one another, and difference cannot be considered in isolation: it inherently implies a comparison. I am not different by virtue of my deafness any more than a hearing person is "different" because he or she can hear. I am different from other deaf people, and I am different from people who can hear. While many aspects of self and other cannot be fully articulated (or even apprehended by individuals themselves), it is with markers of difference that people create, display, and respond to changes in self and other and the perceived relations between them. To acknowledge individuals' yet-to-be-ness is to maintain an openness to one's own and others' identities and to refuse to take identity markers as fixed.

Following from these principles of dynamism and relationality, difference is emergent. It does not exist outside of the interactional moment but, rather, takes shape as individuals make choices about what to reveal about themselves, what to notice or comment upon — or to not notice or comment upon. In order to communicate across difference, people must always be looking to learn what more they do not know about the Other; they must avoid presuming they can know the Other as a totalized and whole consciousness. It is insulting, for example, when students who have taken basic sign language classes try to sign to me instead of speaking, assuming that sign language is the best way to communicate with me simply because I am deaf. To presume to know me is to close off interactional possibilities rather than to hold them open. Bakhtin describes the assumption of wholeness in terms of moments where people step outside of themselves and enter into ("consummate") the Other (*Art*). But just as students cannot literally enter into my mind and "know" me, total consummation can never occur because it would violate the uniqueness of every moment of being. Indeed, this uniqueness is such that people are never even coincident with themselves: I am always yet-to-be, I am always coming to know who I am. I cannot know every aspect of even my own identity and self. As Bakhtin writes, one's life "finds no rest within itself and never coincides with its given presently existing makeup" (*Art* 15).

Because markers are fleeting, often existing only in a single moment, they demand sensitivity to each moment. The ephemerality of markers helps balance the persistence of categories, which sometimes seem to freeze people in time and space. Difference is not "out there" waiting to be found and identified but is always coming-to-be through the here-and-now of interaction. In the moment of interaction, engaging difference is part of a situated activity during which individuals, both consciously and subconsciously, display markers of difference in order to distinguish between themselves and others. When people decide to use a particular marker, that decision is cast against already-existing ideas of how Others may respond to that marker, and interlocutors choose the markers they hope will best accomplish their interactional and relational goals.

In processes of coming to know the Other and coming to know the self, the relationality of difference comes into sharpest focus: it is only through interaction with others that people are able to apprehend themselves. This awareness, subsequently, shapes their consciousness of the markers to which others are orienting and how they take on meaning. This process is akin to what Bakhtin described as "evaluat[ing] our exterior not for ourselves, but *for* others *through* others" (*Art* 33, emphasis in original). Identities are always in flux, always "yet-to-be," so they are never fully known or knowable entities, and knowledge about self comes only through encounters with others. Encountering others in the here and now gives individuals insight into their own selves. When I meet students who ask about my accent, I am reminded that I sound "different" from many nondeaf speakers when I talk, in a way that I am not when speaking with people who are already familiar with my speaking voice. By situating my own understanding against that of others, I am able to make predictions about how the markers I display will be taken up and responded to. While I cannot completely alter my speaking voice to adapt to a particular situation, many times I do make a concerted effort to address any challenges that may be posed by my voice when I anticipate that someone will have difficulty understanding me. Taken together, these three elements — dynamism, relationality, and emergence — constitute a rhetorical presentation of difference in their emphasis on how individuals call attention to — or suppress — difference as well as how they respond to differences displayed by others.

At this point, it will be helpful to distinguish my use of the word *marker* from another common use: to refer to objects or modes that are marked, such as a marked case in linguistics. The marked case is stressed and set apart from unmarked or otherwise un-emphasized cases. For example, when Ruth Frankenberg talks about whiteness as "a set of cultural practices that are usually unmarked and unnamed" and describes the task of her book as that of "exploring, mapping, and examining the terrain of whiteness" (1), she argues that there are salient features of whiteness that can be identified ("marked") even though they are not currently named and discussed. In this context, people may describe practices of "marking difference" that locate difference against an unstated norm, such as when someone might say that my deafness marks me as different. I do not use the term *marker* in this way. To evoke my deafness as a difference, it must be considered relationally — how does my not hearing (of a particular form) make me different from a specific interlocutor? Is this difference taken up by either participant? And if so, how does this marker of difference — whatever it is that cues my deafness or my interlocutor's relationship to my deafness — become salient for each of us?

Thus, in opposition to the way a categorical orientation presumes the significance of a broad label for interactional possibility, these markers show difference as shaped through interaction. For something to be a marker of difference, it must be taken up in a communicative encounter. On its own, a marker has no stable meaning. This is one reason that markers of difference are so deeply rhetorical: they require involvement between a speaker/writer and an audience, and they must be located in their rhetorical context. Markers are used to point to and articulate difference, and some markers are readily engaged while other intended markers may be ignored, suppressed, or disregarded. Category labels can also be used as markers — names with which people mark themselves as, say, members of a particular group.[1] I do this when I describe myself as "deaf" (and, sometimes, as "profoundly deaf," although this more specialized term is only meaningful for particular audiences). It is a rhetorical choice: I do not say "hard-of-hearing" or "partially deaf" or "hearing-aid-wearer," although these terms are used by other people in talking about me. In this way people use categorical terms to mark others as well as assert their own identity claims. Markers of difference provide a mechanism for realizing the ephemerality of difference in interaction while also attending to the categorical representations and signifiers that influence what gets noticed and how meaning gets made.

COMMENTS ON A COMMA: A MARKER-BASED MICROANALYSIS

Moving from the theoretical to the empirical, this section shows how an analysis focusing on markers of difference might proceed. While the preceding discussion drew from general examples of some ways that I negotiate my deafness, I turn here to an excerpt of conversation in which differences in authority emerge between two students through their talk. The distinction between these two examples of marking difference is significant. The former is a set of anecdotal reflections on conscious and purposeful ways that I negotiate language and environment to accomplish communicative goals, while the latter, an examination of recorded classroom discourse, reveals a subtle process of marking difference in an immediate communicative moment. Because marking difference is so intimately tied to the display and recognition of identities, it is an important means by which individuals gauge their willingness (or unwillingness) to engage with another person. Consequently, attention to everyday talk of the sort displayed [in the dialogue on p. 425] is an important resource for teachers as they reflect upon the ways that they and their students build relations with and respond to others within the classroom environment. Before moving into this discussion, I review some background on the study design that informed the data generation and analysis to expose how categorical orientations to difference are deeply embedded within research paradigms.

The design of the study presented here incorporates two central research questions: "How are differences engaged by students in the writing classroom?" and "What role does writing play in the engagement of difference?" When the proposal for this study was under institutional review, feedback from reviewers frequently requested further information on the kinds of differences under investigation — gender, race, class, or the like. Ironically, the mere asking of this question revealed how entrenched the notion of difference as thing-existing-outside-of-the-moment-of-interaction was. Instead of identifying particular differences at the outset, the study focused on what differences became relevant for participants as well as how they became relevant. I expected the study would uncover interactions around difference that spoke to broader categories, such as conversations about race, ethnicity, and gender, or encounters that directly or indirectly invoked identity-related issues, particularly because all of the students in this writing class were also enrolled in a sociology course focused on racial issues in the United States, and because the course was part of one of Midwestern University's major diversity initiatives.[2] However, attention to difference between students rarely involved references to categorical identity signifiers. Students in this writing classroom almost never talked about their own or others' race, ethnicity, gender, disability, or socioeconomic class affiliations. What they did do is work hard to position themselves alongside one another and to construct identities that would be considered persuasive and interesting to others. Similar identity work is performed by teachers crafting their teacherly identities within the classroom. The conversation analyzed [on the following pages] is an everyday occurrence of identity work in which two women each attempt to establish their own interpretive authority by displaying markers of difference that distinguish one's authority from the other's.

At this point, revisiting the difficulty of using categorical description as an entry into analyses of this sort will reinforce the differences between these approaches. A categorical approach might begin by describing the three women — Blia, Lindsey, and Choua — noting that each woman is a first-semester student at the university. It might also use category terms circulating within this particular institutional context to note that Blia and Choua are Southeast Asian American and Lindsey is white. In description of this sort, readers are called upon to notice the women's ages, their gender, and their race-ethnic identifications. Such noticing is heavily influenced by context. There are innumerable other ways these women could have been described. For example, one reader of this essay noted that at universities in the Southwest, a student might choose to self-identify as "Anglo" rather than "white." Or, readers might be asked to notice each student's declared major, or their hometown, or even hair color or clothing style. Yet, even when such descriptions acknowledge that no one can know from the outset what information will be most important for understanding conversation, a key assumption motivating this analytic approach is that "relevant" descriptive information is necessary to contextualize a particular situation or setting. But no matter how detailed or attentive the teacher or analyst is, any noticing presumes the relevance of a particular set of category identifications to the conversation and is limited to what the teacher/analyst is already aware of as potentially significant. As such, these noticings can reveal more about the teacher/analyst's positionality (Rosaldo), rather than about how individuals in this context are orienting to one another.

Reading difference through categories — looking for specific identity markers in order to place people into one category or another — can prevent an analyst or teacher from attending to less apparent differences. It can also prevent them from picking up on what participants themselves may be orienting to in an interaction; what may be evident to one person is not necessarily meaningful to another. Now, I am in no way suggesting that teachers and researchers should ignore how race, ethnicity, age, and gender affect these women's talk. I am also not suggesting — impossible as this would be — that people avoid categorical observation altogether. What I am saying, though, is that until we look at how these women are interacting with one another we cannot presume to know how any particular identity categories or their intersections are influencing how Blia, Lindsey, and Choua are identifying themselves. No descriptions of these women, no matter how rich, can determine or fully account for the differences among them that are brought to bear on the here and now of their peer review work. While some might argue that categorical description is a predictor rather than a determinant of individual positions, understanding categories as predictive is useful only insofar as teachers and researchers have tools for revisiting or revising the meanings attributed to categories. Markers of difference address this gap because the repeated noticing of particular markers or styles of marking can cultivate complex articulations of difference that bring life to relatively inert identity categories. In this way, markers of difference help build reflexivity between teachers and researchers' categorical awareness and the meanings that are ascribed to those categories.

Table 1 provides an overview of questions made available to us by categorical and marker-based orientations to difference. These questions reinforce ways that analyses of difference are shaped by underlying orientations to difference. The analysis below focuses on the second set of questions, emphasizing a perspective that works from participants' communicative work within the interactional moment and seeks to understand how their rhetorical choices respond to, constitute, and direct that moment.

Having emphasized an analytic approach that focuses on interactional activity for what it can reveal about participants' orientations to one another, I now examine a short conversational exchange that took place during a peer review session. This particular excerpt was chosen for several reasons. Thus far to illustrate processes of marking difference, I have primarily drawn on anecdotal examples taken from my personal experiences negotiating my deafness in a variety of teaching situations. This sort of anecdotal reflection forms a significant part of my teaching practice (a point to which I return below), but not all of the differences significant to my interactions with others are as easily recognized and articulated as my deafness. Moreover, because I am attuned to my deafness being an influential element of my discourse with others, I sometimes fail to recognize other differences that are marked

TABLE 1 Questions for Categorical- and Marker-Based Analyses of Difference

Categorical Lens	Markers of Difference
• What differences are present in the classroom?	• How do individuals position themselves alongside others?
• What categories do individuals belong to?	• How are individuals positioned by others?
• What categories can be ascribed to particular individuals?	• How do individuals acknowledge similarities and differences between themselves and others?
• What can we learn about the individuals in the classroom?	• What differences are made salient through classroom interactions?
• What information about the self is being communicated in talk?	• How are students and teachers learning with others in the classroom?

and engaged in those exchanges. With the analysis of this excerpt, then, I aim to show one way that differences take shape through interaction and to encourage greater attention to the nuances and subtleties of individual classroom discourse.

The snippet of talk analyzed here was taken from Blia, Choua, and Lindsey's conversation about one sentence in Choua's draft. The full discussion of this sentence took up nearly one hundred lines of transcript and was the women's longest sustained conversation about a single element of any of their papers.[3] In the ten-line excerpt from this conversation reproduced below, Blia and Choua address Blia's peer review suggestion that Choua add a comma to her sentence, and they engage in a series of affiliative and dis-affiliative moves that enact a complex relationship between them.[4] Details provided within the transcript, such as when Blia and Choua's talk overlapped as well as the volume at which particular words are spoken, provide important clues for considering where and how markers of difference emerge,[5] and they open space for future attention to how markers of difference can be identified in individuals' talk and interaction. The transcript picks up just as Blia reads part of Choua's sentence aloud ("but in the dictionary") and points to her written suggestion that Choua add a comma after the words "dictionary definition" in her essay draft. Choua, rather than simply accepting the suggestion, challenges it, saying "<u>but</u> they don't need commas" (181). The four subsequent conversational turns develop this initial disagreement.

180. BLIA: but in the dictionary [(???)
181. CHOUA: [<u>but</u> they don't need commas
                    because didn't we learn over the summer tha::t
182.   you only put commas when you're separating a fragment
                of two sentences on either side (1.3)
183. BLIA: u::m: I've been taught differently (1.0)
184.   if you're um (0.8)
185. CHOUA: I was taught <u>here</u>::
186.   s[o::
187. BLIA: [oh
188. CHOUA: that's::
189.   but it doesn't matter:: I don't care (2.5)

In lines 181–82, Choua rejects Blia's suggestion, saying, "<u>but</u> they don't need commas." She then attempts to mitigate that disagreement by inviting Blia to share in her assessment: "because didn't we learn over the summer tha::t" (182). While Choua's "we" initially seems to reference a shared learning experience, Blia's response rejects that identification, as she tells Choua, "I've been taught differently" (183). In this turn, Blia's first-person singular pronoun "I" stands in contrast to Choua's use of "we." When Blia asserts her "I", she privileges her own learning over Choua's. Blia also does not respond to Choua's understanding of the rules of comma use, nor does she affirm the position of knowledge Choua attempts to establish. Instead, Blia displays two markers of difference — the words "I" and "differently" — to distinguish herself from Choua (they have not shared a learning experience), as well as to differentiate between what the two women have learned. Choua then pushes back by offering additional information via another marker of difference to re-establish a knowledgeable stance: "I was taught here::" (185), suggesting that place of learning is significant in considering what weight should be accorded to the women's knowledge about punctuation.

The moment Choua asserts the validity of her learning experience "here::" is an especially significant one in terms of the display of markers of difference in this interaction. With this utterance, Choua responds to two previously displayed markers: (a) Blia's verb "taught" and (b) Blia's assertion of having been taught "differently." To the first, Choua's shift from "didn't we learn" (182) to "I was taught" (185) follows Blia's invocation of authority and enables a direct comparison between having been taught here as opposed to somewhere else. To the second, Choua highlights the difference between here and differently. With this marker, Choua resituates the discussion in terms of where she has gained her knowledge. This shifts the difference being marked from authority of person (teacher versus student) to authority of place (proximity versus distance). In other words, Choua's claim is not just about having been taught something (which she and Blia have both experienced), but about the heightened authority that her having been taught might carry in relation to Blia's. Learning *here*, at Midwestern University, Choua might be arguing, has greater influence than some other, more remote learning experience. Blia does not take up this element of Choua's claim, however, and the topic is dropped when Choua abruptly says, "but it doesn't matter:: I don't care" (189). The women do not revisit the comma topic in the remainder of their peer review conversation.

The markers of difference used in this conversation range widely. In just six conversational turns, Blia and Choua have displayed markers that draw on past experiences with writing instruction, positioning cues, explicit differentiation from one another, and punctuation rules as the two women identify themselves in particular ways. It is important to note that the markers displayed and interpreted by Blia and Choua are framed not only by the immediate peer review context in which the conversation is happening but also by broader sociopolitical contexts that motivate and guide the interpretations they each make of the unfolding discourse. Take another look at Choua's utterance "I was taught here:: / s[o::" (185–86) and Blia's subsequent response, "[oh" (187). When Choua makes her claim of having been taught "here::," she evokes an orientation to rules of punctuation that are socially situated and contingent on place or situation. Unlike Choua, Blia may not see punctuation rules as negotiable depending on context. This is one small way that broader sociocultural frameworks, including past experiences with schooling and authority figures, as well as cultural narratives about different types of people intersect with and influence the discourse that takes place within the classroom.

Blia and Choua's peer conversation reveals complex dynamics of disagreement and consensus and shows one way that differences in perception can become material for negotiation among individuals. Such talk exposes some of the power relations that are operating within students' interactions with one another. This episode in particular underscores the stakes involved for students when they share their writing and talk about it with one another: they run the risk of being misunderstood and the risk of being positioned in undesirable ways by others — positions that they may not always be able to directly influence or change. These are not minor concerns for college students negotiating complicated and unfamiliar social environments; nor are they minor concerns for teachers establishing their subject positions in front of a classroom.

IMPLICATIONS OF A MARKER-BASED PERSPECTIVE FOR WRITING TEACHING

How can attention to markers of difference help teachers foster productive classroom environments and teach more effectively? Before entering a specific discussion of ways that markers of difference can enhance teaching and peer review practices, however, it will be useful to re-emphasize the distinction between markers of difference and identity markers more generally. Markers of difference are always situated, negotiable, and part of individual interactions. They are also framed by and interpreted within broader sociopolitical contexts. Markers of difference differ from identity markers because markers of difference do not refer to qualities that characterize particular identities, such as the way skin color may mark a person's racial or ethnic identity or the way clothing choices and hair styles may mark a person's gender, socioeconomic status, or sexuality. Identity markers of this sort *are* important to interaction, as disability theorist Tobin Siebers has pointed out, because they contribute to the identifiability of difference. Identifiability refers not simply to the existence of difference but to the representations and meanings attached to those differences (Siebers 17). As Siebers notes, not all differences are identifiable. Earlier in this essay, for example, I mentioned that I wear glasses. However, "glasses wearing," unlike "hearing-aid wearing," is not a difference often remarked upon or, as Siebers puts it, identified as difference, even between people who do not wear glasses and people who do. Moreover, that a particular difference is identified (gender, for example, is almost always identified in individual interaction) does not in and of itself mean that that difference will be rhetorically engaged or negotiated as a marker of difference in the interaction. Thus, markers of difference do not provide cross-contextual understanding of the meaning associated with any particular identity marker. As a marker of difference, my hearing aids do not have a stable signification outside of an interactional context. So even as my past experiences with making my deafness perceptible affect whether I decide to get neon green or tan hearing aids, there is no dictionary of markers of deafness that I can pull out to understand whether, and how, my hearing aids will become salient in any given interaction. Yet, at the same time that I argue for the contextual and situated nature of markers of difference, markers of difference do inform individuals' awareness of broader cultural categories. Prior experiences of negotiating markers of difference alongside recurring cultural narratives provide material with which people draw more general conclusions about deafness and deaf people.

Given this distinction between the dynamic, relational, and emergent markers that signal individuals' uptake of difference and the general markers that point to identity categories, we can then consider how markers of difference can improve the work of peer review and teaching writing. Such markers can help teachers resist initial or simplistic generalizations and enable the re-examination of texts and interactions for what people choose to highlight or foreground about themselves and others. In forwarding the set of recommendations detailed below, this concept of marking difference is put in conversation with professional discourses about teaching and learning, specifically the "Framework for Success in Postsecondary Writing" (FSPW) developed by the Council of Writing Program Administrators (CWPA), the National Council of Teachers of English (NCTE), and the National Writing Project (NWP). The FSPW puts forth eight "habits of mind" crucial for students' success in writing. These eight habits of mind are also deeply applicable to the work of learning how to teach writing. In the recommendations for paying attention to markers of difference in teaching practice below, I highlight three of these habits of mind: increased *openness* to new information and interpretations; *flexibility* in reinterpreting and re-appropriating classroom discourses and artifacts; and heightened *metacognition* in reflecting upon specific moments of writing, teaching, and learning.

To show how these habits of mind can be cultivated through attention to markers of difference, the remainder of this section suggests practical ways that teachers can attend to markers of difference in their everyday work. Teachers and students use markers of difference to assert their identities and interpretations and to make sense of relationships being established between themselves and others. In the classroom discussed in this article, these identities and self- and other interpretations were prominent during several recurring interactional practices: telling narratives, agreeing and disagreeing with others, and withdrawing from or dismissing a topic. Consequently, these particular dynamics merit special attention from teachers as they consider how markers of difference influence and shape the negotiations that they and their students undertake with one another. I briefly describe each of these dynamics and then turn to specific strategies for attending to the markers of difference displayed therein. Sharing stories is an interactional practice that has received a great deal of attention across several fields of study, most notably in education and sociolinguistics. Elsewhere, I analyze how students exchange narratives in order to solicit details about others and to shore up particular self-identifications. Students' narratives were crafted to highlight particular markers of difference, and students often artfully paralleled markers in their own narratives with those deployed in others' tellings (Kerschbaum). Teachers' narratives display similar elements of creativity. Educational anthropologist Stanton Wortham shows how "participant-examples," a specific type of teacher-narrative in which teachers create hypothetical stories about students in the classroom to illustrate classroom concepts, provide insight into the ways that teachers identify students (*Acting*; *Narratives*). In another vein of research on teachers' stories, educational researchers Lesley Rex and colleagues analyze teachers' pedagogical stories for what models they offer students for success and achievement in the classroom. In these ways, narratives provide rich sources of information regarding how individuals characterize others. In reflecting upon these stories, teachers might ask: What traits, features, and qualities are described or highlighted? How are characters in the narratives portrayed? What plotlines do these characters follow, and what kinds of action or activity are available to them? In what ways are selves and others implicated in these narratives?

Two other interactional patterns — agreeing and disagreeing and withdrawing from or dismissing topics — played a significant role in student and teacher talk. The conversational excerpt from Blia and Choua's peer review session displays both of these dynamics. Blia and Choua actively disagree on the placement of a comma, and Choua ends the topic by withdrawing from it, downplaying the importance of coming to a consensus. Withdrawals of this sort were not uncommon in students' peer review talk. When students disagreed, their reaction was often to agree to disagree or to dismiss the topic. These avoidances and dismissals warrant closer examination: What precipitates someone's decision to drop a topic and avoid further discussion? What markers of difference emerge as individuals collaboratively address issues of topic relevance and importance? These questions are significant not just for what they reveal about what teachers and students deem worthy of discussion, but also for what they suggest regarding topics up for negotiation. Similarly, when individuals express agreement or disagreement, what markers of difference signal to them interpretations that allow them to stake their positions and construct them through discourse?

In turning to specific ways that teachers can attend to these three interactional patterns through the lens of marking difference, this section focuses on how teachers can make more explicit the work that markers of difference do in the course of their everyday practices. In many ways these suggestions are already a part of teachers' careful reflection upon their teaching, but the emphasis here is on developing a heightened sensitivity to the differences already part of everyday discourse as well as to those that others may be bringing to new awareness. Perhaps the most central means for teachers to begin this work is to consider their own teacher identity. They might ask themselves, "How would I characterize myself as a teacher? What choices do I make in presenting this teacher identity to my students?" Examples of this sort of metacognitive reflection have been published in a variety of locations. For instance, Lad Tobin, Deshae Lott, Christina Russell MacDonald, and Mark Mossman each describe their own conscious negotiations in displaying particular teacher roles and identities in their classrooms. This work entails the display of markers of difference that are taken up in a variety of ways by students, and that are rhetorically negotiated and emergent within different classroom settings. Teachers can look across these reflections to consider what kinds of things are chosen in order to signal particular teacher identities as well as to identify how students and other participants have responded to these cues. A second approach for "noticing patterns of noticing" accomplished with markers of difference entails turning the lens away from self-portrayals to other portrayals, asking, How would I characterize my class (or an individual student)? In reflecting on those questions, teachers would attend to the traits, features, or characteristics that are remarked upon, asking further, "What elements are highlighted, and which ones are downplayed or not addressed?" To access the dynamism and change that invariably occur in perception over the course of an academic term or over the course of a teaching career, teachers could perform these activities several times and reflect each time on the features, traits, elements, and practices that are foregrounded and backgrounded in different characterizations. Considered across time, different patterns of observation will emerge, and these patterns will point to both what Rosaldo describes as the analyst/teacher's own positionality and preparedness to notice certain things as well as to the observable cues signaled by those participating in the co-construction of classroom discourse, activity, and writing. For such reflections to be most productive, teachers need to maintain an openness to new and alternate possibilities as they revisit their observations.

Alongside attention to descriptions of self and others, a third strategy is to document the use of participant examples in classroom discourse. In reflecting on classroom practices, or while designing lesson plans, teachers might ask themselves, "Which examples do I (will I) leave abstract, in hypothetical space, and which examples do I (will I) make concrete by invoking specific students to illustrate them? Which students do I (will I) call upon in crafting these examples and why?" It is through such reflection that teachers can become critically aware of how they are mobilizing resources within the classroom, including references to artifacts that they and their students bring with them to class (books, writing implements, computer screens, coffee mugs, clothing) as well as spatial relationships (proximity and distance) to actualize these examples and develop student learning. These reflections can encourage greater flexibility in teachers' appropriation of instructional resources. There are many ways of performing these reflections. I like to annotate my daily lesson plans after each class meeting. Others, such as literacy scholar Morris Young, who shares some of his reflections on teaching in the final chapter of *Minor Re/Visions*, might keep a running journal related to their teaching. In these journals teachers might record feelings, emotions, responses, observations, or even tell stories that offer clues to how they construct classrooms, describe teaching selves, and identify salient classroom elements.

A fourth strategy for tracing the deployment of markers of difference in teaching is to consider responses to student writing. Texts are sites upon which differences are enacted, and these differences become perceptible in both student-to-student feedback (as seen in students' peer review marks on classmates' essays *and* in the talk about those comments) as well as in teacher-student feedback. When are comments made? Why? What kinds? What changes are suggested or implied by these marks? What cues signal differences between the reader's and the writer's perspective? These marks are more than just suggestions for change; they also indicate a reader's stance toward the text and the potential space created for future versions of that text.

A fifth and final recommendation emerging from attention to Blia and Choua's conversation is that of developing a means for recording and revisiting actual moments of classroom discourse. While anecdotal recall and other reflective tools are essential for encouraging metacognition, there is also rich potential in looking at what is actually happening during classroom discussion. In Blia and Choua's writing classroom, for instance, their teacher might look across the peer review conversations for the interactional patterns described above. Key to reexamining classroom performance is the consideration of what new details and differences teachers might become more attuned to. What can students' own talk reveal about the dynamics of difference in classroom spaces? In order to do this work, teachers might take advantage of the technology resources on their campus to make video or audio recordings that can later be revisited.

CONCLUSION: MARKING THE WAY FROM HERE

These teaching methods reinforce two central goals of using markers of difference in teaching writing. First, markers of difference build from the ground up an understanding of differences that are relevant to individuals involved in an interaction. Second, markers of difference enable reflexivity between familiar categories that are already part of conscious identifications and the everyday interactions in which these categories take on greater complexity, resonance, and nuance. Thus, markers of difference are a resource for coming to know others, work that writing scholars have long advocated, even while acknowledging that there are many challenges to cultivating such knowledge. The major contribution that markers of difference make to this conversation is that they resist the impulse to reduce getting to know students to filling out beginning-of-the-semester questionnaires, or to the use of demographic surveys to describe general types of students likely to be found at a particular college or university. Markers of difference answer the question of how demographic knowledge takes on salience by insisting on locating these characteristics and observations within contexts of use, thus providing a valuable pedagogical resource for teachers aiming to cultivate such sensitivity in their everyday teaching practices.

NOTES

1. See, for example, DeFina and West and Fenstermaker for insightful analyses of how individuals use categories in talk to name identities and constitute them interactionally.

2. The school's name as well as participants' names are pseudonyms, and all identifying details have been masked to preserve anonymity.

3. A "line" of a transcript consists of what is spoken between breaths or pauses.

4. Markers of difference take on a variety of forms and can emerge through word choice, emphasis, volume, as well as other verbal cues for signaling meaning. For this reason, I provide a fairly detailed transcript, including information about when students paused or when their talk overlapped or interrupted one another, as illustrated with square brackets indicating the point of overlap/interruption. Considered across time and contexts, the detail in this transcript is designed to enable attention to as many potential markers of difference as possible. Other valuable sources of meaning making not transcribed here include gestures (Wolfe; Godbee) and gaze (Everts), both of which could contribute to interpretations of how students signal and reinforce particular interpretations and cues.

5. In this transcript, pauses longer than half a second are measured in seconds and indicated by a number within parentheses at the end of the line. A left square bracket indicates overlapping talk. An underline indicates words spoken at a higher volume relative to adjacent talk, colons are used to indicate extended sounds, and inaudible words are represented with three question marks within parentheses.

WORKS CITED

Alexander, Jonathan. *Literacy, Sexuality, Pedagogy: Theory and Practice for Composition Studies*. Logan: Utah State UP, 2008. Print.

Bakhtin, Mikhail. *Art and Answerability: Early Philosophical Essays by M. M. Bakhtin*. Trans. Vadim Liapunov. Austin: U of Texas P, 1990. Print.

——. *Toward a Philosophy of the Act*. Trans. Vadim Liapunov. Austin: U of Texas P, 1993. Print.

Burgess, Amy, and Roz Ivanič. "Writing and Being Written: Issues of Identity across Timescales." *Written Communication* 27.2 (2010): 228–55. Print.

Cushman, Ellen. "Toward a Rhetoric of Self-Representation: Identity Politics in Indian Country and Rhetoric and Composition." *College Composition and Communication* 60.2 (2008): 321–65. Print.

De, Esha Niyogi, and Donna Uthus Gregory. "Decolonizing the Classroom." *Writing in Multicultural Settings*. Ed. Carol Severino, Juan Guerra, and Johnella Butler. New York: MLA, 1997. 118–32. Print.

De Fina, Anna. *Identity in Narrative: A Study of Immigrant Discourse*. Philadelphia: John Benjamins, 2003. Print.

Dunn, Patricia. *Learning Re-Abled: The Learning Disability Controversy and Composition Studies*. Portsmouth: Boynton/Cook, 1995. WAC Clearinghouse. Web. 27 Mar. 2011.

Everts, Elisa. "Modalities of Turn-Taking in Blind/Sighted Interaction: Better to Be Seen and Not Heard?" In *Discourse and Technology: Multimodal Discourse Analysis*. Ed. Philip LeVine and Ron Scollon. Washington: Georgetown UP, 2004. 128–45. Print.

Fernheimer, Janice. "Black Jewish Identity Conflict: A Divided Universal Audience and the Impact of Dissociative Disruption." *Rhetoric Society Quarterly* 39.1 (2009): 46–72. Print.

Flower, Linda. "Talking across Difference: Intercultural Rhetoric and the Search for Situated Knowledge." *College Composition and Communication* 55.1 (2003): 38–68. Print.

Flower, Linda, Elenore Long, and Lorraine Higgins. *Learning to Rival: A Literate Practice for Intercultural Inquiry*. Mahwah: Lawrence Erlbaum, 2000. Print.

Fox, Helen. Afterword. In *Social Change in Diverse Teaching Contexts*. Ed. Nancy G.

Barron, Nancy Grimm, and Sybille Gruber. New York: Peter Lang, 2006. 251-66. Print.

"Framework for Success in Postsecondary Writing." Council of Writing Program Administrators, National Council of Teachers of English, and National Writing Project. Jan. 2011. Web. 15 Sept. 2011.

Frankenberg, Ruth. *White Women, Race Matters: The Social Construction of Whiteness.* Minneapolis: U of Minnesota P, 1993. Print.

Glazier, Jocelyn. "Developing Cultural Fluency: Arab and Jewish Students Engaging in One Another's Company." *Harvard Educational Review* 73.2 (2003): 141-63. Print.

Godbee, Beth. "'We're in This Together': Illustrating Potentials for Social Change in Talk about Writing." Unpublished manuscript. Print.

Gomez, Mary Louise, Anne Burda Walker, and Michelle L. Page. "Personal Experience as a Guide to Teaching." *Teaching and Teacher Education* 16 (2000): 731-47. Print.

Gonçalves, Zan Meyer. *Sexuality and the Politics of Ethos.* Carbondale: Southern Illinois UP, 2005. Print.

Gonsalves, Lisa. "Making Connections: Addressing the Pitfalls of White Faculty/ Black Male Student Communication." *College Composition and Communication* 53.3 (2000): 435-65. Print.

Harklau, Linda, Kay Losey, and Meryl Siegal, eds. *Generation 1.5 Meets College Composition: Issues in the Teaching of Writing to U.S.-Educated Learners of ESL.* Mahwah: Lawrence Erlbaum, 1999. Print.

Haswell, Janis, and Richard Haswell. *Authoring: An Essay for the English Profession on Potentiality and Singularity.* Logan: Utah State UP, 2010. Print.

Hawisher, Gail, and Cynthia Selfe, with Yi-Huey Guo and Lu Liu. "Globalization and Agency: Designing and Redesigning the Literacies of Cyberspace." *College English* 68.6 (2006): 619-36. Print.

Herrington, Anne, and Marcia Curtis. *Persons in Process: Four Stories of Writing and Personal Development in College.* Urbana: NCTE, 2000. Print.

hooks, bell. *Talking Back: Thinking Feminist, Thinking Black.* Boston: South End, 1989. Print.

Jung, Julie. *Revisionary Rhetoric, Feminist Pedagogy, and Multigenre Texts.* Carbondale: Southern Illinois UP, 2005. Print.

Juzwik, Mary, Svjetlana Curcic, Kimberly Wolbers, Kathleen D. Moxley, Lisa M. Dimling, and Rebecca K. Shankland. "Writing into the 21st Century: An Overview of Research on Writing, 1999 to 2004." *Written Communication* 26.4 (2006): 451-76. Print.

Kerschbaum, Stephanie. "Classroom Narratives and Ethical Responsibility: How Markers of Difference Can Inform Teaching." *Narrative Discourse Analysis for Teacher Educators.* Ed. Lesley Rex and Mary M. Juzwik. Cresskill: Hampton P, 2011. 77-104. Print.

LeCourt, Donna. *Identity Matters: Schooling the Student Body in Academic Discourse.* Albany: State U of New York P, 2004. Print.

——. "Performing Working-Class Identity in Composition: Toward a Pedagogy of Textual Practice." *College English* 69.1 (2006): 30-51. Print.

Lee, Amy. *Composing Critical Pedagogies: Teaching Writing as Revision.* Urbana: NCTE, 2000. Print.

Lemke, Jay. "Across the Scales of Time: Artifacts, Activities, and Meanings in Ecosocial Systems." *Mind, Culture, and Activity* 7.4 (2000): 273-90. Web. 4 Apr. 2011.

Lieber, Andrea. "A Virtual *Viebershul:* Blogging and the Blurring of Public and Private among Orthodox Jewish Women." *College English* 72.6 (2010): 621-37. Print.

Lillis, Theresa. "Ethnography as Method, Methodology, and 'Deep Theorizing': Closing the Gap between Text and Context in Academic Writing Research." *Written Communication* 25.3 (2008): 353–88. Print.

Lindquist, Julie. "What's the Trouble with Knowing Students? Only Time Will Tell." *Pedagogy: Critical Approaches to Teaching Literature, Language, Composition, and Culture* 10.1 (2009): 175–287. Web. 15 Jan. 2010.

Lott, Deshae. "Going to Class with (Going to Clash with?) the Disabled Person: Educators, Students, and Their Spoken and Unspoken Negotiations." In *Embodied Rhetorics: Disability in Language and Culture*. Ed. James C. Wilson and Cynthia Lewiecki-Wilson. Carbondale: Southern Illinois UP, 2001. 135–53. Print.

Lyons, Scott. "Rhetorical Sovereignty: What Do American Indians Want from Writing?" *College Composition and Communication* 51.3 (2000): 447–68. Print.

MacDonald, Christina Russell. "Imagining Our Teaching Selves." In *Teaching Writing: Landmarks and Horizons*. Ed. Christina Russell MacDonald and Robert L. MacDonald. Carbondale: Southern Illinois UP, 2002. 171–83. Print.

Morris, Amanda Lynch. "Native American Stand-Up Comedy: Epideictic Strategies in the Contact Zone." *Rhetoric Review* 30.1 (2011): 37–53. Print.

Mossman, Mark. "Visible Disability in the College Classroom." *College English* 64.6 (2002): 645–59. Print.

Okawa, Gail. "'Resurfacing Roots': Developing a Pedagogy of Language Awareness from Two Views." In *Language Diversity in the Classroom: From Intention to Practice*. Ed. Geneva Smitherman and Victor Villanueva. Carbondale: Southern Illinois UP, 2003. 109–33. Print.

Ortmeier-Hooper, Christina. "English May Be My Second Language, but I'm Not 'ESL.'" *College Composition and Communication* 59.3 (2008): 389–419. Print.

Ratcliffe, Krista. *Rhetorical Listening: Identification, Gender, Whiteness*. Carbondale: Southern Illinois UP, 2005. Print.

Rex, Lesley, Timothy Murnen, Jack Hobbs, and David McEachen. "Teachers' Pedagogical Stories and the Shaping of Classroom Participation: 'The Dancer' and 'Graveyard Shift at the 7-11.'" *American Educational Research Journal* 39.3 (2002): 765–96. Print.

Ridgeway, Cecilia. *Framed by Gender: How Gender Inequality Persists in the Modern World*. New York: Oxford UP, 2011. Print.

Rosaldo, Renato. *Culture and Truth: The Remaking of Social Analysis*. Boston: Beacon P, 1989. Print.

Royster, Jacqueline Jones. *Traces of a Stream: Literacy and Social Change among African American Women*. Pittsburgh: U of Pittsburgh P, 2000. Print.

Rumsey, Suzanne. "Heritage Literacy: Adoption, Adaptation, and Alienation of Multimodal Literacy Tools." *College Composition and Communication* 60.3 (2009): 573–86. Print.

Schultz, Katherine. *Listening: A Framework for Teaching across Differences*. New York: Teachers College P, 2003. Print.

Siebers, Tobin. *Disability Theory*. Ann Arbor: U of Michigan P, 2008. Print.

Sohn, Kathleen Kelleher. "Whistlin' and Crowin' Women of Appalachia." *College Composition and Communication* 54 (2003): 423–52. Print.

Tobin, Lad. "Self-Disclosure as a Strategic Teaching Tool: What I Do — and Don't — Tell My Students." *College English* 73.2 (2010): 196–206. Print.

Valdes, Guadalupe. "Bilingual Minorities and Language Issues in Writing." *Written Communication* 9.1 (1992): 85–136. Print.

Villanueva, Victor. *Bootstraps: From an American Academic of Color.* Urbana: NCTE, 1993. Print.

West, Candace, and Sarah Fenstermaker. "Accountability in Action: The Accomplishment of Gender, Race, and Class in a Meeting of the University of California Board of Regents." *Discourse and Society* 13.4 (2002): 537–63. Web. 13 May 2010.

Wolfe, Joanna. "Gesture and Collaborative Planning: A Case Study of a Student Writing Group." *Written Communication* 22.3 (2005): 298–332. Print.

Wortham, Stanton. *Acting Out Participant Examples in the Classroom.* Philadelphia: John Benjamins, 1994. Print.

——. *Learning Identity: The Joint Emergence of Social Identification and Academic Learning.* New York: Cambridge UP, 2006. Print.

——. *Narratives in Action.* New York: Teachers College P, 2001. Print.

Young, Morris. *Minor Re/Visions: Asian American Literacy Narratives as a Rhetoric of Citizenship.* Carbondale: Southern Illinois UP, 2004. Print.

Ilona Leki

Meaning and Development of Academic Literacy in a Second Language

As English continues to expand into a global language (Kachru, 1992; Penny-cook, 1994), English learners worldwide experience pressure to develop literacy in English, often a high level of academic literacy. Yet, book titles such as *The Violence of Literacy* (Stuckey, 1991) and references to literacy as genocidal (Purcell-Gates, 1998) point to a growing recognition that literacy is neither innocent nor unproblematic. The potential negative consequences of enforced literacy described by these writers hold ethical implications for those of us involved in English literacy development and require us to examine the issues raised by second- (or third- or fourth-) language literacy and to become more fully aware of the complexity of the enterprise. This complexity entails differing conceptions of the meaning and role of literacy across cultures. It is my hope that such a cross-cultural approach to thinking about literacy will help to engender sympathy and respect for learners of English as an additional language by promoting a better understanding of the task they face in acquiring English academic literacy.

Even from the perspective only of native language literacy (Street, 1995), it is clear that literacy, certainly including academic literacy, is not a single, uniform, unitary skill and that literacy can be properly understood only from the perspective of a social context and not as the possession or personal cognitive ability of a single individual. If literacy is neither a unitary skill nor a personal possession independent of context, then what it means to be academically literate necessarily varies from one culture to the next. Being academically literate in Chinese, for example, means, among other things, having knowledge of thousands of characters and enough familiarity with the works of writers of antiquity to be able to quote them without hesitation in certain contexts. This concept of academic literacy is not the same for English. Attempting to move across cultures and languages into new literacies, academic or otherwise, complicates literacy acquisition qualitatively.

This chapter examines four of the complicating issues raised by the development of academic literacy in English as a second language (ESL): correctness, range, identity, and discourse community values.

This article is reprinted from Brian Huot, Charles Bazerman, and Beth Stroble (eds.), *Multiple Literacies for the 21st century* (Cressowood: Hampton Press, 2004), 115–28.

CORRECTNESS

illiteracies

When I first started teaching, the grammar and vocabulary idiosyncrasies of second language (L2) writers were actually called "illiteracies." In other words, if L2 English learners made grammar and vocabulary errors, no matter how competent they were in their own languages, they were, for some, illiterate. These days most trained teachers of L2 academic literacy think of the language variances of L2 writers either as interlanguage forms (Selinker, 1972; i.e., intermediary grammars that are systematic and rule-governed but exhibit features unlike target language features) or as a type of *contact variety* of English, a term that comes from studies of pidgins and creoles and refers to mediating language forms that develop when people who do not speak each other's languages attempt to communicate.

Whatever such forms are called, questions of correctness do arise, if only in terms of whether or not the contact language forms are comprehensible to the members of an academically literate community. These issues of correctness arise not just in terms of producing text but also in interpreting text. How "correct" does a reading have to be to qualify as an instantiation of academic literacy in an L2? Peirce and Stein (1995) recount a striking case of conflicting instantiations of English academic literacy. A group of Black South African high school students whose first language (L1) was not English were asked to participate in piloting a text to be used in an English language proficiency test for university admissions. The text was based on a newspaper story about a group of 80 monkeys, four of whom were shot in the effort to stop their wild rampage against a home in Durban, where they attacked a boy, two policemen, and the house itself. (The monkeys had apparently become enraged at the entrapment of a mother monkey and her baby.) As one of the White L1 English authors explained, she and her colleagues took the text to be "a simple factual report" about this incident with monkeys in Durban. The Black high school students doing the pilot test, however, regarded the text as racist, one of them interpreting the passage as being "about Black people, who are the 'monkeys' 'on the rampage' in White people's homes" (p. 56). Another said "It's about who owns the land—the monkeys think the land belongs to them but the Whites think they own the land" (p. 56). Although the text was withdrawn as a test item, these students, who hoped eventually to be admitted to the university, were obviously not participants in the same interpretive community as the White test makers. Had the piloting not occurred, the students' "misinterpretation" may well have been read as a simple lack of L2 English academic literacy.

But the issue of correct interpretation can arise at the most basic level. For example, in responding to one student's text written under some time constraints in a composition class, I wrote something like "It's too bad you didn't have more time to finish." He was mortified because as he understood it, I was telling him his paper was bad, "too bad." When issues of correctness and comprehensibility arise, the question becomes, how correct does something have to be to be comprehensible? How distant and unlikely can an interpretive frame be and still qualify as a literate reading in L2? How closely does the reading and writing of an L2 English learner have to match that of other members of an L1 English literate culture, including in terms of grammatical accuracy, and what are the consequences when the mismatch leads to misunderstanding?

RANGE

Range of literate abilities is also a very important issue for L2 English students. Normally, we would probably associate academic literacy with the ability to use and produce texts in a fairly wide range of general academic contexts. This is the meaning of academic literacy that undergirds the undergraduate general education curriculum. But with L2 learners once again we may need a different perspective. For example, one of the participants (Yang) in a research project of mine majored in nursing. Although she was trained as a physician and practiced medicine in the People's Republic of China, when she came to the United States, she was in her middle 30s and had not really studied English beyond high school. She had a great deal of difficulty making herself understood orally and produced contact variety writing. In fact, the first report she wrote for a nursing class was simply returned to her as unacceptable because of the problems her professor noted in language. Yang's general extemporaneous written work never really got much better in the three years of her nursing program, but she eventually graduated with a solid B average because all of her exams in the nursing program were multiple choice; whenever she had to write a paper she always made use of the writing center and of her husband's and her young adolescent daughter's better command of grammar and vocabulary to screen the paper before she turned it in; and much of the writing required of her at the university was in the form of nursing care plans that are written in symbols and abbreviations as incomprehensible to most English users as a foreign language. In sum, the range of her academic literacy was quite narrow although I believe no one would challenge its depth within her field of expertise. Nevertheless, her L2 academic literacy, one that is so narrow and so dependent, again pushes at the margins of what it means to have L2 academic literacy.

IDENTITY ISSUES

Issues of identity arise to some degree in any language learning situation, but the poignancy of the issues are seen most clearly through the example of Fan Shen (1989), whose frequently quoted article appeared in *College Composition and Communication*. As Shen explained, he was a Chinese graduate student studying American literature and having trouble with his writing. His professor told him to stop worrying about being so academic in his writing and to just be himself. That advice made Shen realize that he could not in fact be himself in English because when he was himself, he was Chinese, and when his real Chinese self wrote something, it was not what his American professors were looking for. In order to write what they expected of him, he had to create and pretend to be a different self, an English-speaking self, one that did not mind arrogantly writing in the first person, one who put himself forward as having himself thought up these ideas he wrote and defended, rather than his Chinese self who did not write in the first person and whose native rhetoric required him to look to the authority of other writers and credit them with the ideas he wrote about. He had to pretend to be self-confident and assertive instead of circumspect, tentative, and suggestive as he really was. He managed, but only by becoming someone else, by creating an alter ego, a bold self-centered English-speaking person. Asking that someone create an alter ego is quite a lot to ask in the name of English academic literacy development. Why was it not possible for Shen to remain a Chinese person in his English writing?

Shen was a graduate student and possibly a visa student. That is, enough of his emotional and intellectual development had already taken place in Chinese so that he was able to resist the English assault against his Chinese self productively. The tension between identity and the development of L2 academic literacy presents an even more problematic and painful set of issues for younger students, particularly those who come to the United States as permanent residents. First, Cognitive Academic Language Proficiency (CALP), a concept proposed by Cummins (1979), develops somewhat independently from what Cummins called Basic Interpersonal Communicative Skills (BICS). In other words, although permanent resident students may be quite capable of handling their real-world communicative needs, including everyday reading and writing needs, that proficiency is of a different nature from the kinds of proficiency needed to succeed in academically oriented tasks. CALP takes a relatively long time to develop, long enough so that permanent resident students entering English medium high schools may in fact get to graduation before having developed academic proficiency in English (Collier, 1987). Bosher (1998) further suggests that this situation is exacerbated for refugee students, whose education may be interrupted by stays in refugee camps en route to permanent residences; to complicate matters, these students may not be academically literate in their first language (Fu, 1995; for a less academic perspective on these issues, see also Fadiman, 1997).

When permanent resident students enter college, we sometimes witness the sad and frustrating result of the educational system's response to these students, who communicate well in the everyday world but whose academic literacy is less well developed. In moving and eye-opening research on L2 students' experiences in the transition between high school and college, Harklau (2000) explored the situation of a small group of permanent resident students whose identities were in effect constructed for them by their teachers and classmates in high school, identities that they embraced. The four whom Harklau studied were considered top students in their high schools because they always did their homework as required, they tried hard academically and seemed to think education was important and teachers were to be respected, and they behaved well in class, so unlike native U.S. students with their disregard for schooling, as their teachers said. These L2 students' teachers in high school praised them to the domestic students as models, pointing out how they obviously valued education despite their language "handicaps." With their first semester in college, however, their identities were reconstructed, not as model students, but first and foremost as ESL students, as students who had to be separated out from the other graduates of U.S. high schools because their proficiency in English (presumably in writing) was judged to be insufficient to allow them to take mainstream freshman writing classes. This reinterpretation of their identities was an embarrassment and a humiliation for these students, who had up to this point been taking all their high school classes with the U.S. students; they dressed like them, liked the same entertainments, lived like U.S. teenagers, and had been praised for their efforts in high school despite their language problems. They had become fully invested in their English-speaking identities. Now, after all this time succeeding in English, they were redefined, in the name of academic literacy, as failures in English, not primarily as model students but as ESL students.

ACADEMIC DISCOURSE COMMUNITY VALUES

At least in part, the development of academic literacy entails sharing the values of an academic discourse community, including subscribing to its expressed or tacit assumptions about what it means to be academically literate, that is, what it means to be one of the members of the literacy club, as Smith (1988) said. The academic discourse community in this U.S. culture currently values, among other things, critical thinking, developing "voice," and avoiding plagiarism. It might be useful to examine these values by first looking at different conceptions of what academic literacy means and how it is acquired in different cultures in order to make the point that beliefs about and attitudes toward literacy themselves form a part of literacy and that the acquisition of academic literacy in an L2 can be impeded by clashing culture-bound, often implicitly held values. The point of such an examination is to problematize these values as local and historical rather than universal and eternal. This critique then is intended to underscore the status of L1 English academic values as contingent and so to work against the colonizing of other literacies and concomitant devaluation of the literacy knowledge and practices of L2 English learners.

Although the research exists (see, e.g., Street, 1993), we in the United States have not focused much on research on cross-cultural academic literacy besides the large volume of work on contrastive rhetoric, which is fairly limited in scope, dealing mainly with patterns of text structure, not with values, beliefs, attitudes toward, or development of academic literacy (see also, Carson, 1992). One possible insight from contrastive rhetoric that moves beyond organizational issues appears in the often cited, although perhaps somewhat controversial, work by Hinds (1987) on Reader- and Writer-Responsible text. From his analyses of texts in Japanese and English, Hinds concluded that in some cultures, such as the

United States, the burden of communication falls on the writer. That is, it is the writer's responsibility to make the meaning of a text as transparent as possible for the reader by explicitly explaining what the main point of the text is, how the text is divided, how various parts of the text are related to each other. On the other hand, other cultures prefer Reader-Responsible writing. In this case, it is the reader's responsibility to read between the lines, to intuit the meaning the writer only hints at, to see through disparate parts of the text to their underlying unity. If in fact such cultural preferences exist, it is easy to see why a highly literate reader and writer from a Reader-Responsible academic culture would have some difficulty seeing the value of and thus being willing to take on the habits and preferences of someone from a Writer-Responsible culture, and vice versa. In other words, if Hinds's studies hold up, U.S. reader/writers might find Japanese writing diffuse, suggestive, but unclear; Japanese reader/writers might find U.S. writing lockstep, simplistic, overly specified.

In addition to studying texts across cultures in an attempt to understand the nature of academic literacy, we might look cross-culturally at literacy training. In describing literacy training and practices in Korea, Lee and Scarcella (1992) noted that in grammar school Korean children are encouraged to keep daily journals that are collected once a week though not graded or corrected, that children are regularly asked to write to commemorate special occasions, and that many urban Korean families with children subscribe to special daily newspapers for children that report world, national, and local news, among other things. As adults, Koreans particularly appreciate poetry and short fiction. In fact, Lee and Scarcella reported that Koreans are, amazingly, accustomed to constructing poems on the spot. They refer to an article in the *Los Angeles Times* from 1988 that described a radio talk show host in Korea going out onto the street and randomly asking people to construct poems to express their opinions on the then current government corruption scandal.

However, although the Korean "person on the street" reported on in the article seems able and willing to create poetry, essay writing is not taught in schools and so not practiced much, with the general public apparently feeling, according to these authors, that only experts in a subject area are qualified to write essays on that topic. They also report the comments of a Korean university student who claims that the really good Korean writers spend a great deal of time planning what they will write, gathering their thoughts, and so once an essay is written, writers are unlikely to be inclined to spend time revising it. By contrast, the U.S. literate community seems to hold strong beliefs about the value of revising. Ability and willingness to revise practically define U.S. notions of expertise in writing.

Moving to China for a glimpse of other ways with words, we learn from Kohn (1992) something about reading instruction in the PRC. In Chinese reading classes, children are taught to read slowly and be sure they know each word before moving on; to reread difficult sentences until the meaning is clear; to look up definitions of all unknown words in a dictionary. As Kohn points out, this list of dos and don'ts is almost exactly the opposite of what current reading instruction theory recommends in this country, particularly in the instruction of L2 reading, where learners are encouraged to read fast to get the gist; use background knowledge to guess meaning; focus on main ideas, not details; and guess the meanings of unknown words instead of looking them up right away.

Clearly, attitudes and beliefs about academic literacy and literacy acquisition differ across cultures. With these differences as a backdrop, we might now turn to some of the values and beliefs that undergird academic literacy practices in this culture. One of the currently most pervasive and highly prized stances before text in this culture is that required for critical thinking. Critical thinking appears to mean approaching text with a combination of skepticism and analysis. It also appears to be taken for granted that critical thinking represents a universal good, and it is sometimes argued that for students from countries that value rote memorization in education (with all the negative connotations this term indexes), critical thinking is a skill or attitude that is especially important to teach to L2 students, suggesting that they in particular, because of their educational backgrounds, lack the ability to take such an approach. It is also only recently that writing researchers are finally beginning to examine critical thinking with a bit of critical distance.

Atkinson (1997) links the notion of critical thinking with the glorification of individualism, standing alone against the crowd or against the received wisdom of a particular text. He points out that not all countries have this obsession with the power and importance of the individual above the group that undergirds current notions of critical thinking, and so we should be clear that this notion of critical thinking is culture bound, preferred by some academically literate communities as a way of approaching text at this particular time. It is neither a universal value nor an expression of the universal good. Atkinson's analysis is important for those of us who deal with students who come from cultures where the proper approach to a text is not a critical approach, from cultures that encourage a less individualistic stance before text. His discussion reminds us of the arrogance of believing that, because at this moment in time we feel that a critical approach works well for us, we must require it of every student that comes our way, not as an option but as the only appropriate form of intellectual engagement.

But perhaps more important to remember is that, although the U.S. academic discourse community currently finds the critical thinking approach to text useful and other cultures may find this approach to text less interesting, useful, or appropriate for whatever reason, not adopting a critical thinking stance before a text in an educational context cannot be equated with an inability to think critically. It would in fact be ludicrous to make such an assumption. After all, what culture, what part of the world does not at one time or another witness the political unrest and/or protest that can be one of the consequences of thinking critically, analytically, skeptically? Certainly, L2 English students can and do think critically, without our help, and very often their critical thinking is directed at the United States, at what we do here in general and at what we do in our classes in particular. Those who despair that these students are not critical enough need to have more conversations with them. But approaching a text, especially certain kinds of texts, with a primary view to finding fault with it may simply not be an appropriate stance to take before a text, at least not certain texts and perhaps not in an initial encounter. What might those certain texts be? They might easily be religious texts, but they might well also be academic texts in academic settings, especially on subjects the students do not know much about, and most especially on subjects related to a culture that is not their own (see, e.g., Johns, 1991).

Like critical thinking, another value associated in this culture with academic literacy and taught in writing classes, although mentioned only rarely in disciplinary courses across the curriculum, is the development of an authorial voice. An apparent goal of writing classes in this culture is the development of a sense of individual difference: to set oneself apart from the others, to be unlike other writers, to let individual voices stand out and be heard. Such a stance is open to the criticism, in a post-structuralist context, that it emphasizes to students the discredited notion of the unified, autonomous subjectivity, posits the notion as natural and universal rather than constructed and determined, and thus casts as unnatural anyone for whom such an emphasis on individualism is not automatic.

In addition to reemphasizing our heavy bias toward individualism, the notion of voice appears to be associated, at least to some degree, with a willingness to self-disclose and herein lies another potential problem for L2 writing development. On one hand, not all cultures encourage young people to self-disclose in classrooms, to talk about their personal experiences and opinions; that simply is not what school is for. And on the other hand, in other educational systems, that kind of self-disclosure may in fact be considered very appropriate but exclusively for schoolchildren, not for adults at a university, who would be expected to be able to exercise self-control and to find ways to self-disclose among their family and friends, not in a classroom. *this is somt. true*

In other words, while English writing teachers value voice in student writing, it too must be considered contingent, valued in a particular time and place, but not an essential component of academic literacy and so perhaps not worth hammering on too much in L2 reading/writing classes. (For further discussion of voice in L2 writing, see the special issue on voice in the *Journal of Second Language Writing*, Belcher & Hirvela, 2001.)

And finally, plagiarism. Although critical thinking and voice are relative newcomers to the list of qualities that writers are currently being encouraged to exhibit, the nearly absolute requirement to avoid plagiarism has been around much longer. But not forever. Strictures against plagiarism are neither universal nor ahistorical; they appear to have begun in the English-speaking world during the Renaissance and for specific historical reasons. Pennycook (1996) traces the history of plagiarism in the West and helps us to put into perspective this currently greatest of literacy sins. The reason it is important to see plagiarism as a notion limited to a particular time and place is to blunt the hysteria with which accusations of plagiarism are surrounded. Blunting this hysteria is especially important when dealing with L2 students for at least three reasons. First, in many cultures citing someone else's work without saying who the source is marks the writer as particularly steeped in literate culture. It is a sign of respect toward the reader as well, indicating the writer's belief that the reader is too literate to require a source reference.

The second reason not to exaggerate the importance of plagiarism is related to culturally dependent notions of what it is to learn. For example, in an incident at my school, a group of Malaysian students came to see me in despair that their history teacher was giving them Fs on a recent exam because he was accusing them of plagiarism. As they adamantly maintained, they had not plagiarized. They had simply done what good students do; they had memorized portions of the textbook. During the exam they wrote exactly the correct answer, taken from the textbook word for word, from memory, not copied from the book, which is what they understood we meant here by plagiarism. They had learned the material by heart, which to them meant, really learned it. Clearly, their view of learning clashed with the view the professor had. He had faith in the idea that only if you can more or less say something in your own words can you claim to have learned it. I leave open the question of how well "your own words" are able to accurately retain the meaning of what you might be trying to learn. In any case, this teacher did not want these students to use the textbook author's words.

But the third reason to view plagiarism with a bit more distance is that in a sense L2 students are always using others' words. How can they not? Because of a limited linguistic repertoire in their L2, they may simply have no other way available to them to restate what they just read. They may not be able to tell if an attempted paraphrase in fact paraphrases an original text. Or having limited options themselves, they may find the original captures for them the one best way to say something. As one student said, "If you have a . . . text in perfect English, that's exactly . . . what you should say and this is the best way. Then [because you don't want to plagiarize] you have to find another way. This is funny. . . . So you have to change it and then it gets worse. Kind of sad" (Leki & Carson, 1997, p. 59). This is not to say that L2 English learners do not need to be aware of the great store this culture puts in "using your own words," only that plagiarism elicits emotional reactions from teachers and perhaps others that are entirely out of proportion to the event, and L2 literacy teachers need to be aware of our own deep enculturation on the topic.

To set the beliefs and practices of these different discourse communities in contrast, then, we find some cultures where reading instruction recommends careful focus on detail to understand text and others where the focus is on global approaches to help understand a text; some where poetry is part of everyday life but expressing personal opinion in essays is left to experts in the subject area and others where essay writing, developing individual voice, and expressing personal opinion constitute the quintessence of knowing how to write; some that value implicitness above overexplaining, others that consider implicitness to be vague, maybe even deceitful, and value straightforward, clearly explicit approaches instead.

But how much do these differences matter? Could we not just recognize that there are differences and move on? To try to answer these questions, it might be useful to look at the experience of one more L2 learner, highly literate in her L1, English, and very motivated to develop L2 literacy. Bell (1995) describes her attempt to learn Chinese and explains how implicit clashing assumptions about literacy on her part and on the part of her Chinese tutor led to frustration and feelings of failure. Bell began studying written Chinese at the same time as she began oral Chinese. She felt she progressed well in oral Chinese but began to feel increasingly miserable about what she perceived as her lack of progress in written Chinese. Her Chinese writing tutor would introduce one character at a time, showing how the strokes are made and in what order and Bell would then be asked to practice, practice, practice that same character.

But Cindy, her tutor, was never satisfied; her feedback was consistently that the characters lacked balance and that Bell needed to concentrate more, feedback that became increasingly irritating and incomprehensible to Bell as the months went on and she was still practicing the same characters over and over. She finally came to realize that what was getting in her way were certain basic assumptions she had about learning, deeply held convictions that had made of her all her life an efficient and accomplished learner in her own culture. She examines two particularly striking clashes of assumptions. First, Bell assumed that the characters she was learning could more or less be split into their forms and their content, that her goal was to be able to recognize and generally reproduce a character, and that she could clean up the niceties of reproducing the forms perfectly later. That is, as long as the characters were recognizable for what they were, superficial issues like neatness and attractiveness could be worried about later. But for Cindy, the Chinese tutor, appearance was essential; form was inextricably linked to content; presentation, not just ideas, was crucial. There was no first sloppy draft and then going back to clean it up; in Cindy's view, for Bell to develop the mental discipline to succeed (i.e., to become literate), each character needed to be perfect each time.

The second area in which Bell's and Cindy's assumptions conflicted had to do with learning style. Bell had become a successful academic through her engaged, questioning, active learning style. When she tried to use the same style with Cindy in learning to write Chinese, Cindy told her that "the way to learn is to receive. . . . You do a lot of observing and then you think about it" (p. 698). Cindy is clearly not talking about passive rote learning; you do a lot of observing and then you think about it, she says. But it is possible that the attitude toward learning that Cindy expresses here may be interpreted in U.S. culture as passive, unquestioning, unengaged, and the people, say Chinese, who use this style and believe in this way of learning (and for good reason because they have probably become academically successful using it), these people may well be viewed in U.S. culture as not thinking critically, not developing personal voice, maybe likely to plagiarize by wanting to copy text word for word. As we see in Bell's example, it is difficult to understand cross-cultural literacies without first examining the assumptions of our own L1 literacy and then being willing to challenge or suspend the values tied to it.

The question of academic discourse communities finally presents itself to L2 literacy teachers in two forms. First, if beliefs and attitudes about L1 literacy and about the acquisition of L1 literacy inform approaches and attitudes toward L2 literacy acquisition, L2 literacy teachers need to do more to understand the kinds of literacy expectations and attitudes students bring with them from their families and their home cultures and to build on those expectations. Remaining ignorant of other cultures' approaches to literacy may cause us to misunderstand our students' actions and motivations and to misinterpret the causes of obstacles they may be experiencing in acquiring L2 literacy.

Second, L2 reading/writing teachers need to think long and hard about our own academic discourse community. What is it? Specifically, what community do we belong to? As we introduce L2 students to academic literacy, whose discourse community are we representing to them? In the course of doing research on professors' expectations about writing across disciplines, I learned that in our College of Agriculture, before turning in papers to their professors, students are asked to run a computer check of the length of each of the sentences in their reports. The computers there are programmed to flag any sentences longer than 21 words. I was stunned to learn this. In my L2 writing classes I encouraged students to try to combine short sentences into longer ones, telling them, as I believe, that in English we tend to value embedding at the sentence level; complex sentences lend an air of maturity to writing. Apparently, however, this belief is not shared in the discourse community of the College of Agriculture. There, longer sentences are discouraged as more likely to be confusing than short sentences. Whose discourse community was I representing in what I was teaching my students, my L2 English students who are in college to study engineering, business, agriculture, computer science, math, biology? Clearly, I was representing the English department's discourse community to my students as the very holder of the meaning of what it is to be literate—the English department, the academic discourse community that is the most likely to assign essays to write rather than reports, the one that values personal disclosure to develop a writer's voice, the one that encourages, even requires, students to express personal opinions on topics they may know very little about, the one literacy community that my L2 English students are the very least likely to want to join. I would argue that it is important to keep reminding ourselves that different communities value different aspects of reading and writing, and English department literacy values are not universal and do not define literacy in general. This knowledge, however, puts L2 reading/writing teachers in the odd and conflicted situation of trying to introduce L2 English students to literacy communities we ourselves do not belong to and of belonging to a community they have no reason to be introduced to.

In view of the place of English in the world today and the role it sometimes plays in both empowering and dramatically constraining the lives and futures of people from different L1 backgrounds, I feel an interrogation of the characteristics of L1 English literacy and its place among the other literacies in the world is a task that L1 English literates are morally and ethically obliged to undertake. Given how complex literacy issues in second, third, or fourth languages can become, perhaps the only reasonable stance to take, at least initially, is one of modest flexibility and willingness to learn from others, one in which "You do a lot of observing and then you think about it."

OBSERVE

REFERENCES

Atkinson, D. (1997). A Critical Approach to Critical Thinking in TESOL. *TESOL Quarterly, 31,* 71–94.

Belcher, D., & Hirvela, A. (Eds.). (2001). *Journal of Second Language Writing, 10* [Special issue on Voice in L2 Writing].

Bell, J. (1995). The Relationship between L1 and L2 Literacy: Some Complicating Factors. *TESOL Quarterly, 29,* 687–704.

Bosher, S. (1998). The Composing Process of Three Southeast Asian Writers at the Post-secondary Level. *Journal of Second Language Writing, 7,* 205–241.

Carson, J. (1992). Becoming Biliterate: First Language Influences. *Journal of Second Language Writing, 1,* 37–60.

Collier, V. (1987). Age and Acquisition of Second Language for Academic Purposes. *TESOL Quarterly, 21,* 617–641.

Cummins, J. (1979). Linguistic Interdependence and the Educational Development of Bilingual Children. *Review of Education Research, 49,* 222–251.

Fadiman, A. (1997). *The Spirit Catches You and You Fall Down.* New York: Farrar, Straus & Giroux.

Fu, D. (1995). *My Trouble Is My English.* Portsmouth, NH: Boynton/Cook.

Harklau, L. (2000). From "Good Kids" to the "Worst": Representation of English Language Learners across Educational Settings. *TESOL Quarterly, 34,* 35–67.

Hinds, J. (1987). Reader vs. Writer Responsibility: A New Typology. In U. Connor & R. Kaplan (Eds.), *Writing across Languages: Analysis of L2 Text* (pp. 141–152). Reading, MS: Addison-Wesley.

Johns, A.M. (1991). Interpreting an English Competency Examination: The Frustrations of an ESL Science Student. *Written Communication, 8,* 379–401.

Kachru, B. (1992). *The Other Tongue: English across Cultures.* Urbana: University of Illinois Press.

Kohn, J. (1992). Literacy Strategies for Chinese University Learners. In F. Dubin & N. Kuhlman (Eds.), *Cross-Culture Literacy: Global Perspectives on Reading and Writing* (pp. 113–125). Englewood Cliffs, NJ: Prentice-Hall.

Lee, C., & Scarcella, R. (1992). Building upon Korean Writing Practices: Genres, Values, and Beliefs. In F. Dubin & N. Kuhlman (Eds.), *Cross-culture literacy: Global Perspectives on Reading and Writing* (pp. 143–161). Englewood Cliffs, NJ: Prentice-Hall.

Leki, I., & Carson, J. (1997). "Completely Different Worlds": EAP and the Writing Experiences of ESL Students in University Courses. *TESOL Quarterly, 31,* 39–69.

Peirce, B., & Stein, P. (1995). Why the "Monkeys Passage" Bombed: Tests, Genres, and Teaching. *Harvard Educational Review, 65,* 50–65.

Pennycook, A. (1994). *The Cultural Politics of English as an International Language*. New York: Longman.

Pennycook, A. (1996). Borrowing Others' Words: Text, Ownership, Memory, and Plagiarism. *TESOL Quarterly, 30*, 201–230.

Purcell-Gates, V. (1998, October). *Literacy at Home and Beyond*. Paper presented at Watson Conference on Rhetoric and Composition, Louisville, KY.

Selinker, L. (1972). Interlanguage. *International Review of Applied Linguistics, 10*, 209–231.

Shen, F. (1989). The Classroom and the Wider Culture: Identity as a Key to Learning English Composition. *College Composition and Communication, 40*, 459–466.

Smith, F. (1988). *Joining the Literacy Club*. Princeton, NJ: Princeton University Press.

Street, B. (Ed.). (1993). *Cross-cultural Approaches to Literacy*. New York: Cambridge.

Street, B. (1995). *Social Literacies: Critical Approaches to Literacy in Development, Ethnography and Education*. New York: Longman.

Stuckey, J. (1991). *The Violence of Literacy*. Portsmouth, NH: Boynton/Cook.

Paul Kei Matsuda

The Myth of Linguistic Homogeneity in U.S. College Composition

In "English Only and U.S. College Composition," Bruce Horner and John Trimbur identify the tacit policy of unidirectional English monolingualism, which makes moving students toward the dominant variety of English the only conceivable way of dealing with language issues in composition instruction. This policy of unidirectional monolingualism is an important concept to critique because it accounts for the relative lack of attention to multilingualism in composition scholarship. Yet it does not seem to explain why second-language issues have not become a central concern in composition studies. After all, if U.S. composition had accepted the policy of unidirectional monolingualism, *all* composition teachers would have been expected to learn how to teach the dominant variety of English to students who come from different language backgrounds. This has not been the case. While Geneva Smitherman and Victor Villanueva argue that coursework on language issues (though certainly not a monolingualist approach) should be part of every English teacher's professional preparation (4), relatively few graduate programs in composition studies offer courses on those issues, and even fewer require such courses. As a result, the vast majority of U.S. college composition programs remain unprepared for second-language writers who enroll in the mainstream composition courses. To account for this situation, I want to take Horner and Trimbur's argument a step further and suggest that the dominant discourse of U.S. college composition not only has accepted English Only as an ideal but it already assumes the state of English Only, in which students are native English speakers by default.

That second-language writing has not yet become a central concern in composition studies seems paradoxical given the historical origin of U.S. college composition as a way of "containing" language differences and sealing them off from the rest of U.S. higher education. Robert J. Connors has suggested that U.S. composition arose in response to perceived language differences — texts written by ostensibly some of the brightest native English speakers that included numerous errors in "[p]unctuation, capitalization, spelling, [and] syntax" (*Composition* 128). Susan Miller also points out that college composition "has provided a continuing way to separate the unpredestined from those who belong [. . .] by encouraging them to leave school, or more vaguely, by convincing large numbers of *native speakers* and otherwise accomplished *citizens* that they are 'not good at English'" (74; emphasis added). To a large extent, however, issues that prompted

---

This article is reprinted from *College English* 68.6 (July 2006): 637–51.

the rise of the composition requirement are weak forms of language differences that affect native speakers of English — matters of convention and style as well as performance errors that arise from factors such as unfamiliar tasks, topics, audiences, or genres. While U.S. composition has maintained its ambivalent relationship with those weak forms of language differences, it has been responding to the presence of stronger forms of language differences — differences that affect students who did not grow up speaking privileged varieties of English — not by adjusting its pedagogical practices systematically at the level of the entire field but by relegating the responsibility of working with those differences to second-language specialists (Matsuda, "Composition"; Shuck).

I am not trying to imply that there has not been *any* effort to address second-language issues in composition studies. I recognize that a growing number of writing teachers who face those issues in their classes on a daily basis have developed, often on their own initiative, additional expertise in issues related to language differences. What I want to call into question is why the issue of language difference has not become a central concern for *everyone* who is involved in composition instruction, research, assessment, and administration. I argue that the lack of "a profession-wide response" (Valdés 128) to the presence of strong forms of language differences in U.S. composition stems from what I call the myth of linguistic homogeneity — the tacit and widespread acceptance of the dominant image of composition students as native speakers of a privileged variety of English. To show how the myth of linguistic homogeneity came into being, I examine the early history of various attempts at linguistic containment, which created a condition that makes it seem acceptable to dismiss language differences. My intention is not to argue against all forms of linguistic containment. Rather, I want to problematize its long-term implication — the perpetuation of the myth of linguistic homogeneity — which has in turn kept U.S. composition from fully recognizing the presence of second-language writers who do not fit the dominant image of college students.

THE IMAGE OF COLLEGE STUDENTS AND THE MYTH OF LINGUISTIC HOMOGENEITY

Behind any pedagogy is an image of prototypical students — the teacher's imagined audience. This image embodies a set of assumptions about who the students are, where they come from, where they are going, what they already know, what they need to know, and how best to teach them. It is not necessarily the concrete image of any individual student but an abstraction that comes from continual encounters with the dominant student population in local institutional settings as well as the dominant disciplinary discourses. Images of students are not monolithic; just as teachers incorporate pedagogical practices from various and even conflicting perspectives, their images of students are multiple and complex, reflecting local institutional arrangements as well as the teaching philosophies and worldviews of individual teachers. Although there is no such thing as a generalized college composition student, overlaps in various teachers' images of students constitute a dominant image—a set of socially shared generalizations. Those generalizations in turn warrant the link between abstract disciplinary practices and concrete classroom practices.

Having a certain image of students is not problematic in itself; images of students are inevitable and even necessary. Without those images, discussing pedagogical issues across institutions would be impossible. An image of students becomes problematic when it inaccurately represents the actual student population in the classroom to the extent that it inhibits the teacher's ability to recognize and address the presence of differences. Just as the assumption of whiteness as the colorless norm has rendered some students of color invisible in the discourse of composition studies (Prendergast 51), theoretical practices that do not recognize and challenge other inaccurate images reinforce the marginal status of those students by rendering them invisible in the professional discourse. At the same time, pedagogical practices based on an inaccurate image of students continue to alienate students who do not fit the image.

One of the persisting elements of the dominant image of students in English studies is the assumption that students are by default native speakers of a privileged variety of English from the United States. Although the image of students as native speakers of privileged varieties of English is seldom articulated or defended—an indication that English Only is already taken for granted—it does surface from time to time in the work of those who are otherwise knowledgeable about issues of language and difference. A prime example is Patrick Hartwell's "Grammar, Grammars, and the Teaching of Grammar," a widely known critique of grammar instruction in the composition classroom. In his analysis of a grammar exercise, he writes that "[t]he rule, however valuable it may be for nonnative speakers, is, for the most part, simply unusable for native speakers of the language" (116). While this is a reasonable claim, to argue against certain pedagogical strategies based on their relevance to native speakers seems to imply the assumption of the native-English-speaker norm. Hartwell also claims that "[n]ative speakers of English, regardless of dialect, show tacit mastery of the conventions of Standard English" (123), which seems to trivialize important structural differences between privileged varieties of U.S. English and many other domestic and international varieties of English.

Language issues are also inextricably tied to the goal of college composition, which is to help students become "better writers." Although definitions of what constitutes a better writer may vary, implicit in most teachers' definitions of "writing well" is the ability to produce English that is unmarked in the eyes of teachers who are custodians of privileged varieties of English or, in more socially situated pedagogies, of an audience of native English speakers who would judge the writer's credibility or even intelligence on the basis of grammaticality. (As a practicing writing teacher, I do not claim to be immune to this charge.) Since any form of writing assessment—holistic, multiple-trait, or portfolio assessment—explicitly or implicitly includes language as one of the criteria, writing teachers regularly and inevitably engage in what Bonny Norton and Sue Starfield have termed "covert language assessment" (292). As they point out, this practice is not problematic in itself, especially if language issues are deliberately and explicitly included in the assessment criteria *and* if students are receiving adequate instruction on language issues. In many composition classrooms, however, language issues beyond simple "grammar" correction are not addressed extensively even when the assessment of student texts is based at least partly on students' proficiency in the privileged variety of English. As Connors has pointed out, "the sentence [...] as an element of composition pedagogy is hardly mentioned today outside of textbooks" ("Erasure" 97), and has become a "half-hidden and seldom-discussed classroom practice on the level of, say, vocabulary quizzes" (120). It is not unusual for teachers who are overwhelmed by the presence of language differences to tell students simply to "proofread more carefully" or to "go to the writing center"; those who are not native speakers of dominant varieties of English are thus being held account-able for what is not being taught.

The current practice might be appropriate if all students could reasonably be expected to come to the composition classroom having already internalized a privileged variety of English — its grammar and the rhetorical practices asso-ciated with it. Such an expectation, however, does not accurately reflect the student population in today's college composition classrooms. In the 2003–04 academic year, there were 572,509 international students in U.S. colleges (Institute of International Education, *Open Doors 2004*), most of whom came from countries where English is not the dominant language. Although the num-ber has declined slightly in recent years, international students are not likely to disappear from U.S. higher education any time soon. In fact, many institu-tions continue to recruit international students — because they bring foreign capital (at an out-of-state rate), increase visible ethnic diversity (which, unlike linguistic diversity, is highly valued), and enhance the international reputation of the institutions — even as they reduce or eliminate instructional support programs designed to help those students succeed (Dadak; Kubota and Abels).

In addition, there is a growing number of resident second-language writers who are permanent residents or citizens of the United States. Linda Harklau, Meryl Siegal, and Kay M. Losey estimate that there are at least 150,000 to 225,000 active learners of English graduating from U.S. high schools each year (2–3). These figures do not include an overwhelmingly large number of functional bilinguals — students who have a high level of proficiency in both English and another language spoken at home (Valdés) — or native speakers of tradition-ally underprivileged varieties of English, including what has come to be known as world Englishes. The myth of linguistic homogeneity — the assumption that college students are by default native speakers of a privileged variety of English — is seriously out of sync with the sociolinguistic reality of today's U.S. higher education as well as of U.S. society at large. This discrepancy is especially problematic considering the status of first-year composition as the only course that is required of virtually all college students in a country where, according to a 2000 U.S. Census, "more than one in six people five years of age and older reported speaking a language other than English at home" (Bayley 269).

THE POLICY OF LINGUISTIC CONTAINMENT
IN U.S. COLLEGE COMPOSITION

The perpetuation of the myth of linguistic homogeneity in U.S. college composition has been facilitated by the concomitant policy of linguistic containment that has kept language differences invisible in the required composition course and in the discourse of composition studies. Since its beginning in the late nineteenth century at Harvard and elsewhere, the first-year composition course has been a site of linguistic containment, quarantining from the rest of higher education students who have not yet been socialized into the dominant linguistic practices (Miller 74). While institutions have used the composition course as a site of linguistic containment for nonnative speakers of privileged varieties of English, institutions have found ways to exclude more substantive forms of language differences even from the composition course by enacting several strategies for linguistic containment. The first and most obvious strategy is to exclude language differences from entering higher education altogether by filtering them out in the admission process. Another common strategy, especially when the number of students from unprivileged language backgrounds is relatively small, is to ignore language issues, attributing any difficulties to individual students' inadequate academic preparation. Even when language differences are recognized by the teacher, those differences are often contained by sending students to the writing center, where students encounter peer tutors who are even less likely to be prepared to work with language differences than are composition teachers (Trimbur 27–28).

The policy of containment is enacted most strongly through the placement procedure, which is unique to composition programs in the sense that students do not normally have the option of choosing a second-language section — perhaps with the exception of speech communication courses. The all-too-common practice of using language proficiency tests for composition placement (Crusan 20) is a clear indication that the policy of linguistic containment is at work. Even when direct assessment of writing is used for placement, the use of holistic scoring may lead raters to give disproportionate weight to language differences because "a text is so internally complex (e.g., highly developed but fraught with grammatical errors) that it requires more than a single number to capture its strengths and weaknesses" (Hamp-Lyons 760). Based on placement test results, many students are placed in noncredit "remedial" courses where they are expected to erase the traces of their language differences before they are allowed to enroll in the required composition course. In other cases, students are placed — sometimes after their initial placement in mainstream composition courses — in a separate track of composition courses for nonnative English speakers that can satisfy the composition requirement. These courses, though sometimes costly to students, provide useful language support for them and are necessary for many students who will be entering the composition course as well as courses in other disciplines where the myth of linguistic homogeneity prevails. At the same time, these placement practices also reify the myth by making it seem as if language differences can be effectively removed from mainstream composition courses.

In the remainder of this essay, I examine the emergence of the myth of linguistic homogeneity and the concomitant policy of linguistic containment in the late nineteenth and the early twentieth centuries — the formative years of U.S. college composition. U.S. higher education during this period is marked by several influxes of international students, many of whom came from countries where English was not the dominant language. Each of these influxes was met not by attempts to reform composition pedagogy but by efforts to contain language differences — efforts that continue even today. I focus on developments before the 1960s because it was the period when a number of significant changes took place. Although English had long been part of U.S. higher education, the English language began to take the center stage in the late nineteenth century through the use of English composition as part of the college entrance exam (Brereton 9) and through the creation of the English composition course that tacitly endorsed the policy of unidirectional monolingualism (Horner and Trimbur 596-97). It was also during this period that language differences in the composition classroom became an issue because of the presence of a growing number of international students, and many of the placement options for second-language writers were created (Matsuda and Silva; Silva). My focus is on international students because, until the latter half of the twentieth century, resident students from underprivileged language backgrounds were systematically excluded from higher education altogether (Matsuda, "Basic" 69-72).

WAVES OF INTERNATIONAL STUDENTS AND THE POLICY OF CONTAINMENT

The image of U.S. college students as native speakers of more or less similar, privileged varieties of English had already been firmly established by the mid-nineteenth century. Although the larger U.S. society had always been multilingual (Bayley 269), language differences were generally excluded from English-dominated higher education of the nineteenth century. The assumption of the native-English-speaker norm was, at least on the surface, more or less accurate in the mid-nineteenth century, when access to college education was restricted to students from certain ethnic, gender, religious, socioeconomic, and linguistic backgrounds. As David Russell notes, U.S. colleges before the end of the Civil War were "by modern standards extraordinarily homogeneous, guaranteeing a linguistic common ground" (35). While U.S. higher education began to shift from exclusive, elitist establishment to more inclusive vehicle for mass education during the latter half of the nineteenth century, the traditional image of college students remained unchallenged for the most part. Although the creation of what have come to be known as historically black colleges had provided African American students access to higher education since the early nineteenth century, they did not affect the dominant image because they were physically segregated from the rest of the college student population. In fact, those colleges served as the sites of containment—ethnic as well as linguistic. The Morrill Act, first passed in 1862 and then extended in 1890, gave rise to land-grant institutions across the nation that made college education open to women as well as to students from a wider variety of socioeconomic groups. Yet, native speakers of nonprivileged varieties of English did not enter higher education in large numbers because the ability to speak privileged varieties of English was often equated with racialized views of the speaker's intelligence.

One of the major institutional initiatives that contributed to the exclusion of language differences was the creation of the entrance exam—first instituted at Harvard in 1874 and then quickly and widely adopted by other institutions. The entrance exam at Harvard was motivated in part by "a growing awareness of the importance of linguistic class distinctions in the United States" (Connors, *Composition* 128). Harvard course catalogs during this period indicate that the entrance exam at Harvard included "reading English aloud" or writing with "[c]orrect [. . .] spelling, punctuation, grammar, and expression" (qtd. in Brereton 34). Miller also points out that "forms of this examination became the most powerful instrument for discriminating among students in higher education" (63), effectively excluding students who did not fit the dominant linguistic profile. Even in the nineteenth century, however, the assumption of linguistic homogeneity in higher education was not entirely accurate, and it moved farther and farther away from the sociolinguistic reality of U.S. higher education. One group of students who brought significant language differences were international students who entered U.S. higher education through different admission processes and therefore were not subject to linguistic filtering (Matsuda, "Basic" 71–72).

The history of international ESL students in U.S. higher education goes at least as far back as 1784, when Yale hosted a student from Latin America; in the mid-1800s, students from China and Japan also attended Yale and Amherst College (King 11). The first sizable influx of international students came in the latter half of the nineteenth century, when U.S. higher education began to attract an increasing number of students from other countries as it developed research universities modeled after German institutions. Most of these international students were from Asian countries that were "undergoing modernization with the help of knowledge acquired from Western countries" (Bennett, Passin, and McKnight 26). During the late nineteenth century, European students also came to U.S. higher education "not so much seeking an education that was not available to them at home, as out of a desire to see America, the 'country of the future'" (Institute of International Education, 1955 *Handbook*, 6).

In the late nineteenth century, when many of the international students were sponsored by their governments, language preparation was generally considered to be the responsibility of individual students or their sponsoring governments, and U.S. colleges and universities usually provided little or no institutional support for international students' cultural and linguistic adjustments. For instance, students from China and Japan, most of whom were sponsored by their respective governments, usually received language instruction before coming to the United States. In many cases, however, their language preparation was less than adequate by the standard of U.S. institutions, and they were sent to preparatory schools, where they were "placed in classes with the youngest children" (Schwantes 194). The Japanese government continued to send students to U.S. colleges; however, they were selected by a rigid examination, and their progress was monitored by a supervisor sent by the Japanese government (Institute of International Education, 1955 *Handbook*, 4). By the 1880s, the practice of holding the sponsoring government responsible for providing language preparation became difficult to sustain as the number of government-sponsored students declined, giving way to an increasing number of privately funded students (Bennett, Passin, and McKnight 32).

The second influx came in the early part of the twentieth century, when internationally known research institutions began to attract a growing number of international students, most from countries where English was not the dominant language. Although in 1911 there were only 3,645 international students in U.S. higher education, the number began to grow rapidly after the conclusion of World War I (1914–18). This change was due partly to European students' dissatisfaction "with their own traditions of education" as well as Asian students' need for "new foundations for modern systems of education" (Kandel 39). Another factor that contributed to the growth was the national interest of the United States. The U.S. government's growing concern with post-WWI international relations—especially with European nations—prompted the establishment in 1919 of the Institute of International Education (IIE) with support from the Carnegie Endowment for International Peace. The IIE was successful in "stimulat[ing] interest in student exchange [and] encouraging public and private groups to sponsor international students" (Institute of International Education, 1955 *Handbook*, 7). By 1920, the number of international students had reached 6,163 and was continuing to increase (Institute of International Education, 1961 *Handbook*, 230). In 1930, U.S. colleges and universities reported the presence of 9,961 international students (Darian 105).

The growing presence of international students from non-English-dominant countries became an issue among hosting institutions. Some educators recognized the problem of the traditional pedagogy based on the dominant image of students. Isaac Leon Kandel, for example, wrote that international students did not benefit as much from the instruction not because of their lack of ability but because "courses were organized primarily with the American student, familiar with American ideals, aims, history, and social and political background, in mind" (50). The solution, however, was not to challenge the dominant image but to contain issues of linguistic and cultural differences by providing additional instruction — an approach that might have seemed reasonable when the number of international students was relatively small. To provide linguistic support for those who did not fit the traditional image of college students, institutions began to develop special English-language courses. According to a 1923 survey of four hundred institutions, all but two institutions stated that they had "provision for special language help by official courses or by voluntary conversation classes" (Parson 155). Although it continued to be "a common rule to refuse admission to students who are unable to speak and read English," about 50 percent of institutions offered "special courses for backward students" (155).

In 1911, Joseph Raleigh Nelson in the Engineering College at the University of Michigan created the first English courses specifically designed for international students (Klinger 1845–47), followed by Teachers College of Columbia University, which created special courses for matriculated international students in 1923 (Kandel 54). Harvard University created its first English courses for international students in 1927, and George Washington University and Cornell University followed suit in 1931 (Allen 307; Darian 77). While there were some exceptions — such as the program at Michigan, which continued for several decades — many of these early programs were ad hoc in nature. The initial innovation at Harvard ceased to exist after a while and, by the 1940s, second-language writers at Harvard had come to be mainstreamed into "regular" sections of composition courses with additional help from individual tutoring services (Gibian 157). At George Washington, the separate section of composition "used the same materials as the sections for Americans and [. . .] was conducted by the same teacher"; however, "none of the English instructors really desired to teach that group," and this program was later found to be unsuccessful (Rogers 394). The courses at Columbia, which allowed students to enroll simultaneously in college-level courses, were also found to be ineffective in containing language differences (Kandel 54). Other institutions, especially where the number of international students was relatively small, dealt with language differences "by a process of scattering foreigners through different courses, so that they must mingle freely with others, rather than segregating them for group study in classes where they may persist in using their own language" (Parson 155).

Following the announcement of the Good Neighbor Policy in 1933, the State Department began to bring international students from Latin America to provide them with scientific and technical training, a development that led to the creation, in 1941, of the English Language Institute (ELI) at the University of Michigan. As an intensive program, it separated students from the college-level courses for a period of several months while they focused on developing their English language proficiency. Although the program was initially intended for Spanish-speaking graduate students from Latin America, it later broadened its scope to include undergraduate students and students from other language backgrounds. The Michigan ELI provided a model for intensive English programs throughout the United States and in many other countries, paving the way for the next wave of ESL courses, which were created after World War II (Matsuda, "Composition" 701–06).

Although the number of international students had declined somewhat during the Depression and World War II, the conclusion of the war brought another influx of international students. The international student population surged from less than 8,000 in 1945 to 10,341 in 1946 (Darian 105), when the United States replaced Germany as the most popular destination for international students. The number doubled in the next two years and, by 1949, there were 26,759 international students (Institute of International Education, 1949 *Handbook*, 7, 14). To contain the language differences these students brought with them, an increasing number of institutions—including those that had relatively small but steady enrollments of international students—began to create separate English courses and programs on a permanent basis (Schueler 309). In 1949, Harvard once again created a special noncredit course for small groups of students from Europe, providing a preparation for the required composition course (Gibian 157). At about the same time, Queens College developed a multilevel intensive English language program with its own teaching and testing materials (Schueler 312–14). Tulane University also created a noncredit English course for second-language writers. Sumner Ives reported that all nonnative English speakers at Tulane, unless "individually excused," were required to enroll in a special English course for nonnative speakers before taking the required English course. This program was unique in that the status of the course was determined after the beginning of the semester. Based on a reading test during the orientation, the teacher would decide whether each student should move to a "regular section" or remain in the remedial course. When most of the remaining students had limited English proficiency, the course was taught as a remedial English language course, using the materials developed by the ELI at Michigan. The course became credit-bearing when a large number of students had reached advanced English proficiency, and the textbooks for regular sections of composition courses were used (Ives 142–43).

The number of ESL writing courses continued to grow. In 1953, according to Harold B. Allen, about 150 institutions reported the existence of English-as-a-second-language programs for international students; by 1969, the number had nearly doubled. In addition, 114 institutions reported that they offered summer programs for international students (Allen 308). Initially, many of those courses were offered on a noncredit basis as preparation for a regular English requirement. These courses focused not only on writing but also on reading and oral communication skills. Noncredit English courses for nonnative speakers offered at many institutions adopted the textbook series developed by the ELI at Michigan, and intensive language courses modeled after Michigan's ELI also became widespread, providing systematic instruction before second-language writers were allowed to enroll in regular college-level courses.

Yet a semester or two of extra language instruction was often not enough to help students fit the dominant image—after all, learning a second language is a time-consuming process, especially for adult learners—and they continued to bring language differences to college composition courses. For this reason, institutions began to develop a separate track of required composition courses for second-language writers — courses that were designed to keep language differences out of the required composition course. In 1954, Michigan's Department of English Language and Literature in the College of Literature, Science, and Art created one of the first credit-bearing ESL composition courses that paralleled the sections of English courses for native speakers of English (Klinger 1849). The University of Washington followed suit with a three-credit composition course for second-language writers, which emphasized purposeful cross-cultural communication with an audience rather than the language drills or linguistic analyses commonly used in intensive language programs at the time (Marquardt 31).

EMBRACING LANGUAGE DIFFERENCES AS THE NEW NORM

The assumption of linguistic homogeneity, which was more or less accurate in U.S. higher education institutions of the mid-nineteenth century, became increasingly inaccurate as linguistic diversity grew over the last two centuries. Yet the growing presence of international students did not lead to a fundamental reconsideration of the dominant image of students in the composition classroom. It was not because the separate placement practices were able to eliminate language differences. For a number of reasons, none of these programs was able to contain language differences completely: because language learning is a time-consuming process; because students often come with a wide range of English-language proficiency levels; and because developing placement procedures that can account for language differences is not an easy task. As Ives wrote, "neither a frankly noncredit course for all, nor [NNES students'] segregation into separate but parallel courses, nor their distribution throughout the regular courses is completely satisfactory" (142). Instead, the dominant image of students remained unchallenged because the policy of containment kept language differences in the composition classroom from reaching a critical mass, thus creating the false impression that all language differences could and should be addressed elsewhere. In other words, the policy of unidirectional monolingualism was enacted not so much through pedagogical practices in the mainstream composition course as through delegation of students to remedial or parallel courses that were designed to keep language differences from entering the composition course in the first place.

The policy of containment and the continuing dominance of the myth of linguistic homogeneity have serious implications not only for international second-language writers but also for resident second-language writers as well as for native speakers of unprivileged varieties of English. Many institutions place students into basic writing classes without distinguishing writing issues and language issues partly because underlying language differences are not easily discernible by observing student texts that seem, at least on the surface, strikingly similar to one another (Matsuda, "Basic" 74). As a result, basic writing courses often enroll many second-language writers — both international and resident — although many basic writing courses, like the credit-bearing composition courses, are designed primarily for U.S. citizens who are native speakers of a variety of English (68).

By pointing out the problem of the policy of containment, however, I do not mean to suggest that these placement practices be abandoned. On the contrary, many students do need and even prefer these placement options. As George Braine suggests, many — though certainly not all — second-language writers prefer second-language sections of composition, where they feel more comfortable and where they are more likely to succeed. To deny these support programs would be to further marginalize normative speakers of English in institutions of higher education where the myth of linguistic homogeneity will likely continue to inform the curriculum as well as many teachers' attitude toward language differences. Instead, composition teachers need to resist the popular conclusion that follows the policy of containment — that the college composition classroom can be a monolingual space. To work effectively with the student population in the twenty-first century, all composition teachers need to reimagine the composition classroom as the multilingual space that it is, where the presence of language differences is the default.[1]

NOTE

1. I am grateful to Min-Zhan Lu, Bruce Horner, Dwight Atkinson, and Christina Ortmeier-Hooper for their helpful and constructive comments on earlier versions of this essay.

WORKS CITED

Allen, Harold B. "English as a Second Language." *Current Trends in Linguistics: Linguistics in North America.* Vol. 10. Ed. Thomas A. Sebeok. The Hague: Mouton, 1973. 295–320.

Bayley, Robert. "Linguistic Diversity and English Language Acquisition." *Language in the USA: Themes for the Twenty-First Century.* Ed. Edward Finegan and John R. Rickford. Cambridge: Cambridge UP, 2004. 268–86.

Bennett, John W., Herbert Passin, and Robert K. McKnight. *In Search of Identity: The Japanese Overseas Scholar in America and Japan.* Minneapolis: U of Minnesota P, 1958.

Braine, George. "ESL Students in First-Year Writing Courses: ESL versus Mainstream Classes." *Journal of Second Language Writing* 5 (1996): 91–107.

Brereton, John C. *The Origins of Composition Studies in the American College, 1875–1925: A Documentary History.* Pittsburgh: U of Pittsburgh P, 1995.

Connors, Robert J. *Composition-Rhetoric: Backgrounds, Theory, and Pedagogy.* Pittsburgh: U of Pittsburgh P, 1997.

——. "The Erasure of the Sentence." *CCC 52* (2000): 96–128.

Crusan, Deborah. "An Assessment of ESL Writing Placement Assessment." *Assessing Writing* 8 (2002): 17–30.

Dadak, Angela. "No ESL Allowed: A Case of One College Writing Program's Practices." *Politics of Second Language Writing: In Search of the Promised Land.* Ed. Paul Kei Matsuda, Christina Ortmeier-Hooper, and Xiaoye You. West Lafayette, IN: Parlor, 2006. 94–108.

Darian, Stephen G. *English as a Foreign Language: History, Development and Methods of Teaching.* Norman: U of Oklahoma P, 1972.

Gibian, George. "College English for Foreign Students." *College English* 13 (1951): 157–60.

Hamp-Lyons, Liz. "Rating Nonnative Writing: The Trouble with Holistic Scoring." *TESOL Quarterly* 29 (1995): 759–62.

Harklau, Linda, Meryl Siegal, and Kay M. Losey. "Linguistically Diverse Students and College Writing: What Is Equitable and Appropriate?" *Generation 1.5 Meets College Composition: Issues in the Teaching of Writing to U.S.-Educated Learners of ESL.* Ed. Linda Harklau, Kay M. Losey, and Meryl Siegal. Mahwah, NJ: Erlbaum, 1999. 1–14.

Hartwell, Patrick. "Grammar, Grammars, and the Teaching of Grammar." *College English* 47 (1985): 105–27.

Horner, Bruce, and John Trimbur. "English Only and U.S. College Composition." *CCC* 53 (2002): 594–630.

Institute of International Education. *Handbook on International Study: A Guide for Foreign Students and for U.S. Students on Study Abroad.* New York: Institute of International Education, 1955.

——. *Handbook on International Study: For Foreign Nationals.* New York: Institute of International Education, 1961.

——. *Open Doors 2004.* New York: Institute of International Education, 2005.

Ives, Sumner. "Help for the Foreign Student." *CCC* 4 (1953): 141–44.

Kandel, Isaac Leon. *United States Activities in International Cultural Relations.* Washington, DC: American Council on Education, 1945.

King, Henry H. "Outline History of Student Migrations." *The Foreign Students in America.* Ed. W. Reginald Wheeler, Henry H. King, and Alexander B. Davidson. New York: Association, 1925. 3–38.

Klinger, Robert B. "The International Center." *The University of Michigan: An Encyclopedic Survey in Four Volumes.* Vol. 4. Ed. Walter A. Donnelly. Ann Arbor: U of Michigan P, 1958. 1843–49.

Kubota, Ryuko, and Kimberly Abels. "Improving Institutional ESL/EAP Support for International Students: Seeking the Promised Land." *Politics of Second Language Writing: In Search of the Promised Land.* Ed. Paul Kei Matsuda, Christina Ortmeier-Hooper, and Xiaoye You. West Lafayette, IN: Parlor, 2006.

Marquardt, William F. "Composition in English as a Second Language: Cross Cultural Communication." *CCC* 17 (1966): 29–33.

Matsuda, Paul Kei. "Composition Studies and ESL Writing: A Disciplinary Division of Labor." *CCC* 50 (1999): 699–721.

——. "Basic Writing and Second Language Writers: Toward an Inclusive Definition." *Journal of Basic Writing* 22 (2003): 67–89.

Matsuda, Paul Kei, and Tony Silva. "Cross-Cultural Composition: Mediated Integration of U.S. and International Students." *Composition Studies* 27 (1999): 15–30.

Miller, Susan. *Textual Carnivals: The Politics of Composition.* Carbondale: Southern Illinois UP, 1991.

Norton, Bonny, and Sue Starfield. "Covert Language Assessment in Academic Writing." *Language Testing* 14 (1997): 278–94.

Parson, A. B. "The Foreign Student and the American College." *The Foreign Students in America.* Ed. W. Reginald Wheeler, Henry H. King, and Alexander B. Davidson. New York: Association, 1925. 149–74.

Prendergast, Catherine. "Race: The Absent Presence in Composition Studies." *CCC* 50 (1998): 36–53.

Rogers, Gretchen L. "Freshman English for Foreigners." *School and Society* 61 (1945): 394–96.

Russell, David. *Writing in the Academic Disciplines: A Curricular History.* 2nd ed. Carbondale: Southern Illinois UP, 2002.

Schueler, Herbert. "English for Foreign Students." *Journal of Higher Education* 20 (1949): 309–16.

Schwantes, Robert S. *Japanese and Americans: A Century of Cultural Relations.* New York: Harper and Brothers and the Council on Foreign Relations, 1955.

Shuck, Gail. "Combating Monolingualism: A Novice Administrator's Challenge." *WPA: Writing Program Administration* 30.1–2 (2008): 59–82.

Silva, Tony. "An Examination of Writing Program Administrator's Options for the Placement of ESL Students in First Year Writing Classes." *Writing Program Administration* 18.1/2 (1994): 37–43.

Smitherman, Geneva, and Victor Villanueva. Introduction. *Language Diversity in the Classroom: From Intention to Practice.* Ed. Smitherman and Villanueva. Carbondale: Southern Illinois UP, 2003.

Trimbur, John. "Peer Tutoring: A Contradiction in Terms?" *Writing Center Journal* 7.2 (1987): 21–28.

Valdés, Guadalupe. "Bilingual Minorities and Language Issues in Writing: Toward Profession-wide Response to a New Challenge." *Written Communication* 9 (1992): 85–136.

Bruce Horner, Min-Zhan Lu, Jacqueline Jones Royster, and John Trimbur[1]

OPINION: Language Difference in Writing: Toward a Translingual Approach

Growing numbers of U.S. teachers and scholars of writing recognize that traditional ways of understanding and responding to language differences are inadequate to the facts on the ground. Language use in our classrooms, our communities, the nation, and the world has always been multilingual rather than monolingual. Around the globe, most people speak more than one language. Indeed, they speak more than one variation of these languages. In addition, these languages and variations are constantly changing as they intermingle. The growing majority of English speakers worldwide — including substantial numbers within the United States — know other languages, and, through interaction, the Englishes they use vary and multiply.

Traditional approaches to writing in the United States are at odds with these facts. They take as the norm a linguistically homogeneous situation: one where writers, speakers, and readers are expected to use Standard English or Edited American English — imagined ideally as uniform — to the exclusion of other languages and language variations. These approaches assume that heterogeneity in language impedes communication and meaning. Hence, the long-standing aim of traditional writing instruction has been to reduce "interference," excising what appears to show difference.

We call for a new paradigm: a translingual approach. This approach sees difference in language not as a barrier to overcome or as a problem to manage, but as a resource for producing meaning in writing, speaking, reading, and listening. When faced with difference in language, this approach asks: What might this difference do? How might it function expressively, rhetorically, communicatively? For whom, under what conditions, and how? The possibility of writer error is reserved as an interpretation of last resort.

In calling for a translingual approach, we hope to forward efforts of a growing movement among teacher-scholars of composition and the language arts generally to develop alternatives to conventional treatments of language difference. With this text, we aim to articulate a research-based and generative conceptual approach to language difference in pedagogy, research, and politics. Our call builds on the work of many — only some of whom, given space limitations, we can

---

This article is reprinted from *College English* 73.3 (Jan. 2011): 303–21.

acknowledge here.[2] Most obviously, our approach is aligned with the Conference on College Composition and Communication (CCCC) 1974 resolution declaring "Students' Right to Their Own Language."[3] That resolution defended the right of students (and all other writers) to use different varieties of English. It opposed the common, though inaccurate, view that varieties of English other than those recognized as "standard" are defective. It also opposed the view, just as inaccurate, that speakers of these varieties are themselves somehow substandard. It recognized the logicality of all varieties of English, the meanings to be gained by speakers and writers in using particular varieties of English, and the right of speakers and writers to produce such meanings. Subsequent resolutions, guidelines, and position statements by CCCC and the National Council of Teachers of English (NCTE) have extended and developed the implications of the "Students' Right" document. So, too, have other professional organizations, as well as many teacher-scholars both individually and through groups. These efforts have addressed bilingual education, English as a Second Language (ESL), English Only policies, and related issues.

The translingual approach we call for extends the CCCC resolution to differences within and across all languages. And it adds recognition that the formation and definition of languages and language varieties are fluid. Further, this approach insists on viewing language differences and fluidities as resources to be preserved, developed, and utilized. Rather than respond to language differences only in terms of rights, it sees them as resources.

The translingual approach encourages reading with patience, respect for perceived differences within and across languages, and an attitude of deliberative inquiry. Likewise, a translingual approach questions language practices more generally, even those that appear to conform to dominant standards. It asks what produces the appearance of conformity, as well as what that appearance might and might not do, for whom, and how. This approach thus calls for *more*, not less, conscious and critical attention to how writers deploy diction, syntax, and style, as well as form, register, and media. It acknowledges that deviations from dominant expectations need not be errors; that conformity need not be automatically advisable; and that writers' purposes and readers' conventional expectations are neither fixed nor unified.

The translingual approach asks of writing not whether its language is standard, but what the writers are doing with language and why. For in fact, notions of the "standard English speaker" and "Standard Written English" are bankrupt concepts. All speakers of English speak many variations of English, every one of them accented, and all of them subject to change as they intermingle with other varieties of English and other languages. Likewise, standards of written English are neither uniform nor fixed. What constitutes expected norms — for example, Edited American English — varies over time and from genre to genre. Indeed, these genres themselves change boundaries and intermingle.

This is not to deny the ongoing, dominant political reality that posits and demands what is termed standard, "unaccented" English in speech and "standard" (aka "correct," or "Edited American English") writing.[4] An industry of textbooks and mass media-style pundits, along with their followers, maintains that reality. But a translingual approach directly addresses the gap between actual language practices and myths about language spread through that industry's political work in order to combat the political realities those myths perpetrate. Though dominant ideology is always indifferent to the invalidity of its claims, we need not and should not accept its sway.

Myths of unchanging, universal standards for language have often been invoked to simplify the teaching and learning of language. But these have often resulted in denigrating the language practices of particular groups and their members as somehow "substandard" or "deviant." By contrast, a translingual approach takes the variety, fluidity, intermingling, and changeability of languages as statistically demonstrable norms around the globe. It confronts, as well, the practice of invoking standards not to improve communication and assist language learners, but to exclude voices and perspectives at odds with those in power. It treats standardized rules as historical codifications of language that inevitably change through dynamic processes of use. A translingual approach proclaims that writers can, do, and must negotiate standardized rules in light of the contexts of specific instances of writing. Against the common argument that students must learn "the standards" to meet demands by the dominant, a translingual approach recognizes that, to survive and thrive as active writers, students must understand how such demands are contingent and negotiable.

In short, a translingual approach argues for (1) honoring the power of all language users to shape language to specific ends; (2) recognizing the linguistic heterogeneity of all users of language both within the United States and globally; and (3) directly confronting English monolingualist expectations by researching and teaching how writers can work with and against, not simply within, those expectations. Viewing differences not as a problem but as a resource, the translingual approach promises to revitalize the teaching of writing and language. By addressing how language norms are actually heterogeneous, fluid, and negotiable, a translingual approach directly counters demands that writers must conform to fixed, uniform standards.

RESPONSES TO DIFFERENCE IN LANGUAGE

We can advance the definition of a translingual approach to language difference by setting it against sketches of two types of responses to language difference that historically have prevailed in the teaching of writing in the United States. Although specific teaching practices have deviated from both, and inevitably nuanced them, we use these sketches to represent the terms and expectations for the teaching of writing within and against which teachers have inevitably had to struggle. One type of response, which we referred to earlier as the traditional approach, has sought to eradicate difference in the name of achieving correctness, defined as writers' conformity with a putatively uniform, universal set of notational and syntactic conventions that we name Standard Written

English (or alternatively, Edited American English). This kind of response is problematic in at least four ways. First, it ignores significant differences between world Englishes and between writing practices with English in different genres, academic disciplines, work sites, and life worlds. Second, it ignores historically demonstrable fluctuations in notational and syntactic conventions. Third, it ignores how readers grant or withhold recognition of particular language practices as "correct" or "acceptable" — thereby often helping the powerful rig a game of demonstrating "mastery." And fourth, it ignores the value for ordinary language users and learners of challenging and transforming language conventions to revise knowledge, ways of knowing, and social relations between specific writers and readers. We take this response to be conservative in the root sense of attempting to preserve what is in fact a false ideal of a uniform language and language practice.

A second type of response has sought to distance itself from the eradicationist approach by acknowledging differences in language use; codifying these; and granting individuals a right to them. This response has thus appeared to be more tolerant and accommodating than the first. However, it assumes that each codified set of language practices is appropriate only to a specific, discrete, assigned social sphere: "home" language, "street" language, "academic" language, "business" language, "written" language (aka the "grapholect"), and so on. Despite the appearance of tolerance, this response is problematic on four counts. First, its codifications of language overlook the fluctuating character of each set of language practices. Second, it overlooks the ways in which each of these codified sets interacts with other sets within and beyond a given arena rather than being restricted to one discrete sphere. Third, like the more conservative response, it overlooks the role that readers' responses play in granting, or refusing to grant, recognition to particular language practices as appropriate to a particular sphere. Fourth, it fails to acknowledge the operation of power relations in defining what is appropriate, and often it resigns itself to these — for instance, designating certain English usages as appropriate only for a specific private sphere and thus inappropriate for public discourse. Masking the politics involved in hierarchically ordering these spheres, this response establishes and ranks its own presumably immutable categories and the groups affiliated with them: African Americans speaking "AAVE,"[5] working-class people using "working-class" language, "educated" people speaking and writing "educated" English, and so on. While it is both accurate and useful to identify the language strategies by which specific collectivities have tried to resist domination, the aim should be to honor their linguistic ingenuity and to encourage other innovative strategies — not to reify a set of forms that supposedly have intrinsic power.

Despite their differences, both these kinds of responses are aligned with the ideology of monolingualism by treating languages and language practices as discrete, uniform, and stable. They differ mainly in that, whereas the first assumes the universal applicability of a single language, the second allows for use of a plurality of languages, though each in a discrete site in hierarchical relation to others. Both kinds of response ignore the inevitability and necessity of interaction among languages, within languages, and across language practices. Both also ignore writers' and readers' need to engage the fluidity of language in pursuit of new knowledge, new ways of knowing, and more peaceful relations.

REDEFINING LANGUAGE FLUENCY, PROFICIENCY, AND COMPETENCE

A translingual approach requires that common notions of fluency, proficiency, and even competence with language be redefined. Insofar as any language practice represents a resource, we applaud efforts to increase students' fluency in as many languages and varieties of language as possible. Hence, we stand by the "English Plus" policy endorsed by CCCC, NCTE, and over forty other educational and civil rights organizations. However, in endorsing a translingual approach, we seek to move beyond an additive notion of multilingualism. We call for working to achieve fluency across language differences in our reading and writing, speaking and listening, so that we can become adept at processes of making and conveying meaning—processes that, particularly when they belong to less powerful communities, sometimes appear opaque to individual readers and listeners.

Because languages and language practices not only differ but fluctuate and interact, pursuit of mastery of any single identified set of such practices is inappropriate insofar as it leads language learners to a false sense of the stability of such practices and the finite character of language learning.[6] Instead, we recognize that we are all language learners, and that learning language is necessarily continuous precisely because language is subject to variation and change. Further, we recognize that language learners are also language users and creators. Thus, mastery must be redefined to include the ability of users to revise the language that they must also continuously be learning—to work with and on, not just within, what seem its conventions and confines.

Writers' proficiency in a language will thus be measured not by their ability to produce an abstracted set of conventional forms. Rather, it will be shown by the range of practices they can draw on; their ability to use these creatively; and their ability to produce meaning out of a wide range of practices in their reading. Translingual fluency in writing would be defined as deftness in deploying a broad and diverse repertoire of language resources, and responsiveness to the diverse range of readers' social positions and ideological perspectives. Translingual fluency in reading would be defined as openness to linguistic differences and the ability to construct useful meanings from perceptions of them.

ESL, BILINGUAL EDUCATION, AND FOREIGN LANGUAGE INSTRUCTION

A translingual approach to language differences is aligned with multilingual education insofar as that education aims to develop and broaden the repertoire of students' linguistic resources and to honor the resources of all language users. Thus, it is aligned with those forms of bilingual education that aim not to replace knowledge of one language with another, but to build on students' existing language abilities, including the teaching of English as a second language. However, it rejects the view that so-called English language learners are the only ones in need of language development. In line with the English Plus policy, a translingual approach supports efforts to increase the number of languages and language varieties that students know, and to deepen their knowledge of these. It supports the granting of academic credit to those students adding knowledge of English to their linguistic repertoire. Similarly, it supports efforts to increase English monolingual students' repertoire of languages and to award academic credit for such learning.

We support the rights of all to use the languages of their nurture. We reject discrimination on the basis of language identity and use. We honor the efforts of all who seek to recover and maintain languages in danger of disappearing, for these are crucial to human linguistic diversity and thus to human survival, as well as to the survival of specific collectivities. We are wary, however, of the ease with which historical descriptions of languages can become prescriptions and rationales for social exclusion. We encourage renewed focus by students of writing on the problematics of translation to better understand and participate in negotiations of difference in and through language, including those leading to the position that no translation is possible.

LANGUAGE RIGHTS, IMMIGRATION, AND STATE LANGUAGE POLICY

A translingual approach rejects as both unrealistic and discriminatory those language policies that reject the human right to speak the language of one's choice. The clear impracticality of such policies is demonstrated by those advocating English Only legislation. These advocates fail to define English, and inevitably they have to include exceptions to their stated policies for purposes of public health and safety.

But we also recognize that, in practice, vagueness in defining English can and does get used to justify discrimination against individuals and groups, who may be designated as failing to produce what those in power deign to recognize as "English," or "true English," or "Standard English," or "Edited American English," or "English without an accent." Such policies operate as faux-linguistic covers for discrimination against immigrants and minorities: in place of discrimination on the basis of presumed national, ethnic, racial, or class identity, discrimination is leveled on the basis of language use. In the specific case of English Only policies, the fact that these are advocated in a situation in which English is anything but threatened shows that language is being used as a proxy to discriminate on the basis of race, citizenship status, and ethnicity. This effort is the precise inverse of efforts to preserve those language practices that are, in fact, in danger of disappearing — for example, Native American languages — as a consequence of oppression and decimation of native peoples.

IMPLICATIONS FOR WRITING PROGRAMS

Advancing a translingual approach requires changes to writing programs in the design of writing curricula and in the hiring, training, and professional development of writing teachers.[7] At the very least, it requires making good on long-standing calls for giving all teachers of writing professional development in better understanding and addressing issues of language difference in their teaching. More ambitiously, it may well involve greater collaboration with departments of so-called foreign languages and greater attention to the problematics of translation in teaching writing. Graduate programs in rhetoric and composition need to take more seriously, and be more ambitious in making use of, what is now all too often treated as a token second-language requirement of its graduates. The challenge is to incorporate more multi- and cross-language work into graduate curricula. In short, new work, in which many faculty cannot yet claim expertise, will be demanded of both faculty and their students. That is the challenge of embracing a translingual approach, and its promise: the necessity of working on writing collaboratively with our students, our current colleagues, and those who can become our colleagues amid the realities of a translingual nation and world.

As a means toward advancing our collective efforts to articulate and enact translingual approaches to writing, we include here a selected bibliography of just some of the scholarship we have found helpful in our thinking about translingual work, and a website for a more extended working bibliography to which we invite readers to contribute suggestions. As will be immediately obvious, this work crosses traditional disciplinary boundaries separating composition studies from ESL, applied linguistics, literacy studies, "foreign" language instruction, and translation studies. And as will also be apparent from our bibliography, we are still at the beginning stages of our learning efforts in this project, which by definition will require the ideas and energy of many—including literacy workers using diverse languages, from outside as well as within the Anglo-American sphere.

We preface this set of resources with several questions we anticipate about the challenge we present for U.S. teachers of writing, with our answers, necessarily tentative.

How do monolingual teachers of writing teach a translingual approach? Wouldn't teachers of this approach have to be multilingual themselves?

Knowing more than one language can only benefit teachers of writing who aim to teach a translingual approach (and others). Yet it's also the case that teachers of writing self-identified as monolingual regularly use a mix of varieties of any one language, and that even ostensibly monolingual texts may be found to be more linguistically heterogeneous than is ordinarily recognized. Teachers can use the actual heterogeneity in genre, register, and language of ostensibly homogeneous texts to explore, with their students, the translingual activity that they and other writers are already engaging in, even when that is not ordinarily acknowledged. And although we recognize the benefit to all of expanding one's linguistic resources, the issue here is approach to language difference. Those identified as "monolingual" might nonetheless take a translingual approach to language difference, while some identified as "multilingual" might nonetheless take a monolingualist approach to language difference.

Does translingualism mean there's no such thing as error in writing?

No. All writers make mistakes, and all writers are usually eager to remove mistakes from their writing. Taking a translingual approach, however, means that teachers (and students) need to be more humble about what constitutes a mistake (and about what constitutes correctness) in writing, rather than assume that whatever fails to meet their expectations, even in matters of spelling, punctuation, and syntax, must be an error. For example, we can't assume that a student who writes "spills out" or "stepping stool" where some readers might expect to read "spells out" or "stepping stone" is making mistakes. However, a student (or any other) writer who following the date of this text's publication writes "2009" to identify the year of a letter he or she has just composed is either making a mistake, engaging in subterfuge, or needing to cue readers about the dating system he or she is employing. That the acceptability of notational practices is negotiable demands more responsibility, not less, from both writers and readers.

Does this mean there aren't any standards?

If by "standards" is meant a desire for quality writing, then no: readers expect, even demand, that writers try to do their best to communicate to their readers, just as writers expect, and sometimes demand, that readers work hard to make the best, most generous sense they can of writers' texts. It does mean that we need to recognize the historicity and variability of standards, which change over time, vary across genres, disciplines, and cultures, and are always subject to negotiation (and hence, change). We can and should teach standards, but precisely as historical, variable, and negotiable. This will help to demystify (and lessen confusion among students about) what these standards are, and will make students feel a greater sense of responsibility, as writers, for the writing practices they engage in.[8]

My students are all English monolinguals. Why would they need to learn a translingual approach to writing?

First, it's often difficult to assess students' actual language abilities—students who by some definitions might be English monolinguals might not be by other criteria. Second, virtually all students who are monolingual in the sense that they speak only English are nonetheless multilingual in the varieties of English they use and in their ability to adapt English to their needs and desires. And even if we overlook this resource, it's worth recalling that what we think of as English is itself linguistically heterogeneous in its origins and ongoing formations, as demonstrated by neologisms, the development of world Englishes, and shifting conventions.

Further, even if we were to accept that our students are English monolinguals, they are unlikely to be restricted in their writing, or their speech, to audiences of only other English monolinguals. Others to whom they write, and whose writing they read—including faculty, employers, fellow employees, fellow citizens, and members of their communities—are increasingly likely to know English as a second, third, or fourth language, and to know varieties of English that differ from what some recognize as Standard English or Edited American English. A translingual approach to differences can facilitate writers' interactions with the full range of users of English and other languages.

Finally, while increasing one's linguistic resources is always beneficial, taking a translingual approach is not about the number of languages, or language varieties, one can claim to know. Rather, it is about the disposition of openness and inquiry that people take toward language and language differences. For example, although we take a translingual disposition toward language difference in this text, it is still primarily monolingual by conventional definitions of multilingualism. Students who are identified by conventional standards as monolingual might take a translingual approach to language difference, as demonstrated by their response to unfamiliar ways of using language, while individuals identifiable by conventional standards as multilingual with regard to their own linguistic resources might well approach language differences in ways at odds with a translingual approach.

Don't students first need to learn the basics of writing in one language before taking on the challenges of writing in another language?

No. The problem here resides in assumptions about the basics and fluency. Scholars of basic writing have long since exploded the notion that adult writing students improve their writing by first attempting to master the so-called mechanics of writing before working on what are deemed to be higher-order features of writing. Instead, like all writers, student writers' command of various features of writing fluctuates: they may have more difficulty with issues addressed through copyediting as they attempt to write in different genres or about new topics or to unfamiliar audiences. Likewise, language users' spoken fluency with a particular language—even their "home" language—will fluctuate in relation to the genre and topic and circumstances of the speech situation.

Rather than put off translingual work, students can investigate, in order to make more conscious use of, differences in all features of written language, including syntax, punctuation, formatting, media, organization, and genre, addressing these in terms of their interrelations. They will gain fluency in working across language differences in all these areas, instead of attempting to achieve a chimerical fluency in one language alone.

How will taking a translingual approach to language differences help my students do well academically and in the job market?

The linguistic heterogeneity we speak of applies to all spheres of life, including the academic realm as well as public and private spheres. Except perhaps for professional actors, few walks of life require attaining native-like spoken fluency in a particular variety of a particular language (and even with professional actors, what is achieved is more likely to be simply what it is believed that particular audiences have learned to recognize as representative of a specific language variety). Instead, what is increasingly needed, and even demanded, is the ability to work across differences, not just of language but of disciplines and cultures. This requires changing our predispositions from those of monolingualism to translingualism. Monolingualism teaches language users to assume and demand that others accept as correct and conform to a single set of practices with language and, in multilingual situations, to assume and demand that others accept as correct and conform to multiple discrete sets of practices with language. By contrast, translingualism teaches language users to assume and expect that each new instance of language use brings the need and opportunity to develop new ways of using language, and to draw on a range of language resources. The ability to negotiate differences and to improvise ways to produce meaning across language differences with whatever language resources are available is becoming increasingly necessary, not only to careers and commerce, but to the chances for peace and justice.

I'm intrigued by the notion of taking a translingual approach, but I don't know how to do it. Where can I go for help?

Taking a translingual approach goes against the grain of many of the assumptions of our field and, indeed, of dominant culture. At the same time, it is in close alignment with people's everyday language practices. While we've found the works listed in the selected bibliography that follows to be helpful in thinking through why it is important to take a translingual approach, and what it might mean to do so, we don't claim expertise, nor do we believe it necessary to first acquire such expertise before taking up the important work that is called for. Instead, we believe we can all, teachers and students alike and together, develop ways of taking up such an approach by changing the kind of attention we pay to our language practices, questioning the assumptions underlying our learned dispositions toward difference in language, and engaging in critical inquiry on alternative dispositions to take toward such differences in our writing and reading.

Increasingly, our professional organizations are recognizing the need to take up these alternative dispositions and to cross disciplinary divides. We see this in moves to enable teachers to attend annual conferences of both Teachers of English to Speakers of Other Languages (TESOL) and CCCC (instead of having to choose one or the other). We see it in the work of individual scholars and groups of scholars to address cross-language work, the devotion of special issues of *College English* and *WPA* to scholarship addressing such work, and the ongoing efforts of such venues as the *Journal of Second Language Writing*, the Symposium on Second Language Writing, and the CCCC Language Policy Committee. But we also see this in the efforts of individual teachers and programs to confront the realities of language difference in writing in ways that honor and build on, rather than attempt to eradicate, those realities of difference in their work with their students.

The following teacher-scholars have seconded the project outlined in this text:

Lisa Arnold, University of Louisville
Resa Crane Bizzaro, Indiana University of Pennsylvania
Patricia Bizzell, College of the Holy Cross
Deborah Brandt, University of Wisconsin–Madison
A. Suresh Canagarajah, Pennsylvania State University
Ralph Cintron, University of Illinois at Chicago
Marilyn M. Cooper, Michigan Technological University
Laura Detmering, University of Louisville
Christiane Donahue, Dartmouth College
Matthew Dowell, University of Louisville
Tom Fox, California State University–Chico
Steven Fraiberg, Residential College in the Arts and Humanities, Michigan
    State University
Diana George, Virginia Polytechnic and State University
Keith Gilyard, Pennsylvania State University
Susan M. Griffin, University of Louisville
Jeanne Gunner, Chapman University
Joseph Harris, Duke University
Gail E. Hawisher, University of Illinois at Urbana-Champaign
Suzette A. Henke, University of Louisville
Wendy Hesford, The Ohio State University
David Jolliffe, University of Arkansas
Debra Journet, University of Louisville
Julia Kiernan, University of Louisville
Karen Kopelson, University of Louisville
Tika Lamsal, University of Louisville
Shirley Wilson Logan, University of Maryland
LuMing Mao, Miami University
Paul Kei Matsuda, Arizona State University
Carol Mattingly, University of Louisville
Peter Leslie Mortensen, University of Illinois at Urbana-Champaign
Samantha NeCamp, University of Louisville
Dhruba Jyoti Neupane, University of Louisville
Brice Nordquist, University of Louisville
Malea Powell, Michigan State University
Catherine Prendergast, University of Illinois at Urbana-Champaign
Scott L. Rogers, University of Louisville
Stephen Ruffus, Salt Lake Community College
Eileen E. Schell, Syracuse University
John Schilb, Indiana University–Bloomington
Cynthia L. Selfe, The Ohio State University
Ghanashyam Sharma, University of Louisville
Vanessa Kraemer Sohan, University of Louisville

Christine Tardy, DePaul University
Ryan Trauman, University of Louisville
Victor Villanueva, Washington State University
Bronwyn T. Williams, University of Louisville
Joanna Wolfe, University of Louisville
Xiaoye You, Pennsylvania State University
Morris Young, University of Wisconsin–Madison
Vershawn Ashanti Young, University of Kentucky

NOTES

1. This essay grew out of discussions the four of us had following, and inspired by, an October 2009 symposium at the University of Louisville, sponsored by the Thomas R. Watson Endowment and the Endowed Chair in Rhetoric and Composition. We thank all of those who participated in the symposium, whatever their views toward the ideas presented here, for their insights. We don't intend this essay to represent either the specific views, or the culmination, of the October symposium, at which different perspectives on a variety of issues were aired.

Our essay is neither all-inclusive on the issues it does address, nor the final word. We have developed this piece because we believe it is far past time for the issues it addresses to be engaged more aggressively in our field, and we hope to open a much-needed conversation that will be continued in many places, in many genres and forums, from many different points of view—with an eye toward change in the conceptual, analytical, and pedagogical frameworks that we use here.

At the end of this text, we include a list of colleagues who "second" the idea that we need to have these issues more fully on the table, and who believe, like us, that teaching, discussion, research, and scholarship (past, present, and future) in this area are important and deserve our direct attention. (Time constraints have so far restricted us to approaching only the symposium participants and invited speakers of the 2010 Thomas R. Watson Conference.) We invite those wishing to add their names to this list to contact Bruce Horner.

2. See the selected bibliography for more information on works cited and additional resources on which we've drawn.

3. Reaffirmed in 2003, with an annotated bibliography added in 2006 (CCCC Language Policy Committee).

4. The term *Edited American English* encapsulates the gap between linguistic practices and political realities. As a purely descriptive phrase, "Edited American English" applies to an enormous corpus of writing of incredible diversity: produced by Americans attempting to "write English" which has been subjected to editing. Our essay serves as one tiny contribution to that corpus. And yet, as the anticipated opacity of our text for some readers illustrates, at least some readers will fail to recognize in this text the features that would justify calling it Edited American English, because all of the three terms in the phrase are subject to dispute insofar as they represent not just descriptions but valuations ascribed to which writing should, and shouldn't, have legitimacy conferred upon it by identifying it as edited, American, or English.

5. There is a long and ongoing debate on whether to name the language practices of

African Americans "African American Vernacular English" (AAVE), "African American Language" (AAL), "African American English" (AAE), "Black English Vernacular" (BEV), "Black English" (BE), or "Ebonics" (see DeBose; Mufwene; Smitherman; Young).

6. As the contemporary Martinican writer Raphaël Confiant observes, notions of the stability of the language to be "mastered" often interfere with language learning:

> [A]près cinq ou dix années de scolarité plus ou moins chaotique, l'Haïtien moyen parvient à peine à articuler une phrase correcte en français alors que lorsqu'il émigré aux USA, au bout de six mois, il parle déjà anglais relativement couramment! [...] La raison est la suivante: en français, il est paralysé par l'épée de Damoclès d'une norme rigide, il crève de peur de commettre des fautes alors qu'en anglais, rien de tout cela ne pèse sur lui. Personne ne lui fera de remarque désobligeante sur son accent ou sur telle ou telle faut qu'il pourra inévitablement commettre au cours de son apprentissage.

7. Though we focus on the implications of a translingual approach for writing programs, clearly such an approach has implications for all programs of language study, within and outside "English."

8. Some readers will see our own decision to follow conventional notational practices as evidence that we are failing to practice what we appear to be preaching—shouldn't we be somehow more "translingual" in our spelling, diction, punctuation, syntax? To this, we observe that to include in one's writing recognizable deviations from what is expected in these matters (inserting the occasional "ain't" or "dissin' or "je ne sais quois") does not in itself necessarily demonstrate a translingual disposition toward language difference; for example, in certain instances it might serve only to advertise the breadth of the writer's linguistic repertoire. Conversely, our decision to use "&" instead of either "and" or "et" in our citation of the collection by Zarate, Lévy, & Kramsch (see selected bibliography) represents our effort to negotiate between readers' expectations for and familiarity with each of these options and our responsibility to the three authors. In other words, some readers' sense that we are in fact writing "standard" Edited American English is a product and effect of their reading practices, which we are at pains to persuade them to revise.

9. We plan to post this selected bibliography plus information about additional works online. We invite readers to send us their suggestions for adding to this online bibliography (contact Bruce Horner).

SELECTED BIBLIOGRAPHY[9]

Agnihotri, Rama Kant. "Towards a Pedagogical Paradigm Rooted in Multilinguality." *International Multilingual Research Journal* 1.2 (2007): 79–88. Print.

Alptekin, Cem. "Towards Intercultural Communicative Competence in ELT." *ELT Journal* 56.1 (Jan. 2002): 57–64. Print.

Bamgbose, Ayo. "Torn between the Norms: Innovations in World Englishes." *World Englishes* 17.1 (1998): 1–14. Print.

Bean, Janet, et al. "Should We Invite Students to Write in Home Languages? Complicating the Yes/No Debate." *Composition Studies* 31.1 (2003): 25–42. Print.

Bernabé, Jean, Patrick Chamoiseau, and Raphaël Confiant. *Éloge de la créolité.* Trans. M. B. Taleb-Khyar. Paris: Gallimard, 1989; Baltimore, Johns Hopkins UP, 1990. Print.

Bex, Tony, and Richard J. Watts, eds. *Standard English: The Widening Debate.* London: Routledge, 1999. Print.

Bourdieu, Pierre. *Language and Symbolic Power.* Ed. John B. Thompson. Trans. Gino Raymond and Matthew Adamson. Cambridge: Harvard UP, 1991. Print.

Brandt, Deborah. *Literacy in American Lives.* New York: Cambridge UP, 2001. Print.

Bruch, Patrick, and Richard Marback, eds. *The Hope and the Legacy: The Past, Present, and Future of "Students' Right to Their Own Language."* Cresskill: Hampton, 2004. Print.

Brutt-Griffler, Janina. *World English: A Study of Its Development.* Clevedon: Multilingual Matters, 2002. Print.

Canagarajah, A. Suresh. "Lingua Franca English, Multilingual Communities, and Language Acquisition." *Modern Language Journal* 91.5 (2007): 923–39. Print.

——. "Multilingual Writers and the Academic Community: Towards a Critical Relationship." *Journal of English for Academic Purposes* 1.1 (2002): 29–44. Print.

——. "The Place of World Englishes in Composition: Pluralization Continued." *CCC* 57.4 (2006): 586–619. Print.

Conference on College Composition and Communication. *CCCC Guideline on the National Language Policy. National Council of Teachers of English.* NCTE, 1988; updated 1992. Web. 19 Aug. 2008.

——. *CCCC Statement on Second Language Writing and Writers. National Council of Teachers of English.* NCTE, 2001; revised Nov. 2009. Web. 9 Dec. 2009.

——. *Conference on College Composition and Communication Language Policy Committee. National Council of Teachers of English.* NCTE, 2006. Web. 16 June 2010.

——. *Students' Right to Their Own Language. National Council of Teachers of English.* NCTE, 1974. Web. 31 Aug. 2009.

Confiant, Raphaël. "Créolité et francophonie: Un éloge de la diversalité." Web. 30 Sept. 2007.

Cope, Bill, and Mary Kalantzis, eds. *Multiliteracies: Literacy Learning and the Design of Social Futures.* London: Routledge, 2000. Print.

Coupland, Nikolas. Review article. "Sociolinguistic Prevarication about 'Standard English.'" *Journal of Sociolinguistics* 4.4 (2000): 622–34. Print.

Crawford, James. *Hold Your Tongue: Bilingualism and the Politics of "English Only."* Reading: Addison-Wesley, 1992. Print.

Cronin, Michael. *Translation and Globalization.* London: Routledge, 2003. Print.

Crystal, David. *English as a Global Language.* 2nd ed. Cambridge: Cambridge UP, 2003. Print.

DeBose, Charles. "The Ebonics Phenomenon, Language Planning, and the Hegemony of Standard English." *Talkin Black Talk: Language, Education, and Social Change.* Ed. H. Samy Alim and John Baugh. New York: Teachers College P, 2007. 30–42. Print.

Dubin, Fraida. "Situating Literacy within Traditions of Communicative Competence." *Applied Linguistics* 10.2 (1989): 171–81. Print.

English Plus Movement. "Statement of Purpose and Core Beliefs." *Intercultural Massenglishplus.org.* EnglishPlus Information Clearinghouse. 1987. Web. 16 June 2010.

Fairclough, Norman. *Critical Discourse Analysis: The Critical Study of Language.* London: Longman, 1995. Print.

Fox, Tom. *Defending Access: A Critique of Standards in Higher Education.* Portsmouth: Boynton/Cook Heinemann, 1999. Print.

Gal, Susan, and Judith T. Irvine. "Disciplinary Boundaries and Language Ideology: The Semiotics of Differentiation." *Social Research* 62.4 (1995): 967–1001. Print.

García, Ofelia. *Bilingual Education in the 21st Century: A Global Perspective.* Oxford: Wiley-Blackwell, 2009. Print.

Gentil, Guillaume. "Commitments to Academic Biliteracy: Case Studies of Franco-phone University Writers." *Written Communication* 22.4 (2005): 421–71. Print.

Gilyard, Keith. *Voices of the Self: A Study of Language Competence.* Detroit: Wayne State UP, 1991. Print.

Grosjean, François. "The Bilingual as a Competent but Specific Speaker-Hearer." *Journal of Multilingual and Multicultural Development* 6.6 (1985): 467–77. Print.

Guerra, Juan C. "Cultivating Transcultural Citizenship: A Writing across Communities Model." *Language Arts* 85.4 (2008): 296–304. Print.

Harklau, Linda, Kay M. Losey, and Meryl Siegal, eds. *Generation 1.5 Meets College Composition: Issues in the Teaching of Writing to U.S.-Educated Learners of ESL.* Mahwah: Erlbaum, 1999. Print.

Hesford, Wendy, Eddie Singleton, and Ivonne M. García. "Laboring to Globalize a First-Year Writing Program." *The Writing Program Interrupted: Making Space for Critical Discourse.* Ed. Donna Strickland and Jeanne Gunner. Portsmouth: Boynton/Cook, 2009. 113–25. Print.

Higgins, Christine. "'Ownership' of English in the Outer Circle: An Alternative to the NS-NNS Dichotomy." *TESOL Quarterly* 37.4 (2003): 615–44. Print.

Horner, Bruce, and Min-Zhan Lu. "Resisting Monolingualism in 'English': Reading and Writing the Politics of Language." *Rethinking English in Schools: Towards a New and Constructive Stage.* Ed. Viv Ellis, Carol Fox, and Brian Street. London: Continuum, 2007. 141–57. Print.

Horner, Bruce, Min-Zhan Lu, and Paul Kei Matsuda, eds. *Cross-Language Relations in Composition.* Carbondale: Southern Illinois UP, 2010. Print.

Horner, Bruce, and John Trimbur. "English Only and U.S. College Composition." *CCC* 53.4 (2002): 594–630. Print.

House, Juliane. "English as a Lingua Franca: A Threat to Multilingualism?" *Journal of Sociolinguistics* 7.4 (2003): 556–78. Print.

Jenkins, Jennifer. "Current Perspectives on Teaching World Englishes and English as a Lingua Franca." *TESOL Quarterly* 40.1 (2006): 157–81. Print.

——. *English as a Lingua Franca: Attitude and Identity.* Oxford: Oxford UP, 2007. Print.

——. *World Englishes: A Resource Book for Students.* London: Routledge, 2003. Print.

Kachru, Braj. *The Alchemy of English: The Spread, Functions, and Models of Non-native Englishes.* Urbana: U of Illinois P, 1990. Print.

Kells, Michelle Hall, Valerie Balester, and Victor Villanueva, eds. *Latino/a Discourses: On Language, Identity and Literacy Education.* Portsmouth: Boynton/Cook Heinemann, 2004. Print.

Khubchandani, Lachman M. "A Plurilingual Ethos: A Peep into the Sociology of Language." *Indian Journal of Applied Linguistics* 24.1 (1998): 5–37. Print.

Kirklighter, Cristina, Diana Cárdenas, and Susan Wolff Murphy, eds. *Teaching Writing with Latino/a Students: Lessons Learned at Hispanic-Serving Institutions.* Albany: State U of New York P, 2007. Print.

Kramsch, Claire. "The Privilege of the Intercultural Speaker." *Language Learning in Intercultural Perspective: Approaches through Drama and Ethnography.* Ed. Michael Byram and Michael Fleming. Cambridge: Cambridge UP, 1998. 16–31. Print.

——. "The Traffic in Meaning." *Asia Pacific Journal of Education* 26.1 (2006): 99–104. Print.

Kubota, Ryuko. "Teaching World Englishes to Native Speakers of English in the USA." *World Englishes* 20.1 (2001): 47–64. Print.

Lam, Wan Shun Eva. "L2 Literacy and the Design of the Self: A Case Study of a Teenager Writing on the Internet." *TESOL Quarterly* 34.3 (2000): 457–82. Print.

Lees, Elaine O. "'The Exceptable Way of the Society': Stanley Fish's Theory of Reading and the Task of the Teacher of Editing." *Reclaiming Pedagogy: The Rhetoric of the Classroom.* Ed. Patricia Donahue and Ellen Quandahl. Carbondale: Southern Illinois UP, 1989. 144–63. Print.

Leung, Constant. "Convivial Communication: Recontextualizing Communicative Competence." *International Journal of Applied Linguistics* 15.2 (2005): 119–44. Print.

Leung, Constant, Roxy Harris, and Ben Rampton. "The Idealised Native Speaker, Reified Ethnicities, and Classroom Realities." *TESOL Quarterly* 31.3 (1997): 543–75. Print.

Lippi-Green, Rosina. *English with an Accent: Language, Ideology and Discrimination in the United States.* London: Routledge, 1997. Print.

Lu, Min-Zhan. "An Essay on the Work of Composition: Composing English against the Order of Fast Capitalism." *CCC* 56.1 (2004): 16–50. Print.

——. "Professing Multiculturalism: The Politics of Style in the Contact Zone." *CCC* 45.4 (1994): 442–58. Print.

Lunsford, Andrea A., and Lahoucine Ouzgane, eds. *Crossing Borderlands: Composition and Postcolonial Studies.* Pittsburgh: U of Pittsburgh P, 2004. Print.

Lyons, Scott Richard. "Rhetorical Sovereignty: What Do American Indians Want from Writing?" *CCC* 51.3 (2000): 447–68. Print.

Makoni, Sinfree. "African Languages as European Scripts: The Shaping of Communal Memory." *Negotiating the Past: The Making of Memory in South Africa.* Ed. Sarah Nuttall and Carli Coetzee. Capetown: Oxford UP, 1998. 242–48. Print.

Makoni, Sinfree, and Alastair Pennycook, eds. *Disinventing and Reconstituting Languages.* Clevedon: Multilingual Matters, 2006. Print.

Matsuda, Paul Kei. "Composition Studies and ESL Writing: A Disciplinary Division of Labor." *CCC* 50.4 (1999): 699–721. Print.

——. "Myth 8: International and U.S. Resident ESL Writers Cannot Be Taught in the Same Class." *Writing Myths: Applying Second Language Research to Classroom Teaching.* Ed. Joy M. Reid. Ann Arbor: U of Michigan P, 2008. 159–76. Print.

Matsuda, Paul Kei, Maria Fruit, and Tamara Lee Burton Lamm, eds. *Bridging the Disciplinary Divide: Integrating a Second-Language Perspective into Writing Programs.* Spec. issue of *WPA: Writing Program Administration* 30.1–2 (2006). Print.

Matsuda, Paul Kei, Christina Ortmeier-Hooper, and Xiaoye You, eds. *The Politics of Second Language Writing: In Search of the Promised Land.* West Lafayette: Parlor, 2006. Print.

McKay, Sandra Lee. "Toward an Appropriate EIL Pedagogy: Re-Examining Common ELT Assumptions." *International Journal of Applied Linguistics* 13.1 (2003): 1–22. Print.

Milroy, James. "Language Ideologies and the Consequences of Standardization." *Journal of Sociolinguistics* 5.4 (2001): 530–55. Print.

Modern Language Association Ad Hoc Committee on Foreign Languages. "Foreign Languages and Higher Education: New Structures for a Changed World." *Modern Language Association.* MLA, 2007. Web. 28 Aug. 2009.

Mohan, Bernard, Constant Leung, and Christine Davison, eds. *English as a Second Language in the Mainstream: Teaching, Learning, and Identity.* Harlow: Longman, 2001. Print.

Muchiri, Mary N., Nshindi G. Mulamba, Greg Myers, and Deoscorous B. Ndoloi. "Importing Composition: Teaching and Researching Academic Writing beyond North America." *CCC* 46.2 (1995): 175–98. Print.

Mufwene, Salikoko. "What Is African American English?" *Sociocultural and Historical Contexts of African American English.* Ed. Sonja Lanehart. Amsterdam: John Benjamins, 2001. 21–51. Print.

National Council of Teachers of English. *Position Statement Prepared by the NCTE Committee on Issues in ESL and Bilingual Education. National Council of Teachers of English.* NCTE, 1981; updated 2008. Web. 14 Aug. 2008.

——. *Resolution on Developing and Maintaining Fluency in More Than One Language. National Council of Teachers of English.* NCTE, 1997; updated 2008. Web. 21 June 2009.

——. *Resolution on English as a Second Language and Bilingual Education. National Council of Teachers of English.* NCTE, 1982; updated 2008. Web. 8 Aug. 2008.

——. *Resolution on English as the "Official Language." National Council of Teachers of English.* NCTE, 1986; updated 2008. Web. 8 Aug. 2008.

Nayar, P. Bhaskaran. "ESL/EFL Dichotomy Today: Language Politics or Pragmatics?" *TESOL Quarterly* 31.1 (1997): 9–37. Print.

Nero, Shondel J., ed. *Dialects, Englishes, Creoles, and Education.* Mahwah: Erlbaum, 2006. Print.

——. *Englishes in Contact: Anglophone Caribbean Students in an Urban College.* Cresskill: Hampton, 2001. Print.

Parakrama, Arjuna. *De-Hegemonizing Language Standards: Learning from (Post)Colonial Englishes about "English."* Basingstoke: Macmillan, 1995. Print.

Parks, Steve. *Class Politics: The Movement for the Students' Right to Their Own Language.* Urbana: NCTE, 2000. Print.

Pennycook, Alastair. "English as a Language Always in Translation." *European Journal of English Studies* 12.1 (2008): 33–47. Print.

——. *Language as a Local Practice.* Milton Park: Routledge, 2010. Print.

——. "Performativity and Language Studies." *Critical Inquiry in Language Studies* 1.1 (2004): 1–19. Print.

Pratt, Mary Louise. "Linguistic Utopias." *The Linguistics of Writing: Arguments between Language and Literature.* Ed. Nigel Fabb, Derek Attridge, Alan Durant, and Colin MacCabe. New York: Methuen, 1987. 48–66. Print.

Ramanathan, Vaidehi. "Of Texts AND Translations AND Rhizomes: Postcolonial Anxieties AND Deracinations AND Knowledge Constructions." *Critical Inquiry in Language Studies* 3.4 (2006): 223–44. Print.

Rampton, Ben. *Crossing: Language and Ethnicity among Adolescents.* 2nd ed. Manchester: St. Jerome, 2005. Print.

Rodby, Judith. *Appropriating Literacy: Writing and Reading in English as a Second Language.* Portsmouth: Boynton/Cook, 1992. Print.

Rose, Mike. *Lives on the Boundary: A Moving Account of the Struggles and Achievements of America's Educationally Unprepared.* New York: Penguin Books, 1989. Print.

Royster, Jacqueline Jones. *Traces of a Stream: Literacy and Social Change among African American Women.* Pittsburgh: U of Pittsburgh P, 2000. Print.

——. "When the First Voice You Hear Is Not Your Own." *CCC* 47.1 (1996): 29–40. Print.

Royster, Jacqueline Jones, and Ann Marie Mann Simpkins, eds. *Calling Cards: Theory and Practice in the Study of Race, Gender, and Culture.* Albany: State U of New York P, 2005. Print.

Rubdy, Rani, and Mario Saraceni, eds. *English in the World: Global Rules, Global Roles.* London: Continuum, 2006. Print.

Schroeder, Christopher, Helen Fox, and Patricia Bizzell, eds. *ALT/DIS: Alternative Discourses and the Academy.* Portsmouth: Boynton/Cook Heinemann, 2002. Print.

Scott, Jerrie Cobb, Dolores Y. Straker, and Laurie Katz, eds. *Affirming Students' Right to Their Own Language: Bridging Language Policies and Pedagogical Practices.* New York: Routledge/Urbana: NCTE, 2009. Print.

Severino, Carol, Juan C. Guerra, and Johnnella E. Butler, eds. *Writing in Multicultural Settings.* New York: MLA, 1997. Print.

Silva, Tony, Ilona Leki, and Joan Carson. "Broadening the Perspective of Mainstream Composition Studies: Some Thoughts from the Disciplinary Margins." *Written Communication* 14.3 (1997): 398–428. Print.

Singh, Rajendra, ed. *The Native Speaker: Multilingual Perspectives.* New Delhi: Sage, 1998. Print.

Smitherman, Geneva. "CCCC's Role in the Struggle for Language Rights." *CCC* 50.3 (1999): 349–76. Print.

——. *Talkin that Talk: Language, Culture and Education in African America.* London: Routledge, 2000. Print.

Smitherman, Geneva, and Victor Villanueva, eds. *Language Diversity in the Classroom: From Intention to Practice.* Carbondale: Southern Illinois UP, 2003. Print.

Travis, Peter W. "The English Department in the Globalized University." *ADE Bulletin* 138–39 (2006): 51–56. Print.

Trimbur, John. "The Dartmouth Conference and the Geohistory of the Native Speaker." *College English* 71.2 (2008): 142–69. Print.

Valdès, Guadalupe. "Bilingual Minorities and Language Issues in Writing: Toward Professionwide Responses to a New Challenge." *Written Communication* 9.1 (1992): 85–136. Print.

Venuti, Lawrence. *The Scandals of Translation: Towards an Ethic of Difference.* London: Routledge, 1998. Print.

Villanueva, Victor. *Bootstraps: From an American Academic of Color.* Urbana: NCTE, 1993. Print.

Widdowson, Henry G. "The Ownership of English." *TESOL Quarterly* 28.2 (1994): 377–89. Print.

Williams, Joseph M. "The Phenomenology of Error." *CCC* 32.2 (1981): 152–68. Print.

Working English in Rhetoric and Composition: Global-local Contexts, Commitments, Consequences. Spec. issue cluster of *JAC* 29.1–2 (2009). Ed. Bruce Horner with Min-Zhan Lu, Samantha NeCamp, Brice Nordquist, and Vanessa Kraemer Sohan. Print.

You, Xiaoye. *Writing in the Devil's Tongue: A History of English Composition in China.* Carbondale: Southern Illinois UP, 2010. Print.

Young, Vershawn Ashanti. *Your Average Nigga: Performing Race, Literacy, and Masculinity.* Detroit: Wayne State UP, 2007. Print.

Zamel, Vivian. "Toward a Model of Transculturation." *TESOL Quarterly* 31.2 (1997): 341–52. Print.

Zamel, Vivian, and Ruth Spack. "Teaching Multilingual Learners across the Curriculum: Beyond the ESOL Classroom and Back Again." *Journal of Basic Writing* 25.2 (2006): 126–52. Print.

Zarate, Geneviève, Danielle Lévy, & Claire Kramsch, eds. *Précis du Plurilinguisme et du Pluriculturalisme.* Paris: Editions des archives contemporaines, 2008. Print.

Cynthia L. Selfe

Toward New Media Texts: Taking Up the Challenges of Visual Literacy

How can teachers of composition *begin* working with new media texts—especially when they feel less than prepared to do so? One productive route of approach, I suggest in this chapter, is through visual literacy.

It is not unusual for faculty raised on alphabetic literacy and educated to teach composition before the advent of image-capturing software, multimedia texts, and the World Wide Web to feel inadequate to the task of teaching students about new media texts and the emerging literacies associated with these texts. Many have used computers extensively in the composition instruction they offer students, but most, if not all, of the assignments they favor regularly depend on the alphabetic, demand it as a primary focus, have—in most cases—been limited to it.

In part, faculty may limit their teaching in this way because they lack familiarity with a range of new media texts that they consider appropriate for study in composition classrooms. Given their educational backgrounds and expertise, after all, most faculty remain book readers, primarily. Further, although they may have encountered some new media texts, and may even enjoy these texts in many ways, they may not be convinced that such texts are worth further study in the English composition classroom. In addition, faculty may feel that they lack the analytical skills they need to conduct serious study of these texts, an effective vocabulary and set of strategies for discussing the structure and composition of new media texts, or that they lack expertise with the software packages typically used to create such texts—Macromedia Director™ and Dreamweaver™, Adobe Photoshop™ and Premiere™, Corel Poser™ and Bryce™, among others.

Importantly, operating from these constraints, many English composition faculty realize that they can offer only limited help to students who read new media texts; and they cannot help students who want to compose such texts. And, as the work of scholars as diverse as Manuel Castells, Gail Hawisher, and The New London Group suggests, this illiteracy can be costly in terms of faculty's understanding of the ways in which communication is changing at the beginning of the 21st century. Perhaps more importantly, however, it may have a cost for the students in their classes—individuals who need to learn more about

This article is reprinted from Anne Frances Wysocki, Johndan Johnson-Eilola, Cynthia L. Selfe, and Geoffrey Sirc, *Writing New Media: Theory and Applications for Expanding the Teaching of Composition* (Logan: Utah State University Press, 2004), 67–93.

481

the new media literacies now being used to shape meaning and information as it is composed and exchanged.

To work toward a better understanding of new media texts—and to open composition classes to some of the expanded possibilities suggested by such terms—a good first step may involve focusing on visual literacy and on texts, both online and in print, that depend primarily on visual elements and materials.

My reasoning in suggesting this approach is simple, but then so, too, is my level of skill in this new area: one of the primary elements that make new media texts new for me—and at times difficult to discuss in a composition classroom—is their heavy dependence on visual communication. This is an area in which I, personally, feel less than confident as a teacher of English composition, given our profession's historical focus on alphabetic literacy and uncertainty about whether visual studies is an appropriate focus for composition classrooms (cf., George; Sean Williams). Therefore, like most of my colleagues, I have only limited ability to help students analyze the visual elements of text and even less in helping them create texts composed of such elements.

Given this context, I suspect if we can help teachers become more knowledge-able and comfortable in working with students to read, discuss, and compose texts that depend primarily on visual elements, they will also be increasingly willing and able to apply these understandings to the teaching of new media texts as well. For me, focusing on the visual in composition classrooms is a pro-ductive first step—albeit not the only route—toward the larger goal of focusing on new media texts in the same environment.

This chapter, then, seeks to provide a brief rationale and several specific strat-egies for integrating visual literacy into composition classrooms—both in terms of consumption and production.

SOME WORKING DEFINITIONS FOR THIS CHAPTER

Most teachers thinking about integrating visual literacy into composition classes need some definitional focus for their efforts. And although, as Diana George notes, the definitions of visual literacy—and the related terms of visual com-munication, visual rhetoric, and the visual—remain under formulation in our profession, it may be useful to pose a temporary working definition for some of the key terms in this chapter, while recognizing that the larger professional effort to settle on a formal acceptable definition will continue to go forward.

By visual literacy, then, I will refer to the ability to read, understand, value, and learn from visual materials (still photographs, videos, films, animations, still images, pictures, drawings, graphics)—especially as these are combined to create a text—as well as the ability to create, combine, and use visual elements (e.g., colors, forms, lines, images) and messages for the purposes of communicating (cf. Kress and van Leeuwven, *Reading Images;* Debes and Williams; *The On-line Visual Literacy Project*). And—although I under-stand some of the problems posed by using the lens of alphabetic literacy to understand visual literacy (Wysocki and Johnson-Eilola)—based on the work of scholars such as Brian Street, James Gee, Harvey Graff, Deborah Brandt ("Literacy Learning"), and David Barton and Mary Hamilton, for the purpose of this chapter, I will assume, further, that visual literacy (or literacies), like all literacies, are both historically and culturally situated, constructed, and valued.

By texts that depend primarily on visual elements, visual texts, and visual compositions, I will refer to communications (e.g., visual poems, visual essays, visual messages, visual arguments, collages, multimedia presentations, among other forms) that people compose/design (both online and in print environments) in which visual elements and materials assume the primary burden of communication.

I will also use the term **the visual,** to refer broadly to a focus on visual elements and materials of communication, and the term visual compositions to refer to the texts that individuals or groups design/compose, primarily of visual elements and materials, for the purposes of communicating.

Finally, I will use the term **composer/designer,** instead of "author" or "artist," for instance, to describe an individual who produces or creates a visual text and the term **design/compose** to describe the complex set of activities involved in such a creative and strategic task. To refer to the reader of visual texts, I will use the term **reader/viewer** and, for the complex set of activities associated with understanding and interpreting a visual text, I will use **reading/viewing.** Although I understand these terms have their own limitations, I believe they are suggestive of the richness of visual compositions and will provide teachers some help, even if on a temporary basis, in reading this chapter.

FOCUSING ON THE VISUAL

More About Approach and Avoidance

If focusing visual literacy may be a useful first step in approaching new media texts, it is, itself, not always an easy one for teachers of English composition.

Although we have always acknowledged, at some level, the visual appearance of alphabetic texts (their formatting, their appearance, the spatial presentation of information), both visual compositions and the new media texts on which this book focuses typically privilege such information — depend on and focus on visual images, photographs, animations, multimedia depictions in ways that print texts typically do not.

This emphasis on the visual presentation of information, as Gunther Kress ("'English'") has noted, is manifested broadly in our culture and represents an important "turn to the visual" (66). Alphabetic texts, Kress continues, are being challenged by texts that are more oriented toward visual elements:

> The visual is becoming more prominent in many domains of public communication. From a different perspective this is to realize that written language is being displaced from its hitherto unchallenged central position in the semiotic landscape, and that the visual is taking over many of the functions of written language. (68)

Acknowledging this turn toward the visual—which has occurred in print texts as well as new media texts—scholars have begun to re-examine the role of visual literacy and our understanding of the visual in composition studies. Wysocki and Johnson-Eilola, for instance, have pointed out the limitations of using alphabetic literacy as a lens for understanding the new—and often visually rich—compositions that students are encountering in computer-based communication environments. Geoffrey Sirc has argued that visual compositions may provide teachers a valuable "demographic" that they have, in the past, lacked, one which reveals the "form patterns"—born of poetic expression—that individuals "actually make in their lives" as they try to "live their desire" (11) in a postmodern culture. Diane Shoos and Diana George argue for much broader definition of literacy, composition, and reading, one that takes a critical, visual intertextuality into account, among other things, and that acknowledges the "relationship(s) of texts [visual ads of commercial magazines, film posters, documentaries, television fiction, essays among them] to one another and to their multiple contexts" (124). And this is only a small sampling of the recent work done in composition studies with an emphasis on the visual.

Despite this work, however, as Diana George has recently pointed out, many teachers continue to rely on impoverished approaches to teaching visual literacy in their composition classrooms, introducing visual texts as the less-important and less-intellectual sidekicks of alphabetic texts. Such approaches are deeply sedimented, not only in the cultural, linguistic, and historical practices that privilege alphabetic literacy (cf. Wysocki and Johnson-Eilola; Wysocki, "Impossibly Distinct"; Jay; Kress, " 'English' "), but also in the practices and approaches of our profession. As George reminds us, when English composition teachers have thought to bring visual forms into their classes—a practice which they have carried on for at least forty years—they have typically presented them as second-class texts: either as "dumbed down" (32) communications that serve as "stimuli for writing but [. . .] no substitute for the complexity of language" (22) or as texts related to, but certainly not on an equal footing with, the " 'real' work of the course" (28).

English composition teachers have continued to privilege alphabetic texts over texts that depend on visual elements, I believe, because such texts present familiar forms, forms with which we have developed a comfortable, stable intellectual relationship. We know, for instance—from lots of previous experiences—how to approach a book or a non-fiction essay; we have developed many strategies for reading and understanding such texts, for analyzing and interpreting them, for talking about them. Indeed, we feel confident about teaching students how to compose alphabetic texts primarily because we are so familiar with those forms. Relatively few English teachers, however, feel as comfortable in approaching a visual text unless they have some training in art or design. Given this context, we remain unsure how to approach visual texts, how to explore them, how to understand them, and how to teach them. And we also feel less than competent about composing visual texts ourselves.

Part of the reason this feeling has persisted, of course, has to do with the material conditions of teaching and learning in the United States and the relations of such conditions to technologies of production and composition. Many of us, for instance, had our last art class in elementary school and have learned since that time to pin our hopes for academic and professional success on alphabetic texts. As a result, we have also learned to use and value technologies — pens, pencils, typewriters, ditto machines, books, journals, and, more recently, computers and word-processing packages — for the ease they afford us in creating alphabetic texts. It is only recently — in conjunction with the cultural turn to the visual, I believe — that increasing numbers of composition teachers have had some access to technologies which allow for the production of texts highly dependent on visual elements (color photocopiers, digital scanners; computers that contain page-layout, photo-manipulation, animation, multimedia software, etc.). Many of these technologies, however, are still expensive — and, thus unevenly distributed in schools along the axis of material resources — as well as relatively difficult to access and learn.

Finally, I would suggest, many English composition teachers have downplayed the importance of visual literacy and texts that depend primarily on visual elements because they confront us with the prospect of updating our literacies at the expense of considerable work, precious time, and a certain amount of status. Teachers continue to privilege alphabetic literacy over visual literacy, in other words, because they have already invested so heavily in writing, writing instruction and writing programs — and because we have achieved some status as practitioners and specialists of writing. Undertaking the study of literacies based in visual studies, learning to analyze and talk about and compose these texts — especially with a high degree of technological sophistication will take time and effort — may also force us to acknowledge gaps in our own literacy sets.

Recently, however, our single-minded focus on alphabetic texts in composition classes has come to seem outdated, even obdurate, in the face of practical realities. Global communications, for example — exchanged via increasingly complicated computer networks that stretch across traditional geographic and political borders and that include people from different cultures who speak different languages — increasingly involve texts that depend heavily, even primarily, on visual elements (New London Group). Moreover, with the ongoing expansion of global markets, political systems, and communication networks, such an emphasis is sure to continue, if not increase.

Given the pace and scope of changes accruing from this set of circumstances, if our profession continues to focus solely on teaching alphabetic composition — either online or in print — we run the risk of making composition studies increasingly irrelevant to students engaging in contemporary practices of communicating. Students already, as Diana George reminds us, have a "much richer imagination for what we might accomplish with the visual" than we ourselves have (12).

By continuing a single-minded focus on alphabetic literacy — and failing to give adequate attention to visual literacy — as Sean Williams points out, we not only unnecessarily limit the scope of composition studies, both intellectually and practically:

> Restricting composition to verbal media and reproducing the verbal bias in our classrooms is perilous [...] because it contradicts the critical thinking skills that we as composition teachers strive to teach.[...I]f composition's role is to help students acquire skills to lead a critically engaged life—that is to identify problems, to solve them, and to communicate with others about them—then we need to expand our view of writing instruction to include the diverse media forms that actually represent and shape the discursive reality of students. The verbal bias, then, reveals two closely interwoven perils;
>
> - a political one that reinscribes a conclusion-based rationality, and
> - a rhetorical one that ignores the possibility that different media function more or less effectively in different contexts. (25)

As Kress and van Leeuwen (*Reading Images*) put the case, then, it may be time to rethink what "literacy" ought to include, and what should be taught under the heading of "writing" in schools (32).

By adding a focus on visual literacy to our existing focus on alphabetic literacy, we may not only learn to pay more serious attention to the ways in which students are now ordering and making sense of the world through the production and consumption of visual images, but we may also extend the usefulness of composition studies in a changing world.

WHERE DO WE GO FROM HERE?

Individual teachers and programs, surely, will differ widely in their willingness to experiment with the challenges of visual composition, to take personal and intellectual risks as they learn to value visually-oriented texts, and to engage in composing texts that combine the visual as well as the alphabetic.

The following pages provide examples of assignments designed to provide teachers a range of approaches to visual texts, even when instructors have no formal coursework or professional preparation in this area.

1. The assignments connect what is—at least for some teachers—the less-familiar realm of visual composition with the more-familiar realm of alphabetic composition.
2. Most of the assignments deal at some level with a combination of both visual and alphabetic literacies. Most—following the lead of scholars such as Susan Hilligoss, Sean Williams, Clay Spinuzzi—use a rhetorical approach to analyzing the audience, purpose, and messages conveyed by a visual text—employing questions that many instructors already

use in teaching students how to compose more conventional alphabetic texts.

3. And most of the assignments do not require teachers or students to use sophisticated computer environments as contexts for visual assignments.

4. Importantly, I would add that most of the assignments involve teachers and students as co-learners in the project of paying increased attention to visual texts. As a result, they do not require teachers to begin with a great deal of information or background on visual literacy. Through the completion of the assignments, both teachers and students will acquire some basic conceptual vocabulary that they can use to discuss the reading/viewing and composing/designing of texts that rely primarily on visual elements. For those colleagues who feel more comfortable approaching such assignments with some background reading under their belts, I can suggest Kress and van Leeuwen's *Reading Images: The Grammar of Visual Design*.

The topics of the following assignments are far less important than their focus on the visual, and so teachers are also encouraged to revise them to fit specific courses. For example, the first assignment is currently designed for an undergraduate course on literacy issues. It asks students to create a visual essay that describes their general development as readers and writers over the course of their lifetimes. However, in another course focused on the American novel, the same assignment could be revised to ask students to trace a more specific line: focusing on their family's history in America. Similarly, the second assignment — currently designed for a first-year English course focused on the relationship between humans and robots/cyborgs — asks students to make a visual argument about what this relationship will look like in 2050. In a course focusing on issues of race, this same assignment could be revised to ask students to make a visual argument based on their stance toward affirmative-action programs.

Ultimately, the goal set for these assignments is both modest (in that the general process will be familiar to most teachers of composition) and exceedingly challenging (in the attempt to focus primarily — although not exclusively — on the visual), and one I hope many teachers of composition can embrace: to help students and ourselves better understand the communicative power and complexity of visual texts by reading and looking at them, by thinking seriously about these texts and analyzing their components, by talking to other people about our interpretations of them, by composing visual texts ourselves, by sharing our efforts at composing with other author/designers, and by reflecting on the compositions we create and exchange with others as complex symbolic instantiations of the human need to communicate.

ACTIVITY 1: A VISUAL ESSAY

Teachers' Notes

Goals

- To involve students in reflecting on and representing
  - the range of the literacies they have developed in their lifetimes (both online and in-print).
  - the development of these literacies.
  - their feelings about/values toward various forms of literacy.
- To help students understand how much tacit knowledge they have about visual composition.
- To provide students some basic vocabulary they can use in talking about and analyzing visual compositions.

Time Required

- one homework assignment to compose visual essay (1 week for out-of-class work).
- 30 minutes in class for viewing and reflecting on visual essays
- 30 minutes in class for discussion of successful strategies for:
  - creating overall visual coherence
  - visually identifying 2–4 of the essay's most important points
  - visually indicating pattern(s) of organization
- one homework assignment focused on comparing author/designers' reflections and audience/viewers' reflections

Sequence

1. **Creating a visual essay.** As a homework assignment, each student creates a visual essay on the range of literacies (both on and off computers) they have developed over their lifetimes and their feelings toward literacy.
2. **Viewing and Reflection Session.** In class, students form teams of three for a 30 minute *Viewing and Reflection Session*. During this session, teams do three rounds of reflection. During each round, the team views a visual essay for 10 minutes and reflects on a series of questions. Composer /designers reflect on what they tried to accomplish; readers/viewers write about what the visual essay communicates to them.
3. **Discussion.** In class, the teacher asks students to point out the successful strategies that authors/designers used in their essays to:
    1. impart visual impact
    2. create an overall sense of coherence
    3. indicate the importance of 1–4 major points
    4. create pattern(s) of organization
4. **Comparing Author/Designers' Reflections with Audience/Viewers' Reflections.** As a homework assignment, each composer/designer com-

pares his/her own answers on the reflection questions to those provided by the audience viewers. Each author/designer will summarize
areas of agreement and disagreement.

Useful Vocabulary

from Kress and van Leeuwan's *Reading Images: The Grammar of Visual Design*

- **Visual impact:** The overall effect and appeal that a visual composition
  has on an audience.
- **Visual coherence:** The extent to which visual elements of a composition
  are tied together with color, shape, image, lines of sight, theme, etc.
- **Visual salience:** Importance or prominence of a visual element.
- **Visual organization:** Pattern of arrangement that relates the elements of
  the visual essay to one another in a way that makes them easier for readers
  /viewers to comprehend.

VISUAL ESSAY

HOMEWORK

Assignment (Homework)

Objectives

- To reflect on the entire range of literacies (both online and print) you have developed over your life; the practices, understandings, and values that make up your literacies; where these practices, understandings, and values came from; how you have developed them; and who has helped you become literate.
- To represent this information as richly as possible in a visual essay.
- To provide you practice in documenting images.

Task

- Compose a visual essay that represents and reflects on

  1. the range of different literacy practices, values, and understandings you have developed over your lifetime (from birth to now)
  2. how you have developed these literacies (where, how, who helped)
  3. your feelings about these literacies

- The audience for this essay is other students in the class. The purpose is to show the range and extent of your own personal set of literacies, their development over time, and your feelings toward literacy at various points of your life.
- For the purposes of this essay, we will define literacy broadly — not only as your reading and writing skills but also the values and understandings that go along with these skills. For instance, you might (but don't have to) include, such activities as reading and writing in print contexts (books and magazines, writing stories and plays), on computers (designing Web sites, reading gaming situations, writing in chat rooms), on television (reading the texts of television programs), in church (reading the Bible, writing for your church bulletin), at home (writing letters, reading directions), in school (reading lab reports, collaborating with a group to compose a report).
- The essays should demonstrate a high degree of visual impact.
- The essay should demonstrate an overall coherence (elements of the essay should be linked by color, shape, theme, arrangement, etc.).
- The essay should identify 2–4 major points as particularly important (using strategies to make these points prominent and stand out from other elements: size, color, contrast, placement, etc.).
- Use some pattern of organization to help viewers to comprehend your essay (arrange elements along a timeline, a path, a trail, or some other metaphor that represents your life; separate your computer and your book-based literacies or connect them if they are related).

Format

- Your essay can take any number of forms. Be creative in your thinking and representation: create your own literacy path or trail, a diagram of human development annotated with images of your literacy activities, a scrapbook with "snapshots" of your literacy development; a map of your literacy landscape; a literacy game board; a literacy Web.
- Compose this essay either on a Web page that you create online or on a poster board that you purchase at the college bookstore.
- If you create a Web page, compose your essay from images that you find or create online. Before you download an image from another Web site, carefully check to make sure the Web site does not prohibit the copying of images.
- If you use poster board, create your collage from images you cut out of magazines or from family photographs.
- Include at least 15 images in this essay.
- Document the source of each image using the formats below.

Web Essays & Documenting Images from an Online Source

- Create a Web page for your essay.
- Create a separate Web page for each image's bibliographic citation.
- Link each image in your essay to the appropriate Web page containing its bibliographic entry. Here is a model, with an example:

Artist (if given). Title of file. <Web site from which image was taken> (date on which you accessed Web site).

Example: Doe, Jane. SpottedPig.jpg. <http://www.spottedanimal/pigs/#22> (Accessed 22 June, 2002).

Poster Board Essays & Documenting Images from Print/Photographic Sources

- Create your essay. Number each image.
- Create a bibliography page. List entries in numerical order, numbering each entry to correspond to an image: [15] "Drink Milk." Time 20 September 2002: 15.
- Attach this page to the back of your essay.

Artist (if given). "Title of image" (if given). *Magazine Title* or Photograph Collection Day Month Year: page number (if applicable).

Example from a magazine: [15] "Drink Milk." *Time* 20 September 2002: 15.

Example from a photograph: [15] Doe, John "Me and My Mother." Personal photograph collection. Taken 9 August 1978.

VISUAL ESSAY

CLASSROOM WORK

Reflection Sheet

(Composer/Designer)

Composer/designer _____

Objective

- To articulate and reflect on what you are trying to convey about your literacies, literacy development through/in your essay.
- To identify what parts of your essay worked well and what parts worked less well.
- To reflect on your attempt to create visual coherence, salience (prominence/importance), and organization in your essay.

Task

Take 10 minutes to reflect on the first three questions that follow. For homework, reflect on the last four questions and hand in this page—along with the reader/viewers' Reflection sheets from your team—at the beginning of next class. *Do not speak about or explain your visual essay to your readers/viewers.*

During Class

- What were you trying to convey about your literacies/literacy development in this essay?
- What parts of this essay worked the best? Had the most effect impact? Why?
- What parts of this essay worked less well in your opinion? Had the least effective impact? Why?

For Homework

- What specific techniques did you use to establish visual coherence in your essay?
- What specific strategies did you use to identify each of the 2–4 major points you were trying to make in this essay and to lend them visual salience (make them prominent to the reader/viewer)?

VISUAL ESSAY

CLASSROOM WORK

Reflection Sheet

(Reader/Viewer)

Essay composed/designed by _____

Essay read/viewed by _____

Objective

- To articulate what the visual essay conveyed to you as a reader/viewer.
- To reflect on what parts of the essay worked well/had great impact for you and what parts worked less well/had low impact for you.

Task

Take 10 minutes to reflect in writing on the following questions. Do not talk to the composer/designer.

- What did the essay convey to you about the composer/designer and his/her literacies? His/her development as a reader/viewer or composer/designer? List at least five impressions you got.
- What parts of the essay worked the best for you — had the highest impact?
- What parts of this essay worked least well for you — had the lowest impact?
- Below, please identify the 2–4 main points you think the composer/ designer wanted to make in the essay.

VISUAL ESSAY

Sample Evaluation

Composer/designer _____

1: OVERALL EFFECT OF THE VISUAL ESSAY

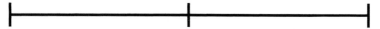

Essay's overall   Essay has moderate   Essay has exceptional
impact is low &   level of overall impact   overall impact and
presentation is   and presentation is   presentation is highly
less than effective.   moderately effective.   effective.

Comments:

2: COMPOSER/DESIGNER'S DEVELOPMENT/FEELINGS

Essay provides modest   Essay provides adequate   Essay provides exceptional
information about   information about   information about
composer/designer's   composer/designer's   composer/designer's
development/feelings.   development/feelings.   development/feelings.

Comments:

3: VISUAL COHERENCE

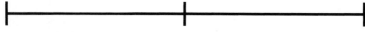

Essay needs more   Essay is visually   Essay demonstrates
visual coherence.   coherent.   exceptional visual
                                                   coherence.

Comments:

4: VISUAL SALIENCE

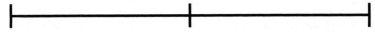

Essay doesn't
identify 2–4 major
points (visual
salience).

Essay does identify
2–4 major points
(visual salience).

Essay is exceptionally
clear in identifying
2–4 major points
(visual salience).

Comments:

5: ORGANIZATION OF THE ESSAY

Essay's organization
is unclear or
confusing.

Essay's organization
is helpful and clear.

Essay's organization
contributes in
exceptional ways to
its overall effects.

Comments:

6: DOCUMENTATION OF IMAGES

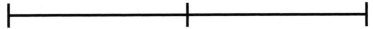

Images are not
correctly documented.

Images are generally
correctly documented.

All images are
documented correctly.

Comments:

7: REFLECTION

Reflection is less
than fully elaborated
and thoughtful.

Reflection is elaborated
and thoughtful.

Reflection is robustly
elaborated and
exceptionally
thoughtful.

Comments:

VISUAL ESSAY

CLASSROOM WORK

Sample Evaluation (a model)

Composer/designer   *Michelle Sarinen*

1: OVERALL EFFECT OF THE VISUAL ESSAY

Essay's overall impact is low & presentation is less than effective.

Essay has moderate level of overall impact and presentation is moderately effective.

Essay has exceptional overall impact and presentation is highly effective.

Comments: *Very complete rendition of literacy activities, but not designed for a high level of impact. All the events are shown at essentially the same level of impact. Is this possible?*

2: COMPOSER/DESIGNER'S DEVELOPMENT/FEELINGS

Essay provides modest information about composer/ designer's development/feelings.

Essay provides adequate information about composer/ designer's development/ feelings.

Essay provides exceptional informa- tion about composer/ designer's development/ feelings.

Comments: *The essay doesn't give me a sense of you. It could be about almost anyone in this class. Can you give some visual emphasis to the details/ events that really helped you form your identity?*

3: VISUAL COHERENCE

Essay needs more visual coherence.

Essay is visually coherent.

Essay demonstrates exceptional visual coherence.

Comments: *I think you could make more effective use of color and line to make your points and get your essay to hang together. For instance, why not color-code the print-based events in your childhood to differentiate them from the computer-based events in your adolescence?*

4: VISUAL SALIENCE

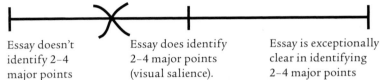

| Essay doesn't identify 2–4 major points (visual salience). | Essay does identify 2–4 major points (visual salience). | Essay is exceptionally clear in identifying 2–4 major points (visual salience). |

Comments: *I really didn't get a sense of which elements/events were most important in your life...*

5: ORGANIZATION OF THE ESSAY

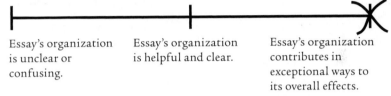

| Essay's organization is unclear or confusing. | Essay's organization is helpful and clear. | Essay's organization contributes in exceptional ways to its overall effects. |

Comments: *Yes – The organization is clear: it's chronological.*

6: DOCUMENTATION OF IMAGES

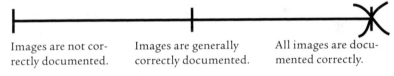

| Images are not correctly documented. | Images are generally correctly documented. | All images are documented correctly. |

Comments: *Yes, complete.*

7: REFLECTION

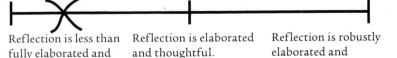

| Reflection is less than fully elaborated and thoughtful. | Reflection is elaborated and thoughtful. | Reflection is robustly elaborated and exceptionally thoughtful. |

Comments: *It doesn't seem as though you've reflected too much on what specific literacy events have shaped you as a person. Or, at least, I can't see it...*

ACTIVITY 2: VISUAL ARGUMENT ASSIGNMENT*

Teachers' Notes

Goals

- Involve students in identifying effective strategies composers/designers have used in their arguments to establish visual impact, coherence, salience, and organization.
- Introduce some new vocabulary for discussing the concepts of visual impact, coherence, salience, and organization.

Below, we list some of the possible strategies that students may identify for establishing visual impact, coherence, salience, and organization. However, such strategies work differently in combination and within the context of specific arguments. Encourage students to identify unusual strategies that generate innovative and surprising effects — especially if those effects succeed.

Discussion Questions

After students have completed the assignment on the following pages, look together at all the arguments they've made. Get the class talking by asking the following questions. The questions are set up around the vocabulary from the previous assignment.

Questions About Visual Impact

VISUAL IMPACT is the overall effect and appeal that a visual composition has on an audience.

- *Which arguments that you looked at exhibited the highest overall impact/effect? Why?* Ask the team members to identify the strategies they think the particular author/designer employed to establish visual coherence. Ask students on other teams to identify additional arguments that succeed in establishing overall coherence. Encourage students to identify strategies that are unusual, unexpected; that generate surprising (and yet successful) effects; that are innovative.

Students might mention these strategies for creating visual impact:
- author/designer employed an overall concept
- author/designer used images that were especially effective
- author/designer used lots of details
- author/designer used color effectively
- author/designer composed an especially creative visual design
- author/designer used elements that the audience could relate to

---

* I am indebted to Dr. Diana George for the concept of visual arguments. She describes several such arguments created by students at Michigan Technological University in her article "From Analysis to Visual Design."

Questions About Visual Coherence

VISUAL COHERENCE is the extent to which the various elements of a visual composition are tied together, represent a unified whole.

- *Which essays demonstrated an effective sense of visual coherence? Why?*
Ask the team members to identify the strategies they think the particular composer/designer employed to establish visual coherence. Ask students on other teams to identify additional essays that succeed in establishing overall coherence. Encourage students to identify strategies that are unusual, unexpected; that generate surprising (and yet successful) effects; that are innovative.

Students might mention these strategies for creating visual coherence:
- composer/designer linked elements by using patterns or color
- composer/designer linked elements through similar shapes
- composer/designer created coherence with unifying pictorial graphics (lines, arrows, paths, etc.)
- composer/designer tied elements together using proximity, overlapping, or juxtaposition
- composer/designer tied elements together using a shared visual theme (images of books, pens, or computers)
- composer/designer balanced major elements to create cohesion

Questions About Visual Salience

VISUAL SALIENCE is the relative prominence of an element within a visual composition. Salient elements catch viewer's eye; they are conspicuous.

- *Which arguments demonstrated an effective sense of visual salience?*
Ask the team members to identify the strategies they think the particular composer/designer employed to establish visual salience. Ask students on other teams to identify additional arguments that succeed in establishing salience. Encourage students to identify strategies that are unusual, unexpected; that generate surprising (and yet successful) effects; that are innovative.

Students might mention these strategies for creating visual salience:
- composers/designers increased the size of major elements
- composers/designers sharpened the focus for major elements
- composers/designers increased the contrast (darker, lighter, more saturated colors) of major elements
- composers/designers positioned major elements in the center
- composers/designers positioned major elements in the foreground
- composers/designers highlighted major elements with color
- composers/designers used pictorial graphics (lines, arrows, etc.) to point toward major elements
- composers/designers used/angled other elements to direct the viewer's eye toward a major element

Questions About Visual Organization

VISUAL ORGANIZATION is the pattern of arrangement that relates the elements of the visual essay to one another so that they are easier for readers/viewers to comprehend.

- *Which arguments demonstrated an effective sense of visual organization?*
  Ask the team members to identify the strategies they think the particular author/designer employed to establish effective patterns of visual organization. Ask students on other teams to identify additional arguments that succeed in establishing effective patterns of visual organization. Encourage students to identify strategies that are unusual, unexpected; that generate surprising (and yet successful) effects; that are innovative.

  Students might mention these strategies for creating visual organization:
  - composer/designer linked elements by using patterns of color
  - composer/designer linked elements through similar shapes
  - composer/designer created coherence with unifying pictorial graphics (lines, arrows, paths, etc.)
  - composer/designer tied elements together using proximity, overlapping, or juxtaposition
  - composer/designer tied elements together using a shared visual theme (images of books, pens, or computers)
  - composer/designer balanced major elements to create cohesion

VISUAL ARGUMENT

HOMEWORK

Creating a Visual Argument

Objectives

- To engage students in reflecting on the relationship between humans/ robots/cyborgs and constructing this relationship actively through visual representation.
- To provide students practice in identifying and visually representing a line of argument.
- To provide students practice in analyzing visual arguments and evaluating their effectiveness.
- To provide students practice in documenting images

Task

During this term, we have read Karel Capek's play *R.U.R.*, and Isaac Asimov's *I, Robot,* and we have watched Ridley Scott's *Bladerunner.* In discussing these works, we have asked the following questions, among others:

Are humans already cyborgs?
Can robots have a soul?
Why do humans guard intelligence so jealously?
Why do humans craft robots in their own image?
Why do humans fear robots?

With these readings and questions in mind, create a visual argument on the following topic:
By the year 2050, I think humans and robots will become more alike, become increasingly different, or should establish the following relationship: _____

- You may want your argument to address questions like these: *Will robots have a soul? Should robots have emotions? Should robots/cyborgs be able to love/ marry/inherit property/become a citizen/raise children? Will most humans become cyborgs? Should humans respect robots as living beings? Will humans be able to download their brains into robots? Should such robots be considered cyborgs?*
- Your audience is a group of ordinary citizens, one of whom will be selected (by lottery) to sit on a national panel of robot/cyborg ethics that will make decisions on the kind of robot/cyborg research that can/should go on in this country. Your purpose is to persuade these individuals to adopt the most productive possible understanding of the human/robot/cyborg relationship.
- In your essay, make sure you identify the premise(s) of the argument and provide adequate evidence for the position you are representing. Choose evidence that will be persuasive to your audience.

Format

- Compose your essay either on a Web page that you create online or on a poster board that you purchase at the college bookstore.
- If you create a Web page, compose your essay from images that you find or create online. Before you download an image from another Web site, carefully check to make sure the Web site does not prohibit the copying of images.
- If you use poster board, create your essay from images you cut out of magazines.
- Include at least 15 images in this essay.
- Document the source of each image using the formats below.

Web Essays & Documenting Images from an Online Source

- Create a Web page for your essay.
- Create a separate Web page for each image's bibliographic citation.
- Link each image in your essay to the appropriate Web page containing its bibliographic entry. Here is a model, with an example:

Artist (if given). Title of file. <Web site from which image was taken> (date on which you accessed Web site).

Example: Doe, Jane. SpottedPig.jpg.
<http://www.spottedanimal/pigs/#22> (Accessed 22 July, 2002).

Poster Board Essays & Documenting Images from Print/Photographic Sources

- Create your essay. Number each image.
- Create a bibliography page. List entries in numerical order, numbering each entry to correspond to an image: [15] "Drink Milk." Time 20 September 2002: 15.
- Attach this page to the back of your essay.

Artist (if given). "Title of image" (if given). Magazine Title or Photograph Collection Day Month Year: page number (if applicable).

Example from a magazine: [15] "Drink Milk." Time 20 September 2002: 15.

Example from a photograph: [15] Doe, John. "Me and My Mother." Personal photograph collection. Taken 9 August 1978.

VISUAL ARGUMENT

IN-CLASS WORK

Review and Reflection (Reviewers' Sheet)

Composer/designer _____

Reviewer _____

Objectives

- To give you practice in analyzing visual arguments and evaluating their effectiveness.

Task

Form review teams of three people. For each essay in your group (two essays per person), take 10 minutes to reflect in writing on the questions that follow. *Do not ask the composers/designers to explain their essays.*

- Provide a title for this essay that speaks to the argument and the position it represents.

- In one sentence, identify the premise(s) of this essay.

- Identify the evidence that the composer/designer provides for this argument.

- Does this argument depend primarily on logos? Pathos? Ethos? Explain your answer.

- Rate the visual impact/effectiveness of this essay from 1 (least effective) to 5 (most effective). Explain the reasons for your rating with specific reference to parts of the visual essay/strategies that the author used in composing the argument.

VISUAL ARGUMENT

IN-CLASS WORK

Review and Reflection (Composer/Designer's Sheet)

Author/designer _____

Objective

- To involve composer/designers in reflecting on their success in presenting an argument.
- To provide students practice in analyzing visual arguments and evaluating their effectiveness.

Task

For your own essay, take 10 minutes to reflect in writing on the first five questions that follow. *Do not explain your essay to reviewers.* For homework, answer the last two questions. Hand in both the reviewers' comments on your essay and your own reflections at the beginning of the next class period.

In Class

- Provide a title for this essay that speaks to the argument and the position it represents for you.
- In one sentence, identify the premise(s) of this essay.
- Identify the evidence that you provide for this argument.
- Does your argument depend primarily on logos? Pathos? Ethos? Explain your answer.
- Rate the effectiveness of your essay from 1 (least effective) to 5 (most effective). Explain the reasons for your rating with specific reference to parts of the visual essay.

For Homework

- What are the most effective parts of your argument? Why?
- What are the least effective parts of your argument? Why?

VISUAL ARGUMENT

IN-CLASS WORK

Evaluation

Composer/designer _____

1: OVERALL EFFECT OF THE VISUAL ARGUMENT

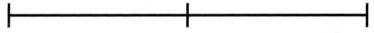

Argument's
overall impact is
low & presenta-
tion is less
than effective.

Argument has
moderate level of
overall impact and
presentation is
moderately effective.

Argument has
exceptional overall
impact and presenta-
tion is highly effective.

Comments:

2: THE PREMISE OF THE VISUAL ARGUMENT

The premise of the
argument is not
clearly identified.

The premise of the
argument is identified.

The premise of
the argument is
clearly identified.

Comments:

3: SUPPORTING EVIDENCE FOR THE ARGUMENT

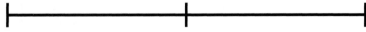

The supporting
evidence is less
than persuasive.

The supporting evi-
dence is persuasive.

The supporting
evidence is highly
persuasive.

Comments:

4: REFLECTION

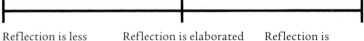

Reflection is less
than fully elaborated
and thoughtful.

Reflection is elaborated
and thoughtful.

Reflection is
robustly elaborated
and exceptionally
thoughtful.

Comments:

5: DOCUMENTATION OF IMAGES

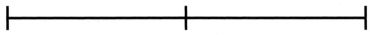

Images are not cor-
rectly documented.

Images are generally
correctly documented.

All images are docu-
mented correctly.

Comments:

Anne Frances Wysocki

awaywithwords: On the Possibilities in Unavailable Designs

INTRODUCTION

You have assigned a research paper in a graduate class you teach. Under what conditions would you accept a paper handwritten in crayon on colored construction paper?

If you can imagine no conditions whatsoever, then for you color of paper and technologies of print typography are like water or stones: things whose natural properties (seem to) necessarily constrain how we can use them. We do not attempt to make soup from stones nor do we imagine early hominids attacking mammoths by throwing water at them. If paper and typography are similar in having such inherent constraints, then it is the neat rows of typographically clean letters on letter-size white paper that are necessary for serious thought.

But.

My claim about the limitations of water, at least, are incorrect, for we can and do use water as weapon, as when police used high-pressure hoses on 1960s Civil Rights marchers in the southern United States. The lesson is that things can be put to many uses, often neither just nor humane. And were we in our classes to study the pressurized water-as-weapon as an example of such use, we would not focus on what it was about water alone that allowed it to be used so against bodies; although one could argue that it was precisely the natural qualities or constraints[1] of water that allow it to be pressurized and so used, were we to talk about this situation only in terms of the water we could rightfully be criticized for acting as though it is ever reasonable to exclude considerations of human life and rights from our work. Instead, in examining this use, we might question what in the context and purposes of the police allowed them to use water in such a way. We might develop an intriguing study into contemporary relations among technologies of water use, law enforcement, and White imaginations about Black bodies. In such a study, we might also learn about the resistances, actions, and particular understandings of material things like water that encourage change in relations among people.

In the preceding paragraphs I am, obviously, trying to use water and its varied applications as an analogy for the materials we use in building communications. If our particular uses of water as weapon — or as soup, swimming place, trash receptacle (as the lake on which we live was used in the nineteenth century),

---

This article is reprinted from *Computers and Composition* 22 (2005): 55–62.

energy generator, scarce natural resource—cannot be separated from the relations that hold among people in particular places and times, then how can we believe that whatever we put on paper or the different screens we use—or the paper or screen itself—can be so separated? If how we conceive of water is unseparable from place and time, how can our communication materials, for which we can make no similar claim to naturalness as we can with water, be otherwise?

My desire in this writing, then, is to push at the edges of where Gunther Kress (2005) directs our attentions in many of his writings. I am in happy agreement with him on the need to encourage a rhetorical focus in our teaching—

> In this social and cultural environment, with these demands for communication of these materials, for that audience, with these resources, and given these interests of mine, what is the design which best meets these requirements? (Presented at CCCC)

—for my experiences working on interdisciplinary software development teams, or with artists working in a range of media, or with people in classes developing instructional materials, have taught me that the question he asks above—entwining context, purpose, audience, and communication strategies (including material choices)—is an approach that helps people working both within and across disciplines or materials to produce effective communication. But there is an addition—or an expansion—that I want to foreground here: I have learned in the process of developing communications that it is always worth asking how our materials have acquired the constraints they have and hence why, often, certain materials and designs are not considered available for certain uses.[2] As with water, constraints of communication materials are often social and historical; to ask after the constraints as we teach or compose can help us understand how material choices in producing communications articulate to social practices we may not otherwise wish to reproduce. That is why, then, I wish to question what becomes unavailable when we think of word and image as Kress has suggested we do, as bound logically and respectively with time and with space.

Did you read my title as "a way with words" or "away with words"? The potential ambiguity, I think, shows how a particular visual space has become natural to how we now read. Space between words has not always been a function of written texts in the West. Our current practices of spacing text on a page developed over hundreds of years, catching on only slowly—as Paul Saenger (1997) has demonstrated through close analysis of manuscripts from throughout Europe—from the seventh through the twelfth centuries and developing out of (Saenger argued) particular practices in Irish monasteries. The development of consistent spacing of words—of a consistent notion of what constitutes a "word" on a page and hence conceptually—seems to have accompanied a shift from the social reading of texts to silent and individual readings. Saenger wanted to argue, also, that it is space between words on a page that—precisely because it allowed or encouraged individual silent reading—gave rise to notions of individuality and so to individual political responsibility (pp. 264–276). I am not willing to go that far with him, because his arguments (like those of McLuhan) tend to technological determinism, where it is simply and only the shape of what is on the page or of a book itself that causes immense shifts in human behavior, but Saenger's arguments, like the much simpler example of my title, do ask us to acknowledge that how we use space on pages affects how we read and understand. Saenger's arguments also asked us to acknowledge that space on pages both shapes and grows out of how we understand what words, texts, and reading are: Are they objects and practices embedded (for example) in the shared vocal work of monasteries or in the silence of a far library carrel?

The spaces of pages can also articulate with our larger sense of the spaces within which we read. In a study that entwines captivity narratives from the earliest days of the United States with details of the publication of Emily Dickinson's poetry, Susan Howe (1993), for example, has argued that editing practices that constrain punctuation and unconventional uses of spacing in writing correlate to an American desire to tame space by shaping wilderness into a bright, tight comprehensible regularity — whether wilderness be the dark forest at one's door or the imagined darkness of women's internal lives.[3]

When we speak of the various kinds of space we can use when we shape alphabetic text, then — when we speak of the tops and bottoms of pages, and of the left and right, and the placement of textual elements — we tie into other spatial understandings we have of our embodied worlds, as Kress and Theo van Leeuwen (1996) or Keith A. Smith (1995), for example, have argued that in addition to what I've described above. There is also the front of a book and its back, and all the spatial issues of orientation within a text that so vexed early (and ongoing) developers of hypertext as readers complained that they could not find their ways back to a particular page or could not remember where a text was because onscreen texts did not provide the same learned spatial memory cues as pages in books.

To say then, as Kress does, that what we need to ask when we read is "What are the salient events and in what (temporal) order did they occur?" is not wrong, but I believe — based even on the little I have written about space and words above — it is incomplete. If we are to help people in our classes learn how to compose texts that function as they hope, they need consider how they use the spaces and not just one time that can be shaped on pages. They also need to question how they have come to understand the spaces of pages so that they can, if need be, use different spaces, potentially powerful spaces that — as Howe, for example, has described — have been rendered unavailable by naturalized, unquestioned practice.

When Kress claims that words are governed by a "temporal and sequential logic," his next move is predictable. Because he has implicitly accepted another logic, that of dichotomous splitting, he must, when he grants certain qualities to words, grant the opposite qualities to what he opposes to words — what he names "image-representations." "Image-representations," therefore, must be governed by a "spatial and simultaneous logic."

There is much to question about using a logic of dichotomies in thinking about the possibilities of multimodalities.

There is, of course, the general questioning of dichotomies and dichotomous thinking that has sparked so much late-twentieth and early twenty-first century writing. There ought to be no need for me to repeat what others have written as they have detailed how, since at least the time of Pythagoras, the engine of dichotomies has driven what many now consider most problematic in western thought.[4]

But for the particular dichotomy with which Kress spends so much time, that of word and image, I think it is probably worth mentioning how W.J.T. Mitchell (1986), for example, has examined the historical dance of word and image in the writings of theorists like Lessing, Locke, and Edmund Burke. Mitchell argued that the separation between these two terms is often the same separation — with all its implications for how we conceive of and so treat each other — that holds between male and female, reason and emotion, civilized and barbarian.[5] To treat the realm of modalities as so divided would seem to me to be inviting us in directions we might otherwise want to question. Instead, we should acknowledge that when we work with what is on pages or other surfaces, alphabetic text is always part of what must be visually arranged and can be designed to call more or less visual attention to itself (with the current academic and literary convention to be that of calling less attention to itself).[6]

It is also worth considering what happens when "image" is used to represent all that is not made exclusively of words. First, even if I were to pretend that the repertoire of communication materials available to us has nothing to do with other practices that shape what we do in the world, I think that "images" — if by that term we mean what many of us implicitly imagine when the term is used, a page-sized or no more than 3″ by 3″ realistically representational photograph, drawing, or painting — nonetheless exceed logics of space. Such images can appear to be moments pulled out of sequential time because we can apparently see what is in the image all at once, given the angles of vision afforded by our human eyes and, importantly, given the particularly designed compositions of many such objects. In a painted portrait or photograph of a single person or a small group that fills the frame of the image, we see the composition as singular, and then — in looking at the image's elements to understand better how the composition works — we see how the elements relate to each other, what is at top, what is at bottom, what is at left, what is at right: We notice how the elements have been arranged so that we see them in some ordering. What has the composer emphasized for us to see first and what elements are treated so as to retreat into the background to be noticed later, if at all? Notice, then, too, that temporal strategies of composition are very much present even in images that we can apparently perceive all at once. But even visually designed objects that fit the definition I have given of image can more emphatically emphasize how time can be variously present in such objects: think of any painting by Brueghel, such as "Children's Games" or "The Black Death," which are small paintings and yet they give us no way to see what is in them all at once; they require considerable time for separating out the elements and finding compositional structure.

But perhaps more importantly, were we to consider "word" in this same commonsensical way as "image" is here, limiting it to a particular size and to a set of compositional strategies and means of production, it would be as though we were asking people in our classes to go out into the world believing that the only writing everyone everywhere ever does is the academic research essay. We certainly do

encounter innumerable visual representations that follow the commonsense definition of image I gave above: We find such images in our wallets, magazines, CD
racks, and photo albums, as well as on the walls of our homes and museums
and on computer monitors. But it does not take much additional looking to see
films, billboards, decorated fingernails, sculptures, typography, the Gilmore Girls,
abstract non-representational paintings or animations, the backs of shampoo
bottles or the fronts of T-shirts, maps, Amy's or Kristin's tattoos, advertising on
the sides of trucks, *USA Today*'s illustrated graphs, the interiors of churches and
schools and conference presentation rooms, Carole Maso's repeated use of a
Giotto fresco in a novel, any car . . . ; you will undoubtedly have thought of more.

To compare just two of the visually designed objects I listed above, for example
a tattoo and a film, is to quickly see that their particular uses of time and space
and their social functionings — how different people in different places and times
understand what they do — are different. And so to use image to name some class
of objects that function in opposition to word is thus either to make an arbitrary
cut into the world of designed visual objects or to try to encompass a class so
large the encompassing term loses function. To say that all these objects rely on a
logic of space is to miss their widely varying compositional potentials.

Like Kress, I too want to understand what is gained and what is lost through
any communication practice, especially as computer technologies heighten
our awareness of the visuality of texts — but I also want to understand what is
possible. If human practices do entwine, as I have been arguing, to the extent
that the spacing of lettershapes on a piece of paper reflects and helps continue
unquestioned restrictions on behavior or that a habit of understanding words
and images as opposites reflects and helps continue beliefs about relations
between men and women, then it is possible that trying new spaces on pages or
exploring the visuality of alphabetic text can be seeds for changes in such practices and beliefs. But we can only do this if we look beyond what appear to be
constraints. As we analyze and produce communications, we need to be asking
not only what is expected by a particular audience in a particular context but
also what they might not expect, what they might not be prepared to see. It is
in the apparently unavailable designs — Emily Dickinson's idiosyncratically
punctuated handwriting that has only recently been published as she spaced it
on the page or a graduate-level essay composed in crayon on colored paper — that
we can see what beliefs and constraints are held within readily available, con-
ventionalized design. By focusing on the human shaping of material, and on
the ties of material to human practices, we might be in better positions to ask
after the consequences not only of how we use water but also of how we use
paper, ink, and pixels to shape — for better or worse — the actions of others.

NOTES

1. I have purposefully avoided using "affordance" here to avoid using the time of
this paper to debate or attempt to fix definitions, even though what affordance exists
to fix is precisely what is at stake in what I write. What is at stake is the independent

life of things—whether those things are water or the shapes of ink on paper: What in any thing is a quality independent of human action and what results from human action and habit? James Gibson's (1979) original discussion of affordance (he said of the term at the time, "I have made it up" [p. 127]) was meant to "impl[y] the complementarity of the animal and the environment" (p. 127), and that "affordances are properties of things taken with reference to an observer but not properties of the experiences of the observer" (p. 137). Gibson acknowledged, "these are slippery terms that should only be used with great care, but if their meanings are pinned down to biological and behavioral facts the danger of confusion can be minimized" (p. 137). Twenty years later, Donald Norman (1999) wrote, "I introduced the term affordance to design in my book 'The Psychology of Everyday Things' ... The concept has caught on, but not always with true understanding. Part of the blame lies with me: I should have used the term 'perceived affordance,' for in design we care much more about what the user perceives that what is actually true." Norman went on to differentiate among real and perceived affordances as well as among physical, logical, and cultural constraints (and sometimes he replaced "constraints" with "conventions" when he discussed what develops out of culture); in spite of or perhaps because of these careful delineations, Norman also wrote that "I suspect that none of us know all the affordances of even everyday objects." The slipperiness of "affordance"—as of "biological and behavioral facts" or even of "convention"—results precisely from our inability to fix, with any finality, what the things of our world are capable of doing as we use them within the complex contexts in which we live. And so I have tried with purpose in this paper to use terms like "constraint" and even "convention" that (I hope) are less fixed in our language practices, to hold onto the messiness of how we live with things that both resist and work with us and to hold on, therefore, to considering our communication materials as things whose possibilities we should be trying to open and understand rather than fix.

2. My use of "unavailable designs" rests, obviously and with thanks, on the New London Group's (2000) highly useful notion of "available designs." As I understand the term, available designs, the "resources for Design" (p. 20), are what communicators can observe in use around them as they prepare to design new communications; as examples, the New London Group (NLG) mentioned the "'grammars' of various semiotic systems" and "orders of discourse," which include "particular Design conventions" such as "styles, genres, dialects, and voices" (p. 21). As the NLG described the design process, communicators draw on available designs in designing (which also includes "reading, seeing, and listening" [p. 22]), which involves re-presenting and recontextualizing available designs in order to develop the redesigned, which is always a "transformed meaning," "founded in historically and culturally received patterns of meaning" (p. 23). This process can imply certain circularity, with the redesigned then becoming itself an available design for the next go-round. I am curious about how we can break this circle—should we need to—given (as I argue here) how unquestioned, naturalized communication habits can reproduce (another circular process) social practices we might not want. As I argue in this paper, the notion of "unavailable designs" helps get at this by encouraging us to explore unconventional or outsider designs, which might allow of richer transformation—as long as we figure out strategies for helping audiences understand why we do such experimenting. But that is the subject of other writing.

3. For a perspective that focuses on using textual practices to tame social classes rather than genders, see Adrian Johns (1998) (pp. 408–428), for a discussion of seventeenth century British attitudes toward—and considerations of how to use reading to control—enthusiasm.

4. Oh heck, let's see: see almost anything by Donna Haraway or by Derrida, for starts.

5. For another perspective on how differing approaches to representation—roughly sketched as the verbal and visual—are historically shaped and situated, see Wendy Steiner (1982). For other arguments on social consequences of how we have at this time distinguished words from visual work, see Robert Romanyshyn (1989, 1993).

6. For discussion of the development of pages that call little visual attention to themselves, pages in which tightly regulated lettershapes are the bulk of what is visible, see, for example, Kress and van Leeuwen (1996) concerning the work done by ruling classes in the late nineteenth century to preserve their cultural position by claiming the "densely written page" as their own while shaping layout and variety for "'the masses,' or children" (pp. 185–186). See also Joanna Drucker (1994) on "unmarked pages" and how such pages develop closely alongside practices of industrialization and standardization; Robin Kinross similarly argued that dreams of neutrality in page layout—dreams of pages whose layout has nothing to do with contemporary ideologies—are tied to specific social structurings.

REFERENCES

Drucker, Joanna. (1994). *The visible word: Experimental typography and modern art, 1909–1923.* Chicago: The University of Chicago Press.

Gibson, James J. (1979). *The ecological approach to visual perception.* Boston: Houghton-Mifflin.

Haraway, Donna. (1991). *Simians, cyborgs, and Women: The reinvention of nature.* New York: Routledge.

Howe, Susan. (1993). *The birth-mark: Unsettling the wilderness in American literary history.* Hanover, NH: Wesleyan UP.

Johns, Adrian. (1998). *The nature of the book: Print and knowledge in the making.* Chicago: University of Chicago Press.

Kinross, Robin. The rhetoric of neutrality. *Design Issues, II*(2), 18–30.

Kress, Gunther, & van Leeuwen, Theo. (1996). *Reading images: The grammar of visual design.* London: Routledge.

Kress, Gunther. (2005). *Gains and losses: New forms of texts, knowledge, and learning.* Computers and Composition, 22(1).

Mitchell, W. J. T. (1986). *Iconology: Image, text, ideology.* Chicago: University of Chicago Press.

Norman, Donald A. *Affordances and design.* Retrieved August 15, 2004, from <http://www.jnd.org/dn.mss/ affordances-and-design.html>.

Romanyshn, Robert. (1989). *Technology as symptom and dream.* London: Routledge.

Romanyshn, Robert. (1993). The despotic eye and its shadow: Media image in the age of literacy. In David Michael Levin (Ed.), *Modernity and the hegemony of vision* (pp. 339–360). Berkeley, CA: University of California Press.

Saenger, Paul. (1997). *Space between words: The origins of silent reading.* Stanford, CA: Stanford University Press.

Smith, Keith A. (1995). *Text in the book format.* Rochester, NY: Keith A. Smith Books.

Steiner, Wendy. (1982). *The colors of rhetoric: Problems in the relation between modern literature and painting.* Chicago: University of Chicago Press.

The New London Group. (2000). A pedagogy of multiliteracies: Designing social futures. In Bill Cope & Mary Kalantzis (Eds.), *Multiliteracies: Literacy learning and the design of social futures* (pp. 9–37). London: Routledge.

Cheryl Glenn

2008 CCCC Chair's Address: Representing Ourselves

It's a great privilege to stand here with my friends and colleagues at this, our fifty-ninth annual convention of the Conference on College Composition and Communication. I'm delighted to help launch the inspiring program of events that Chuck has so ably put together around the theme of "Writing Realities, Changing Realities." In many ways, my remarks, "Representing Ourselves," will extend Chuck's timely theme.

As I prepared for this morning, my thoughts ran through the cascade of CCCC conventions I've attended since my very first one in Atlanta some twenty-one years ago. That's where I met my husband. It was Jon Olson's first CCCC, too. And in the years since then, Jon and I have celebrated mutual support, commitment, and passion. My thoughts also turned to all the past CCCC Chairs, especially those who have extended their support and friendship to me. In addition, I thought of the other CCCC officers, with whom I share an intellectually stimulating, progressive, and compassionate working friendship. All of these relationships embody for me the eloquent declaration of Frances Ellen Watkins Harper: "We are all bound up together in one great bundle of humanity" (149). Thanks to you all.

Twenty-one years ago, then, my first convention was both exciting and auspicious. David Bartholomae had prepared a compelling program, entitled "Language, Self, and Society." And Miriam Chaplin, who was standing before us as Chair, eloquently addressed the issues of that decade: adjunct labor, the job market, a range of misinformed attitudes toward our discipline, and standardized testing that allegedly measured both student ability and teacher quality. As I listened to her, I never imagined that the issues she stared square in the face that morning would persist into the twenty-first century. But persist they have.

Since my first convention, I've followed closely the issues that other Chairs have presented to us: Andrea Lunsford called for us to compose ourselves; Bill Cook, for us to write in the spaces left; and Jackie Royster, for us to operate on codes of better conduct. Wendy Bishop demanded that we act as agents more often than as the acted upon; Shirley Logan that we make ourselves visible and audible; and Doug Hesse that we take ownership of the teaching of writing. In the course of my remarks this morning, I will pick up strands of previous Chairs' addresses and weave them through the fabric of my remarks. What I hope will give sheen to the fabric is my entreaty that we conceive of new ways

This article is reprinted from *College Composition and Communication* 60.2 (Dec. 2008): 420–39.

of working together across differences in order to represent our professional selves strategically.

I don't think I'm asking too much.

After all, a number of CCCC Chairs have emphasized the enduring challenge of how we might best represent ourselves. "We have a lot to solve," Keith Gilyard admonished, prodding us to make our discussions about identity "serve a critical, democratic project." Duku Anokye called for the construction of a "public voice" as purchase for political power. Cindy Selfe warned us about the "perils of not paying attention." And Kathi Yancey reminded us that "we have a moment." So in this moment, I want to consider some of the rich possibilities of coalescing and representing ourselves as we face the issues of our decade, our century.

> With whom do you believe your lot is cast?
> from where does your strength come? (Rich, "IV" 6)

So asks Adrienne Rich, one of the many feminists with whom I have cast my lot, from where my strength comes. These feminist writers (male and female alike) have helped move the feminist project beyond its initial position (that sustained focus on women) into a position of seeking out coalitions: strategic, provisional coalitions constructed across *acknowledged* differences of class, culture, nationality, religion, race, sexual orientation, and, of course, gender.

Building coalitions across differences is never easy, but as Toni Morrison reminds us, "The difference is all the difference there is" (84). Besides, as Audre Lorde encourages, "It is the work of feminism to make connections, to heal unnecessary divisions," and to "pay attention to the voices we have been taught to distrust, [to] articulate what they teach us, and [to] act upon what we know" (qtd. in Bereano 8, 11). Employing feminism to this end means "doing the unromantic and tedious work necessary to forge *meaningful* coalitions, . . . recognizing which coalitions are possible and which coalitions are not" (Lorde, "Learning" 142, emphasis added). Coalition building within and across the CCCC, then, is "the name not of the solution but of the challenge" (Appiah xv).

So in my call for coalescing across differences, I want to be clear that I am *not* arguing for consensus, *not* for post-identity politics, *not* for the suppression of critical and dissenting voices, and *not* for a homogenizing professional narrative of harmonious pluralism. Instead, mine is a feminist call for us to mobilize an organizational identity that can be used for strategic representation. Mine is a reminder that such coalitions are contingent, fragile, and often uncomfortable, particularly when they are put into service for a common goal.

Therefore, we must (as Cindy would have us do) pay attention. We must pay attention to the issue of diversity as both a challenge and a resource, to the diversity of ourselves as complex individuals who come together *as* the CCCC and to the diversity of our equally complex students. We must pay attention to legislation and policies that represent what others imagine to be improvements in our professional lives. And we must pay attention to the ways we could be representing ourselves strategically as CCCC.

I don't think I'm asking too much.

One place to look at the ways we currently represent the diversity within our organization is in the CCCC convention program itself, where all our complementary and competing identities are taxonomized into twelve strands of over 500 panels, nearly 50 workshops, and nearly 50 special-interest groups. We are American citizens and international scholars of every race, cultural-ethnic background, sociopolitical bent, religion, institution, commitment, and combination thereof. Generally speaking, within a membership of over 6,000 writing teachers, administrators, and graduate students (most of whom are white and middle aged), around 20 percent of us teach at two-year colleges and 20 percent at doctoral-granting universities. The rest of us teach in four-year, MA-granting, or other institutions (CCCC, "General"). Well over 30 percent of us are tenure track and have been teaching for over twenty years, while nearly 15 percent of us have been teaching for fewer than five years.

The diversity of who we are, what we think, how we act, and where we teach makes for a dynamic organization, that's for sure, but it also provides us with a rich intellectual opportunity.[1] The nearly 4,000 college writing teachers who come to our convention every year can tap the energy of that diversity by leveraging the following strengths: the invitational activism of our CCCC Newcomers' Orientation Committee; the recruitment and mentoring projects of the various CCCC networks, coalitions, and consortia; the recognition programs of the Scholars for the Dream, the Tribal Fellowships, Chairs' Memorial Fellowships, and Professional Equity Program; and, of course, inspiring the political commitments of our Black, Latino, Asian/Asian-American, American Indian, Jewish, and Queer caucuses. We already have in place systems of hope for nourishing and diversifying our organization even further, not only in terms of age, institution, and experience, but also in terms of a membership that more closely reflects the ethnic-racial demographics of college-level writing teachers and their students all across the nation.

Yet that same diversity that offers us so much opportunity sometimes renders us divided. Instead of rhetoric and composition, we sometimes become "rhetoric and 'competition'" (Hutcheon 522). Instead of publish or perish, we sometimes think "publish and punish," of academic assassinations right out of David Lodge novels. As though she were targeting Lodge's own Morris Zapp, Jane Tompkins writes, "In veiled language, . . . we accuse one another of stupidity, ignorance, fear, envy, pride, malice, and hypocrisy. . . . We feel justified in exposing these errors to view . . . because we are right, so right, and they . . . are wrong, so wrong" (588). Thus, too often we allow ourselves to become divided when a decision to transcend our disagreements at that moment might allow us to leverage our diversity into a strategic representation of the CCCC as an intellectual community with professional force and public influence over those external powers who want to fashion who we are or what we should do.

Ironically, even when experiencing that division, even when we're not strategic in our representation, we still believe that we have much to learn from and teach one another. Last year's post-CCCC convention survey results revealed that "respondents were less likely to be drawn to prestigious speakers" and more likely to value the new ideas and research of their colleagues (CCCC, Officers' Conference Call). In fact, networking with colleagues is one of the main reasons we say we attend our annual convention. That survey also revealed that nearly every one of us comes because we're interested (still) in sessions that focus on "practices of teaching writing" (CCCC, "General").[2] We seem to be holding on to the hope that our teaching and our students' writing will make a difference.

Hope is one value we can coordinate to get things done together, that's for sure. But in hope, as in everything else, each of us must start from where we are. And where we are today is New Orleans, a city still recovering from Hurricane Katrina, the biggest natural disaster (one compounded by human and governmental error) the United States has ever experienced, leaving tens of thousands of former Gulf Coast residents still displaced.[3] Nevertheless, at the center of that disaster shines hope, in the bodies of two writing teachers, Jim Randels and Kalamu ya Salaam, who, along with their writing students, have created an "intentional community" called "Students at the Center."

Students at the Center is a New Orleans–based writing project that trains high school students to become writing mentors for peers and to use writing as a way to improve their schools and communities. Randels teaches students to write with words; ya Salaam, a videographer, to "write with light." Recently named "People of the Year" by the *New Orleans Tribune*, Randels, ya Salaam, and their students explain that "through writing and sharing their writing, there is hope in a classroom" ("Jim Randels" 4).

Indeed, there *is* hope in the classroom. Graduating senior Nadja Tilstra (student of my old friend Molly Travis) delivered the following words in her Tulane University commencement address just last spring: "We have been told that we have the power to change the world . . . [but] we have had the unique opportunity to live in a world that has changed us[, that has] forced us to . . . bec[o]me more aware citizens . . . [and] to give back to this amazing city that has inspired us" (Tilstra). For Randels, ya Salaam, Students at the Center, and Tilstra, then, "Hope Is to Create," like Kathleen Raine's poem of the same name:

> Hope is to create
> in possibility
> . . . . . .
> Therefore I hope for hope (339)

As we come together here in New Orleans, we do so with the hope of creating more and better possibilities for students and ourselves.

Still, the gap between the hopes we discuss here and the material conditions of our daily lives is too often vast, leaving us vulnerable to cognitive dissonance. As Michelle Cliff reminds us, "Because every little piece of reality exists in relation to another little piece, our situation [is] not . . . simple" (64). And in those relations lie the biggest of our challenges.

I've already described the ways the relation among our diverse professional selves challenges our daily lives at the same time that it offers one of our greatest resources. So how might we strategically transform any divisiveness into a resource when state, local, and national legislation so often modifies our shared goals or dismantles those goals altogether?

We writing teachers are no strangers to diversity, to the ways it simultaneously complicates and enriches our lives. Every day we take into careful consideration the diversity of our students. Over the past thirty-five years, for instance, the CCCC position on *Students' Rights to Their Own Language* has provided us pedagogical guidelines for handling linguistic diversity. Yet all the while you and I are working to honor the diverse languages and dialects our students bring to our classrooms, the U.S. Senate is working to beef up the (as yet unpassed) Senate Immigration Reform Act by including English-only language. Without any reference to the CCCC Position Statement on "The National Language Policy" or any consultation with the CCCC Committee on Language Policy (that I know of), Amendment 4073 (which did pass, 58–39) declares "that English is the common and unifying language of the United States" (U.S. Congress).[4] Whether it is intended to be pro-American or anti-Mexican, the amendment is nevertheless "odd," Dennis Baron notes, given that the 2000 Census confirms that "94% of Americans [already] speak English" ("English").[5]

Yes, diversity does bring challenges to both the national and local scene. But too many schools across the United States have responded to the challenges of linguistic *and* racial diversity by easing along that well-worn groove known as "segregation." In *The Shame of the Nation*, Jonathan Kozol reveals a bleak picture of public education in the United States:

> Schools that were already deeply segregated 25 or 30 years ago ... are no less segregated now, while thousands of other schools that *had* been integrated either voluntarily or by the force of law have since been rapidly resegregating both in northern districts and in broad expanses of the South. (18, emphasis in original)[6]

Kozol drapes his indignation on New York, Michigan, Illinois, and California, the "four most segregated states for black students," but he nails his grievances on New York and California, in particular, where "only one black student in seven goes to a predominantly white school," and where a segregated inner-city school is "almost six times as likely" to be a school of concentrated poverty as is a school that has an overwhelmingly white population (21).

The segregation of the rich from the poor and the white from nonwhite is further aggravated by federal legislation. Perhaps the most important federal education law in our nation's history is the "remarkably ambitious and unusually intrusive" (Ryan 937) 2002 No Child Left Behind Act (NCLB). The purpose of NCLB is twofold: (1) to increase the academic achievement of all K–12 students, ensuring that students "disadvantaged" by socioeconomic class, race, ethnicity, ability, and home language meet the same achievement targets as their more advantaged counterparts, and (2) to attract quality teachers. Both are admirable intentions, to be sure.[7]

But the actual consequences of the act are just the opposite. Law professor James E. Ryan incisively pares the prose from the substance of the act, writing that, in its implementation, NCLB "creates incentives for states to lower academic standards," "to increase segregation," "to push low-performing students out of school," to "divert [some teachers] from the most challenging of classrooms," and "to deter [other teachers] from teaching altogether" (934).[8]

You might wonder, "Why is NCLB a challenge for the Conference on College Composition and Communication? After all, this legislation hasn't touched us directly." Well, as Doug Hesse warned us a few years back, "Teachers may only whisper how well their students . . . do . . . ; [while] the shout is left to No Child Left Behind" (458).[9]

Still our challenges don't end with NCLB.

Already stressed by the apartheid of class and race and pressured by threats of endless assessments, our entire educational system now rests precariously on a fault line of social and financial neglect — yet another huge challenge we face as parents, as professionals, and as an organization. As you may well know, America has the highest incarceration rate in the world — and the biggest prison buildup in history to prove it. In the last three decades, state budgets have been "funding prisons at the expense of education," at the rate of 5 to 1 (Ambrosio and Schiraldi 1).[10] Thus, as financial support has been leached away from colleges and universities, tuitions rise, and the financial burden of going to — and staying in — college falls on students and their families.

Keep in mind that just as the ever-rising cost of going to college falls back on individuals and their families, the average American family is losing its spending power in nearly every other way. Economist Robert B. Reich writes that "America's median hourly wage is barely higher than it was 35 years ago, adjusted for inflation. The income of a man in his 30s is now 12 percent below that of a man his age three decades ago" (par. 5).[11] Paul Krugman writes that more children live below the poverty line now than they did when LBJ launched his War on Poverty.[12] And the National Coalition on Health Care has announced that nearly 20 percent of Americans have no health insurance, with our students (young adults between the ages of 18–24) the least likely of any age group to have health insurance.[13] Even the GI Bill lags nearly 25 percent in terms of what it actually costs for a veteran to attend a public four-year university.[14] Little wonder, then, that many veterans use their enlistment bonus checks for motorcycles, trucks, or flat-screen TVs — hardly the best investment of their well-deserved bonus.

Apartheid schooling, cell blocks versus classrooms, haves and have-nots, and a chronic achievement gap between the two groups — what a treacherous landscape we are asking our students, their parents, and ourselves, their teachers, to travel. How might we, as a professional organization, address these inequalities, this betrayal of an entire generation of students?[15] What are the chances we can build a landscape in higher education that we and these students might want to travel together?[16]

I doubt an official CCCC Position Statement will do the trick. Who would read it even if we wrote it? I believe that our only course of action is to follow Duku's charge for us to "pull together our troops, raise our voices in unison . . . [and] demand our voices be heard" (Anokye 274). We need to develop our voice and represent ourselves, that's for sure. But we also need to consider what we would use that voice for. We must define our common desires, identify the specific forces that frustrate those desires, and work together to envision what is humanly possible.

Our biggest challenge, then, is to define what is humanly possible. And a good place to start might be by concentrating on what is humanly possible on our own campuses, in our own writing programs, and in our own classrooms. For instance, how might we coalesce professionally in order to influence the local forces who control the conditions under which writing is taught, those who ignore the CCCC "Statement of Principles and Standards for the Post-secondary Teaching of Writing"?

Published nearly twenty years ago, this statement recommends that "departments offering composition and writing courses should rely on full-time tenured or tenure-track faculty members who are both prepared for and committed to the teaching of writing" (sec. I). The position statement also calls special attention to class size and teaching loads, arguing for no more than twenty (ideally, only fifteen) students in any writing class, with each "English faculty member" teaching no more than sixty writing students each term (sec. II).

Yet, two decades later, this document carries little weight, given the fact that more writing courses than ever are taught by part-time and adjunct labor or by graduate students. In doctoral departments, 94 percent of first-year writing is taught by non-tenure-track faculty; in MA-granting departments, it's 80 percent (Laurence, "MLA" 216). According to the latest MLA survey, 63.7 percent of all English instructors in higher education are non-tenure-track faculty, and an average of 72 percent of those instructors teach first-year writing.[17] We (our departments and programs) are complicit in these numbers, having moved far beyond our support of graduate students in our use of non-tenure-track faculty. Furthermore, most of us here this morning teach writing courses with more than twenty students in each class. And far too many of us teach more than sixty writing students a term. When, at last year's CCCC convention, Lois Powers revealed the results of her workload survey of community college instructors, members of her audience were agitated, but not surprised. Powers's findings reveal that "more than 20 percent of writing instructors at community colleges teach between 111 and 130 students each semester. And 9 percent report teaching 131–150 students a semester" (Jaschik, par. 3).

As you are all well aware, the workload differential exacerbates a pay differential. The disjunction between those of us who teach two courses a semester and those of us who teach twice that many (if not more) is aggravated by a pay differential between full professor-rank English faculty, who earn an average of $74,000, and instructor-rank faculty, who earn about half that amount ($37,573)![18] I don't have time this morning to go into the issue of professional support or fringe benefits between the two ranks, except to say that 69 percent of tenure-track faculty receive financial support to attend a professional convention like this one, while only 26 percent of non-tenure track faculty receive such support.[19] These differences separate us into the "haves" and the "have-nots" in our profession, prompting one adjunct to write, "I love my students; I love what I do . . . [, but] colleges hire custodians for just less than what I earn — and custodians get health care benefits!" (Confused).[20]

Yes, despite these inequalities, there is still love — as well as hope.

Most of us do love what we do, despite any material and psychic hardships in our daily lives. We love our teaching; we say it often. That's fortunate because our teaching is often the only thing our students want from us anyway. Good thing it's the best thing we have to offer them. We've long known that most of our students come to us with the same hope we have long held for our own, better-educated selves: that education — that our teaching — will change their lives. After all, when all is said and done, teaching isn't about our own scholarly achievement or our students' lack thereof; rather, it is about our movement between worlds, arms out, changing students' lives at the same time that they change ours, making the connections that count.

To be sure, economics, class size, teaching load, and No Child Left Untested pose serious challenges — for our students, their parents, our colleagues, and our hopeful selves. It's unfortunate, then, that I can so easily enumerate additional constraints to the connections that count, to the hope that brings teachers and students together. Those constraints include the devaluation of a college degree (while expensive online degrees are proliferating); the lure of the semi-skilled workplace; the seduction of parties and bars; the limited resources families have for an ever more costly education; and the overt restrictions and hidden injuries of class bias, racism, physical ability-ism, and heterosexism in the classroom. Any one of these constraints gives us a good reason to coalesce and strategically represent ourselves as CCCC. But I would be remiss if I didn't mention the biggest constraint to coalitions of hope — and that is violence.

We real cool. . . .
. . . .
. . . . We
Die Soon. (Brooks, 608-9)

The violence of daily life, writ globally and locally, cuts our connections and fetters our hope.

One way and another, on every continent, a war has raged for three thousand years.[21] As I write this, Benazir Bhutto has been buried, along with the nearly thirty others who were killed as a result of her assassination, and her nineteen-year-old son has been tapped to carry on the work of the Pakistani People's Party. If we ever thought systematic genocide was over and done, we have only to look to Kenya (long considered the most peaceful and prosperous African nation), where ethnic violence, killing over 1,000 people and displacing nearly 300,000, has continued unabated, after what can only be described as "deeply flawed" elections.

Writing from the Agha Khan Academy in Nairobi, Kenya, where he teaches, David Wandera (Bread Loaf School of English student) describes the high price the urban poor and "countryside folk" have paid for internecine warfare:

> The eruption of the tribal time bomb [in the Rift Valley province] was immediate;
> ...the frenzied looting, the avenged killings, the wanton destruction....
> [B]ands of youth armed with crude weapons...erected road blocks...sieving
> out those from "undesirable tribes"...[who] would be beaten, raped, [and]
> bludgeoned to death....So intense was this hatred that a rabid group of arson-
> ists pursued a displaced community [who had taken refuge in] a church....
> They waited outside after setting the church on fire and killed those who tried
> to run out. The result was over 35 women and children dead.

The most horrific feature of David's report is that the violence is neither shock-
ing nor unspeakable. Violence is part of our daily lives.

It might have been tempting to think of Columbine as an isolated incident,
but with the tragic shootings at Virginia Tech and more recently at Northern
Illinois, we must embrace the fact that such violence doesn't occur in a vac-
uum. After all, the Northern Illinois shooting was the fifth school shooting in
the United States that week.[22] In the UK, an average of 197 people die each year
from shooting; in Japan, it's 83. But in the United States, we shoot and kill
14,054 people a year.[23] Seven U.S. children aged nineteen and under die from
gunfire each day—that's a Columbine High School massacre every other day
or a Virginia Tech massacre every five days.[24]

We and our students inhabit a school culture of physical danger. Even on
the most placid campuses, gays, lesbians, and heterosexual women remain the
targets of sexual harassment and physical violence, acts that are too often and
too easily blamed on alcohol (think back to gay victim Matthew Sheppard).
But alcohol was not to blame when fifteen-year-old Lawrence King was shot to
death by a junior high classmate in Oxnard, California, a couple of months
ago. Lawrence was shot and killed because he admitted that he was gay.[25]

We live in a world where the ethical fenders threaten to fall off the wheels.

Still, there is hope—or (as Kathleen Raine would say) hope for hope. If that
were not the case, we wouldn't be here—and we sure as heck wouldn't get up
early to hear (let alone give) a Chair's address. As Adrienne Rich reminds us,
it's folks like us—professional intellectuals, writers, and teachers—who must
make and write history through the "sheer power of a collective imagining of
change and a sense of collective hope" ("Arts" 167). After all, the strength of CCCC
is the rich and complex nature of our membership. We are a 6,000-member collective of pedagogical activists, artists, and poets; of intellectual projects; and
of political commitments. And together, we could be (but we are not yet) a force
to be reckoned with. To that end, we have some serious and very hard work to
do if we are to represent the CCCC as a coalition. We must mobilize a collective
imagining that is both relevant to the material conditions of our daily lives as
well as politically responsive to wrong-headed power and bad-faith judgments.

I want department heads, deans, and college and university presidents to
worry about what we think, what position we have taken. I want every legisla-
tor to worry that if she doesn't consult with us, work with us, listen to us (and
we'll listen to her, too), that she might not get reelected. I want to inhabit a future
of Doonesbury cartoons that feature a Capitol Dome with a president wondering

what the CCCC membership thinks, what we might do, how we might vote as
a strategic block. I want a president who welcomes the opinions of a thoughtful,
engaged secretary of education, someone like Kathi Yancey, for example. I want
us to focus our attention against the damaging economic, political, educational,
and social forces that we—as an organization—have the potential to dismantle.

"And just how might we do this work," you may be thinking, "when we're not
all the same, when we don't all agree?" Well, as one of Anne Gere's writing group
participants declared, "We can disagree with each other's views but the point . . .
is to do the work" ("Kitchen Tables" 248). In fact, the work will be richer, more
ethical, and more effective if we don't all agree, if our work is the result of our
understanding rather than persuading one another. We can, as Sojourner Truth
once said, "Keep the thing going while things are stirring."

This world is ours. We make of it what we will. One of the things I've liked
about getting older is taking responsibility for my own life, for my own choices.
As any self-conscious adult knows, we create our own lives at some considerable cost. So we must consciously be willing to live our lives—and think about
leaving them. We rarely imagine ourselves evaporating in a split second or dis-
patched by violence. If you're like me, you imagine yourself lying on your death-
bed, very old, surrounded by your loved ones, realizing, finally, the "right" frame
of mind. We're not going to lie there wishing we'd been even meaner, been more
right more times, or had the last word. So if ever we're going to understand one
another, if ever we're going to be more generous, better listeners, better respect-
ers of difference, better strategic collaborators, why not start now? Why wait
until we reach our end?

Now and together, we must orchestrate our future so that it is shared; we
must metabolize our experience into something that is useful, lasting, effective.

As I work toward a closing, I want to quote Audre Lorde one last time:

> To refuse to participate in the shaping of our future is to give up. . . . Each of us
> must find our work and do it. . . . You do not have to be me. . . . I do not have to be
> you. . . . What we must do is commit ourselves to some future with the particu-
> lar strengths of our individual identities. And in order to do that we must allow
> each other our differences at the same time as we recognize our sameness. ("Learn-
> ing" 141–42)

So as you walk through the convention, talking *and* listening to the colleagues
you understand and those you don't, to those you like and those you don't,
try with me to deploy empathy and difference so that together we can move
into a CCCC culture of strategic representation, a coalition of acknowledged
differences in pursuit of transformation. Let us do this without grandiosity
or false humility—but with hope—as we steadily write and teach our way
through this twenty-first century, imagining and shaping a world we all want
to share.

I don't think I'm asking too much.

It's up to us.

Our future is what we imagine it to be. The greatest tragedy that can befall
us is that we leave our future *un*imagined. For that reason, we must work together

for the good of a world that none of us may ever know but that our children and grandchildren might gladly enter.

NOTES

1. Journalist Sam Roberts writes that "managing the nation's unprecedented diversity may be the greatest challenge facing America as it begins the 21st century" (112).

2. The survey revealed other features of our collective identities as well. Most of us teach in mid-sized or large cities (with populations between 25,000 and 250,000), and 25 percent of us teach in English departments, as opposed to teaching in separate writing or humanities programs (CCCC, "General"). We're mostly female (68 percent) (with only twenty-one female CCCC chairs in our fifty-nine-year history), mostly middle-aged — and still mostly white at 92 percent (though I hasten to say that the efforts to diversify and thereby enrich our membership continue unabated) (ibid.). Most of us (71 percent) come to the convention because we're interested in sessions focusing on "practices of teaching writing" (ibid.).

3. Hurricane Katrina displaced more than a million people when it struck in August 2005, and tens of thousands of Gulf Coast residents remain displaced two years and five months later ("New Report").

4. The second half of the amendment proposes "to preserve and enhance the role of the English language," prompting Dennis Baron to wonder if those were votes *for* English or *against* Mexico ("Word," emphasis in original).

5. In *Language Death*, David Crystal tells us: "The human brain has the natural capacity to learn several languages, and most members of the human race live in settings where they naturally and efficiently use their brains precisely this way. Half the human race is known to be at least bilingual, and there are probably half as many bilinguals again in those parts of the world where there have been no studies, though cultural contacts are known to be high. People who belong to a predominantly monolingual culture are not used to seeing the world this way because their mindset has been established through centuries of being part of a dominant culture, in which other people learn your language and you do not learn theirs" (45).

6. Quoting the findings of Harvard University's Civil Rights Project, Kozol goes on to write: "Almost 'three fourths of black and Latino students attend schools that are predominantly minority,' and more than two million, including more than a quarter of black students in the Northeast and Midwest, attend schools which we call apartheid schools' in which 99 to 100 percent of students are nonwhite" (19).

7. Schools and their students that maintain "adequate yearly progress" (AYP) are rewarded by additional federal funding; schools and their students that fail to meet their goals "face increasingly harsh sanctions for every year that they fail" (Ryan 933).

8. Ryan is William L. Matheson and Robert M. Morgenthau Distinguished Professor at the University of Virginia School of Law. In a recent study of Texas's public school accountability system (a proto-NCLB system), researchers at Rice University and the University of Texas at Austin found: "The loss of growing numbers of students actually led to improvements in how public schools were rated by the state. That's because most of the students who left schools were low-achieving — and a disproportionate share were black or Hispanic, or spoke English as a second language — which meant that their departure led to an increase in the schools' average test

scores and created the appearance that the school was closing the test-score gap between white and minority students" ("Texas Study," par. 2).

9. Since "teaching for the test" and "assessment" are the fuel that makes NCLB run, many of us in CCCC wonder if testing and assessment will become the fuel for funding higher education. As I write this, Kathi Yancey has posted on the WPA-listserv that "NCLB is not coming to higher ed after all, or not anytime soon" ("Spellings," par. 1). I hope she's right.

10. Through the 1980s into the twenty-first century, corrections' piece of the state and local pie has increased by 104 percent, while higher education's share has dropped by 21 percent ("Cellblocks"). Adrienne Rich writes that prisons have become "holding pens for youth, disproportionately for young African American men" ("Arts" 157). But women (of all colors) are the "fastest growing incarcerated group, two-thirds being mothers of dependent children." The bottom line, though, is that prison terms, like bad schools, are tabulated to race.

11. Reich served as the twenty-second secretary of labor under President Bill Clinton. At present, he is professor of public policy at the Goldman School of Public Policy at the University of California at Berkeley. A prolific writer, Reich works at the intersection of economic and social policy, with sympathy for the poor, the untrained, and the uninsured. He writes that "most of what's been earned in America [in the past three decades] has gone to the richest 5 percent" (par. 5).

12. "In 2006, 17.4 percent of children in America lived below the poverty line, substantially more than in 1969" (Krugman, par. 6).

13. Over 30 percent of all young adults have no health insurance. Only 32.6 percent of people of Hispanic origin have health insurance (National Coalition, par. 4).

14. The American Association of State Colleges and Universities reports that the "$9,909 annual benefit for former active duty service members covers only about three-quarters of the average total cost of attendance at public four-year universities ($13,145)" (Redden, par. 3).

15. In "Arts of the Possible," Adrienne Rich describes "an imaginative, highly developed educational system that would serve citizens at every age — a vast, shared, public schooling in which each of us felt a stake, as with public roads, there when needed, ready when you choose to use them — [which] would mean changing almost everything else" (162–63).

16. Former Harvard president Derek Bok, who applies continuous pressure on higher education to improve itself, writes about the positive consequences of educational diversity at every level. Despite the controversies and pain that are bound to occur when students live together and work together across divisions of race, culture, and gender, he writes, those students improve their "powers of critical thinking" when they respond to "different values and perspectives." In addition, they become "civically active," "inclined to help others," and "committed to improving their communities" (195). The ensuing benefits to society are immeasurable, for the development of "tolerance and mutual respect from different groups within [a] citizenry . . . contain[s] the religious and ethnic tensions that have riven so many countries around the world."

17. The percentage of first-year writing taught by non-tenure-track faculty falls into the following categories: doctoral departments, 94.0 percent; MA-granting departments, 79.9 percent; BA-granting departments, 57.8 percent, and AA-granting departments, 55.2 percent (Laurence, "MLA" 216). MLA's David Laurence is currently updating this employment picture but assures me that the 2001 results still provide an

accurate picture (email to author). Anne Ruggles Gere, who has read the draft of that current MLA survey, tells me that "English is in much worse shape than other disciplines" with regard to the rise of non-tenure-track faculty and declining numbers of tenure-track faculty, adding that "much of this is due to what has been happening in comp" ("Numbers"). Anne urged me to make "the profession at large more aware of this creeping decline."

18. According to the latest *Chronicle of Higher Education* report on salaries, the average English faculty salaries at four-year institutions are as follows: professor, $74,040; associate professor, $57,598; assistant professor, $47,724; and instructors, $37,573 ("Average" 25).

19. The CCCC Committee on Part-time/Adjunct Issues reports that the professional support provided for non-tenure-track and part-time non-tenure-track faculty in freestanding writing programs differs markedly from that of their tenure-track counterparts: 89.47 percent of part-time non-tenure-track (NTT) share their office (compared to 31.25 percent of tenure track [TT]), 78.95 percent of NTT share computer access (18.75 percent for TT); 47.37percent of NTT receive regular salary increases (81.25 percent of TT); 26.32 percent of NTT receive support to travel to professional meetings (68.75 percent of TT); and 15.79 percent of NTT have access to institutional research grants (56.25 percent of TT) (342). In terms of fringe benefits, the gap is even wider, with only 21 percent of part-time non-tenure-track faculty being eligible for a health plan paid by both the institution and themselves; only 26 percent eligible for a retirement plan, and only 21 percent eligible for life insurance (343).

20. In response to the online question "Do Adjuncts Earn a Living Wage?" Confused explained: "Last fall, I taught six classes for two districts at four different locations. . . . I taught five courses in the spring, and the max of three in the summer term. As an adjunct I earn nothing for prep time or grading. My annual earnings? Just over $32,000. This is not a living wage in my part of the country. . . . I love what I do and the particular kind of student I encounter at my community colleges. [But I] question the wisdom of putting so much heart into a profession that our culture so clearly undervalues."

21. The hovering threat of renewed al-Qaida attacks and the ongoing wars in Iraq, Afghanistan, Turkey, and Iran are hardly news. The U.S. military death toll in Iraq has exceeded 4,000, with over 33,000 wounded. Despite this continued violence and death, Mitt Romney pronounced that a Democratic presidency "would mean attacks on America, launched from safe havens that would make Afghanistan under the Taliban look like child's play. About this, I have no doubt" ("Mitt"). About his claim, I shudder. Can he really believe in one last war?

22. Twenty-two students were shot, and six were killed, including the perpetrator at Northern Illinois University. A nineteen-year-old was shot by a classmate in the Mitchell High School cafeteria in Memphis, Tennessee; another Memphis student was shot in the leg during algebra class at Hamilton High School; a female student shot dead two female students before killing herself at Louisiana Technical College at Baton Rouge, and an estranged husband shot his wife in front of her fifth-grade students at Notre Dame Elementary School in Portsmouth, Ohio.

23. The major broadcast networks average about five acts of violence every hour in their prime-time programming (that's one violent act every twelve minutes), an alarming figure given that the visual media have become a fact of cultural life. By the age of eighteen, the average American college freshman has witnessed 40,000 simu-

lated murders on television and 200,000 acts of violence. These never-ending images of violence seem to cancel out the actual experience and suffering of all the children who are killed daily.

24. In case you didn't already realize it, the large-scale problems with guns in school have invariably come from white, suburban neighborhoods. Imagine all the killings, attacks, assaults, sex offenses, robberies, burglaries, motor vehicle thefts, arsons, hate crimes, murders, and manslaughters that have been reported as occurring on school grounds. Then try to imagine the number of crimes that went *unre-ported* — or imagine adding all of the school-related killings, hostage situations, stalkings, and bullying that have occurred in just the past few weeks.

25. Fourteen-year-old Brandon McInerney has been charged as an adult with the hate crime of premeditated murder and gun possession, for killing Lawrence King in the computer lab at E. O. Green Junior High School. "If convicted, he faces a sentence of 52 years to life in prison" (Cathcart, par. 13). Given the levels of school violence, many parents, concerned about "safety, drugs, and negative peer pressure" are homeschooling (Princiotta, Bielick, and Chapman iv). According to the latest survey (2003, published in 2006), 1,096,000 students are homeschooled in the United States, a 29 percent increase from the estimated 850,000 students who were being homeschooled in 1999 (iii). The homeschooling rate "rose from 1.7 percent in 1999 to 2.2 percent in 2003," with parents citing "religious and moral instruction" as the second reason they homeschool (iii). Seventy-five percent of homeschooled students are white, non-Hispanic, compared with 65 percent of nonhomeschooled students (1).

WORKS CITED

Ambrosio, Tara-Jen, and Vincent Schiraldi. "From Classrooms to Cell Blocks: A National Perspective." Justice Policy Institute Policy Report. Washington, DC: Justice Policy Institute, Feb. 1997. 1–30.

Anokye, Akua Duku. "Voices of the Company We Keep." *College Composition and Communication* 59.2 (Dec. 2007): 263–75.

Appiah, Kwame Anthony. *Cosmopolitanism: Ethics in a World of Strangers.* New York: Norton, 2006.

"Average Faculty Salaries by Selected Fields and Rank at 4-Year Institutions, 2006–7." *Chronicle of Higher Education* 31 Aug. 2007: 25.

Baron, Dennis. "The English Language Unity Act of 2007: It Takes More Than a Language to Unify a Nation." *Web of English* 22 Feb. 2007. 27 Aug. 2008 <http://illinois.edu/blog/view?topicId=581>.

——. "The Word of the Year for 2007 Is English." *Web of English* 16 Dec. 2007. 15 Feb. 2008. 27 Aug. 2008 <http://illinois.edu/blog/view?topicId=1299>.

Bereano, Nancy K. Introduction. Lorde 7–11.

Bishop, Wendy. "Against the Odds in Composition and Rhetoric." Roen 383–94.

Bok, Derek. *Our Underachieving Colleges.* Princeton, NJ: Princeton UP, 2006.

Brooks, Gwendolyn. "We Real Cool." *A Book of Women Poets from Antiquity to Now: Selections from the World Over.* Ed. Aliki Barnstone and Willis Barnstone. 1980. New York: Schocken, 1992. 608–9.

Cathcart, Rebecca. "Boy's Killing, Labeled a Hate Crime, Stuns a Town." *New York Times* 23 Feb. 2008. 23 Feb. 2008 <http://www.nytimes.com/2008/02/23/us/23oxnard.html>.

"Cellblocks or Classrooms? The Funding of Higher Education and Corrections and Its Impact on African American Men." Washington, DC: Justice Policy Institute, Aug. 2002. 27 Aug. 2008 <http://www.nationalinstituteofcorrections.gov/Library/017941>.

Chaplin, Miriam T. "Issues, Perspectives, and Possibilities." Roen 156–68.

Cliff, Michelle. "If I Could Write This in Fire, I Would Write This in Fire." *The Graywolf Annual Five: Multicultural Literacy 1988.* Ed. Rick Simonson and Scott Walker. St. Paul: Graywolf P, 1988.

Conference on College Composition and Communication (CCCC). "General University Profile." Urbana: NCTE, 2008.

——. "The National Language Policy." 1988. *CCCC Position Statements.* Rev. 1992. National Council of Teachers of English. 14 Feb. 2008 <http://www.ncte.org/cccc/resources/positions>.

——. "Statement of Principles and Standards for the Postsecondary Teaching of Writing." 1989. *CCCC Position Statements.* National Council of Teachers of English. 19 Feb. 2008 <http://www.ncte.org/cccc/resources/positions>.

Conference on College Composition and Communication (CCCC), Committee on Part-Time/Adjunct Issues. "Report on the Coalition on the Academic Workforce/CCCC Survey of Faculty in Freestanding Writing Programs for Fall 1999." *College Composition and Communication* 53.2 (Dec. 2001): 336–48.

Conference on College Composition and Communication (CCCC), Officers' Conference Call. 18 July 2007.

Confused. "Do Adjunct Instructors Earn a Living Wage?" Response to Jaschik (27 March 2007) 14 Feb. 2008 <http://www.insidehighered.com/news/2007/03/27/workload>.

Cook, William W. "Writing in the Spaces Left." Roen 228–47.

Crystal, David. *Language Death.* Cambridge, UK: Cambridge UP, 2000.

Gere, Anne Ruggles. "Kitchen Tables and Rented Rooms: The Extracurriculum of Composition." Roen 248–66.

——. "A Numbers Question." Email message to the author, 21 Feb. 2008.

Gilyard, Keith. "Literacy, Identity, Imagination, Flight." Roen 370–82.

Harper, Frances Ellen Watkins. "We Are All Bound Up Together." *Available Means.* Ed. Joy Richie and Kate Ronald. Pittsburgh: U of Pittsburgh P, 2001. 147–50.

Hesse, Douglas. "Who Owns Writing?" Roen 457–74.

Hutcheon, Linda, "Presidential Address 2000." *PMLA* 116.3 (May 2001); 518–30.

Jaschik, Scott. "The Overflowing Composition Classroom." *Inside Higher Ed* (27 March 2007) 14 Feb. 2008 <http://www.insidehighered.com/news/2007/03/27workload>.

"Jim Randels, Kalamu ya Salaam, and Students at the Center: Our People of the Year." *New Orleans Tribune* 24.1 (Dec. 2007/Jan. 2008): 4, 7, 8–9.

Kozol, Jonathan. *The Shame of the Nation.* New York: Three Rivers P, 2005.

Krugman, Paul. "Poverty Is Poison." *New York Times* 18 Feb. 2008. 18 Feb. 2008 <http://www.nytimes.com/2008/02/18/opinion/18krugman.html>.

Laurence, David. Email message to author. 22 Feb. 2008.

——. "The MLA Survey of Staffing in English and Foreign Language Departments." *Profession* (2001): 211–24.

Logan, Shirley Wilson. "Changing Missions, Shifting Positions, and Breaking Silences." Roen 418–29.

Lorde, Audre. "Learning from the 60s." *Sister Outsider.* New York: Quality, 1984. 134–44.

Lunsford, Andrea A. "Composing Ourselves: Politics, Commitment, and the Teaching of Writing." Roen 185–200.

"Mitt Romney Suspends Campaign." *New York Times* 7 Feb. 2008. 9 Feb. 2008 <http://www.nytimes.com/2008/02/07/us/politics/08romney-transcript.html>.

Morrison, Toni. *The Bluest Eye*. London: Chatto and Windus, 1979.

National Coalition on Health Care. "Health Insurance Coverage." 2008. 15 Feb. 2008 <http://www.nchc.org/facts/coverage.shtml>.

"New Report, Top UN Official Say [sic] Katrina Response Still Not Meeting U.N. Human Rights Standards." *Louisiana Weekly* 21 Jan. 2008. 22 Jan. 2008 <http://www.louisianaweekly.com/weekly/news/articlegate.pl?20080121m>.

Princiotta, Daniel, Stacey Bielick, and Christopher Chapman. "Homeschooling in the United States: 2003." Washington, DC: National Center for Education Statistics, 2006.

Raine, Kathleen. *The Collected Poems of Kathleen Raine*. Washington, DC: Counterpoint, 2001.

Redden, Elizabeth. "Best You Can Be without a Degree." *Inside Higher Ed* 14 Feb. 2008. 14 Feb. 2008 <http://www.insidehighered.com/news/2008/02/14/veterans>.

Reich, Robert B. "Totally Spent." Op-Ed. *New York Times* 13 Feb. 2008. 13 Feb. 2008 <http://www.nytimes.com/2008/02/13/opinion/13reich.html>.

Rich, Adrienne. "Arts of the Possible." *Arts of the Possible: Essays and Conversations*. New York: Norton, 2001. 146–68.

———. "IV." *Your Native Land, Your Life*, New York, Norton: 1986. 25.

Richie, Joy, and Kate Ronald, eds. *Available Means*. Pittsburgh: U of Pittsburgh P, 2001.

Roberts, Sam. *Who We Are Now: The Changing Face of America in the 21st Century*. New York: Times Books, 2004.

Roen, Duane, ed. *Views from the Center: The CCCC Chair's Addresses, 1977–2005*. Boston: Bedford/St. Martin's P and NCTE, 2006.

Royster, Jacqueline Jones. "When the First Voice You Hear Is Not Your Own." Roen 284–97.

Ryan, James E. "The Perverse Incentives of the No Child Left Behind Act." *New York University School of Law–Law Review* 79.3 (2 July 2004): 932–89. 14 Feb. 2008 <http://www.law.nyu.edu/journals/lawreview/issues/vol79/no3/NYU303.pdf>.

Selfe, Cynthia L. "Technology and Literacy: A Story about the Perils of Not Paying Attention." Roen 323–51.

Students' Right to Their Own Language. Spec, issue of *College Composition and Communication* 25 (Fall 1974): 1–32.

"Texas Study Suggests 'No Child Left Behind' Could Hurt High-School Graduation Rates." *Chronicle of Higher Education* 14 Feb. 2008. 15 Feb. 2008 <http://chronicle.com/news/article/3957/texas-study-suggests-no-child-left>.

Tilstra, Nadja. "Tulane Commencement Address." Unpublished ms. 2007.

Tompkins, Jane. "Fighting Words: Unlearning to Write the Critical Essay." *Georgia Review* 42.3 (1988): 585–90.

Truth, Sojourner. "Keeping the Thing Going While Things Are Stirring: Address to the First Annual Meeting of the American Equal Rights Association, May 9, 1867." 3 Feb. 2008 <http://www.pacifict.com/ron/Sojourner.html>.

U.S. Congress. Senate. S. Amdt. 4073, 109th Cong., 2nd sess. *Congressional Record* 109 (18 May 2006): S 4811.

Wandera, David. "Surmounting the Tribal Challenge in Kenya." Unpublished ms. 8 Jan. 2008.

Yancey, Kathleen Blake. "Made Not Only in Words: Composition in a New Key." Roen 430–56.

———. "Spellings," Online posting. 2 Feb. 2008. WPA-listserv.

Acknowledgments

Wendy Bishop. "Helping Peer Writing Groups Succeed." From *Teaching Lives: Essays and Stories*, pp. 14–24. Copyright © 1997 by Utah State University Press. Reprinted by permission of Utah State University Press.

Amy J. Devitt, Anis Bawarshi, and Mary Jo Reiff. "Materiality and Genre in the Study of Discourse Communities." From *College English* 65.5 (May 2003): pp. 541–58. Copyright © 2008 by the National Council of Teachers of English. Reprinted with permission.

"Diagram of Four Elements." From *The Mirror and the Lamp*, by M.H. Abrams. Copyright © 1971. Reprinted by permission of Oxford University Press, USA.

Douglas Downs and Elizabeth Wardle. "Teaching about Writing, Righting Misconceptions: (Re)Envisioning 'First-Year Composition.'" From *College Composition and Communication* 58.4 (June 2007): pp. 552–85. Copyright © 2007 by the National Council of Teachers of English. Reprinted with permission.

Cheryl Glenn. "Representing Ourselves: 2008 CCCC Chair's Address." From *College Composition and Communication* 60.2 (December 2008): pp. 420–39. Copyright © 2008 by the National Council of Teachers of English. Reprinted by permission.

Muriel Harris. "Talking in the Middle: Why Writers Need Writing Tutors." From *College English* 57.1 (January 1995): pp. 27–42. Copyright © 1995 by the National Council of Teachers of English. Reprinted with permission.

Bruce Horner, Min-Zhan Lu, Jacqueline Jones Royster, and John Trimbur. "Opinion: Language Difference in Writing: Toward a Translingual Approach." From *College English* 73.3 (January 2011): pp. 303–21. Copyright © 2011 by the National Council of Teachers of English. Reprinted by permission.

Stephanie L. Kerschbaum. "Avoiding the Difference Fixation: Identity Categories, Markers of Difference, and the Teaching of Writing." From *College Composition and Communication* 63.4 (June 2012): pp. 616–44. Copyright © 2012 by the National Council of Teachers of English. Reprinted by permission.

Ilona Leki. "Meaning and Development of Academic Literacy in a Second Language." From *Multiple Literacies for the 21st Century*, edited by Brian Huot, Beth Stroble, and Charles Bazerman, pp. 115–28. Copyright © 2004. Reprinted with permission of Hampton Press, Inc.

Gerald Locklin. "Amphibians Have Feelings Too." From *In Praise of Pedagogy*, edited by Wendy Bishop and David Starkey. Copyright © 2000 by Heinemann. Reprinted by permission of Gerald Locklin.

Andrea A. Lunsford and Karen Lunsford. "'Mistakes are a Fact of Life': A National Comparative Study." From *College Composition and Communication* 59.4 (June 2008): pp. 781–806. Copyright © 2008 by the National Council of Teachers of English. Reprinted with permission.

Paul Kei Matsuda. "The Myth of Linguistic Homogeneity in U.S. College Composition." From *College English* 68.6 (July 2006): pp. 637–51. Copyright © 2006 by the National Council of Teachers of English. Reprinted by permission.

Ruth Mirtz. "You Want us to do WHAT? How to Get the Most Out of Unexpected Writing Assignments." From *Elements of Alternate Style: Essays on Writing and Revision*, by Wendy Bishop.

Index

Abbott, Robert, 310
ABCD Books, 44
Abels, Kimberly, 452
Abrams, M. H., 215
absenteeism, 16–17, 33, 83–84
academic language, learning in tutorial
    instruction, 326–30
accumulation, for creative nonfiction
    essays, 203
Ackerman, John M., 278, 329
Adams, Heather, 246
Adisa, Opal Palmer, 407, 409
Adler-Kassner, Linda, 9
advertiser's stance, 216
African American voice, 401–10
    inquiry/discovery, need for, 402–5
    multiple voices, authenticity of,
        407–8
    new paradigms, need for, 408–10
    voice within, importance of, 405–7
Alexander, Jonathan, 413
Alfano, Christine, 250
Allen, Harold B., 457–58
Allen, Nancy, 321
Alred, Gerald, 324, 330
alternate styles, 227–31
    in classroom, 228–30
    evaluating and grading, 230–31
    student errors unrelated to, 358–59
alternativity, transitional words for,
    208
Ambrosio, Tara-Jen, 519
American English. See English language
analogy
    elements of, 168
    topical invention for, 169
Angel, 8, 68
Anokye, Ajua Duku, 515, 519
anthologies, 6
Anzaldúa, Gloria, 225, 408

appeals
    emotional, 195, 197–98
    types of, 197–98
Appiah, Kwame Anthony, 515
a priori fallacy, 168
arguments
    arrangement for, 193–94, 201–2
    as assignments, historical trend,
        353
    and invention, 165–66
    visual argument activities, 498–506
Aristotle
    classical invention, 167–72
    and four elements, 215
    on four-part arrangement, 192–94
    on three-part arrangement, 188–90
Arnold, H. J., 385, 391
arrangement, 186–210
    for arguments, 193–94, 201–2
    for cause and effect analysis, 201
    classical forms of, 188–99
    for classification and division, 200
    for comparison and contrast, 201
    for creative nonfiction essays, 202–4
    for definition, 201
    for descriptions, 200
    for exemplification, 200
    invention linked to, 204
    and multimodal writing, 204–5
    for narratives, 200
    and outlines, 205–7
    for process analysis, 201
    relationship to form, 186–88
    transitions in, 208–9
Asons, Iveta, 78
assignments, 95–124
    blogs, creating, 118
    creating, 119
    explaining to students, 119–20
    good assignment, features of, 97–99

assignments (*cont.*)
  information for students in syllabus, 19–25
  oral presentations, 115–16
  research assignments, 100–114
  revision, 120–23
  sequences. *See* assignment sequences
  at student-teacher conferences, 82
  from textbooks, 96
  visual essays, 117–18
  Web design projects, 114–15
  Web sites on, 124
assignment sequences
  Bain sequence, 99
  multimedia rhetoric analysis assignment, 249–50
  using, steps in, 99–100
Atkinson, D., 442
attendance, information for students in syllabus, 12, 16–17
attention deficit disorder (ADD), 5
audience
  and delivery, 247–48
  and style/formality level, 217–18
Axelrod, Rise, 236

Bacon, Nora, 226
Bain, Alexander, 99
Bakhtin, Mikhail, 418–20
Ball, Arnetha, 5, 223, 252
Balthazor, Ron, 347
Barnes, Douglas, 322, 323
Baron, Dennis, 518
Bartholomae, David, 514
Barton, David, 483
Basic Interpersonal Communicative Skills (BICS), 439
basic writing (BW) program, 4
bathos (laughable emotional appeal), 195
Bawarshi, Anis, 365, 372
Bayley, Robert, 453, 454
Bazerman, Charles, 252, 280, 373, 374, 375–77
Beach, Richard, 307
Beason, Larry, 284
Beaufort, Anne, 264, 282, 298
Beaven, Mary, 133–34, 310
Becker, Alton L., 164

behavioral approach, writing course, influence on, 383–85
behavioral-emotional issues, reporting, 5–6
Belanoff, Pat, 70, 146, 147
Belcher, D., 443
Belk, John, 125
Bell, J., 445
Bennett, John W., 455–56
Benton, Steve, 297
Bereano, Nancy K., 515
Berkenkotter, Carol, 278, 280, 284
Berlin, James, 383
Bernard-Donals, Michael, 240
Bernhardt, Steve, 299
Bhabha, Homi K., 408
Bilsky, Manuel, 168
Bishop, Wendy, 72, 96, 101, 221, 224, 228, 230–31, 309, 319, 376, 514
Black, Laurel, 146
Blackboard, 8, 68
blackboard prompts, 29–30
Blair, Hugh, 197
Bleich, David, 376, 379
blogs
  creating, as assignment, 118
  as journal, 173, 176–77
body of essay, in three-part arrangement, 189–90
Bok, Derek, 342
book fairs, 6–7
Booth, Wayne, 215–16
Boothman, Nicholas, 46
Bosher, S., 439
Bosse, Bob, 280
Braine, George, 460
brainstorming, 178–79
  in classroom, 178–79
  for research topics, 103
Brande, Dorothea, 181
Brandt, Deborah, 483
Brannon, Lil, 328, 334
Brereton, John C., 455
Bridgeford, Tracy, 69
Broad, Bob, 280
Brooke, Collin Gifford, 204–5
Brookfield, Stephen D., 60, 63–64
Brown, Laura Michael, 261
Bruch, Patrick, 5
Brueggeman, Brenda Jo, 5, 86

Bruffee, Kenneth, 310, 322
Buffon, Georges de, 212
Burgess, Amy, 416
Burke, Kenneth, 188, 276
Burkland, Jill, 328

Calfree, Robert, 146
Callahan, Raymond, 384
Campbell, George, 239
Campus Compact, 44
cancelled classes, alternate plans
     for, 84–85
capitalization errors, 356–57
Carson, J., 440, 444
Castells, Manuel, 481
causativity, transitional words for, 208
cause and effect analysis
  arrangement for, 201
  consequence, topic of, 168
CCCC (Conference on College
     Composition and Communication),
     261, 280, 464, 472
  chair's address (2008), 514–26
  on digital environments, 7
  Students' Right document, 464
cell phone policy, 18, 36–37, 85
Chaplin, Miriam, 514
Chapman, Marilyn, 377
Chatman, Seymour, 212
Christian, Barbara, 406
chronological order
  for narratives, 200
  for process analysis, 201
  reverse, 201
Cicero, 167, 197, 218, 246
Clark, Irene, 319
classical arrangements, 188–99
  four-part, 192–97
  six-part, 197–99
  three-part, 188–91
classical invention, 167–72
  for analogy, 168–69
  for consequence, 168, 170
  for definition, 168–69
  main/subordinate theses
       generation, 171
  origin of, 167–68
  teaching guidelines, 170–72
  for testimony, 169–70

classical rhetoric
  classical arrangements, 188–99
  on delivery, 246
  historical basis of, 167
  topical invention. *See* classical
       invention
classification and division
  arrangement for, 200
  outline for, 206–7
classroom management, 83–87
  absenteeism, 83–84
  cancelled classes, 84–85
  disruptive students, 60, 85–86
  late assignments, 84
  lateness, 83–84
  personal technology, rules for, 85
  plagiarism, 87–93
  students with learning disabilities,
       86–87
classroom space, delivery in, 257–59
Cliff, Michelle, 517
clustering, 179–180, 237
Code of Academic Integrity, 18
coherence, transitional words for, 208–9
collaborative learning
  criticisms of, 310
  introducing, activities for, 70–71
  peer writing groups, 308–17
  teaching concept of, 314
collective memory, 240–41
Collier, V., 439
Comley, Nancy, 177
comments of teachers. *See* evaluation of
       student writing
commonplace books, 173
communication materials, word/image
       and design of, 507–11
communication triangle, 215
community, writing-related programs,
       9–10
comparison and contrast, arrangement
       for, 201
composition
  and computers, readings on, 271–72
  rhetorical cannons. *See* rhetorical
       practices
  suggested readings on, 268–69
  theory and practice, Web sites on,
       266–67

composition/rhetoric study, 261–67
　book series on, 262
　critical concerns in field, 263–65
　journals of, 262
　professional organizations, 261–62
　suggested readings on, 267–74
　Web sites related to, 266–67
Composition Studies, 6
computer literacy, 253–56
　as concept, teaching, 254–56
　critical, 253
　functional, 253
　rhetorical, 254
　of students, assessing, 69–70
computer-supported classrooms
　class routines in, 66–70
　computer literacies, considering, 69–70
　course-management systems, 7
　e-mail, use of, 8
　evaluation of essays, 132
　first-time teachers in, 67
　online peer response, 77
　online textbooks/materials, 8
　online writing labs (OWLs), 7
　pedagogical goals as focus, 68–69
　Web-based discussion pages, 8, 67
conclusativity, transitional words for, 208
conclusion
　in four-part arrangement, 194–95, 197
　thesis in, 190, 198
　in three-part arrangement, 190
Condon, William, 147
Conference on Computers and
　　Composition, Language and
　　Learning across the Curriculum
　　(LALAC), 261
conferences with students. *See* student-
　　teacher conferences
confirmatio (proof of the case), 197–98
confirmation, in four-part arrangement,
　　193–94, 196
congenital word blindness, 389
Connor, Ulla, 78
Connors, Robert J., 128–29, 135–36, 168,
　　188, 192, 221, 234, 328, 342–354,
　　449, 452, 455
consequence
　elements of, 168
　topical invention for, 170

containment, linguistic containment
　　methods, 453–56
content, standards of, 129–31
contract grading, 144–46
Cook, Bill, 514
CoolArchive, 115
Cooper, Anna Julia, 407
Cooper, Charles, 236
coordination, transitional words for,
　　208
Corbett, Edward P. J., 168, 188, 192–93,
　　198, 211, 212, 221, 234
corrective introduction, 193
course-based grading, 138–39
course calendars, syllabus information
　　about, 14, 25–29, 37–42
course-management systems software, 8
creative nonfiction essays, arrangement
　　for, 202–4
critical computer literacy, 253
Croce, Benedetto, 212
Crocean aesthetic monism, 212–13
Crooks, Robert, 9
Crowley, Sharon, 235, 237–39, 280
Crusan, Deborah, 453
Cubberley, Ellwood, 384
cultural diversity, and peer response
　　groups, 78–79
cultural literacy, 392
Cummins, J., 439
Curry, Wade, 297
Curtis, Marcia, 416
Curzan, Anne, 46–47, 60, 93, 125, 134
Cushman, Ellen, 413
custom-published textbooks, 6

Dadak, Angela, 452
Daedalus Integrated Writing
　　Environment Overview, 44
Daiker, Donald, 328
Damour, Lisa, 46–47, 60, 93, 125, 134
D'Angelo, Frank J., 199
Danis, Francine, 310
Darian, Stephen G., 456, 457, 458
Davis, Barbara Gross, 46–47, 53, 125
Davis, Ken, 297
Davis, Lennard, 5
Dawkins, John, 284
De, Esha Niyogi, 414

Deans, Thomas, 9
definition
    arrangement for, 201
    elements of, 168
    topical invention for, 169
deliberative topics, 195
delivery, 246–60
    and audience, 247–48
    and changing nature of writing/texts,
        247–48, 252
    classical rhetoric on, 246
    in classroom spaces, 257–59
    and computer literacy, 253–56
    elements of, 247
    multimodal texts, 248–52
Delpit, Lisa, 223
DePeter, Ronald A., 202
descriptions, arrangement for, 200
descriptive responding, 70
Desire2Learn, 68
Desmet, Christy, 347
Devitt, Amy J., 365–66, 372, 374
Dew, Debra, 297
diagnostic essay, 50–54
Dickinson, Emily, 511
Dickson, Marcia, 146
Didion, Joan, 104–5
difference, addressing. *See* diversity
        and difference
Dillard, Ann, 222–23
Diller, Christopher, 278, 280
Diogenes, Marvin, 248–49
disabilities
    general guidelines, 86–87
    of learning. *See* learning differences
discourse blocs, 208
discourse communities, 365–80
    and ethnography, 375–79
    and legal genre, 366–72
    and medical history form, 372–75
discussions in class, 61–65
    functions of, 62
    leading, by teacher, 62–64
    online alternative. *See* Web-based
        discussion pages
    questions, asking, 63–64
disruptive students, handling of, 60,
        85–86
diversity and difference, 412–31

among peer writing groups, 311–12
areas of exploration, 413–17
categories, redefining, 415–16,
        423–24
critical concerns in field, 264–65
difference, interactional approach,
        417–22
fixing difference, 414
learning-based. *See* learning
        differences
marking difference, 414, 420–31
second language-based. *See* ESL
        students
suggested readings on, 270–71
writing class, microanalysis, 422–27
diviso (partition, division), 197–98
Doctorow, E. L., 236, 239
documentation of sources, 88, 107
Dowdy, Joanne Kilgour, 223
Downs, Douglas, 263, 278
drafting, research assignments, 107–10
DuBois, W. E. B., 247, 405
Duhamel, P. Albert, 168
Dunn, Patricia, 413
Durst, Russel K., 147
dysgraphia, 5
dyslexia, 5

Ede, Lisa, 163, 211
educational psychology, writing course,
        influence on, 383–85
Elbow, Peter, 70, 126, 129, 133, 136,
        144–45, 147, 164–65, 176, 182,
        202, 225–26
Eldred, Janet M., 66–67
Elias, David, 321
e-mail
    connecting with students, 8
    peer-response in, 77
    syllabus information about, 34–35
emotional appeals, 195, 197–98
English as a second language (ESL). *See*
        ESL students
English language
    English Only policies, 468
    as skill, approach to teaching, 386–88
    standard, problems of, 464–67
    Students' Right document, 464
    varieties of, 222–24

English Language Institute (ELI), 457–58

Enoch, Jessica, 9, 14–15, 99

entertainer's stance, 216

entrance exams, and linguistic
    containment policy, 455–56

epilogue (conclusion), 194–95

e-portfolios, 146–48

errors in student writing, 342–64
    coding process, 351–52
    coding rubric for study, 349–51
    error studies (1986–2006), 346–47
    institutional review board (IRB)
        research, 347–48
    syntactic errors, 128
    teacher comments on. *See* evaluation
        of student writing
    top ten errors lists, historical view,
        343–46
    twenty most common errors (Lunsford
        and Connors), 344–46, 358
    twenty most common errors (Lunsford
        and Lunsford), 128, 354–58
    word-level errors, 128

ESL students, 436–47
    academic community values, problems
        of, 440–46
    in colleges, historical view, 454–59
    contact language forms, 437
    and critical thinking approach,
        442–43
    English Plus policy, 467
    evaluating writing, focus of, 130–31,
        134
    identity issues, 438–40
    international students, influx to
        colleges, 455–58
    L2 population, size of, 452–53
    language differences, common
        responses to, 465–66
    language variety, teaching awareness
        of, 224–25
    learning style, 445–46
    linguistic containment methods,
        453–56
    and linguistic homogeneity myth,
        449–60
    literate abilities, range of, 438
    misinterpretations of text by, 437–38
    and peer response groups, 78–79

placement procedure, past view,
    453–54

plagiarism, 443–44

standard English, problem with
    concept, 464–67

Students' Right document, 464

translingual approach to, 463–475

and voice, 443

writing programs for, historical view,
    457–59, 464, 468

essays
    diagnostic essay, 50–54
    strategy words, 119–20
    visual essay activities, 488–97

ethnography
    in composition studies, 376–79
    genre theory analysis, 375–79

etymological meanings, 168

evaluation of student writing, 125–60,
    333–40
    alternate-style texts, 230–31
    alternative methods, need for, 338–40
    electronic tools for, 354
    errors in essays. *See* errors in student
        writing
    of ESL students, 130–31, 134
    grading, 137–59
    improvement as goal of, 126–27,
        333–34
    marginal comments, 133–35
    by peers. *See* peer-response groups
    of peer writing groups, 316–17
    routines, general, 131–32
    standards, formal, 127–29
    standards of content, 129–31
    and teacher appropriation of text,
        334–36
    teacher comments, past/present
        comparison, 353–54
    teacher comments, research findings
        in, 334–40
    teacher comments, student view of,
        126
    teacher comments as vague directives,
        337–38
    terminal comments, 135–37
    of visual texts, 494–97, 505–6

Evans, Rick, 284

everyday journals, 173

exemplification, arrangement for, 200
exordium (introduction), 197–98
experience, writing from, 239–40
extratextual space, delivery in, 256–57

Fadiman, A., 439
Faery, Rebecca Blevins, 202
Faigley, Lester, 297
Faris, Michael J., 95
Farmer, Frank, 221
Farmer, Robert, 342
Fernheimer, Janice, 413
film structure, comparing to nonfiction
    essays, 202–3
final grades, 154–58
    mathematical systems for, 155–57
first class, tasks during, 45–49
first-year writing (FY), 5, 278–99. *See also*
    writing course
    academic language, learning, 326–30
    assignments, historical trends, 352–53
    critical concerns in field, 263–65
    essay assignments, change over time
        (1917–2006), 352–53
    evaluation/grading criteria, 139
    expected outcomes, 280–81
    imitation exercises, 221–22
    Introduction to Writing Studies as
        alternative. *See* writing-about-
        writing courses
    journal writing issue, 174
    length of essays, historical trends, 352
    peer-response groups, 72–79
    peer writing groups, 309–17
    realistic goal for, 282
    strategic knowledge needs in, 322–25
    style issues in, 217–19
    suggested readings on, 273
    syllabus for, 11, 15–30
    transfer of skills issue, 281–82
    typical practices, 278–82
    universal assumptions in, 280–82
Fish, Stanley, 280
flashbacks, 200
Flower, Linda, 252, 284, 291–93, 298,
    320, 324, 329, 413
Flynn, Elizabeth, 310
focus, narrowing, for research topic,
    105–6

Fontaine, Sheryl I., 202
forensic topics, 195
form. *See also* arrangement
    relationship to arrangement, 186–88
    rhetorical, 187–88
formal evaluation, 127–29
formality level, and audience, 217–18
Forster, E. M., 206
four-part arrangement, 192–97
Fox, Helen, 413
Freedman, Aviva, 376, 379
freewriting, 180–84
    benefits of, 183
    in classroom, 181–83
    freewriting diary, 176
Frey, James, 236
Fu, D., 439
Fulkerson, Richard, 353–54
functional computer literacy, 253
FY course. *See* first-year writing (FY)

Gates, Henry Louis, Jr., 225
Gay, Pamela, 126
Gee, James, 284, 483
Geertz, Clifford, 378
genre
    genre sets, 374
    roots of term, 373
    as social action, 373
genre theory
    areas of exploration, 365–66
    context and study in, 376
    ethnography, 375–79
    legal genre, 366–72
    medical history form, 372–75
George, Diana, 312–13, 482, 484
Gere, Anne Ruggles, 9, 310, 523
Gibian, George, 458
Gilyard, Keith, 223
Giovanni, Nikki, 342
Glaser, Joe, 227
Glazier, Jocelyn, 413
Glenn, Cheryl, 163, 199–201, 211,
    514–24
    CCCC conference address (2008),
        514–26
Goldblatt, Eli, 252
Golden, James, 198
Gomez, Mary Louise, 416

Gonsalves, Lisa, 414, 416
Gorrell, Donna, 221
Goswami, Dixie, 252
grading, 137–59
    alternate-style texts, 231
    B fallacy, avoiding, 138
    contract grading, 144–46
    course-based criteria, 138–39
    final grades, 154–58
    information for students in syllabus,
        13, 17
    paper load, handling, 153–54
    portfolios, 151, 153
    revised versions, 123
    rubrics, creating for, 139–44
    syllabus information about,
        33–34
Graff, Harvey, 483
Graham, Janet Gorman, 297
Graves, Richard, 214
Gray, William S., 390
Green, David F., Jr., 211
Green, Roberta, 343–46
Greene, Stuart, 286, 288
Gregory, Donna Uthus, 414
Grimm, Nancy, 328
group ethos, 59–60
Guiler, W. S., 384

Haas, Christina, 284, 291–93
Hager, Elizabeth, 297
Haley, Alex, 409
Hall, Donald, 189
Hamilton, Mary, 483
Hampl, Patricia, 236
Hamp-Lyons, Liz, 147, 453
handbooks, 6
Harklau, Linda, 414, 439, 452
Harris, Muriel, 318, 322, 330
Hartwell, Patrick, 451
Harvard University
    entrance exams and linguistic
        containment, 455
    ESL writing courses, first, 458
    first composition course, 382
Haswell, Janis, 416
Haswell, Richard H., 46, 53, 93, 135, 280,
        297, 346–47, 416
Hawisher, Gail E., 7, 69, 416, 481

Hayes, John R., 284, 298
Hayes, Mary, 328
Healy, Dave, 318
Heath, Shirley Brice, 252
Herrington, Anne, 416
Herzberg, Bruce, 9, 10, 372
Hesse, Doug, 514, 519
heuristics
    for invention, 164, 166–67
    memory as, 235
Higgins, Lorraine, 413
Hilligoss, Susan, 486
Hinds, J., 440–41
Hinshelwood, James, 389
Hirvela, A., 443
Hjortshoj, Keith, 282
Hodges, John C., 343–45
Hogan, Coun, 59
Holdstein, Deborah, 299
Hongo, Garrett, 223
honors composition, syllabus, sample of,
        31–42
hooks, bell, 225, 408, 413
Horner, Bruce, 449, 463
Howard, Rebecca Moore, 281
Howe, Susan, 509
Huckin, Thomas N., 278, 284
Hughs, Gail F., 297
Hughs, Richard P., 168
Hull, Glynda, 281
Huot, Brian, 137, 264
Hurston, Zora Neale, 225
Hurtgen, James R., 297
Hutcheon, Linda, 516
Hyland, Ken, 280, 281
hyphenation errors, 357

illiteracy. *See also* literacy
    inappropriate claims of, 392–94
    use of term, problem of, 393–94
imitation, style, developing by, 220–22
inclusativity, transitional words for,
        208
individualistic monism, 212–13
inquisitive introduction, 193
insinuato, 198
instant messaging (IM), 358–59
institutional review board (IRB), student
        errors research, 347–48

International Society for the History of Rhetoric (ISHR), 261
Internet
  plagiarism, 92–93
  sources of information on. *See* Web sites
introduction
  in four-part arrangement, 192–93, 196
  in six-part arrangement, 197–98
  in three-part arrangement, 189
  Whately's types of, 193
Introduction to Writing Studies. *See* writing-about-writing courses
invention, 163–85
  arrangement linked to, 204
  brainstorming, 178–79
  classical invention, 167–72
  classroom uses of, 164–66
  clustering, 179–80
  defined, 163
  freewriting, 180–84
  heuristic systems of, 164, 166–67
  journal writing, 172–78
  memories, accessing, 237–38
  for research topic, 104–5
  Web sites on, 185
Irmscher, William, 182
Ivanic, Roz, 416
Ives, Sumner, 458

Jaschik, Scott, 520
Jewell, Ross M., 297
Johns, A. M., 443
Johnson, Mark, 284
Johnson, Roy Ivan, 343–46
Jordan, June, 223
Journal of Teaching Writing, 6
journal writing, 172–78
  blog as, 173, 176–77
  for creative nonfiction essays, 203
  evaluating, avoiding, 177–78
  for freewriting, 176
  FY problems, 174
  journals, types of, 172–73
  by teachers, 177
  by writing teachers, 262
Jung, Julie, 416

jury instructions, 368–71
  legal genre, layperson's understanding of, 368–71
juxtaposition, for creative nonfiction essays, 203
Juzwik, Mary, 415

Kachru, B., 436
Kain, Donna, 299
Kandel, Isaac Leon, 456–57
Kantz, Margaret, 284, 286
Kaufer, David S., 278
Kellerman, Paul M., 14, 31
Kent, Thomas, 263
Kerschbaum, Stephanie L., 412
King, Henry H., 455
Kitalong, Karla, 69
Klaus, Carl, 202
Kleine, Michael, 287
Klinger, Robert B., 457, 459
Knoblauch, C. H., 328, 334
knowledge, acquisition, in tutorial situation, 322–25
Kohn, J., 441
Kozol, Jonathan, 518
Kress, Gunther, 482–83, 486–87, 489, 508–10
Krugman, Paul, 519
Kubota, Ryuko, 452

labyrinthine sentences, 229–30
Lakoff, George, 284
Lang, Albert, 390
Langer, Ellen J., 298
language differences. *See* ESL students
language variety
  English, examples of, 222–24
  student awareness, facilitating, 224–26
  style, developing with, 222–26
  syntax, varying, 226–27
Lanham, Richard, 219, 228
laptops in classroom, 85
Lardner, Ted, 5, 223
Larson, Richard, 131, 186
late assignments, 84
lateness to class, 17, 83–84
Lauer, Janice, 163–64, 166
Laurence, David, 520

learning differences
  historical view, 389–90
  learning disabilities, 5, 86, 390
  medical model, 389–90
  teacher attention to, 86–87
learning style, ESL students, 445–46
LeCourt, Donna, 413, 417
lectures, limiting, 61
Lee, Amy, 416
Lee, C., 441
legal genre, 366–72
  jury instructions, 368–71
  laypersons contact with, 367
Leki, Ilona, 5, 79, 436, 444
lesson plans, 54–58
  sample plans, 55–58
Levin, Samuel R., 212
Levine, Adina, 78
Lewiecki-Wilson, Cynthia, 5, 86
library research, 105
Lieber, Andrea, 413
Lillis, Theresa, 415
Lindquist, Julie, 417
Lindsley, Philip, 395
linguistic homogeneity myth, 449–60
  versus historical facts, 454–59
  and image of college students, 450–52
  L2 population, size of, 452–53
  language differences as new norm,
    459–60
  linguistic containment methods,
    453–56
listening, teaching by, 306–7
literacy
  community-based projects, 9–10
  computer. *See* computer literacy
  definitional issues, 392–93, 436
  functional literacy, 392
  L2 literacy. *See* ESL students
  and new media texts. *See* visual literacy
  study of, suggested readings on,
    269–70
Lives on the Boundary (Rose), 9
Lodge, David, 516
Logan, Shirley, 514
logical fallacies, 168
logs, writing, 172
Long, Elenore, 413
Lopez, Barry, 104–5

Lorde, Audre, 407, 515, 523
Losey, Kay, 414, 452
Lott, Deshae, 429
Lovitt, Carl, 252
Lowe, Charles, 118
Lunsford, Andrea A., 50, 88, 93, 128–29,
    134, 135–36, 150, 163, 190, 211,
    223, 241–44, 248–49, 328, 342,
    342–362, 514
Lunsford, Karen J., 50, 128, 342, 355–362
Lyons, Scott, 413
Lyons, William, 281
lyric essays, 202

McCarthy, Lucille, 282, 284
McCorkle, Ben, 246
MacDonald, Christina Russell, 429
MacDonald, Susan Peck, 278, 281
McKnight, Robert K., 455–56
McPhee, John, 105
Macrorie, Ken, 164, 174, 176–78, 181,
    216
Mahiri, Jabari, 252
Mahony, Patrick, 235
Marback, Richard, 5
marginal comments, 133–35
markers for differences, 414, 420–431
  students, microanalysis, 422–27
  and teaching writing, 428–431
Marquardt, William F., 459
Martin, Gerald R., 297
Mathieu, Paula, 9, 252
Mathis, Joel, 368
Matsuda, Paul Kei, 449–50, 454–55,
    458, 460
medical history form, genre theory
    analysis, 372–75
medical model, learning differences,
    389–90
Mellix, Barbara, 225
memoir. *See* personal writing
memory, 234–45
  collective memory, 240–41
  and composition studies, 235–36
  connection to effective writing,
    235–36
  personal writing, 236–40
  Web sites on, 245
Milic, Louis T., 212–13

Miller, Carolyn, 280, 373, 376
Miller, Susan, 449, 453
Min-Zhan Lu, 46, 53, 93, 223, 463
Mirtz, Ruth, 228
Mitchell, W. J. T., 510
Modern Language Association (MLA), 261
Mohanty, Chandra Talpade, 406, 408
Moodle, 8, 68
Morgan, W. Pringle, 389, 391
Morrill Act (1862), 455
Morris, Amanda Lynch, 413
Morrison, Toni, 515
mosaic essays, 202–3
mosaic plagiarism, 90–91
Moss, Beverly, 252, 365, 377–78
Mossman, Mark, 429
multimodal learning technologies. See computer-supported classrooms
multimodal projects, 9
    arrangement for, 204–5
    blogs, creating, 118
    delivery, 248–52
    goals for, establishing, 248–49
    memoir, 243–44
    textbooks on, 250
    and visual literacy, 481–506
    Web design projects, 114–15, 205
Murphy, Sandra, 146
Murray, Donald M., 284, 305

narratio (statement of facts), 193, 197–98
narrative introduction, 193
narratives, arrangement for, 200
National Commission on Writing in America's Schools and Colleges, reports of, 280
National Council of Teachers of English (NCTE), 3, 261–62, 464, 518–19
National Service-Learning Clearinghouse, 44
National Writing Centers Association (NWCA), 261
National Writing Project Resources, 44
Native American languages, 468
negative analogy, 168
Nelson, Jennie, 286
Nelson, Joseph Raleigh, 457
Newkirk, Thomas, 263

new media texts. See multimodal projects; visual literacy
nonfiction essays, arrangement for, 202–4
nonlinear forms, creative nonfiction essays, 202–4
note-taking, in research process, 106–7

Oates, Scott F., 278, 280
objective tests, 384
O'Brien, Alyssa, 250
observativity, transitional words for, 208
Oded, Brenda, 78
Odell, Lee, 252
O'Hara, Jessica, 186
Okawa, Gail, 413
Olsen, Tillie, 405
O'Neill, Peggy, 137, 264
Ong, Walter, 247
online writing labs (OWLs), 7
Onore, Cynthia, 322
oral presentations, 115–16
    revising text for, 116
    rhetorical elements in, 115–16
order in classroom, 59–60. See also classroom management
    and group ethos, 59–60
organization. See also arrangement
principles of, 190
Ortmeier-Hooper, Christina, 415
Orton, Samuel, 389–90
Osborne, Alex, 178
Ostrom, Hans, 96, 220–21
outlines, 205–7
    topic outline, 206–7
    topic-sentence outline, 206

Page, Michelle L., 416
Palmeri, Jason, 7
Paradis, James, 280
paradoxical introduction, 193
parallelism, for creative nonfiction essays, 203
paraphrase
    introducing, 107
    plagiarism by, 89–90
Paré, Anthony, 375, 377
Parson, A. B., 457
Passin, Herbert, 455–56

pathos (emotional appeal), 195, 198
Patient Medical History Form (PMHF),
     genre theory analysis, 373–74
patterning, for creative nonfiction
     essays, 203
pedant's stance, 216
peer editing, 71
peer-response groups, 72–79
  cultural/language differences in,
     78–79
  evaluating, 78
  guidance for students, 75–77
  membership and size, 72–73
  online peer response, 77
  positive aspects of, 72
  response techniques for, 70–71
  tasks for, 73–74
peer writing groups, 309–17
  differences among, 311–12
  efficacy, research on, 310
  evaluation of, 316–17
  failure, reasons for, 313
  monitoring during work, 316
  naming groups, 315
  planning/preparing for, 314–15
  positive aspects of, 310
  success, reasons for, 313
  training of, 315–16
Peirce, B., 437
Penn State Public Writing Initiative, 9, 44
Pennycook, A., 436, 443
Perelman, Chaim, 217
Perfumo, Pam, 146
Perkins, David N., 282, 298
Perl, Sondra, 284
peroratio (conclusion), 194, 197–98
personal writing, 236–40
  arrangement for, 202
  assignments, examples of, 241–44
  experience, writing from, 239–40
  memory in, 236–38
  research for, 238–39
Petraglia, Joseph, 278, 282
Phelps, Louise, 323–24, 327
Pike, Kenneth L., 164
Pitkin, Willis, 208
plagiarism, 87–93
  confronting students, 93
  defining, 87–88

and ESL students, 443–44
  Internet plagiarism, 92–93
  mosaic plagiarism, 90–91
  by paraphrase, 89–90
  Penn State Guide, 88–93
  policy, communicating to students,
     12, 36
  preventing, teaching toward, 92
  Web sites on, 94
  word-for-word, 88–89
point-by-point order, 201
Polanyi, Michael, 61
portfolios, 146–53
  benefits to use, 147–48
  cover letters, 148–49
  e-portfolios, 146–48
  evaluation of, 150–51
  expectations, handout for, 148–50
  grading, 151, 153
  table of contents, 151–53
post hoc, ergo propter hoc fallacy, 168
Postman, Neil, 253
Potts, Joseph, 147
Powers, Lois, 520
practice pads, 384
Pratt, Mary Louise, 327
Prendergast, Catherine, 451
preparatory introduction, 193
Preskill, Stephen, 60, 63–64
Pressey, Luella Cole, 384–85
principium, 198
process analysis, arrangement for, 201
proem (before the song), 192
professional organizations
     journals of, 262
     list of, 261–62
psychological services, reporting
     students, 5–6
public writing initiatives, 9
Purcell-Gates, V., 436

Quaas, Francie, 202
quantification, writing course, influence
     on, 383–85
questions
  discussions in class, stimulating,
     63–64
  heuristic of invention, 164, 166–67
Quintilian, 167, 193, 197, 246

Raines, Kathleen, 517, 522
Randels, Jim, 517
Ransom, Grace, 384
Ratcliffe, Krista, 415
reading, in writing-about-writing
    courses, 284–85, 294
reading centers, 5
reading journals, 172
Redd, Teresa M., 5
Redman, Nathan, 163
refutation, in six-part arrangement,
    197–98
Reiff, Mary Jo, 365, 375
Reither, James, 280, 287
remedial classes
    historical view, 388–91
    medical model, 389–90
    and transience myth, 396
reprehensio (refutation), 197–98
research assignments, 100–114
    five-week model for, 103–11
    ideas, brainstorming for, 103
    preparing students for, 101–2
    in writing-about-writing courses,
        285–87, 291–95
research journals, 173
research process
    note-taking, 106–7
    for personal writing, 238–39
    sources, types of, 105
revision, 120–23
    exercise for, 110–11
    grading revised version, 123
    problems related to, 122–23
    by students, benefits of, 120–23
    systems for, 121–22
Rex, Lesley, 429
Reynolds, John Frederick, 235
Reynolds, Nedra, 150–51
rhetorica ad herrenium, 192
rhetorical choices, for style, 213–14
rhetorical computer literacy, 254
rhetorical dualism, 212–13
rhetorical form
    classical. *See* classical rhetoric
    elements of, 187
rhetorical methods
    arrangement for, 200–204
    classical. *See* classical rhetoric

rhetorical practices
    arrangement and form, 186–210
    delivery, 246–60
    invention, 163–85
    memory, 234–45
    style, 211–33
    suggested readings on, 267–68
    Web sites on, 266–67
rhetorical stance, 215–17
    imbalances related to, 216
rhetorical theory, suggested readings on,
    267–68
Rhetoric Society of America (RSA), 261
rhetorics/textbooks, 6
Rice, Rich, 150–51
Rich, Adrienne, 515, 522
Rico, Gabriele Lusser, 179–80
Ridgeway, Cecilia, 416
Riffaterre, Michael, 212
Roemer, Marjorie, 147
Rogers, Gretchen L., 457
Rood, Craig, 234
Roorbach, Bill, 214, 226–27, 236
Root, Robert L., Jr, 202
Rosaldo, Renato, 416
Rose, Mike, 9, 330, 381
Roswell, Barbara, 9
routines, classroom. *See* writing course
    routines
Royster, Jacqueline Jones, 401, 413, 463
rubrics
    for grading, 139–44
    Penn State first-year standards for,
        140–44
Rudman, Mark, 202
Rudolph, Fredrick, 394
Rumsey, Suzanne, 416
Rupiper, Amy, 263
Russell, David R., 278, 280–83, 373, 454
Ryan, James E., 518
Ryle, Gilbert, 281

Saenger, Paul, 508
Salaam, Kalamu ya, 517
Salomon, Gavriel, 282, 298
sayback technique, 70
Scarcella, R., 441
Scharton, Maurice, 297
Schick, Kurt, 263

Schiraldi, Vincent, 519
Schryer, Catherine, 365
Schueler, Herbert, 458
Schultz, Lucille M., 147
Schutz, Aaron, 9
Schwantes, Robert S., 456
scripting, student-teacher conferences,
    81–82
second class, tasks during, 49–53
segmented essays, 202–4
Selber, Stuart, 7, 253–54
Selfe, Cynthia L., 7, 69, 74, 117, 416,
    481, 515
Selfe, Dick, 69
Selinker, L., 437
Selzer, Jack, 252
sentence structure errors, 357–58
sequentiality, transitional words for, 208
service learning, 9
Shamoon, Linda, 281
Sharp, Michael, 368
Shaughnessy, Mina, 127–28, 183, 346
Shen, F., 438–39
Shoos, Diane, 484
Siebers, Tobin, 427
Siegal, Meryl, 414, 452
Silva, Tony, 454
Sirc, Geoffrey, 484
six-part arrangement, 197–99
skills approach, English as skill, 386–88
Sloan, Gary, 346
Slocombe, John, 297
Smart, Graham, 377
Smit, David, 280–81, 298
Smith, Frank, 307, 440
Smith, John A., 144
Smith, Keith A., 509
Smith, Louise Z., 329
Smitherman, Geneva, 223, 225, 449
social media, as freewriting diary, 176
Sohn, Kathleen Kelleher, 413
Sommers, Nancy, 52, 126, 134, 137, 177,
    284, 289, 292, 333
sources
    documentation, type of information, 88
    note-taking from, 106–7
    not giving credit. *See* plagiarism
    student errors related to, 356
spatial order, descriptions, 200

spell-checkers, and wrong word errors, 356
Spinuzzi, Clay, 486
Spivak, Gayatri Chakravorty, 408
Spivey, Nancy Nelson, 286
spreadsheet, for final grades, 156–57
Standardized English. See English
    language
standards
    of content, 129–131
    formal, 127–29
Starfield, Sue, 452
Starkey, David, 221
statement of fact, in four-part
    arrangement, 193, 196
Stein, Gertrude, 220–21
Stein, P., 437
Steingraber, Sandra, 104–5
strategy words, 119–20
Straub, Richard, 134, 137
Street, B., 436, 440, 483
Stuckey, J., 436
student evaluations
    of teacher, supplying form for, 158–59
    of tutor, 320
students
    academic level and abilities of, 4–5
    diagnostic essay for, 50–54
    initial information gathering about,
        4–6, 48–49
Students' Rights document, 464
student-teacher conferences, 79–82
    assignments during, 82
    best uses of, 80
    information for students in syllabus,
        13, 17
    positive aspects of, 80–81
    scripting, 81–82
    syllabus information about, 34
style, 211–33
    alternate styles, 227–31
    audience considerations, 217–18
    developing, imitation exercises, 220–22
    evaluation of, 130
    formality, levels of, 218–19
    and language variety, 222–26
    Milic's theories of, 212–14
    for research assignment, 109–10
    rhetorical choices, teaching of, 214–15
    rhetorical stance, choosing, 215–17

subordinate theses, 171
summary, of source information, 107
Summers, Sarah, 3
Sunstein, Bonnie, 147
Swales, John M., 281, 284, 372
syllabus, 10–42
  distributing, 48
  functions of, 10–11
  outline/information needed, 11–14
  sample syllabi, 14–42
syntactic errors, 128
syntax, varying, stylistic aspects, 226–27

table of contents, portfolios, 151–53
Tan, Amy, 222, 224–25
Tate, Gary, 263
Taylor, Todd, 257
Teachers of English to Speakers of Other
    Languages (TESOL), 261, 472
teachers of writing. *See* writing teachers
technology
  in the classroom. *See* computer-
    supported classrooms
  and composition, readings on, 271–72
  online technology. *See* Internet; Web
    sites
  and student projects. *See* multimodal
    projects
  workshops for teachers, 68
terminal comments, 135–37
testimony
  elements of, 169
  topical invention for, 170
textbooks
  assignments from, 96
  choosing for course, 6–7
  companion Web sites for, 8
  custom-published, 6
  historical view, 384
  information sources about, 6–7
  on multimodal texts, 250
  online, 8
  syllabus information about, 12, 16, 31
  types of, 6
Thelen, Erik, 324, 330
theory of ornate form, 212–13
thesis
  classical topical invention for, 169–71
  in classification and division, 200

in conclusion, 190, 198
in exemplification, 200
formulating, 108–9
and invention, 165–66
main and subordinate, 171
in six-part arrangement, 198
in three-part arrangement, 189–90
third class, tasks during, 53–54
Thomas, Lewis, 104–5
Thonus, Terese, 330
Thoreau, Henry David, 410
Thorndike, E. L., 383
three-part arrangement
  for arguments, 201
  elements of, 188–91
Tilstra, Nadja, 517
Tobin, Lad, 263, 429
Tompkins, Jane, 516
topic outlines, 206–7
topics
  generating. *See* invention
  narrowing focus of, 105–6
topics (seats of argument). *See* classical
    invention
topic-sentence outlines, 206
Towns, Cheryl, 327
Track Changes, 77, 132
Trainor, Jennifer Seibel, 5
transfer of skills, and FY courses, 281–82
transience myth, 394–98
  and educational system, 394–95
  socio-political factors, 395–96
transitional words and phrases,
    relationships created with, 200,
    208–9
translingual approach, 463–75
  and bilingual education, 467–68
  CCCC resolution compatibility with, 464
  versus common response to
    differences, 465–66
  endorsements for, 473–74
  English Plus policy, 467–68
  errors, approach to, 470
  fluency/proficiency redefined by, 467
  human rights addressed by, 468
  and monolingual students, 470–72
  and monolingual teachers, 469–70
  orientation of, 463–65
  resources for, 472

translingual approach (*cont.*)
  standards, approach to, 470
  writing programs, types of changes to, 469–72
Travis, Molly, 517
Trimbur, John, 449, 453, 463
Tufte, Virginia, 226
tutorial instruction, 318–30
  academic language learning in, 326–30
  affective concerns of students, addressing, 325–26
  collaborative talk, 321–22
  and strategic knowledge acquisition, 322–25
  student information gained from, 319–20
  student positivity toward, 320–22
  tutor, role of, 318–20

Ulmer, Gregory, 165, 234, 240

Valdes, Guadalupe, 414, 450, 452
Vandament, William E., 297
van Leeuwen, Theo, 482, 486–87, 489, 509
Villaneuva, Victor, 413, 449
visual arguments, 498–506
visual essays, 117–18, 488–97
visual literacy, 481–506
  assignments, requirements for, 486–87
  avoidance by teachers, 484–86
  defined, 482–83
  evaluating assignments, 494–97, 505–6
  scholarly examination of, 484
  visual argument activities, 498–506
  visual essay activities, 488–97
visual texts, software tools for, 481
vocabularies of errors concept, 384
voice, 401–10
  African American, dimensions of, 401–10
  and ESL students, 443
  and invention, 164–65

Walker, Alice, 225
Walker, Anne Burda, 416
Walker, Carolyn, 321
Walvoord, Barbara, 282
Wandera, David, 521–22
Wardle, Elizabeth, 263–64, 278, 281, 283, 287, 294

Watkins, James Ray, Jr., 5
Watters, Ann, 9
Weathers, Winston, 214, 220, 227–28, 359
Weaver, Christopher C., 125
Web-based discussion pages, 8
  routines for, 67
  syllabus information about, 32–33, 35–36
Web design projects, 114–15
  arrangement for, 205
  teaching guidelines, 114–15
  Web sites on, 124
Weber, Susan, 45
Web sites
  on blogs, creating, 124
  on field of rhetoric and composition, 266–74
  on invention, 185
  on memory, courses on, 245
  on plagiarism, 94
  textbook companion sites, 8
  on Web design, 124
  writing-related, 44
Weeber, Susan, 45
weighing, final grades, 155–56
Weiser, Irwin, 146
Welch, Kathleen, 234
Welch, Nancy, 252
Wells, Ida, 406
West, Cornel, 408
Whately, Richard, 192–93
White, Edward M., 50
Williams, Joseph, 360
Williams, Patricia, 409
Williams, Sean, 482, 485–86
Williams, Terra, 118
Williams, Terry Tempest, 104–5, 223
Winterowd, W. Ross, 208, 211
Witte, Stephen, 297
Witty, Paul, 343–46
word-for-word plagiarism, 88–89
word-processing programs, 67
  peer-response use of, 77
  Track Changes, 77, 132
workshops, 70–72. *See also* peer-response groups
  pre-collaboration activities, 70–71
  whole-class, techniques for, 71–72
Wortham, Stanton, 416

Writer's Workbench software, 334
writing center (WC), 4
  information for students in syllabus, 18
  tutors in. *See* tutorial instruction
writing course
  activities. *See* writing course routines
  assignments. *See* assignments
  basic information about, 3–6
  calendar/schedule. *See* course
    calendars
  community links to, 9–10
  course-management systems
    software, 8
  departmental structure for, 4
  essay assignments, change over time
    (1917–2006), 352–53
  first class, 45–49
  first-year. *See* first-year writing (FY)
  lesson plans, 54–58
  management of classroom. *See*
    classroom management
  multimodal learning technologies, 7–9
  order and group ethos, 59–60
  second class, 49–53
  student evaluations on, 158–59
  syllabus for, 10–42
  textbooks, choosing, 6–7
  third class, 53–54
  university, historical view. *See* writing
    course, past perspective
writing course, past perspective, 381–98
  educational psychology, influence of,
    383–85
  English as skill approach, 386–88
  first course, 382
  illiteracy concerns, 392–94
  position in American curriculum, 382
  remediation courses, 388–91
  transience myth, 394–98
writing course routines, 60–79
  in computer-supported classrooms,
    66–70
  discussions, 61–65
  lectures, limiting, 61
  peer-response groups, 72–79
  student-teacher conferences, 79–82
  workshops, 70–72
  writing in-class, 65–66
writing in-class, 65–66

writing program administrator (WPA),
  3, 7, 10, 86
writing teachers
  concerns related to teaching writing,
    263–65
  evaluation of student writing. *See*
    errors in student writing;
    evaluation of student writing
  good, traits of, 46
  journals for, 262
  journal writing by, 177
  listening, teaching by, 306–7
  pedagogy-related readings, 273–74
  professional organizations for,
    261–62
  revealing, teaching by, 307–8
  student evaluations of, 158–59
  suggested readings for, 267–74
  telling, teaching by, 305–6
  visual literacy teaching, avoidance of,
    484–86
writing-about-writing courses, 283–99
  benefits, student feedback on, 293–95
  challenges related to, 295–97
  critiques about, 297–98
  outcomes for students, examples of,
    287–93
  presentation assignments, 287
  principles and goals of, 283–84
  readings for, 284–85
  reflective assignments for, 285
  research assignments, 285–87,
    291–95
wrong word errors, 355–56, 358
Wurt, Adrian, 9
Wysocki, Anne Frances, 7, 69, 205

Yagelski, Robert, 252
Yagoda, Ben, 211
Yameng Liu, 164
Yancey, Kathleen Blake, 146, 247, 256,
  353–54, 515, 523
Young, Morris, 413, 416, 430
Young, Richard, 164, 278

Zak, Frances, 125
Zapp, Morris, 516
Zemliansky, Pavel, 101
Zinsser, William, 190, 206